POLITICS IN RUSSIA: A READER

For CMO and ARO, for keeping me whole.

POLITICS IN RUSSIA: A READER

Joel M. Ostrow, editor

Los Angeles | London | New Delhi
Singapore | Washington DC

Los Angeles | London | New Delhi
Singapore | Washington DC

FOR INFORMATION:

CQ Press

An Imprint of SAGE Publications, Inc.

2455 Teller Road

Thousand Oaks, California 91320

E-mail: order@sagepub.com

SAGE Publications Ltd.

1 Oliver's Yard

55 City Road

London, EC1Y 1SP

United Kingdom

SAGE Publications India Pvt. Ltd.

B 1/I 1 Mohan Cooperative Industrial Area

Mathura Road, New Delhi 110 044

India

SAGE Publications Asia-Pacific Pte. Ltd.

3 Church Street

#10–04 Samsung Hub

Singapore 049483

Printed in the United States of America

Library of Congress Cataloging-in-Publication Data

Politics in Russia: a reader / [edited by] Joel M. Ostrow.

p. cm.
Includes bibliographical references and index.

ISBN 978-1-60871-650-0 (pbk.)
1. Russia (Federation)—Politics and government—1991-
I. Ostrow, Joel M.

JN6695.P6537 2013
320.947—dc23   2012007493

This book is printed on acid-free paper.

Acquisitions Editor: Elise Frasier
Associate Editor: Nancy Loh
Production Editor: Brittany Bauhaus
Copy Editor: Pam Schroeder
Typesetter: C&M Digitals (P) Ltd.
Proofreader: Eleni-Maria Georgiou
Cover Designer: Stefan Killen Design
Marketing Manager: Chris O'Brien

SFI° Certified Sourcing
www.sfiprogram.org
SFI-00453

12 13 14 15 16 10 9 8 7 6 5 4 3 2 1

CONTENTS

Preface   ix

Acknowledgments   xv

1. **An Introduction to the Soviet Political System   1**

   1.1 MARY MCCAULEY, "Introduction," from *Soviet Politics, 1917-1991*   7

   1.2 MERLE FAINSOD, "Terror as a System of Power"   16

   1.3 SEWERYN BIALER, "Soviet Stability and its Sources"   44

2. **The Collapse of the Soviet Union   65**

   2.1 KATHERINE VERDERY, "What was Socialism and Why Did it Fall?"   70

   2.2 JOEL M. OSTROW, "Glasnost Gutted the Party, Democratization Doomed the State: Political Liberalization and the Soviet Disintegration"   84

   2.3 ALEXANDER DALLIN, "Causes of the Collapse of the USSR"   115

3. **Core Tasks for Postcommunist Russia   134**

   3.1 JOEL M. OSTROW, GEORGIY A. SATAROV, AND IRINA M. KHAKAMADA, "Crucial Junctures and the Demise of Democracy in Russia"   139

   3.2 ZVI GITELMAN, "The Democratization of Russia in Comparative Perspective"   149

   3.3 DAVID FOGLESONG AND GORDON M. HAHN, "Ten Myths About Russia: Understanding and Dealing with Russia's Complexity and Ambiguity"   163

4.   The Economy: Market Capitalism or Institutionalized Corruption?   181

   4.1   ANDREI SHLEIFER AND DANIEL TREISMAN, "A Normal Country: Russia after Communism"   187

   4.2   LILIA SHEVTSOVA, "The Triumph of Bureaucratic Capitalism"   203

   4.3   STEVEN HANDLEMAN, from "Comrade Criminal" and "The Criminal State"   212

5.   The Executive and the Legislature   234

   5.1   LILIA SHEVTSOVA, "Liberal Technocrats as an Adornment of the State"   239

   5.2   OL'GA KRYSHTANOVSKAYA AND STEPHEN WHITE, "Inside the Putin Court: A Research Note"   242

   5.3   PAUL CHAISTY, "Majority Control and Executive Dominance: Parliament–President Relations in Putin's Russia"   253

6.   Political Parties   268

   6.1   VLADIMIR GEL'MAN, "Party Politics in Russia: From Competition to Hierarchy"   273

   6.2   VLADIMIR GEL'MAN, "Political Opposition in Russia: A Dying Species?"   290

   6.3   STEPHEN WHITE, "Russia's Client Party System"   306

   6.4   M. STEVEN FISH, from "Symptoms of the Failure of Democracy in Russia"   331

7.   Elections   333

   7.1   JOEL M. OSTROW, GEORGIY A. SATAROV, AND IRINA M. KHAKAMADA, from "Corrupting the Elections: Enter the Oligarchs" and "Abandoning Democracy: Anointing a Successor"   337

7.2   MISHA MYAGKOV AND PETER C. ORDESHOOK, "Russian Elections: An Oxymoron of Democracy"   373

7.3   M. STEVEN FISH, from "Symptoms of the Failure of Democracy in Russia"   389

8.   Nationalism and Chechnya   405

8.1   RAFAEL KHACHATURIAN, "The Specter of Russian Nationalism"   409

8.2   ANNA POLITKOVSKAYA, "Chechnya: A Dirty War 1999-2002"   418

8.3   MARLÈNE LARUELLE, "[Conclusion]"   434

9.   The Media   444

9.1   JOEL M. OSTROW, GEORGIY A. SATAROV, AND IRINA M. KHAKAMADA, "Dictatorship Becomes the Only Game in Town"   448

9.2   M. STEVEN FISH, from "Symptoms of the Failure of Democracy in Russia"   455

9.3   MASHA LIPMAN, "Constrained or Irrelevant: The Media in Putin's Russia"   463

9.4   OLEG PANFILOV, "Russia: Why Do Journalists Die?"   473

9.5   OLEG PANFILOV, "Rebirth of Russian Nationalism"   476

9.6   DAVID SATTER, "Remembering Paul Klebnikov: Journalism of Intimidation"   482

9.7   DMITRY SIDOROV, "All the News the Kremlin Thinks is Fit to Print"   485

About the Editor   488

PREFACE

As this volume goes to press, a smattering of diffuse hints at change dot the Russian political landscape. In response to widespread reports of vote fraud in the elections for the Russian State Duma, the national legislative body, several thousand people took to the streets in Russia's major cities. Most of the reports were on Internet blogs, as the government heavily censors the traditional electronic and print media. Internet censorship in Russia is more spotty.

From one perspective, the protests are puzzling. Russia's elections have been marred by fraud both subtle and blatant since the suspect adoption of the new constitution in December 1993. The reality is that Russia has yet to have a free and fair, competitive election that has been free of widespread fraud. But the Russian public has seemingly tolerated this reality in every election since the collapse of communism. What makes 2012 different?

Nothing, really. Leadership change at the top has been pre-arranged by the leaders themselves, just as Russia's first president, Boris N. Yeltsin, handed power to Vladimir V. Putin in 2000 and Putin handed power to Medvedev in 2008. There is no open competition for legislative seats, as opposition parties and politicians continue to be systematically excluded, with many exiled or eliminated over the past decade. So, even when Putin's United Russia garners fewer votes than anticipated based on past votes, the groups that increased their tally can hardly be classified as true opposition. United Russia is a statist and quasi-nationalist group. The Liberal Democratic Party is a xenophobic nationalist group. Just Russia is a socialist-nationalist grouping. And then there is the Communist Party. These groups and their members are all from the same spectrum of the Russian political landscape, which is why they are allowed to stand in the elections in the first place under Putin's closed system.

The fact that the odds are overwhelmingly against those who would seek political change does not mean that it can not happen. However, one must be impressed with the resources the regime commands to befuddle any such attempts. Whether one speaks of ideals or labels, notions of liberalism and democracy remain thoroughly discredited among the Russian public. Even if there are signs of a people tiring of the era of Putin and United Russia, there is little evidence to suggest a people moving to embrace anything remotely resembling open politics. This is a tribute to Putin's aggressive dismantling of what was a free and independent media and his destruction of independent political opposition as a legitimate enterprise.

This volume brings together some of the best work on the Russian political system as it developed in the two decades after the Soviet collapse. Together, it describes the system as it exists as Putin returns to the presidency and how it became the system that it is. Russia continues to be not only a fascinating state, but one that is intensely important for regional and global political and economic security. Russia has the longest border in the world including a border with China, the most rapidly growing economy and the largest population in the world, that has long been contested. Russia is a major supplier of petroleum products to Europe, and has used that as leverage in its foreign policy. Russia maintains important strategic and political interests in the Middle East, where some of the most intractable and violent disputes continue to vex diplomats and policymakers. And, of course, Russia maintains the second-largest stockpile of nuclear weapons in the world and an ability to project its military power around the globe. For these reasons and more, Russia is and will remain central to all discussions about political, economic and military stability around the world.

However, it is equally true that, some two decades after the end of communist rule, serious questions remain about Russia's internal political and economic stability, and therefore about its objectives and behavior internationally. At the onset of World War II, British Prime Minister Winston Churchill famously described the USSR, as "a riddle, wrapped in a mystery, inside an enigma." While Russia in the 21st Century is not nearly so opaque, it is nevertheless one of the most widely misunderstood countries, politically, in the world. This volume, if it does anything, seeks to shed some light on how experts understand and mis-understand Russia, a state that remains vitally important to European and, indeed, global political stability.

Hopes that Russia would develop into a liberal, capitalist democracy and join the West, hopes that many held with the final lowering of the Hammer and Sickle flag in late-1991, have all but disappeared. Although nearly a decade late, the conventional wisdom finally seems to have caught on to the reality that Russia's political system today is not, by any reasonable definition, a democracy nor does it have much in common with the central components of democracy. In a recent book, my co-authors and I define democracy as, "a system that ensures popular control over the state. This subsumes such aspects critical to a functioning democratic political system as transparency, accountability, open competition that includes but goes beyond formal elections, to encompass a con-tinuing role for the polity."[1] In an earlier book, I defined democracy as a set of political institutions that peacefully manage, channel, and regulate political con-flict, that constrain conflict by providing incentives for promoting its peaceful resolution.[2] Russia is neither of these, nor is it an "adjectival democracy" – electoral, partial, managed or otherwise.

Russia's political system more resembles a dictatorship than a democracy. Throughout his two terms as President from 2000, when he was handed the presidency, to 2008, when he handed the office to Dmitriy Medvedev and himself slid into the office of prime minister, Vladimir Putin brought changes that torpedoed any hopes for democracy in Russia. Elections lost meaning, and for governors and the most important mayors were ended altogether. Those positions are filled from Moscow. The free press disappeared with the restoration of censorship in the media, including total state control over electronic media. He similarly ended real political competition, organization, and association by instilling fear into any with resources who might deign to pretend to have an independent political voice. Putin did not consolidate democracy in Russia; if anything he consolidated the restoration of dictatorship.

When he engineered his move to the prime ministership and Medvedev's assumption of the presidency, only those misunderstanding Russia viewed Medvedev as the leader. Any who ignorantly did so need only review the events of September 24, 2011, when Medvedev "proposed" at a conference of the ruling party United Russia that Putin run for president in 2012. The latter, of course, "accepted" as it had been planned long in advance. He is likely to serve as president through 2024. Whether this was decided when Putin first left the office of the presidency in 2008, or on the day of the announcement, or at some time in between is irrelevant. It is irrelevant because anyone paying attention would know that nothing in Russia changed when Putin became prime minister and nothing will change when he regains his former title. He rules the Russian political system, and had done so since Boris Yeltsin resigned and handed him the office on New Year's Eve 1999. While technically he must "run" and be "elected," nobody anywhere had any doubt about his guaranteed overwhelming victory; there was no real competition. Putin assured that fact roughly two years into his first term in the office.

Consequential decisions about Russian politics are made in secret, and ultimately by a single individual. These decisions include who will hold supreme political authority. There is no scrutiny, there is no contestation, there is no accountability to anyone except to Putin. The polity has little voice and less authority.

It is these realities that propelled at least some of the protesters to the streets in December 2011. Whether they will remain in the streets demanding change, and what sort of change they would demand, are entirely open questions as this book goes to press. However, this is a dynamic combination of factors that should keep Russia at the forefront of consciousness, for that state has the capacity to be either a cause of major global problems or source of solutions for those problems. Given the country's importance and the questions about its direction, it is rather distressing that Russia has remained largely off the journalist and academic radar. But this is in fact the case. With the Soviet collapse has come a dramatic rise in focus on China and its role in the global economy and as a global political actor. With the terrorist attacks on the United States on September 11, 2001, the emphasis on security has shifted to the Middle East and Central Asia. The de-emphasis on Russia is an unfortunate and potentially dangerous mistake.

The collapse of the Soviet Union that marked the end of the Cold War and triggered in Russia massive political, economic and social challenges also triggered a dramatic decline in public, media and academic interest in that country. In the heady months between the summer of 1989 and winter of 1991, there was a sense of triumphalism in the democratic world, a Kantian sense, as articulated by Francis Fukuyama, that history was ending.[3] The euphoria sparked a complacency, fueled by an assumption that Russia was on an inexorable path to democracy. A misguided notion was prevalent that with communism gone, in essence the story was over. Those who challenged the underlying assumptions, who dared to suggest both Russia and the world faced problems that would severely test both Russia and the liberal West – those who questioned "endism" – were largely ignored or scoffed at.[4]

But those who questioned "endism" have been proven to be right. A stable, liberal, capitalist democracy was never the most likely trajectory for Russia, and no reasonable person in 2012 can argue that these words describe Russia today. This reality presents serious challenges that require attention and understanding, not delusions and wishful thinking. Russia's stability has a direct impact on global stability; understanding what is happening in Russia is not merely an esoteric exercise, for Russia holds a key for every state's political and economic development.

Owing to the decline both of the country and of interest in it, over the last two decades few quality textbooks about Russian politics have been published. Of course, Russia has been something of a moving target, and books can be out of date by the time they are published. However, Russia's importance in world affairs demands an attempt to teach about that country, and that demand requires an effort to present the best material available to explain and understand contemporary Russia.

This book seeks to fill the void as a core text for introductory courses in Russian Politics. It assumes of the reader no prior knowledge about the country. The volume is comprised of works by leading scholars and observers of Russia, on many of the most important and controversial issues. The selections here are works previously published elsewhere. Most are reprinted in full, some are lightly excerpted. Most of the authors are widely recognized as leading authorities on their particular subject, and the selections included in this volume are among their very best published works. Students who complete this book should come away with a solid background on the major problems facing the Russian Federation and with knowledge of various perspectives on how to understand and interpret those challenges.

This approach to an introductory textbook carries with it certain drawbacks. While this volume strives to be comprehensive, because it contains reprinted material, considerations of both length and cost required difficult choices to be made in terms of both content and organization. Some of the choices I have made will be controversial, and it is worth noting here that every one of them was difficult to make. The editor is fully cognizant of the fact that most experts and instructors will have some bone to pick, because of the simple fact that there are more pressing problems facing Russia than a single volume of this sort can encompass. It is also the fact that no semester-length course can address all of the important problems, and as a result no two syllabi on Russian politics are the same. Add to these realities the fact that there are more quality publications and worthy authors on each of the topics that are included than could be presented in the contents of this volume, and one sees the dilemma. On both axes – issues and approaches – people differ about what is "most important," "most interesting," or "most convincing." Personal preferences and inclinations, academic and otherwise, would lead to different choices along each of these axes.

These simple and indisputable facts mean that choices had to be made on what to include and what to leave out. A book that included everything would see much go unused in any normal course while at the same time being prohibitively costly. Users of this volume may long for more emphasis on the Soviet period, or regret a lack of specific attention on Russian foreign policy, or wish for coverage of demographic and social issues relating to health and gender in particular, or find insufficient depth on problems such as the Chechen wars or the dynamics of federalism in Russia. However, a choice to exclude all mention of the Soviet period, or glance over the myriad problems with Russia's elections, or ignore the quirky aspects of the development of political parties, or to leave out the restoration of censorship in the media and its consequences would have rendered the book not viable. The hope is that most introductory courses will use the resultant book in full, or very nearly in full, while understanding that instructors will supplement with additional material as deemed desirable.

The fact is that individual instructors are likely to vary on which of the topics omitted here they would include in their courses, or which ones deserve lengthier and more in-depth treatment, and the expectation is that all will supplement with additional readings or topics to suit their particular expertise and interests. Likewise, students are encouraged to explore in greater depth when a particular reading or topic captures their interest. For each article included in this volume, half a dozen or more were excluded that address the same topic from a different angle or from a different viewpoint entirely. The suggestions for additional reading throughout are drawn from sources readily available either over the Internet or through virtually any library, and are all worthwhile and thought-provoking works that will expand your understanding of Russia and of matters of political and economic development.

The hope is that you will come away from this book appreciating the myriad contradictions and complexities that are the current reality in Russia, and with a context for understanding developments into the future. An awareness of the important role that Russia plays, and of the dilemmas facing decision makers in the public and private sectors alike who deal with that country, will improve understanding that can only increase hopes for the future.

NOTES

1. Ostrow, Satarov and Khakamada (2007), *The Consolidation of Dictatorship in Russia* (Praeger), Chapter 1, p. 6. See also Fish (2005), *Democracy Derailed*, (Cambridge University Press), Chapter 1.

2. Ostrow (2000), *Comparing Post-Soviet Legislatures: A Theory of Institutional Design and Political Conflict*, (Ohio State University Press), Chapter 1.

3. Francis Fukuyama, *The End of History and the Last Man*, Penguin Books, 1992.

4. A compelling, prescient, and largely overlooked objection was Ken Jowitt, "A World Without Leninism," in *New World Disorder: The Leninist Extinction*, University of California Press, 1992. Also, more widely recognized but understandably confusing coming from the man who coined the notion of ever-growing and accelerating "waves" of democracy, see Samuel P. Huntington, "The Errors of Endism," *The National Interest*, Fall 1989.

ACKNOWLEDGMENTS

I wish first and foremost to thank Elise Frasier at CQ Press for believing in this project and being such a faithful advocate, but even more for being such a patient editor. I faced a steep learning curve on this project, as what must have seemed like my endless questions made fairly clear. There is not a more able editor, nor one more delightful to work with. I also thank Pam Schroeder and Brittany Bauhaus at CQ Press, for their quick turnarounds and helpful corrections during copy editing.

Of course, I am also indebted to all of the authors and publishers who consented to having their works reprinted in this volume. Without that cooperation, this book would never have been possible. Sharon Lazich, my research assistant on this project, worked tirelessly and efficiently through the process of gaining these permissions, and she proved an effective negotiator with the less willing publishers.

The parameters of this volume were set and tweaked during my many semesters of teaching Russian Politics at UC Berkeley, Georgia State University, LaGrange College, Loyola University Chicago, and at Benedictine University. Over the years, many students, and especially my PLSC-222/322 students at Benedictine, have provided quite helpful feedback on readings essential and less so. I also thank all of the students in Russian Politics over the years, for their reactions to the material on my syllabi shaped and continue to shape my approach to the subject, and much of their direct and indirect feedback finds its way into this volume.

Various colleagues, including several anonymous reviewers, provided invaluable input on the contents. However, of my colleagues I must above all thank Valerie Sperling, whose generosity (and over-extension!) sent CQ to me in the first place. For that I am forever grateful, even if I did not find a way to include a chapter on women and social movements in this book; I agree, it is a shortcoming! Brian Taylor and Robert Moser at various stages also made suggestions for content that appear in the final version, or that do not appear but caused me sufficient doubt and angst as to boost my confidence that what is in this volume is indispensable.

The professors who taught me, Peter Shearman, Donald L. M. Blackmer, Loren Graham, Gail Lapidus, George Breslauer, Andrew Janos and Ken Jowitt, whose courses and syllabi provided the essential backbone for this book and in particular on the Soviet period, kind and wise people who shaped the scholar I have become, also deserve special mention. So, too, do all of the students with whom I sat in those courses! I also must anonymously and collectively thank the literally dozens of professors of Russian politics courses, past and present, whose online syllabi I learned from and poached from.

I thank, once again, my co-authors Georgiy A. Satarov and Irina M. Khakamada, as excerpts of several chapters from our *The Consolidation of Dictatorship in Russia* appear in the chapters of this book.

The idea was to produce a book that most will find both valuable and easy to incorporate into their courses, while leaving ample space to add according to one's individual preferences, quirks, or interpretations of what is important about politics in Russia. I, of course, accept full responsibility and beg forgiveness, for any errors of omission or commission that remain.

1

An Introduction to the Soviet Political System

On November 7, 1917, Vladimir I. Lenin led the Bolshevik Party takeover of power in Russia, setting in motion the creation of the first socialist state, The Union of Soviet Socialist Republics (USSR), or the Soviet Union. The Party's expressed goal was to achieve the communist utopia that Karl Marx and Frederich Engels envisioned in their *Communist Manifesto* more than half a century earlier. Lenin's triumphant return from exile following the fall of the Tsarist regime and the ascendance of the Bolsheviks heralded a new era that promised the liberation of oppressed workers and peasants as well as equality, advancement, peace, and social justice for all. The actual political system that emerged, of course, diverged radically from that utopian dream. What materialized instead was one of the most closed, repressive, and unequal—not to mention violent—regimes the world has ever known. Politically and economically, Russia's communist system dominated, often violently, both its own people and those of the empire that it controlled. It ultimately served as a model for all communist regimes that arose around the world during the twentieth century.

For a half century after World War Two, the Soviet Union and the United States occupied opposing positions in a bipolar international system: two superpowers balancing power in a cold war, which if it had turned hot, would likely have had terrifying global consequences. And then, suddenly and shockingly, both the Soviet Empire and the Soviet Union itself disintegrated, and communism dissolved as a meaningful ideal for other revolutionary leaders.[1]

If we wish to understand the difficulty that postcommunist leaders had in trying to achieve their goals after the fall of communism, we must first grasp the essential impact that the Soviet system had and how its legacy continues to affect the politics and the people of Russia. Soviet political development was a standard course in undergraduate and graduate political science programs for much of the 20th century, and textbooks and readers abound that reflect divergent ways of understanding the Soviet Union. In the most general sense, the Western view of the Soviet Union is split in half. Until the late 1950s, the vast majority of studies described the Soviet Union as a rigid monolith, a violent totalitarian state lacking in dynamism and flexibility.[2] By the 1960s, a shift began with increasing portrayals of the Soviet Union as responsive, flexible and inclusive.[3] The reality, of course, lay somewhere in between. There can be no doubt whatsoever that, upon Stalin's death in 1952, the level of internal violence decreased, terror eased, and a quiet stability of bureaucratic rule accurately described the day-to-day political atmosphere.[4] Yet, this in no way negates the fact that the gulag prison system, rule by fear, and the arbitrary application of that rule all remained as central features of Soviet power.

As a general overview, Soviet political history from 1917 to 1991 may safely be categorized into distinct periods. The early years of 1917 to 1921 was the revolutionary period, when the new Bolshevik regime, headed by Lenin, was focused on securing Communist Party control over the vast Russian territory while defeating counterrevolutionary movements during the Civil War. At the same time, the new radicals in power experimented with the rapid introduction of some of their most utopian ideas during this period of "War Communism," including abolishing money, mostly with disastrous results. The result was chaos; some areas were plagued by famine, others by virtual anarchy, while others felt the first hints of a crushingly oppressive dictatorship that would eventually consume the entire country.

The wreckage of War Communism led to what historians consider a tactical retreat by Lenin and the Party in a pragmatic series of policies designed to restore stability and growth. These were known as the New Economic Policy (NEP). The backtracking from radical Marxist ideas in these years, which provided the ideological basis for a future period of reform in the late 1980s, encouraged entrepreneurial innovation in an effort to jump-start economic growth and development. The NEP lasted only a few years, however.

Lenin's untimely death in 1924 sparked a violent internal leadership struggle during which Stalin engineered a series of purges, first against the left wing of the Party and then against the right wing, ultimately leaving himself at the top of the Party and state as the unchallenged, supreme leader. While one can identify various policy initiatives, such as revolution from above, collectivization and industrialization (1927–1932), the Great Terror (1932–1938), World War II (1939–1945), and late Stalinism (1945–1953), it is fair to refer to the entire period from 1927 to 1953 as Stalinism. As McAuley summarizes, Stalinism featured the institution of an enormous and overlapping party–state bureaucratic apparatus, a command economy, a pervasive secret police, and a personality cult around the supreme leader overseeing arbitrary rule. The *mature* Stalinist system was an administrative-command structure encompassing all of these features consolidated during Stalin's rule, and it remained fairly stable through the early 1980s.[5]

However, the system underwent important changes from the perspective of the Soviet people both inside and outside the Communist Party apparatus. Nikita Khrushchev's Secret Speech in 1956, which exposed and denounced many of the crimes committed under Stalin, opened a thaw in Soviet internal politics, prompting a period of de-Stalinization and relaxing of terror. While there were swings between openness and retreat, innovation and conservatism, the period from Khrushchev's ascension to Brezhnev's death was a period of stability under the administrative-command system of the Soviet socialist state, which political scientist Seweryn Bialer has masterfully detailed. It was also a period of great technological advancement with the advent of the space age, the emergence of the global reach of Soviet power, and the height of the Cold War.

Even during periods of relative openness, however, it is a reasonable characterization that, at least from Stalin's consolidation of power in the late 1920s through the mid-1980s, the party–state apparatus tolerated no opposition to or deviation from the "correct line" as established by the Party leadership on any given issue at any given time. Through its Central Committee organizations and approved by the apex of power in the Politburo, the Communist Party of the Soviet Union (CPSU) dictated the "truth" that was compulsory for all.[6] From economic output parameters established in the central plans to the maintenance of tight censorship of a wide range of subjects in all media, the Soviet Union was, in many aspects, an inflexible and highly controlled society in which a pervasive secret police enforced adherence to the directives from on high. A rigid, vertical power structure culminating with the General Secretary of the Communist Party yielded clear lines of authority, and those above wielded myriad sources of power over those at levels below in enforcing order. Fear pervaded society from arbitrary application of those rules, which could change at any time. An atomized society was the result.

It is these general aspects that support the totalitarian image of the nature of Soviet power from at least Stalin's consolidation of power until the very last years of the regime. It was not, however, the only image of the USSR in the scholarly community.[7] From roughly the time of the internal political thaw under Nikita S. Khrushchev in the late 1950s, a contending image saw the post-Stalin Soviet Union as a modern political system, striving to meet the needs of a people while maintaining internal stability in the context of the Cold War competition. Such approaches emphasized the degree to which the regime was flexible, allowed for upward mobility and opportunity, and met the needs of the people. It focused on achievements from the dramatic, as in the first explosion of a hydrogen bomb and winning the race to outer space, to the mundane, as in the expansion of availability of and improvements in quality of consumer goods, or to put it differently, in the degree to which it was able to put food on the table.

Much of the basis for these judgments about the internal stability and strength of the Soviet Union, we now know, relied heavily upon Soviet economic data, which in fact, proved to be wildly unreliable. Party and state functionaries had enormous incentives to "cook the books" in ways that suggested growth and efficiency, thereby masking gross inefficiencies and flaws in the command economy. Nevertheless, it is absolutely the case that few scholars saw deep-seated instability and fragility in the regime in the mid-1980s. Most were impressed with the "sources of stability," to use Bialer's phrase, as evidenced by these military, scientific, and other achievements.

Regardless of the lens through which scholars viewed the regime, all described an overlapping party–state bureaucracy with duplication in every sphere. Where there was a government ministry for agriculture, there was a Party Central Committee Department for the same. Indeed, for every sector of activity, whether mining, forestry, heavy and light industry, etc., in the economy or the press, youth, the arts, etc., in social affairs, there existed a CPSU department and a government ministry to establish and implement the correct line at all times. At every factory, publishing house, theater, etc., the KGB "Fourth Department" officer monitored compliance and behavior—cast the shadow of fear that ensured order throughout society. Such was the design of the mature Stalinist system that long outlived its namesake and was replicated in every Soviet client state as well. It set the rules and maintained compliance over the vast majority of activities affecting the vast majority of individuals in the vast majority of circumstances. And, lest we forget, it was the system that cast so much fear over the West for its perceived successes and achievements, indeed its perceived superiority, in terms of internal stability, economic growth, and scientific and military advancement.

The Soviet Union was a serious challenger ideologically, politically, militarily, and economically to the democratic–capitalist West throughout most of the 20th century. It projected power globally, with aspirations for expansion that were every bit as universal as those of the United States and a conviction every bit as strong that the system was ideal for people everywhere. The system was built on lofty revolutionary ideals, and the implementation of those ideals was understood as an experiment whose success would generate emulation, much as the founders of the United States understood their project in the late eighteenth century.

The selections that follow provide a brief overview of Soviet political history, of the system of fear that so uniquely characterized the political system, and of the nature of Soviet stability, which most scholars saw in the 1980s, that made the collapse at the end of that decade such a shock to many. The chapter by Mary McAuley is the introduction to her masterfully concise synopsis of Soviet political history. Anyone wishing to have a basic knowledge of that empire ought to read her *Soviet Politics 1917–1991*, which consists of her lectures in her Introduction to Soviet Politics course at Oxford. The introduction included here elaborates on the periods suggested above, with more background. The second selection is from Merle Fainsod's classic, *How Russia is Ruled*. His student, Jerry Hough, in the 1980s, transformed this book, preserving his mentor as coauthor, in *How the Soviet Union Is Governed*. The difference in approach was fundamental; it was truly a different book. Fainsod's was the most widely read and the most thorough approach to Soviet politics in the totalitarian school. Any number of sections would have served to convey the essence of that approach. His chapter on terror, however, serves best to demonstrate both how the political system was constructed and how fear played such an essential role to its operation both within the Party and throughout society. Fear was the backbone, and in describing the backbone, Fainsod also portrays the body. The reader will need to read between the lines a bit to get the full picture or get a hold of Fainsod's book and read more. Finally, Bialer's chapter on Soviet stability details how the political system functioned through the two decades prior to Gorbachev's introduced fundamental reforms. Fear remained, but terror was gone, and the system settled in. Even those who anticipated change with a new generation of leaders were compelled, as was Bialer, by the resilience, the success, and the future stability of the Soviet political system. His was the dominant view in the mid-1980s, and reading his chapter today is essential to understanding the effect Gorbachev had and in evaluating Gorbachev as a leader. One must conclude that the Soviet collapse was hardly preordained!

For Further Reference

Books

Seweryn Bialer, *The Soviet Paradox*, Knopf: 1987.

Seweryn Bialer, *Stalin's Successors*, Cambridge University Press: 1980.

Robert Conquest, *The Great Terror*, Oxford University Press: 1991.

Sheila Fitzpatrick, *The Russian Revolution*, Oxford University Press: 1982.

Geoffrey Hosking, *The First Socialist Society: A History of the Soviet Union*, Harvard University Press: 1992.

Peter Kenez, *A History of the Soviet Union from the Beginning to the End*, Cambridge University Press: 2006.

Mary McAuley, *Soviet Politics 1917–1991*, Oxford University Press: 1992.

Roy Medvedev, *Let History Judge*, Columbia University Press: 1989.

Novels

Arthur Koestler, *Darkness at Noon,* Bantam: 1984.

Boris Pasternak, *Doctor Zhivago,* Vintage: 1957.

Anatoli Rybakov, *Children of the Arbat*, Little Brown & Co: 1988.

Alexander Solzhenitsyn, *One Day in the Life of Ivan Denisovich*, Farrar, Straus and Giroux: 2005

Films

Battleship Potemkin
Burnt by the Sun
East/West
Kommisar

NOTES

1. The best, and most concise, political history of the Soviet Union remains Mary McAuley's *Soviet Politics 1917–1991* (Oxford University Press, 1992).

2. As a leading example, see Merle Fainsod, *How Russia is Ruled* (Harvard University Press, 1963). Also Philip Selznick, *The Organizational Weapon: A Study of Bolshevik Strategy and Tactics* (The Rand Corporation, 1952); T. H. Rigby, "Politics in the Mono-Organizational Society," in *Authoritarian Politics in Communist Europe* (University of California Berkeley, 1976); and Carl J. Friedrich and Zbigniew Brzezinski, *Totalitarian Dictatorship and Autocracy* (Praeger, 1961).

3. Jerry Hough rewrote and retitled Fainsod's account, though preserving him as a coauthor, in *How the Soviet Union is Governed* (Harvard University Press, 1979). Also see Sewereyn Bialer, *Stalin's Successors* (Cambridge University Press, 1980).

4. Ken Jowitt describes this *routinization* in *New World Disorder* (University of California Press, 1992).

5. See Bialer, "The Mature Stalinist System," in *Stalin's Successors.*

6. I still find the best explication of the correct line and its role in Soviet rule to be Jowitt, *New World Disorder*, pp. 8–11.

7. George Breslauer has published a thought-provoking postmortem on the field of sovietology, laying out the main trends and the strengths and weakness of those trends. See his "In Defense of Sovietology," *Post-Soviet Affairs,* Vol. 8, No. 3 (October–December 1992), pp. 197–238.

1.1

Introduction

Mary McCauley

In January 1917 the Russian Empire stretched from Vladivostok in the east to Poland in the west, from the frozen Arctic Circle down to the arid lands of Central Asia. A population of roughly 125 million inhabited the huge continent, a population whose dominant group of Slavs, centred in Russia and the Ukraine, had spread out east and southwards to all parts of the Empire. More than 100 different nationalities—Armenians, Innuits, Germans, and Kazakhs, to name but a few—lived within its boundaries and, in terms of religion, Orthodox Russians were joined by Muslims in the south, Lutherans and Catholics in the west. Eighty per cent of the population were peasants, and illiterate. By the turn of the century, however, and certainly by January 1917, industry had made its appearance; the railways had spread their network across the country, large industrial centres and huge shipyards employed both skilled and raw unskilled labour, and modern technology was operating alongside wheelbarrows. The country was ruled by Tsar Nicholas II, whose brutal autocratic regime was supported by an aristocracy happier speaking French than Russian, by the army with its smart officer corps, and by the Russian Orthodox Church. Rule was carried out through the state bureaucracy centred in St Petersburg, the capital of the Empire, and in the provinces governors ruled with the help of the army, and new local government institutions.

In February 1917 Tsarism collapsed, brought down when the soldiers joined the women protesting in the bread queues. Nine months of turmoil followed. Revolution gathered speed as social and economic conflict deepened; an attempt to replace the old Tsarist autocratic regime with constitutional rule ended with the Bolsheviks taking power in the capital, and the revolution spread across the country. The Bolsheviks, a working-class party with a small group of intellectuals among its leadership, came to power in the major industrial centres with the support of the rank and file soldiers and the industrial workers. They, as a socialist party, were committed to replacing private ownership with social ownership, and to a society of equality run by workers and peasants, a society without coercion and without a legal system because crime would be no more. Freedom, creativity, and science would be its hallmarks, religion would fade away, and new forms of

---

Source: Mary McCauley, "Introduction," *Soviet Politics,* 1917–1991. Oxford University Press, 1992. 1–11.

Note: Notes and references have been removed from this article.

art and culture would emerge. A new international morality would inform the socialist world order from which war would disappear.

In Western eyes Russia in January 1917 was a primitive sleeping giant, a force to be reckoned with, a Great Power with whom alliances should be made, but a sadly illiberal regime who, it was hoped, might one day move towards a more enlightened form of government. With the coming to power of the Bolsheviks, Western opinion divided. The established governments were fearful: if Bolshevik aims were realized, it was the end of the system of power, privilege, and wealth which existed in Western society. This was a time when the upper classes were looking nervously over their shoulders at their own working classes as they too, began to claim their rights. In England wealthy members of society put their jewels in strong-boxes in Brighton so that they could move across the Channel to safer places should the revolution occur in London, Liverpool, or Manchester. The Western press portrayed the Bolsheviks as inhuman monsters, and stressed the Jewish origins of their leaders, and their unnatural ideas. But if unnatural, then came the argument that the ideals were unrealizable, and that here was a hopeless experiment bound to fail. This view was held initially by members of the old order inside Russia too. Very different was the response from the labour movement in the West, a response which resulted in a split within its ranks. Some saw the Bolsheviks as the standard-bearers of socialism and thereafter gave their support to the (Bolshevik) Communist Party in the Soviet Union; others were far more sceptical or hostile.

Let us now jump twenty years to November 1937. What did Russia look like in 1937 and what of the aims and hopes of 1917? A new Union of Soviet Socialist Republics had replaced the original Russian Empire, but it was still a single social-ist state, ringed by a circle of hostile capitalist countries. Private ownership had gone. Whether we are talking of industry, now under nationalized state owner-ship, of retail trade and services, or of agriculture where collective (co-operative) and state farms had replaced family farms, private ownership of productive assets was no more. But far from withering away, the state had grown: a huge central-ized state machine, consisting of commissariats (as the ministries were called)—for heavy industry, defence, education, justice—operated out of the new capital, Moscow. In place of that dream of popular participation, of an end to bureaucracy and hierarchy, there were state institutions, run on a hierarchical basis, issuing orders and instructions to the industrial enterprises and the institutions which themselves were organized on the basis of one-man management. The soviets, the councils elected by workers and peasants and soldiers, although they existed in name, had long ceased to be active bodies running local affairs. In 1935 a new Constitution was announced which gave pride of place to a legislature called the Supreme Soviet. On paper its provisions looked remarkably like those of a Western constitution: a federal system of eleven republics (each based on a key language group), with direct elections of deputies to the Supreme Soviet on the basis of universal suffrage. But the elections were not envisaged as elections between competing parties; rather the electorate turned out to cast their votes for a single candidate in each constituency, thus reaffirming their support for the order in which they were living, and the federal arrangements masked a system in which all key decisions, both on policy and personnel, were made in Moscow.

The key political institution in 1937 was the Communist Party and in particular its apparatus, an inner core of full-time party functionaries, directed from Moscow, and controlling all the republics. They were the ones with an authoritative voice, with the power to issue orders which were obligatory for all. By 1937, however, the party apparatus was under threat from the NKVD, the People's Commissariat for Internal Affairs, the secret police. The year 1937 saw the height of the Great Purges—terror, show trials, arrests of old Bolsheviks, of new commissars, members of the new élite, and of the general public. The Gulag, a network of labour camps, stretched across the country. And, standing above the Communist Party apparatus, the large state bureaucracy, and the NKVD, was the figure of Stalin, cloaked in an extraordinary cult of the wise leader—Stalin to whom hymns were sung, Stalin whose light burned in the little Kremlin window so that the citizens of Moscow would know that the great leader was always awake, always thinking and caring about them.

What though of society in 1937? Here the picture is a confusing one. On the one hand there was rapid social mobility: hundreds of thousands, even millions of peasants and industrial workers, of society's poor, had obtained an education and moved up to office-work, to positions of authority, and management. By 1937 there were factory directors who in 1917 had been apprentices, there were women who had escaped from the drudgery of home and sweat-shop, and become engineers, architects, doctors, and NKVD officials. This mobility, however, had been accompanied by a gradual reimposition, the reintroduction of hierarchy and privilege. By 1937 an élite had emerged with access to scarce goods, new apartments, and special shops. But this was only part of the picture. The campaign to collectivize the countryside from 1929 to 1932 had resulted in the deaths of millions of peasants, and millions more of the urban population were now in the camps. For some the 1930s meant achievement, a life their parents could never have dreamed of; for others, the old intellectuals, it was a time of confusion and anxiety; and for many of all strata it brought death in the labour camps.

Western attitudes were still divided between those who now saw the Soviet Union as the promised land and those who were more sceptical. For some everything that took place in Soviet Russia was good, a new civilization had taken root. But even their conservative opponents were much more positive than they had been twenty years earlier. The quality press referred approvingly to 'the sensible Mr. Stalin', who was perceived as greatly preferable to such heady and foolish Bolsheviks as Lenin and Trotsky. Mr Stalin had introduced a Constitution, brought Russia into the League of Nations, and, probably the most important factor, Russia was a potential bulwark against Fascism, and Hitler's Germany.

Forty years later takes us to 1977. In the intervening period the Second World War had devastated the western part of the country, and 20 million had died. From 1917 through to 1945 the whole period was one of trauma, of death, of tragedy, turmoil, and headlong speed. It was followed by an unprecedented period of peace, and social calm. By 1977 there were still 100 nationalities, speaking different languages, in a population of more than 260 million, of whom more than half now lived in towns. The old peasant society had yielded to an industrial one. In the previous twenty years, from 1957 to 1977, huge strides in education, in health, and housing had been made, and in the standard of living in general. Those years saw a rapid improvement in the provision of consumer durables and also in the food supply. But the pattern of provision did not reflect that found, even twenty years earlier, in the industrialized West. The Soviet Union still had a very large agricultural sector and a very inefficient one, short on skill and technology. Lacking a transport system, lacking storage facilities, even a good harvest did not guarantee food in the shops. There were no supermarkets, few cars, no shopping centres of the kind which dotted Europe and North America. It was still a society in which one sent jam made from berries picked in the forest through the post to relatives in other parts of the country who might not have any sugar in the winter. Industry had its advanced sectors, particularly in the military sphere, but also a pool of poorly qualified, unskilled labour, and by 1977 the technology gap with the West was no longer closing. This meant, for example, that a Soviet fridge might need seven times as much electricity to run as its Western counterpart, that a pair of spectacles was twice as heavy to wear. In terms of quality, new products, and technological performance, Soviet industry by 1977 was falling behind. The catching up process was slowing down. Militarily, however, by 1977 the Soviet Union had obtained parity with the United States: it was one of two superpowers. And not only that. It was now the dominant figure in the world Communist-movement, flanked to the east by the Communist Party states of Eastern Europe, to the west by the Chinese republic (albeit a difficult socialist relation), and courted by Third World countries.

What kind of a political system existed in 1977? Political authority rested with the Communist Party of the Soviet Union: the single political Party that was allowed, as stated in the new Constitution of 1977, to be the leading political organization in society. The General Secretary of the party, and also head of state, was Leonid Brezhnev, a cautious politician, who had made the Politburo, the leading party organ, into the cabinet of the system. This small body of leading party officials and ministers, chaired by the General Secretary, and staffed by the party Secretariat, took the key policy decisions. Thereafter the party apparatus of full-time officials, stretching from the Secretariat down to the localities, was responsible for ensuring that the appropriate state institutions executed the decisions emanating from the centre. The mass membership of the party now stood at approximately 16 million; many of its members' views were indistinguishable from those of non-members but they were obliged to carry out the instructions and decisions taken by the higher party organizations. Many worked, in different capacities, in the huge state apparatus which was growing visibly year by year, as ever more institutions, ministries, and state committees encrusted the overblown centre of the empire. Coercion was still there, but in the background rather than to the fore. The KGB was still responsible for surveillance and control but it was no longer operating a system of terror, of arbitrary arrest and repression. By 1977 citizens knew what was and was not permissible.

We are talking then of a highly centralized system of political control over all major activities, the economy, the media, and social activities. The key values of the system, by 1977, had become those of patriotism, stability, and order. As an example, let us take the initiation ceremony at which 9-year-old children joined the Young Pioneers, the youth organization. They would be given their red ties, their little badges of Lenin, and, during the ceremony, introduced to individuals who represented the heroes of Soviet society, past and present. The person they would have wished most of all to have present was, of course, Lenin. By then he was a sacred figure, the father figure, the person who had made the revolution and made life ever better for children not only in the Soviet Union but throughout the world. Given this was impossible, it was desirable to find an old Bolshevik, someone who had known Lenin, preferably someone who had touched him, at the least someone who had seen him and would be able to tell the children what he or she had thought and felt on hearing Lenin speak. A second individual would be a veteran of the Second World War, someone who had defended the motherland and who could talk of the fight against the fascists, and a third would be a hero of socialist labour, a worker with an outstanding production record. Ideally he or she would be a *young* hero of socialist labour whose father or mother and grandparents before that had worked in the same factory—the representative of a labour dynasty. Here then were three figures signifying the system: Lenin—the revolution; the war veteran—patriotism; and a hero of socialist labour—the working class.

Western attitudes were by now far more ambivalent, both those of the establishment and those within the labour movement. The Soviet Union had been an ally in the Second World War, but then came the Cold War, and the spread of Communism throughout the world. In the 1950s the American public could still be swayed by anti-Communist hysteria, while Communist candidates won elections in Europe. But Khrushchev's denunciation of Stalin's dictatorship in 1956, the Soviet government's use of force in Hungary in 1956 and Czechoslovakia in 1968, and the United States' inability to portray, even to itself, the Vietnam war as a fight for freedom, made the old convictions less secure. The 1970s saw *détente* and new co-operation between the world's two great nuclear powers, but civil rights still dogged the agenda. As ideological passion gave way to cautious conservatism in the Soviet Union, so in the West defenders and critics voiced their convictions less stridently. The European Communist parties began to distance themselves from Moscow and when, in the 1980s, Ronald Reagan tried to re-create 'the evil empire' the theme had little resonance, even in the United States.

In 1988, as Reagan left the White House, the Soviet Union had an energetic new Communist Party leader, Mikhail Gorbachev, who was speaking out on the need for economic and political reform, but no major changes had yet taken place. Brezhnev, who died in 1982, would have disapproved of many of Gorbachev's statements, and counselled against such rash adventurism, but he would have recognized the system as the one he knew. By the end of 1991, within the space of three years, both his and Gorbachev's world had gone for ever, with momentous and unpredictable consequences not only for the peoples of the Soviet Union but for the world as a whole.

It was not simply that what had appeared to be a stable, authoritarian regime in an increasingly conservative society found itself forced to adapt to unexpected pressures for change, but that the political system fell apart, the empire disintegrated, and the economy collapsed. Even arrangements that had pre-dated the revolution of 1917 bit the dust. It was not just that the countries of Eastern Europe gained their independence, and the Baltic states which had been incorporated into the Soviet Union at the time of the Second World War became sovereign states, but that, on the territory of the original Russian Empire which had formed the basis for the subsequent Union of Soviet Socialist Republics, a new Commonwealth of sovereign states was announced. When the heir to the Tsarist throne, Grand Duke Vladimir, flew in from Paris in November 1991 for the celebrations to mark the renaming of Leningrad as St Petersburg, he arrived in a Russia which no longer ruled the Ukraine, Georgia, Armenia, and those lands of Central Asia which had belonged to his forefathers. These new sovereign states now had popularly elected parliaments or presidents, some of whom, such as Yeltsin in Russia and Kravchuk in the Ukraine were old Communist Party politicians, while others, such as Gamsakhurdia in Georgia (shortly to be ousted by force) or Landsbergis in Lithuania, were 'dissidents' or newcomers to politics. The Communist Party of the Soviet Union had been dissolved, and its republican organizations banned in most republics.

As political authority had slipped away, during 1990 and 1991, from the central institutions to the republics, and the Communist Party lost its power and position, the centre had grown weaker and weaker. By August 1991 there was a black hole: a President with the power to issue decrees that were not implemented, left only with control over the still centralized means of coercion, the military, KGB, and Ministry of Internal Affairs, although the degree of central control over the latter two was already in doubt. An attempted coup by some of Gorbachev's ministers sought to reimpose some kind of control over a territory, the old Empire, in which central political authority had evaporated. With its failure the republican governments began, in keeping with their political autonomy, to claim the responsibility for the defence of their territories. The nakedness of the Presidency became all too apparent: the existence of the nuclear arsenal its only remaining rationale. By December 1991 both the Presidency and other central institutions had been wound up, and the question of who should control the armed forces came to the fore.

The breakneck political change was not accompanied by economic reform and, as the centrally planned economy broke down and failed to provide the goods, the central government printed more money and raised wages, while the economy spiralled ever downwards. With the abolition of the centre, the new republican governments became responsible for those resources that traditionally came under the jurisdiction of the central ministries, and for the worsening economic situation. All that had been agreed by the end of 1991, and to varying degrees by the different republican governments, was that state ownership and central planning must be replaced by some kind of a private-ownership market system if their economies were ever going to compete with the advanced industrial countries of east and west.

The key resources of the media were no longer centrally controlled, indeed they were hardly controlled at all. In liberal democratic systems the degree of state control and censorship varies, as does the control over editorial policy by those who own radio, television companies, and the press. But in the Soviet Union, as central government control began to slip, an extraordinary situation developed in which those who spoke for the media became responsible to no one but themselves. They still drew their salaries because the bureaucratic state machine still trundled on; the constraints were those of the availability of paper and of equipment, and the whims of producers, the journalists themselves, and, for local media, the local authorities. Soviet television became perhaps the freest medium in the world.

If 1917 saw a revolution that changed the face of the world for the next fifty years, 1989–91 witnessed a phenomenon of equal significance: the disintegration, in the space of three years, of probably the most powerful empire the world has known. The world Communist movement, the movement whose aim had been to bury capitalism, was no more. It is too early even to guess the repercussions. We suggested earlier that Western reactions to 1917, to Stalinism, and to the

Soviet Union under Brezhnev had varied, and were strongly influenced by factors in the home environment. The reader might like to pause, and consider why the press and the politicians of the late 1980s adopted the positions they did towards the reform process, and the collapse of Communist Party rule. Are Western perceptions in 1990 any better informed than those of 1917, and what are the interests involved? A concern for democracy and human rights, or for strategic weapons and the balance of power in the world, fear of the repercussions of economic chaos, or the chance to plunder the rich resources of a huge continent? How will a future generation assess the West's reaction to the end of Communist Party rule? One thing is for certain: the collapse owed nothing to the politics of Western powers (technological progress was perhaps a different matter), but the continued support for the Gorbachev leadership may have accentuated the economic crisis and therefore contributed to the subsequent political instability.

Our aim is to try to make sense of the developments since 1985: to show how and why the system fell apart. This requires an understanding of the historical context of the drama, and of the Soviet political system, and also of the way in which, more generally, political change occurs. What is the relationship between economic development (or stagnation) and political change, if any? Do social change or cultural traditions influence political outcomes? Why *does* political change occur? Do key individuals play a part under some circumstances, and, if so, which? Explanations differ, sometimes dramatically.

How then should we begin? We want to arrive at a position from which we can analyse and understand recent and current political developments in what was the Soviet Union. It will help if we bear in mind certain key factors that are relevant to the establishment and maintenance of political regimes in the modern world. Politics, it is often said, is about the exercise of power within society. But such a statement is too broad: there are many kinds of power we would not want to describe as political. It is better to think in terms of a particular type of power: that associated with *ruling*, with the ability to determine the rules for a society, and to back up their implementation with force, if need be. Authority and control of the means of coercion are the key attributes of rulers. That does not mean that there are not instances when those in control possess nothing but their weapons, but this is an unstable basis for rule because the *right* to rule, the authority of those in power, is not recognized. Hence rulers are anxious to acquire authority, which may rest on different bases: it may, for example, be seen as God given, to stem from tradition, or from an election. This has the consequence that those who possess political power are always sharply observant of those who control the means of communication, of culture and education: in older times the Church, today the media and education. They may be content to observe, to intervene at the edges, if their authority is not threatened; they may move in to censor or take over.

Similarly they will be concerned with the use of economic resources. If the rulers are to maintain an army to defend the territory against outsiders and order within it (perhaps their basic task), they need to raise taxes; they may also decide they require revenue to provide themselves with the lifestyle to which they feel entitled, or to carry out certain projects. Now a poor economy not only provides a weak tax base, but is likely to increase the discontent of those who have to pay. Hence economic prosperity is desirable, and even more desirable if the rulers acquire the obligation to provide education or welfare. They may well feel the need to strike a delicate balance between allowing those who own and dispose of the economic resources to exploit them as they wish, and ensuring that the consequences do not create a level of social discontent that jeopardizes their own safety as rulers. Hence those who control the political resources (authority and coercion) will be very aware of those who control economic resources and may, for different reasons, move in to share or limit the rights of ownership.

There are then resources which provide those who possess them with power: the means of coercion, the attribute of authority, control of knowledge and ideas, the ownership of economic resources. Control over the means of coercion is the most important because it will decide the outcome of an issue if it cannot be resolved by other means; it is the most powerful resource of all. In analysing political regimes we take that for granted, then turn our attention to the relationships between the holders of political office (and authority), the citizenry, and those who 'own' and control the other key resources. These will determine the key contours of the state—society relationship. Coercion, authority, economic resources, and the means of communication all featured in the thumbnail sketches of 1917, 1937, 1977, and 1991, and the changing relationship between them will run like a motif through the following chapters.

If a major objective is to make sense of developments in the Soviet Union as *perestroika* turned into the collapse of Communist Party rule, the other is to cast light on the extraordinary period 1917–91 as a whole. There was a revolution, the creation of a new state, an unprecedented experiment at crash industrialization and social mobility, a dictatorship and mass terror, its replacement by a system of conservative state control, and then the swift collapse of the state, the end of empire, and embryonic attempts to create a new political order, All pose interesting and difficult problems of analysis in their own right. All raise important political issues. To mention but two: what are the causes and consequences of terror, and what are the pre-conditions for the establishment and maintenance of a democratic order? As we shall see, there are no easy answers. The chapters that follow, while providing a minimal narrative account of the political history of the period, each address a different and important political topic. We begin with revolution.

1.2

Terror as a System of Power

Merle Fainsod

Every totalitarian regime makes some place for terror in its system of controls. Whether exercised on a massive scale by a Stalin or held in reserve by a Khrushchev, an awareness of its potentialities conditions the behavior of the totalitarian subject. Under Stalin, the pervasive fear of the informer and the secret police made the air heavy with suspicion and distrust. Under Khrushchev, Soviet citizens breathe and talk more freely, but the knowledge that the police remain vigilant serves as a brake on those who remember the past.

This does not mean that coercion is the only method by which a totalitarian regime maintains itself in power. Loyalty and devotion must also be elicited. The skillful totalitarian dictator weaves a complex web of controls in which social pressures and incentives have their appointed places and indoctrination plays a key role. Agitation and propaganda may rally fanatic support, and appeals to self-interest may enlist the energies of the ambitious and bind their fortunes to the regime. When discontent accumulates, "loyalty" to the regime may be consolidated by providing scapegoats on whom frustrated aggression may exhaust itself. The shrewd totalitarian dictatorship may go further and permit ventilation of grievances of a nonpolitical and nonorganized character. It may even institutionalize such expression as the Soviet dictatorship does when it sanctions criticism of bureaucratic malpractice or inefficiency. Such criticism may play a constructive role in strengthening the regime since it accomplishes the triple function of draining off aggression on the part of its subjects, prodding the bureaucracy to improve its performance, and sustaining the belief that the supreme leadership is genuinely concerned about popular complaints and vexations.

Yet ultimately the totalitarian dictatorship must depend on terror to safeguard its monopoly of power. The instrument of terror can always be found, ready for use when needed, operative, above all, even when not visible by the mere fact that it is known to exist. Because the totalitarian regime provides no legitimate channel for

---

Source: Merle Fainsod, "Terror as a System of Power," *How Russia is Ruled.* Harvard University Press, 1963. 421–462.

Note: Notes and references have been removed from this article.

the expression of political dissent, its constant concern is to prevent or eliminate its illegal existence. To accomplish this purpose, it recruits its specialists in surveillance and espionage and uses fear as a political weapon. The task of the secret police is to serve as the eyes and ears of the dictator, to perform a prophylactic as well as a punitive function. It must not only hear what people say; it must also be prepared to diagnose their souls and plumb their innermost thoughts. It must transform every citizen into a potential watchdog and informer, not merely to paralyze the activities of "imperialist agents," but also to uncover "unstable Soviet people who have erred and fallen under alien influence." It must, as N. Mironov, the head of the Central Committee Department of Administrative Organs, put it, "rear Soviet people in a spirit of revolutionary vigilance," for only vigilance can be trusted to protect the regime against those who seek to "harm" and "undermine" it.

The Defense of Terror

The practice of totalitarian terror generates its own underlying theoretical justifications. The role of terror in Communist ideology furnishes a prime example. Violence is accepted as implicit in the class struggle. As Lenin said in defending the dissolution of the Constituent Assembly, "Violence when it is committed by the toiling and exploited masses is the kind of violence of which we approve." This instrumental attitude toward violence prepares the way for its sanctification when employed by the Party in the name of the working class and by the Party leadership in the name of the Party.

The rationalization of terror embraces two central propositions. The first emphasizes the safety of the revolution as the supreme law. In the words of Lenin, "The Soviet Republic is a fortress besieged by world capital . . From this follows our right and our duty to mobilize the whole population to a man for the war." The second emphasizes the intransigence of the enemies of the revolution, the necessity of crushing them completely if the revolution itself is not to be destroyed. "What is the 'nutritive medium',," asks Lenin,

> which engenders counterrevolutionary enterprises, outbreaks, conspiracies, and so forth? . . . It is the medium of the bourgeoisie, of the bourgeois intelligentsia, of the kulaks in the countryside, and, everywhere, of the "non-Party public, as well as of the Socialist Revolutionaries and the Mensbeviks. We must treble our watch over this medium, we must multiply it tenfold. We must multiply our vigilance, because counterrevolutionary attempts from this quarter are absolutely inevitable, precisely at the present moment and in the near future.

In essence, Stalin's defense of terror, delivered in an interview with visiting a foreign workers' delegation on November 5, 1927, covers much the same ground, though with notably less frankness. [. . .]

> . . . We are a country surrounded by capitalist states. The internal enemies of our revolution are the agents of the capitalists of all countries . . . In fighting against the enemies at home, we fight the counterrevolutionary elements of all countries . . .

> No, comrades, we do not wish to repeat the mistakes of the Parisian Communards. The GPU is necessary for the Revolution and will continue to exist to the terror of the enemies of the proletariat.

The real significance of Stalin's theory did not become fully manifest until the period of the Great Purge in the thirties. The liquidation of the Old Bolsheviks made it altogether clear that the salient role of terror in Stalinist ideology was to serve as a bulwark of defense for his own monopoly of Party leadership. Since this involved establishing a regime of terror within the Party, Stalin was faced with the problem of reconciling his innovation with the traditional notion that terror was reserved for the class enemy. The problem was neatly and ruthlessly solved by identifying any form of opposition to Stalin with counterrevolution and foreign espionage. The formula of capitalist encirclement proved elastic enough to embrace the enemy inside the Party as well as the enemy outside. Stalin put it as follows:

> It should be remembered and never forgotten that as long as capitalist encirclement exists there will be wreckers, diversionists, spies, terrorists, sent behind the frontiers of the Soviet Union by the Intelligence services of foreign states . . .

> It should be explained to our Party Comrades that the Trotskyites, who represent the active elements in the diversionist, wrecking and espionage work of the foreign intelligence services . . . have already long ceased to serve any idea compatible with the interests of the working class, that they have turned into a gang of wreckers, diversionists, spies, assassins, without principles and ideas, working for the foreign intelligence services.

> It should be explained that in the struggle against contemporary Trotskyism not the old methods, the methods of discussion, must be used, but new methods, methods for smashing and uprooting it.

After the Great Purge, Stalin again faced the problem of reconciling the retention of these strong-arm methods with the claim that antagonistic classes had ceased to exist in the Soviet Union. In his report to the Eighteenth Party Congress in 1939,

Stalin addressed himself to the issue, "It is sometimes asked: We have abolished the exploiting classes: there are no longer any hostile classes in the country; there is nobody to suppress; hence there is no more need for the state; it must die away— Why then do we not help our socialist state to die away? . . . Is it not time we relegated the state to the museum of antiquities?" Again Stalin rested his case for the retention of the terror apparatus on the allegation of capitalist encirclement:

> These questions not only betray an underestimation of the capitalist encircle-
> ment, but also an underestimation of the role and significance of the bour-
> geois states and their organs, which send spies, assassins and wreckers into
> our country and are waiting for a favourable opportunity to attack it by
> armed force. They likewise betray an underestimation of the role and signifi-
> cance of our socialist state and of its military, punitive and intelligence organs,
> which are essential for the defense of the socialist land from foreign attack.

At the height of the purge in 1937, Stalin had sought to justify mass terror on the ground that the internal class struggle was becoming more and more acute as the Soviet Union moved toward socialism. Khrushchev condemned this theory in his secret speech to the Twentieth Party Congress, but he did not reject that part of Stalin's formulation which stressed the danger from without. "It must not be forgotten," Khrushchev declared, "that enemies have always tried and will go on trying to hinder the great work of building communism. The capitalist encirclement sent many spies and saboteurs into our country. It would be naive to suppose that our enemies will now give up their efforts to harm us in every way . . . We must therefore raise the revolutionary vigilance of the Soviet people and strengthen the state security agencies in every way." Addressing the Twenty-First Congress, he repeated: "The state security agencies, which direct their spearhead primarily against agents sent into the country by imperialist states, must be strengthened, as must other agencies which have the mission of blocking the provocational actions and intrigues of our enemies from the impe-rialist camp. Our enemies are spending enormous sums on subversive work against the socialist countries. How, then, can we abolish agencies which have the duty of safegarding the security of the socialist state! That would be foolish and criminal." Behind these latter-day rationalizations lies the conviction that the Soviet regime cannot dispense with surveillance, even though the mass inci-dence of terror has been greatly curbed.

The Creation of the Cheka

The genealogy of the Bolshevik terror apparatus reaches back to the first weeks after the seizure of power. In prerevolutionary days, the Bolsheviks had occasion to acquire an intimate familiarity with the operations of the Tsarist *Okhrana* or secret police; the lessons they learned then were later to be applied and amplified. [. . .] Workers, soldiers, and peasants were instructed to inform the Cheka "about organizations and individual persons whose activity is harmful to the Revolution." At the same time, a system of revolutionary tribunals was established to investigate and try offenses which bore the character of sabotage and counterrevolution. The judges of the revolutionary tribunals were to fix penalties in accordance with "the circumstances of the case and the dictates of the revolutionary conscience."

In the confusion of the first months of the Bolshevik Revolution, terror was far from being a monopoly of the specialists in terror. The Cheka was still in its organizational phase, and its regime was singularly mild compared with what was to come. Acts of violence against the bourgeoisie were common, but they were usually committed by revolutionary mobs and undisciplined sailors and soldiers and were not ordinarily officially authorized and inspired. The early death sentences of the Cheka were imposed on bandits and criminals. As the White forces began to rally their strength, the Cheka spread its net more widely and turned to sterner measures. On February 22, 1918, the Cheka ordered all local soviets "to seek out, arrest, and shoot immediately all members . . . connected in one form or another with counterrevolutionary organizations . . . (1) enemy agents and spies, (2) counterrevolutionary agitators, (3) speculators, (4) organizers of revolt . . . against the Soviet government, (5) those going to the Don to join the . . . Kaledin-Komilov band and the Polish counterrevolutionary legions, (6) buyers and sellers of arms to equip the counterrevolutionary bourgeoisie . . . all these are to be shot on the spot . . . when caught red-handed in the act."

The terror began to gather momentum. Gorky's newspaper *Novaya Zhizn'* (New Life) reported, "Executions continue. Not a day, not a night passes without several persons being executed." On the night of April 11, 1918, the Cheka staged a mass raid on anarchist centers in Moscow; several hundred were arrested and approximately thirty were killed while resisting arrest. Though the curve of Cheka activity was rising, its operations still remained on a limited scale.

The terror was given a sharp impetus by the effort of the Left SR's to seize power in Moscow soon after the assassination of German Ambassador Mirbach on July 6, 1918. Large-scale arrests of Left SR's followed, and at least thirteen were shot. As the punitive actions of the Cheka increased, the SR's replied in kind. On August 30, 1918, Uritsky, the head of the Petrograd Cheka, was assassinated, and Lenin was seriously wounded. The attacks on Uritsky and Lenin unleashed mass reprisals. In Petrograd alone, more than five hundred "counterrevolutionaries and White Guards" were immediately shot. The slaughter in Moscow included "many Tsarist ministers and a whole list of high personages."

The president of the Provincial Soviet of Penza reported, "For the murder from ambush of one comrade, Egorov, a Petrograd worker, the Whites paid with 152 lives. In the future firmer measures will be taken against the Whites." The prominent Chekist Latsis declared;

> We are no longer waging war against separate individuals, we are exterminating the bourgeoisie as a class. Do not seek in the dossier of the accused for proofs as to whether or not he opposed the soviet government by word or deed. The first question that should be put is to what class he belongs, of what extraction, what education and profession. These questions should decide the fate of the accused. Herein lie the meaning and the essence of the Red Terror.

The demonstrative massacres which followed the attack on Lenin were designed to strike fear into the hearts of all opponents of the Bolsheviks. The terror was mainly directed against the former nobility, the bourgeoisie, the landowners, the White Guards, and the clergy. But it was by no means confined to these groups. The SR's and Mensheviks, too, felt its sharp edge, and peasants who resisted the requisitioning of grain or who deserted from the Red Army were also among its victims. The Red Terror had its counterpart on the White side; the victims in this grim competition were numbered in the tens of thousands and perhaps hundreds of thousands.

As the Cheka broadened the scope of its activities, it also jealously resisted any interference with its claimed authority. Its tendency to set itself above and beyond the law aroused concern even in Bolshevik circles. At the Second All-Russian Conference of Commissars of Justice held in Moscow on July 2–6, 1918;

> Comrade Lebedev . . . pointed out that granting the necessity for the existence of the Extraordinary Commissions, it was nevertheless important to delimit their sphere of activity . . . Otherwise we shall have a state within a state, with the former tending to widen its jurisdiction more and more . . .

> Comrade Terastvatsaturov said that . . . in the provinces the question of the activities of the Extraordinary Commissions is a very acute one. The Commissions do everything they please . . . The president of our Cheka in Orel said: "I am responsible to no one; my powers are such that I can shoot anybody."

The reply of Krestinsky, the Commissar of Justice, emphasized the difficulty of imposing restraints on the Cheka. "So long as the Cheka functions," concluded

Krestinsky, "the work of justice must take a secondary place, and its sphere of activity must be considerably curtailed." The Cheka was vigorous and effective in asserting its prerogatives both against local soviet authorities and the Commissariat of Justice. The Chekist Peters put it bluntly, "In its activity the Cheka is completely independent, carrying out searches, arrests, shootings, afterwards making a report to the Council of People's Commissars and the Soviet Central Executive Committee."

After the end of the Civil War and the inauguration of the NEP, an effort was made to impose legal limits and restraints on Cheka operations. On the initiative of V. M. Smirnov, an Old Bolshevik of the Left Opposition, the Ninth Congress of Soviets, meeting in December 1921, adopted a resolution, which, after expressing gratitude for the "heroic work" of the Cheka "at the most acute moments of the Civil War," recommended that curbs be imposed on its powers.

The GPU

On February 8, 1922, the VTsIK (the All-Russian Central Executive Committee) issued a decree abolishing the Cheka and its local organs and transferring its functions to a newly created State Political Administration (GPU), which was to operate "under the personal chairmanship of the People's Commissar for Interior, or his deputy." The following tasks were assigned to it: "(a) Suppression of open counterrevolutionary outbreaks, including banditry; (b) Taking measures to prevent and combat espionage; (c) Guarding rail and water transport; (d) Political policing of the borders of the RSFSR; (e) Combating contraband and crossing of the borders of the republic without proper permission; (f) Executing special orders of the Presidium of the VTsIK or of the Sovnarkom for protecting the revolutionary order." Special army detachments were placed at the disposal of the GPU, and the field organization was made directly subordinate to the central GPU. Although the GPU was given full authority to undertake searches, seizures, and arrests, procedural restraints were imposed on it. Arrested prisoners were to be supplied with copies of their indictments not later than two weeks after their arrest. [. . .]

Although uneasiness over the arbitrary authority exercised by the GPU was widespread even in Party circles, Lenin was persuaded that the regime could not dispense with terror. On May 17, 1922, he wrote Kursky with reference to the Criminal Code, "The Courts must not do away with terror; to promise such a thing would be either to fool ourselves or other people." In the eyes of the Party leadership, the OGPU had become indispensable; its *de facto* authority to take summary action against enemies of the regime was a weapon which the regime showed no disposition to relinquish. [. . .]

During the NEP, most prisons and "corrective labor colonies" were outside the jurisdiction of the OGPU. The concentration camps directly administered by the OGPU were reserved for hardened criminals, so-called counterrevolutionaries, and politicals. The Northern Camps of Special Designation (SLON), of which the most notorious were located on the Solovetski Islands, formed the primary base of the OGPU detention network. According to one former inmate, in 1925 the Solovetski Monastery housed about 7,000 prisoners. "Two or three years later the prisoners totalled well over 20,000." Prisoners at first worked solely to meet camp needs. The system of large-scale exploitation of prison labor in lumbering, mining, and construction of public works had its antecedents in NEP experiments, but during the middle twenties its operations were still on a limited scale.

With the abandonment of the NEP and the decision to proceed with a program of rapid industrialization and agricultural collectivization, the OGPU began to play a much more prominent role. Its energies were concentrated on three targets: the Nepmen or private traders, who had been permitted to flourish under the NEP; the old intelligentsia, who were made the scapegoats for early failures and difficulties in the industrialization drive; and the kulaks, who offered active or passive opposition to the collectivization program. As a result of the cumulative impact of these campaigns, the OGPU became the intimate caretaker of the destinies of millions instead of tens of thousands.

The roundup and repression of the Nepmen assumed intensified form as the NEP period drew to a close. At the height of the NEP in 1924, the number of privately owned shops totaled 420,368. The proprietors of these shops became a special object of OGPU attention. There is no way of knowing precisely how many were incarcerated, how many were condemned to administrative exile, and how many succeeded in eluding the OGPU by shifting their occupations and disappearing into the anonymity of the rapidly expanding industrial labor force. Many were caught up in the drive which the OGPU spearheaded to accumulate gold and other sources of foreign exchange (*valuta*) in order to finance the purchase of machinery abroad. Nepmen, members of the former well-to-do classes, and other persons suspected of hoarding gold or other valuables were arrested in large numbers and their property confiscated.

The persecution of the old intelligentsia, which revived in intensity after the beginning of the five-year plan, was inspired by doubt of their loyalty to the Soviet regime. As hardships mounted and living conditions deteriorated, the Party leadership utilized the old intelligentsia as a scapegoat to divert popular discontent and frustration. Every breakdown in production tended to be treated as an act of sabotage for which some old-regime engineer was held personally responsible. The acts of "sabotage" were in turn magnified into conspiracies to overthrow Soviet power in which foreign capitalist enemies of the USSR were alleged to be deeply involved.

The OGPU was given the responsibility of preparing a series of show trials which would lend plausibility to these flimsy accusations. The production lag in the Donets Coal Basin in 1927–28 led to the widely advertised Shakhty prosecution of Russian technicians and old-regime engineers who were alleged to have conspired with the Germans to commit acts of sabotage and espionage. In the autumn of 1930, forty-eight specialists in the food industry were arrested and shot for alleged membership in a counterrevolutionary organization charged with sabotaging the workers' food supply. In December 1930 came the famous *Prompartiya* (Industrial Party) trial in which Professor Ramzin and seven other prominent Soviet engineers were accused and convicted of organizing a secret political party, committing acts of sabotage, and conspiring with Franco to overthrow the Soviet regime. Six of the defendants received death sentences which were subsequently reprieved; the two others were given ten-year terms of imprisonment. In March 1931 another trial was dramatically staged. Fourteen professors and officials were convicted of counterrevolutionary activity and sabotage in conspiracy with the Mensheviks abroad. One of the main culprits was Professor Groman of the Gosplan, whose real sin apparently lay in insisting that the targets of the First Five-Year Plan were unrealistically high.

The drive against the intellectuals was not limited to show trials. As Sidney and Beatrice Webb observed in a volume notable for its generally friendly tone to Soviet achievements:

> This much-discussed prosecution of Professor Ramzin and his colleagues inaugurated a veritable reign of terror against the intelligentsia. Nobody regarded himself as beyond suspicion. Men and women lived in daily dread of arrest. Thousands were sent on administrative exile to distant parts of the country. Evidence was not necessary. The title of engineer served as sufficient condemnation. The jails were filled. Factories languished from lack of technical leadership, and the chiefs of the Supreme Economic Council commenced to complain "that by its wholesale arrests of engineers the GPU . . . was interfering with industrial progress."

On June 23, 1931, Stalin called a halt to the policy of specialist-baiting. Having accomplished his purpose of frightening the intellectuals into submission, he now faced the necessity of utilizing their indispensable skills. The new line announced by Stalin was soon echoed and re-echoed by lesser dignitaries. Soltz, a member of the Central Control Committee of the Party, proclaimed, "We are not accustomed to value the human being sufficiently. To withdraw men from important posts in industry and civil service by arresting and sentencing them without adequate justification has caused the state tremendous loss."

In the period immediately after Stalin's pronouncements, a substantial number of engineers were released from prison or recalled from exile. Ramzin, the convicted "agent" of the French General Staff, resumed his lectures at the Institute of Thermodynamics. Other engineer "traitors" and "saboteurs" received similar treatment. Encouraged by the promise of a more liberal dispensation, the old technical intelligentsia again began to take its place in industry, to recover its courage, and to assume the "production risks" out of which so many earlier charges of wrecking had developed.

The liberal interlude was not destined to be prolonged. With the sharp deterioration of living conditions in the winter of 1932–33, scapegoats again became necessary, and a new wave of persecution engulfed the old intelligentsia. In January 1933 another show trial was staged, this time directed against six British Metro-Vickers engineers, ten Russian technicians, and a woman secretary who had been associated with them. All were charged with sabotage of power stations and the usual accompaniment of conspiracy and espionage. Two months later, the OGPU announced the discovery and punishment of a large-scale conspiracy in the People's Commissariat of Agriculture and State Farming. The accused were charged with using their authority to wreck tractors and to disorganize sowing, harvesting, and threshing in order "to create a famine in the country." Thirty-five of the alleged culprits were shot; twenty-two received ten-year sentences; and eighteen were ordered confined for eight years. The victims were all alleged to be descended "from bourgeois and landowning classes." The pall of terror enveloping the old intelligentsia was lifted slightly after the favorable harvest of 1933. In July 1934 Andrei Vyshinsky, then deputy state prosecutor, ordered local prosecutors to cease their policy of indiscriminate prosecution of engineers and directors for administrative failures.

The mass incidence of OGPU arrests during the period of the First Five-Year Plan was most widely felt in the countryside. The commitment to collectivize and mechanize agriculture involved a decision to liquidate the kulaks as a class, on the ground that they were inveterate enemies of Soviet power and could be counted on to sabotage collectivization. Stalin estimated in November 1928 that the kulaks constituted about 5 per cent of the rural population, or more than one million of the twenty-five million peasant families. The OGPU was assigned the task of ejecting them from their land, confiscating their property, and deporting them to the north and Siberia. Some of the more recalcitrant were shot when they resisted arrest or responded with violence to efforts to dispossess them. The great majority became wards of the OGPU and were sentenced to forced labor in lumber camps or coal mines, or on canals, railroads, and other public works which the OGPU directed. At one stroke, the OGPU became the master of the largest pool of labor in the Soviet Union. Its own enterprises expanded rapidly to absorb them; those for whom no work could be found in the OGPU industrial empire were hired out on contract to other Soviet enterprises encountering difficulty in mobilizing supplies of free labor.

The mass deportation of the kulaks meant a tremendous growth in the network of forced-labor camps. At the same time, the jurisdiction of the OGPU over ordinary criminals was enlarged. All prisoners serving sentences of more than three years were transferred to OGPU care, even if the crimes were not of a political character. No official statistics were made available on the population of the camps in the early thirties, but some indication of the magnitudes involved is provided by the fact that Belomor, the canal project connecting Leningrad and the White Sea, alone utilized more than two hundred thousand prisoners. By the end of the First Five-Year Plan, forced labor had become a significant factor in manning the construction projects of the Soviet economy.

The NKVD and the Great Purge

The powers of the OGPU were concurrently enhanced. It was given authority to enforce the obligatory passport system introduced in large areas of the Soviet Union at the end of 1932. In July 1934 the OGPU was transformed into the People's Commissariat of Internal Affairs, or NKVD. The enlarged activities of the NKVD included responsibility for state security, all penal institutions, fire departments, police (militia), convoy troops, frontier guards, troops of internal security, highway administration, and civil registry offices (vital statistics). The reorganization of 1934–35 involved a consolidation of the repressive machinery of the Soviet state. For the first time, all institutions of detention were placed under one jurisdiction. The secret police and their supporting military formations were united with the ordinary police. A formidable structure of power was cemented.

[. . .]

Before 1934 the victims of the OGPU-NKVD were largely former White Guards, the bourgeoisie, political opponents of the Bolsheviks, Nepmen, members of the old intelligentsia, and kulaks. During the late twenties and early thirties, some members of the Trotsky-Zinoviev and Right oppositions were also arrested by the OGPU and condemned to administrative exile or confinement in political *isolators;* but as Anton Ciliga, who was sentenced to one of the latter, records, the political prisoners received "special treatment," had books at their disposal, held meetings and debates, published prison news sheets, and lived a relatively privileged existence compared with the wretched inhabitants of the forced-labor camps. Until 1934, the Party was largely exempt from the full impact of the OGFU-NKVD terror; the relatively few oppositionists who were confined in OGPU prisons were still treated with comparative humanity.

In December 1934, when Kirov was assassinated by Nikolayev, allegedly a former member of the Zinoviev opposition, a new era in NKVD history opened. The "liberal" regime which the imprisoned oppositionists enjoyed came to an abrupt end. The concentrated power of the NKVD was now directed toward uprooting all actual or potential opposition in the Party. For the first time, the Party felt the full brunt of the terror.

The murder of Kirov was followed by drastic reprisals. Nikolayev and a group of his alleged confederates were charged with having formed a so-called Leningrad Center to organize the assassination and were condemned to death. More than a hundred persons who had been arrested prior to Kirov's death as "counterrevolutionaries" were promptly handed over to military commissions of the Supreme Court of the USSR for trial were found guilty of preparing and carrying out terrorist acts, and were instantly shot. This demonstrative massacre was accompanied by the arrest and imprisonment, on charges of negligence, of twelve high NKVD officials in Leningrad. In the spring of 1935, thousands and perhaps tens of thousands of Leningrad inhabitants who were suspected of harboring opposition sentiments were arrested and deported to Siberia. In the sardonic nomenclature of exile and concentration camp, they came to be referred to collectively as "Kirov's assassins."

Zinoviev, Kamenev, and all the principal leaders of the Zinoviev group were also arrested and transferred to the political isolator at Verkhne Uralsk During the summer of 1935, Zinoviev, Kamenev, and an assortment of lesser figures were secretly tried for plotting against the life of Stalin. According to Ciliga, "Two of the prisoners were shot: one collaborator of the G.P.U. and one officer of the Kremlin Guard. The others escaped with sentences ranging between five and ten years. Stalin; in addressing the graduates of the Red Army academies at the Kremlin on May 4, 1935, observed;

> These comrades did not always confine themselves to criticism and passive resistance. They threatened to raise a revolt in the Party against the Central Committee. More, they threatened some of us with bullets. Evidently, they reckoned on frightening us and compelling us to turn from the Leninist road.
>
> We were obliged to handle some of these comrades roughly. But that cannot be helped. I must confess that I too had a hand in this.

During 1935 the purge gathered momentum, but its proportions were still relatively restricted. The dissolution of the Society of Old Bolsheviks on May 25,

1935, was an ominous portent of things to come. On May 13, some two weeks earlier the Party Central Committee had ordered a screening of all Party documents in order to "cleanse" the Party of all opposition elements. As Zhdanov stated in a report at the plenum of the Saratov kraikom, "Recent events, particularly the treacherous murder of Comrade Kirov, show clearly how dangerous it is for the Party to lose its vigilance . . . I have to remind you that the murderer of Comrade Kirov, Nikolayev, committed his crime by using his Party card." By December 1, 1935, 81.1 per cent of all Party members had been subjected to screening, and 9.1 per cent of these were reported as expelled. On December 25 the Central Committee of the Party, dissatisfied with the modest results of the verification of Party documents, ordered a new purge. Beginning February 1, 1936, all old Party cards were to be exchanged for new cards; the issuance of new Party documents was to serve as the occasion for a rigorous unmasking of enemies who had survived the earlier screening. The bite of the first phase of the purge is indicated by the striking decline of Party membership from 2,807,786 in January 1934 to 2,044,412 in April 1936. In a little over two years, more than one out of every four members and candidates disappeared from the Party rolls. Their fate can be inferred from the diatribes which the Soviet press of the period directed against "wreckers, spies, diversionists, and murderers sheltering behind the Party card and disguised as Bolsheviks."

The Great Purge readied its climax in the period 1936–1938. Its most dramatic external manifestation was the series of show trials in the course of which every trace of Old Bolshevik opposition leadership was officially discredited and exterminated. The first of the great public trials took place in August 1936." Zinoviev, Kamenev, Ivan Smirnov, and thirteen associates were charged with organizing a clandestine terrorist center under instructions from Trotsky, with accomplishing the murder of Kirov, and with preparing similar attempts against the lives of other Party leaders. All sixteen were executed. In the course of the trial, the testimony of the accused compromised many other members of the Bolshevik Old Guard. A wave of new arrests followed. On August 23, 1936, Tomsky, hounded by a sense of impending doom, committed suicide.

In January 1937 came the trial of the Seventeen, the so-called Anti-Soviet Trotskyite Center, which included such prominent figures as Pyatakov, Radek, Sokolnikov, Serebryakov, and Muralov. [. . .] The prisoners in the dock fought for their lives by playing their assigned role in a drama designed to destroy Trotsky's reputation. Radek and Sokolnikov were rewarded with ten-year prison sentences. Two minor figures were also sentenced to long prison terms. The remaining thirteen were shot.

On June 12, 1937, *Pravda* carried the announcement of the execution of Marshal Tukhachevsky and seven other prominent generals of the Red Army "for espionage and treason to the Fatherland." This time no public trial was held. The Party press merely declared that the executed generals had conspired to overthrow the Soviet government and to re-establish "the yoke of the landowners and industrialists." The conspirators were alleged to be in the service of the military intelligence of "a foreign government," to which they were supposed to have indicated their readiness to surrender the Soviet Ukraine in exchange for assistance in bringing about the downfall of the Soviet government. [. . .] The execution of Tukhachevsky and his associates was the prelude to a mass purge of the Soviet armed forces in the course of which the top commanding personnel was particularly hard hit.

Speaking to the Twenty-Second Party Congress, Khrushchov "rehabilitated" them and explained what happened: "Such outstanding military commanders as Tukhachevsky, Yakir, Uborevich, Kork, Yegorov, Eideman, and others fell victim to the mass repressions . . . A rather curious report once cropped up in the foreign press to the effect that Hitler, in preparing the attack on our country, planted through his intelligence service a faked document indicating that Comrades Yakir and Tukhachevsky and others were agents of the German General Staff. This "document," allegedly secret, fell into the hands of President Bones of Czechoslovakia, who, apparently guided by good intentions, forwarded it to Stalin. Yakir, Tukhachevsky, and other comrades were arrested and then killed. Many splendid commanders and political officials of the Red Army were executed . . . " *Pravda*, October 20, 1961.

The slaughter of the Old Guard continued with the Trial of the Twenty-One, the so-called Anti-Soviet Bloc of Rights and Trotskyites, in March 1938. Among the prisoners in the dock were Bukharin, Rykov, and Krestinsky, all former members of the Politburo; Yagoda, the former head, of the NKVD; Rakovsky, the former chairman of the Council of People's Commissars in the Ukraine and Soviet ambassador to England and France; Rosengoltz, the former People's Commissar of Foreign Trade; Grinko, the former People's Commissar of Finance; and Khodjayev, the former chairman of the Council of People's Commissars of Uzbekistan. The indictment against them embraced the usual combination of treason, espionage, diversion, terrorism, and wrecking. The bloc headed by Bukharin and Rykov was alleged to have spied for foreign powers from the earliest days of the revolution, to have entered into secret agreements with the Nazis and the Japanese to dismember the Soviet Union, to have planned the assassination of Stalin and the rest of the Politburo, and to have organized innumerable acts of sabotage and diversion in order to wreck the economic and political power of the Soviet Union. If the testimony of Yagoda is to be believed, he not only murdered his predecessor in office, Menzhinsky, but also tried to murder his successor, Yezhov; he facilitated the assassination of Kirov, was responsible for the murder of Gorky, Gorky's son, and Kuibyshev; he admitted foreign spies into his organization and protected their operations; he planned a palace coup in the Kremlin and the assassination of the Politburo.

If these lurid tales strain the credulity of the reader, they nevertheless represent the version of oppositionist activity which Stalin and his faithful lieutenants found it expedient to propagate. Without access to the archives of the Kremlin and the NKVD, it is doubtful whether the web of fact and fancy behind the show trials will ever be authoritatively disentangled. Khrushchev's secret speech to the Twentieth Congress and the revelations of the Twenty-Second Congress left no doubt that the charges were unfounded, but he was singularly silent about the show trials themselves, and no tears were wasted on the oppositionists who were destroyed.

How then explain the confessions of guilt in open court? It is important to recall that the great majority of the executed, including all the military leaders, were tried on *camera*; presumably, despite the pressure to which they were exposed, they could not be persuaded to confess publicly to the crimes with which they were charged. The prisoners who appeared in the show trials represented a small handful of the accused, though they included a number of the leading figures of the Leninist epoch of the Party. What inspired them to pour out their guilt and to confess to deeds of which they were patently incapable? Why did only one of them, Krestinsky, use the opportunity of the public trial to repudiate the admissions of guilt which he had made in his preliminary examination, and why did he return the next day to repudiate his repudiation? Were Krestinsky and the rest shattered by the continuous interrogations and tortures of the NKVD examiners? Did they perform the roles assigned to them in the show trials in the desperate hope of winning clemency for themselves or their families? Were they inspired by a twisted sense of Party loyalty in which the ritual acknowledgment of crimes they had not committed and recantation of sins they were not guilty of served as an act of atonement for earlier breaches of Party unity? Was their attachment to the Communist dream so strong that their own capitulation and debasement appeared as a minor perversion in the glories and achievements of Soviet construction? Did they genuinely believe, as Bukharin claimed in his final plea, that "everything positive that glistens in the Soviet Union acquires new dimensions in a man's mind? This in the end disarmed me completely and led me to bend my knees before the Party and the country."

The answers to these questions are buried with the dead. From Stalin's point of view, the motivations of the repentant sinners at the show trials were irrelevant. What counted was the creation of a legend which stamped the oppositionists irrevocably as spies and traitors to the Soviet cause. To liquidate the whole generation of Old Bolsheviks without pre-text or explanation would have represented too naked an exposure of the mechanics of a regime in which any form of dissidence had become a sufficient ground for extermination or imprisonment.

The role of the show trials was to demonstrate to the Soviet public and to the world that the Bolshevik Old Guard had become a fifth column which was desperately seeking to undermine and dismember the Soviet state and that the Great Purge had its ultimate justification in considerations of national security and defense. Behind the camouflage of this myth, Stalin proceeded with ruthless determination to consolidate his own power by eliminating every actual or potential rallying point for an alternative government. [. . .]

The course of the purge can be conveniently divided into three periods. The first dates from the assassination of Kirov to the removal of Yagoda as head of the NKVD in late September 1936. During this period, the purge was gathering momentum, but its sharpest edge was reserved for the remnants of the Trotsky-Zinoviev group and other left-wing oppositionists inside and outside the Party. The symbol of this phase of the purge was the Zinoviev-Kamenev trial in August 1936. In this period, Stalin appeared to be settling accounts with the left, and, though the victims were by no means confined to Old Bolsheviks suspected of harboring sympathies for Trotsky or Zinoviev, they constituted a primary target. The public signal for the widening of the purge was given at the Zinoviev-Kamenev trial; the prearranged testimony implicated the right as well as the left in the "plot" to wipe out Stalin. The whole Bolshevik Old Guard appeared compromised. [. . .]

The crescendo of the Great Purge was reached in the second period, which extended from September 1936, when Yezhov took command of the NKVD, until the end of July 1938, when Lavrenti Beria was designated as Yezhov's deputy and eventual successor. The announcement of Yezhov's removal did not come until December, but meanwhile Beria assumed *de facto* command of the NKVD organization, and early in 1939 Yezhov disappeared and was liquidated.

The period of the Yezhovshchina involved a reign of terror without parallel in Soviet history. Among those arrested, imprisoned, and executed was a substantial proportion of the leading figures in the Party and governmental hierarchy. The Bolshevik Old Guard was destroyed. The roll of Yezhov's victims included not only former oppositionists but many of the most stalwart supporters of Stalin in his protracted struggle with the opposition. No sphere of Soviet life, however lofty, was left untouched. Among the purged Stalinists were three former members of the Politburo, Rudzutak, Chubar, and S. V. Kossior, and two candidate members, Postyshev and Eikhe. An overwhelming majority of the members and candidates of the Party Central Committee disappeared (see Chapter 6). The senior officer corps of the armed forces suffered severely. According to one sober account, "two of five marshals of the Soviet Union escaped arrest, two of fifteen army commanders, twenty-eight of fifty-eight corps commanders, eighty-five of a hundred and ninety-five divisional commanders, and a hundred and ninety-five of four hundred and six regimental commanders." [. . .] Almost every commissariat was deeply affected.

The purge swept out in ever-widening circles and resulted in wholesale removals and arrests of leading officials in the union republics, secretaries of the Party, Komsomol, and trade-union apparatus, heads of industrial trusts and enterprises, Comintern functionaries and foreign Communists, and leading writers, scholars, engineers, and scientists. The arrest of an important figure was followed by the seizure of his entourage. The apprehension of members of the entourage led to the imprisonment of their friends and acquaintances. The endless chain of involvements and associations threatened to encompass entire strata of Soviet society. Fear of arrest, exhortations to vigilance, and perverted ambition unleashed new floods of denunciations, which generated their own avalanche of cumulative interrogations and detentions. Whole categories of Soviet citizens found themselves singled out for arrest because of their "objective characteristics." Old Bolsheviks, Red Partisans, foreign Communists of German, Austrian, and Polish extraction, Soviet citizens who had been abroad or had relations with foreign countries or foreigners, and "repressed elements" were automatically caught up in the NKVD web of imprisonment. The arrests mounted into the millions; the testimony of the survivors is unanimous regarding crowded prison cells and teeming labor camps. Most of the prisoners were utterly bewildered by the fate which had befallen them. The vast resources of the NKVD were concentrated on one objective — to document the existence of a huge conspiracy to undermine Soviet power. The extraction of real confessions to imaginary crimes became a major industry. Under the zealous and ruthless ministrations of NKVD examiners, millions of innocents were transformed into traitors, terrorists, and enemies of the people.

How can one explain the Yezhovshchina? What motives impelled Stalin to organize a blood bath of such frightening proportions? In the absence of revealing testimony from the source, one can only venture hypotheses. Stalin's desire to consolidate his own personal power appears to have been a driving force. The slaughter of the Bolshevik Old Guard may be viewed partly as a drastic reprisal for past insubordination; it was more probably intended as a preventive measure to end once and for all any possibility of resistance or challenge from this direction. The extension of the purge to the Stalinist stalwarts in the Party and governmental apparatus is much more difficult to fathom. It is possible that many fell victim to the system of denunciations in the course of which their loyalty to Stalin was put in question, that a number were still involved in official or personal relationships with former oppositionists, that some were liquidated because they displayed traces of independence in their dealings with the Supreme Leader, that others were merely suspected of harboring aspirations toward personal power, and that still others simply furnished convenient scapegoats to demonstrate the existence of a conspiracy reaching into the highest circles.

Implicit in any understanding of the Yezhovshchina is a theory of the role of terror in Stalin's formula of government. The consolidation of personal rule in a totalitarian system depends on the constant elimination of all actual or potential competitors for supreme power. The insecurity of the masses must be supplemented by the insecurity of the governing elite who surround the dictator. The too strongly entrenched official with an independent base of power is by definition a threat to the dictator's total sway. The individuals or groups who go uncontrolled and undirected are regarded as fertile soil for the growth of conspiratorial intrigue. The function of terror thus assumes a twofold aspect. As a preventive, it is designed to nip any possible resistance or opposition in the bud. As an instrument for the reinforcement of the personal power of the dictator, it is directed toward ensuring perpetual circulation in the ranks of officeholders in order to forestall the crystallization of autonomous islands of countervailing force.

The manipulation of terror as a system of power is a delicate art. A dictator in command of modern armaments and a secret police can transform his subjects into robots and automatons, but, if he succeeds too well he runs the risk of destroying the sources of creative initiative on which the survival of his own regime depends. When terror runs rampant, as it did at the height of the Yezhovshchina, unintended consequences follow. Fear becomes contagious and paralyzing. Officials at all levels seek to shirk responsibility. The endless belt of irresponsible denunciations begins to destroy the nation's treasury of needed skills. The terror apparatus grows on the stuff it feeds upon and magnifies in importance until it overshadows and depresses all the constructive enterprises of the state. The dictator finds himself caught up in a whirlwind of his own making which threatens to break completely out of control.

As the fury of the Yezhovshchina mounted, Stalin and his intimates finally became alarmed. Evidence accumulated that the purge was over-reaching itself and that much talent sorely needed by the regime was being irretrievably lost. [. . .]

The third and final phase of the Great Purge involved the purging of the purgers. In late July 1938 Yezhov's sun began to set when Beria took over as his deputy. In December, Yezhov was ousted as head of the NKVD and appointed Commissar for Inland Water Transport, from which post he soon disappeared unmourned but not forgotten. During the same month came the sensational announcement of the arrest, trial, and shooting of the head of the NKVD of Moldavia and a group of his examiners for extracting false confessions from innocent prisoners. The enemies of the people, it now appeared, had wormed their way into the NKVD apparatus itself and had sought to stir up mass unrest and disaffection by their brutal persecution of the guiltless.

It was now the turn of Yezhov and his collaborators to play the role of scape-goat for the excesses of the purge. A wave of arrests spread through the NKVD organization. The prisons began to fill with former NKVD examiners; many pris-oners who had been tortured by these same examiners had the welcome experi-ence of greeting their former tormentors as cellmates in prisons and labor camps. The Great Change, as it was soon to become known, was marked by a substantial amelioration in prison conditions and examining methods. According to Beck and Godin, "Prisoners were released by the thousands, and many were restored to their old positions or even promoted." A new era appeared to have dawned.

Stalin now presented himself in the guise of the dispenser of mercy and justice. Excesses of the purge were blamed on subordinate officials who had exceeded their authority, saboteurs who had tried to break the indissoluble link which bound leader and people, and careerists and counterrevolutionaries who had insinuated themselves into the Party and NKVD organizations in order to sub-vert and undermine the Soviet regime. [. . .]

Thus, the pressure of the purge was temporarily relaxed as Stalin sought to enlist the energies and loyalties of the new governing elite which he had pro-moted to positions of responsibility over the graves of its predecessors. Again, as in the collectivization crisis earlier, Stalin demonstrated his remarkable instinct for stopping short and reversing course at the brink of catastrophe.

The full circle of the Great Purge offers a remarkable case study in the use of terror. Arrests ran into the millions. The gruesome and harrowing experiences of the victims blackened the face of Stalinist Russia. The havoc wrought in leading circles appeared irreparable. Yet despite the damage and the hatred engendered, the dynamic momentum of the industrialization program was maintained. The arrests of responsible technicians and officials frequently produced serious set-backs in production, but, as their replacements acquired experience, order was restored and production began to climb again. While many functionaries reacted to the purge by shunning all responsibility, others responded to the fear of arrest by working as they had never worked before. Terror functioned as prod as well as brake. The acceleration in the circulation of the elite brought a new generation of Soviet-trained intelligentsia into positions of responsibility, and Stalin anchored his power on their support. Meanwhile, Stalin emerged from the purge with his own position consolidated. The major purpose of decapitating the Bolshevik Old Guard had been accomplished. Every rival for supreme power who was visible on the horizon had been eliminated. The Party and the nation were thoroughly intimidated. The purgers had been purged and the scapegoats identified. The ancient formula of protecting the infallibility of the Leader by punishing subordi-nates for their excessive ardor was impressively resurrected.

The moving equilibrium on which Stalin balanced his power structure entered a new phase. The temporary lifting of the blanket of fear was designed to restore morale, to revive hope and initiative, and to reforge the bonds between regime and people which the purge had dangerously strained. But the mitigation of the terror involved no abandonment of the system. The Stalinist refinement on the use of terror as a system of power involved oscillating phases of pressure and relaxation which varied with the dictator's conception of the dangers confronting him. The essence of control was never abandoned. At the same time, when the pressure became too great, a mirage of security and stability was held out in order to enlist the energy and devotion of the oncoming generations. It is a system which devours many of its servants, but, as in games of chance, since the winners and survivors are highly rewarded and cannot be identified in advance, the ambitions of the players are periodically renewed and the regime bases its strength on their sacrifices.

As the Great Purge drew to a close, the major efforts of the NKVD were concentrated against elements which might prove unreliable in the event that the Soviet Union became involved in war. After the Soviet-Nazi pact and the partition of Poland, the NKVD undertook wholesale arrests in the newly occupied areas. The victims ran into the hundreds of thousands and included whole categories of people whose "objective characteristics" could be broadly construed as inclining them to anti-Soviet behavior. The great majority were deported to forced-labor camps in the north, from which the survivors were amnestied by the terms of the Polish-Soviet pact concluded after the Nazi attack on the Soviet Union. The Soviet occupation of the Baltic states in June 1940 was also followed by large-scale NKVD arrests and deportations of so-called anti-Soviet elements.

After the Nazi invasion, the NKVD engaged in widespread roundups of former "repressed" people and others whose records aroused suspicion of disloyalty to the Soviet regime. The Volga-German Autonomous Republic was dissolved, and its inhabitants were dispatched to labor camps or exile in the far reaches of Siberia. With the turning of the tide at Stalingrad and the advance of the Soviet armies westward, the NKVD found new victims among the population of the reoccupied areas. Many were arrested on the ground of actual or alleged collaboration with the Germans, and the forced-labor camps reaped a new harvest. A number of the national minorities served as a special target of NKVD retribution because of their alleged disloyalty. The Crimean Tatars were penalized for their "traitorous" conduct by the abolition of the Crimean Autonomous Republic. As Khrushchev later acknowledged: "Already at the end of 1943 . . . a decision was taken and executed concerning the deportation of all the Karachi from the lands on which they lived. In the same period, at the end of December 1943, the same lot befell the whole population of the Autonomous Kalmyk Republic. In March 1944 all the Chechen and Ingush people were deported and the Chechen-Ingush Autonomous Republic was liquidated. In April 1944, all Balkars were deported to far away places from the territory of the Kabardino-Balkar

Autonomous Republic. The Ukrainians avoided meeting this fate only because there were too many of them, and there was no place to which to deport them. Otherwise, he [Stalin] would have deported them also." Meanwhile, German war prisoners accumulated, and the NKVD took over the responsibility of running the camps in which they were confined.

After the capitulation of the Nazis, the NKVD confronted the vast new assignment of sifting the millions of Soviet citizens who found themselves in Germany and Austria at the end of the war. Most of them were war prisoners and *Osterbeiter* who had been shipped west by the Germans as forced laborers. Some, however, had retreated with the German armies in order to escape Soviet rule. Others had fought in Nazi military uniform or in separate anti-Soviet Military formations such as the Vlasov Army. The latter when caught received short shrift; the great majority were executed. All of these groups on whom the NKVD could lay its hands were rounded up at assembly points and subjected to intensive interrogations before being shipped back to the Soviet Union. The NKVD followed a calculated policy of treating the "returnees" as contaminated by their contact with the West. In order to isolate them from the Soviet populace, large numbers were dispatched to labor camps on suspicion of disloyalty or traitorous conduct. Mass deportations were also reported from the border areas of Esthonia, Latvia, Lithuania, Karolia, and the western Ukraine; the native population was shifted to remote areas in Siberia and replaced by Russians, frequently war veterans, brought in from other regions.

After the war, according to Khrushchev, "Stalin became even more capricious, irritable and brutal; in particular his suspicion grew." The MGB, successor organ to the NKVD, fed "his persecution mania" by manufacturing new enemies who had to be suppressed. The so-called Leningrad Case which occurred shortly after the death of Zhdanov on August 31, 1948, involved a thoroughgoing purge of his entourage. Among its victims were Politburo member N. A. Voznescensky; A. A. Kuznetsov, the Central Committee secretary who had been entrusted by Stalin himself with the supervision of state security organs; M. L. Rodionov, chairman of the RSFSR Council of Ministers; P. S. Popkov, first secretary of the Leningrad Party organization; and many others. The circumstances of the case remain mysterious. Khrushchev, in his speech to the Twentieth Congress, acknowledged that it was fabricated from beginning to end; according to him, "the elevation of Voznesensky and Kuznetsov alarmed Beria," who took advantage of Stalin's suspicion to destroy his political rivals. In the same speech Khrushchev also revealed that the so-called case of the Mingrelian nationalist organization of 1951–1952 in Georgia represented still another MGB invention. In Khrushchev's words, "On the basis of falsified documents, it was proven that there existed in Georgia a supposedly nationalistic organization whose objective was the liquidation of the Soviet power in that Republic with the help of imperialist powers. In this connection, a number of responsible Party and Soviet workers were arrested in Georgia . . . As it developed, there was no nationalistic organization in Georgia. Thousands of innocent people fell victim to willfulness and lawlessness."

There were other areas of MGB activity in the postwar period which Khrushchev chose to ignore. One of the most notable was the anti-Jewish campaign of the years 1948–1952, which began with a sweeping denunciation of rootless cosmopolitans and culminated in 1952 with the execution of several dozen leading Jewish writers. Khrushchev did, however, denounce the "doctors' plot" of 1952–1953 as a fabrication, although without mention of its anti-Semitic connotations. Of this affair, which involved an alleged conspiracy of Kremlin doctors (mainly Jewish) to cut short the lives of Zhdanov and Shcherbakov and to destroy the health of leading Soviet military personnel, Khrushchev observed:

> Actually there was no "Affair" outside of the declaration of the woman doctor Timashuk, who was probably influenced or ordered by someone (after all, she was an official collaborator of the organs of state security) to write Stalin a letter in which she declared that doctors were supplying supposedly improper methods of medical treatment.

> Such a letter was sufficient for Stalin to reach an immediate conclusion that there were doctor-plotters in the Soviet Union. He issued orders to arrest a group of eminent Soviet medical specialists . . . Present at this Congress as a delegate is the former Minister of State Security, Comrade Ignatiev. Stalin told him curtly, "If you do not obtain confessions from the doctors we will shorten you by a head."

> Stalin personally called the investigative judge, gave him instructions, advised him on which investigative methods should be used these methods were simple—beat, beat and, once again, beat.

> . . . When we examined the "case" after Stalin's death, we found it to be fabricated from beginning to end.

The tense atmosphere which prevailed in high Kremlin circles at the time of the doctors' plot, an atmosphere reminiscent of the period of the Great Purge, is suggested by still another of Khrushchev's revelations. According to him, Stalin had plans "to finish off the old members of the Politburo." Andreyev was ejected from the Politburo; Voroshilov was forbidden to attend meetings, was spied upon, and was accused by Stalin of being an English agent. Molotov and Mikoyan were under suspicion, and the decision to create a Presidium of twenty-five members after the Nineteenth Congress was intended as a cover "for the future annihilation of the old Politburo members." If Khrushchev's testimony is to be credited, only Stalin's fatal illness averted a blood bath in the very highest Kremlin circles.

Post-Stalinist Reforms

After Stalin's death, steps were taken to mitigate the terror. The amnesty decree of March 27, 1953, was widely saluted as the beginning of a new dispensation. On April 3 the Kremlin doctors were released, and a *Pravda* editorial three days later promised that all cases of official "high-handedness and lawlessness" would be rooted out and that constitutional rights would be safeguarded. A wide-ranging series of reforms unfolded, involving among others, a curbing of the extrajudicial powers of the security police, a reassertion of Party control over the police, the dismantlement of the security police's economic empire, the release of hundreds of thousands of prisoners from the forced-labor camps, and the rationalization of the system of criminal justice. [. . .]

The measures marked a significant reduction in the incidence of Stalinist terror, but they did not mean its complete abolition. The fate of those released from the forced-labor camps is instructive. Some were completely rehabilitated and permitted to return to their homes. Others were either required to remain in the area of their previous incarceration or were confined to certain districts which they were not permitted to leave without express permission. There they remained under police surveillance; indeed, even some former political prisoners allowed to return home were also required to report to the local police officials at regular intervals. [. . .]

The Organization of the Police Apparatus

The KGB is particularly important in terms of its surveillance functions. Its responsibilities include the protection of high Party and governmental officials, the enforcement of security regulations, the conduct of espionage abroad, the tracking down of foreign intelligence agents in the Soviet Union, the censorship of correspondence within the Soviet Union and with foreign countries, and the supervision of a network of informers to detect disloyalty or political instability and to report on the attitudes of the Soviet populace toward the regime.

The KGB is organized on the pattern of a union-republic ministry with the main organization at the center and branches in each of the fifteen republics. Its extensive field organization, which is subject to more highly centralized control than is customary in the usual union-republic ministry, extends down to the regional, city, and district levels. In a report to the Twenty-Second Party Congress, Shelepin, then the KGB Chief, stated that its size had "been cut down substantially," but perhaps understandably, no data were provided.

Although authoritative current information on the internal structure of the KGB is unavailable, the organization of its predecessor agency in the NKVD has been extensively described in the reports of escapees who served in it or who had occasion to familiarize themselves with its operations. A number of accounts compiled by different informants agree in identifying many of the same basic subdivisions, usually described in Soviet terminology as main administrations. A special administration was concerned with the security of high Party and governmental leaders, The Economic Administration (EKU) was responsible for coping with wrecking, sabotage, production failures, and other "counterrevolutionary" activity in Soviet industry and agriculture. All personnel occupying responsible positions in Soviet economic life had to be investigated and cleared by the EKU, which operated through special sections located in all industrial enterprises of any importance, The EKU was also responsible for the collection of economic information from foreign countries. The Secret Political Administration concentrated its fire against members of the Trotsky-Zinoviev and Right oppositions, former Mensheviks, SR's, and members of other anti-Bolshovik parties, leaders of the church and religious sects, national deviationists, and members of the intelligentsia whose devotion to the Soviet regime was in question. The Special Section was concerned with the loyalty of the armed forces. Its representatives were assigned to all military and naval formations and constituted an elaborate special hierarchy with its own independent channel of command responsible directly to the NKVD. The Counter-intelligence Administration directed its efforts toward combating foreign intelligence agents operating within the USSR. Its responsibilities included surveillance of foreign visitors and foreign embassies and consulates on Soviet soil. The Transport Administration focused its activities on the protection of goods in transit, the fulfillment of state plans for freight move-ments, and protection against sabotage or other damage to the transporta-tion network. The Foreign Administration devoted its primary efforts to espionage activity outside the Soviet Union. Its responsibilities included the control of Soviet personnel stationed abroad, the penetration of Russian anti-Soviet émigré organizations, the collection of intelligence of value to the Soviet leadership, and the recruitment of foreign Communists, sympa-thizers, and others as agents in the Soviet spy network. [. . .]

The meager information which is available on the recruitment and training of professional security personnel is derived largely from reports of former mem-bers of the Soviet secret police. Before the Great Purge, the higher circles of the NKVD organization were still dominated by Old Chekists who had won their spurs during the Civil War period and who had supported Stalin in his struggle with the Right and Left oppositions during the twenties. New officials of the NKVD were recruited almost exclusively from trusted Party members who were assigned to NKVD work by the cadre sections of the Secretariat of the Party Central Committee and lower Party organs. The purge of Yagoda and his entourage was also accompanied by the elimination of many Old Chekists from responsible positions. Rapid promotions from the ranks became the order of the day. At the same time, the NKVD was compelled to resort to widespread mass recruiting of new personnel in order to cope with the burdens of Yezhovshchina. Again, the selection and assignment process was handled through Party channels. Under orders transmitted through the Central Committee Secretariat, quotas were imposed on local Party and Komsomol organizations, and Party and even Komsomol members who were deemed trustworthy were transferred to NKVD work. The purge of Yezhov and his followers created another personnel crisis for the NKVD. Again upward mobility was rapid, and the vacancies were filled by the designation of Party personnel for NKVD assignments. Under Beria, more emphasis was placed on professional qualifications in recruiting NKVD personnel. The new employees were used to control sectors of Soviet life with which they were familiar. Particularly noteworthy was the use of engineers for work in the special sections of industrial enterprises. The purge of Beria and his group was followed by a new infusion of Party personnel into the security organs. As Shelepin pointed out to the Twenty-Second Congress, "The Party has assigned a large contingent of Party, Soviet, and Komsomol workers to positions in them."

During the Great Purge, the training of professional NKVD personnel had to give way to the urgencies of speeding new recruits into operative work. Even in this period, a network of special schools was maintained to instruct those who had been selected for NKVD duty. Courses were accelerated, and the training of lower-ranking personnel was concentrated in "inter-krai" schools located in Moscow, Leningrad, Kharkov, Kiev, Odessa, Baku, Tiflis, and other large centers. At these schools students were exposed to a combination of political indoctrination, military training, and instruction in criminal law and procedure, investigation, intelligence and counterintelligence. NKVD officials who were slated for promotion to responsible positions in the apparatus were dispatched to the central NKVD school in Moscow where more intensive training was given in specialized aspects of NKVD work.

The NKVD encountered no difficulty in attracting recruits. The privileges which it commanded marked it out as an elite service. A major in the state-security organization had the rank and perquisites of a commander of an army brigade; a colonel of state security was on the same level as the commander of an army division. In a scarcity economy, the NKVD officialdom inhabited an island of plenty. The advantages of affiliation were not lost either on the cynical careerists or the fanatics among Soviet youth. The Party leadership depended on the NKVD as one of its primary pillars of support. The rewards which were held out were designed to bulwark the edifice of NKVD loyalties.

The Methods of the Secret Police

During the Stalinist era the apparatus of the secret police reached directly into every organized formation in Soviet society. The head of the special section in the factory, the plenipotentiary of the secret police in the regiment, the chief of the raion office in rural areas, all operated under the same mandate to keep the Soviet populace under the most careful observation. This did not mean that every Soviet citizen was equally exposed to police surveillance. Certain categories were singled out for special attention. Among them were one-time members of hostile social classes or political parties, former oppositionists, "repressed people," and others whose political sentiments were regarded as particularly dubious. Certain areas of Soviet life were subject to more intensive supervision than others. The armed forces, military plants, industries of strategic military significance, transport, the universities and institutes, and the intelligentsia were scrutinized particularly closely. [. . .]

During the Great Purge almost all arrests were made in the dead of night. Agents presented themselves at the home of the victim with an order authorizing them to make the arrest and search the premises. All material regarded as compromising was confiscated; at the same time, a list was made of the articles appropriated and a receipt given for their detention. Once the search was finished, the agents escorted the accused to the place of detention, where his money and any articles on his person which he could use to harm himself were expropriated. Again, receipts were punctiliously given for the money and goods expropriated. The accused was then put in a cell to await the pleasure of the examiner assigned to his case. During the Great Purge, this waiting interval sometimes stretched out to several weeks or even several months.

When the prisoner was finally called out for interrogation, usually at night, the examiner ordinarily began by trying to persuade the prisoner to make a voluntary admission of guilt. The examination was almost invariably based on the assumption of the guilt of the accused; the primary task of the examiner was therefore to extract a confession from the prisoner and to compel him to disclose the names of all accomplices with whom he was involved. If the accused proved unamenable to persuasion, the examiner resorted to intimidation, threats, or physical violence. The prisoner might be warned that failure to confess would lead to retaliation against his family; the longer the accused held out, the more severe would be the penalty. If the prisoner still proved recalcitrant, he would be subjected to the nerve-wracking ordeal of continuous interrogations which might stretch over a period of weeks. During this period "on the conveyor" as it was called, the accused would be deprived of sleep, interrogated constantly by a rotating team of examiners, made to stand at attention while the questioning was going on, and beaten or slapped into consciousness when he collapsed from exhaustion. All but the iron-willed succumbed to this incessant bombardment. At the end, a "confession" would be signed, and the accused would be ready for trial or sentencing. [. . .]

The Hazards of Terror

The reliance on terror as an instrument of dominion has its elements of danger. It is not easy to control. A secret police develops its own laws of growth. The more discord it discovers or unfolds, the more indispensable it becomes. Its tendency is always to extend its own sovereignty, to emancipate itself from external controls, to become a state within a state, and to preserve the conditions of emergency and siege on which an expansion of its own power depends. From the viewpoint of the leadership, there is an even greater worry, the fear that the secret police will become a menace to the security of the highest Party leaders themselves. It is a risk of which the leadership has been aware and against which it takes precautions. Every effort is made to subordinate the KGB to central Party controls. Responsible employees are required to be Party members. Appointments and promotions must be cleared with the Department of Administrative Organs of the Central Committee Secretariat, which maintains a particularly close watch over the KGB. The secretaries of Party organizations in the KGB are used as the eyes and ears of the Central Committee. Special groups in the Party-State Control Committee are assigned to observe the KGB. In these and perhaps other ways, the Party leadership seeks to safeguard itself against the possibility that "the avenging sword of the revolution" may turn against the revolutionary leadership itself.

Thus far, no head of the Soviet secret police has succeeded in using his position as a platform from which to strike out for supreme power. The first director of the Cheka and OGPU was Felix Dzerzhinsky, an Old Bolshevik of unimpeachable idealism whose whole career documented the proposition that there is no fanaticism so terrible as that of the pure idealist. Dzerzhinsky gave no evidence of Napoleonic ambitions and died in 1926 without attaining Politburo status. His successor, Menzhinsky, was a much lesser figure, and though he continued as head of the OGPU until 1934, he never moved beyond the second rank of Party leaders. Yagoda, who came next was removed from office in 1936 and executed in 1938. His successor, Yezhov, was relieved of his duties in 1938 and disappeared in 1939. Neither Yagoda nor Yezhov could be counted in the front ranks of Party leaders. Beria, who succeeded Yezhov, was the first head of the NKVD to enter the Politburo, where he became a leading figure. But he too was executed in the succession struggle after Stalin's death). His successors were two professional police officers Kruglov, the MVD chief, and Serov, head of the KGB, neither of whom seemed to pose any real danger to the ruling group. But they too were soon replaced by two Party functionaries, Dudorov and Shelepin, both then outside the Presidium circle of top Party leaders. In late 1961, Shelepin was promoted to a Central Committee secretaryship and yielded his KGB post to Semichastny, former Komsomol first secretary. Thus far, the vigilance of the Party leadership has been proof against all dreams of utilizing the police apparatus as the road to supreme power.

Even if the Party leadership is successful in controlling the secret police, there are other disadvantages in a regime in a police surveillance, which are not so amenable to skillful manipulation. A system which puts large-scale reliance on a secret police is wasteful of manpower. The atmosphere of suspicion which surveillance breeds is not ordinarily conducive to creative thinking and displays of individual initiative. There is always the hazard that the secret police will run amok, as it did during the Great Purge, and do serious and perhaps unintended harm to the productive and administrative machinery of the state. It is no easy task to apply terror and at the same time to hold it in leash.

Perhaps the most subtle danger posed by police surveillance is its effect on political decisions at the very highest levels. The KGB is an important source of intelligence regarding both domestic and international dangers. Since the KGB apparatus lives and grows on emergency and crisis, its justification hinges upon the maintenance of a state of siege. Consequently, the intelligence that filters through the KGB to the top political leadership is apt to emphasize the storms that are brewing, the plots against the regime, and sinister threats at home and abroad. The risk which the Party leadership faces is that it too will become the unconscious victim of the Frankenstein's monster which it has created. The ultimate hazard of terror as a system of power is that it ends by terrorizing the master as well as the slave. To read Khrushchev's secret speech to the Twentieth Party Congress is to sense the extent to which Stalin was trapped by his own suspicions and fears. In turning his back on the Stalinist legacy of mass terror and in bridling the KGB, Khrushchev may well be building his power on a more rational and ultimately more secure base.

1.3

Soviet Stability and its Sources

Seweryn Bialer

The pronounced tendency in journalistic and even academic accounts of the Soviet Union to dwell on difficulties, troubles, and unresolved issues goes far to color and distort our perceptions of conditions within the country. What major aspect of Soviet reality has not been associated with a "problem"? There is the "problem" of the economy, the "problem" of nationalities, the "problem" of technological lag, the "problem" of rising popular expectations. In the last fifteen years more has been written about the "problem" of dissent than about any other single subject. One could only think that dissent is the overwhelming fact of life in the Soviet Union and decisively shapes internal politics and policies. There is, of course, no doubt that all these and other aspects of Soviet life are truly "problem" areas, points of genuine and recognized vulnerability and potential crisis; but what has been most surprising during the Brezhnev era is not the presence of these genuine problems but rather that they did not create any semblance of a systemic crisis whether separately or in combination.

Among more serious observers of the Soviet Union there are some who regard the system as inherently unstable owing to an alleged lack of legitimacy and others who focus on the persistence of crisis situations, some quite profound, which fail to yield durable solutions despite repeated efforts and mobilization of resources. To the former one can for the moment observe that a line of reasoning which admits to no other stability of the regime than its survival over the last quarter-century assigns to stability a very narrow, almost grotesque meaning, while its questioning of Soviet legitimacy is extremely exaggerated and one-sided. It almost equates legitimacy, with the existence of constitutional democratic regimes. To the latter one should point out that political stability cannot simply be equated with a lack of crisis situations and challenges to the system but rather with the political regime's ability to resolve these crises, to neutralize or even to ignore them, and to adjust to periods of prolonged coexistence with them.

The overwhelming feature of the Brezhnev era is the sociopolitical stability of the country which has accompanied and sustained the stability we have clearly

Source: Seweryn Bialer, "Soviet Stability and its Sources," Stalin's Successors. Cambridge University Press, 1980. 141–183.

Note: Notes and references have been removed from this article.

demonstrated among political leadership and elites. The Soviet political system shows no signs of political fragmentation. The centralization of its administrative structure at the present time is if anything greater than at the beginning of the Brezhnev era. The divisive pull of interest groups, while strong, is manageable for the process of unified policy making; the pressures of participation are containable. The aggregating and coordinating functions of the party apparatus are still pronounced. The centrifugal forces of ethnic self-identification and assertiveness in the multinational Soviet state have not only failed to produce symptoms of political disintegration, but no single situation has developed in the last fifteen years that can be described as a serious challenge to Moscow's ethnic policies.

Alone among the industrially developed states the Soviet Union has avoided the political consequences of a cultural generational chasm. While one can speak of the developing youth culture, especially in large metropolitan centers, one can hardly postulate a politically meaningful youth revolution that actively counters the values of older generations. The Soviet Union has not escaped the wave of rising popular expectations, but these have not evolved into the well-known vicious-circle pattern of exaggerated, unfulfillable, and conflicting hopes which overload and undermine the political process. It is highly significant, moreover, that the rising popular expectations are almost entirely confined to the material sphere and scarcely encroach directly on cultural and political areas.

One feat of the Soviet authoritarian system, so amazing to observers and critics because of its unexpectedness, has been the ability to contain the political consequences of widespread intellectual dissent movements, the first in Soviet history. Surprising was the fact that this containment did not entail resort to mass political terror or to satisfaction of any of the dissenters' demands but the most marginal politically and harmless domestically. The Soviet elite exhibited greater flexibility, self-confidence, and cunning in dealing with dissent than any of its critics had anticipated. Today the international impact and repercussions of dissent far exceed any domestic consequences.

The stability of the Soviet system stands out against the background of events and trends in developed industrial democracies over the last fifteen years. As recently as a decade ago, Samuel Huntington began his major work, *Political Order in Changing Societies,* with the following proposition:

> The most important political distinction among countries concerns not their form of government but their degree of government. The differences between democracy and dictatorship are less than the differences between those countries whose politics embodies consensus, community, legitimacy, organization, effectiveness, stability, and those countries whose politics is deficient in these qualities. . . . The United States, Great Britain,

and the Soviet Union have different forms of government, but in all three systems the government governs.

Just a few years ago, however, in the superb report to the Trilateral Commission entitled *The Crisis of Democracy* (1975), to which Huntington contributed, the question was posed: Are democracies governable? No such question is being asked about the Soviet system. To be sure a multiplicity of small and large crises afflicts the Soviet Union. As a matter of fact its entire history constitutes an unending chain of crisis situations, primarily in the economic area but also to some extent in social, cultural, and political areas. There is adequate evidence to argue that the dominant style of Communist politics was and remains to a large extent "crisis politics"; the dominant style of its political leadership was and remains largely that of emergency leadership. The increased institutionalization of the Soviet political order was and remains to a large extent the institutionalization of this type of politics and style of leadership. Indeed, far from entering a post-mobilizational state, as some postulate, this leadership is still associated with and committed to high levels of mobilizational effort.

While some serious students have suggested that a process of decay and debilitation is eroding the Soviet political system, even they regard its destructive effects as a long-range potential rather than as a clear and present danger to existence and effectiveness. All would certainly hesitate to proclaim the "crisis of communism in power" or even to raise the question of the "governability" of the Soviet Union. Indeed, the principal author of the Trilateral Commission's report on the "governability of democracies," recently made a strong argument that "to date . . . the Soviet system has certainly demonstrated the ability to contain or protect itself from extrinsic challenges. None of the challenges which are identified for the future, moreover, appear to be qualitatively different from the challenges which the Soviet system has demonstrated the ability to deal with effectively in the past."

Whatever the future of the Soviet system may be, it projects internally the image of a society of law and order and externally the image of a growing world power which is just beginning to assert an influence to match its strength. This image contrasts with the realities of an unstable world where an unending stream of coups and rebellions and transitions undermines old and new autocratic regimes and where popular disillusionment, lack of effective leadership, and unprecedented challenges engulf even the most successful industrial democracies.

The purpose here is not to analyze and test the validity of various claims concerning the supposed future of the Soviet system but to examine the almost quarter-century of post-Stalinist development and especially the Brezhnev era. And here, despite wide differences of opinion about the present state of the Soviet system and the even greater disagreement about its possible futures, there does exist a basis for consensus regarding the proposition that the Soviet political system has remained and remains as yet *politically stable* in the Brezhnev era, regardless of disputes concerning the nature and sources of this stability.

By any meaningful standards, the Soviet social and political system during the Brezhnev era has displayed a high level of stability and governability. Surprise has been one ingredient in the reaction to this state of affairs. Not only did such an outcome contradict the expectations of a majority of Western analysts when Brezhnev came to power. Not only did it contrast strikingly with the situation in a majority of Western industrial nations. The element of surprise resulted also from the expectation that certain changes that have occurred in the Soviet system during the post-Stalin period as well as the persistence of certain challenges, some of them clearly unresolved, should normally have yielded destabilizing effects.

Those changes include first and foremost the patent and extensive, if uneven, weakening of mass and elite controls; the acquisition of a relatively higher degree of professional autonomy by the expert and managerial classes; and the greater freedom of access to the decision-making process by elite and subelite groups and institutions. Those past and present challenges that could be expected to undermine the stability of the system include the traumatic shock of the anti-Stalin campaign and the continued questioning of the Soviet past which lingers even after the official closing of the campaign; the novel wave of dissent which seized a small but vocal segment of the intelligentsia; the probably more important newly developing attitude among larger segments of the creative intelligentsia of withdrawal from official life, of internal emigration, at best of neutrality toward the official goals of the regime; the explosion of the massive and unprecedented Jewish emigration drive after decades of assimilation; the shocks in Soviet relations with Eastern Europe which could have brought into question the very principles on which these relations are based; the highly accelerated modernization of many aspects of Soviet life and almost all regions, with the attendant material and spiritual dislocations and displacements-indeed, all the "problems", which commentators have enumerated and which retain their reality and seriousness.

That the extent of systemic stability under Brezhnev has been so unexpected is in part a legacy of implications of the totalitarian model which for so long governed the study of the nature and future of the Soviet state and in part a consequence of our cumulative experience with modernizing authoritarian regimes. According to the totalitarian model, the abolition of mass terror, personal dictatorship, and the most extreme forms of the transformation-mobilization push of the regime should have weakened the intrinsic ability of the system to survive, should have left it without an internal raison d'être, without a control mechanism to assure its replication. If, on the other hand, the Soviet Union can best be understood as a highly authoritarian but not totalitarian regime, as most students would agree our experience with the history of such regimes—whether exclusionary, inclusionary, or even Communist—argues for the exceptionality of prolonged and high levels of stability, especially when accompanied by economic growth, social transformation, and particularly political systematic change, the case with the Soviet regime. Our experience with modernizing authoritarian regimes on the contrary calls for recurring crises of legitimacy, participation, and governability. Given the weight of the reasons adduced to anticipate destabilization, it becomes enormously important, for both practical and theoretical considerations, to attempt an explanation of the remarkable stability enjoyed by the Soviet system in the Brezhnev era.

The most general and immediate explanation of Soviet stability is obvious and valid. The Soviet leaders and elites who direct the system work very hard to make the system stable. If there is any single value that dominates the minds and thoughts of the Soviet establishment from the highest to lowest level, it is the value of order; if there is any single fear that outweighs all others, it is the fear disorder, chaos, fragmentation, loss of control. This fear supports the world's most extensive and methodical police-state machinery which derives its principal strength less from the extent of actual punitive action than from the extraordinary attention paid to preventive action against any form of social deviance, an effort soldiered by untold millions of informers. This enormous coercive effort—potential and actual, preventive and punitive—is augmented by an extensive attempt to inculcate positive socialization through the educational process, massive propaganda efforts, the elimination of competing ideas, and so forth. How is it, though, that these efforts have apparently proved effective for so long?

Part of the reason rests with the fact that fear of disorder and attachment to orderly society are valued not only by political leaders and elites but find strong resonance in the Soviet popular mind. This is to a large extent a historical phenomenon; the mechanism and process of conditioning in this direction are impossible to trace. Undeniably, the Russian people in all walks of life fear the chaos and disorder they sense directly below the surface of their lives; they fear the potential of elemental explosions of violence and rage that mark their historical past and occupy a central place in their history textbooks; they prize and yearn for strong government, the *khoziain* or boss who will ward off the *smuta,* the time of troubles."

It is noteworthy that this fear pervades the communities of Soviet dissidents, most of whom urge evolutionary, incremental change and have a horror of contributing to the unleashing of spontaneous and destructive forces in Russian society. Pavel Litvinov, the dissident grandson of Stalin's foreign minister Maxim Litvinov, has remarked:

> Under the czars we had an authoritarian state and now we have a totalitarian state but it still comes from the roots of the Russian past. You should

understand that the leaders and the ordinary people have the same authoritarian frame of mind. Brezhnev and the simple person both think that might is right. That's all. It is not a question of ideology. It's simply power. Solzhenitsyn acts as if he thinks this has all come down from the sky because of Communism. But he is not so different himself. He does not want democracy. He wants to go from the totalitarian state back to an authoritarian one.

A second ingredient of the explanation for Soviet stability may be found in the largely noncumulative nature of the problems faced by the Soviet leadership. There are very different priorities among the dissatisfactions and demands expressed by Soviet "public opinion." These are not expressed simultaneously; they often contradict rather than reinforce one another. One has only to think of the aspirations of Russians versus those of other minorities (and particularly the large Russian minorities in non-Russian areas); the anti-authoritarianism and desire for creative freedom among intellectuals versus the managers' desire for greater autonomy and for more stringent discipline of workers; and the aspirations of both intellectuals and managers versus the egalitarian goals of workers and their anti-intellectualism. [. . .]

To go to the core of the explanation for Soviet stability, the effectiveness of the regime's massive efforts to maintain order, one must turn to a number of deeper processes and undercurrents in Soviet society. These have frequently been overlooked as a consequence of the coincidence of certain aspects of official Soviet and Western analysis that often leads to a distortion of Soviet reality and inhibits the deeper understanding of the system's social processes and mechanisms of functioning. The Soviet version of this parallel portrayal is best expressed in describing the society as "planned," as evolving in accordance with the law of "planned, proportionate development." The Western version of Soviet society is often not very different. To take but one example, Charles Lindblom makes the following comparison of the polyarchic, market societies of the West with their Communist counterparts:

> In their reach into every aspect of life and in the weakness of major social constraints on their scope and ambition, rulers of these [communist] systems go far to substitute—deliberately—formal organization for the complex social structures found in noncommunist societies. *Formal organization supercedes a variety of other forms of social coordination:* ethnic solidarity, religious belief, market, family, and moral code.

There is undoubtedly a strong element of truth in these parallel images. The issue range of centralized political decision making in the Soviet system is clearly broader, the scope of deliberate decision making consciously directed at managing the society is clearly larger than in Western democratic societies. The role of the "invisible hand" of market and social forces is more dominant in the democratic systems as compared to the Soviet system where there is a pronounced stress on the "visible hand" of coordinated organizations, regulations, and detailed social policies. Despite the increased complexity of Soviet society on the one hand and the increased role of the state and progressing bureaucratization of Western societies on the other, it would still be correct to argue the unequal weight and significance in both societies of formal organizations as compared to social organization. Relative to one another, the stability and legitimacy of the democratic systems rest and depend much more on the latter and the Soviet system on the former. It is easy to forget, however, that the differences here are only relative, those of degree.

The parallel Western and Soviet images of Soviet society that we have described tend to exaggerate the "visible hand" features of the Soviet system with its stress on formal organizations and to underestimate the "invisible hand" aspects of systemic processes with their stress on social organization. In so doing, they yield a number of consequences which skew our understanding of the Soviet system.

In the first place this picture tends to minimize the elements of spontaneity, the degree of give-and-take in the Soviet political process itself. It exaggerates the planning dimension of Soviet policy making, the phase of adopting decisions and policies, and undervalues the phase of policy implementation in which adopted, "deliberate" policies usually lose their original shape in the cross current of conflicting interests and forces. Second, this picture underestimates the significance and scope of the unintended consequences of Soviet policies. It tends to exaggerate the degree to which Soviet policies even at their inception are deliberate attempts to shape societal environment according to long-range plans rather than continuous reactions to the shape and influence of political and social forces beyond the policy makers' control. Third, and most important for our theme, this picture tends to exaggerate the role of the formalized and guided control mechanism in securing the stability and legitimacy of the regime and to ignore the significant role of social mechanisms and processes in the attainment of these ends.

The analysis of the sources of the stability of the Soviet regime during the Brezhnev era in this chapter will seek therefore to explore some of those processes. It will address four sources of Soviet stability: the performance of the Brezhnev leadership; the nature of rising popular expectations; the relation between the institutionalization of Soviet politics and popular participation; and the effect of social and political mobility.

The Performance of the Regime

There can be little doubt that a regime's performance in areas which citizens deem important, and especially those which touch on their everyday lives, is directly related to stability. This does not necessarily mean that bad or indifferent performance creates or deepens instability, for the time gap between performance and citizens' response may be quite wide, especially in a society of the Soviet type where social controls are strong and communications are highly managed and manipulated. What it does mean clearly is that good performance contributes to the stability of the regime.

The major question is what one selects to evaluate and how one evaluates the performance. From the vantage point of the Western analyst, the comparison of technological progress in the Soviet Union and the West, for example, may be considered a crucial point of evaluation of Soviet performance over the last fifteen years. Or one can survey the dreary wasteland of Soviet culture in this period and note the forced emigration of some of Russia's most talented and creative writers and artists. By either of these standards one would hardly judge the Brezhnev era a success. I would argue, however, that in order to gauge the regime's stability, the only legitimate vantage point is that of Soviet citizens themselves. And here the crucial sphere is the domestic economy, and the point of reference for judging performance is the comparison with the immediate Soviet past. By this standard the regime's performance in the Brezhnev era can be judged a success. [. . .]

The key successful projects of the Brezhnev era five-year plans—among them the Kama power complex, the Togliatti automobile factory, the Samotlor oil field, the Kama truck plant, the "Friendship" pipeline through the Urals, the chemical fertilizer plants, the Soviet fishing and merchant fleets, the Orenburg natural-gas pipeline, the metallurgical complex at Kursk, the Baikal-Amur Railroad—all are fitting symbols of Soviet economic accomplishments. Yet from the point of view of our interest the most important and impressive change and the most salient characteristic of Soviet economic performance has occurred in the consumer goods sector with the raising of the standard of living. Brezhnev spoke the truth with regard to the raising of Soviet living standards when he proclaimed at the Twenty-fifth Party Congress that the "history of our country has not known such a broad social program as that fulfilled in the period for which I give the report." [. . .]

The Soviet regime has by and large been able to deliver the goods; it has generally been able to satisfy popular expectations for higher standards of living. The indices which we used to reach this conclusion have been aggregate figures for the entire population. From the point of view of our interest in how the regime's performance influences Soviet stability, it is questionable, however, whether one can draw inferences for political stability from aggregate figures. It can be argued that these figures must be disaggregated to get at the political problems. In other words, what is most important to stability are sudden changes or discontinuous drops in living standards (such as changes in work norms or sudden price increases) and other matters of equity for given groups; because even when aggregate standards rise, the situation of some group or groups may decline. Similarly, one should probably make regional breakdowns, since any region which feels disadvantaged by the system may harbor resentments which could erupt into political disturbance. In sum, factors which affect the standards or relative position of specific groups are more important in triggering political disruptions than are slow, continuous changes in the aggregate measures. Moreover, while in decentralized market systems resentment is diffused, in the centralized systems of the USSR and Eastern Europe it is channeled to the center, since economic problems are necessarily blamed on the government and lower authorities usually lack power to act.

The availability of economic data does not permit a detailed disaggregation of the comprehensive indicators by groups and regions. A few well-grounded impressions based on what data do exist, however, would strongly argue that with regard to the main groups of the population and the main regions a disaggregation of indices would not alter the basic conclusion that Soviet performance under Brezhnev in the area of living standards does contribute to the stability of the regime.

First of all, the data indicate that all major groups of Soviet society have participated in the general improvement of living conditions. Although their respective shares were unequal, no group was left out. The improvement affected both the urban and rural populations, the skilled and unskilled workers, the managers and professionals, the students and pensioners. White-collar workers, clerks, typists, etc. probably profited least from the increase in the living standard, but this group from the point of view of political weight in the society, past record of causing trouble, ability to organize, and so forth is the least sensitive for the Soviet regime to deal with.

Second, all major regions, that is, primarily the republics, benefited from the improvement. Regional differences did exist, but they followed the normal, long-standing pattern that the greatest improvement in production and consumption related inversely to the level of the region's development. If differences among regions have therefore somewhat narrowed, the prevailing ranking of the regions has not changed.

Third and most important, by far the greatest improvement in living conditions was felt by the most unprivileged groups in Soviet society, those who were probably most dissatisfied with their lot. Minimum wages rose by about 50 percent;

pensions were substantially increased; the peasants were included in the social security system; collective farms were covered by a state insurance system against bad harvests. In the decade 1965–75 the number of people with a monthly income of 100 rubles or more per family member increased eight and one-half times, a virtual income revolution embracing tens of millions of people.

Fourth, the government in this period pursued a very cautious policy with regard to raising norms or increasing prices, that is, the steps which would lead to a drop in the standard of living of specific groups. As a matter of fact, it is the level of prices of basic consumer goods, supported by enormous subsidies and the sometimes absurdly low and unchanging level of industrial norms of production, to mention two of many items, which account to a large extent for the strong inflationary pressures in the Soviet market and for the glaring inefficiencies and low productivity of the Soviet worker. It is virtually certain that this policy of caution betrays exactly the regime's concern over the possible destabilizing effects of any other alternative—a view which the bitter experiences with raising norms and prices in Poland could only have reinforced.

Fifth, the rise in the living standard was achieved in part through a channel which, from the point of view of its contribution to stability, is probably the most advantageous to the regime, namely, through social mobility. Improvement in this area is the most satisfactory, most drastic and most immediate of all forms of improvement in the standard of living and, incidentally, requires the least investment from the state. I am thinking here not only of the regular channels of mobility through higher education but primarily about mobility from rural to urban occupations and from unskilled to skilled labor. [. . .]

The Nature of Rising Popular Expectations

Stability of the regime cannot be discussed apart from the question of the nature and level of popular expectations. As we have mentioned, the most important aspect of the rise of popular expectations to date is its confinement largely to the material sphere. No doubt the rise of nonmaterial expectations would present dangers to the system's stability.

It seems clear that the nonmaterial expectations and aspirations of various Soviet groups and the population at large differ today in many respects from what they were twenty or twenty-five years ago. All groups now expect a secure life, free from capricious harassment and from terror. All aspire to live in a state which preserves a respectable level of legality in daily contacts with citizens. The creative intelligentsia–writers, artists, directors–expect greater artistic freedom;

they aspire to a state of being where they can, within limits, experiment and err. They expect to continue the often enjoyed advantage to opt out, to engage safely in artistic pursuits which are neutral to the goals of the regime.

The creative and technical intelligentsia as well as the various elites share the expectation and strong desire never again to be isolated from the main streams of non-socialist world culture and progress. Professional groups expect a greater degree of professional autonomy and aspire to extend still further the limits of this autonomy, to gain greater access to information and data about their own and other societies, to be able to address the areas of their expertise more freely if only in closed discussion and publications of limited circulation.

The émigré dissident Valery Chalidze has contended that active dissent in the Soviet Union represents only a tip of the iceberg, that behind each *active* dissenter there are scores of *hidden* dissenters among the intelligentsia and even within the elites who share the ideas but lack the courage or ability or opportunity or desire to act openly. We cannot know whether Chalidze is correct. In all probability he accurately describes those groups of dissenters who hold the most moderate views. Even if Chalidze were right, however, from the point of view of the regime's stability, the point to be made is that the distinction between a small active dissent movement and a large inactive dissent group is a crucial one. The small active dissent movement can be fought with relative ease; it can be frag- mented, isolated, neutralized. Where *conditions of stability* already exist, it suf- fices at most to identify for further reference the larger inactive dissent sympathy mood and then to ignore it. *Inactive dissent does not produce instability: its danger to the regime lies in the possibility of its activation under conditions of instability.*

Yet one may also argue, as this author does, that Chalidze exaggerates the extent of the inactive dissent by identifying it incorrectly as dissent. In light of what has just been said about the raised nonmaterial expectations and aspira- tions of various groups in Soviet society, it is more probable that what we observe is the partial coincidence of these aspirations and some of the views of the dis- senters. What is crucial about the coincidence of shared aspirations, however, is, first, that for the dissenters the aspirations of these strata, especially in scope and intensity, represent only a small part of their program and, second, that for the dissenters their program is to be achieved through systemic change, while the various other groups aspire to realize their goals within the system by means of pressure that results in policy relaxation.

The nondissident groups and strata then do not expect a change of system but seek accommodation within it. Moreover, their expectations and, within limits, their aspirations are not neglected by the system's directors. As a matter of fact, their very expectations are based on changes which have already taken place in the post-Stalin era with the willing or grudging support of the leadership. These changes–toward greater professional autonomy, greater freedom of expression, greater contacts with the non-socialist world—did not endanger the regime's stability. Indeed, their implementation owed perhaps less to pressures from the various groups than to the coincidence of those pressures with some interests of the leadership itself. The leadership slowly became convinced that such changes, when controlled and kept within limits, could serve to enhance the effectiveness and performance of the system or were even necessary to that end. The crux of the matter is to contain the aspirations within limits so as not to impinge on issues which the regime considers crucial to its survival.

It now seems that despite the partial coincidence of the aspirations of these groups and strata with those of active dissidents the former do not pose a threat to the system as long as they do not share the dissidents' broader goals and selection of means for their attainment. In addition, as long as the regime has the opportunity and these strata show the willingness to trade off nonmaterial aspirations for material demands—and this is what the regime has also been doing throughout the Brezhnev era—the regime is well prepared to cope with those aspirations.

In this connection the following proposition of Walter Connor holds true not only for the relations between the elite and the population at large but for relations between the regime's leadership and all important strata of the Soviet, particularly Russian Soviet, society:

> The political culture links the bureaucratic elite and the "masses" more closely than it links the dissidents to either. The institutional framework that emerged in the Stalin era "fitted" relatively well with the antecedent political culture of tsarist Russia at the most critical points, and to all appearances the *contemporary* Soviet political culture still "fits" this relatively unchanged institutional pattern quite well.

Under Brezhnev the rise in the expectations and aspirations of Soviet citizens of high and low status has been most noticeable in the material sphere. In the last fifteen years a fever of materialism has seized the Soviet population of all classes and stations, a visible and all-pervasive drive to acquire goods, to live better, to enjoy. What is more striking, however, especially when compared to the situation in the West, is first that in absolute terms these expectations are very modest for an industrial nation and second that they are not far removed from what is realistically possible, though often unrealized, in Soviet conditions. To put it differently, although material expectations remain in advance of reality, one doubts whether there is a widening gap between expectations and reality.

The rising material expectations of the Soviet population do not get out of hand. They do not create a vicious circle which narrows restrictively and increasingly the leadership's ability to impose its own set of priorities on the society, which creates unbearable inflationary pressures and, by translating rising expectations into political pressures, overloads the entire system of government. The Soviet situation under Brezhnev, the combination of rising material expectations on the one hand and their limits on the other, has led to a partial reordering of the regime's priorities in the direction of consumerism. At the same time the system's directors have retained enough flexibility to decide the order of priorities, free from society's dictation. [. . .]

The rise in material expectations of the Soviet public requires no explanation. More problematical is why rising expectations have not developed into a vicious-circle pattern. Of the major reasons for this untypical state of affairs, we should like to introduce four.

1. The attitude and behavior of the Soviet population, especially of the middle and older generations, is largely shaped by the past. The restraint in popular expectation is striking in a system which for decades overindulged in utopian promises, but it is exactly the overindulgence which partly explains the restraint. Soviet society was and is a society in which the regime's promises are as quickly devalued as they are issued. Past performance tempers both the expectations for the future and the countervailing influence usually associated with the betterment of the living standard which has occurred recently.

People believe in what they get now and what they can get; they fantasize little about what they will have or may get. A Soviet saying expresses this attitude well: "Please God, may it not get better" — ("Bozhe, chtoby ne bylo luchshe"). This mood is akin, though much stronger, to the feelings of the American generation which experienced the Great Depression and lived long after with the fear that things might again go wrong. The memories and fears act to dampen rising expectations and to keep them from escaping control.

2. By the measuring rod of industrially developed societies, the standard of living in the Soviet Union, even after many years of significant improvements, remains very low.

The consequences of this situation from the point of view of the level of expectations are significant. In a society where food still constitutes over 50 percent of the family budget, where starches still account for about two-thirds of the food consumed, where fresh vegetables, not to mention fruits, are a rarity in urban areas, where regular meat deliveries to the stores are an exception, where a pair of shoes wears only a few months before disintegrating and a suit of clothes looks as though it was confected at the turn of the century, and where the pattern of building and inhabiting communal apartments with shared kitchens and bathrooms has only recently been abandoned, the "normal" consumer expectations are unimaginative and modest. They are likely to remain so in a society which displays before the public no examples of conspicuous luxury and mounts no advertising campaigns directed to the consumer. The modesty of consumer expectations thus renders them attainable under Soviet conditions long before they become economically and politically difficult to handle. From the existing base any step forward in the quantitative and especially the qualitative indicators of consumer supply will continue to be welcome as a real improvement.

An extremely important dimension in evaluating one's standard of living and setting one's expectations concerns the reference point used as the base. It is our contention that for the average Soviet consumer this reference point is neither the West nor even East European Communist countries but his own past. We often exaggerate tremendously the effects that opening the Soviet Union to the West in the last ten to fifteen years has had on the general Soviet public, given both the long history of isolation and the relative narrowness of the present opening. True, many "normal" Soviet citizens in metropolitan areas see foreigners and even have sporadic contacts with them. At the same time they are denied comprehensive and visual information about life in the West and are bombarded, if anything at a greater rate than before, with distorted data and images of life in the West. Travel to the West of course is enjoyed almost entirely by representatives of elites and subelites as a major ingredient of their privileged position.

For the "normal" Soviet citizen who suspects the official version, life in the West has nevertheless no reality of its own. It cannot and does not in my opinion serve as a reference point of his rising expectations. That point is provided by his own and his peer group's past, which, it should be stressed, is very often a peasant past, even in urban areas. Comparison with this past can only heighten approval of ongoing improvements and temper expectations.

The situation differs for elites and subelites and part of the professional classes. Their notion of the Western standard of living acquires plasticity thanks to their access to literature, their contacts with foreigners, their personal travel, or the accounts of friends. To counter potential disaffection the authorities assure these groups a standard of living much closer to the West and infinitely higher than the Soviet average. These beneficiaries contrast their superior lot to their less fortunate fellow citizens and enjoy it with some gratitude and even some guilt.

The picture we conveyed would not be correct were it to depict simply a harmonious society with modest expectations and high levels of satisfaction. If, as we contend, the basic background is that of modest expectations, the situation is more complex. The level of satisfaction of various Soviet publics is not normally high because the attainment of even modest expectations comes at the cost of constant gripes, dissatisfaction with what is available, and the unceasing competition for it. The point is, however, that the dissatisfaction and unfulfilled expectations with rare exceptions find expression in ways that may be unpleasant and injurious to the system but not dangerous. Discontent is funneled through specifically designated channels which tend to deflect criticism from central authorities to local bureaucracies. (The principal channel for complaints is the local soviet, the authority closest to the citizen.) One senses that expressions of dissatisfaction function for the regime not only as a safety valve but as a pressure on subordinate bureaucracies. Deviant *individual* behavior (alcoholism, absenteeism, and the like) serves as another channel of expression.

Needless to say, dissatisfaction is almost never expressed in more drastic and independent ways through the organization of autonomous groups or actions like strikes, given the stringent controls over nonofficial communication and organization. Restrictions on the articulation of grievances are an essential means by which Soviet authorities manipulate popular expectations. Where they failed to work, as in Poland, the industrial working class achieved a virtual veto over the government's economic policies. The Soviet Union in this regard has very far to go.

Paul Hollander in his excellent comparison of Soviet and American societies has remarked: "The key to the stability of the Soviet system lies in its management of expectations rather than in the powers of the KGB." As long as Soviet citizen's focus their expectations on material achievements, as long as the rising spiral of expectations remains relatively modest and partly satisfied, as long as the articulation of dissatisfaction follows traditional Soviet channels, the Soviet regime will be able to maintain this major pillar of its stability.

Institutionalization and Popular Participation

The question of stability in the Soviet Union under Brezhnev requires consideration of the interconnections among three processes or characteristics of Soviet society: political apathy, political participation, and professionalization of social and political management. (Only those aspects of these vast topics that relate to stability will be examined here, while the matter of participation will be treated at greater length when I discuss legitimacy.) One of the most accepted and well-tested propositions in the study of political stability concerns the relation between institutionalization and participation. What has been convincingly argued may be summarized as follows: While a modern polity in the process of socioeconomic and political modernization produces and requires an increase in the intensity and scope of political participation, it requires as well a high level of political institutionalization which will keep pace with the increased participation. Political instability inevitably results if the level of political institutionalization is not high enough to absorb the increased pressures of the participation.

Analysts have frequently alleged that in contrast to the Khrushchev period, the succeeding Brezhnev period is characterized by the decline of participatory politics. It is our contention that the level of political participation today seems, if anything, to be higher than in the immediate post-Stalin decade, that what has changed involves some emphases, directions, moods, and forms of political participation but not its level.

The two periods differ most in our opinion in the relation between participation and institutionalization. One may suggest that in the Khrushchev period the levels of participation and institutionalization did not keep step and, indeed, that their respective directions ran counter to one another. Khrushchev, in his attempt to shake up the system, destabilized political institutions. He may be said to have deinstitutionalized Soviet politics somewhat at the very same time that he conducted a partially successful effort to increase popular political participation. In our view participation increased also during the Brezhnev period and went less noticed because the institutionalization of Soviet politics matched its pace of development.

Both periods share the un-Stalinist attitude of encouraging criticism, feedback, and initiative, that is, a positive commitment to expanded participation. Yet, while the tendency of the Khrushchev approach was to equalize the political status of full-time officials and the participatory *aktiv*, Brezhnev seeks successfully to reconcile the expanded political participation of nonbureaucrats with a strong commitment to the political and bureaucratic autonomy of Soviet officialdom. (In the apt phrase of George Breslauer, Khrushchev's approaches to achievement, participation, and authority building may be labeled "organizational," "populist," and "confrontational"; Brezhnev's as "financial," "rational-administrative," and "corporate.")

If, as we noted above, expanded participation often produces the danger of destabilization, a degree of political apathy in society, an element of apolitization is not undesirable *from the systemic point of view,* as Huntington suggested. It does, after all, provide a stabilizing cushion, a safety valve. Exactly this is taking place in Soviet society. Contradictory as it may sound, the expanded participation of the Brezhnev era goes hand in hand with the retention of one of the most characteristic features of major Soviet social groups—their high level of apolitization.

In order to understand this apolitization, a major distinction has to be made between "high politics" and "low politics." The former involves the principal political issues of society, the abstract ideas and language of politics, the decisions and actions of the societal leadership. The latter involves the decisions that directly touch the citizen's daily life, the communal matters, and the conditions of the workplace.

The average Soviet citizen is apolitical, indifferent, apathetic with regard to "high politics." Lacking curiosity and interest, he suffers his routine encounters with "high politics," unavoidable in Soviet conditions, but he remains untouched by them. The language is rich in sayings that convey this attitude: for example, "The bosses know best" ("Nachal'stvo luchshe znaet") or "That's none of my business" ("Moia khata s kraiu"). The average person considers politics a separate way of life, a profession for which one is trained and paid. He customarily regards dissenters who risk their lives and careers for "high politics" as abnormal and aberrant or simply as trouble-makers. Nowhere is this attitude toward high politics more prevalent than among youth, so often the most politically volatile of all groups, but who in the Soviet Union, according to most competent observers, orient their lives toward careers and leisure. Former Soviet citizens recall from their experience as Komsomol members that the organization from the point of view of "high politics" was very nonpolitical.

By contrast, "low politics" regularly involves a very high proportion of Soviet citizenry. As we shall restate later in our discussion of legitimacy, "low politics" constitute the very substance of the Soviet system of political participation. Very seldom under Soviet conditions do the "low" and "high" dimensions of Soviet politics intersect. When they do, it is a matter of the objective *effects* of the "low politics" of mass political participation on "high politics," and not as a consequence of the conscious *actions* of citizens. In all probability only a major shock or a prolonged crisis could provoke such actions.

This form of political apathy, while obviously an important element of political stability in the Brezhnev era, equals or perhaps even yields in significance as a factor of stability to the element of the increased institutionalization of Soviet politics. Increased institutionalization manifests itself in a number of ways—in the stability and streamlining of organizations active in Soviet politics, in the depersonalization of Soviet politics as compared to the Khrushchev period, in the establishment and adherence to long-range procedures in decision making, and so forth. Yet the major and to a large extent the new factor of this institutionalization is the heightened professionalization of all aspects of Soviet politics and administration. [. . .]

Social and Political Mobility

Of all the social processes in the Soviet Union there is one that provides the crucial safety valve against discontent and a key basis for the positive identification of various social strata with the regime. It is the process of social mobility in general and, more especially, the process of political mobility. There would appear to be no necessary relation between the degree of democracy within a given political system and the openness of recruitment into its elites and sube-lites. If one measures the openness of recruitment by the ease of access of diverse social strata to positions of a political and administrative power, that is to say, by intra- and intergenerational political and administrative mobility, one must con-sider highly democratic society like Great Britain to possess a fairly closed, nondemocratic system of recruitment and, by contrast, a highly authoritarian society such as the Soviet Union to display the most open, democratic system of recruitment of all developed societies.

Soviet society exhibits vast inequalities of class, status, and power. The revo-lutionary Bolshevik egalitarian ideal is farther from fulfillment today than it was in the first postrevolutionary decade. These inequalities remain firmly-embedded-in-the fabric the of Soviet society, despite the appreciable rise in living standards and improvement in the level of political participation during the post-Stalinist and especially the Brezhnev periods. Yet they should not distract attention from the high degree of political mobility within the society, that is to say, from the degree to which the elite system is open, accessible to recruitment from the lower strata of the society.

The original Bolshevik elite came from the intelligentsia or middle class. From the 1930s and especially from the Great Purge until today, however, the over-whelming majority of the national Soviet leadership as well as the leading offi-cials of the various functional bureaucracies are working class in origin. This holds especially true for officials on all levels of the most exclusive and powerful bureaucracy, the party apparatus, as Table 1 illustrates. In this respect the present and the past are differentiated by the type of mobility that has brought individu-als of working-class origin into the elites. In the past it was partly intergenera-tional mobility but to a large extent also intragenerational mobility; today it is primarily or predominantly intergenerational mobility.

To say it differently, those individuals who entered the elite in the late 1930s, 1940s, or even 1950s were very often not only of working-class origin but had actually engaged in physical labor in their youth. Those individuals who entered the elite more recently may still derive predominantly from working-class ori-gins, but their own social position prior to joining the political world was much less frequently that of worker or peasant. The decline in intragenerational mobil-ity reflects the changes which have taken place in the typical lifestyle pattern of educationally mobile working-class youth in Russia in the last few decades, espe-cially with the advent of mass middle education.

The openness of recruitment into Soviet political and administrative elites and subelites results in part from deliberate policies and in part from the functioning of spontaneous social processes. First of all, it can occur only in an ideological atmosphere that encourages the advancement of individuals of working-class origin into the elites and subelites. The official Soviet ideology with its symbolic cult of the working classes creates a propitious environment which supports the aspirations of working-class individuals to enter the elite and propitious conditions for their competition with individuals of other social origins.

Table 1. Social origin of leading Soviet cadres, 1956–66.

Cadres	No.	% of worker and pleasant origin
Top party and state leaders		
(Politburo Secretariat, Presidium of Council of Ministers, Presidium of Supreme Soviet)	67	87
Central Committee apparatus	48	73
Council of Ministries	107	76
Provincial and republican party-state		
Leaders	276	82
Key economic managers	185	72
Key military commanders	65	74

Source: Calculated on the basis of the author's personal files. The two major official sources of data on the social origins of Soviet high officials—*Deputaty Verkhovnogo Soveta SSSR, Piatoi sozyv* (Moscow: Izd. Izvestiia, 1958) and *Deputaty Verkhovnogo Soveta SSSR, Shestoi sozyv* (Moscow: Izd. Izvestiia, 1962)—provide the following picture: Of 581 officials listed in those sources, data concerning social origin are provided for 364 individuals (62.6 percent). Of these, 344 officials (94.5 percent) are listed as being of worker or peasant origin.

Second, the dominant working-class origin of the Soviet elites is widely publicized in the Soviet Union precisely because it is ideologically attractive to Soviet rulers and because it confirms the claim that Soviet authority is derived from the people. This too encourages individuals of working-class origin to advance into the elite. Studies of mobility in Western countries have reinforced the axiom that people, as a rule, strive primarily for what they consider attainable and avoid what they consider, rightly or wrongly, unattainable.

Third, the easiest means to recruit individuals of nonworking-class origin into the elites would obviously be to coopt members of the families of the elites and subelites themselves. Such cooptation, however, is officially and strenuously discouraged at all levels of the administrative ladder. Party policy was and remains directed against it for fear of populating the functional bureaucracies and geographical regions with family cliques whose personal loyalties would resist the penetration and supervision of superior authority and create a diffusion of central power. Party policy vigorously encourages recruitment into elites and subelites from families of party members and discourages it from families of elite members.

Fourth, the main precondition of recruitment into elites and subelites is educational achievement, and education constitutes the main channel of entrance. As many studies have shown, the higher educational process in the Soviet Union favors groups of nonworking-class origin, despite official efforts to the contrary. One discerns the discriminatory class element in Soviet higher education, however, only when one examines the relative group representation of various classes in the student body and especially among graduates of the various Soviet institutions of higher learning. But from the point of view of the availability of working-class candidates for recruitment into the elite, the absolute pool of Soviet graduates of working-class origin is so large as to make irrelevant the relative class representation among the graduates.

Fifth and finally, a crucial factor in the advance of working-class individuals into the elites and subelites is on the one hand the attractiveness of this type of career for these individuals and on the other hand the pronounced reluctance of individuals of professional and "upper class" origin (with the notable exception of the military elite) to embark on a road which would lead them directly to such careers. This is especially true with regard to the political elite in the strict sense of the word, the party apparatus. Were this not the case, one would suspect more obstacles in the path of advancement by working-class individuals.

The degree to which the children of professional and especially elite families are disinclined to choose a political career is striking. A number of reasons may account for such reluctance in addition to the previously mentioned official discouragement of the practice. In the case of individuals from professional families, the attraction of their parents' profession, whether doctor, engineer, or scientist, may be of overwhelming importance. In the case of individuals from elite and subelite families, the force of the negative example of their parents' careers combined with the relative ease of their own advance into the "free" professions or arts or diplomacy thanks to family backing may be crucial.

Parents for their part want their children to have a "better" future than an administrative or political career, the pitfalls and difficulties of which they know so well. They consider it one of the perquisites of office to be able to direct their children along different, attractive, high-status paths. The children, for their part, have an opportunity to observe the tedium, insecurity, and extreme hard work associated with their parents' careers. While taking for granted and even regarding as hereditary the privileges of status, they are at the same time drawn to other high-status careers.

By contrast, ambitious individuals of working-class origin face very stiff competition from better-prepared and better-backed children from professional and elite families in the striving for high-status, nonpolitical, and nonadministrative careers. Moreover, they perhaps idealize the realities of political and administrative careers while coveting the material benefits and power that accompany political elite status.

Whatever accounts for the pattern of recruitment, however, the high level of working-class intergenerational mobility into the political and administrative elites has highly significant consequences for the system, For the working classes, the high levels of social mobility in general and mobility into the elites in particular provide one of the most tangible and visible stakes in the system.

Probably there are few families in the Soviet Union where either the nuclear or extended family has no member who can be identified with a ruling group, whether as an officer of the armed forces or the police, a manager of an enterprise, a functionary of the party, or an official of a ministry. There are probably few working-class families where parents fail to hold aspirations for their children's future career and with the reasonable expectation of realization. The Soviets have long provided opportunities of advancement for the working classes, a circumstance which could not fail to influence at least in part a positive identification with the regime and to dilute significantly any feelings of opposition to the regime.

There is yet another important sense in which upward mobility and the predominantly working-class origin of the leadership and elites bear on the legitimacy of the regime. Well before the revolution in Russia and to the present day, society has exhibited a pronounced "we" versus "they" syndrome. Usually we contrast "we," the simple "normal" people, with "they," the power holders on all levels, the *nachal' stvo*. Yet the reality and genuineness of this division may conceal a phenomenon no less real and for questions of stability even more significant. It is the sense of cultural community between "we" and "they," where the "we" represents the working classes. After all, they both come from the same social stuff; they share much the same life histories; they resemble one another culturally to an amazing degree, as witness their sentimentalism, basic nationalism, mannerisms, artistic and literary preferences, language, and all the rest. The world of privilege may separate "we" and "they" in Soviet society, but origin and culture unite them. It is in this sense and only in this sense that one should understand the observation of a Russian writer in a conversation with me, "Our power is a genuinely popular power" ("U nas nastoiashchaia narodnaia vlast'").

To this point the discussion has focused on a number of processes which underlie the stability of the Soviet regime in the Brezhnev era. The argument can be further developed in two directions. First I propose to analyze the question of the legitimacy of the Soviet system, a central ingredient in our understanding of the nature and mechanism of its stability. Then I propose to demonstrate some of my propositions concerning stability by studying in more detail the most serious long-range domestic challenge to Soviet stability at the present time, the national problem.

2

The Collapse of the Soviet Union

It is safe to say that when Mikhail S. Gorbachev became General Secretary of the Communist Party of the Soviet Union in March 1985, no serious scholar anticipated the imminent collapse of communist rule in Eastern Europe, much less the disintegration of the Soviet Union itself. Yet, in less than five years, the Soviet empire was gone, and by the end of 1991, the CPSU and the USSR itself were relegated to the dustbin of history.[1]

Over the next two years, as Gorbachev initiated economic and political reform under the slogans *glasnost* (openness), *perestroika* (restructuring), and *demokratizatsiya* (democratization), Western observers predictably engaged in debate over the likelihood those reforms would prove successful. These reforms were Gorbachev's response to the years of "stagnation," as both Russian and Western experts referred to the decline in the Soviet economy that began in the late 1970s. It was not just a stagnation of economic growth but also of ideas and of the officials who clung to them. Change and innovation had become anathema to every aspect of Soviet rule. Gorbachev, sensing a looming, systemic crisis, initiated his reforms to reinvigorate what had become a stagnant system through and through.

Some, who continued to see the totalitarian underpinnings of the system Stalin created, predicted utter failure due to that system's basic inflexibility.[2] Any attempt to upset the apple cart was doomed to failure, and Gorbachev would suffer the same fate—removal from his post—as the earlier reformer Khrushchev.[3] They did not, as a rule, forecast that these efforts would topple the party and the regime itself. Rather, they anticipated an era of retrenchment internally and hostility toward the West externally.

These were a distinct minority in the West, however. The vast majority of experts on the Soviet Union were swept away by a general infatuation with the idea of the reforms and with the leader himself, who projected an innovative, dynamic, modern image. Gorbachev's image in the West, enhanced by media and academic accounts alike, was of a brilliant renaissance man, a liberal akin to the American Founding Fathers. He stood not just for peace with the West but for real integration with the liberal, democratic, and capitalist world. Hard to believe in retrospect, but this was the public perception of him and was reflected in his receipt of the Nobel Peace Prize in 1989.[4] Though widely scorned and even hated at home at all ends of the political spectrum, he was beloved in the West.

I witnessed this disconnect personally in October 1990, when working as an accredited Moscow correspondent for Crain's Communications, a news and media group specializing in business and trade publications. At a banquet in the most exclusive hotel restaurant in Moscow, to support the fledgling advertising and public relations industry just emerging in Russia, I was seated next to the company's matriarch, Gertrude Crain, then in her late seventies. On the other side of me sat a twenty-something female Muscovite, an artist and aspiring advertising designer, sporting a nose ring and short, spiked purple hair. Gorbachev had been awarded the Nobel Peace Prize earlier that day, and a positively ecstatic Mrs. Crain asked whether everyone in Russia was excited by the news. Turning to the hip, young woman on my left, I asked dryly, "She wants to know what people here think about Gorbachev's receiving the Nobel."

Her large eyes bugging out and shaking her head, she simply stated, *"Uzhasniy koshmar."*

I translated for Mrs. Crain, "She says it is a terrible nightmare."

The look of utter incomprehension on the face of this powerful, stately woman was one I shall never forget. The local experience with Gorbachev was chaos and breakdown brought about by half measures and unfulfilled promises. This initial exchange triggered a fascinating education of a news powerhouse by a wannabe punk artist on the intricacies of the late-Soviet socioeconomic milieu. For, by October 1989, the Soviet Empire in Eastern Europe was spinning out of control as the communist regimes were falling like dominos. Across Russia, the masses found their earnings had become largely worthless, while store shelves were becoming barren. Hour-long lines for meager basics were the norm as black-market prices topped unreachable levels for most of the Soviet people. Where Gorbachev had promised growth, modernity, and the strengthening of the country, the people experienced exactly the opposite while observing their leader being indecisive, erratically switching course, and generally demonstrating incompetence. The attempt at educating the wealthy, American media mogul failed entirely. After about twenty minutes, a flabbergasted Mrs. Crain shook her head and, ending the conversation, stated, "It does not make any sense. He has made everything so much better. He has brought so much change for these people and peace to the world."

Perhaps the normative bias in the West regarding the direction of events in the USSR, reflected in Gertrude Crain's incomprehension, blinded people to the harsh realities that the mass of the Soviet population experienced as the demise of the empire and the collapse of the country approached. While we in the West were celebrating the end of the Cold War and the triumph of liberal, capitalist democracy, we failed to grasp the realities of systemic collapse in Russia. People were in fear during hyperinflation in the late 1980s and early 1990s that they would go hungry, that there would be another famine. It was existential fear.

But what is, in retrospect, truly bewildering is that the total and rapid demise of all of the communist regimes across Eastern Europe in the second half of 1989 did not shake the widespread perception of Gorbachev's success, much less raise anticipation of a pending collapse of the Soviet political system. Gorbachev was making the world more peaceful with unilateral force cuts, troop withdrawals, and accelerated arms control negotiations with the United States. His reforms advanced within the Soviet Union the cherished Western liberal ideals of political and economic freedoms. These domestic and international changes produced euphoria in the West—things were changing in ways that the United States and its allies wanted. Writers, musicians, and artists were free to produce and disseminate their work. How vibrant the cultural space was becoming! People were able to espouse their political views without fear. How dynamic the political space was becoming! The military standoff between East and West was receding. How peaceful the world was becoming! It was understandably easy to get carried away and to equate all of these changes with success.

And so, the abrupt demise of the Soviet Union following the unsuccessful coup against Gorbachev in August 1991 came as a shock to virtually everyone in the West. The coup, in which eight government officials, including Gorbachev's Vice President, Interior Minister, KGB Chief, Minister of Defense, and the head of the parliament, petered out as the erstwhile leaders and the army units deployed into Moscow lacked the resolve to open fire on the group of citizens and politicians, including Russian President Boris Yeltsin, who gathered in protest of the action. In the wake of the Soviet collapse, scholars have surveyed where the study of that country went wrong and why so few foresaw the end.[5] These discussions probed the interesting question of whether any reform strategy in a Soviet-type political system could have succeeded or whether such systems were immutable to reform and, if there were paths to reform that could have succeeded, why other choices were made.

The following selections provide an overview of the myriad challenges the Soviet Union faced in its final years, a review of the reforms Gorbachev initiated that sought to address these challenges, and explanation of why that attempt so spectacularly failed. Most of these analyses directly link to the wider literature on "transitions to democracy", as Gorbachev's response to systemic crisis was a series of reforms designed to "open up" the Soviet system, to ease controls, and to provide a wider scope for individual action and individual responsibility. They were liberalizing measures designed to resolve crisis that instead triggered an explosion of antisystem sentiment. Because the Western expectation was that these measures would succeed in transforming the Soviet Union, the ultimate collapse sparked inquiries attempting to explain the failure. Katherine Verdery, in "What Was Socialism and Why Did it Fail?" offers a compelling overview of the failure of the Soviet political economy as it was first and foremost economic failure that sparked Gorbachev's reformist orientation. Verdery's is a thorough analysis of why Soviet-style economies fell behind so catastrophically, with insights into both the internal and external challenges that made the situation so dire. By contrast, Alexander Dallin, in "Causes of the Collapse of the USSR" offers an overview of various political explanations for the causes of the Soviet collapse. My own piece, "Glasnost Gutted the Party, Democratization Destroyed the State," seeks to reevaluate the role of Gorbachev himself, evaluating his leadership, the decisions he made, and the forces he unleashed in an attempt to demonstrate how far the results deviated from his own goals. In the end, one comes away impressed that the systemic, circumstantial, and individual variables all contributed substantially to the unraveling of the Soviet political system, to the disintegration of the empire, and to the dismemberment of the state.

For Further Reference

Books

Valerie Bunce, *Subversive Institutions: the Design and the Destruction of Socialism and the State,* Cambridge University Press: 1999.
Mikhail S. Gorbachev, *Memoirs,* Doubleday: 1996.
Ken Jowitt, *New Word Disorder,* University of California Press: 1992.
Boris Kagarlitsky, *The Disintegration of the Monolith,* Verso: 1992.
Yegor Ligachev, *Inside Gorbachev's Kremlin,* Pantheon Press: 1993.
Michael McFaul, *Russia's Unfinished Revolution,* Cornell University Press: 2001.
Steven Skolnick, *Stealing the State: Control and Collapse in Soviet Institutions.* Harvard University Press: 1998.
Gale Stokes, *The Walls Came Tumbling Down: The Collapse of Communism in Eastern Europe,* Oxford University Press: 1993.
Ronald Suny, *The Revenge of the Past: Nationalism, Revolution, and the Collapse of the Soviet Union,* Stanford University Press: 1993.

Journal Articles

Journal of Cold War Studies special issues on "The Collapse of the Soviet Union," Vol. 5, No. 1 (2003); Vol. 5, No. 4 (2003).

Novels

Slavenka Drakulic, *How We Survived Communism and Even Laughed,* Harper: 1993.
David Remnik, *Resurrection,* Vintage: 1988.

Films

Little Vera
Repentance
Taxi Blues

NOTES

1. The phrase was coined by early Bolshevik leader Leon Trotsky, who hurled it at less radical socialist competitors in Russia who walked out on a meeting of communists during the Revolution in 1917. "You are pitiful isolated individuals; you are bankrupts; your role is played out. Go where you belong from now on into the dustbin of history!" Trotsky shouted at them. (See Leon Trotsky, *History of the Russian Revolution* Vol. 3 [Chicago: Eastman], ch. 10.)

2. Most famous and controversial among these was Z [Martin Malia], "To the Stalin Mausoleum," *Daedalus,* Vol. 119, No. 1 (1990), pp. 295–344.

3. Marshall Goldman, in particular, routinely predicted in public talks that Gorbachev would be removed from power within six months. He began making this prediction in mid-1987. See an account in *Los Angeles Times,* December 7, 1987, titled "The Washington Summit: Enigmatic Gorbachev Taxes Kremlinologists' Skills."

4. This was clearly the dominant position in the West, with far too many representative sources to identify as leading. Stephen Cohen and Katrina vanden Heuvel's *Voices of Glasnost* (WW Norton, 1991); Seweryn Bialer's *Inside Gorbachev's Russia: Politics, Society and Nationality* (Westview Press, 1989); and Ed A. Hewett and Victor H. Winston's *Milestones in Glasnost and Perestroika* (Brookings, 1991) are all edited volumes with selections of leading scholars of Soviet politics, economics, and society, who without exception hailed the dawning of a new age.

5. For a nice exchange laying out varying approaches to the Soviet crisis and their strengths and weaknesses, see George Breslauer, "In Defense of Sovietology," in *Post-Soviet Affairs,* Vol. 8, No. 3 (October–December 1992), pp. 197–238; and Ken Jowitt, "Really Imaginary Socialism," in *East European Constitutional Review,* Vol. 6, No. 2–3 (Spring/Summer 1997), pp. 43–49.

2.1

What was Socialism and Why Did it Fall?

Katherine Verdery

The startling disintegration of Communist Party rule in Eastern Europe in 1989, and its somewhat lengthier unraveling in the Soviet Union between 1985 and 1991, rank among the century's most momentous occurrences. Especially because neither policy-makers nor area specialists predicted them, these events will yield much analysis after the fact, as scholars develop the hindsight necessary to understanding what they failed to grasp before. In this essay, I aim to stimulate discussion about why Soviet-style socialism fell. Since answers to the question require understanding how socialism "worked", I begin with a model of this; I then suggest how it intersected fatefully with certain features of the world-system context.

What was Socialism?

The "formerly existing" socialist states of Eastern Europe and the Soviet Union differed significantly from each other—for instance, in the intensity, effectiveness, and span of central control, in the extent of popular support or resistance, and in the degree and timing of reforms. I opt nevertheless for a single model of them. The resemblances within socialism were more important than its variety, for analytic purposes, much as we can best comprehend French, Japanese, West German, and American society as variants of a single capitalist system. Acknowledging, then, that my description applies more fully to certain countries and time periods than to others, I treat them all under one umbrella.

For several decades, the analysis of socialism has been an international industry, employing both western scholars and eastern dissidents. This industry has lately received a massive infusion of new raw materials, as once-secret files are opened and translations appear of research by local scholars (especially Polish and Hungarian) into their own declining socialist systems. My own taste in such theories is "indigenist": I have found most useful the analyses of East Europeans concerning the world in which they lived. The following summary, which is subject to revision as new material appears, owes much to that work. Given

Source: Katherine Verdery, "What was Socialism and Why Did it Fall?" Contention. Vol.3, No. 1, 1993, p. 223.

Note: Notes and references have been removed from this article.

temporal and spatial constraints, I will compress elements of a larger analytical model. I will emphasize how production was organized and the consequences of this for consumption and for markets, themes that afford the best entry into why Party rule crumbled much faster than anyone expected.

Production

Socialism's fragility begins with the system of "centralized planning," which the center neither adequately planned nor controlled, Central planners would draw up a plan with quantities of everything they wanted to see produced, known as targets. They would disaggregate the plan into pieces appropriate for execution, estimating how much investment and how many raw materials were needed if managers of firms were to fill their targets. Managers learned early on, however, that not only did the targets increase annually, but the materials required often did not arrive on time or in the right amounts. So they would respond by bargaining their plan: demanding more investments and raw materials than the amounts actually necessary for their targets. Every manager, and every level of the bureaucracy, padded budgets and requests in hopes of having enough, in the actual moment of production. (A result of the bargaining process, of course, was that central planners always had faulty information about what was really required for production, and this Impeded their ability to plan,) Then, if managers somehow ended up with more of some material than they needed, they hoarded it. Hoarded material had two uses: it could be kept for the next production cycle, or it could be exchanged with some other firm for something one's own firm lacked. These exchanges or barters of material were a crucial component of behavior within centralized planning.

A result of all the padding of budgets and hoarding of materials was widespread shortages, for which reason socialist economies are called *economies of shortage*. The causes of shortage were primarily that people lower down in the planning process were asking for more materials than they required and then hoarding whatever they got. Underlying their behavior was what economists call *soft budget constraints*—namely, if a firm was losing money, the center would bail it out. In our own economy, with certain exceptions (such as Chrysler and the Savings and Loan industry), budget constraints are hard: if you cannot make ends meet you go under. But in socialist economies, it did not matter if firms asked for extra investment or hoarded raw materials; they paid no penalty.

With all this padding and hoarding, it is clear why shortage was endemic to socialist systems; and why the main problem for firms was not whether they could meet (or generate) demand but whether they could procure adequate supplies. So while the chief problem of economic actors in western economies is to get profits by *selling* things, the chief problem for socialism's economic actors was to *procure* things. Capitalist firms compete with each other for markets in which they will make a profit; socialist firms competed to maximize their bargaining power with suppliers higher up. In our society, the problem is other sellers, and to outcompete them you have to befriend the buyer. Thus, our clerks and shop-owners smile and give the customer friendly service because they want business; customers can be grouchy and it will only make the clerk try harder. In socialism, the locus of competition was elsewhere: your competitor was other buyers, other procurers, and to outcompete them you needed to befriend those higher up who supplied you. Therefore, in socialism it was not the clerk—the provider, or "seller"—who was friendly (they were usually grouchy) but the procurers, the customers, who sought to ingratiate themselves with smiles, bribes, or favors. The work of procuring generated whole networks of cozy relations among economic managers and their bureaucrats, clerks and their customers. We would call this corruption, but that is because getting supplies is not a problem for capitalists: the problem is getting sales. In a word, for capitalists salesmanship is at a premium; for socialist managers, the premium was on acquisitionsmanship, or procurement.

Among the many things in short supply in socialist systems was labor. Managers hoarded labor, just like any other raw material, because they never knew how many workers they would need. Fifty workers working three eight-hour shifts six days a week might be enough to meet a firm's targets—*if* all the materials were on hand all month long. But this never happened. Many of those workers would stand idle for part of the month, and in the last ten days when most of the materials were finally on hand the firm would need 75 workers working overtime to complete the plan. The manager therefore kept 75 workers on the books, even though most of the time he needed fewer; and since all other managers were doing the same, labor was scarce. This provided a convenient if unplanned support for the regimes' guaranteed employment.

An important result of labor's scarcity was that managers of firms had relatively little leverage over their workers. Furthermore, because supply shortages caused so much uncertainty in the process of production, managers had to turn over to workers much control over this process, lest work come to a standstill. That is, structurally speaking, workers under socialism had a somewhat more powerful position relative to management than do workers in capitalism. Just as managers' bargaining with bureaucrats undercut socialist central power, so labor's position in production undercut that of management.

More than this, the very organization of the workplace bred opposition to Party rule. Through the Party-controlled trade union and the frequent merger of Party and management functions, Party directives were continually felt in the production process—and, from the workers' viewpoint, they were felt as unnecessary and disruptive. Union officials either meddled unhelpfully or contributed nothing, only to claim credit for production results that workers knew were their own. Workers participated disdainfully—as sociologist Michael Burawoy found in his studies of Hungarian factories—in Party-organized production rituals, such as work-unit competitions, voluntary work-days, and production campaigns; they resented these coerced expressions of their supposed commitment to a wonderful socialism. Thus, instead of securing workers' consent, workplace rituals sharpened their consciousness and resistance. Against an official "cult of work" used to motivate cadres and workers toward fulfilling the plan, many workers developed an oppositional cult of *non*-work, imitating the Party bosses and trying to do as little as possible for their paycheck. Cadres often found no way around this internal sabotage, which by reducing productivity deepened the problems of socialist economies to the point of crisis.

The very forms of Party rule in the workplace, then, tended to focus, politicize, and turn against it the popular discontent that capitalist societies more successfully disperse, depoliticize, and deflect. In this way, socialism produced a split between "us" and "them," workers and Party leaders, founded on a lively consciousness that "they" are exploiting "us." This consciousness was yet another thing that undermined socialist regimes. [. . .]

Surveillance and Paternalistic Redistribution

Ruling Communist Parties developed a variety of mechanisms to try to obscure this fact of their nature from their subjects, mechanisms designed to produce docile subject dispositions and to ensure that discontent did not become effective opposition. I will briefly discuss two of these mechanisms; the apparatus of surveillance, and redistribution of the social product. [. . .]

In each country, some equivalent of the KGB was instrumental in maintaining surveillance, with varying degrees of intensity and success. [Networks of informants and collaborators] formed a highly elaborate "production" system parallel to the system for producing goods—a system producing *paper*, which contained real and falsified histories of the people over whom the Party ruled. Let us call the immediate product "dossiers" or "files," though the ultimate product was political subjects and subject dispositions useful to the regime. This parallel production system was at least as important as the system for producing goods, for producers of files were much better paid than producers of goods. My image of this parallel production system comes from the memoirs of Romanian political prisoner Herbert Zilber:

> The first great socialist industry was that of the production of files . . . This new industry has an army of workers: the informers. It works with ultramodern

electronic equipment (microphones, tape recorders, etc.), plus an army of typists with their typewriters. Without all this, socialism could not have survived . . . In the socialist bloc, people and things exist only through their files.
All our existence is in the hands of him who possesses files and is constituted by
him who constructs them. Real people are but the reflection of their files.

The work of producing files (and thereby political subjects) created an atmosphere of distrust and suspicion dividing people from one another. One never knew
whom one could trust, who might be informing on one to the police about one's
attitudes toward the regime or one's having an American to dinner. [. . .] The
existence of this shadowy system of production could have grave effects on the
people "processed" through it, and the assumption that it was omnipresent contributed much to its success, in some countries, in repressing unwanted opposition.

If surveillance was the negative face of these regimes' problematic legitimation, its positive face was their promises of social redistribution and welfare. At
the center of both the Party's official ideology and its efforts to secure popular
support was "socialist paternalism," which justified Party rule with the claim that
the Party would take care of everyone's needs by collecting the total social product and then making available whatever people needed: cheap food, jobs, medical care, affordable housing, education, etc. Party authorities claimed, as well,
that they were *better able* to assess and fill these needs than were individuals or
families, who would always tend to want more than their share. Herein lay the
Party's paternalism: it acted like a father who gives handouts to the children as
he sees fit. The Benevolent Father-Party educated people to express needs it
would then fill, and discouraged them from taking the initiative that would
enable them to fill these needs on their own. The promises—socialism's basic
social contract—did not go unnoticed, and as long as economic conditions permitted their partial fulfillment, certain socialist regimes gained legitimacy as a
result. But this proved impossible to sustain.

Beyond its effects on people's attitudes, paternalism had important consequences for the entire system of production discussed above and for consumption;
here I shift to the question of why consumption was so central in the resistance to
socialism. A Party that pretends to meet its citizens' needs through redistribution
and that insists on doing so exclusively—that is, without enlisting their independent efforts—must control a tremendous fund of resources to redistribute.
Nationalizing the means of production helped provide this, and so did a relentlessly
"productionist" orientation, with ever-increased production plans and exhortations to greater effort.

The promise of redistribution was an additional reason, besides my earlier argument about shortages, why socialism worked differently from capitalism. Socialism's
inner drive was to accumulate not (as in capitalism) *profits*, but *distributable resources*.

This is more than simply a drive for autarky, reducing dependency on the outside: it aims to increase dependency of those within. Striving to accumulate resources for redistribution involves things for which profit is totally irrelevant. In capitalism, those who run lemonade stands endeavor to serve thirsty customers in ways that make a profit and outcompete other lemonade stand owners. In socialism, the point was not profit but the relationship between thirsty persons and the one with the lemonade—the Party center, which appropriated from producers the various ingredients (lemons, sugar, water) and then mixed the lemonade to reward them with, as it saw fit. Whether someone made a profit was irrelevant: the transaction underscored the center's paternalistic superiority over its citizens, i.e., its capacity to decide who got more and less lemonade.

Controlling the ingredients fortified the center's capacity to redistribute things. But this capacity would be even greater if the center controlled not only the lemons, sugar, and water but the things they come from: the lemon trees, the ground for growing sugar beets and the factories that process them, the wells and the well-digging machinery. That is, most valuable of all to the socialist bureaucracy was to get its hands not just on resources, but on resources that generated *other* usable resources, resources that were themselves further productive. Socialist regimes wanted not just eggs but the goose that lays them. Thus, if capitalism's inner logic rests on accumulating surplus-value, the inner logic of socialism was to accumulate *means of production*.

The emphasis on keeping resources at the center for redistribution is one reason why items produced in socialist countries so often proved uncompetitive on the world market. Basically, most of these goods were not being made to be sold competitively: they were being either centrally accumulated or redistributed at low prices—effectively given away. [. . .] In fact, the whole point was *not* to sell things: the center wanted to keep as much as possible under its control, because that was how it had redistributive power; and it wanted to give away the rest, because that was how it confirmed its legitimacy with the public. [. . .] Instead, "efficiency" was understood to mean "the full use of existing resources," "the maximization of given capacities" rather than of results, all so as to redirect resources to a goal greater than satisfying the population's needs. In other words, what was rational in socialism differed from capitalist rationality. Both are stupid in their own way, but differently so.

Consumption

Socialism's redistributive emphasis leads to one of the great paradoxes of a paternalist regime claiming to satisfy needs. Having constantly to amass means of production so as to enhance redistributive power caused Party leaders to prefer heavy industry (steel mills, machine construction) at the expense of consumer industry (processed foods, or shoes). After all, once a consumer got hold of something, the center no longer controlled it; central power was less served by giving things away than by producing things it could continue to control. The central fund derived more from setting up a factory to make construction equipment than from a shoe factory or a chocolate-works. In short, these systems had a basic tension between what was necessary to *legitimate* them—redistributing things to the masses—and what was necessary to their *power*—accumulating things at the center. [. . .]

Each country addressed this tension in its own way. For example, Hungary after 1968 and Poland in the 1970s gave things away more, while Romania and Czechoslovakia accumulated things more; but the basic tension existed everywhere. The socialist social contract guaranteed people food and clothing but did not promise (as capitalist systems do) quality, ready availability, and choice. Thus, the system's mode of operation tended to sacrifice consumption, in favor of production and controlling the products. This paradoxical neglect of consumption contributed to the long lines about which we heard so much (and we heard about them, of course, because we live in a system to which consumption is crucial).

In emphasizing this neglect of consumption as against building up the central resource base, I have so far been speaking of the *formally* organized economy of socialism—some call it the "first" or "official" economy. But this is not the whole story. Since the center would not supply what people needed, they struggled to do so themselves, developing in the process a huge repertoire of strategies for obtaining consumer goods and services. These strategies, called the "second" or "informal" economy, spanned a wide range from the quasi-legal to the definitely illegal. In most socialist countries it was not illegal to moonlight for extra pay— by doing carpentry, say—but people doing so often stole materials or illegally used tools from their work place; or they might manipulate state goods to sell on the side. Clerks in stores might earn favors or extra money, for example, by saving scarce goods to sell to special customers, who tipped them or did some important favor in return. Also part of the second economy was the so-called "private plot" of collective farm peasants, who held it legally and in theory could do what they wanted with it—grow food for their own table or to sell in the market at state-controlled prices. But although the plot itself was legal, people obtained high outputs from it not just by virtue of hard work but also by stealing from the collective farm: fertilizer and herbicides, fodder for their pigs or cows, work-time for their own weeding or harvesting, tractor-time and fuel for plowing their plot, etc. The second economy, then, which supplied a large part of consumer needs, was parasitic upon the state economy and inseparable from it. It developed precisely because the state economy tended to ignore consumption.

It is clear from what I have said that whereas consumption in our own society is considered primarily a socioeconomic question, the relative neglect of consumer interests in socialism made consumption deeply political. [. . .]

The system's organization exacerbated consumer desire further by frustrating it and thereby making it the focus of effort, resistance, and discontent. Anthropologist John Borneman sees in the relation between desire and goods a major contrast between capitalism and socialism. Capitalism, he says, repeatedly renders desire concrete and specific, and offers specific—if ever-changing— goods to satisfy it. Socialism, in contrast aroused desire *without* focalizing it, and kept it alive by deprivation.

As people became increasingly alienated from socialism and critical of its achievements, then, the politicization of consumption also made them challenge official definitions of their needs. They did so not just by creating a second economy to grow food or make clothes or work after hours but also, sometimes, by public protest. Poland's Communist leaders fell to such protest at least twice, in 1970 and in 1980, when Polish workers insisted on having more food than government price increases would permit them. Less immediately disruptive were forms of protest in which people used consumption styles to forge resistant social identities. The black markets in western goods that sprang up everywhere enabled alienated consumers to express their contempt for the system through the kinds of things they chose to buy. You could spend an entire month's salary on a pair of blue jeans, for instance, but it was worth it: wearing them signified that you could get something the system said you didn't need and shouldn't have. Thus, consumption goods and objects conferred an identity that set you off from socialism, enabling you to differentiate yourself as an individual in the face of relentless pressures to homogenize everyone's capacities and tastes into an undifferentiated collectivity. Acquiring objects became a way of constituting your selfhood against a deeply unpopular regime. [. . .]

Why Did it Fall?

My discussion of socialism's workings already points to several reasons for its collapse; I might now address the question more comprehensively. To do this requires, in my view, linking the properties of its internal organization (discussed above) with properties of its external environment, as well as with shorter-term "event history." This means examining the specific conjuncture of two systems— "capitalist" and "socialist," to use ideal types—one encompassing the other.

In event-history terms, the proximate cause of the fall of East European and Soviet socialism was a public-relations gambit by the Hungarian government on the eve of a visit by President George Bush: the dismantling of the barbed wire between Hungary and Austria. This enabled some East German tourists to extend their tour, and thereby—because Gorbachev refused to support Honecker with Soviet troops—to bring down the Berlin Wall. We still need to explain, however, the conjuncture in which Hungary could score its public-relations coup and Gorbachev could decide to refuse his troops. For that, we must wind up the static model I have offered and set it in its international context. This includes asking how socialism's encounter with a changing world capitalism produced or aggravated factional divisions within Communist Parties.

My discussion of socialism indicated several points of tension in its workings that affected the system's capacity for extended reproduction. Throughout their existence, these regimes sought to manage such tensions in different ways, ranging from Hungary's major market reforms in the 1960s to Romania's rejection of reform amid its heightened coercive extraction. In all cases, managing these tensions involved decisions that to a greater or lesser degree opened socialist political economies to western capital. The impetus for this opening—critical to socialism's demise—came chiefly from within, as Party leaders attempted to solve their structural problems without major structural reform. Their attitude in doing so was reminiscent of a "plunder mentality" that sees the external environment as a source of booty to be used as needed in maintaining one's own system, without thought for the cost. This attitude was visible in the tendency of socialist governments to treat foreign trade as a residual sector, used to supplement budgets without being made an integral part of them. Because of how this opportunistic recourse to the external environment brought socialism into tighter relationship with capitalism, it had fateful consequences.

The critical intersection occurred not in 1989 or 1987 but in the late 1960s and early '70s, when global capitalism entered the cyclical crisis from which it is still struggling to extricate itself. Among capitalists' possible responses to the crisis (devaluation, structural reorganization, etc.), an early one was to lend abroad. This enabled recipients to buy capital equipment or to build long-term infrastructure, thereby expanding the overseas markets for western products. The loans became available just at the moment when all across the socialist bloc the first significant round of structural reforms had been proposed, half-heartedly implemented, and, because profitability and market criteria fit so poorly with socialism's rationale, largely abandoned. Instead of reforming the system from within, most Party leaderships opted to meet their problems by greater articulation with the surrounding economy: importing western capital and using it to buy advanced technology (or, as in Poland, to subsidize consumption), in hopes of improving economic performance. Borrowing, then, became a substitute for extensive internal reforms that would have jeopardized the Party's monopoly over society and subverted the inner mechanisms of socialism. Thus, the internal cycles of two contrasting systems suddenly meshed.

The intent, as with all the international borrowing of the period, was to pay off the loans by exporting manufactured goods into the world market. By the mid 1970s it was clear, however, that the world market could not absorb sufficient amounts of socialism's products to enable repayment, and at the same time, rising interest rates added staggeringly to the debt service. With the 1979–80 decision of the western banking establishment not to lend more money to socialist countries, the latter were thrown into complete disarray. [. . .]

In these circumstances, the balance of power tilted toward the faction within the Communist Party that had long argued for structural reforms, the introduction of market mechanisms, and profit incentives, even at the cost of the Party's "leading role." The choice, as Gorbachev and his faction saw it, was to try to preserve either the Soviet Union and its empire (by reforms that would increase its economic performance and political legitimacy), or collective property and the Party monopoly. He was ready to sacrifice the latter to save the former, but ended by losing both.

While western attention was riveted on the speeches of policy-makers in the Kremlin, the more significant aspects of reform, however, were in the often-unauthorized behavior of bureaucrats who were busily creating new property forms on their own. Polish sociologist Jadwiga Staniszkis describes the growth of what she calls "political capitalism," as bureaucrats spontaneously created their own profit-based companies from within the state economic bureaucracy. Significantly for my argument that socialism's articulation with world capitalism was decisive in its fall, the examples she singles out to illustrate these trends are all at the interface of socialist economies with the outside world—in particular, new companies mediating the export trade and state procurement of western computers. She sees as crucial the factional split between the groups who managed socialism's relations with the outside (such as those in foreign policy, counterintelligence, and foreign trade), and those who managed it internally (such as the Party's middle-level executive apparatus and the KGB). Forms of privatization already taking place by 1987 in Poland and similar processes as early as 1984 in Hungary show the emerging contours of what Staniszkis sees as the reformists' goal: a *dual* economy. One part of it was to be centrally administered, as before, and the other part to be reformed through market/profit mechanisms and selective privatization of state property. The two were to coexist symbiotically.

These forms of "political capitalism" arose in part by economic managers' exploiting the shortages endemic to socialism—shortages now aggravated to crisis proportions. In the new hope of making a profit, "political capitalists" (I call them "entrepratchiks") were willing to put into circulation reserves known only to them—which they would otherwise have hoarded—thus alleviating short-ages, to their own gain. As a result, even anti-reformist Soviet and Polish bureau-crats found themselves acquiescing in entrepratchiks' activities, without which, in Staniszkis's words, "the official structure of the economic administration was absolutely unsteerable." Contributing to their tolerance was rampant bureau-cratic anarchy, a loss of control by those higher up, rooted in the "inability of superiors to supply their subordinates (managers of lower level) with the means to construct a strategy of survival." Since superiors could no longer guarantee deliveries and investments, they were forced to accept whatever solutions enter-prising subordinates could devise—even at the cost of illicit profits from state reserves. Entrepratchiks soon began to regard the state's accumulations much as Preobrazhensky had once urged Soviet leaders to regard agriculture: as a source of primitive accumulation. They came to find increasingly attractive the idea of further "privatization," so important to western lenders.

It is possible (though unlikely) that socialist regimes would not have collapsed if their hard-currency crisis and consequent intersection with capitalism had occurred at a different point in capitalism's cyclicity. The specifics of capitalism's own crisis management, however, proved unmanageable for socialist systems. [. . .]

Thus, I submit, it is not simply socialism's embrace with capitalism that brought about its fall, but the fact that it happened to embrace a capitalism of a newly "flexible" sort. David Harvey's schematic comparison of "fordist modernity" with "flexible post-modernity" clarifies things further; socialist systems have much more in common with his "fordist" column than with his "flexible" one.

Let me add one more thought linking the era of flexible specialization with socialism's collapse. Increasing numbers of scholars note that accompanying the change in capitalism is a change in the nature of state power; specifically, a num-ber of the state's functions are being undermined. The international weapons trade has made a mockery of the state's monopoly on the means of violence. Capital's extraordinary mobility means that as it moves from areas of higher to areas of lower taxation, many states lose some of their revenue and industrial base, and this constrains their ability to attract capital or shape its flow. Capital flight can now discipline *all* nation-state governments. The coordination of global capitalism by finance capital places a premium on capital mobility, to which rigid state boundaries are an obstacle.

This has two consequences for the fall of socialism. First, within socialist coun-tries those groups whose structural situation facilitated their fuller participation in the global economy now had reasons to expand their state's receptivity to capital—that is, to promote reform. Second, the extent to which socialist states controlled capital flows into their countries may have made them special targets for international financial interests, eager to increase their opportunities by undermining socialist states. These internal and international groups each found their chance in the interest of the other. It is in any case clear from the politics of international lending agencies that they aim to reduce the power of socialist states, for they insist upon privatization of state property—the basis of these states' power and revenue. Privatization is pushed even in the face of some economists' objections that "too much effort is being invested in privatization, and too little in creating and fostering the development of new private firms"— whose entry privatization may actually impede.

No Time for Socialism

Rather than explore further how flexible specialization compelled changes in socialism, I will summarize my argument by linking it to notions of time. Time, as anthropologists have shown, is a fundamental dimension of human affairs, taking different forms in different kinds of society. The western notion of a linear, irreversible time that consists of equivalent and divisible units, for instance, is but one possible way of conceptualizing time and living it. A given cultural construction of time ramifies throughout its social order, as calendars, schedules and rhythms establish the very foundations of daily existence (which is why elites, especially revolutionary ones, often manipulate them) and affect how people make themselves as social beings.

Capitalism exists only as a function of time—and of a specific conception of it. Efforts to increase profits by increasing the velocity of capital circulation are at its very heart. Thus, each major reorganization of capitalism has entailed, in Harvey's terms, "time-space compression": a shrinking of the time horizons of private and public decision-making, whose consequences encompass ever-wider spaces owing to changed communications and transport technology. The inner logic of socialism, by contrast placed no premium on increasing turnover time and capital circulation. Although the rhetoric of Stalinism presented socialism as highly dynamic, for the most part Soviet leaders acted as if time were on their side. (When Khrushchev said "We will bury you," he was not too specific about the date.) Indeed, I have argued that in 1980s Romania, time—far from accelerating—was being gradually *slowed down*, flattened, immobilized, and rendered non-linear.

Like the reorganization of capitalism at the end of the 19th century, the present reorganization entails a time-space compression, which we all feel as a mammoth speed-up. Yet the socialism with which it intersected had no such time-compressing dynamic. In this light, the significance of Gorbachev's perestroika was its recognition that socialism's temporality was unsustainable in a capitalist world. Perestroika reversed Soviet ideas as to whose time-definition and rhythms were dominant and where dynamism lay; no longer within the socialist system but outside it in the West. Gorbachev's rhetoric from the mid 1980s is full of words about time: the Soviet Union needs to "catch up," to "accelerate" its development, to shed its "sluggishness" and "inertia" and leave behind the "era of stagnation."

> [By] the latter half of the seventies . . . the country began to lose momentum. . . . Elements of stagnation . . . began to appear. . . . A kind of "braking mechanism" affect[ed] social and economic development. . . . The inertia of extensive economic development was leading to an economic deadlock and stagnation.

Change has suddenly become an "urgent" necessity. These are the words of a man squeezed by the compression of space and time.

Even as he spoke, new time/space-compressing technologies were wreaking havoc on the possible rhythms of his and other leaders' control of politics, as Radio Free Europe made their words at once domestic and international. Soviet leaders could no longer create room for themselves by saying one thing for domestic consumption and something else for the outside world: they were now prisoners of simultaneity. The role of western information technology in undermining socialism was evident in the spread of Solidarity's strikes in 1980, news of which was telephoned out to the West and rebroadcast instantly into Poland via Radio Free Europe and the BBC, mobilizing millions of Poles against their Party. The revolutions of 1989 were mediated similarly.

I am suggesting, then, that the collapse of socialism came in part from the massive rupture produced by its collision with capitalism's speed-up. If so, it would be especially useful to know something more about the life-experience of those people who worked at the interface of these two temporal systems and could not help realizing how different was capitalism's time from their own. Bureaucrats under pressure to increase foreign trade and foreign revenues, or importers of computer equipment would have discovered that failure to adapt to alien notions of increased turnover time could cost them hard currency. They would have directly experienced time-annihilating western technologies, which effected a banking transaction in milliseconds as opposed to the paper-laden hours and days needed by their own financial system. Did the rise of "profitability" criteria in the command economy owe something to such people's dual placement? Did they come to experience differently their sense of themselves as agents? My point, in short, is that the fall of socialism lies not simply in the intersection of two systems' temporal cycles but rather in the collision of two *differently constituted temporal orders*, along with the notions of person and activity proper to them.

If socialist economies had not opened themselves to capital import and to debt servicing, perhaps their collision with capitalist speedup would have been less jarring—or would at least have occurred on more equal terms. But the capitalist definition of time prevailed, as socialist debtors bowed to its dictates (even while postponing them), thereby aggravating factional conflicts within the elite. Because its leaders accepted western temporal hegemony, socialism's messianic time proved apocalyptic. The irony is that, had debtor regimes refused the definitions imposed from without—had they united to default simultaneously on their western loans (which in 1981 stood at over $90 billion)—they might well have brought down the world financial system and realized Khrushchev's threatening prophecy overnight. That this did not happen shows how vital a thing is a monopoly on the definition of social reality, and it should give pause to those impatient to move beyond capitalism.

2.2

Glasnost Gutted the Party, Democratization Doomed the State: Political Liberalization and the Soviet Disintegration

Joel M. Ostrow

Discussing the role of political liberalization in the collapse of the USSR is almost like discussing the role of the collapse in the collapse of the USSR. Regardless of the issue under consideration, authors turn to political liberalization to explain why things in the Soviet Union spun so horribly out of control. Whether focusing on the economic catastrophe, ethnic conflict and nationalism, the demise of the Communist Party, or virtually any other factor related to the collapse of the Soviet Union, political liberalization is the spark that caused that particular issue to spin out of control. It is not that economic decline, Party decay, and other issues did not contribute to the Soviet collapse—they most certainly did! But in early 1987, prior to Gorbachev's initiation of reforms to Soviet political institutions, none of these problems appeared on the verge of deteriorating so badly. Indeed, in some areas, including economic performance, modest improvements were being recorded. Gorbachev's political liberalization, however, so aggravated each of these problems that the state itself disintegrated.

Thus Schroeder argues that the economy could have continued to putter along, that the economic problems "were chronic rather than critical in nature," until Gorbachev's political liberalization began "undermining the key institutions" producing "destabilization and deterioration."[1] Similarly, Tuminez reveals that ethnic and national tensions, though lingering underneath the surface, remained quiet only until political liberalization enabled and incited their rise. Taylor shows that military discipline and subordination only came under serious doubt when "Gorbachev's far-reaching political reforms endangered Soviet military interests."[2] And Bunce argues political liberalization in effect "forced" political elites in the Soviet federal system to become nationalists seeking independence, the death knell for the federation.[3]

Political liberalization did more than exacerbate all of these problems—it exacerbated them all at the same time. The problems fed off of each other, creating a spiral of chaos propelling the country to disintegration. For this, Mikhail S. Gorbachev must bear overwhelming responsibility. Political liberalization was, if not his idea, his policy. "Demokratizatsiya" could not even have been uttered as a slogan were it not for the General Secretary's initiative and approval. Gorbachev initiated political liberalization, rammed it through the leadership and the Party in spite of repeated, diverse, and vociferous warnings against doing so by many of his closest associates. He did so in spite of objective factors about the nature of Soviet socialism of which he most certainly should have been aware. While Gorbachev may not have been responsible for the country's economic ills—these predated his ascension to the position of General Secretary—political liberalization made the economic situation critical, as it did such problems as inter-ethnic relations, military discipline, and social order. He is responsible for that political liberalization, and thereby he is responsible for his country's demise. If indeed he is correct that "The Union Could Have Been Saved," who else to blame but Gorbachev for not doing so?[4]

History, if historical analysis is to have any value, must judge Gorbachev as one of the most spectacular failures ever to lead a country. Yet Western analysts, journalists, and casual observers routinely give Gorbachev hero's credit for his political reforms, for "opening up" the Soviet Union. It is not just remaining members of the Communist Party or Russian nationalists who should lambast Gorbachev for the disintegration of the U.S.S.R. Those who credit Gorbachev for initiating liberalization policies should also consciously and explicitly lay historical blame for the demise of his country on that same Gorbachev, and recognize that this should place him at the bottom of history's rankings of political leadership.

Let me be clear—I was ecstatic when communism collapsed. I was overjoyed, for example, for Estonia and the other Baltic states when they gained their independence. I believe the Soviet socialist system was inhumane and grossly oppressive for the vast majority of the people who had to live under it. From a world historical perspective, I believe it is a good thing that communism in the Soviet Union collapsed. But this is not the point. We in the West may favor liberal capitalism and hail the dissolution of the Soviet empire, the dismemberment of the Soviet Union, and the death of communism. Gorbachev, though, never embraced any of these; indeed they were his worst nightmares! For him such outcomes were tragic. This comes through clearly enough in his memoirs and speeches. Everything Gorbachev did, he thought he was doing not merely to save but to strengthen his country. Yet everything he did sped the country to its destruction, brought consequences diametrically opposite to those he intended and expected. He was a leader lacking a vision for his country's future, lacking a strategy to move the country forward, lacking a basic understanding of the nature of his country's political system, political dynamics, and political culture, and lacking the ability to make authoritative decisions on policy matters of the greatest importance and to stick with them. Such qualities are the definition of political ineptitude and leadership failure, and history should, on this basis, judge Gorbachev's leadership as a spectacular failure.

Western analysts tend to evaluate Gorbachev's leadership according to Western standards and normative desires. We like Gorbachev because he ended the Cold War and destroyed communism. Such analyses, though, are not evaluations of the leader, but about how the author in question feels about that leader. Historical evaluation of leadership requires sensitivity to the societal context being analyzed. Understanding others, including their performance in a job, demands sensitivity to the subjective meanings those individuals give to their own behavior and experience.[5] Because such evaluations of Gorbachev's leadership are lacking, this analysis of political liberalization's role in the Soviet collapse will include also evaluation of Gorbachev's role in introducing and instituting the policies that led to his country's destruction. My evaluation, therefore, is not inconsistent with my personal delight that Gorbachev proved to be so incompetent, or my overall satisfaction with the consequences of that incompetence.

Most astounding is that even today Gorbachev does not seem to accept that his brand of political liberalization was incompatible with the very existence of his country. His naivete and ineptitude continue to dog him. History is replete with examples of authoritarian regimes crumbling in the wake of liberalization policies.[6] Tocqueville was hardly the first to observe that

> When people who have long endured an oppressive regime without complaint suddenly find it relaxing its pressure, they rise up violently against it. . . . the most dangerous moment for a bad government usually comes when it begins to reform itself.[7]

Yet nowhere in Gorbachev's memoirs do we find any evidence of his appreciation of this danger or how to deal with it, while in the memoirs of his Politburo colleagues we find repeated frustration over his incapacity to grasp the essence of their warnings to this effect.

A single chapter cannot hope to elaborate the entirety of the impact of Gorbachev's political liberalization. All it can hope to accomplish is to argue that the processes and dynamics glasnost and democratization ignited were the underlying cause of the Soviet Union's demise. The discussion begins with an elaboration of the articulated goals of political liberalization. The remaining sections demonstrate how the political changes fueled disorder and the collapse of the Party, executive authority, the economy, and ultimately the state itself. The discussion throughout confronts Gorbachev's political incompetence, naivete, and outright failure.

Gorbachev's Goals for Political Liberalization

It is no simple task to explain just what the goals of political liberalization were. It is now axiomatic that Gorbachev never developed or articulated a clear strategy to give meat to any of his reform slogans of "perestroyka," "glasnost" and "demokratizatsiya". Indeed, this inability to devise a clearly-defined strategy or program of action was perhaps Gorbachev's most tragic failing. The record of Gorbachev's leadership is one of unpredictability, incoherence, and tentativeness in policy making. Still, it is possible from speeches and memoir records to piece together a plausible argument for where political liberalization fit into Gorbachev's reform scheme, and what he hoped it would accomplish. The characterization of the goals for political liberalization presented in this section reflect those at the time of their initiation, roughly speaking in 1986 and 1987.

What is often forgotten in the West is that glasnost and democratization were not initially aimed at changing the country's political institutions. Their purposes, as stated and understood by the Party leadership, were very limited. Gorbachev saw glasnost as a "tool of perestroyka," his slogan for economic reform or "restructuring."[8] As he later acknowledged in his memoirs, "At first, perestroyka meant for us only economic reform."[9] It was only after his first economic measures failed that he turned to political reforms as well, but the political reforms were explicitly justified in terms of advancing economic reform. Gorbachev introduced political liberalization, first glasnost in the press and later democratization in economic and political institutions, to bring about the "acceleration" and then the "restructuring" he was calling for in the economic sphere. Glasnost or openness in the press, Gorbachev believed, was needed to "activate" the system, and the people, to make officials more responsible, to restore "discipline and order," to root out corruption and "end stagnation."[10] Political liberalization, then, was intended purely as a means to overcome the "inertia" of the entrenched Party bureaucracy, seen as dragging its feet on economic reform.[11] It was a tactical move, subordinate to and part of the goal of economic rejuvenation, but not an end in itself.

The initial emphasis was on political liberalization in the press. Glasnost, or openness in the media, was to expose corrupt, inefficient, and/or alcoholic managers and bureaucrats by name, pinning personal responsibility for economic failure on those officials as a means to pressure them to reform their behavior or to force them out of their positions.[12] The primary targets, and subject matter, were ineffective factory managers and undisciplined workers.[13] When first conceived, then, political liberalization was far from all-encompassing. It had nothing to do with the political system, and was to be focused specifically on economic inefficiency and resistance to change in economic behavior. It appeared to be a campaign, not very unlike earlier Soviet campaigns to expose and punish individuals responsible for behavior inimical to the leader's current priorities.

It is important to note that this is precisely how the rest of the Soviet leadership viewed the policies when approving them in the Politburo. The Chairman of the Council of Ministers, Nikolay Ryzhkov, had a very clear understanding:

> We believed glasnost would be limited to criticism of several workers and collective farms, bureaucrats, corrupt lower-level officials, and pertain to those social problems such as crime, violence, alcoholism and similar obvious, open problems.[14]

Several Politburo members echo this understanding of the purpose of glasnost, and explain Gorbachev's "betrayal" according to his betrayal of this understanding of the limits of political liberalization.[15] They believed he was initiating a new Party-led, Party-defined campaign, and had absolutely no reason to believe otherwise.

As with all of the reforms during Gorbachev's tenure as leader, however, political reform policies were conceived of and introduced haphazardly, at times in reaction to a crisis or some disappointment or difficulty in the economic sphere, at times to undermine his opponents, at times to gather to himself more personal power, and at other times simply spontaneous, poorly thought out ideas that had not been fleshed out with the rest of the political leadership. But when Gorbachev unleashed the first steps towards glasnost and democratization, when he placed political liberalization on the agenda, there was a unanimous understanding among the broader leadership of the Party and state, echoed in Gorbachev's own statements and writings, that political liberalization was to serve and be limited to serving the advancement of economic reform. The problem was, he never actually devised a proper "campaign" or strategy, only the catchy slogans.

Glasnost and the Relativization and Demise of the Communist Party

Although the two processes obviously interacted with each other, it is not too much of an oversimplification to say that glasnost caused the collapse of the Communist Party, while democratization caused the collapse of the Soviet state. This section examines the role of glasnost in the demise of the Party. This most certainly was not the effect Gorbachev had in mind when he first pronounced and advocated glasnost, nor was it the objective of any of his colleagues in the

Soviet leadership who approved of the new policy of openness. As noted above, however, the Soviet case is only the most recent historical case supporting the contention that an "opening up" of the ideological realm is incompatible with one-party, authoritarian rule.

That the Soviet Union was a one-party, authoritarian system is hardly disputable. This was the definition of Soviet Socialism! The Party-controlled monopoly on power, conceived of by Lenin and solidified by Stalin, established the primacy of politics over economics in all aspects of Soviet life. The interlocking of both economic and social-cultural spheres of life with the political structures of the Party was the essence of Soviet socialism.[16] The Party leadership sent down the "correct line," the unquestionable truth for the Party membership, and through the Party for all of Soviet society. The correct line was "an exclusive ideological-political statement that must be adopted and adhered to" by everyone.[17] It gave the Party its semi-mystical status of the holder of the truth, and by compelling adherence to the correct line and brooking no deviation from it, the Party held the Soviet Union together. The correct line was essential to running the country, because the Party was physically involved in running virtually every aspect of life in the country, from government organizations to economic enterprises to social organizations.[18]

The burden of argument would seem to rest with anyone who would suggest that political liberalization in such a state could be contained, whether to economic or any other limited purposes. Gorbachev's initial belief that glasnost could be limited to the purpose of jump-starting the economy was flawed from the start. Glasnost was to bring open criticism of economic inefficiency and intransigence to reform of economic practices. But this meant criticizing Party officials, be they the heads of factories or of regional Party committees. Direct criticism of the Party undermined its control over ideology and political thought, by destroying the myth of the Party's exclusive claim to the truth. It undermined the Party's ability to rule, by destroying its claim to unquestioned obedience and authority. It meant stressing the procedural over the charismatic, in the case of the Soviet Union the charisma residing in the all-knowing Party. It meant stressing individual responsibility and initiative over the organizational infallibility of the Party. It meant stressing empirical reality over ideological purity.[19] In every respect, it attacked the absolute status of the Party. Because the Communist Party was an absolutist party, that meant attacking its very reason for being.

This is precisely Jowitt's point when he argues Gorbachev "relativized" the Party. The pillars of Soviet socialism were the correct line and the exclusivity of the Party as the sole political leadership defining that correct line. Political liberalization in the form of glasnost relativized both the Party's message and the Party as the purveyor of the message.[20] Most simply, it exposed the Party to challenge: perhaps it could do wrong; perhaps its economic policies were not working; perhaps the institutions it created and methods it employed were not the most efficient.

Encouraging criticism of Party officials automatically presented the scenario that the Party could be fallible, and one did not have to think too long in the mid-1980s to find reasons to criticize the Communist Party of the Soviet Union! For seven decades the Soviet state had been held together by methods of coercion and fear. Given an opportunity, people will rebel against such a system—you cannot make legitimate that which is fundamentally illegitimate. Indeed, the horrors of the Stalinist period were still in the memories of enough people that openness and criticism of the Party unleashed a flood of attacks, exposing "the comprehensive failure and brutality of the entire system."[21] That flood shook the very top, as anything Party officials did was in the name of the correct line handed down by the highest Party leadership, and it shook all the way down, as the Party was so interpenetrated into all aspects of Soviet life.

By destroying the notion of a single truth embodied in and by the Party, Gorbachev's liberalization destroyed the need for a single party altogether. If there is no unquestioned leading ideology, then why an unchallengeable leading party? Similarly, the competitive elections both within the Party and representative institutions, brought societal control over the cadres. Again, this fundamentally eroded, or relativized, the position of the Party in the polity. If the people control the cadres, then why the cadres in the first place? As McCauley put it, "what did one need the Party for?"[22]

Political liberalization, therefore, automatically spelled the death of the Party's "leading role," and as such spelled the collapse of the Party itself. No leader could contain glasnost to focus merely on ineffective economic managers. What made those managers ineffective? Where were their ineffective orders coming from? What created the incentive structures that led to corruption, to lack of and even outright resistance to innovation, to the anecdotal repeated ad nauseam, "they pretend to pay us and we pretend to work"?

Gorbachev from the start did not understand that such criticism would quickly focus on the Party itself and the system it had created. This was no minor oversight! He could have known, he should have known, he had a duty to know! Writers and intellectuals who had been given a taste of greater creative freedom during Khrushchev's "thaw," only to be frustrated when the door was shut during eighteen years of Brezhnev's rule, seized the new opportunity and broke out far more critically than they had before. The Party lost control over parts of the press, and the opening unleashed a torrent of unofficial and uncontrollable leaflets and circulars from all corners of the political spectrum. Samizdat was now in the open. The Party could no longer claim that it's truth was unquestionable—it was being openly questioned everywhere, in myriad ways.

Gorbachev's second failure was in not seizing the opportunity to reign in glasnost.[23] That opportunity came with the publication of Nina Andreyeva's article, "I Cannot Forgo My Principles," on March 13, 1988 in *Sovetskaya Rossiya*. This article criticizing the extent to which glasnost had gotten away from the purpose of economic reform, and the sharp Politburo debate it sparked, gave Gorbachev the chance either to define limits or to reverse course. Several Politburo members argued for the need to control the press, to control attacks on the Soviet past. Others argued the press needed to be prevented from launching anti-perestroika attacks. But Gorbachev heeded neither of these warnings, choosing to see the manifesto as one of those opposing all reform, rather than one of those trying to defend the leading role of the Party and thus the survival of the Soviet state.[24]

The April 5, 1998 publication of a rebuttal to Andreyeva in *Pravda* marked the end of the Party's control over political thought in the country. First, it was obvious that Andreyeva's article was published with the assistance of someone in the upper echelons of the Party, perhaps even the second ranking party member, Yegor Ligachev. A split at the highest levels of the Party revealed once and for all the fallacy of a single truth, and "there can be no doubt about the importance of faith for the cohesion of a regime that had chosen to make its ideology so central and weighty a core of the system."[25] That faith was gone for good. Second, it signaled that there would not be limits on openness, that all areas could be questioned in the press, including the policies of the Party and its leader. The Party leadership was split, and people could choose sides. The Party's "leading role" was a thing of the past. With this step, Gorbachev began to lose the trust of a large portion of the leadership at all levels of the Party.

Gorbachev of course bears responsibility for this, because he initiated glasnost in the media. It could not have happened without the personal initiative of the General Secretary, nor could such a response to the Andreyeva letter have been published in Pravda other than on orders of the Party leader. Gorbachev allowed the release of dissidents such as Andrei Sakharov, the publication of previously-banned books, like *Children of the Arbat*, and the reappearance of such controversial authors as Yevtushenko and Solzhenitsyn. He is the one who allowed the airing of previously-banned movies, like *Repentance*. All of these steps brought intensified and expanded challenges to the Party's central role in the Soviet Union, to the system it had created, and by extension to the Party's very existence.

Gorbachev rested his belief that political liberalization would move both the Party and the country forward on one fundamentally flawed assumption. He believed that by trusting the people with glasnost, the people would respond with adoration for him, for the Party, and for perestroyka. He believed, as Reddaway put it, "in an entity which has scarcely existed . . . the 'Soviet people.'"[26] He believed in the Soviet equivalent to the American national "myth." Embodied in America by such phrases and concepts as "We the people," "Liberty and justice for all," the "American Dream," the Bill of Rights, and the Fourth of July, the Soviet myth presumably embraced "communism," "friendship of the peoples," Lenin, October, and the Great Patriotic War. Most important, Gorbachev "assumed an identity between a Soviet national myth and Party ideology," and a "Soviet people" who "accept the basic features of a Leninist regime."[27]

If there is any doubt that Gorbachev actually believed this, one need only heed his own words, uttered on countless occasions. During the Politburo discussion of the Andreyeva letter, for example, he said:

> I have said this again and again . . . and repeat it again because it is of prin-
> ciple importance. If we do not expand the democratic process, that means
> we do not trust and are afraid of our own people. That we don't believe in
> them and their responsibility and wisdom . . . not one [demonstrator] has
> raised slogans against perestroyka, against Soviet power, against socialism
> or against the USSR. These don't exist![28]

But they did exist, and more! That Gorbachev did not recognize the shallowness of the "myth" in Soviet society was yet another of his fatal flaws, one that led him to continue pursuing his disastrous course.

Why did the Politburo leadership go along? The answer to this remains murky, even after publication of the memoirs of several of his colleagues. The closest explanation comes from Ryzhkov and Vorotnikov, who describe how Gorbachev exerted great political capital convincing the rest of the leadership to support these initiatives, convincing them in the process that they were part of a larger strategy. Even Gorbachev's harshest critics give him credit not only for being a "master of maneuver," but for gathering supporters by "giving the illusion of confiding" in them.[29] But his initiatives were not and never were backed by any coherent strategy. They were reactive, spontaneous, frequently unthought out and undiscussed in the Politburo.[30] He reacted to glasnost's spiraling out of control by authorizing more glasnost. When it became clear there was no strategy there to defend the Party, the Party and society split, into those who sought to challenge and undermine the Party itself, those who believed Gorbachev's path was the one to preserve and strengthen the Party, and those who opposed Gorbachev and continued political liberalization, believing a change of course was needed to save the Party from destruction. This split of the Party and society into at least these three identifiable groupings spelled the end of Communist Party authoritarian rule, and ultimately of the Party itself.

Democratization of Political Institutions and the Collapse of Executive Power

While glasnost relativized and divided the Communist Party, democratization tore apart the Soviet state. It fragmented executive power and sent the government into chaos. It hindered economic reform and sent the economy into a tailspin. It fueled separatist movements in the republics that destroyed the federation. While one can debate whether the Soviet Union's political structures could have been changed in a way consistent with preservation of the state, there can be no doubt that a haphazard and inconsistent democratization of Soviet-style authoritarianism, conducted by a leader with no clear strategy and no clear vision for the future, could only breed chaos. Gorbachev's erratic and unpredictable behavior regarding political reorganizations so irked his colleagues that it is not only his detractors who criticize him for ill-conceived, inadequate reforms of the Soviet Union's political institutions. Even those who continue to rank among his supporters acknowledge that his initiatives in reforming the political system were inadequate and poorly thought out.

Gorbachev's initiatives frequently shocked and dismayed his Politburo colleagues, who felt at best not consulted, at worst outright deceived. His impromptu structural changes divided and brought confusion and breakdown to executive power, and brought conflict and division to the top leadership. As Ryzhkov notes, fewer than three months passed between the Second Congress of People's Deputies (CPD), at which the idea of instituting a Presidency was not even discussed, and the Third CPD, at which Gorbachev not only raised the idea of creating such an office, but rammed it through in accelerated fashion and had himself elected to the post in an uncontested vote! Besides the fact that such actions hardly seemed in the spirit of "democratization," prior to that Third Congress, Gorbachev had vigorously rejected the suggestion by the Inter-Regional Deputy Group and others that he should create a presidency.[31]

Such sudden and unannounced reversal of direction was typical of a leader lacking an overall vision or strategy. In 1988, Gorbachev introduced the idea of creating the new CPD, and this body was elected in March of 1989 and convened in May. At the same time, Gorbachev reorganized the governmental apparatus, creating the position of Prime Minister. Less than a year later, in March 1990, he suddenly introduced the presidency, along with a Federation Council and Presidential Council. Then in December 1990, he created a Vice Presidency, abolished that Presidential Council, and disbanded the Council of Ministers in favor of a new Cabinet of Ministers and Security Council. Ryzhkov reflected with exasperation, "In just a year and a half, three cardinal changes were contrived to the power structures in the country."[32]

It isn't just that there was a lot of change, but that the changes did not make sense. The continuous turmoil kept the executive branch in confused disarray, always waiting and preparing for the next reorganization. In the meantime it was impossible for the government to get anything done, because it was unclear exactly what "the government" was! As Ryzhkov puts it, "a completely idiotic situation arose, in which two executive branches worked simultaneously—the presidency and the Council of Ministers."[33] This situation arose because Gorbachev never discussed with his own Prime Minister how powers and responsibilities would be divided between them when drafting the laws creating the new presidential structures. Even more disruptive over the long run, he never held such a discussion with Ryzhkov even after the presidency was created, and the duplication and confusion had become obvious! Gorbachev never allowed serious thought to go into "how to change, who to change, what will be needed tomorrow, who is needed and where are they needed."[34] The result was a flood of resolutions, instructions, decrees and other policy documents, often at odds with each other, being issued simultaneously by the ministries and the office of the President, as no lines of communication and cooperation were ever formally established between the two entities.[35] It is no surprise, then, that even those who supported Gorbachev to the bitter end lamented that he was "inadequate in creating presidential structures."[36]

It began to seem that "any change in executive structures, any change, became a goal in itself," and for this reason Gorbachev bears responsibility for the decline in governmental effectiveness that occurred as a result of his reforms to the political system under the "democratization" slogan.[37] Such an attitude regarding the structures of government by a head of state could only cause turmoil and breakdown. It is difficult today to disagree with Ryzhkov's assessment of Gorbachev's leadership style and his character as that of a man "rushing too fast for the next great future . . . to break down the door instead of calmly inserting the key." He was driven by "a love of words instead of deeds," and his constant "improvisation" betrayed a "lack of priorities," other than that of "gathering more and more power into his own hands."[38]

The story surrounding Gorbachev's switch from opposing to forcing creation of a presidency is familiar enough. Having reconstituted the Supreme Soviet, and making the party leaders the heads of the soviets, his goal presumably was to give himself new authority at the center as head of both the Party and the national legislature, and to give his Party bosses around the country similar authority. At the same time, he hoped to gain greater popular legitimacy by way of periodic elections. But Gorbachev created this new "democratic" legislature without having considered what it would or should actually do. If he thought by chairing it he could control it and gain a new power base, he instead found himself chairing daily sessions of a legislature and spending endless time mediating procedural and agenda disputes, instead of running the country. Moreover, the legislators laid their own claim to a basis to rule. The people had elected them. They had formal supremacy to rule in the Constitution. With the Party having suffered serious losses in the elections, and the soviets taking primacy in policy formation, Gorbachev and the Party had actually suffered a decline in power.

It was only when he grasped this reality that he turned to the idea of creating a presidency. Seeing that his innovation had not gone as hoped, Gorbachev tried "to gather more power into his own hands" than being the head of the legislature and head of the Party had given him. He sought to bypass both, first by creating the presidency, and then by trying to pull the ministries under his control.[39] But to everyone else it looked like Gorbachev was flailing. Suddenly embracing the idea of a presidency after months of consistently opposing the idea, and having created the new legislative structures instead, made Gorbachev appear even less decisive, even less in control, and most important even less with a strategy and vision for the direction the country was headed, than had previously been the case. The leadership and the people around the country began to lose trust in both Gorbachev and the center, for the center appeared to have no idea what it was doing.

Why these structural changes would grind government effectiveness to a halt becomes clearer when one remembers that even before Gorbachev added the presidency to the system, the executive branch in the Soviet Union already could be described as a dual-channel design. The Communist Party Central Committee had a department for overseeing every sector of the economy, paralleling the ministries and departments in the Council of Ministers, and duplicating many of their information-gathering and policy-setting functions.[40] However, because the Party and government channels were tightly linked, and because Party dominance was unquestioned, the two channels worked together and managed and minimized conflict between them.

The creation of the new presidential apparatus threw everything into turmoil, not merely because of its creation but because of the spontaneous way Gorbachev introduced it. No thought was given to how the different branches would fit together. The presidency added a new channel of executive authority, but one entirely unlinked from the other. It competed with the Party and the ministries, in collecting information, setting policy, and implementing policy. It competed for the loyalties of those around the country responsible for implementing policy and running the economy. Even if one accepts that by 1990 the Party had been withdrawn from overseeing the economy, a controversial contention in itself, what the new presidency created was an unlinked, dual-channel executive branch. Such a design inevitably produces unmanageable conflict, chaos, and breakdown.[41] For example, after being elected President, Gorbachev created the Presidential Council. Some on the Council were ministers, others were simply members, some coming from outside organizations or institutions. Gorbachev appointed Medvedev to be responsible for foreign economic relations. But there was already a department within the Council of Ministers responsible for this, and with a huge staff. Neither Gorbachev nor the Constitution nor any law offered guidance regarding the relationship between the two channels, or regarding lines of responsibility and authority. All could go directly to Gorbachev with information and advice, and all could go to officials around the country with the same.[42] With no boundaries, no clear authority, and no links binding the channels together, conflict erupted over responsibilities and jurisdiction. A war of decrees and instructions ensued, with ministries, party committees, and Presidential aides all claiming and fighting to gain control over government policy.

Even the Congress of People's Deputies and Supreme Soviet claimed executive powers! As the Constitutionally supreme "organs of power" in the country, they had a formal claim to such powers. Ryzhkov had warned of this problem prior to the 19th Party Conference, when discussing the proposal for introducing this new body:

> This will weaken executive powers. This is impermissible! Let us clearly separate the functions between the three classical forms of power. Let us at least clearly determine the boundaries of the spheres of activity of each. Or, if the idea of all-powerful Soviets is so dear to you, then at least give them all powers. It is another matter whether they can handle it. I think not. And that will mean the state could become ungovernable . . . [43]

Neither Gorbachev nor the Politburo heeded his advice, and indeed government fell into chaos.

Because the responsibilities and boundaries between the different branches and powers were never drawn clearly, and because it was not obvious to middle and lower level officials around the country to whom they should listen or to whom they were responsible, confusion and inaction were the principle by-products of this competition at the top. History, after all, showed that acting contrary to Party officials, particularly local ones, could have very painful costs. But now frequently inconsistent or directly contrary instructions were coming from the Party, the President's Administration, the Council of Ministers and the Supreme Soviet! Inconsistency, disorder, lack of direction were the only way to characterize the highest organs of political power at the center. Given that the economy was already plunging into a deep crisis, this was the least desirable outcome of political reforms, at exactly the wrong time.

Political Reform and Economic Collapse

This breakdown of authority at the center wreaked havoc on the economy. For one thing, the political reforms introduced at the 19th Party Conference were the wrong shift of focus at the wrong time. After two years of half-hearted, haphazard economic reforms, a constant stream of promises from the leadership, and the rising euphoria generated by glasnost, expectations were high for economic improvement, but results were few indeed. The one thing the Conference needed to accomplish was to approve and unite behind a plan for economic development, and in retrospect the Conference probably marked the final opportunity for the Gorbachev leadership to devise, adopt, and gain support for a coherent national plan for economic reform. Instead, though, Gorbachev shifted gears, wrenching the Conference to focus on reform of the political system. Vorotnikov grasped the implications of this shift:

> Political reorganization diverted attention from economic reform. Without preparation of a legal and economic base, without an account of the traditions and fundamentals of the country, such a radical change from economic to state-political reform was one of the basic reasons for the destruction of horizontal and vertical lines of communication, both in state and in economic structures.[44]

The governmental crisis this produced, the breakdown of authority at the top, came at exactly the wrong time for the economy. It caused a system-wide breakdown of "lines of communication" that sent the Soviet economy reeling, just as central planning was being withdrawn and responsibility for economic performance was being shifted to lower levels. These disruptive changes in economic behavior around the country demanded political coherence and direction at the top, in the form of a coherent plan for economic development. Such was not forthcoming. The political reorganizations tore apart the party and executive branch at the top, as discussed above. The neglect registered in economic performance: the modest economic gains registered in 1985 to 1987 quickly disappeared.[45]

Focus on the economy was diverted because the political reforms were so sweeping and simply demanded time to prepare and adjust to. Political elite around the country were forced to become "wrapped up in the organizational process of political reform," particularly in preparing for and conducting elections at all levels.

> [It] required explaining to the people the reasons for the changes. All Party and Soviet energy was put to this work. As a result, we not only did not help the economy, but more important we put economic problems to the side, becoming embroiled in the verbal and written battles. In short, we neglected the economy.[46]

But all this energy and focus in the end produced an executive branch so divided and unable to manage conflict within its own ranks that no economic reform program was ever forthcoming, even after focus supposedly shifted back to the economy. The neglect and disorder continued.

It did not help that the people were also divided. Gorbachev sought to use political reform to influence economics, to get the people involved and identifying with the changes. But it was too much change too soon and in too many directions. Rather than uniting the people behind improving economic efficiency, the new and highly visible political division at the top, combined with the opening to criticize and question both the system and its policies, divided society in a polarizing political battle. The masses became activated, but in the form of fragmented political action, not united economic action. This polarization and emphasis on big political issues "distracted people from resolving concrete economic problems."[47]

The tumult at the top filtered all the way down the economy, as could be expected in an economy that had been centrally controlled for more than five decades. "Local party leaders found that the center was no longer sending instructions."[48] This was no small problem for a Leninist system! The onus was suddenly on local Party officials and even individual enterprises, to figure out input needs, production objectives, distribution patterns, and even pricing. But they had little idea what to do, and even less of an idea of what was expected.[49] The organizational backbone of the economy had been ripped out, and nothing put in its place. The new soviets, for their part, were so fiercely divided and the members so inexperienced that they had no hope of introducing coherence or gaining control even at the most local of levels, much less at the center. As Medvedev put it, the first session of the CPD made clear that "an active position in reforming and reviving the economy had been lost."[50] Gorbachev's political reforms destroyed much, but created little.

The 19th Party Conference was the last real chance for adoption of a coherent economic plan that could be implemented, precisely because the political changes caused such fierce division and competition, so thoroughly fragmented the executive branch. After the reorganizations began, it was unclear who was responsible for the economy, and all of those who believed they were began devising plans that radically differed from each other. This was true of the presidency as it was true of the Council of Ministers. As a result, not only the central plan but the center itself was being withdrawn, but no plan for economic reform or development was ever adopted.

Several players sought control. The President had a team working on a plan. The Council of Ministers developed its plan. The Supreme Soviet sought to develop a plan. And by then independent teams of economists were making

public their own plans. One can sympathize with the Prime Minister for implor-
ing Gorbachev, "Why don't you trust those who have worked long and learned
much in the economy, who went from the bottom to the top?"[51] What he meant
was, "Why don't you trust your Prime Minister!" Gorbachev failed to respond
to Ryzhkov at this Politburo session. Gorbachev never entrusted the Council of
Ministers to formulate and implement an economic strategy, instead keeping the
process in the Party, in his own circle of advisors. All the Council was to do was
draft a plan and submit it for consideration.

The problem with this was that although Gorbachev had amassed so much
formal powers to himself with the creation of the presidency, he proved as incapable in that post of making policy decisions as he had proven as General Secretary
and as Supreme Soviet Chairman. He could wrench the country along the path of
political reorganization after political reorganization, and he could speak in lofty
slogans and convincing generalizations, but when it came to making a policy decision, particularly one requiring a long-term vision such as an economic program,
he was lost. Ryzhkov made the point most succinctly:

> [Gorbachev] hated making authoritative decisions, preferring long discus-
> sion of problems, carefully listening to many opinions and arguing. He eas-
> ily and astutely avoided making final decisions, hiding his 'for' and 'against'
> in hidden tangled words. He never wanted to take on himself any respon-
> sibility or guilt for mistakes on any decision.[52]

He enthusiastically "preached" an array of lofty slogans about perestroyka, self-
management, responsibility, and improving efficiency, but he never embraced
any policy program.

When it came to policy issues, Gorbachev relished long discussion and argument, always calling for "more detailed analysis", but avoiding making a final
decision.[53] The familiar story surrounding his commissioning of, accepting, and
then abruptly abandoning the Shatalin-Yavlinskiy "500 Day" economic reform
program in 1990 was only the most publicly visible sign of his waffling, indecisive
decision-making style. His half-measures only further demoralized the Party and
disjointed the state system.[54] He was one constantly trying to compromise with
uncompromising foes, "to reconcile irreconcilable interests."[55] This he tried to
do even with radically different plans for economic reform, ordering a reconciliation between the radical "500 Days" plan and Ryzhkov's more gradual approach.
The only effect was to prevent any action from being taken, as these plans could
not be reconciled!

As a result, Gorbachev's reforms created a supremely fragmented executive
branch, and a critical vacuum of authority at the very top. The "democratization"

political reforms fragmented executive powers and undermined and divided the Party. The opportunity was certainly there for Gorbachev to seize control as a uniting force. But this would have required a leader with a strong vision of the future and an elaborate strategy for getting there. Gorbachev lacked both of these. With fragmentation and chaos at all levels of the political system and a vacillating, indecisive leader at the top, the struggling economy in whose name all of the changes were nominally being made simply had no hope of recovering.

The failure of the political liberalization reforms to improve the economy, indeed their exacerbating the economic crisis, was particularly destabilizing. It reflected an interlocking web of misjudgement and errors by the country's leadership, and a chronic inability of the system to correct or reverse those errors. First, the leadership implicitly admitted the failure of its calls for economic "acceleration" and improvements in economic efficiency by introducing glasnost, placing responsibility on the people for improving the economy. But it proved incapable of keeping glasnost focused on economic improvement and reform. So it turned to reform of political structures as a means of replacing personnel and bringing in fresh enthusiasm to the cause. But the political reforms brought division and decay, both to the political system and to the economy. And thanks to glasnost, not only was all of this obvious, but people could speak and write about it, and do so in terms of the failure and lack of direction of the country's top leadership. Everything it had tried had failed to bring about anything close to the intended results. The economic disaster that worsened as a result of political liberalization was the final piece of evidence that the leadership had no idea what to do to stabilize the country, to improve the lives of the people.

Democratization and Dismemberment of the State

Gorbachev's "democratization" initiatives revealed that he "did not sufficiently understand the nature of the regime he was attempting to reform."[56] The Soviet Union was not Spain or Chile. Embarking on political liberalization without first implementing an economic reform program that would create new economic and societal interests doomed the state. Those interests needed to be created in the Soviet Union, because the Party so thoroughly dominated the economy and society, and for decades had prevented the formation of such interests independent of the Communist Party and its correct line. The only potential non-Party interests that continued to exist in the Soviet Union were ethnic-national interests, as the federation was designed along national-ethnic lines. Political liberalization revived precisely these interests, which quite naturally tore apart the Union.

These had been so thoroughly repressed during decades of fear and control, that even the top political leaders in the country were deceived by their own slogans about a "Soviet nationality," a "Soviet people" having been created, that "the nationality problem was solved."[57] Motyl was wrong to write, "it would be naive to think that Gorbachev believes all he says about the indissoluble friendship of peoples;" it was and remains naive to think he did not believe them![58] Gorbachev's declaration to a Central Committee Plenum in 1988, was one he repeated in many forms in Politburo meetings and conversations with his colleagues: "Soviet patriotism is our most prized value!"[59] Gorbachev was of course not alone, the entire leadership believed the slogans, and "simply did not want to know" that they were false.[60]

It was on the basis of this self-deception and naivete that Gorbachev pursued liberalization policies that ultimately destroyed the state. As Bunce has argued, by introducing political liberalization in a "federalized socialist" state, Gorbachev unleashed "the political opportunity" for challenges to the system itself. It gave elites in the republics the opportunity to press old ethnic-based claims and grievances, and to develop new interests and demands that had nothing to do with and everything to undermine the Party, perestroyka, and preservation of the Union. They made those challenges against a state and a system that had become severely weakened in its capacity to respond, weakened by precisely the same set of political reforms![61]

Motyl explained the peril Gorbachev was placing the Soviet state in at the same time Gorbachev was praising "Soviet patriotism." Democratization and economic decentralization in a Soviet-type federal state "forces peripheral elites to pursue *only* their own interests . . . compels peripheral elites to focus their energies on the territorial unit they administer."[62]

Democratization meant devolution of power to the local levels, and perestroyka generally called for the same regarding economic decisionmaking. This combination forced nationalist thinking because local elites were suddenly made responsible for the economic well-being of their federal territories, which in the Soviet Union were ethnically defined. "Local elites need not be nationalists" prior to liberalization, as Motyl notes, but liberalization creates incentives to focus on "enhancing the prosperity and modernity of one's own republic and, thus, automatically neglecting the all-union context."[63]

The "proclivity" of non-Russians, demonstrated in the 1929s, and 1960s, has always been "to defend their interests and to go their own way whenever Moscow permits them to do so." That is why preventing non-Russian nationalism was always "the main purpose of Soviet policy toward the non-Russians," and why any nationalist behavior was "always repressed by the Soviet authorities, quickly and usually violently."[64] Put differently, the Kremlin held the Soviet

Union together, maintained communist regimes in the republics, through a combination of force, fear and intimidation. Gorbachev's predecessors understood that "there were Russians, Ukrainians, Georgians and Lithuanians, but not very many 'Soviets' in the Soviet Union."[65] Motyl understood all of this. Gorbachev and his colleagues, incredibly and inexcusably, did not.

It is one thing to crack down on nationalist separatists. It is a far more difficult problem when the Party's own elites in the republics began to think and act in a nationalist manner, when the incentives they faced propelled them in that direction.[66] But this was the inevitable consequence of Gorbachev's fits and starts at political liberalization. His policies "had the effect of leaving republican elites stranded. They were forced to build authority and collect resources from the bottom up." Reform shifted resources and power to the republics, but left on their own they needed the authority to use those resources without the fear of consequences from the "outside." This meant they had to demand, first autonomy, and then independence. The result was that "deregulated state socialism was a contradiction in terms, and state socialism, as a result, collapsed."[67] Having already undermined and divided the Party, continued political liberalization in the Soviet Union's federal system caused the breakup of the state itself. Liberalization in a Soviet federal state encourages nationalist separatist movements; democratization combined with economic decentralization "logically leads to the breakup of the Soviet system."[68]

Why did Gorbachev continue to pursue decentralization and liberalization policies right up to the Soviet collapse? It appears that Gorbachev did not understand the severity of the problem, and the rest of the leadership could not believe that he did not understand. Consider his comment at a 1988 Politburo discussion of the eruption of the Nagorno-Karabakh conflict between Armenia and Azerbaijan:

> That the people took to the streets does not mean they threaten Soviet power, internationalism, or the CPSU. After all, it is said there were no anti-Soviet slogans. On the contrary, they appealed to Moscow to resolve the problem.[69]

Gorbachev chose to see the Karabakh and other ethnic problems around the country as challenges to perestroyka, but they were, as Ryzhkov argues, attacks on the state itself. "The breakup of the Union gradually began when the center did not want or couldn't manage to hear the Karabakh 'bell'."[70] When Gorbachev told a subsequent Politburo gathering, "we will oppose any action threatening to destroy our Union," he never specified what actions were unacceptable and never outlined what sort of counteraction was forthcoming.[71] Neither Gorbachev nor the Politburo ever made any decision either about the boundaries of acceptable action or about what response violations of such boundaries would bring on. Indeed, there was scarcely even discussion along these lines, at least none evident in the published memoirs of several Politburo members at the time.[72]

Gorbachev's colleagues, however, were clearer than their leader about the reality of the dangers republican nationalism spelled for the Union. They warned Gorbachev repeatedly, but he proved incapable of understanding. Ryzhkov mused at a 1989 Politburo meeting regarding the Tbilisi massacre that the Politburo was abdicating its leadership function, and the country appeared leaderless before its own people and the world. At the same meeting, Medvedev warned regarding the Baltic states:

> The so-called flexible maneuvering of the leadership is leading to continuous tensions . . . and reflects poorly on the strength of the Party . . . The republic leadership desperately needs help and moral-political support from [the Politburo.][73]

Gorbachev's answer was silence, and his message to the republic leaders was, "It is all up to you. . . . The center's interests are few: the army, the apparat, and science. All else is the Republics' responsibility." It is difficult to believe that a man who had lived his entire life in the Soviet Union, and whose only career had been in the Party apparat in leading positions around the country, could have said these words about the Soviet Union. It reflected a fundamental misunderstanding of the nature of Soviet federalism, a misreading that doomed the country.

This essentially remained Gorbachev's stand, even against continued warnings and opposition by his colleagues. While Gorbachev was saying "The Soviet people share one fate," Vorotnikov and others warned against embracing the concept of sovereignty for the republics: "What is this sovereignty? Self-determination all the way to secession? Re-thinking the Union Treaty? I wouldn't mess with this!" Shevardnadze blasted Gorbachev for lacking "any clarification" of his ideas on reforming the federation, saying in the middle of 1989, "If two years ago we simply said we needed to reform the federation, that would have been interesting."[74] As Reddaway argued, nationalism could perhaps have been stopped at the first warnings of their stirring in Alma-Ata and Riga in late 1986, if the leadership had acted "decisively and got out ahead of the nationalists by sponsoring a new Union Treaty *early*."[75] But by 1989 it was already too dangerous to raise such a prospect, and Gorbachev was still opposed to the idea, only grudgingly coming around to the idea in 1991.

In 1989 Gorbachev was still talking in terms of patchwork "laws" to reform the federation, and Shevardnadze had to repeat three times for Gorbachev to understand that any document regarding reform of the federation had to spell out in writing that secession would not be allowed. Perhaps the most lucid example came in an exchange in the Politburo in January 1990:

> Gorbachev: For three years we have been talking about the universal interests of all people, and national processes continue on their own course to the point where Armenia and Azerbaijan have formed their own armies.
>
> Vorotnikov: We need to throw all of these laws on autonomy into the trash. They are no good.
>
> Gorbachev: The first law we need to develop is a mechanism for secession from the Soviet Union. The second is on autonomy.[76]

As this exchange reveals, Gorbachev was incapable of choosing between two objectives that in a Soviet state were contradictory: pursuing the unity of the country versus strengthening the sovereignty of the union republics. It seems he never even grasped that the two objectives were indeed contradictory. He repeated both as priority objectives first as General Secretary and then as President. But both objectives could not be pursued. Even after the coup, Gorbachev never grasped why the republics perceived the choice as "either there be independence, in which case there is not and cannot be a center, or the center remains, but then goodby independence."[77] Indeed, even his second memoir, "The Union Could Have Been Saved," fails to recognize how political liberalization prior to implementation of coherent economic reform spelled doom for a Soviet federal state.

The greatest danger in fueling republican autonomy demands was that it would fuel similar demands in Russia. Russian autonomy raised a plethora of system-destabilizing processes. Demands for a Russian Communist Party meant "turning the CPSU from a united Party into a union of parties," and by extension turning the USSR from a united state into a union of states. Gorbachev failed to recognize until too late that the processes set off in the Baltic, Central Asian and Caucusus republics would also hit the Slavic republics, including Russia, and when they did hit his actions betray a lack of understanding of those processes and their significance. His own colleagues were frustrated that he "did not pay enough attention" to either Russian level CPD elections or other events related to the Russian Party and government. Gorbachev ignored repeated warnings from Medvedev and others to nominate prominent candidates for the Russian CPD, the result being there were no candidates "who could reasonably contest Yeltsin" for the leadership of the republic. This inattention relegated the communists in Russia to the opposition, which sent Russia on an immediate course towards sovereignty and independence from the Soviet center.[78]

Gorbachev was at his peak of incompetence when dealing with politics and processes in Russia. First he was too late in paying attention to the Russian elections to have any influence over the outcome. When he finally did pay attention, every act he took worked directly against his explicit objectives. First and foremost, he sought to prevent Yeltsin's election as Chairman of the Russian Supreme Soviet. When Yeltsin fell a few votes shy of gaining the post, Gorbachev delivered a scathing speech before the Russian legislature sharply attacking Yeltsin and his support for Russian sovereignty, and warning of dire consequences if they elected Yeltsin. The result, of course, was that the deputies rallied to prevent Yeltsin, exactly the opposite of Gorbachev's intended outcome.

It was clear Gorbachev learned absolutely nothing from his bungled attempt to prevent Yeltsin's election to head the legislature. Less than one year later, after Yeltsin had delivered a televised national speech personally attacking the Soviet President, the Russian Congress convened a special emergency session with one issue on the agenda: a motion to remove Yeltsin from his post as Chairman of the Russian Supreme Soviet. The overwhelming sentiment among the deputies was hostile to Yeltsin, and his political career was most in jeopardy. But an incomprehensible act by Gorbachev again saved Yelstin. The deputies awoke March 28, 1991 to find the center of Moscow, including the Kremlin where the deputies were to meet, surrounded by troops and armored vehicles. It was not clear to anyone what they were doing there, but the deputies took it as a clear and direct threat to Russian sovereignty. In the corridors, as the deputies made their way into the session, they had completely forgotten about their quarrel with Yeltsin. All the deputies were talking about in the corridors was the illegality of Gorbachev's actions in Moscow, and the need to defend Russia's sovereignty. And that is precisely what they did: the Congress became a rally in defense of Russian sovereignty, against Gorbachev! It was perhaps the luckiest moment of Yeltsin's political career. He emerged as a heroic leader.

It was simply astounding that a man with such little political aptitude could have ascended to the top position in the Soviet Union. Gorbachev had no conception of the dynamics of elite politics in Russia, or the consequences of the political reforms he himself had initiated. Had he paid attention to the Russian elections, perhaps a stronger candidate could have been put forth to challenge Yeltsin for the Chairmanship. Having failed this, had Gorbachev let the Congress be, it might never have elected Yeltsin in 1990. Had he let the Congress alone in March 1991, there is little reason to doubt the deputies would have removed Yeltsin from the chairmanship, which could have effectively ended his political career. Instead, Gorbachev's lack of understanding of processes in the republics, including the Russian Republic, led him to actions that decreased trust among the top political elite in his authority and competence, expanded broader opposition to his leadership and policies, and fueled rather than quieted autonomy and secessionist sentiments.

As if these domestic consequences of political liberalization were not enough of a threat to the Soviet state, the policies triggered convulsions in Eastern Europe that completely surprised the Soviet leadership. These in turn had consequences in the Soviet Union for which the Soviet leadership was entirely unprepared. Unfortunately, Western analysts, Soviet observers, and former Soviet officials rarely give serious consideration to this matter when analyzing the Soviet collapse, but it demands substantial examination far beyond what can be done here. Suffice it to say that the collapse of communist regimes across Eastern Europe in 1989 virtually guaranteed the end of the Soviet Union, they dealt a blow from which the Soviet Union was unable to recover, and it is for this reason that the bulk of events and processes discussed in this chapter precede 1990. I consider the death sentence for the Soviet Union to have been sealed by New Year's Day, 1990.[79]

Gorbachev, Medvedev, and Ryzhkov remain all but silent regarding events in Eastern Europe, and what should have been done. Vorotnikov briefly addresses the issue in his memoirs, but he doesn't really address why the upheaval in the Warsaw Pact countries was important domestically. All he offers are observations of Gorbachev's attitude. After the January 1987 Party Plenum, he reveals, Gorbachev put off the issue of how perestroyka would affect relations with Eastern Europe, saying "We'll figure that out later."[80] When the street demonstrations and emigration waves began in East Germany, Vorotnikov argues only that "Either Gorbachev did not understand how the people in the USSR would painfully react, or he consciously distanced himself from the events."[81] Either way, by that point a conscious response was needed opposite from the one needed in 1987—this time for a domestic audience regarding the implications of events in Eastern Europe for the Soviet Union! As in 1987, however, no such response, no recognition of the significance of events in Eastern Europe, was forthcoming from the Soviet leader or leadership.

That political liberalization would mean the end of communism in Eastern Europe certainly ought to have been obvious, or at least occurred to Gorbachev, even if we accept his naivete regarding the "Soviet people." The significance of 1956 Hungary, 1968 Czechoslovakia, or 1980 Poland should have been clear enough to signify the tentative legitimacy at best of the regimes in those countries. If NATO could reasonably doubt whether East Germans would fire on West Germans, whether Czechs would fire on Germans, or whether Poles would fire on the French if it came to that, certainly Moscow must have shared the concern that they would have turned their fire on Russians instead. It took Soviet force and threats of force, both implicit and explicit, to preserve the regimes in Eastern Europe after World War II. Political liberalization in Moscow meant the end of communist regimes in Eastern Europe. Once it became clear that Moscow would not send tanks to crush anti-communist demonstrations, the people of Eastern Europe took to the streets in droves, flushing out the regimes in a matter of weeks.[82]

The demonstration effect this had was clear, and it was powerful. It proved the regimes could be overthrown, and with minimal if any violence. It proved Moscow would not use force to prevent massive anti-communist demonstrations. From the vantage point of, say, Estonia, the reasoning was, "If they are not going to shoot Czechs, they are not going to shoot us." This message was received the same way in the other Baltic States, in the Caucusus, and most significantly in Russia itself. Both the people and the elites must have been shocked by Gorbachev's inaction. But it appeared he meant what he said when he told the republics everything was in their hands. What they heard when he said this was, the Union is history.

Conclusions

Political liberalization thus underlies all of the centrifugal processes that splintered the Soviet Union. Glasnost relativized and divided the Party, destroying its myth of being the holder of truth and dislodging it from its leading role in society. The structural reorganizations to the political system under the label "democratization" fragmented executive powers and incapacitated government, distracted from and hindered economic reform, and incited nationalist separatist tendencies that dismembered the federal state. Gorbachev's personal initiatives were the only way these policies could have been introduced, and they reflected his flawed understanding of the nature of his state and society, and his general lack of vision and strategy, that is, his ineptitude as a political leader.

The question remains, could a leader have introduced reform in the Soviet Union without threatening the very survival of the state? I share the skepticism of Bunce and others on this score. However, we also need not act as if brainwashed by Gorbachev's repeated declarations that there were "no alternatives" to perestroyka, to glasnost, to democratization, to himself. I do not accept that repression and violence from the Party and state were necessary to preserve the Soviet Union. The most obvious alternative is somewhat beyond the scope of this chapter. Gorbachev was too impatient with economic reform. A more enlightened leader would have followed something closer to the "Chinese path," focusing on economic reforms without reorganizing the state's political institutions and without significant political liberalization. After the first initial, tentative steps of

1985 and early '86, then, instead of giving up and turning to political reform as a way to influence the economy, a different approach would have been to concentrate efforts on developing a comprehensive plan for economic reform and development, adopt it, and implement it. Rhetoric notwithstanding, explanations when offered (rarely!) fail to convince that economic reform in the Soviet Union necessarily required reform of the state's political institutions. There is simply no reason to believe the Soviet Union could not have introduced such initiatives as allowing for multiple forms of ownership, introducing market mechanisms and competition, even in agriculture, allowing obsolete enterprises to go bankrupt, and creating incentives to stimulate consumer goods production, without gutting the Party and fragmenting the government and state.

Such measures might have brought successes to the Soviet economy as it has to the Chinese. Adoption of such a strategy would have indicated a united leadership with a vision for the future and a plan for getting there. It would have involved a plan giving people greater economic freedom. While it may not have suddenly made the people love and trust the Party, it is not at all clear they would have necessarily risen up against it, had such a plan been introduced and implemented beginning in 1986 or '87. Such reforms could have begun to create interests in society independent of the Party, yet not based on ethnic-national distinctions, that is, they could have begun to create a middle class. Again, we see this happening in China. Were political liberalization introduced after an extensive period of coordinated economic reforms along these lines, things might have gone differently for the Soviet Union.

Of course, China brutally massacred peaceful demonstrators in 1989, just as Moscow was allowing such demonstrations in the Soviet Union and Eastern Europe. The question, then, is whether non-repressive political reforms could have succeeded. Was there a path to liberalization that could have worked? Could political liberalization have been carried out in a way that would have helped to bring a rejuvenated economy and society while preserving at least the state and perhaps the Party's leadership as well? While serious doubts exist, and I remain skeptical, one thing is abundantly clear: any alternative path, to be successful, would have required leadership from one with a vision of the future, a strategy for getting there, and a will to carry out that strategy. In other words, it would have required someone other than Mikhail S. Gorbachev. This, of course, would not necessarily have been good for the United States in particular or the West in general. Indeed, if it would have meant a continued Communist Party monopoly on political power, it seems reasonable to say it would have not been good for the people of the Soviet Union either. This, however, does not negate the possibility that there were indeed options for political reform for the Soviet Union that might have had a better chance at meeting the goals of the Soviet leadership.

First, and perhaps most important of all, any strategy for political liberalization needed to be aiming at creating rather than destroying, it needed to have a positive rather than a negative justification. Almost all of Gorbachev's reforms were negative: overcoming conservatism, rooting out old officials and old thinking, eliminating inefficiency and lack of innovation.[83] One of the problems with piecemeal reforms is they are usually reactive, and thus in response to one or another current problem. A leader with vision, though, could have taken the opportunity to introduce a comprehensive and sweeping political reform. For example, in preparing for the 19th Party Conference, Gorbachev could have commissioned a re-drafting of the Constitution, implementing a complete restructuring of the country's political institutions. This would have forced a choice between forming a parliamentary or a presidential type system, and would of necessity had to have addressed the question of the division of responsibilities between the various branches. In particular, it would have required reconstituting the government to provide for a unified executive branch. It seems less significant exactly what form this reconstitution would have taken, presidential, parliamentary, semi-presidential. What was needed above all from political reorganization from Party rule to something else, regardless of the particular answer, was to resolve the questions of who holds what power, and who is subordinate and responsible to whom. In Gorbachev's partial reforms, these answers were never forthcoming, indeed the confusion became ever-greater.

The advantages gained would have been several. First, after the reorganization, political reform would not have remained an open book. It would have been a decisive, bold step and a sweeping one. The door on further change could then reasonably have been closed, and focus could have been turned again to resolving the pressing economic and social problems. Second, it would have forced a solution to the problem of the locus of executive power, thereby bringing the potential of order and coherence to subsequent management of the economy. Spheres of power would have been clearly drawn, and the ambiguity and confusion regarding lines of authority and responsibility could have been avoided. Third, it would have cast the leadership in a strong, self-assured, active light, rather than a reactive, tentative, disorderly light that surrounded Gorbachev's half measures. Such a leadership could have reasonably expected a "honeymoon" period in the new system, and enjoyed a measure of confidence from the people. With Gorbachev's reforms, the Party remained fused into the power structures—the party First Secretaries headed the Soviets. There was no confidence that anything had really changed, or that there was any order or vision at the top.

It does seem clear that political liberalization was incompatible with Communist Party rule. An opening up to freedom of expression and political criticism destroyed the Party's exclusive hold on information, its mythical role as holder of the single truth. However, it is just as equally clear that the Communist Party could have survived in some form, as indeed it has to this day as one of many competing partisan organizations. Communist Party rule, though, in the sense of its continued "leading role," was dead with the introduction of political liberalization no matter what form such liberalization were to take.

However, the state need not have disintegrated. A comprehensive approach as outlined above could have been implemented across the Soviet space, particularly if combined with or including reconsideration of the nature of the federation. Again, actions needed to be comprehensive and decisive, rather than half-hearted and drawn out. At the first sign of ethnic unrest, then, a decisive response would have been to gather all of the republic leaders in Moscow and, as Reddaway argues, get ahead of the processes by getting those leaders to agree to a new Union Treaty early on. This was needed certainly by 1987, rather than hemming and hawing until 1991. Once agreed on, a willingness of the center to use force if necessary to then uphold that treaty would have needed to be clear to all participants. There is no objective reason to deem this repressive. The will to defend the sovereignty and security of the state should be the first and unswerving duty of any political leader, as the West accepted regarding events in Chechnya in 1995.

The reason for continued skepticism, however, that political liberalization of any kind in the Soviet Union could have succeeded, rests with the reaction of the Baltic States and Eastern Europe. I see this as a single question, because as argued above the two fates were integrally linked. Moreover, I find it difficult to conceive of any means of allowing the three Baltic States independence, regardless of the circumstances, that could have been consistent with the continued survival of the Soviet Union. Had the type of constitutional changes I suggest been introduced in, say, 1987 or 1988, there is little reason to doubt that the Baltic States would have been a part of those changes. However, the reaction of Eastern Europe to even this approach to political liberalization in the Soviet Union remains a trickier question. My own guess is it would likely have been the same as it was in 1989. If this is true, then the fate of the Soviet Union would have remained grim. As long as Eastern Europe was allowed to go independent and re-align with the West, the Baltic States would not be far behind in the same direction. This, in turn, could only imperil the overall integrity of the Soviet Union. Therefore, it seems clear that the Soviet leaders also would have had to consider, as part of their domestic constitutional changes and political liberalization, some form of new, revitalized confederation with the states of Eastern Europe. Whether any such arrangement could have been found, or could have survived for long, is an open question.

To rephrase the point, there does indeed seem to have been a domestic alternative to Gorbachev's haphazard political liberalization, one consistent with preservation of the Union. However, the external consequences of *any* liberalization may well have been too great, and fed back into the Soviet Union processes that were incompatible with the continued survival of the state. If this is true, then any Soviet leader introducing political liberalization while believing such policies would strengthen the Party and state would have to go down as a failure.

NOTES

1. Schroeder, "The Economy and the Fate of the USSR" (June 1997 version, pages 14, 28, 32). This point echoes those made in the '80s by such observers as Timothy Colton, *The Dilemma of Reform in the Soviet Union*, (New York: Council on Foreign Relations, 1986); and Seweryn Bialer, *Stalin's Successors*, (Cambridge: Cambridge University Press, 1980). Although Schroeder accepts that "political reforms were essential to carrying out a successful economic reform," she seems to accept this repeated assertion by Gorbachev on faith, as do most other Western scholars. However, it is a controversial assertion, to say the least, one that was and remains challenged by many of Gorbachev's Politburo colleagues. Events would seem to have borne out the doubts of those colleagues, as this paper argues.

2. Taylor, "The Soviet Military and the Disintegration of the USSR" (March 1997 version, page 10).

3. Bunce, "Subversive Institutions: The End of the Soviet State in Comparative Perspective" (n.d., esp. pages 21–26).

4. The title of Gorbachev's second memoir, *Soyuz Mozhno Bylo Sokhranit*, (Moscow: April-85).

5. Max Weber, *Basic Concepts in Sociology*, (New York: Citadel Press, 1964), p. 29. This is the crux of Weber's *Verstehen*, or interpretive understanding. One may also call it, interpretive sensitivity.

6. For an interesting interpretation of the fall of Rome, see Ramsay MacMullen, *Enemies of the Roman Order: Treason, Unrest and Alienation in the Empire*. (London: Routledge, 1966).

7. Alexis de Tocqueville, *The Old Regime and the Revolution*, Trans. Alan S. Kahan, (Chicago: University of Chicago Press, 1998), p. 222.

8. *Pravda* February 14, 1987, translated in *Current Digest of the Soviet Press*, vol. 39 no. 7, p. 6.

9. M. S. Gorbachev, *Gody trudnykh resheniy* (Years of Difficult Decisions). (Moscow: Alpha-Print, 1993), p. 6.

10. Ibid., pp. 29, 33, 44.

11. *Pravda*, September 25, 1988, translated in *Current Digest of the Soviet Press*. Vol. 40, no. 39, p. 7.

12. See Vera Tolz, "The Soviet Press Under Gorbachev," *Radio Liberty Research Report* no. 38/86.

13. See Gorbachev's speech in *L'Humanite*, published in Russian in *Moskovskaya pravda*, February 8, 1986, pp. 1–2.

14. N. I. Ryzhkov, *Perestroika: Istoriya predatelstv.* (Perestroyka: The History of Betrayal). (Moscow: Novosti, 1992). p. 199.

15. See, for example, Vadim Medvedev, *V Komande Gorbacheva: Vzglyad iznutry.* (On Gorbachev's Team: An Inside View). (Moscow: Bylina, 1994); and V. I. Vorotnikov, *A Bylo Eto Tak. . . .* (This is How it Was). (Moscow: Sovet Veteranov Knigoizdaniya, 1995).

16. Martin Malia (Alias "Z") offered a nice summary of Soviet-style "totalitarianism" in his "To the Stalin Mausoleum," *Deadalus*. vol. 119 no. 1 (Winter 1990), pp. 295–344). See esp. pp. 301–319.

17. Ken Jowitt, "The Leninist Phenomenon" in *New World Disorder*, (Berkeley: University of California Press, 1992), esp. pp. 8–11.

18. Theodore Draper, "Who Killed Soviet Communism?" in *New York Review of Books*. vol 39 no 11, (June 11, 1992) pp. 7–14.

19. See Jowitt, "Gorbachev: Bolshevik or Menshevik?"in *New World Disorder*, esp. pp. 230–231.

20. Ibid, pp. 238–240; and Jowitt, "The Leninist Extinction" in *New World Disorder*, esp. p. 258.

21. Reddaway, "The Quality of Gorbachev's Leadership," p. 433.

22. Mary McCauley, *Soviet Politics 1917–1991*. (Oxford: Oxford University Press, 1992), p. 93.

23. It bears repeating that I am not lamenting his failure to end glasnost, nor do I think the people of the former Soviet Union would be better off had glasnost been terminated in 1987 and reforms ended. I am strictly suggesting that continued pursuance of glasnost was directly inconsistent with the survival of the Party, and Gorbachev was intensely in favor of the Party's continued survival!

24. See Gorbachev, *Gody Trudnykh Resheniy*, pp. 98–106, for documents from the Politburo sessions. See also the accounts of Medvedev, *V Komande Gorbacheva*, pp. 62–71; and Vorotnikov, *A Bylo Eto Tak . . .* , pp. 198–203.

25. Alexander Dallin, "Causes of the Collapse of the USSR," in *Post-Soviet Affairs*, vol. 8, no. 4, p. 287.

26. Peter Reddaway, "The Quality of Gorbachev's Leadership," in Ed Hewett and Victor Winston, eds., *Milestones in Glasnost and Perestroika*, (Washington, D.C.: The Brookings Institution, 1991), p. 433.

27. Jowitt, "Gorbachev: Bolshevik or Menshevik?", pp. 238–240, 248. See also Stephen Hanson, "Gorbachev: The Last True Leninist Believer?" in Daniel Chirot, ed. *The Crisis of Leninism and the Decline of the Left*, (University of Washington Press, 1991).

28. Gorbachev, *Gody Trudnykh Resheniy*, pp. 108–109.

29. Vorotnikov, *I Eto Bylo Tak . . .* pp. 40–42. Also Ryzhkov, *Perestroyka: Istoriya Predatelstv*, pp. 93–95.

30. Ibid. Interviews with several confidential sources in 1990 and 1991 revealed that Gorbachev had consistently rejected as early as 1988 the urging of his political advisor, Georgiy Shakhnazarov, to create a Presidency. He then submitted the proposal at the Third CPD on his own, without carefully considering what such an office would look like and what responsibilities it would have related to other branches of the governing system. See discussion below.

31. Ryzhkov, *Perestroyka: Istoriya Predatelstv*, p. 345.

32. Ibid., pp. 26–28.

33. Ibid., pp. 20–21.

34. Ibid., pp. 20–21, 345.

35. Ibid.

36. Medvedev, *V Komande Gorbacheva . . .* , p. 165.

37. Ryzhkov, *Perestroyka: Istoriya Predatelstv*, p. 21.

38. Ibid, pp. 113–115, 161–162.

39. Ryzhkov provides a particularly convincing analysis along these lines. See *Perestroyka, Istoriya Predatelstv*, pp. 113–114, 167–171, and 345–346.

40. For a full elaboration of dual-channel institutional designs and their consequences, see Joel M. Ostrow, *Comparing Post-Soviet Legislatures: A Theory of Institutional Design and Political Conflict* (Ohio State University Press, 2000).

41. See Ibid., and Ostrow, "Procedural Breakdown and Deadlock in the Russian State Duma: The Problems of an Un-Linked, Dual-Channel Institutional Design," *Europe-Asia Studies*, June 1998.

42. See Medvedev, *V Komande Gorbacheva* . . . , pp. 165–166.

43. Ryzhkov, *Perestroyka: Istoriya Predatelstv*, pp. 274–275.

44. Vorotnikov, *A Bylo Eto Tak* . . . , p. 103.

45. See Schroeder's review of the sudden decline in economic performance, pp. 32–33. Both Vorotnikov (pp. 118–120), and Kotz and Weir (pp. 73–82) provide evidence for an argument that the first two years of perestroyka actually did bring modest economic improvements. The break came with the turn to political reform.

46. Vorotnikov, *A Bylo Eto Tak* . . . , pp. 120–121.

47. Ibid., pp. 220–221.

48. Kotz and Weir, p. 105.

49. Ibid.

50. Medvedev, *V Komande Gorbacheva*, p. 103.

51. Ryzhkov, *Perestroyka: Istoriya Predatelstv*, p. 167.

52. Ibid., p. 364.

53. Medvedev, *V Komande Gorbacheva*, pp. 70–73.

54. Draper, "Who Killed Soviet Communism?" p. 8.

55. McCauley gives a nice summary of this characteristic in *Soviet Politics 1917–1991*, p. 109–110.

56. Andranik Migranyan, "Gorbachev's Leadership: A Soviet View," in Hewett and Winston, *Milestones in Glasnost and Perestroyka, pp. 460–461*. For similar views see Jowitt, "Gorbachev. Bolshevik or Menshevik," Reddaway, "The Quality of Gorbachev's Leadership," and Hanson, "@@

57. Ryzhkov admits to the collective naivete of the Politburo leadership, but argues persuasively that Gorbachev, if he ever opened his eyes to the fallacy, was the last to do so. See *Perestroyka: Istoriya Predatelstv*, pp. 199–200.

58. Motyl, 160.

59. Gorbachev, *Soyuz Mozhno Bylo Sokhranit*, p. 17.

60. Ryzhkov, *Perestroyka, Istoriya Predatelstv*, p. 199.

61. Bunce pp. 19–20.

62. Alexander J. Motyl, "The Sobering of Gorbachev," in Seweryn Bialer, ed., *Politics, Society and Nationality Inside Gorbachev's Russia*, (Boulder. Westview Press, 1989), *pp. 166–168*.

63. Ibid.

64. Ibid., pp. 151–152.

65. Jowitt, "Gorbachev: Bolshevik or Menshevik?" p. 248.

66. See Motyl, "The Sobering of Gorbachev," p. 152.

67. Bunce, pp. 24–26.

68. Ibid., pp. 168–169. Motyl was of course wrong in his conclusion that the system's survival was not in doubt. It was a strange conclusion from his analysis, all of which powerfully suggested that the Soviet state was on its last legs.

69. Gorbachev, *Soyuz Mozhno Bylo Sokhranit*, p. 20.

70. Ryzhkov, *Perestroyka: Istoriya Predatelstv*, p. 207–208.

71. Gorbachev, *Soyuz Mozhno Bylo Sokhranit*, p. 41.

72. Oddly, even Gorbachev's harshest critics do not suggest boundaries that should have been set or concrete actions that should have been taken in the republics, even retrospectively.

73. Gorbachev, *Soyuz Mozhno Bylo Sokhranit*, p. 51–52.

74. Gorbachev, *Soyuz Mozhno Bylo Sokhranit*, pp. 61–62.

75. Reddaway, "The Quality of Gorbachev's Leadership," pp. 435. Emphasis in the original.

76. Ibid., pp. 92–93.

77. Gorbachev, *Soyuz Mozhno Bylo Sokhranit*, pp. 228–229.

78. Medvedev, *V Komande Gorbacheva*, pp. 137–142.

79. When I left for Moscow in December 1989, I went with the conscious purpose of watching the regime collapse. Once the regimes had fallen in Eastern Europe, the writing was on the wall for the Soviet Union.

80. Vorotnikov, *A Bylo Eto Tak . . .* , p. 130.

81. Ibid., p. 321.

82. Still the most engaging account of the fall of Eastern European Communism is Timothy Garton Ash, *We the People,* (London: Granta Books, 1990).

83. See on this point Motyl, pp. 156–157; and Hanson, p. 84.

2.3

Causes of the Collapse of the USSR

Alexander Dallin

In awe, amazement, and disbelief, the world witnessed the collapse of the Soviet Union, which swept away the Soviet system of government, the erstwhile superpower, the communist belief system, and the ruling party.

Why did the Soviet system disintegrate? In the first year since its collapse, several conflicting and controversial "theories" have been proposed in explanation. A sharp line may be drawn between explanations that focus on particular aspects of the Soviet system—operations (as indicated by the slowdown of the economy, for example), institutions or personalities—and those which find the cause of the collapse in the essence of the Soviet regime.

Essentialist Arguments

The "essentialists," whose moral absolutism was at the root of the famous identification of the Soviet Union, barely ten years ago, as the "evil empire," make three claims regarding the origins of Soviet collapse:

(1) The original seizure of power by the Leninists in 1917 was illegitimate, and this illegitimacy and a peculiar "genetic code" remained attached to the ruling party and the regime. And much as a form of original sin, they could not be shed or overcome; thus, the system was in some sense doomed from the start.

(2) Throughout its history, the Soviet system was essentially unchangeable: whatever the alterations in institutions, policies, and personalities, these were relatively trivial; as throughout it was and remained an "ideocracy" and a "partocracy."

(3) The Soviet system was "intrinsically unreformable": efforts to tinker with it, including those of the Gorbachev era, were intended only to rescue and strengthen it, whereas the system needed to be demolished and a new system built from scratch on a different foundation.

Source: Alexander Dallin, "Causes of the Collapse of the USSR," *The Soviet System in Crisis*, Westview Press, 1991. 673–695.

Note: Notes and references have been removed from this article.

The essentialists themselves break down into those who see the Soviet Union as the quintessence of the worst of Russian political culture and those others who see the source of evil—its totalitarianism—in ideology and organization, that is, in Marxism-Leninism and the Communist Party. In fact, the differences between these two camps are not at all insignificant.

We may take the recent writings of Martin Malia as the most explicit, most elegant, and most systematic exposition of the neo-totalitarian approach, which moreover does claim to provide an explanation for what he calls the "implosion" of the Soviet order. Precisely because this argument risks becoming an ideology of its own—and because it is based on assumptions that this observer considers thoroughly misguided—the following is an attempt to provide a different set of propositions to explain the Soviet collapse.

Against Predetermination

Identifying the sources of historical events is a notoriously chancy and disputed business. We have no experimental method, nor proof that would stand up in a scientific court of law. Etiology—the search for causes—is not a science, nor is there any reliable technique for weighing the relative importance of different inputs. The archives will reveal no documents that will conveniently spell out the causes of the Soviet collapse. Moreover, the assessment of causes may well change with the distance in time from the events. Finally, as with an earthquake, at times subterranean processes are at work without our being able to track them in advance of their eruption.

Research will help, as will a commitment to making assumptions explicit. At the very least, it is often possible to tell who has gotten it wrong, without being sure who has gotten it right. But, ultimately, we have to rely on an individual analyst's scholarly intuition and empathy, and on his or her implicit philosophy of history. It is only fair to indicate that my own inclination is to distrust both conspiracy theories and flukes, and to be suspicious of all manner of determinism and inevitability, mysterious "essences" and broad a priori philosophical schemes. It is far better, I would maintain, to examine the empirical evidence without prejudging the case.

I find no grounds for arguing that the outcome—the disintegration of the Soviet system—was predetermined, let alone inscribed in the "genetic code" that went back to October 1917 and the origins of that system. How do we know what, if anything, was preordained? More concretely, the system withstood many tests far more severe than what it experienced in the 1980s (for example, in the first Five-Year Plan and in World War II) and survived: its institutions and controls were scarcely brittle then, and popular attitudes—admittedly, difficult to probe in retrospect—scarcely bore out the neo-totalitarian argument that the regime never had any legitimacy in the eyes of the population.

Of course the seizure of power in 1917 was illegitimate. But it is impossible seriously to derive the events of 1991 from that fact. It is far more sensible and far more persuasive to argue that what we see in the Soviet collapse is the product of unintended results, both of socioeconomic development and of earlier policy choices. According to the neo-totalitarian argument, the Soviet Union remained totalitarian after Stalin—not because the reality of Soviet life was so, but because of a continued commitment of the decision-makers to a totalitarian vision. By the same token, it is precisely the extent to which Soviet reality diverged from that vision that provides evidence of social autonomy—of what is properly referred to as unintended consequences.

What we are really puzzling over is how as thoroughly controlled, as tightly disciplined, as rigidly programmed, and as heavily indoctrinated a system as the Soviet managed to fall apart, unravel so easily and so completely, and in the process prompt in its citizenry an utter scorn for authority, and a disregard for laws and regulations.

The answers, I believe, have to go beyond social psychology, for they centrally involve political institutions and behavior. They involve both broad secular changes and particular individual choices. There is, I suggest, a cluster of interrelated developments that together, and in their interaction, formed the essential preconditions—necessary but not sufficient—for what occurred in the 1990s. In brief, they are: (1) the loosening of controls; (2) the spread of corruption; (3) the erosion of ideology; (4) the impact of social change on values and social pathologies; (5) the growing impact of the external environment on Soviet society and politics; and (6) the consequences of economic constraints. Against these background conditions, certain decisions of the Gorbachev regime, in turn, appear decisive as catalysts for collapse.

The Loosening of Controls

One thing that held the Soviet Union together, exacted obedience and compliance, and provided the framework for its *sui generis* development, was the sweeping Stalinist system of controls. Stalin died in 1953. In retrospect, what we see during the following 30 years is a gradual, unheralded loosening and then breakdown of these controls.

An essential part of the control structure and process was the terror that had reached unbelievable proportions and exacted such an incredible cost in the Stalin years. In the Khrushchev years it was the abandonment of mass political terror that provided the conditions for reducing the scope of controls. It ended the atomization, the silencing of that society—with an impact that did not become fully apparent until a generation later. As T. H. Rigby, an astute analyst of the Soviet scene, observed, in differentiating between active and symbolic, covert and overt elements that presaged the emergence of a civil society a generation later:

> The most interesting developments came in the covert active elements. I am not thinking so much of the shadow economy and clientelist networks, although these also thrived mightily, especially during the Brezhnev years. Of far greater importance for the future of the civil society was the profuse blossoming of what I have called the covert "market in ideas," a blossoming vastly greater than what was apparent publicly. The key facilitating factor here was the curbing of the political police after Stalin's death. . . . People gradually found they could get away with a great deal in the way of unorthodox opinions and behaviour in private [. . .] The rehousing program helped here, because tens of millions of city dwellers now acquired some real privacy as they moved from so-called communal apartments to little family flats. The Soviet population was acquiring "freedom of speech in one kitchen."

[. . .] In the Brezhnev years a remarkable change in mood became apparent. Whether or not it accurately reflected reality, Soviet observers began to speak—rather more candidly than before—of stagnation and the leadership's failure to come to grips with urgent problems, and foreigners noted the change. Thus the economist Joseph Berliner was struck by the contrast between 1958 and 1967. By the later date;

> there was in fact an air of gloom in the comments of economists I talked to. Perhaps my impression was heightened by the contrast in their tone with that during my earlier visit to the USSR [in 1958] . . . the USSR was riding the crest of a period of rapid economic growth. Consumption levels had risen rapidly following Stalin's death, and rates of investment were high. . . . There was a mood of exuberance and confidence in the vitality of the Soviet economic system. All this had changed by 1967. One found a candid admission that the economy was facing some nasty problems. [. . .]

And Dusko Doder recalled:

> When I arrived in Moscow on temporary duty in the summer of 1978, it was apparent that incremental changes had taken place over the past decade. . . . In the narrow circle of my friends I found something that was new, or at least more pronounced than before—the quest for the comforts of middle-class life: a car, a place in the country, a tiled bathroom, a Japanese stereo, a chance to travel abroad—at least to Bulgaria.

By the early 1980s it was apparent to him that;

> Brezhnev's stable regime had produced an amazing proliferation of corruption, a cynicism that undermined all enterprise. An air of stagnation, the timeless inertia of the bureaucracy, a crisis of spirit—all characterized a system that seemed to have accompanied the aging leaders into exhaustion and debility.

These comments touch on the principal arenas in which critical changes were indeed taking place. To what extent the Communist Party itself was affected was not yet apparent, and of course large bureaucratic organizations are capable of conducting routine operations regardless of the morale or enthusiasm, or lack thereof, of their personnel. But something else was becoming evident: what had been aptly described as a "mono-organizational" system was showing cracks. Party, state, and police officials were working the system for their own benefit.

Blair Ruble has suggested that (by analogy with Quebec) what was taking place was a sort of "quiet revolution"—with the informal emergence of a second economy, a second culture, even a second politics alongside, and in full recognition of the continuing limits imposed by, the official ones. What added to the toleration of the new ambiguities was the fact that the second economy had its functional aspects insofar as performance was concerned. So, it has been argued, had the crystallization of rival patronage networks cultivated by various Soviet leaders. While the emergence of patron-client relations is a virtually ubiquitous development in all complex societies, John Willerton posits convincingly that, insofar as it promotes individual needs or interests, it undercuts the centrality or priority of government (or party) norms and goals.

The Spread of Corruption

Far more serious is the massive spread of corruption, in all its many aspects, as a way of life. In a powerful account based on personal experience and replete with well-documented anecdotes, Konstantin Simis, in his *USSR: The Corrupt Society,* is compelled to conclude:

> The Soviet Union is infected from top to bottom with corruption—from the worker who gives the foreman a bottle of vodka to get the best job, to Politburo candidate Mzhavanadze who takes hundreds of thousands of rubles for protecting underground millionaires; from the street prostitute, who pays the policeman ten rubles so that he won't prevent her from solic-iting clients, to the former member of the Politburo Ekaterina Furtseva, who built a luxurious suburban villa at the government's expense—each and everyone is afflicted with corruption. [. . .]

Especially in the late Brezhnev years, scandalous examples multiplied, from the appearance of feudal baronies in Uzbekistan or in the Urals, where high offi-cials were able to operate with impunity, to the involvement of Brezhnev's daughter, Galina, and her lover with a crowd of circus crooks, the theft of jewels, and the entanglement of high secret-police officials. [. . .]

Much of this "quiet revolution" became possible because the end of mass terror also meant an end to the individual's paralyzing fear, and because bureaucratic actors saw opportunities for self-aggrandizement with minimal risk or cost. But in Stalin's time, in addition to both outer constraints and often simply the lack of opportunity for autonomous corruption, there had been psychological inhibitions on many well-placed individuals, rooted in their belief in the system and in the cause in the name of which it was all being done. Later, with a change of generations and apparently a change of values, one began to observe an erosion of ideological commitments and a more single-minded pursuit, and at times also a more explicit articulation, of personal priorities.

Perhaps the most interesting conceptualization of this phenomenon is to be found in Ken Jowitt's writings. Stressing the disappearance of the party's overriding combat task—or transformation agenda—of earlier years, he remarked in the 1980s: "Today what impresses one about the Soviet Union is the party leadership's inability and/or unwillingness to devise a credible and authoritative social combat task capable of sustaining a distinction between the regime elite's particular status interests and the party's general compe-tence and interest . . . ." What is remarkable, he finds, is the increasing ten-dency of individual members to be "oriented to personal, familial, and mate-rial concerns." In Jowitt's post-Weberian vocabulary, "the subordination of office charisma to the incumbents' particular interests" is then identified pre-cisely as "corrupt routinization."

The Erosion of Ideology

Beginning at an earlier point but most explicit and tangible in the post-Stalin years, some of the millions of communists who made up the Soviet elite, and who were slated to become the regime's next generation of leaders, experienced an unadvertised but far-reaching crisis of identity and self-doubt.

One facet of this crisis was the subtle erosion of faith in the future and of the belief that the Bolsheviks alone had all the answers. This disillusionment, greatly intensified by Khrushchev's anti-Stalin campaign, was accompanied by an unheralded transformation in the dominant orientation: a shift from the pursuit of the millennium to compromising with reality. Seweryn Bialer was one of those who remarked on the withering of utopianism in the Brezhnev years. Wherever the faithful looked, the traditional prophecies had failed to come through: world revolution had not occurred, crime had not vanished, nationalism and religion had not disappeared with the passing of capitalism, as had been predicted. To be sure, the orthodox formulae continued to be reprinted *ad nauseam*, but inspiration had turned into ritual, and especially in the Brezhnev years there was no longer any serious effort made to reconcile conflicting articles of faith and observation.

Strikingly, a similar decline may be noted in the rulers' self-confidence concerning their right to rule. Unwittingly, memoirs such as those of Khrushchev's son Sergei and of others close to the leadership testify to this point. A number of former Soviet academics have privately related their difficulties in coming to terms with the Stalin phenomenon. How had it been possible in the first place, and how could Stalinism now be explained to the next generation? What were the implications for the Soviet experiment? Within the limits of the permissible, serious questions were raised from within the Marxist-Leninist tradition: for instance, on the nature of "contradictions" under socialism, and the phenomenon of bureaucracy.

A good example is also provided by General Dmitriy Volkogonov, who recently recalled that in the 1970s:

> I was an orthodox Marxist, an officer who knew his duty. I was not part of some liberal current. All my changes came from within, off on my own. I had access to all kinds of literature. . . . I was a Stalinist. I contributed to the strengthening of the system that I am now trying to dismantle. But latently, 1 had my ideas. I began asking myself questions about Lenin, how, if he was such a genius, none of his predictions came true. The proletarian dictatorship never came to be, the principle of class struggle was discredited, communism was not built in fifteen years as he had promised. None of Lenin's

major predictions ever came true! I confess it: I used my position, I began gathering information even though I didn't know yet what I would do with it.

Yet there can be no doubt about the importance of faith for the cohesion of a regime that had chosen to make its ideology so central and weighty a core of the system.

Indeed, it was during the Brezhnev years that we witnessed an unprecedented surge of dissident literature—not from people who had never shared the regime's values or goals but from prominent individuals well within the system's elite. In retrospect, the number of dissidents appears to have been greater than was commonly assumed at the time. In 1970, Andrey Sakharov, Roy Medvedev, and Valeriy Turchin addressed a letter to the Soviet leadership, arguing in favor of far-reaching democratization.

> Over the past decade menacing signs of disorder and stagnation have begun to show themselves in the economy of our country. . . . The population's real income in recent years has hardly grown at all; food supply and medical and consumer services are improving very slowly, and with unevenness between regions. The number of goods in short supply continues to grow. . . . What is the source of all this trouble? The source lies in the antidemocratic traditions and norms of public life established in the Stalin era, which have not been decisively eliminated to this day. Noneconomic coercion, limitations on the exchange of information, restrictions on intellectual freedom, and other examples of the antidemocratic distortion of socialism which took place under Stalin were accepted in our country as an overhead expense in the industrialization process.

Whether or not this had been justified in the first rush of industrialization, they wrote, there is no doubt that these had now become serious handicaps. [. . .]

And in 1983 the famous "Novosibirsk memorandum" found its way abroad. In it, Tat'yana Zaslavskaya, was telling the authorities:

> Over a number of decades, Soviet society's economic development has been characterized by high rates and great stability. . . . However, in the past 12–15 years a tendency towards a noticeable decline in the rate of growth of the national income began to make itself felt in the development of the economy of the USSR. . . . This does not provide for either the rate of growth in living standards that is required for the people, or for the intensive technical retooling of production. . . . In our opinion, [the cause

of this is] the inability of this system to make provision for the full and sufficiently effective use of the labour potential and intellectual resources of society.

While written in a style entirely loyal and conforming to official Soviet norms, the memorandum does point to a number of changes that have occurred in Soviet economy, society, and technology that require recognition and changes in institutions, attitudes, and practices. [. . .]

As discussed below, the increasing acquaintance and fascination with foreign norms, styles, and practices—and goods—would, in their own way, further contribute to the erosion of commitments to official Soviet orthodoxy.

Social Change

The Soviet era witnessed a remarkable process of social change. In some measure it had begun even before the 1917 revolutions: urbanization and higher educational attainments are the universal by-product of economic development. To a significant degree, this was ideologically welcome to the Leninists as it promoted "proletarianization" at the expense of the peasantry. Later, the "liquidation of the kulaks as a class" was a conscious policy decision buttressed by ideological, economic, and security considerations (whether spurious or not). Similarly, the massive employment of female labor, the wholesale resettlement and migration, as well as the expansion of labor camps and forced settlements, were willed by the regime. And to some extent, the new social stratification was the inevitable by-product of choices made on behalf of rapid industrialization, bureaucratization, and centralization. But, whether willed or not, these developments had unforeseen, unintended, and (from the regime's point of view) often undesirable consequences.

The magnitude of the transformations is suggested by Soviet census figures: the urban share of the population rose from some 18 percent in 1926 to about 65 percent in 1985. The number of "specialists"—the so-called intelligentsia—grew from some 2 million before World War II to over 30 million in the 1980s, of whom more than half had specialized training or higher education. The government, party, police, and military bureaucracies grew at a comparable pace.

The resulting sociography of the Soviet Union still awaits thorough study. For instance, the attitudes and values of the working class—and regional variations—remain to be better understood. What is clear, however, is that, in so far as they involved the formation of a new intelligentsia (the equivalent of an urban middle class), and the crystallization of new values, priorities, and aspirations within it, these transformations had profound effects in generating a new sociopolitical force. So, inevitably, did the appearance of a new, postwar generation of citizens, possessed of rising expectations, and whose members had not shared in the hopes and sufferings of earlier years.

An additional factor in the 1970s and early 1980s was the (accurate) perception, spreading in urban society, that the previously axiomatic opportunities for upward social mobility were no longer there. With the slowdown of economic growth, the more or less stable size of administrative and military cadres, the end of massive purges (and the widespread retention of older officials in office), it was plausible that there should be fewer vacancies to be filled. The resulting effect on morale, especially among ambitious younger people, was obvious.

We find then an unmistakable spread of skepticism and widespread cynicism, particularly in the 1970s. Along with the "weakening belief in ideals," cited above, observers pointed to a career-mindedness and materialism, and a combination of consumerism and consumer pessimism. Moreover, it was pointed out, "because economic performance has been so central to sociopolitical stability, the consequences of this stagnation are potentially serious". There was also a lack of fit between educational opportunities and career needs; and high aspirations combined with a disdain for manual labor to create further tensions. High rates of labor turnover, low productivity, and low worker morale were additional indicators of growing problems.

The loss of optimism and the loss of purpose readily led to a change of attitude. This was reflected, for instance, in the jocular remark, "We pretend to be working, and they pretend to be paying us," as well as in the middle-class view of corruption reported by Bushnell: "It's a crime *not* to steal from them," which is revealing also for the use of "them" for the authorities. It easily spilled over into antisocial behavior. Alcoholism, in particular, became even more of a severe problem than before, with manifest consequences from industrial accidents to family life. Lying and cheating seemed to become pandemic in Soviet society. [. . .]

Students of Soviet society concluded, even prior to the accession of Gorbachev, that the potential for instability was greater then than at any time since World War II.

> Possibly the most dramatic change of recent years, and one with profound
> implications for the legitimacy and stability of the Soviet system, has been
> a shift in attitudes within the Soviet population during the past two decades
> [i.e., 1960s and 70s]. Most visible within the middle class and intelligentsia

but extending to the working class as well, it involves growing pessimism about the Soviet future, increasing disillusionment with official values, and an accompanying decline in civic morale.

As Geoffrey Hosking, a well-qualified observer, remarked: "There has been evidence for more than two decades that society and politics were out of phase with one another, that society was starting to outgrow the crude and rigid integument of the party-controlled political system."

These attitudes and values need not have been dangerously incongruent with the existing regime. In fact, in large part the new middle class as well as the workers were dependent on that regime for their own advancement and careers, a circumstance that importantly distinguishes Soviet "classes" from their counterparts in liberal-democratic societies. For better or for worse, Soviet citizens had been accustomed—at whatever price to themselves—to distinguish between their private and their public personae and not to give voice to impolitic desires. Moreover, the existence of unorthodox attitudes does not, and need not, readily translate into political demands or action programs. Yet, it turned out, especially the new middle class—in and out of the Communist Party—provided a fertile breeding ground and, later, a social base, first for the "reformers" and then for the "democrats."

As Zbigniew Brzezinski concluded:

> the Stalinist system endured [in the Brezhnev years] not only because Brezhnev and his immediate comrades benefited from it and remained loyal to it. It survived because it had become a vast structure of overlapping privileges, controls, rewards, and vested interests. . . . Most important, Stalinism both endured and stagnated because it was a political system without real political life within it. That stagnation could not be forever ignored. Already by the later years of the Brezhnev era, a sense of malaise was developing within a portion of the upper Soviet elite. An awareness of decay, of ideological rot, of cultural sterility was setting in. It began not only to permeate the intellectual circles but also to infect some members of the political elite.

The International Environment

There has been discussion in the West, more of it political than scholarly, about the extent to which the international environment, and more explicitly, American policy, can take credit for the collapse of the Soviet system. In regard to explicit policy by Western powers, it is impossible to find direct evidence of its destabilizing impact on Soviet society or polity, though at least three factors can be assumed to have played some role: (1) the unintended consequences of the inclusion of "Basket 3" (on human rights) in the Helsinki accords of 1975; (2) a heightening of the fear of nuclear war; and (3) almost certainly the strains imposed by the defense burden, discussed below. On the other hand, it remains to be studied whether or not a "tough" Western posture tended to reinforce a siege mentality within the Moscow elite. But, quite distinct from Western policy and conduct, there is good evidence of the importance of simply the existence of the outside world as a challenge to and as a reference group for comparisons by Soviet observers.

The years up to 1985, when Gorbachev came to power, saw a significant increase in the Soviet elite's familiarity with alternative political and socioeconomic systems and with life abroad, a result of both technology and détente. While on the surface that early détente was a political failure, it worked certain important changes in information and attitude that are relevant to our discussion, by strengthening pro-reform images.

Thus, after many years of imposed isolation, Soviet specialists were allowed to travel abroad, correspond with professional colleagues, read foreign journals and magazines. Tourists began to visit other countries; we saw Soviet exchange scholars and students in the U.S. wandering through supermarkets and reading books that had been forbidden back home. In fact, at a time of growing middle-class *veshchizm* (crass consumerism), rapidly expanding tourism even to Eastern Europe stimulated provocative comparisons.

What is more, new technology could be enlisted on behalf of the curious citizenry (and not solely, as George Orwell had posited, on behalf of the regime). Direct-dialing telephones put them in easier touch with émigrés and colleagues abroad, gave them a chance to realize how far behind they were, and stimulated questions about regime policies and the assumptions that had prompted them. Audio cassettes, television, and VCRs (video-cassette recorders) made both information and ideas more accessible.

Nor should we dismiss this new acquaintanceship as trivial or marginal. We know the importance of reference groups from numerous studies. And we know of historical instances where exposure to other civilizations wrought havoc, be it China's acquaintance with the West as a result of the Opium Wars, or the intrusion of Islam into the Mediterranean civilization; or for that matter, the impact of television—showing how people lived elsewhere—on the American civil rights movement in the 1960s and on French Quebec.

Economic Decline

Specialists told us that the Soviet economy needed structural reform long before 1985. Above all, the central command economy had failed to keep up its previously impressive growth rate, the GNP plummeting (by Western estimates) from some 6 percent growth rates in the 1960s to perhaps 2 percent or less in the early 1980s. Per capita real income declined as well. One reason was that earlier on, inputs—capital, labor, energy—had been ample and cheap. By the 1970s this was no longer so, and it was necessary to switch from a strategy of extensive development to an intensive one. Moreover, productivity was low, and the system failed to provide adequate incentives for harder work or for technological innovation. If anything, the technological gap and lag behind the West were increasing. Typically, the quality of production and services was substantially below world standards. This reduced Soviet ability to export goods and also added to consumer dissatisfaction, given the rising expectations of the new elite.

This was also the one area where U.S. policy may have had an impact. Given the Soviet leadership's commitment after the Cuban missile crisis of 1962 to catch up with American military might, including R&D in advanced technology, a totally disproportionate share of Soviet GNP (clearly over 15 percent, by some estimates a lot more) was allocated for the arms race—in an economy whose total product was a good deal less than that of the U.S. The result of these investments was to seriously distort the economy at precisely a time when the decline in its growth rate required cuts in allocations to other parts of the economy, including welfare, services, and consumption.

Here then we have a combination of inherent trends and disastrous policy choices by the Soviet leadership. In addition to objective problems that the Soviet economy presented, the trends sketched above were bound to impact subjective perceptions as well. Not only was the unquestioned priority of defense expenditures becoming more apparent, but the resulting "defense burden" no longer went unchallenged. In addition, the implications of the slowdown not only affected other sectors of the economy but also led to questions concerning the axiomatic effect of continued economic growth on the perceived legitimation of the Soviet system. For some years short-term successes (as well as economic and social problems abroad) had concealed the structural inadequacies of the Soviet economic mechanism, but by the early 1980s profound doubts about it had matured, particularly as Soviet observers increasingly tended to judge the system by its performance rather than by its promises.

Interaction Among the Variables

All this adds up to a subtle change in the relationship of state and society on the eve of the Gorbachev years. Society gains greater autonomy, grievances and expectations become more critical and more overt, and there occurs an implicit shift to some expectation of accountability. If there is an increasing inclination to judge the regime by its performance, in the 1980s the regime falls short. And, more immediately important in 1985, it is essentially this perception of the same trends that shaped the conviction of Mikhail Gorbachev and his friends that "things cannot go on like this."

I have argued that none of the trends we have examined was the prime motor in this process of change. It is precisely the interaction among these variables that was critical. While we cannot "replay" the events with one variable left out, some inferences as to relative weights are plausibly strong. Thus, had the whole control structure not loosened up, much of the articulation of grievances could not have occurred, acquaintance with the outside world would have been far more modest, and the assertion of autonomy in various venues could neither have been undertaken nor succeeded to the degree that it did. Similarly, the effect of the loosening up on the spread of corruption, the perception of stagnation, and contact with the West all facilitated the erosion of ideological commitments. So manifestly did the social pathologies, the value shift and the rising expectations among the new urban middle class erode the faith among officials and non-officials alike.

True, the economic constraints alone should have been enough to engender doubts, comparisons, and grievances. However, the true economic facts were not widely known; indeed, some "derogatory" facts were scarcely known even in the highest leadership circles. Furthermore, at earlier times of economic difficulty—be it 1930 or 1946—there had been no such articulation, essentially because both the actors and the political environment had been so different. We must then conclude that the cluster of trends we have focused on provided a set of necessary conditions for the changes that ensued.

The Gorbachev Factor

Taken together, the trends and developments discussed above suggest a number of serious flaws and fragilities in the Soviet system. But there are no grounds for arguing that they doomed it. If we had seen them as clearly as we do now in, say, 1984, would we have been led to conclude that a collapse of the Soviet Union was inevitable in the foreseeable future? I think the answer has to be "no."

In that case, do we mean to say that, had Gorbachev and his associates *not* come to power, the Soviet Union would have hobbled along, and might have continued to muddle through without overt instability? That is the only possible conclusion. If we reach that conclusion, based on those premises, then we must give serious weight to the proposition that the much-touted "collapse of communism" was perhaps not nearly so inevitable and surely not necessarily so imminent as it has been made out to be.

There is room for counterfactual speculation, and I think the most responsible answer is that, while we cannot be sure, at the very least Moscow might have gained considerable time, might have avoided the destabilization and delegitimation that the Gorbachev years brought, and might have shaped the domestic and international environment very differently from what in fact occurred. What comes to mind as one scenario is something like the evolution of Turkey or Mexico, which experienced radical regimes and transformations in the first quarter of this century, but where revolutionary zeal petered out without an overthrow of governments.

One could point to problems with this sort of scenario, born of differences between the Soviet Union and Mexico or Turkey. Specifically, the Soviet regime propagated an explicit, mandatory ideology based on the notion of two adversary world systems. That ideology, among other things, provided the justification for the inordinately burdensome effort to match the United States in defense expenditures and weapons research. One could argue, therefore, that drastically cutting the military effort—for a nuclear superpower, at that—would have required a fundamental reorientation of the image of the enemy and the whole ideological mind-set. (Moreover, even such a major restructuring of the Soviet budget probably would not have sufficed to address the structural disorders that ailed the Soviet economy.)

This argument is compelling, though not entirely convincing. True, rational policy choices are constrained by dos and don'ts rooted in beliefs. But was this true under Brezhnev? To some extent, yes; but it was becoming less so. Precisely the Brezhnev years had been a great exercise in fudging issues and overtly denying realities. Such behavior both reflected and deepened the disillusionment and uncertainty about ideological verities within the political establishment. But precisely because of that change in perspectives, the doctrine became even more pragmatically malleable. With a little semantic effort, Brezhnev's successors, had they been so inclined, could surely have managed to cut defense without giving up such parts of the residual communist vision as they wished to protect and preserve. Thus, they could have made policy adjustments while continuing to legitimize their right to rule by reference to other components of the ideology. They would have sacrificed some measure of credibility in the process. But that is not the same as losing the ability to maintain elite unity against challenges to the system.

If my argument has merit, the implication is that the Gorbachev years, and what is now called *katastroyka*, are an essential part of the explanation of the collapse. They are not sufficient by themselves to explain it, but they are, ironically or tragically, a vital link in the chain of destabilization, delegitimation, and disintegration that led from the superpower status of the 1970s to the new, shrunken, confused, and impoverished Russian Federation of the 1990s.

Unlike some of the earlier trends that we can label impersonal or secular, in the Gorbachev period we are dealing with very distinct acts of will, acts that in retrospect should deaden any temptation to agree with those who seek to transform history and politics into mathematical formulae of rational choice. It did make a lot of difference that these particular individuals, beginning with Gorbachev and soon Yakovlev and Shevardnadze, were the ones taking charge in Moscow. Suffice it to contemplate counterfactual scenarios in which, say, Chernenko remained in office for another five years, or was succeeded by Grishin or Romanov: how different would the country have looked?

Those who see the Soviet period and the dominant Leninist ideology as a seamless web have difficulty explaining how a Gorbachev and his cohort could have emerged in charge of such a system in the first place. Whatever happens elsewhere, here personalities have certainly played a significant part. The fact that they, and not any others, came to power in 1985 also serves to torpedo the "inevitable collapse" argument. To claim that the Soviet system was bound to crash amounts to committing what Reinhard Bendix (1964, p. 13) called "the fallacy of retrospective determinism"—denying the choices (however constrained) that the actors had available before acting.

But what was it about the Gorbachev policies—so many of which were brilliant—that contributed to the system's collapse? First and foremost, Gorbachev put an end to the claim that there was one single truth and therefore one single party that was its carrier. In association with this argument, he fostered *glasnost'*, an end to censorship, an end to widespread political repression, and an end to the official monopoly on rewriting the past. In terms of sociopolitical impact, all this brought about a remarkable sense of having been lied to, of having been deprived of what the rest of the world had had access to, a "desacralization" of the system and delegitimation of the authorities, a transformation of the Communist Party from the unchallenged clan of privilege to a hollow institution without a rational task other than self-preservation. This in turn opened the floodgates to massive and varied grassroots organization and articulation outside the party.

The other major arena in which the new policy of *glasnost'* had an impact was the republics. From Estonia to Azerbaijan, *glasnost'* mobilized opinion around issues of ethnic identity, beginning with language, school, or culture, and ending with national-liberation fronts. And while there had obviously been some sense of national consciousness that had been stifled earlier on, some of its growth was another unintended consequence of the Soviet experience. The organization of the federation by Union republics, each with its dominant nationality, the ethnic identification of all Soviet citizens in their passports, and the promotion of national cultures and histories (in however circumscribed a fashion) all served to nurture memories and identifications that would be mobilized and reshaped later, when conditions permitted.

Yet, one may hypothesize, the big impetus came precisely from the new doubts about, and the newly perceived challengeability of, the Soviet system. For once their identities as Soviet citizens or communists faded, people looked around for alternative loci of loyalty and identity, and the most powerful "imagined communities" were the ethnonational ones. Thus (to oversimplify a complicated process) *glasnost* made possible the political mobilization of doubting, contemptuous, and newly emboldened publics, and the invention of new organizations. These acquired an additional ethnic coloration because of the discrediting of alternative identities, which brought to the top of the political agenda the question of the future of the Soviet federal system. That transformation did not come soon enough to avoid the polarization between the centralist "coup plotters" of August 1991 and the separatists at the other end of the center/periphery spectrum. A year later, Gorbachev admitted that his failure fully to recognize the seriousness of the "nationality question" had perhaps been his most serious error in office.

In arguing that the liberalization of the system from 1985 to 1991 was part of the explanation for its collapse, I am *not* agreeing with the proposition that the system could not be reformed. That argument comes from both ends of the political spectrum, though it is made with divergent purposes in mind. The Stalinists in Moscow insist that *any* attempt to "reform" the Soviet system—to alter or abandon its Stalinist cast—was bound to subvert it and therefore must at all costs be avoided; Molotov's critique of Khrushchev's policy in the 1950s came close to this view. Likewise, we hear from those at the other extreme that the Soviet system could not be reformed step by step but needed to be totally demolished before a democratic and healthy system could be erected from scratch. The experience of the Gorbachev regime does not answer the question whether its errors— say, on the nationality question or in economic policy—were avoidable or not. I believe they were, as they were errors of individual judgment, not inherent and inescapable trends. While there are many significant differences between the two cases, the "Chinese option" also suggests that—in the regime's own terms—certain reforms could succeed.

Finally we must ask what, in this setting, provided the trigger for the outward collapse of what remained of the Soviet Union. Here Boris Yel'tsin and his successful "second coming" deserve a little credit (or blame). His re-emergence in 1990 in the context of competitive elections was a product of the unraveling of the system and in turn contributed to the shift in the locus of power and popular support away from the old center. His declaration of Russian sovereignty legitimated the other republics' posture against the "center" and momentarily united democrats and nationalists. His election as president of Russia in June 1991 and, two months later, his stand against the "coup plotters" dramatized both his strength and Gorbachev's weakness. Yel'tsin chose to magnify that asymmetry, and in December he decided to torpedo what remained of the "Union" structure and to erect the improvised "Commonwealth" framework in its place.

Yel'tsin could not have pulled off these changes if the system had not already been badly injured. Still, he made the most of it, for himself as well, and in the process permitted the collapse of the Soviet Union itself. Identifying him as the final catalyst of the collapse may be the easiest part of this exercise.

Conclusion

It is perhaps natural for us to seek simple explanations, single causes, and yes-or-no answers. More often than not, in real life, things are far more complex. We must take care not to introduce retrospectively a clarity, let alone inevitability, where there was contingency and complexity. A retrospective view should underscore the dynamic and variable character of many Soviet policies and institutions. While it is no doubt true that "the party" or "the secret police" or "the dictator" was an ever-present power in the Soviet state, the limits of each changed over time. If corruption was a perennial feature, its scope varied greatly. So did dissent and deviance.

And so did legitimacy. From the manifest fact that the Soviet regime, by 1991, was not widely perceived as legitimate by the population, it is important not to draw the inference that the Soviet regime had been perceived as illegitimate at all earlier times—during the NEP, at the end of World War II, or in the 1960s and

1970s, for instance. The recognition of this fact helps us understand why it is not the case that the Soviet system could have collapsed at any given moment during its 74-year history (though, of course, factors other than a lack of legitimacy could have brought about its demise). It turned out that its end required the maturation, as well as the interaction, of the several trends identified above. It also required the particular, albeit understandable, blind spots in the perceptions and policy choices of the Gorbachev leadership.

3

Core Tasks for
Postcommunist Russia

In January 1992, Russia's new leaders were nearly as surprised as observers in the West that there was no longer a Soviet Union. They suddenly found themselves having to figure out how to rebuild Russia as an independent state. Led by President Boris Yeltsin, Russia's leaders, like the new leaders across Eastern Europe in 1989 and 1990, proclaimed their intention to create a capitalist democracy out of the ashes of the communist collapse. There is no reason whatsoever to believe that Yeltsin was anything but sincere in this intent, and the same can be said about most of his closest advisors. That said, they had at best a fuzzy understanding of what a capitalist democracy was, even less clarity about how to create one, and widely varying commitment to this general goal. Still, they were clear in the broadest sense about the direction in which they saw the country to be headed. Among Russia's most influential leaders at the time, there was broad consensus that, in rebuilding the ruined economy, the aim should be to create a system based on free market principles; in addressing the political system, the goal should be to entrench the principles of freedom and of choosing leaders through competitive elections.

Outside of Russia, that Russia's future was as a liberal, capitalist democracy was assumed and accepted without question. This was certainly the approach of the overwhelming majority of those studying Russia. The only question was what strategy would be employed to achieve that end and what sort of bumps would be encountered along the way should a less-than-ideal path be chosen. Different authors had different conclusions on the ideal strategy, but there was wide agreement on the outcome. An assumption that a transition to democracy in Russia was underway universally dominated virtually every analysis of politics in that country from 1992 onward. Works with titles such as *Democracy from Scratch, Russia's Unfinished Revolution,* and *The Rebirth of Russian Democracy*[1] were typical of the dozens of books and hundreds of journal articles published in the 1990s and 2000s embracing the same assumption. That assumption, embodied in accounts of the transition taking place in Russia, was that democracy was an inevitable endpoint; it was firmly embedded in the entire transitions approach.[2] The assumption itself was routinely applied to the "lessons" supposedly learned in Russia about what makes "the transition" succeed.[3]

One must seriously question now whether "the transition" ever existed at all. Political scientists with expertise in southern Europe and Latin America had developed by the mid-1980s a transitions-to-democracy framework detailing a series of steps that prodemocratic leaders must take to overthrow authoritarian leaders and reform their political systems to embrace democratic ideals and procedures. The clear implication in that literature, and certainly in applications of it, was that, by merely following these steps, democracy will inevitably result. This framework, developed by scholars of Latin America, was never appropriate to the Russian situation. For one thing, in Latin America and southern Europe, the changes were confined to the political system from closed and authoritarian to competitive and electoral; the framework had nothing to say about the economic system because those were already market capitalist systems with long traditions of private ownership and entrepreneurship. The situation in Russia was entirely different, and for that reason, the explanatory framework was entirely lacking.

A few, rare, early approaches to Russia's postcommunist political turmoil had the insight to emphasize the extensive disconnect between Russia's situation and those from which the transitions framework emerged. Most significant among these differences was that, unlike the Latin American cases, Russia had no surviving traditions of private enterprise, private property or capitalist exchange. Under conditions of total economic collapse, what Russia faced was not in any way, shape, or form a political "transition" but, instead, a simultaneous political and economic transformation. Politically there were, again unlike in Latin America, no surviving political party organizations, outside of the Communist Party, and socially no existing experience with independent political organization. The creation of a liberal, capitalist democracy in this environment would require not a transition but a total transformation.[4] If the transitions framework could usefully be applied anywhere, it nevertheless seems that it was inappropriate for efforts to understand the challenges facing post-Soviet Russia.[5]

As a result of the wide disconnect between the hopes and assumptions on the one hand and the results on the other, much of the literature even by the mid-1990s and certainly by the 2000s adopted a baffled, disappointed, or frustrated tone. The lesson to this day has not sufficiently been learned either by postsovietologists or by comparativists generally that merely calling a state democratic does not make it so. It is hardly trivial to recall that Boris Yeltsin and most of the cabinet-level ministers, not to mention the overwhelming majority of mid-level government officials and legislators, were all communists reared in communist politics and practices. Nor does a declaration of intent to create a democratic system guarantee the success of that effort. While luck has a role, it does not all come down to luck either; at a minimum, the effort requires committed and honest leaders with integrity and perseverance to implement critical structural changes in the face of enormous obstacles, opposition, and personal opportunity that all work against realization of the democratic and capitalist ideals.

Consider Russia's basic milieu at the time of the disintegration of the USSR. The economy was in total collapse with rampant hyperinflation and a currency so devalued that it was essentially worthless. Indeed, for a time in 1992, the ruble was of such little value and toilet paper was so scarce—and therefore costly—that many around the country found it rational to use the worthless money rather than to shop for hours for the expensive product. Political parties were nonexistent, and the notion of a party itself was offensive to a people after seven decades in which the Party controlled so much of everyday life. Political ideals and divisions lacked even a semblance of organization, and no agreement on structures or processes existed. Indeed, the divisions were hostile and increasingly so. The notion of individual responsibility was virtually absent in the culture, while at the same time, there was zero trust in government or institutions—a particularly debilitating combination. Politically, economically, and socially, Russia was in ruins.

While observers either advocated the transitions formula or judged Russia's progress against that formula, Russia itself essentially muddled through. One laudable aspect of the use of the transitions framework was the conscious effort to study the changes in Russia in a true comparative perspective rather than treating Russia as unique. After all, whether the purpose of the political scientist is to understand, explain, predict, or prescribe, one common requirement is reference points. How can we understand Russia other than in reference to or relative to other environments and circumstances? Without the comparative approach, all we can really do is describe. If we can predict in one place, the same variables should help us to predict in another place. However, it may well be the case that the transitions approach, developed in one setting, lacked the comprehensiveness to render it applicable anywhere else.

The debate about whether Russia is *sui generis* or best understood comparatively is a long-standing divide in the field of Russia studies.[6] It is related to the question of whether it is desirable or even possible to develop models or theories out of one country's experience that would have relevance for explanation or prediction elsewhere. The selections in this chapter offer a flavor of the variety of approaches springing from a variety of these orientations, revealing the strengths and weaknesses of each for understanding of just what Russia faced and how it dealt with those challenges in the wake of communism's demise. Zvi Gitelman, in "The Democratization of Russia in Comparative Perspective," offers a survey of the transition approach as applied to Russia in a comparative perspective. David Fogelsong and Gordon Hahn, in "Ten Myths About Russia" address popular myths in the West about Russia in an effort to provide some clarity of thought about Russia's political realities. Joel M. Ostrow, Georgiy Satarov, and Irina Khakamada, in "Critical Junctures and the Demise of Democracy in Russia," offer a general framework for understanding the tasks facing new leaders who seek to diverge from an authoritarian past and create a democratic future and analyze the major decisions of Russia's leaders against that framework in an effort to explain the departure from the hoped-for democratic path.

For Further Reference

Books

Ruth Berins Collier and David Collier, *Shaping the Political Arena*, University Of Notre Dame Press: 1991.

Larry Diamond and Marc F. Plattner, eds., *Consolidating the Third Wave Democracies*, Johns Hopkins University Press: 1997.

Larry Diamond and Marc F. Plattner, eds., *Democracy After Communism*, Johns Hopkins University Press: 2002.

Jon Elster, ed., *Institutional Design in Post-Communist Societies*, Cambridge University Press: 1998.

M. Steven Fish, *Democracy Derailed in Russia: The Failure of Open Politics*, Cambridge University Press: 2005.

Michael McFaul, *Russia's Unfinished Revolution: Political Change from Gorbachev to Putin*, Cornell University Press: 2002.

Michael McFaul and Kathryn Stoner-Weiss, eds., *After the Collapse of Communism: Comparative Lessons of Transition*, Cambridge University Press: 2010.

Sven Steinmo and Kathleen Ann Thelen, *Structuring Politics: Historical Institutionalism in Comparative Analysis*, Cambridge University Press: 1992.

NOTES

1. M. Steven Fish, *Democracy from Scratch: Opposition and Regime in the New Russian Revolution* (Princeton University Press, 1995); Michael McFaul, *Russia's Unfinished Revolution* (Cornell University Press, 2001); Nicolai Petro, *The Rebirth of Russian Democracy* (Harvard University Press, 1995).

2. The transitions framework developed out of studies of the experience of Spain, and scholars in Latin American area studies extended it in the 1970s to that continent. See Dankwart Rustow, Transitions to Democracy: Toward a Dynamic Model, *Comparative Politics*, Vol. 2,

No. 3 (1970), pp. 337–363; Guillermo O'Donnell, Philippe Schmitter, and Lawrence White-head, eds., *Transitions From Authoritarian Rule* (Johns Hopkins University Press, 1986); and Juan Linz and Alfred Stepan, *Problems of Democratic Transition and Consolidation: Southern Europe, South America and Post-Communist Europe* (Johns Hopkins University Press, 1996). See also Samuel P. Huntington, *The Third Wave: Democratization in the Twentieth Century* (University of Oklahoma Press, 1991).

3. Among a multitude, the best representative article embracing the notion of a demo-cratic future in Russia is McFaul, "Lessons from Russia's Protracted Transition From Com-munist Rule," *Political Science Quarterly*, Vol. 114, No. 1 (1999), pp. 103–130.

4. One of the most forceful and convincing cautionary notes was Claus Offe, "Capitalism by Democratic Design? Democratic Theory Facing the Triple Transition in East-Central Europe," *Social Research*, Vol. 58, No. 4 (1991), pp. 893–902. A more retrospective and combat-ive critique of transitology came from Thomas Carothers, "The End of the Transition Para-digm," *Journal of Democracy*, Vol. 13, No. 1 (2002), pp. 3–21.

5. See Valerie Bunce, "Comparing East and South," Journal of Democracy, Vol. 6, No. 3 (1995), pp. 87–100; and Bunce, "Rethinking Recent Democratization: Lessons From the Post-communist Experience," *World Politics*, Vol. 55, No. 2 (2003), pp. 167–192. Also see Ken Jowitt, "The Leninist Legacy" and "A World Without Leninism" in *New World Disorder* (University of California Press, 1992).

6. Breslauer nicely surveys this divide in "In Defense of Sovietology," *Journal of PostSoviet Affairs*, Vol. 8, No. 3 (1992).

3.1

Critical Junctures and the Demise of Democracy in Russia

Joel M. Ostrow, Georgiy A. Satarov, and Irina M. Khakamada

Journalists and politicians critical of the government are murdered, and no arrests are made, nobody is brought to justice. Businessmen who take an interest in politics are arrested, exiled or sentenced to hard Labor, and have their assets seized by the state. The Kremlin controls the media, which operates under conditions of direct and indirect censorship. Political officials are appointed, or, where elections are held, the outcomes are predetermined. The parliament is a mechanical rubber stamp filled with secret security agents. Corruption and bribery are institutionalized throughout government, at all levels. In the one-party regime, all substantial decision-making is centralized in the hands of the leader in the Kremlin. Serious, organized opposition has been eliminated. The old Soviet Union? No, this is the "new Russia."

It is not just that it is inappropriate today to describe Russia's political system as a "democracy." It may never have been appropriate and certainly has not been since the late-1990s. While Western analysts trumpeted democracy, Russia's leaders at each critical moment made decisions that were either explicitly anti-democratic or gravely impeded the development of a democratic system. Even after the undemocratic hand over of the presidency to KGB officer Vladimir V. Putin, academics and journalists alike have continued to use the term; authors who should know better have misled their readers. A normative bias encouraged many in the West, particularly in the United States, to cling to the term democracy, modified with myriad adjectives that do more to confuse than clarify. Whether "electoral" "limited" or "partial", "managed," or the ever-popular "transitional," analysts employing these modifiers always begin with the assumption that Russia is a democracy. The "democracy" part of the compound label is rarely if ever explained or justified, much less questioned or challenged. Even many who have seemed to question whether Russia under Putin can be called a democracy with any sort of modifier at all conclude, as if out of nowhere, that there is something "hybrid" about the regime. Whether or not any of these

Source: Joel M. Ostrow, Georgiy Satarov, and Irina Khakamada, "Crucial Junctures and the Demise of Democracy in Russia," *Consolidation of Dictatorship in Russia.* Praeger, 2007. 1–14.

Note: Notes and references have been removed from this article.

modifiers or the assumption ever offered accurate descriptions of Russia, today any use of the word democracy applied to Russia requires grotesque concept stretching.

How and why did this happen, when there was so much promise for and so many promises of a democratic outcome? Boris N. Yeltsin left a lasting image of a triumphant, wildly popular leader when he climbed down from that T-72 tank in August 1991. He had turned the military to the side of the demonstrators opposing the hard-line communist coup against hapless Soviet leader Mikhail S. Gorbachev, and led the defeat of the coup plotters. That victory marked the end of Communism and, shortly thereafter, of the Soviet Union itself. Three people died, crushed by tanks during the resistance, but Yeltsin's efforts were critical in persuading the military not to fire on the demonstrators, avoiding massive bloodshed, defeating the coup leaders, and bringing an end to the communist regime. He had won, decisively so, and was clearly ascendant over Gorbachev in appearances before parliament and other meetings over the next several weeks. In that capacity, he promised to lead Russia to a new, democratic and market-oriented future.

The August 1991 coup was traumatic, if brief. It was traumatic for the world, as it brought to an end the division between the liberal, democratic West and communist East that had defined international relations since the end of the Second World War. It triggered a reconfiguration of world politics, of alliances, and of internal state politics across the globe that continues as this book was being written. The hope was that a unified world of free, market-oriented democracies, with the United States and Russia in partnership, would emerge.

Boris Yeltsin was the unquestioned leader of Russia, and he had a team of reform-minded leaders who proclaimed democracy as their goal. They had the world open to them, and Yeltsin's popular legitimacy to rule was overwhelming. Indeed, it appeared that Russia had emerged as a new state and could chart a new course, for its transcendent leader had made a number of booming proclamations to the world of his and his country's democratic intentions, and that he would not repeat the indecisiveness and half-measures that marked Gorbachev's tenure and spelled his political doom. Although the difficulties of such a project were obvious to everyone, there was also hope that a democratic outcome would be a reality. After all, Russia had many examples and lessons to learn from. The varied experiences across Eastern Europe since the domino collapse of communism in 1989 provided clear evidence of the importance of this brief window of opportunity for demolishing the old political system and creating a new one, and of seizing this opportunity if democracy was the objective. They set the example by demonstrating the obstacles that a democratizing state emerging from communism must overcome, and the steps needed in overcoming them that would move the country in a democratic direction. And the United States and its allies in the West stood ready to help their former enemy transform into a political and economic ally and partner. The year 1992, in short, opened with optimism for a democratic future for Russia. [. . .]

None of these hopes were realized. Russia is once again a one-party dictatorship, and an increasingly violent one at that. The roots of this reality lay in decisions made when communism collapsed and in decisions made at each critical moment for the future of Russia's political system after that collapse. [. . .]

A Brief Word About Words

A long school of thought from Schumpeter to Dahl to Huntington defines "democracy" as a set of institutions, governmental and societal, that ensure open, competitive elections to select leaders who will make political decisions and protect basic rights and freedoms. The theoretical literature on democracy is as voluminous as it is interesting. Some authors adopt a minimalist definition that equates elections with democracy. We prefer a more comprehensive definition, agreeing with Fish, who in his recent review of this literature in the Russian context adopts a broad definition of democracy as a system that ensures popular control over the state. This subsumes such aspects critical to a functioning democratic political system as transparency, accountability, and open competition that includes but goes beyond formal elections, to encompass a continuing role for the polity. [. . .] Elections are formal events, and democracy certainly requires free, competitive elections, but democracy also requires more to ensure popular control over the state and protections from the state. Even by this minimalist definition, however, Russia falls far short of democracy.

It is inconceivable that one would apply the term to today's Russia, yet many Western academics have continued to insist that Russia has "a limited form of democracy." Even recent studies bemoaning the failure of democratization in Russia fall short in their analysis of the reality of the current regime. Russia is again an autocracy, even if not in the pure sense of a single individual ruling. No modern state meets or can meet that ideal type, by the very nature of ideal types. Russia is what is commonly called an authoritarian regime, and more accurately a dictatorship, and it serves no useful purpose to shy away from the term.

What Russia has consolidated since Communism's demise is dictatorship, not democracy. There are surprisingly few clear definitions of "dictatorship" or "authoritarianism" in the political science literature, with most authors using the terms in contradistinction to "democracy." One source-book defines authoritarianism as a system in which values and decisions are imposed on those who lack the right to respond or react freely, and dictatorship as rule by one person. The former is plausible though incomplete, the latter is not even plausible.

When one can say of a country that how politics are conducted is determined by a single individual, where that individual makes decisions and imposes them on a populace that is denied the political freedom to organize, compete, and hold leaders accountable electorally or otherwise, that country is a dictatorship. The word democracy has no place. This certainly describes Russia under Putin, and is the definition we embrace for dictatorship. Putin has used the virtually unlimited powers of his office and the precedents set by Yeltsin to wipe out hopes for a democratic Russia for the foreseeable future. Politics are closed in dictatorships; political freedoms are minimal; political activity is severely circumscribed for individuals and groups alike. The nature of the system, whether it is benevolent or malign, depends exclusively upon the personal predilections of the leader.

Such is the case in Russia today. Of course, there are dictators, and there are dictators. Putin's is not rule by state terror, he is no Caligula, no Stalin, no Pol Pot. Russia is not again a totalitarian state. Yet there have been hundreds of unsolved murders of political figures critical of, investigating, or in opposition to Putin, his government and his policies. Putin is a dictator reared in and intensely loyal to the KGB, now the FSB, one of the most secretive and brutal government organizations the world has ever known. He has promoted fellow officers to an extent far surpassing that which existed in the Soviet period. He has systematically eliminated all significant sources of political competition or opposition, while consolidating immense powers into his own hands. His is rule through consistent harassment of and often violent crackdown against organized political opposition, against individual opponents or critics, and against the media. Putin has effected the elimination or extreme isolation of alternative political parties at all levels, national, regional and local, and the return of one-party rule. [. . .] The gap between the hopes of 1991 and the reality is startling and saddening for those who worked for democratic political development in Russia after the fall of communism.

Critical Junctures

[. . .] Russia has been, is, and will continue to be a vital player in European and global security and stability. What happens there matters, and because it matters it needs to be understood. That means knowing both the "what" and the "why". Calling Russia a democracy simply because we want it to be one is not just wrong, it is potentially dangerous. [. . .] Because the key points in the story of

Russia's postcommunist political development have commonalities across the postcommunist environment, we offer a framework for explaining the keys to successful democratization. The framework, the authors believe, can be used to explain successes or failures elsewhere, and to offer guidance to other countries. Russia's leaders made choices at important moments and on important decisions that held real consequences for future political developments. The lessons of those choices are not just lessons for Russia. They are lessons for any country attempting to make a transformation from authoritarian rule to democracy.

We identify several "critical junctures" through which, we argue, all postcommunist states pursuing democratic political development must pass. Indeed, any democratizing regime, it seems to the authors, must confront each of these junctures and resolve the inherent problems in a pro-democratic direction if a democratic outcome is to be likely. The choices leaders make at each of those junctures will either enhance or impede the establishment of a stable democracy. Put differently, each juncture has different potential paths that result from various possible decisions available to leaders. Only some decisions, or resultant paths, will be beneficial to the creation of a stable democracy, whereas some will directly impair the development of a democratic political system. One can, therefore, trace a state's path through these critical junctures, or major decision points, identifying each as one in which the prospects for a democratic outcome hangs in the balance, explaining the factors that led to one or another decision, and analyzing the consequences of each outcome for the future.

Our use of the term "critical junctures" adopts but also adapts somewhat the most well-known and cited application of the concept by David Collier and Ruth Collier. We embrace the basic premise that decisions made in response to a problem at one point in time "establish distinct trajectories within which [quoting Paul David], 'one damn thing follows another.'" Anyone familiar with any of the stories of postcommunist democratic reform can appreciate this observation. By their definition, however, historians a century and more hence would define the decade or two following Communism's demise in 1989, or in Russia's case in 1991, as a single critical juncture, with the problem or outcome explained being the creation (or not) of a liberal democratic regime. Whether or not a country developed a stable, liberal democratic regime as an outcome of this juncture would determine other outcomes over the following several decades. Indeed, the critical juncture the Colliers analyze, the rise of labor movements in Latin America, and the effects on regime dynamics, in some cases spanned several decades. While the Colliers offer that critical junctures may be brief or stretch over long periods of time, the demands of their schematic make it a bit difficult to conceive of how one could be brief. Be that as it may, their framework has certainly proved valuable and has inspired insightful research in a number of different directions.

We are similarly inspired by their research. However, we find it not only unreasonably limiting but also unreasonable logically to consider the attempt to create a democratic political system as a single event. It is not particularly useful to conceive it as such, because doing so robs us of the ability to explain the success or failure of the project. We seek to "reach inside" and consider the critical decisions made that, in Russia's case, set it on a nondemocratic path. Democratic transformation is a project involving multiple processes with varying requirements that depend upon, among other things, the political, social, and economic preconditions. If we want to explain comparatively the relative success or failure of democratization, we need to identify the most important common aspects of that project, and an analytic basis for explaining varying outcomes. Despite its tendency toward gross misapplication and wildly unrealistic assumptions and predictions, the voluminous literature on "transitions" has identified some important legacies of Communism and tasks of democratization with which postcommunist elites attempting democratic political reconstruction have had to grapple. The list is familiar and lengthy: drafting new constitutions, defining the polity, establishing borders, instituting political competition, creating the rule of law, creating market economies, creating and protecting the institution of private property, and establishing basic freedoms are just a few of the tasks that have faced states embarking on democratization in the wake of the communist collapse. A postcommunist state attempting to create a new democratic political system may encounter a range of problems, and each state's political leaders and the political elite more generally must make decisions about how to solve these problems.

While the particular problems of democratization will vary from state to state, there are at least a few issues that every postcommunist state attempting democratic change will encounter. How it navigates those issues will affect the prospects for democracy either positively or negatively. When these issues pop up, the regime is faced, if not with a crisis, then with a series of difficult decisions. They become a dominant concern. Whether they realize it or not, and often they do not, the choices leaders make at these critical junctures will shape both the immediate and the long-term prospects for the creation of a stable democracy. In other words, leaders frequently have no idea that the problem they are confronting is in fact critical in this sense. This, it seems to the authors, is the essence of the phrase "critical juncture," for some decisions taken may unintentionally undermine entirely the prospects for democracy. The appearance of each of these problems represents a critical juncture for that state, for its leaders, and for the people, for some decisions and actions make democracy a more likely outcome, while others may impede or completely derail a democratic future. It is not necessarily the case that the leadership recognizes a situation as critical in this sense. It is also not necessarily the case that they see alternative solutions either; indeed, in some instances the characteristic seems to be ignorance of or even conscious denial of the existence of alternatives.

We identify four critical junctures that, we believe, are common to all post-communist states, and likely to all states embarking on democratic transformation. We address them as they appeared chronologically in Russia, though this order may not be fixed. First is the question of what to do with the legacy institutions of the communist (or prior) political system. In short, the issue becomes when and how to eliminate them. Second is the issue of when and how to adopt a new constitution. Third, how will the state approach the new problem of political competition, including the rise of new political actors and interests. Fourth, how will the system handle the problem of leadership change. How the new leaders handle each of these problems as they present themselves will influence the options available for addressing the subsequent tasks when they arise. Indeed, particular decisions at point A will impede the ability to make certain types of decisions at point B in ways that may narrow the likelihood of creating a stable democratic regime. Although they may not recognize the fact, decision makers do have alternatives available to them for addressing these tasks. It is precisely the importance of each task for all subsequent tasks on the list, and the availability of distinct alternatives, that makes the process of resolving the issue a critical juncture in the country's development, and absolutely critical to the success of creating a democratic political system.

At each critical juncture, Russia's postcommunist leaders have consistently made choices that have undermined rather than furthered the prospects for democracy, and in some cases those choices have been unambiguously antidemocratic in nature. Agency, that is individual decisions of individual leaders, matters. So do institutions and structures, for individuals make decisions in the context of the institutional settings in which they act. While individuals are constrained by their institutional environment, their decisions also can serve to shape that environment at critical junctures. Russia's postcommunist leaders made antidemocratic choices at each critical juncture, choices that paved the way to the consolidation of dictatorship under Putin. This reality today is a consequence that can be traced to decisions made over how to demolish the communist political system, when and how to adopt a new constitution, how to respond to political competition, how to respond to new political actors and interests, and how to handle leadership change. [. . .]

[In 1992, Russia's new leaders made] the now difficult to comprehend decision [. . .] to ignore political reform. In other words, on the question of when and how to destroy the ancient regime, they simply ignored the question altogether. Most important was what to do with the existing legislature, the

Supreme Soviet. Yeltsin and his advisors thought that the Supreme Soviet, having supported them before, would continue to serve Yeltsin into the future. It was a tragically flawed assumption that guided them, that democracy would develop on its own and they could focus exclusively on economic reform. However, attempting market reform in the absence of any of the institutions of democracy or Capitalism brought rampant corruption and a system that used conflict rather than compromise to resolve disputes. [A] wide range of options [were]clearly available. [. . .] In May 1993, Yeltsin had another chance to deal with the matter of existing institutions. A national referendum on the question of the locus of political power and trust in the leaders that gave the president wide authority provided an opportunity to resolve the deepening standoff with the Supreme Soviet. Although the questions put to the public were entirely vague, after the referendum Yeltsin again had the opportunity to use the results in his favor to take decisive action regarding the political system. He again squandered this chance, and blood in the streets was the ultimate result. Why did the Kremlin, which still claimed to have democratization as a highest goal, fail to seize the opportunity to create democratic institutions and use a democratic process in doing so? The failure cast a deepening cloud over democracy's hopes in Russia. This first critical decision seems incredible in retrospect. It seriously undermined democratic hopes going forward.

[. . .] After the second coup, in which the president bombed the Supreme Soviet out of existence, Russia's leaders made a conscious decision to hedge against democracy, and they did so in the most important aspects of the new constitution. After eliminating the Supreme Soviet and prior to election of a new legislature, Yeltsin ruled unchallenged and unchecked. The test was and the future of democracy in part hinged upon what he did with the unlimited power he held. Yeltsin's team had the potential and promised to create a democratic political system from above. Their actions, however, betrayed the hollowness of their promises.

It is generally forgotten and has not been explained why the constitution that was adopted in December 1993 deviated from the one published in the summer. Hundreds of people from all walks of life, civil servants, academics, politicians, and business people, had convened to draft a new constitution. They reached agreement, and the president approved it for presentation to the public. That draft envisioned a presidential system balanced by real legislative and judicial powers. However, after the armed confrontation, a small group of advisors, with the president's approval, introduced several subtle amendments to the version brought to referendum for adoption. Those changes opened the door to dictatorship by stripping the legislature of most of its authority and autonomy, and vesting in the presidency wide-ranging power over virtually all policy and personnel matters. This opened the way for an individual so inclined to seize virtually unlimited power into the presidency. A more balanced draft constitution was available and had been approved by the president. Why did that draft not go forward? [. . .] [T]he story of the intrigue and machinations around the constitution is a story critical to understanding Russia's path toward authoritarianism.

[Regarding competition], Yeltsin and his team [in 1996] could not resist the urge to squelch real political opposition and competitive elections. The decisions made in 1996 set terrible precedents that accelerated the demise of basic democratic principles. As Boris Yeltsin's first term neared its end, his approval rating plummeted. The new superrich elite, whose wealth was without exception possible only through shady, often murderous practices, feared a return to power by the communists would endanger their wealth and, possibly, more basic interests. A group of these "oligarchs", led by two who owned independent media outlets, approached Yeltsin's top advisors with a proposal to guarantee his reelection in return for privileges, access, and protection after the victory. The cost of not allowing a real political competition and a truly free campaign proved to be the very demise of democracy itself. The welcoming of the oligarchs into the closest circles of power and the gross violations of election and campaign laws brought corruption and criminality directly into the presidency, and presaged the crackdown on independent media and political opposition that was to come.

[In the] final blow, the decision to abandon democracy altogether rather than allowing for electoral competition to decide the direction of leadership change when Yeltsin's second term came to a close, the sitting president decided to hand power to a chosen successor. There were some in the West who praised the coronation of former KGB spy Vladimir Putin as president as constitutional democracy in action. While it is true that the Russian Constitution has procedures for succession following the resignation, death, or incapacitation of a president, Boris Yeltsin was the first Russian president. Precedent matters. Yeltsin was the first Russian president to face the question of how to handle his exit from power. Yeltsin studied George Washington; he liked to refer to him. His speechwriter and close political advisors knew this. He had to have known his purported role model's example. Imagine if Washington, rather than staying on the sidelines while a spirited and at times brutal campaign raged for his successor, had intervened, chosen a successor, and resigned to hand the office over to that successor.

Yeltsin did just that, and more. He chose to invoke the extraordinary measures in the constitution before the normal procedures had ever been given a chance to work. He handed the presidency to a man virtually unknown, with no political base, and with no history of political activity or stated political program, a man whose career flourished in the most hated and feared agency of communist power, the KGB. The resignation reduced the campaign from 6 months to 90 days, a reality that compelled all of the leading contenders to drop out or to wage symbolic campaigns with no hope of success. Moreover, Putin used Yeltsin's example from 1996 to control media access and coverage of that truncated, farcical campaign—he and he alone dominated the airwaves.

Why resign? Why Putin? Why not allow an electoral system in place determine leadership change at the top? The requirement of leadership change as Yeltsin's second term came to an end offered a chance to resurrect some hope for democratic politics in Russia, and set a precedent that the constitution could promote democracy. A freewheeling campaign was just what Russian democracy needed, and it was just beginning to develop as Yeltsin announced his resignation. Why Russia's first president decided on one of the most nondemocratic methods of leadership change begs explanation, as does his choice of the shady KGB operative Vladimir Putin to assume the post of president.

[. . .] President Putin has ended open politics in Russia, restored a hypercentralized political vertical, eliminated competitive politics, made a farce of elections, restored censorship, and emasculated economic rights. [. . .] In short, the regime has all the signature trademarks of a dictatorship, and the arrests and political intolerance show every sign of increasing, rather than declining.

The seeds of this system were sown in the prior decade, when the opportunity to create democratic institutions was lost, and then squandered again after an unlikely second chance. The door was opened with the creation of a severely unbalanced constitution that vested supreme powers in an unchecked presidency. An example was set with executive branch meddling in elections and undermining the principle of political competition. The fate of democracy was sealed with a noncompetitive hand over of power to an individual schooled in the harshest institution ever created for the suppression of freedom of political expression, the KGB. We should not be surprised that this individual has used this constitution to create a strong authoritarian system. [. . .]

3.2

The Democratization of Russia in Comparative Perspective

Zvi Gitelman

Contrary to what most residents of English-speaking countries might assume, democracy has not been and is not now the 'normal' form of government. Democracy made its first appearance in the modern world only a little over two hundred years ago when first the American and then the French revolutions inaugurated it. A look at a map of today's world shows that democracy is the dominant form of government in the twentieth and twenty-first centuries only in North America and Western Europe, Oceania, India, Israel, but in very few countries in Asia, Africa and Latin America. According to Samuel Huntington, in 1990 about two-thirds of the countries of the world did not have democratic regimes. Beginning in the mid-1970s, as Huntington sees it, a 'third wave' of democratization has swept over southern and Eastern Europe as well as Latin America. (The first two 'waves' were in 1828–1926 in Europe and the United States, and in 1943–62 in Europe, East Asia and parts of Latin America.) Nevertheless, despite the collapse of authoritarian communist regimes the proportion of democracies has not grown appreciably. It remains true that across both time and space, democracy has been the exceptional form of government rather than the rule.

Democracy, like other forms of government, should not be seen as an absolute, but as a spectrum. Political systems are not easily classified as either democratic or non-democratic. There are more and less democratic political systems and organizations, and the same system may vary over time in the extent to which it is democratic. For example, the gradual expansion of the franchise in England in the mid-nineteenth century, granting women the right to vote in the United States after the First World War and the passage of the Civil Rights Act of 1964 granting African-Americans full legal equality and protection of the law moved those countries toward the more democratic end of the spectrum.

The idea that democratic forms of government are expandable and retractable is crucial for our discussion of Russia or any other postcommunist country. Especially after only a little more than a decade of postcommunist political life, preceded by

---

Source: Zvi Gitelman, "The Democratization of Russia in Comparative Perspective," from Stephen White, et al. *Developments in Russian Politics: 6*, Duke University Press, 2005. 241–256.

Note: Notes and references have been removed from this article.

seven decades of communism and centuries of tsarist autocracy, the proper question is not so much whether Russia *is* democratic or not, but whether it is *becoming* more or less democratic. There has been considerable debate over whether the Russian Federation has evolved into a democratic state. When the communist regimes of the Soviet Union and Eastern Europe collapsed in 1989–91, many in the West made the facile assumption that democratic systems would replace them, as if there were no alternatives to communism other than democracy. In hindsight, we realize that no single type of system has replaced communism and that the formerly communist states in Eastern Europe and the territories of the former Soviet Union range from those that seem fully democratic to the distinctly undemocratic. Some have been admitted to the European Union, while others seem to be a way off from meeting the criteria for admission, which include commitments to democratic practices as defined by the Union's members. One scholar maintains that while 28 states have abandoned communism, only nine have become liberal democracies. What explains why some postcommunist states have moved considerable distances toward democracy (Poland, Hungary, the Baltic States and most recently Georgia as well as others) while other countries (Azerbaijan, Belarus, Romania, the Central Asian republics) have not, and still others have moved only hesitantly in this direction (Moldova, Albania, Armenia)? What, after all, is democracy? How and why among a group of states, all of which started from the same communist base, do some appear to be democracies today and others do not?

What is Democracy?

Democracy is a system of government that meets three essential conditions: (i) meaningful, extensive and non-violent competition for power at predictable intervals; (ii) the opportunity for all to participate in politics; (iii) civil and political liberties 'sufficient to ensure the integrity of political competition and participation'. What differentiates democratic governments or organizations from others is that anyone can aspire to leadership, and can dissent from leaders' opinions and preferences. Moreover, leadership is responsive to the rank and file.

A more elaborate set of criteria for democracy is posited by Robert Dahl. These are: freedom to form and join organizations; freedom of expression; the right to vote; eligibility for public office; the right to compete for electoral support; alternative sources of information; free and fair elections; and institutions for making government policies depend on votes and other expressions of preference. Both definitions encompass the sources of authority for government, the purposes served by government, and the procedures for constituting it. These are the critical issues for democracies. Huntington, like many before him, believes that what distinguishes democracy from other forms of government is the emphasis on procedure—contestation and participation. To have genuine contestation and participation a system must provide for freedom of expression and assembly, for without such freedoms, genuine contestation and participation cannot occur.

Transition, Democratization and Consolidation

Analysts have identified three stages of post-1991 politics in Russia and other formerly communist states: transition, democratization and consolidation. There is no consensus on the importance or utility of any of the three terms. Some argue that while a transition from communism has been made, it is not clear to what the transition has been. Others point to the return to power in Hungary, Poland, Lithuania and Central Asia of former communists—though by the twenty-first century they had once again lost power in the first three—and the vigorous competition given to Boris Yeltsin by a coalition of Communists in the 1996 Russian presidential election and their dominance of the Duma until President Putin gained the overwhelming support of the Duma in recent elections as evidence that the transition from communism is by no means assured. Communist or quasi-communist parties remain competitive in several of the postcommunist states and it is not impossible that they will return to power through democratic means. While some claim that the transitions from communism are paralleled by transitions from authoritarian governments in southern Europe (Greece, Portugal, Spain) and Latin America (Argentina, Brazil) and that there are critical features common to these transitions, others argue that the transitions are different in important ways. For example, in southern Europe the only issue was democratization, whereas in Eastern Europe and the former Soviet Union it has been the creation of a new economy, class systems, international relations and even states themselves.

There are similar disagreements over the most effective way of 'democratizing' a political system. Should economic and political reform be introduced simultaneously, and, if not, which should come first? What is the most effective and long-lasting way of democratizing—by agreement among elites, by pressures 'from below' (among ordinary people), or by some combination of these? What should be the role of external actors—states, international organizations, private groups—in spurring the growth of democracy? Can democratization be accomplished in a relatively short period, or does it require slow, organic growth over many years if it is to be firmly implanted? Obviously, these issues are relevant to many parts of the world. For example, these questions would presumably be highly relevant to the current American administration's purported attempt to bring democracy to Iraq, or to the Palestinian Authority which is wrestling with the legacy of corruption and authoritarianism bequeathed to it by Yasser Arafat.

Analysts realize that democratization may be temporary and superficial. Therefore, they have considered how and when a democracy can be 'consolidated'. Some reject the very notion that there is some point at which a democracy can be assumed to be permanent or 'consolidated'. After all, the argument goes, if democracy is a process and not a result, 'if the democratic project can never be completed, then how can we understand the term "consolidation" with its implication of democracy as an end state? What are the measuring rods of consolidation—the absence of large-scale protest against the system or presence of relatively durable coalitions, and widespread support for the institutions and procedures of democracy? Concretely, how would an observer know whether Ukraine, Moldova, Albania or Russia—or Iraq and Afghanistan—can be considered viable democracies where democratic systems will persist for a very long time?

Huntington suggests that a democracy is consolidated when citizens learn that 'democracy rests on the premise that governments will fail and that hence institutionalized ways have to exist for changing them. . . . Democracies become consolidated when people learn that democracy is a solution to the problem of tyranny, but not necessarily to anything else'. In other words, when people persist in supporting a democratic system even though the particular government is not meeting their expectations, democracy is consolidated. More concretely, Huntington proposes a 'two-turnover test' for measuring democratic consolidation. If the party or group that takes power in the initial election loses a subsequent election but turns over power peacefully, and if the new winners, in turn, surrender power to the winners of the next election, the democratic system can then be considered consolidated. [. . .]

The Prospects for Democracy in Russia

Though there is a broad consensus on *what* democracy is, there is no agreement on *how* a system becomes democratic. What are the prospects of Russia becoming democratic? This, too, is a matter of considerable debate. The debate centres on the importance of economics and of political culture, that is, a group or nation's subjective orientation towards and understanding of politics. Nearly half a century ago, Seymour Martin Lipset argued that democracies emerge only in societies that are relatively prosperous. He continues to believe that 'economic well being comes close to being a necessary condition for democracy. The poorer a polity, the less amenable its leaders . . . will be to giving up power, their only source of status and wealth'. Potentially always one of the world's richest countries, Russia remains poor by European standards and her economic status should not be conducive to democracy.

Nevertheless, as a Russian political scientist points out, India, a poor country, is a democracy, while Singapore, a rich one, is not. Moreover, due to the steep increase in world petroleum prices, Russia has been able to take advantage of its being first or second in the world in the volume of oil production and has greatly increased its national income, curbed inflation, and raised the standard of living of many of its citizens, though Russia's new wealth is heavily concentrated in Moscow and in the hands of relatively few people. [. . .] Thus, country-wide a middle class that is said to be the social backbone of democratic systems is emerging only slowly and thus far it has not acquired a distinctive political profile or voice.

Lipset suggests that relatively high levels of education and low income disparities are other requisites for the emergence of democracy. In addition, he sees democracy requiring 'a supportive culture, the acceptance by the citizenry and political elites of the principles underlying freedom of speech, media and assembly; rights of political parties, rule of law, human rights, and the like. Such norms do not evolve overnight'.

Some believe that culture is quite stable and puts its stamp on state institutions, creating an inertia difficult to reverse. They would argue that in the light of Russia's autocratic past, there is a 'natural tendency' towards non-democratic forms of government. Others see political culture as more malleable. As William Zimmerman points out, there are two variants of this approach, one holding that 'the core attitudes that constitute a political culture are driven by societal and technological change and evolve as society changes'. The other variant stresses the role of institutions and incentive structures. 'If the institutions are right, political culture follows, rather than drives, successful institutionalization. . . . Change the institutions, change the political culture'. Institutional change was seen as the way to democratize Germany after the First World War, but it proved insufficient to overcome that country's authoritarian heritage. Following the next world war, the Allies attempted to change not only Germany's (and Japan's) institutions but also its political culture, including family patterns and attitudes towards authority and towards peoples of different religions, races and cultures. This attempt to alter the political culture directly, rather than relying on institutions, seems to have been more effective. Perhaps it was so because, unlike the aftermath of the First World War, Allied troops occupied the country and supervised the transformation of its political culture.

The German experience may provide some lessons for those interested in changing Russian political culture in a more democratic direction. Constitutional lawyers, political scientists, educators and human rights activists, from within Russia and without, have been attempting to alter both Russia's institutions and, to a lesser extent because it is much more difficult and a longer-term undertaking, its political culture. But, unlike Germany and Japan in 1945, Russia has not had democratic rule imposed on it by occupying powers who invested a great deal in the political resocialization of the population. Militating against rapid democratization are Russia's history and traditions of authoritarian rule; disunity among democratic politicians who have not been able to unite in a single electoral list, let alone a political party, over the course of several parliamentary and presidential elections; prolonged economic crisis; and the training and experience of most of the leaders of the formerly Soviet states. As one observer points out, despite the collapse of the Soviet state and its economy, there has been 'remarkable elite stability'. Unlike Poland, Hungary, the Czech Republic, Slovakia and the Baltic states—but like the Central Asian states, Romania, Serbia and other states that have not moved very far towards democracy—the postcommunist leadership in Russia has come largely from the former elites and not from the democratic opposition. [. . .]

Moreover, unlike Hungarian, Polish and even Czech Communists, Russian Communists did not have several years of experience in negotiating with an opposition and at least partly accommodating it. Thus, their authoritarian reflexes were largely undisturbed. One of the criticisms of Boris Yeltsin's rule was that under a democratic veneer it was quite authoritarian. But, some argued, presidential power and dominance of the other branches of government was needed in a period of transition to democracy because only a strong presidency could push Russia along the road away from its authoritarian past. Yet, when Yeltsin resigned in favour of Vladimir Putin, the latter took advantage of the ongoing conflict in Chechnya to rationalize the need for an extension of presidential power. Since late 1999, little has been heard of limiting that power. Instead, Putin went after the few media that were critical of him and his government by arresting Vladimir Gusinsky, head of the largest independent media conglomerate, and by curbing the power of the regional governors. Gusinsky, like other oligarchs such as Boris Berezovsky and Leonid Nevzlin, fled abroad to avoid what they consider to be political persecution under the guise of legal prosecution. In October 2003, Federal Security Bureau officers in Novosibirsk pulled Mikhail Khodorkovsky, chairman of the Yukos oil company and reputedly Russia's richest man, from his charter plane and arrested him. He was charged with seven counts of tax evasion and embezzlement, acts supposedly committed in the early 1990s when Russian laws were poorly defined. Ironically, it was widely agreed that Yukos was the most transparent among Russia's major companies and that Khodorkovsky had done more than any other oligarch to bring order to Russian business practices and to eliminate corruption. Many suggested that the real reason for Khodorkovsky's arrest was that he was financing politicians opposed to Putin and that he himself had ambitions of running for the presidency of the Russian Federation.

President Putin has attempted several times and in different ways to limit the powers of the regional governors. To be sure, many of the latter rule their regions like feudal fiefs, but Putin's drive to reduce the number of Russian regions, and to curb the powers of the governors, was designed to enhance central power, not to democratize the regions. Following the atrocity at Beslan in the Caucusus in September 2004 in which over 300 people, including many children, were killed in the clash between Chechen hostage-takers and Russian forces, Putin proposed replacing popular elections and other regional leaders with people appointed by the federal government in Moscow. Like President Bush in the United States, Putin argued that the threat of terrorism demanded more centralized government and a stronger executive. It should be noted that in Holland, Spain, France and Britain, where terrorist actions have also occurred, there have been similar calls to limit such rights as freedom of expression and of assembly. It seems that peoples who are terrorized are willing to put more power in the hands of a leader, as George Bush's advisers realized in the 2004 presidential campaign when they correctly counted on Americans 'feeling safer' with a single-minded leader than with one who would weigh alternatives.

Certainly, Putin projects strength and determination. His proposals and actions have gone much further than those of American and West European leaders. Thus, if we measure Russia under Putin against criteria for democracy such as free and open competition for office and power, and civil and political liberties 'sufficient to ensure the integrity of political competition and participation', the Russian Federation falls short. Moreover, where once the Duma was controlled by the Communists and thus presidential power would run into some, at least symbolic, opposition, in 2003 the party supporting Putin, United Russia, secured more than 37 per cent of the party-list votes for the Duma, nationalist parties had about 20 per cent, and the Communists only about 13 per cent, whereas they had been the largest single party in the Dumas of the 1990s. Liberal parties such as Yabloko and the Union of Right Forces failed to pass the 5 per cent threshold and won very few single-member seats. At least in the short run, the government would hear fewer dissenting voices and independent opinions.

Putin's steadily high ratings in opinion polls, even in the wake of the *Kursk* submarine disaster in the summer 2000, the seizure of a Moscow theatre by Chechen terrorists in October 2002 resulting in the deaths of more than a hundred, as well as the Beslan massacre indicate that a large number of Russians favour a strong and even somewhat dictatorial leadership. Moreover, disunity among democratic politicians has not only weakened their influence in the institutions of governance, but has diminished their appeal as people worthy of support and of office-holding.

The authoritarian traditions of Russia and most of the other Soviet successor states mean that people are not used to democratic behaviours and values, such as welcoming pluralism in thinking and behaving, tolerating dissent, and supporting seemingly less efficient methods of democratic decision-making. They do not easily see the advantages of debate, discussion and non-conformity, and not defer-ring to a class of 'superiors'. Recent surveys certainly show that Russians have far less favourable attitudes towards democracy than people in scores of other coun-tries. [. . .] The World Survey [which] compares over 60 counties, found in 1999–2000 that whereas over all the countries 89 per cent of respondents gave a positive account of democracy, in Russia only 56 per cent did so. Russians were very dis-satisfied with their government's performance; they were less trusting and toler-ant, less healthy and less happy than people in many other countries. Inglehart finds that such attitudes are correlated with scepticism about democracy. 'Culture seems to shape democracy far more than democracy shapes culture. This is bad news for anyone seeking a quick and easy solution to the problems of democratiza-tion.' Since, he argues, 'cultural factors are ultimately more decisive than economic ones' in bringing democracy about, an improvement in the Russian economy would not by itself substantially increase the prospects for democracy.

The Russian Federation has failed to develop stable, respected and vigorous political institutions such as political parties, non-commercial interest groups, an independent judiciary and an effective legislature. Much of this may be attribut-able to the desire of Yeltsin and especially Putin, both of whom made their careers in the Soviet apparatus, for personalistic regimes. Second, there are no precedents in the living memory of Russians for such democratic institutions, unlike the Czech Republic and even Poland and Hungary. Third, many Russian citizens have a deep-rooted cynicism about political life, a rational response to Soviet circumstances, and this has led them to adopt apolitical postures. For example, in the elections to the governorship of St Petersburg and to the gover-norship of the Leningrad region, only 29 per cent of eligible voters cast a ballot, and 11 per cent of those who did vote selected 'against all candidates'. Moreover, citizens' post-Soviet experiences of widespread corruption, self-serving and cyn-ical politicians, and political murders have reinforced their belief that little changes or can change. The euphoria of 1988–90 when people listened atten-tively to debates in the Supreme Soviet and took a genuine interest in political life was dissipated by coup attempts, an inebriated and ineffective president and, very importantly, widespread corruption.

But there are forces that could impel Russia in the other direction. They include the revulsion that is felt by many about the communist political and economic systems; Western pressure for democratization and the desire by many to be accepted as part of 'Europe'; growing exposure to the cultures and political sys-tems of the West; and the democratic strains in the Russian political tradition upon which even Russian nationalists can draw. Indeed, most surveys taken in Russia in the last decade show that democratic attitudes and support for a market economy are strongest among the young, those who have had the least experience of communism and the most of the West. Roughly speaking, younger cohorts are more inclined towards pluralism of opinions, are sceptical about the existence of a 'single truth', optimistic about the future of democracy in Russia and reluctant to return to communist practices in economics, culture and politics. The university-educated are also more likely to support democratic values than those with less education. They tend to be more favourable towards the market economy, and more willing to gamble that political and economic change will be ultimately for the better. They are less inclined to retain an oppressive but familiar political system and a stagnant but minimally providing economic system. On the other hand, middle-aged men, farm workers, the unemployed and underemployed, and those dependent for their livelihood on one of the enormous industrial 'dinosaurs' that can no longer be justified in economic terms are understandably desperate. It is among such people that the 'solutions' proffered by non-democratic politicians such as Vladimir Zhirinovsky or Gennadii Zyuganov, or a variety of nationalists and even neo-fascists find their greatest appeal. Some have concluded, therefore, that since it is among the younger people that support for democracy is strongest, all other things being equal, time is working in favour of broader mass support for democracy in Russia.

Huntington lists several factors that influence whether or not a country will go in a democratic direction. These include prior democratic experience; a high level of economic development; a consensual and non-violent transition; and absence of severe social and economic problems. Russia has had only fleeting prior democratic experience. On economic development Russia would rank much higher than the Central Asian successor states, and ahead of Moldova, Belarus and Ukraine and the republics of the Caucusus, but behind the three Baltic republics. Indeed, those people who are worse off economically within Russia are generally the least favourable towards reform and democracy. The transition in Russia was largely consensual, though both in 1991 and 1993 some violence accompanied major changes. Unfortunately, Russia continues to face serious problems, including crime, corruption, capitalist-style poverty, homelessness, dramatic increases in the gap between the rich and poor, high rates of divorce and alcoholism—the latter contributing to a shocking decline in longevity, especially among men—and unemployment. To the extent that these are associated with 'democracy', as opposed to communism—in other words, that people believe that these social and economic problems appeared only with the dissolution of the Soviet state—popular support for political democracy is weakened.

Moreover, the prolonged, demoralizing and costly war in Chechnya is a multifaceted problem: the Chechens have humiliated the armed forces and political leadership, divided Russia's politicians, thrust the vexed problem of the nature of the federation and centre—periphery relations into the forefront of Russians' consciousness and, worst of all, cost thousands of lives. The humiliation of Russia has another dimension, the loss of empire and of control over a huge multi-republic state. Not only has Russia lost her status as a world superpower, but she has lost control of Eastern Europe and of the roughly 140 million non-Russians in the old Soviet Union. Perhaps this is why President Putin intervened openly in Ukraine's presidential election in 2004, backing the preferred choice of that country's Russian-speaking population. [. . .] Such a position appeals to Russians' pan-Slavism and their desire to stand up to the USA and restore their international dignity. Not surprisingly, they are also interested in securing what they regard as a pro-Russian government in Ukraine and the other countries of the 'near abroad'.

Democratization in Russia in Comparative Perspective

Analysts agree that Russia is not a consolidated democracy, but there is no consensus on how to 'label' its political system. Many point to the 'hybrid' nature of a regime that exhibits both democratic and non-democratic characteristics. One scholar describes Russia not as a democracy but as a system with a 'durable division of power among a fairly stable group of elite actors,' though this was written before Putin began his campaign against the oligarchs and regional governors. Other writers have called the Russian system 'soft Bonapartism', a 'personalist, populist, plebiscitary regime that rests on the administrative and coercive apparatuses of the state and that by seemingly elevating itself above society, acts as an arbitrator and preserver of the new bourgeoisie's interests as a whole'. Should Putin continue successfully to erode the power of the 'new bourgeoisie' and other elites, analysts may begin to perceive the system in different terms.

Obviously, it is very difficult to predict how the Russian system will evolve even in the near future. Can one extrapolate from the experiences of other democratizing societies in order to make an educated guess about the direction in which Russia will go? Some have suggested that the way in which the transition from authoritarianism was made originally is critical to the prospects for democracy. Transitions may be led by existing elites or by the opposition. They may result from the overthrow of the regime or from its collapse from within. They may be consensual ('pacted') or produced by conflict. Elite-led transitions are less likely to lead to democratization since the elites were the leaders of an authoritarian system, and this is certainly the case in Russia and many of the other successor states, as noted earlier. The transition in Russia was not exclusively the result of an internal collapse, though that was the long-term cause, but violence was rather limited and the process of transition did not leave the deep scars it might have. This is, of course, propitious for democracy. The transition also had elements of both conflict and consensus. Therefore, the transition process itself does not point clearly towards or away from the consolidation of democracy in Russia.

According to Linz and Stepan, in order to become consolidated democracies need five interacting areas: a lively civil society, a relatively autonomous 'political society' (institutions and procedural rules), the rule of law, a functioning state bureaucracy, and an 'economic society' (norms, institutions and regulations that mediate between the state and the market). A democracy is 'consolidated' when no major group tries to overthrow the democratic system, a strong majority of the public believes that democratic procedures and institutions are the most appropriate way to govern collective life, and conflicts are resolved within the democratic process.

Once again, the evidence from Russia is mixed. Some observers see a civil society emerging, one in which autonomous groups mediate between the state and the citizenry, though the most powerful groups seem closely tied not just to state but to a particular government and even a particular person, whether Yeltsin or Putin or a local ruler. One element of civil society is stable, visible political parties that serve to aggregate and articulate the political interests of the citizenry. With the possible exception of the weakened Communist Party, Russian political parties seem to be ad hoc coalitions of electoral candidates. They lack permanent structures, clear ideologies and programmes, and stable constituencies. Political institutions are still being moulded, as might be expected. The shape of the executive and legislature, relations between the nearly ninety units of government and the federal centre, and other basic institutional arrangements are not yet stabilized. The rule of law seems to be taking hold, though as in most other spheres, few would assert that it is firmly established. The state bureaucracy is problematic for several reasons: Soviet-era habits are still prevalent, and corruption is widespread, although apparently less than in Ukraine and other postcommunist states. Relations between the state and the market seem to be volatile, especially as the market is not yet fully developed. Local and foreign businessmen complain of what they see as capricious economic regulation and exploitative taxation, favouritism, and irrational and unpredictable state economic policies.

Part of the problem of both political and economic institutionalization may lie in the choice made between parliamentary and presidential forms of democracy. Linz and Stepan argue that the choice of parliamentary or 'semi-presidential' constitutions in Greece, Spain and Portugal gave those new democracies 'greater degrees of freedom' than if they had chosen American-style presidentialism as their constitutional framework. Parliamentarism is generally more conducive to democratic consolidation than presidentialism because it gives the political system greater efficacy, the capacity to construct majorities and the 'ability to terminate a crisis of government without it becoming a crisis of the regime'. Hungary, the Czech Republic and Slovenia have adopted the parliamentary system and 'it is perhaps no accident' that they are closer to consolidation than any postcommunist country with a directly elected president who has significant powers. The three major Slavic republics of the former Soviet Union, Russia, Ukraine and Belarus, all have presidential forms, as do the Central Asian states.

In addition to the choice of presidentialism, there are other choices made by Russia which have militated against rapid democratization. Several policies of the late Soviet period weakened the state but did not create new democratically legitimated central state structures. Gorbachev's programme of *perestroika* and *glasnost* was one of these. The previously hollow institutions of Soviet federalism provided the framework for the political mobilization of ethnicity. That was more effective than ideological mobilization in a state in which political alternatives had not been open to discussion for the better part of a century. Appealing to one's 'primordial' ethnic identity was a far more effective short-term strategy than trying to win support for a new, complicated political programme, even had such programmes existed. Moreover, many of the nationalisms which emerged from under the facade of Soviet 'proletarian internationalism' and 'friendship of the peoples' were exclusivist, militant and intolerant, and not very compatible with democratic thinking and acting. Local and regional elections shifted the focus from civic to ethnic issues, spurring the disintegration of the state. Most of the successor states have put independence ahead of democratization and have therefore emphasized collective over individual rights, and economic ahead of political restructuring. According to Linz and Stepan, had political reform and consolidation preceded economic reform, the state would have been stronger and better able to implement the economic reforms.

This raises the question of whether the sequencing of political and economic reform influences the success of democratization. Linz and Stepan argue that in Spain, the primacy of political reform, followed by socioeconomic reform and only then economic reform, was probably the optimal sequence for the consolidation of democracy. However, most analysts of the postcommunist states argue for the simultaneity of economic and political reform as the optimal strategy. Linz and Stepan feel that political reform should precede economic reform because democracy legitimates the market, not the reverse. Democratic regulatory state power is needed to make the market work. 'Effective privatization . . . is best done by relatively strong states that are able to implement a coherent policy . . . Effective privatization entails less state scope but greater state capacity . . . A state with rapidly eroding capacity simply cannot manage a process of effective privatization'. Furthermore, if there is a strong popular commitment to the new democratic forms of government, this can be a cushion against the blows of economic restructuring. The postcommunist Polish system seems to have enjoyed this advantage. Painful economic restructuring was tolerated by a public firmly committed perhaps not so much to democracy as to not returning to communist dictatorship. By now, it is clear that the Polish economy has succeeded in making the transition to the market, and economic success now serves as legitimation of the political system with which it is associated. Support for specific achievements of a system can grow into 'diffuse support', that is, a generalized support of the system which gives it the slack to survive temporary setbacks.

Comparable survey data show that the postcommunist polities of Hungary, Poland and the Czech Republic get much more popular support than do those of Russia, Belarus and Ukraine. [. . .]

Thus, it seems reasonable to conclude that democracy is better established in the northern tier of East Central Europe (Poland, Czech Republic, Hungary), in the three Baltic states and in Slovenia than it is in Russia, but in this respect Russia is ahead of Belarus, the Central Asian states, and perhaps other former Soviet republics. Even where reform communists have returned to power, they have accepted the rules of the game both in the elections themselves and in the way they have been exercising power. They have been accepted by the parties they defeated and by the public and thereby strengthened confidence in the fairness of democratic procedure. But more than the East European parties, a Russian communist party or coalition is likely to revert to practices of earlier times. Some even advocate a return to Stalinism.

There is no reason to assume either that democracy can never be firmly established in Russia or that it must inevitably be. It is reasonable to expect that postcommunist states will reach different degrees of democratization or not democratize at all. We come back to the idea that democracy is a spectrum, and the states emerging from the Soviet Union, though they all seemed to start at the same point, are likely to range themselves across this spectrum. Scholars will continue to debate the determinants of democracy and why one country reaches one point on the spectrum and another reaches a different point. Political culture, level of economic and cultural development, external influences and social problems are all factors in the equation. But perhaps the most important is elite choices. Precisely in periods of transition, elites make fateful choices among alternative directions in which they can lead their countries. As Linz and Stepan note, 'Democratic institutions have to be not only created but crafted, nurtured and developed'. Russia seems to have been halted, at least temporarily, at the creation stage. This is due in large part to the contradictory nature of Yeltsin's impulses, which alternated between those of a populist democrat and those of the provincial party boss he once was. A range of freedoms never enjoyed by Russia's citizens was not only introduced but has been more or less maintained, but neither

Yeltsin nor Putin has even tried to form an institutionalized constituency for democracy (a party, for example). Yeltsin's seemingly arbitrary hiring and firing of assistants, advisers and ministers was more reminiscent of a royal court than of a modern democracy. Putin's intolerance of political competitors and growing appetite for control have moved Russia further away from consolidated democracy, at least for now. If one were to draw up a balance sheet of democratization in Russia to date, on the positive side one might list broad freedom of expression but not in the most popular public media; the right to organize; a broad franchise; no ethnic discrimination emanating from the government and governmental tolerance and sometimes even support for non-Russian cultures; freedom of travel and of emigration; and the lifting of most restrictions on private economic activity. On the other side of the balance sheet would be presidential control of much of the media, especially television; the imbalance of power within the federal government which gives the president overwhelming power *vis-à-vis* the legislature; the '*nomenklatura* privatization' which gave favoured individuals privileged access to vast resources; and the too close ties between many interest groups and the government. The preoccupation with Chechnya, the genuine though perhaps waning strength of the communist constituency and the failure of the democrats to unite and articulate a clear and appealing programme are other roadblocks on what might otherwise have been a smoother path to democracy.

Over 150 years ago, the Russian novel *Dead Souls*, written by Nikolai Gogol, whom Ukrainians claim as one of their own, concluded with this by now well-known observation:

> And you Russia—aren't you racing headlong like the fastest troika imaginable . . . And where do you fly to, Russia? Answer me! . . . She doesn't answer. The carriage bells break into an enchanted tinkling, the air is torn to shreds and turns into wind; everything on earth flashes past, and, casting worried, sidelong glances, other nations and countries step out of her way.

At the beginning of the twenty-first century it is still not clear where Russia is racing. While outsiders continue to cast 'worried, sidelong glances' they cannot permit themselves to merely 'step out of her way'. Though no longer a superpower, Russia remains the largest state in the world, a country of some 145 million, and a great power with which the rest of the world is still obliged to come to terms.

3.3

Ten Myths About Russia: Understanding and Dealing with Russia's Complexity and Ambiguity

David Foglesong and Gordon M. Hahn

SINCE the collapse of the Soviet Union in 1991, American thinking about Russia has been distorted by at least ten major myths. Both conservatives and liberals, Russophobes and Russophiles, have clouded understanding of Russia by promoting unrealistic expectations about a rapid transformation, oversimplifications of Russia's history, essentialist ideas about its political culture, and exaggerated notions of a threat to American interests. The illusions that have clouded U.S.-Russian relations during the last decade must be dispelled if the present shaky cooperation [. . .] is to lead to a more stable partnership.

Myth 1

A Popular Revolution, Led by Liberal Democrats, Overthrew the Communist System and Launched Russia on a Speedy Journey to Democracy and a Free Market Economy

Early accounts of the demise of the Soviet Union depicted a miraculous transfiguration of the Russian people, who had suddenly cast off the fearful habits of the past, courageously resisted hard-line communist efforts to re-impose totalitarian oppression, and enthusiastically embraced the Western model of democracy and free enterprise. Along with many politicians and journalists, political scientists were caught up in the early euphoria about the supposed victory of Russian civil society against an oppressive state. Many espoused the transitology approach, presuming that Russia had made a radical break with Soviet institutions and embarked on an inexorable "transition" to democracy. This democratic teleology became dogma for those who interpreted the dissolution of the Soviet communist regime as a struggle between state and society. Even some critics of the transition paradigm joined in the widespread tendency to interpret the *perestroika*

Source: David Foglesong and Gordon Hahn, "Ten Myths About Russia: Understanding and Dealing with Russia's Complexity and Ambiguity," *Problems of Post-Communism*, Vol. 49, No. 6. Nov/Dec 2002. 3–15.

Note: Notes and references have been removed from this article.

era as a long "struggle with state institutions" waged by an "insurgent political society" and "the organized, independent, revolutionary opposition."

Although there are elements of truth in such portrayals, they greatly exaggerate the level of popular participation in the demise of the Soviet regime. In fact, prior to the August coup attempt, Mikhail Gorbachev and Boris Yeltsin had led efforts to dismantle the Soviet regime. Gorbachev's reforms and nascent transitional policies, combined with the powers Yeltsin gained as leader of the Russian Soviet Federated Socialist Republic (RSFSR), eroded the authority of the Communist Party of the Soviet Union (CPSU). From 1985 to 1991 the party-state was increasingly incapacitated as the regime split three ways: regime soft-liners like Gorbachev, opposition moderates like Yeltsin, and hard-line conservatives with considerable influence in the organs of coercion and the Party apparat.

In 1990, Yeltsin and his allies took control of the Russian republic's Party machinery and used it to undermine the dominance of the CPSU. They expanded Gorbachev's efforts to partially separate the Party from the state and to decentralize the Union's relations with its republics, ultimately breaking the Soviet party-state's control over the Russian republic's bureaucracy, finances, and natural resources. These revolutionaries-from-above mobilized society for additional support, but the mobilization was minimal and society's resources were limited. Thus, societal opposition played only a limited role in destroying the old order and building the new. Demonstrators in Moscow, St. Petersburg, and several other large cities, in relatively small numbers, actively resisted the attempted coup of August 1991, but across the country most Russians remained on the sidelines. The coup's failure resulted from the three-way regime split, which by 1991 had extended to the party-state, the power ministries, and the Party *apparat*. After the coup collapsed, the final destruction of the Soviet state and the construction of a new Russian regime were actually led by former Communist Party officials (including Yeltsin), opportunistic state bureaucrats, and younger members of the privileged *nomenklatura* class. In sum, the revolution was a bureaucrat-led, state-based "revolution from above" far more than a popular revolution from below.

Moreover, Yeltsin and his cohort were quick to demobilize societal opposition, restraining the development of civil society and a multi-party system in Russia. They soon cut a deal with the Soviet-era economic elite to co-opt the opposition emerging from the more partocratic element in the new ruling alliance against the domestic "neo-liberalism" and "pro-American" foreign policy of the young radicals. Old apparatchiks and young members of the former *nomenklatura* divvied up Party and state property, excluding society from the great Soviet going-out-of-business sale. In addition to the oligarchic-bureaucratic economy, the federal and political systems were constructed on the basis of intra-elite agreements. For example, the Russian Federation was built on the basis of bilateral treaties and agreements between the federal and regional executive branches that divided state property and finances among groups of bureaucrats. The political system was constructed in large part by incorporating Soviet state institutions (and apparatchiks) into the Russian state.

The mistaken view of the revolution as one generated from below, and merely another case in a "third wave" of global democratization, led to a cascade of unrealistic and false expectations, East and West, about the fate of Russia's third revolution in the twentieth century. The fall of the *ancien régime*, it was presumed, would lead almost inevitably to the consolidation of democracy and the market. This democratic teleology reinforced and sustained the view among decision-makers that Russia could integrate into the West and the global economy with limited political and economic assistance. Like Estonia or Hungary, Russia, too, would find its way without anything akin to a Marshall Plan. The West could expand NATO without fear of provoking Moscow, because Russia was already on its way westward. If Moscow turned back, Russia and its culture were entirely to blame. The West would bear no responsibility for failure, which was unlikely anyway because a strong democrat was leading the transition.

Myth 2

Yeltsin Was a Democrat

Yeltsin has been lionized as the bold, white-haired leader who mobilized the Russian people from atop a tank. In reality, he was a semi-democratic, semi-authoritarian personalistic ruler, schooled in the ways of bureaucratic intrigue by years of working in the Party machinery. Aside from those memorable three days in August 1991, Yeltsin fought the Soviet party-state more with presidential decrees, government instructions, and Russian state institutions than with demonstrations or general strikes. To be sure, he skillfully used the growing popular opposition to win concessions from Gorbachev's increasingly divided party-state. Deploying a tactical populism, Yeltsin appealed to the people when he needed to exert greater pressure on the regime to advance his revolutionary takeover of state institutions and Party resources.

However, after defeating the bumbling coup plotters, Yeltsin and his aides stifled the development of a multiparty system and civil society. Yeltsin refused to lead or even join a political party. He postponed promised regional elections and instead appointed regional governors until 1996. He co-opted any and all willing party-state apparatchiks into the state bureaucracy, regardless of their past records or attitudes toward developing democracy and a market economy.

Few members of Yeltsin's administration—including Yeltsin himself—had more than a limited understanding of how a market economy functions. He made deals with former Soviet economic elites to reduce their opposition to the pro-American economic and foreign policies advocated by his more liberal advisers. This approach reached its logical conclusion in December 1992, when Prime Minister Egor Gaidar, the architect of market reforms, was replaced by the communist soft-liner Viktor Chernomyrdin, who had served Gorbachev as fuel and energy minister and a Central Committee member. Then, in 1993, Yeltsin forced the Russian legislature into a corner, abolished it, and ordered tanks to bombard the parliament building. After crushing the October 1993 rebellion, he closed down all the regional soviets. Although he finally held elections to a new federal parliament, the results of the simultaneous referendum on the new constitution may well have been falsified. When public approval of his government's painful and failing policies fell below 10 percent in 1996, Yeltsin came exceedingly close to canceling the scheduled presidential elections. He was able to secure victory only by buying votes with state funds and handing over the state's most valuable enterprises to oligarchs like Boris Berezovskii.

While it is inaccurate to portray Yeltsin as a principled democratic leader, it is equally misleading to paint him as the embodiment of oppressive Russian authoritarianism. Despite his declining popularity, he refused to curb freedom of association, and he accepted the revived Communist Party of the Russian Federation. Although he sometimes manipulated and tried to intimidate the mass media, he tolerated substantial criticism of his policies from journalists. In short, Yeltsin was a hybrid figure—personalist and populist, authoritarian and democratic all at once. In terms of this internal contradiction, he was not unlike the country he ruled.

Myth 3

Russia Is Subject to Universal Laws of Development

Over the last decade, many policy advisers and scholars posited that Russia's inevitable destiny is to conform—or succumb—to the universal process of modernization. According to these arguments, Russia has no choice but to belatedly follow the paths to democracy and capitalism blazed decades or centuries ago by more advanced Western countries.

In fact, Russia is not just another country to be plugged into preconceived formulas. It has a number of peculiarities that must be taken into account both to understand its "non-conformity" and to help transform it where possible. The main peculiarities include Russia's vast size, its geostrategic location, and the residual Soviet impression on its economic geography.

Russia's size has significant implications for both domestic and foreign policy that no other state can claim. By far the largest country in the world, Russia counts ten countries as neighbors. Its border with Kazakhstan alone is the same length as the boundaries of the continental United States. Russia's extensive borders and seacoasts require a large standing army and navy, which burden the budget and deplete economic manpower. These costs and the reality of a territorial expanse spanning eleven time zones would make it difficult for the federal government to build and maintain infrastructure (roads, railroads, bridges, power lines, etc.) even without the challenges of economic transformation. [. . .]

Geostrategically, Russia is the only country in the world that borders the European, Asian, and Muslim worlds. This places special burdens on its foreign and security policies. Russian national security strategists argue (sometimes with hyperbole) that the threat from each of these worlds is arguably growing. In the east, the sleeping dragon is awake. In the south, the Muslim world is in turmoil, leading to terrorist jihads against the West and Russia, assistance for Chechen militants, and a threat to the stability of reasonably friendly secular regimes in Central Asia. In the west, NATO is expanding ever eastward, apparently to Russia's borders with the Baltic states, and eventually perhaps to Ukraine and Georgia. Any exacerbation of Russian security concerns in the three regions could set back progress on reforming the economy and post-Soviet institutions.

Russia's economic geography also hinders the conversion and modernization of its once heavily militarized industries. Russia has the only post-communist economy that consists of hundreds of one-company towns that, in many cases, dominate half the budgets of regions several times larger than medium-sized European countries. Closing, privatizing, or selling the company to foreigners will affect an entire region that is likely to be located hundreds of miles from any other population center. This constrains Russian willingness to engage in uncontrolled large-scale privatization, especially in the outlying regions. With the privatization of large enterprises, oligarchs came to dominate regional economies. Many are now parlaying their economic power into political power, becoming governors and senators. They seek office not to lobby for development aid for their regions, but to gain favors for their firms and immunity from prosecution.

These factors make it inadvisable to force a one-size-fits-all Western model on Russia. Transitology envisaged a rapid, almost automatic, transformation from hostile, autarchic Soviet totalitarianism to a Western-style Russian democracy and market. This mindset led to the belief that overhauling Russia's inefficient economy would not require massive Western financial assistance or new approaches tailored to Russian conditions.

Myth 4

Russia's Unique Culture Dooms It to Eternal Backwardness

When the illusions of sweeping overnight reforms failed to pan out, they gave way to disappointment, disenchantment, and disdain for Russia's alleged inability to change for the better. Bruce Clark, a British correspondent who stressed "Russia's sheer incomprehensibility," was one of the first to argue that the "Eastern Church" was a major obstacle to the Westernization. A little later, the political scientist Samuel Huntington defined Russia as the core of an inscrutable Orthodox civilization that was almost impossible to change. More recently. Matthew Brzezinski, another journalist, attributed the "loss" of the country to Russians' congenital corruption, their peculiar "Slavic soul," and their scheming, non-Western leaders.

Such gloomy views were the opposite of the earlier euphoric universalism. While the zealous optimists had been overconfident about rapidly converting Russia, the pessimists wrongly disparaged Russians as irredeemably averse to Western values. As some pessimists exaggerated the influence of the Orthodox Church (despite seventy years of atheist persecution), others vented a racially tinged scorn for supposedly innate Russian traits (e.g., superstition, laziness, dishonesty). Overreacting to specific setbacks, especially the financial collapse of August 1998, the doomsayers prematurely wrote off Russia's ability to develop a prosperous economy.

Myth 5

Russia Lacks the Cultural Requisites for Democracy and a Market Economy

After Russian voters elected an alarming number of communists and xenophobic nationalists to parliament in 1993 and 1995, many Western journalists and scholars began to voice gloomy appraisals of the incorrigible authoritarianism of "eternal Russia." In 1993, they exaggerated the election outcome as a victory for the quirky quasi-fascist Vladimir Zhirinovskii's Liberal Democratic Party (63 deputies) and the communists. In fact, the party of liberal pro-Western Egor Gaidar took a plurality of seats (76 deputies) in the Duma, and democratic and centrist parties took a majority of the Duma seats (51.7) after deputies elected in majoritarian single-member districts were factored in. Such Russophobic pessimism faded in some circles when Yeltsin triumphed over his communist opponent in the 1996 presidential election and when the Russian stock market became bullish the following year. However, after Yeltsin handed over the presidency to former KGB officer Vladimir Putin at the end of 1999, there was a resurgence of scornful views of Russia as an impenetrable, irredeemable land of cruel masters and servile subjects. In the first days of Putin's presidency, for example, one relatively sophisticated correspondent declared: "Russians have been crushed for so long that they have learned to respond only to an iron fist."

In fact, there has been a recessive but nonetheless rich liberal-democratic substrain in Russian political culture that is too often ignored. While Russian political history has indeed been dominated by authoritarianism and totalitarianism, there have been numerous revolts against despotism and brief periods of quasi-democratic government that might have been more lasting had circumstances been more favorable. The liberal Provisional Government of February—October 1917, in particular, might have been able to establish the foundations for democracy if Russia had not been entangled in World War I. Even in the darker periods of tsarist and Soviet rule, Russians formed revolutionary or dissident organizations, secretively circulated banned publications, and gained knowledge about the outside world from smuggled books or partially jammed radio broadcasts. [. . .]

Even as Russophobes in the West reproduce the myth that Russians are genetically antagonistic to democratic values, public opinion polls and in-depth interviews show that Russians have grown deeply attached to democratic processes and principles, despite their frequently acute disappointment with post-Soviet leaders and institutions. Although the word *demokratiia* has acquired pejorative associations with corruption and foreign imposition, a recent in-depth survey conducted by the Carnegie Endowment for International Peace shows that the overwhelming majority of Russians treasure free elections (87 percent), freedom of expression (87 percent), freedom of the mass media (81 percent), freedom to choose place of residence (75 percent), and freedom of religion (70 percent). Other recent polls show also a growing sense of economic well-being among Russians, an important prerequisite of middle class democratic attitudes. According to one survey, over the last three years the number of survey respondents who regard the situation in Russia as catastrophic has fallen from 51 percent to 14 percent. [. . .]

Contrary to the tendency of cultural essentialists to view Russians as passive, Russia now possesses a civil society that is a reasonably active, autonomous force. There are tens of thousands of non-governmental labor, business, environmental, anti-war, and other organizations that employ hundreds of thousands of citizens and represent the interests of around 20 million people. Some can already point to victories. Russia's trade unions recently forced the Duma to amend a draft Labor Code before passage. To be sure, Russian society could be more highly mobilized and better organized. But the enormous size of the country makes building nationwide organizations a difficult, expensive task, and with 80 percent of the capital concentrated in the city of Moscow, the overwhelming majority of Russians are too resource starved for optimally effective self-organization. However, this is an argument not for dismissing the capacity of Russians for democratic activity, but for increasing Western aid to non-governmental organizations.

Even under current conditions, Russians manage to express their grievances and demand changes. On February 9, 2002, for example, 500 residents of Krasnoiarsk braved the Siberian winter to block a railroad used to import nuclear waste for processing in their region. At the same time, small business organizations protested tax hikes and other governmental decisions in regions across Russia. In response, the federal government modified its tax policy to ease the burden on small businesses. There is also a strong social movement to institute alternatives to military service, and several regions began experimenting with such a system. Although the administration halted these illegal experiments, and stubborn military opposition forced the Putin administration to back, and the Duma to pass, an alternative service bill that requires a three and a half year commitment, the first step has been taken. Moreover, the mayor of Nizhnii Novgorod recently reinstated his city's experiment after the Duma vote and vowed to support an NGO court challenge to the federal ban on regional versions of alternative service.

Myth 6

Putin Is a Dictator

Since the end of 1999, when he assumed the Russian presidency, Western commentators have asserted that the wellspring of Vladimir Putin's politics is his background as a KGB officer from the 1970s to the 1980s and as head of the Federal Security Service (FSB) in the late 1990s. Simplistically labeled a "former KGB operative," Putin is accused of seeking to return Russia to a "police state" and "dictatorship" by centralizing political control, suppressing the independent media, and cracking down on dissent. In July 2000, for example, only months after his inauguration, two American national security analysts asserted that "Putin is now building a police state using primarily the police organs of the Federal Security Service, known as the FSB, and the army to seize all key power positions in Russia, eliminate dissent and attack both internal and external enemies." Similarly, *New York Times* columnist William Safire alleged that Putin planned to follow China's model and crush all democratic tendencies, and he implied that Putin would make himself "president for life."

Such nightmarish predictions are one-sided and ill-informed. An accurate portrait of Putin, like that of Yeltsin or of Russia as a whole, must see him in all his complexity. The simplistic assumption that anyone formerly associated with the KGB must possess the very worst totalitarian impulses of the old regime and be incapable of countenancing democratic reforms reflects an ignorance of history. For example, Gorbachev ascended to the Soviet leadership with support from a former KGB chief, Iurii Andropov, and key KGB leaders played critical roles in the defeat of the August 1991 putsch by refusing orders to assault democratic forces. [. . .]

More important, the cynical view of Putin as first and last a KGB man ignores his tenure in the democratic government of St. Petersburg, an experience that exerts considerable influence on his political makeup. Like many *apparatchiki* in the Gorbachev era, Putin soon shifted from being a supporter of the sinking Soviet regime to a moderate revolutionary. In 1990, he effectively left the KGB and returned to St. Petersburg State University, where he had earned a law degree. There he became an assistant to rector in charge of international liason at St. Petersburg State University, where USSR People's Deputy Anatolii Sobchak was still a law professor a leading moderate democrat, was elected mayor of St. Petersburg later that year. During the attempted hard-line coup of August 1991, Putin reportedly played a key role by negotiating with the commander of the Baltic Military District to prevent troops from entering the city. After the Soviet collapse, the St. Petersburg administration, with Putin as Sobchak's top deputy, followed Yeltsin's lead in banning the CPSU, abolishing the Soviet Union, and privatizing state property. (This also meant that Putin became involved with the corruption that was part-and-parcel of the economic revolution from above.)

After Sobchak lost his re-election bid in 1996, Putin jumped to Yeltsin's presidential administration, where he eventually became intimately familiar with one of the lending alleged state inside traders of the Yeltsin era. As deputy to Kremlin property manager Pavel Borodin, Putin probably was privy to at least some of Borodin's financial and property machinations and the Kremlin's dirty dealings with oligarchs. Later, as chief of the administration's State Control Directorate, he monitored implementation of laws and presidential decrees. Putin saw firsthand the regions' disdain for federal law as well as the institutional chaos at the federal level created by the flood of presidential decrees, governmental orders, and other normative documents that were often self-contradictory and ignored by competing bodies. This is a source of Putin's efforts to re-centralized power in Moscow, harmonize regional law with federal law, and make federation institutions more efficient.

Putin and his cohort of pragmatic former Soviet officials are neither solely authoritarian nor purely democratic. Although Putin has condemned violations of the law by KGB officers in the Soviet era, he has also stated his opposition to declassifying files and his abhorrence at having a democrat, Vadim Bakatin, head the post-Soviet FSK after the 1991 coup. While Putin and his associates respect the democratic processes (mainly free elections) established in the 1990s that serve to legitimate their power, they were disturbed by the drastic decline of federal authority in the Yeltsin era and the degeneration of Russia to near lawlessness.

Since his election as president in March 2000 with 53.44 percent of the vote, Putin has centralized federal power at the expense of the formerly wayward regions, consolidated several centrist parties into one large party, "United Russia," united factions in the Duma, and sought to co-opt into state-organized corporatist structures members and groups previously organized in autonomous association. His authoritarian measures have been undertaken with a soft sleight of hand rather than an iron fist, as in the effort to remove the NTV and TV-6 television stations, respectively, from the control of the oligarchs, Vladimir Gusinskii and Berezovskii. Putin has tolerated oligarchs as long as they limit their clandestine political activities, forgo building independent media empires, and perform economic tasks for the state. Here, he seems to be caught between two of his formative political experiences: his rise to power with the help of oligarchs like Borodin and Berezovskii, and his disdain for the oligarchs' corrupting effect on the state.

The more liberal Petersburg experience in Putin's political biography also informs his presidency. Putin has taken some quasi-democratic political positions, such as ignoring numerous calls, many from governors themselves, for regional governors and republic presidents to be appointed rather than elected. He has also twice quashed efforts to lengthen presidential terms from four to seven years. In economics, Putin has taken important steps to cut taxes and business regulations, encourage foreign investment, and begin reforms of the judiciary, procuracy, and military. In sum, neither Putin's pre-presidential background nor his policies as president match the caricature of him as an untrustworthy KGB spook turned would-be dictator.

Depictions of Yeltsin as a bold, heroic democrat and Putin as a sneaky, sinister autocrat are therefore seriously misleading and mask the important continuities between the Yeltsin and Putin eras. Both manipulated democratic processes and showed some authoritarian tendencies while blocking a totalitarian restoration. [. . .]

Myth 7

Russians Are Inherently Anti-Western and Anti-American

Outbursts of anger and bitterness by nationalist and communist demagogues because of harsh economic policies and Russia's declining global prestige have led many in the West to conclude that xenophobia is implanted in the bones of Russians like some long-lived radioactive isotope. However, most increases in Russian anti-Western sentiment have been provoked by Western policies and actions.

To some extent, the rise of anti-American feeling in the mid-1990s was a predictable counterpart to the naive idealization of the United States between 1989 and 1992. With the downfall of the Soviet Union, many urban Russians vaguely hoped that their country would magically become as prosperous as the United States, and they expected massive financial aid as a reward for overthrowing the "evil empire." When no Marshall Plan for Russia materialized and the economic reforms pushed by American advisers brought widespread hardship, many became disillusioned and embittered.

While anti-American attitudes were held by roughly 30–40 percent of Russians in 1993, the figure doubled later in the decade in reaction to the expansion of NATO into Eastern Europe, the NATO bombing of Bosnian Serbs in 1994, and the NATO bombing of Serbia in 1999 When 60–70 percent of Russian respondents say that the United States or NATO poses a threat to Russia, it should be understood as a reflection of the history of military invasions of Russia from the West and the emotional tribulations Russians have undergone over the last decade more than an inherited cultural paranoia. It is also not a completely irrational response to such Western policies as the expansion of NATO up to Russia's borders, the increase in the number of Russian cities listed as potential targets of U.S. nuclear missiles, and the challenges to Russia's right to a sphere of influence in the Commonwealth of Independent States.

Unlike the rabidly anti-American extremists who have drawn disproportionate media coverage, an overwhelming majority of Russians have either a friendly or an ambivalent attitude toward the United States and the West. Among those who are ambivalent, opinion is subject to abrupt changes of attitude in response to specific events. For example, the terrorist attacks of 9/11 induced a wave of sympathy for America from Russians who believe their own country has been the victim of terrorist raids and bombings by Chechen rebels. [. . .] In early 2002, anti-Americanism became more pronounced, partly because many believed that Russian competitors had been victimized by unfair judging and scapegoating at the Salt Lake City Olympic Games. [. . .]

Like President Putin, who emphatically declares "we are Europeans," many Russians, especially in the younger generations, believe that Russia is or should be a part of Europe. But if Russians feel humiliated, insulted, and excluded by the West, they will be more likely to look for allies in the East and to define themselves as Eurasian.

Myth 8

Russia Is an Expansionist, Neo-Imperialist Menace

Despite the drastic decline of Russian power since 1991, Russophobes like the *New York Times* columnist William Safire have repeatedly charged Russia with harboring its "old imperialist urge." Even as Russia provided much valuable intelligence to assist the U.S. war in Afghanistan, one American think tank deployed its experts to denounce the Northern Alliance's occupation of Kabul as part of a grand Russian "military strategy" and an "ominous gambit" to expand Russian influence in South Asia. Stratfor director George Friedman went a step further, warning that Russia's cooperation with the West in Afghanistan was paving the way for Russia's resurgence and the next war, which would pit Russia against the West. Such views perpetuate reflexive cold war suspicions and wrongly draw a straight line from the nineteenth-century "Great Game" through the alleged Soviet quest for a warm-water port on the Indian Ocean to the new Russia's supposed expansionist aims in Central and South Asia. Proponents seem to have forgotten that Russia was but one of several players in the Great Game, as it was in the much older European game of partitioning Poland.

The projection of cold war antagonism into the post-cold war era rests, in part, on a shallow historical perspective. In more than 200 years of Russian-American relations, the two countries' vital interests rarely clashed before the cold war. When the United States expanded across the North American continent in the nineteenth century, Russia withdrew from settlements in the Pacific Northwest and then sold Alaska for pennies an acre. As American commerce expanded in Northeast Asia around 1900, Theodore Roosevelt and others briefly feared that Russia's prolonged occupation of Manchuria jeopardized the Open Door policy, but between the Japanese thrashing of Russia in 1904–5 and VJ Day in 1945, most U.S. leaders realized that Russia was actually a potential ally against the most formidable threat to U.S. interests, across the Pacific. A long-range view of American-Russian relations thus suggests that collisions are more likely to stem from the expansion of U.S. commercial interests and security commitments than from rampant Russian imperialism.

In more recent years, the specters raised by Russophobic analysts have repeatedly failed to materialize. Putin's turn to the West after September 2001 was a ruse, they warned—Russia would use the "alliance" against terror to bolster its oil and gas pipeline dreams, and then exploit its resulting enhanced international status to challenge American hegemony. Despite the alarms raised by Russophobes, the deployment of Russian Emergency Ministry forces to build a high-tech field hospital and re-establish a Russian embassy in Kabul generated no challenge to U.S. policy in Afghanistan. Indeed, Putin later revealed that the Russian descent on Kabul was carried out with the aid of U.S. forces.

Beyond Afghanistan, there have been few major Russian challenges to U.S. initiatives. [. . .] Even if the Russian government wanted to pursue a sustained imperialist foreign policy, it lacks sufficient military and economic power to do so. An economy no larger than that of the Netherlands is barely capable of supporting imperialist aspirations in Eurasia, much less beyond. Russia has been unable to invigorate the Commonwealth of Independent States (CIS) as a viable international organization, much less as a precursor to a renewed economic union. Only Belarus, Tajikistan, Kyrgyzstan, and Kazakhstan have joined the CIS Customs Union, and these are the states that are least viable and most dependent on Russia to begin with.

All of Russia's seeming neo-imperialist gambits in the post-Soviet era have been either exaggerated by Western analysts or episodic in implementation, intended to manipulate weak bordering states rather than re-incorporate them into a revived Soviet Union. Russia has played a clearly positive role by stationing the 201st Division in Tajikistan, thereby deterring Islamic incursions from Afghanistan and stabilizing the weak and corrupt—but secular—regime of Imomali Rokhmonov in Dushanbe. Western critics of the involvement of Russian forces in Georgia and Transdniestr have ignored the financial costs Russia will incur by withdrawing its troops and equipment, as well as the instability that might result. In Central Asia, where Russian national security really is threatened, weak regimes like Tajikistan, Kazakhstan, and Kyrgyzstan have not been pressured to join a political union with Russia. The so-called Russia-Belarus Union is largely a fiction, even as an economic union. The two sides cannot agree on a common currency, and even the customs agreement has been the subject of repeated disputes between the parties. Any prospects of a real Belarus-Russia Union are minimal until President Aleksandr Lukashenka leaves the scene, since the economies of the two states are vastly different, with Russia having implemented economic liberalization far beyond the virtually unreformed Soviet-style Belarusian economy.

Myth 9

Russia Is No Longer an Important International Player

Many so-called realists believe that Russia is so weakened that it is no longer a serious international player whose interests need be taken into account when planning American foreign policy. For example [. . .] journalist Jeffrey Tayler called Russia "Zaire with Permafrost" and argued that its history doomed the country to shrink, decay, and disintegrate.

Although Russia has experienced a breathtaking decline in its fortunes since the cold war, when the Soviet superpower confronted the United States around the world, it is not so weak that it no longer counts as a great power, and its problems are not necessarily permanent or irremediable. Russia's possession of thousands of nuclear weapons is not the only factor that explodes the myth of its insignificance. Besides the United States, Russia is the only country that is a major player in Europe, the Pacific, South and Central Asia, and the Middle East simultaneously. Because of its geostrategic position and relatively high level of technological development, Russia is a major player in the global energy market as well as in several other natural resource exports. It maintains a faltering but still major space program that is matched only by NASA.

To be sure, Russia's economy is small compared not only with other major powers in the Group of Seven (G-7), but also with many smaller states. However, Russia's vast natural resources, strong human capital, and potential for investment growth represented by the hundreds of billions of dollars secreted in foreign bank accounts suggest, taken together, that a fairly rapid revitalization is possible. With the right policies in these areas, including investors' rights, banking reform, and money-laundering, anti-corruption, and anti-crime laws, a Russian economic revival is quite conceivable. In the last three years, Russia's economy has experienced steady, substantial growth, and Moscow has taken important steps to reverse capital flight, encourage foreign investment, and overhaul its financial system. Russia recovered from its earlier "times of troubles" (in the seventeenth century, during the Crimean War, and during the civil war of 1917–21). It may now be on the way to recovery again.

Myth 10

Russia and the United States Are Strategic Allies

The newest myth is that the United States and Russia became strategic partners, even allies, after the events of September 11, 2001. To be sure, 9/11 reshuffled international affairs in general, and Russian-American relations in particular—at least temporarily. The terrorist attacks highlighted the previously ignored mutual interest in combating militant Islam and international terrorism that Washington and Moscow have shared since the end of the cold war. But there is no guarantee that this common interest will remain clear or paramount to Russian and American policymakers.

Some leaders on each side read developments in Afghanistan as justifying a suspicion that the other country is pursuing selfish gains at the expense of their own country. Thus, certain American actions reinforced the suspicions of some Russians that the United States is seeking to parlay the war against terror into a war for control of oil, gas, and pipeline routes. American special operations forces and marines were first deployed mainly in the south among the Pashtun, who make up the majority of the population of Pakistan, and the United States has had good relations with Pakistan since the cold war. The Pashtun also make up the bulk of the Taliban, who, Russian analysts have long suspected, were backed by Washington to counter Russian interests in Central Asia. The United States inserted Afghan Pashtun leader Abdul Haq into southern Afghanistan in order to entice local Pashtun leaders and Taliban commanders to defect from Osama bin Laden. This was viewed by Russian commentators as an effort to rally Pashtuns around a charismatic leader against the Afghan minorities of Uzbeks, Tajiks, and Khazaris that make up the Northern Alliance, backed for years by Russia, Iran, and India. [. . .]

Back in Washington, some experts claimed that Moscow's outward show of cooperation masked an effort to utilize American power for its own ulterior purposes. For example, Toby Gati, a State Department official in the Clinton administration, declared that Putin "had the Americans doing his business in Afghanistan and he was fighting to the last American." In a similar vein, Russia's dispatch of Emergency Ministry personnel to Kabul to set up a hospital was variously interpreted as a second Pristina, the beginning of Russian troop deployments, and an intelligence operation.

As of the summer of 2002, potential ruptures have been averted or smoothed over by a division of labor. The Russians are working closely with the largely Tajik and Uzbek Northern Alliance, providing assistance for infrastructure and military development, while the United States maintains close ties to the Pashtuns and leads the military struggle against the terrorists in the south. However, there is no guarantee that there will be no friction in the future. [. . .]

In short, it is premature to be celebrating a Russian-American strategic partnership.

Beyond the Myths: Understanding and Dealing with Russia

To have a stable and positive relationship with Putin's Russia, the United States must move beyond the myths and polarized perspectives of the past decade. It is dangerous for both U.S.-Russian relations and international security for Washington to see Russia through monochromatic glasses, either dark or bright. Like the overly optimistic assessments of Russia's progress toward democracy and capitalism in the 1990s, the rosy views of a strategic partnership with the United States may produce a new round of disappointment and disdain. On the other hand, excessively pessimistic or alarmist views of Russia's supposedly failed democratization, innate authoritarianism, and imperialism can undermine Russian-American cooperation and close off opportunities to influence Russia's political and social evolution. To avoid falling into the over-reaction trap once more, we must have a clear, nuanced, and balanced view of Russia.

Russia is a kaleidoscope of interacting positive and negative trends. These must be detected and sorted out by way of objective analysis free of political science preconceptions, historical simplifications, and Russophobic prejudices. The contradictory trends in this sprawling country cannot be captured by crude stereotypes or rigid transition paradigms. Russia, like many other states, is stuck somewhere between a predominantly authoritarian and predominantly democratic order. It can be moving in two directions at once in different spheres, creating a hodge-podge of trends that is difficult to understand, much less model. Thus, Moscow's economic strategy involves greater openness to Western investment and deeper integration into the global economy, but the government's prosecution of critics and scientists for selling classified documents has discouraged open discussion and contacts with foreign colleagues. Russia has adopted a new legal code with many amendments modeled on practices in the United States and Western Europe, yet Putin's vision of a "dictatorship of law" simultaneously entails moving away from Western conceptions of liberty and justice. Important electoral reforms have been implemented, but political parties have been stagnating or losing adherents. Russian judges have gained greater independence, but that independence has not dramatically improved the criminal justice system. Not only have Putin's federal reforms re-centralized power in Moscow, they are also forcing the regions to rescind many of their undemocratic laws. Given such complicated and surprising developments, Western analysts must consciously refrain from extrapolating disappointment over negative trends in one area onto the Russian government or people as a whole.

The pessimists and the optimists share a presumption that Russia's historically determined fate or natural evolutionary endpoint can be seen in advance. The first step in escaping the bipolar swings in American views of Russia is to abandon prophetic pretensions and jettison teleological hubris. Instead of focusing on forecasting the future and constructing (or tinkering with) abstract paradigms, students of post-communist Russia should concentrate on careful empirical study of developments and dynamics in its politics, business, culture, and society. Scholars should spend more time investigating what is really happening and less time judging how the transition measures up according to some predetermined finish line.

While Russophobic essentialists write as if cultural prerequisites were the key, if not sole, determinant for the development of democracy and markets, transitologists tend to eschew culture as an explanatory factor. Both are wrong. Cultural values are one of several important elements facilitating or obstructing democratic and market development. Contrary to the assumptions of Russophobes in the West and Slavophile nationalists in Russia, cultures are not monolithic. They are malleable under the influence of external forces, especially in the era of globalization. This does not mean that Americans can easily complete the cultural transformation and democratization of Russia by launching cold war-style propaganda programs to exploit the presumed gap between the supposedly pro-American Russian people and the obdurate Russian government. It does mean that Western (especially American) culture has strongly affected post-Soviet Russia, though often not in the ways or to the extent Westerners might wish.

Although propaganda campaigns based on an adversarial relationship to the Russian government are unlikely to be very successful (and may actually backfire), there are many ways that Westerners might exert a modest positive influence on Russia's development. This is not the place for a full set of proposals, but a few examples of practical initiatives can be mentioned. While being humbly cognizant of financial misconduct in Western businesses and governments, Western advisers (as Larry Diamond has suggested) can encourage and support the establishment and strengthening of corruption watchdog bodies in Russia, such as an Independent Counter-Corruption Commission and the Audit Chamber. Western non-governmental organizations can promote the establishment of human rights ombudsmen in each of Russia's regions (at present they are set up in perhaps one-third of the regions) and the expansion of their powers so that they can more effectively investigate complaints regarding violations of press freedom and national minority rights.

Finally, the United States and American corporations can expand their cooperation in the development of energy resources and economic infrastructure in Siberia and the Far East, eventually including a trans-Bering rail tunnel for passenger and oil transport. This would simultaneously boost Russia's economic growth, earn the revenue its government needs for projects such as the modernization of schools and hospitals, and reduce Western dependence on energy resources from Arab and Muslim states. To reinforce this strategy, Russia can be brought into the International Energy Association, and the IEA can be reformed to function as a counter to the OPEC cartel, as Ira Strauss has proposed.

These prescriptions do not presume that Russia is already an ally because of Putin's demonstrated support for the United States in the war against Islamic terrorists. They do suggest some ways to assist the evolution of Russia's domestic institutions and to facilitate a closer international partnership. They should be complemented by other measures, such as gradually deepening Russia's relationship with NATO and its integration into the World Trade Organization, the Asia-Pacific Economic Community, and the Group of Eight (the Group of Seven since Russia's inclusion) to take advantage of the new opening for Russian-Western relations. Russian involvement in these international institutions will ease changes in its political culture, economy, and strategic thinking that will in turn alleviate Western fears and undermine Western stereotypes. Thus, a more stable basis for a Russian-American partnership can be established.

4

The Economy: Market Capitalism or Institutionalized Corruption?

The depths of Russia's economic collapse at communism's end is, in retrospect, hard to fathom for those who did not experience it firsthand. The Soviet Union was a superpower, after all, the other "pole" in the bipolar world that defined international relations for more than four decades. Here was the leader of a military, political, and economic empire in a state of total collapse. Hyperinflation—real price increases of 50 percent a month—gripped the economy, with scarcity the norm for even the most basic goods. Shops everywhere closed because their shelves were literally empty.

As a poignant example, on one July afternoon in 1991, Europe's largest bakery, not far from Moscow's historic Arbat district, featured a single basket of half loaves of day-old bread, rock hard, on the first floor. Dozens of other shelves dedicated to a variety of loaves, rolls, and buns all stood empty. The situation on the second floor was even more desperate and gut-wrenching. In what was once a bustling cavernous space offering an array of cakes, pastries, and candies stood thirty-six frowning women in blue aprons before counters devoid of anything for sale—there was not a single piece of candy to be had. This was a depressing sight, one which employees assured had become standard in recent weeks at the store, and spoke to the depths of the economic calamity facing the country. Elsewhere, those who did have items to sell priced their goods in dollars rather than in rubles, which had become virtually worthless. Across the country, the people were rejecting their own country's currency. Exchange rates experienced convulsive changes; on some days the ruble lost as much as 25 percent of its value in a single hour to the point where it was unwise to change more dollars than one was to spend within a few hours. Currency exchanges, reflecting this reality, categorically refused to sell dollars; most were open only for short spells and would only buy dollars, not sell. The country was, to put it bluntly, in the throes of an economic catastrophe.

While the depth of the collapse and size of the economy differed from those of the East-Central European postcommunist states, advisors and officials prescribed "shock therapy" for Russia's postcommunist economic reform, the highly controversial strategy for turning the rubble of the socialist economic system into a market economy. Shock therapy was employed to varying degrees and with varying results across East-Central Europe. It mandated an immediate lifting of all wage and price controls, rapid privatization of all state assets, the withdrawal of all meaningful state subsidies in and regulation of the economy including massive cuts in social spending, and the lifting of most trade barriers. In short, it amounted to applying a strict neoclassical formula for pure market capitalism virtually overnight, to shock the system and the people out of socialist practices and into an idealized version of market capitalism.

Debates on whether shock therapy was a success or failure in the postcommunist experience continues to this day.[1] It was a set of policies recommended by a group of neoclassical liberal economists with powerful academic credentials working as independent consultants and through organizations like the International Monetary Fund. This orientation was dominant in the halls of the International Monetary Fund and the World Bank, reflecting the so-called Washington Consensus against state intervention in the economic sphere. The approach rejected a half-century of success of Keynesian principles and became the standard for imposing structural adjustment policies in return for promises of debt relief across the developing world. Those policies translated to convulsions of political and social instability in many countries and generated much resentment against both capitalism and democracy, yet they became and have remained a requirement for integration into the newly-dubbed "globalized" economy.[2]

For Russia, the stringent austerity measures were required for any international support of the monumental economic transformation, which absolutely required such support. The economy was the primary focus of Russia's new leaders in 1992. Indeed, what the international economic officials and consultants failed to communicate and, seemingly, failed even to comprehend was that, in countries such as Poland, Hungary, and the Czech Republic, a total transformation of the political system along with new constitutions came simultaneously with economic change. Yeltsin and his team, however, allowed the existing political institutions to stand while they attempted to transform the economy. They proceeded with a program that included an overnight lifting of all price controls save on a few basic goods on January 2, 1992, allowing full convertibility of the currency, the most rapid privatization of enterprises in history, and an austerity program of spending cuts including in education, health, and subsidies to the elderly and veterans. Over the next thirty-six months, prices rose more than two thousand times their levels prior to price liberalization, when the economy already was in the throes of hyperinflation.[3]

Some, such as Andrei Shleifer and Dan Triesman, in the selection in this chapter, hailed the implementation of their ideas as signaling the success of Russia's economy, proclaiming its return as a "normal country."[4] Others branded the radical approach "cookbook capitalism" and warned of dire consequences.[5] The Great Depression that consumed the developed world in the 1920s and 1930s, ultimately leading to World War II, had long since discredited the view that self-regulated markets can be efficient or stable, that states should refrain from any involvement in the economy. Such an approach led to dramatic global failures, instability, and insecurity and put peoples' very lives at risk. While the extent of application of Keynesian principles, of the appropriate level of state intervention and regulation in the economy, varied widely across capitalist economies in the eight decades since the Depression, it had been universally accepted that some state involvement was required. Suddenly in the late 1980s, however, radical economic theorists who rejected this consensus became the dominant voice, including the dominant voice advising Russia.

In East-Central Europe, most notably in Poland, Hungary, and the Czech Republic where the political systems had also undergone dramatic transformation, the new politicians quickly stepped in, intervening to temper the radical neoclassical prescriptions. Their approach succeeded in stabilizing their economies while protecting the most vulnerable in society, combating the predictable corruption and mitigating threats to the security of the most vulnerable segments of the population. However, in Russia, no such political transformation had taken place. This is a fact that remains grossly underappreciated by most studies of Russia.

In Russia, the entire approach to the economy hearkens back to the "campaigns" of the early years of communist rule and of Stalin's combination of heroism and hysteria in the 1920s and 1930s. The air of panic, of extremism, and of experimentation was all too familiar. The results similarly diverged from the ideals and promises of the propaganda and left massive problems in their wake. It was a Bolshevik approach in terms of strict, top-down rigidity. The stinging irony is that the Bolshevik approach was mandated by economic consultants and advisors from the West. This, combined with the failure to institute political changes at the outset, carried massive implications. With no rules established in the legal or political arenas to establish norms of accountability and transparency, the result in the economy was, as one critical account branded it, "market bolshevism."[6] Such critics warned of the extent and dangers of rampant capital flight out of the country, seeing not entrepreneurship in the rush to privatization so much as extraction, pillaging and theft.[7] This view tends to see not a functioning market economy but rather institutionalized corruption, and the selection from Handelman's *Comrade Criminal* in this chapter explains the rise of this corruption that remains an essential feature of the Russian economy to this day.[8] His analysis also predicted the rise of the old KGB to power and institutionalized corruption.

When Vladimir Putin took the reigns as president in 2000, a dozen or so "oligarchs," as the wealthiest (and most corrupt) new entrepreneurs became known, wielded enormous influence over Russia's economic and political systems, even as they waged battle among each other through organized criminal rings that periodically surged with explosive violence in the streets of major cities[9]. Putin promised, among other things, to clean things up. However, rather than cleaning up, he simply quieted things down by closing the political system. The message he conveyed was powerful and clear: Stay out of politics, leave security to the state, follow instructions when the government issues them, and you can continue to rake in billions of dollars however you wish. Using tactics derived from his career as a KGB officer, within short order, he had two of the most visible figures—Boris Berezovsky and Vladimir Gusinsky—exiled out of the country with their assets frozen and a third, the ambitious Mikhail Khodorkovsky, arrested and put on a public show trial culminating in the state seizing his assets and his imprisonment in Siberia.[10] The message was clear to those left standing: Politics was a closed arena; if you fund politicians other than Putin and his associates, pursue any policies independent of the state, or seek office yourself, you face arrest, imprisonment, and exile.

Those who see success and those who see structural dangers do agree that the Russian economy today is primarily based on commodity resources, such as oil and gas, lumber, and minerals, and heavy industry, such as steel production. Economic status is based largely on informal rules resulting from individual connections, one of unequal favors and access in an environment in which state involvement in the economy is greater than in the 1990s. Putin's authoritarian rule mandated that all follow the state's priorities or face reprisals. As in most commodity-based economies, freedom is mostly a facade. All of this, combined with the institutional corruption, may well prove to be unstable and an untenable formula. There is every reason to expect another deep economic crisis in the near future.[11]

The selections here present varying interpretations of what Russia's economy in fact is today and how it got to this place. Some see Russia's as a "normal" market economy, as one of its architects, Andrei Shliefer contends. Others, such as Handelman, see a fundamentally flawed, corrupt system inconsistent with the principles of openness and freedom central to democratic ideals. It is a large economy whose stability is critical to European and global security alike. The stakes are indeed high.

For Further Reference

Books

Anders Aslund, *Building Capitalism: The Transformation of the Soviet Bloc,* Cornell University Press: 2001.

Chrystia Freeland, *Sale of the Century: Russia's Wild Ride From Communism to Capitalism,* Crown: 2000.

Marshall Goldman, *The Piratization of Russia: Market Reform Goes Awry,* Cambridge University Press: 2003.

Stephen Handelman, *Comrade Criminal: Russia's New Mafia,* Yale University Press: 1997.

Paul Klebnikov, *Godfather of the Kremlin: Boris Berezovsky and the Looting of Russia,* Harcourt: 2000.

Adam Przeworski, *Democracy and the Market: Political and Economic Reforms in Eastern Europe and Latin America,* Cambridge University Press: 1991.

Peter Reddaway and Dmitri Glinski, *The Tragedy of Russia's Reforms: Market Bolshevism Against Democracy,* United States Institute of Peace: 2001.

Janine Wedel, *Collision and Collusion: The Strange Case of Western Aid to Eastern Europe: 1989–1998,* St. Martin's: 1998.

Novels

Mark Ames and Matt Taibbi, *The Exile: Sex, Drugs, and Libel in the New Russia,* Grove Press: 2000.

Andrew Meier, *Black Earth: a Journey Through Russia After the Fall,* WW Norton: 2004.

M. I. Quandoor, *The Last Hunt: A Novel of the New Russia,* iUniverse: 2008.

Susan Richards, *Lost and Found in Russia: Lives in the Post-Soviet Landscape,* Other Press: 2010.

Film

Eastern Promises

NOTES

1. See, for example, Vladimir Popov, "Shock Therapy Versus Gradualism Reconsidered: Lessons From Transition Economies After 15 Years of Reforms," *Comparative Economic Studies,* Vol. 49 (2007), pp. 1–31; Theodore P. Gerber and Michael Hout, "More Shock Than Therapy: Market Transition, Employment and Income in Russia, 1991–1995," *The American Journal of Sociology,* Vol. 104, No. 1 (July 1998), pp. 1–50; Andrei Shleifer, "Government in

Transition," *European Economic Review*, Vol. 41, No. 3–5 (April 1997), pp. 385–410; Thomas W. Hall and John E. Elliott, "Poland and Russia One Decade After Shock Therapy," *Journal of Economic Issues*, Vol. 33 (1999); Anders Aslund, *How Russia Became a Market Economy* (The Brookings Institution, 1995); and John Marangos, "Was Shock Therapy Consistent With Democracy?" *Review of Social Economy*, Vol. 62, No. 2 (2004), pp. 221–243.

2. A thorough discussion of the Washington Consensus and related policies is beyond the scope of this volume; however, the principles and ideas were and remain important for Russia and the world. See Joseph E. Stiglitz, *Globalization and its Discontents* (WW Norton, 2002) and Stiglitz, *Making Globalization Work* (WW Norton, 2006).

3. Paula de Masi and Vincent Koen, "Relative Price Convergence in Russia," *IMF Staff Papers*, Vol. 43, No. 1 (1996), pp. 97–122.

4. See the Shleifer and Triesman selection in this chapter. Also see Anders Aslund, "Russia's Success Story," *Foreign Affairs*, Vol. 73, No. 4 (1994), pp. 58–71.

5. David Stark was skeptical from the beginnings of shock therapy programs in Eastern Europe for the same reasons. See his scathing attack on neoclassical economic programs in his "Path Dependence and Privatization Strategies in East Central Europe," *East European Politics and Societies*, Vol. 6, No. 1 (1992), pp. 17–54.

6. Peter Reddaway and Dmitri Glinski, *The Tragedy of Russia's Reforms: Market Bolshevism against Democracy* (U.S. Institute of Peace Press, 2001).

7. There was extensive activity of all three types. See especially Andrew Barnes, "Comparative Theft: Context and Choice in the Hungarian, Czech, and Russian Transformations: 1989–2000," *East European Politics and Societies*, Vol. 17, No. 3 (2003), pp. 533–565. Also see Enrico Perotti, "Lessons From the Russian Meltdown: The Economics of Soft Legal Constraints," *International Finance*, Vol. 5, No. 3 (2003), pp. 359–399; Mark Kramer, "Capital Flight and Russian Economic Reform," Program on New Approaches to Russian Security, Policy Memo 128 (2000); Vladimir Tikhomirov, "Capital Flight from Post-Soviet Russia," *Europe-Asia Studies*, Vol. 49, No. 4 (1997), pp. 591–615; and Marshall Goldman, *The Piratization of Russia: Russian Reform Goes Awry* (Routledge, 2003).

8. Steven Handelman, *Comrade Criminal: Russia's New Mafia* (Yale University Press, 1995). See also David Satter, *Darkness at Dawn: The Rise of the Russian Criminal State* (Yale University Press, 2003).

9. See Paul Klebnikov, *Godfather of the Kremlin: The Decline of Russia in the Age of Gangster Capitalism* (Harcourt, 2000). Klebnikov, the founding editor of *Forbes Russia* in Moscow, was murdered in Moscow in 2004. No arrest was ever made, and it is widely accepted that the government was involved in his execution.

10. Richard Sakwa, *The Quality of Freedom: Khodorkovsky, Putin and the Yukos Affair* (Oxford University Press, 2009). See also Ostrow, Satarov, and Khakamada, *The Consolidation of Dictatorship in Russia: An Inside View of the Demise of Democracy* (Praeger, 2007), pp. 108–114.

11. Philip Hanson, "The Russian Economic Puzzle: Going Forwards, Backwards or Sideways?" *International Affairs*, Vol. 83, No. 5 (2007), pp. 869–889.

4.1

A Normal Country: Russia after Communism

Andrei Shleifer and Daniel Treisman

During the 1990s, Russia underwent extraordinary transformations. It changed from a communist dictatorship into a multiparty democracy in which officials are chosen in regular elections. Its centrally planned economy was reshaped into a capitalist order based on markets and private property. Its army withdrew peacefully from eastern Europe and the former Soviet republics, allowing the latter to become independent countries. Twenty years ago, only the most naïve idealist could have imagined such a metamorphosis.

Yet the mood among Western observers has been anything but celebratory. By the turn of the century, Russia had come to be viewed as a disastrous failure and the 1990s as a decade of catastrophe for its people. Journalists, politicians and academic experts typically describe Russia not as a middle-income country struggling to overcome its communist past and find its place in the world, but as a collapsed and criminal state.

In Washington, both left and right have converged on this view. To Dick Armey, then Republican House majority leader, Russia had by 1999 become "a looted and bankrupt zone of nuclearized anarchy." To his colleague, Banking Committee Chairman James Leach, Russia was "the world's most virulent kleptocracy," more corrupt than even Mobutu's Zaire. Bernard Sanders, the socialist congressman from Vermont, described Russia's economic performance in the 1990s as a "tragedy of historic proportions"; liberal reforms had produced only "economic collapse," "mass unemployment" and "grinding poverty."

More recently, a glimmer of optimism returned. President Bush, in late 2003, praised President Putin's efforts to make Russia into a "country in which democracy and freedom and the rule of law thrive." But the happy talk did not last long. When Russian prosecutors arrested the oil tycoon Mikhail Khodorkovsky in October 2003, *New York Times* columnist William Satire reported that Russia was now ruled by a "power-hungry mafia" of former KGB and military officers, who had grabbed "the nation by the throat." When the pro-Putin United Russia Party was announced to have won more than 37 percent of the vote in the December

Source: Andrei Shliefer and Daniel Triesman, "A Normal Country: Russia after Communism," *Journal of Economic Perspectives*. Vol. 19, No. 1 Winter 2005. 151–174.

Note: Notes and references have been removed from this article.

2003 parliamentary election, Safire lamented the return of "one-party rule to Russia," and declared the country's experiment with democracy "all but dead."

Are conditions in contemporary Russia as bad as the critics contend? In this article, we examine the country's recent economic and political performance, using a variety of data on growth, macroeconomic stability, income inequality and company finances, as well as reports of election monitors and surveys of business people and crime victims. We find a large gap between the common perception and the facts. After reviewing the evidence, the widespread image of Russia as a uniquely menacing disaster zone comes to seem like the reflection in a distorting mirror—the features are recognizable, but stretched and twisted out of all proportion.

In fact, although Russia's transition has been painful in many ways, and its economic and political systems remain far from perfect, the country has made remarkable economic and social progress. Russia's remaining defects are typical of countries at its level of economic development. Both in 1990 and 2003, Russia was a middle-income country, with GDP per capita around $8,000 at purchasing power parity according to the UN International Comparison Project, a level comparable to that of Argentina in 1991 and Mexico in 1999. Countries in this income range have democracies that are rough around the edges, if they are democratic at all. Their governments suffer from corruption, and their press is almost never entirely free. Most also have high income inequality, concentrated corporate ownership and turbulent macroeconomic performance. In all these regards, Russia is quite normal. Nor are the common flaws of middle-income, capitalist democracies incompatible with further economic and political progress.

To say that Russia has become a "normal" middle-income country is not to overlook the messiness of its politics and economics or to excuse the failures of its leaders. Most middle-income countries are not secure or socially just places to live. Nor are all middle-income countries alike. None of the others has Russia's nuclear arms or its pivotal role in international affairs. Yet other countries around Russia's level of income—from Mexico and Brazil to Malaysia and Croatia—face a common set of economic problems and political challenges, from similarly precarious vantage points. Russia's struggles to meet such challenges closely resemble those of its peers. In the next section, we provide a brief review of key events in Russia's transition, before plunging into a more detailed examination of the facts.

Russia After Communism

In June 1991, Boris Yeltsin became Russia's first elected president. In December, following a failed putsch by communist hardliners that August, Yeltsin agreed with the leaders of Ukraine and Belarus to dissolve the Soviet Union, leaving

Russia independent. Yeltsin's elevation followed several years of partial reform under the last Soviet leader, Mikhail Gorbachev. The previous two years had seen declines in output, worsening shortages and fears of a complete economic and political collapse. In 1989, the average citizen spent 40–68 hours a month standing in line. By April 1991, fewer than one in eight respondents to an opinion poll said they had recently seen meat in state stores, and fewer than one in 12 had seen butter. In fall 1991, CNN predicted starvation that winter.

Once in power, Yeltsin introduced radical economic reforms. In January 1992, most prices were liberalized. Queues disappeared and goods reappeared in stores. A mass privatization program, implemented during 1993–1994, transferred shares in most firms from the government to their managers, workers and the public. By mid-1994, almost 70 percent of the Russian economy was in private hands. In 1995, with the help of the International Monetary Fund, Russia stabilized the ruble. Enacting these reforms proved extremely difficult. The parliament, the unreformed and well-organized Communist Party, and entrenched industrial interests resisted almost every measure.

In 1995, Yeltsin tried to broaden his support ahead of the 1996 presidential election, which the Communist Party leader, Gennady Zyuganov, was expected to win. As part of this political campaign, and in an attempt to balance the budget, Yeltsin agreed to a "loans-for-shares" program, whereby some valuable natural resource enterprises were turned over to major businessmen in exchange for loans to the government. This highly controversial program accelerated the consolidation of a few large financial groups, led by so-called "oligarchs", who enjoyed great political and economic influence. The oligarchs helped Yeltsin with sympathetic coverage on the television networks and in the newspapers they owned.

Despite suffering a heart attack, which was concealed from the voters, Yeltsin won a second presidential term. He accomplished the goal of his life: to prevent communists from regaining power in Russia. But he was a sick man, lacking political and popular support, and much of his focus was on finding a successor. Political gridlock made it hard for the government to collect taxes. As oil prices collapsed in 1997–1998, so did the federal budget, and the financial turmoil that had started in east Asia spread to Russia. The crisis led to a Russian debt default and a sharp depreciation of the ruble; yet, contrary to the expectations of most pundits, it was followed by a rapid economic recovery. [. . .]

Yeltsin ultimately found a successor, Vladimir Putin, whom he appointed Prime Minister in 1999. On January 1, 2000, Yeltsin resigned and Putin became Acting President, subsequently winning the presidential election in March of that year. Over the following four years, Russia's economy grew rapidly, helped by increases in oil prices and the continuing benefits of exchange rate depreciation. By 2003, the Russian government was borrowing money in world markets long term at an interest rate of around 7 percent, indicating significant investor confidence. Most forecasts for Russia's economic growth had turned highly optimistic.

Economic Cataclysm?

The Output "Collapse"

Russia started its transition in the early 1990s as a middle-income country. The United Nations International Comparison Project, which calculates cross-nationally comparable income figures, estimates that Russia's per capita GDP as of 1989 was $8,210—around the level of Ukraine, Argentina, Latvia and South Africa. (By 1991, when Gorbachev left office, it had fallen to $7,780.) This level was higher than Mexico and Brazil, but only about 65–75 percent of that in poorer west European countries such as Portugal, Greece and Spain; less than half the level of France or Italy; and just over one third that of the United States.

That Russia's output contracted catastrophically in the 1990s has become a cliché. According to official Goskomstat statistics, Russian GDP per capita fell about 39 percent in real terms between 1991, when Gorbachev left office, and 1998, when the economic recovery started.

Yet there are three reasons to think that Russia's economic performance in the 1990s was actually far better. First, official statistics greatly exaggerate the true value of Russia's output at the beginning of the decade. Much of recorded GDP under the Soviet Union consisted of military goods, unfinished construction projects, and shoddy consumer products for which there was no demand. In the early 1990s, military procurement dropped sharply. With the introduction of markets, firms also stopped making consumer goods they could not sell. Cutting such production reduces reported economic output, but does not leave consumers any worse off. Moreover, much of reported output under the Soviet system was simply fictitious. To obtain bonuses, managers routinely inflated their production figures. With the end of central planning, managers now wished to *under*report output so as to reduce their tax bill. Consequently, Russia's economic decline was probably smaller than officially reported.

Second, Russia's unofficial economy grew rapidly in the 1990s. Estimating unofficial activity is difficult. But one common technique for measuring the growth of the whole economy—both official and unofficial—is to use electricity consumption, on the theory that even underground firms must use electricity. Figure 1 shows the trend in reported GDP, deflated for price rises, between 1990 and 2002, alongside figures for electricity consumption. While official GDP fell 26 percent in this period, electricity consumption fell only 18 percent. This

Figure 1. Measuring Economic Change in Russia, 1990–2002

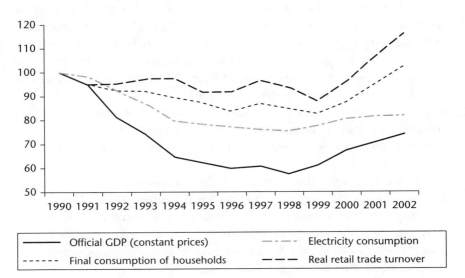

Official GDP (constant prices)	Electricity consumption
Final consumption of households	Real retail trade turnover

Source: Goskomstat Rossii, *Rossiiskiy Statisticheskiy Yezhegodnik 2001, 2003, Rossia v Tsifrakh 2002,* *Goskomstat updates.*

suggests that Russia's output decline in the 1990s was not as sharp as the official statistics indicate. Since under market conditions firms are likely to use electricity more rationally, even the observed decline in electricity consumption may overstate the output drop.

Third, other statistics suggest that average living standards fell little during the decade, and, in some important respects, improved. Retail trade (in constant prices) rose 16 percent between 1990 and 2002, as shown in Figure 1. Goskomstat's figures for final consumption of households (in constant prices) rose by about 3 percent during 1990–2002. Average living space increased from 16 square meters per person in 1990 to 19 in 2000, and the share of this living space owned by citizens doubled during the decade, from 26 to 58 percent. The number of Russians going abroad as tourists rose from 1.6 million in 1993 to 4.3 million in 2000. The shares of households with radios, televisions, tape recorders, refrigerators, washing machines and electric vacuum cleaners all increased between 1991 and 2000. Private ownership of cars doubled, rising from 14 cars per 100 households in 1991 to 27 in 2000, with large increases occurring in almost all regions. At the same time, however, consumption of some previously state-provided or state-subsidized services—trips to the movies, theaters, museums and state-subsidized summer camps for children—fell.

Russia has, without doubt, experienced an increase in inequality (as we discuss below). But some indicators suggest improvement also toward the bottom of the social pyramid. Since 1993 (when comprehensive figures begin), the proportion of Russia's housing with running water has increased from 66 to 73 percent; the share with hot water grew from 51 to 59 percent; and the percentage with central heating rose from 64 to 73 percent. Since 1990, the proportion of apartments with telephones has increased from 30 to 49 percent.

One indicator often taken as evidence of a catastrophic decline in living standards is the sharp drop in Russian life expectancy in the 1990s. Between 1990 and 2000, average life expectancy fell by about four years, from 69.2 to 65.3. [. . .]

Most specialists agree that the rise in mortality in the early 1990s, concentrated as it was among middle-aged men, had much to do with increasing alcohol abuse. This may have been stimulated by a sharp drop in the relative price of vodka in these years. For the average monthly income, Russians could buy 10 liters of vodka in 1990, but 47 in 1994. Several causes of death that increased dramatically have been associated with binge drinking. Stress induced by the economic transition may also have contributed, as Brainerd and Cutler argue. Either way, there is little sign the increased death rate was caused by falling income. As per capita GDP rose by about 30 percent between 1998 and 2002, life expectancy again dropped by 2.2 years.

A close look at Figure 1 also casts doubt on the popular theory that Russia's economic decline was caused by misguided government policies pursued in the 1990s, especially Yeltsin's privatization program and his "loans-for-shares" scheme. As Figure 1 makes clear, most of the fall in both Russia's official GDP and electricity consumption occurred prior to 1994, before the significant part of the mass privatization program was completed and before the "loans-for-shares" program was even contemplated.

Comparing Russia's economic performance in the 1990s to that of other post-communist countries suggests two additional points, illustrated in Figure 2. First, officially measured output fell in all the postcommunist economies of eastern Europe and the former Soviet Union, with no exceptions. It declined in new democracies, such as Russia and Poland, and in continuing dictatorships, such as Belarus and Tajikistan; in rapid reformers, such as the Czech Republic and Hungary, and in very slow reformers, such as Ukraine and Uzbekistan. The universality of the contraction suggests common causes. One possibility is a universal decrease in military and economically useless activities that were previously counted as output. A second is the temporary dislocation that all countries experienced as their planning systems disintegrated. Consistent with both these explanations, officially measured output began to recover after a few years almost everywhere. Second, the depth of the measured contraction was greater in some countries than in others. Generally, it was smaller in eastern Europe and the Baltic states than in the rest of the former Soviet Union. Russia's official output fell slightly less than average for the 14 former Soviet republics for which figures are available.

The patterns of decline in the postcommunist countries challenge another common theory about the output contraction. Some argue that excessive speed of reform exacerbated the decline and compare the "gradualism" of China's economic policies favorably to the "shock therapy" of Russia's. In fact, among the east European and former Soviet countries, there is no obvious relationship between speed of reform and change in official output. Comparisons across these countries must be tentative since the quality of statistics varies, and the uneven impact of civil disorder and war complicates drawing connections between economic policy and performance. However, among the countries that contracted least according to the official figures are both rapid reformers (Estonia, Poland, Czech Republic) and slow or nonreformers (Belarus, Uzbekistan). Those with the largest declines also include both nonreformers (Tajikistan, Turkmenistan) and some that tried to reform (Moldova). A comparison of Russia with Ukraine is particularly instructive (see Figure 2). Ukraine had a large population (about 52 million), an industrial economy, significant natural resources and a "culture" similar to Russia's prior to transition. Unlike Russia, it retained the old communist leadership, albeit renamed, and pursued more cautious reforms, keeping a much larger share of the economy in state hands. Yet Ukraine's official drop in per capita GDP of 45 percent between 1991 and 2001 was almost twice as large as Russia's.

In comparison with other nations of eastern Europe and the former Soviet Union, Russia's economy performed roughly as one might have expected. Our best estimate is that its genuine output drop between 1990 and 2001 was small and probably completely reversed by 2003 (Aslund, 2003). Considering the distorted demand, inflated accounting and uselessness of much of the prereform output, Russians today are probably on average better off than they were in 1990.

Financial Crises

The 1990s was a decade of extreme macroeconomic turbulence for Russia. Between December 1991 and December 2001, the ruble's value dropped by more than 99 percent against the dollar. Three years after the authorities managed to stabilize inflation in 1995, a financial crisis led to a devaluation of the ruble and a government moratorium on foreign debt payments.

But such financial crises are common among emerging market economies. Bad as the 99 percent drop in the ruble's value sounds, an examination of the IMF's *International Financial Statistics* (April 2002) shows that eleven other

Figure 2. Official GDP Per Capita in Postcommunist Countries, First 10 Years of Transition

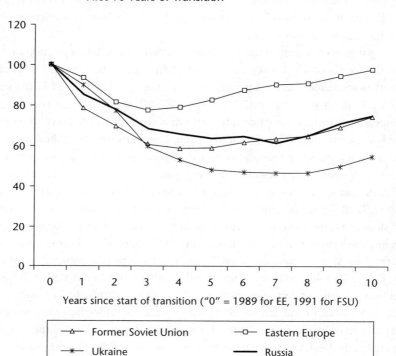

Years since start of transition ("0" = 1989 for EE, 1991 for FSU)

—△— Former Soviet Union   —□— Eastern Europe
—＊— Ukraine   —— Russia

Source: Calculated from World Bank, *World Development Indicators 2003* and EBRD *Transition Report. 1997.* Eastern Europe: unweighted average of Albania, Bulgaria, Hungary, Poland, Romania, Slovakia, Slovenia. Former Soviet Union: unweighted average of Armenia, Belarus, Estonia, Georgia, Kazakhstan, Kyrgyzstan, Latvia, Lithuania, Moldova, Russia, Tajikistan, Turkmenistan, Ukraine, Uzbekistan. Data unavailable for Azerbaijan.

countries—including Brazil, Turkey, Ukraine and Belarus—suffered even larger currency declines during the 1990s. In the 1980s, depreciations this large were even more frequent, with larger ones recorded by Peru, Argentina, Bolivia, Brazil, Uruguay, Nicaragua, Vietnam, Lebanon and even Poland, later seen as the greatest success story of transition from socialism. [. . .]

Economic Inequality

Russia's economic reforms are said to have exacerbated economic inequality, with privatization often fingered as the primary culprit. The European Bank for Reconstruction and Development wrote: "[U]nder the 'shares-for-loans' scheme implemented in 1995, many of the key resource-based companies fell into the hands of a small group of financiers, the so-called 'oligarchs.' This has led to very sharp increases in wealth and income inequality—by 1997 the Gini coefficient for income in Russia was around 0.5."

Inequality *has* increased sharply in Russia since the fall of communism. There is some question about the precise numbers, but no dispute about the trend. Russia's official statistical agency, Goskomstat, shows the Gini coefficient for money incomes rising from .26 in 1991 to .41 in 1994, after which it stabilized at about .40 through the end of the decade. The World Bank, in various issues of the annual *World Development Reports* and *World Development Indicators,* gives figures for Russia's Gini for expenditure of .496 in 1993, .480 in 1996, .487 in 1998, and .460 in 2000. For comparison, the Goskomstat figure of .41 is almost exactly the same as that for the United States (.408 in 1997). The higher World Bank estimate of .496 is about that of Malaysia (.492) or the Philippines (.462), but below that of Hong Kong (.522), Mexico (.531), South Africa (.593) or Brazil (.607).

The trouble with the claim that privatization caused inequality is that inequality came first. Russia's Gini coefficient rose sharply between 1991 and 1993, and peaked in 1994, before any effects of privatization could possibly materialize. Nor is unemployment responsible. In 1992–1993, unemployment remained below 6 percent. It was in 1994–1998 that it grew to 13.2 percent, while inequality declined slightly. The growth of entrepreneurial income also played at most a limited role. Branko Milanovic of the World Bank finds that 77 percent of the inequality increase can be attributed to growing dispersion of wage incomes. While some Russians worked in successful firms that rapidly benefited from free prices and open trade, others remained in declining firms and in the state sector. Unfortunate as the growth of inequality has been, it is largely the result of the upheavals associated with rationalizing economic activity.

Oligarchical Capitalism

Russia's economic reforms are often said to have fueled the rise of a small class of "oligarchs," who stand accused of stripping assets from the companies they acquired. This, in turn, is said to have depressed investment and economic growth.

Russia's big business is certainly dominated by a few tycoons, as Guriev and Rachinsky argue in their contribution to this symposium. However, in this Russia is quite typical. In almost all developing capitalist economies and even in most developed countries, the largest firms are either state or family controlled, with a few dominant families often controlling a large share of national production

through financial and industrial groups. [. . .] Following the Asian financial crisis of 1998, this system of political ownership and control has been pejoratively
rechristened "crony capitalism," even though it has been associated with some
of the most rapid growth ever seen, as well as a remarkable recovery from crisis
in Malaysia and South Korea. Such patterns of ownership have also emerged in
transition economies from Latvia to the central Asian states.

Have Russia's oligarchs depressed economic performance? Russia's tycoons,
like those elsewhere in the developing world (not to mention America's robber
barons of the nineteenth century), grew rich in part through deals with the government. But the claim that this accounts for poor growth in Russia makes little
sense. Russia's sharp decline in official output came before—not after—the oligarchs emerged on the scene in 1995–1996. A few years of stagnation followed
and then rapid growth. Oligarch-controlled companies have performed extremely
well, and far better than many comparable companies that remained controlled
by the state or by their Soviet-era managers. They are responsible for much of
the dramatic increase in output in recent years, as well as the amazing stock
market boom.

Consider three of the most notorious cases. In "loans-for-shares," Mikhail
Khodorkovsky (now in jail) obtained a major stake in the oil company Yukos. Boris
Berezovsky (now in exile), won control of the oil company Sibneft along with his
then-partner Roman Abramovich. Vladimir Potanin acquired the nickel producer
Norilsk Nickel. Between 1996 and 2001, the reported pretax profits of Yukos,
Sibneft and Norilsk Nickel rose in real terms by 36, 10 and 5 times, respectively.
Their stock market valuations also soared (those of Yukos and Sibneft rising by
more than 30 times in real terms). This performance is markedly better than that
of the gas monopoly Gazprom or the electricity utility UES, which stayed under
state control, or of major private companies, such as Lukoil, that remained controlled by preprivatization management.

Have the oligarchs stripped assets from the companies they acquired in privatization? The audited financial statements of these companies suggest they actually invested, especially since 1998. Yukos' assets rose from $5.3 billion in 1998 to
$14.4 billion in 2002, although this might reflect in part higher world oil prices
(see Table 1). Norilsk Nickel's assets rose from $6.6 billion in 1999 to $9.7 billion
in 2002. Sibneft's assets did fall from 1996 to 1999, in part due to an accounting
change (which might reflect asset stripping). But since 1999, they have increased
from $4.3 billion to $7.5 billion in 2002. Recently, the major oligarchs have been
investing hundreds of millions of dollars annually in their companies. In 2002,
Yukos invested $1.26 billion in property, plant, and equipment, and Sibneft made
capital expenditures of $959 million. Guriev and Rachinsky, in a systematic study
of the performance of oligarch-controlled companies in 2001, found that such

companies invested significantly more that year than firms controlled by other Russian owners.

In contrast, the greatest asset stripping scandals have concerned companies that remained under state control. Gazprom's former management has been accused of stealing assets via complicated networks of trading companies. The state-owned airline Aeroflot's reported assets dropped between 1998 and 2001. By and large, the companies privatized to the oligarchs performed far better than those left under state control. That the leading oligarch-controlled oil companies generally outperformed other oil firms such as Lukoil, which remained under Soviet-era management, suggests that their success was due to better management and not only to rising oil prices. [. . .]

In fact, the claim that the oligarchs privatized companies in order to strip their assets and are impeding economic growth has it precisely backward. The oligarchs stripped assets from *state*-controlled companies in order to buy others in privatization. Indeed, the concern with such theft from state firms was one of the reasons to accelerate privatization in 1992. The oligarchs also tried to buy assets in privatization at the lowest possible prices, often offering politicians various deals. Once in control, they attempted to increase their ownership stakes, both legally and illegally. But once oligarchs became full owners, they acted as

Table 1. Total Assets and Investments of Three Leading Russian Companies

	1996	1997	1998	1999	2000	2001	2002
Yukos							
Total assets, bn US $	4.7	5.2	5.3	6.0	10.3	10.5[e]	14.4[e]
Investment,[a] mn US $				226	589[e]	954[e]	1263[e]
Sibneft							
Total assets, bn US $	7.6	5.6[d]	5.0	4.3	4.6	5.7	7.5
Investment,[b] mn US $			154	129	231	619	959
Norilsk Nickel							
Total assets, bn US $				6.6	7.2	10.9[c]	9.7
Investment,[b] mn US $				168	638	510[c]	351

Sources: Audited financial statements and annual reports.

[a] Additions to property, plant and equipment.
[b] Capital expenditures.
[c] Restated in 2002 Annual Report.
[d] Assets reduced by $1.3 bn because of accounting change.
[e] As in 2002 Annual Report.

economic theory predicts: they invested to improve their companies' performance. This is what oligarchs have done in every other country—from J.P. Morgan and John D. Rockefeller to Silvio Berlusconi and the owners of Korean chaebol.

In sum, Russia's economy is not a model of capitalism that one finds in introductory textbooks. Like other middle-income countries, Russia suffers from inequality, financial crises and a large unofficial sector. Economic and political power are intimately intertwined. Nonetheless, Russia started the 1990s a disintegrating, centrally planned economy and ended it a market system in a burst of rapid growth. [. . .]

Corruption

In the late 1990s, the then Chairman of the U.S. House Banking Committee, James Leach, wrote that he had made a study of the world's most corrupt regimes, including the Philippines under Marcos, Zaire under Mobutu and Indonesia under Suharto. Bad as these were, each was outdone by the "pervasiveness of politically tolerated corruption" in postcommunist Russia. Other perceptions of corruption in Russia are equally grim. The anticorruption advocacy group Transparency International (TI) compiles annual ratings of countries' "perceived corruption," based on a range of business surveys. The World Bank has compiled a similar composite rating. Both of these make use, predominantly though not entirely, of surveys of business people or ratings by business consultancies based outside the relevant countries. In both ratings, Russia scores toward the bottom. For instance, in the 2001 version of the World Bank's "graft" index, Russia was 142 out of 160 countries. In TI's 2002 corruption perceptions index, Russia ranked 71 out of 102 countries.

But what about sources less dependent on the perception of outsiders? In summer 1999, the World Bank and the European Bank for Reconstruction and Development (EBRD) conducted a survey of business managers in 22 postcommunist countries. They asked respondents to estimate the share of annual revenues that "firms like yours" typically devoted to unofficial payments to public officials "in order to get things done." Such payments might be made, the questionnaire added, to facilitate connection to public utilities, to obtain licenses or permits, to improve relations with tax collectors or in relation to customs or imports. They also asked respondents to what extent the sale of parliamentary laws, presidential decrees, court decisions and such had directly affected their business, in the hope of measuring the extent to which policymakers were co-opted by business interests.

Comparing Russian business managers to their peers in other postcommunist countries, Russia falls in the middle on both the "burden of bribery" and "state capture" dimensions. If one graphs per capita GDP on the horizontal axis and these measures of corruption on the vertical axis, Russia is almost exactly on the ordinary least squares regression line in both cases. Administrative corruption is very high in the really poor countries, such as Uzbekistan, Armenia and Azerbaijan, lower in Russia, Bulgaria and Lithuania, and lower still in the relatively rich Hungary and Slovenia, as shown in Figure 3.

How does corruption in Russia affect individuals? The United Nations conducts a cross-national survey of crime victims. In 1996–2000, it asked urban respondents in a number of countries the following question: "In some countries, there is a problem of corruption among government, or public officials. During—*last year*—has any government official, for instance a customs officer, a police officer or inspector in your country asked you, or expected you, to pay a bribe for his service?" The proportion of respondents saying they had experienced demands for or expectations of bribes in the last year in Russia (16.6 percent) was lower than that in Argentina, Brazil, Romania or Lithuania, as shown in Table 3. Again, a simple regression shows that the rate for Russia is almost exactly what one would expect given its per capita **GDP**.

Figure 3. Administrative Corruption in Postcommunist Countries, EBRD Survey of Business Managers, 1999 (BEEPS)

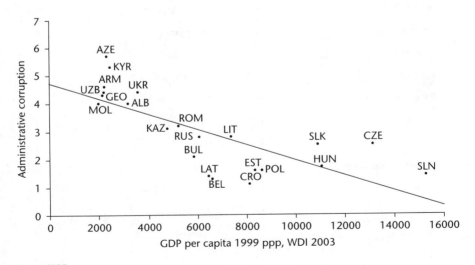

Source: EBRD.
Note: "Administrative corruption" = percentage of revenues paid in bribes by "firms like yours."

Looking at crime in general, the reported victimization rate in Russia is not particularly high. Only 26 percent of Moscow respondents said in 2000 that they had been victimized the previous year by property crimes, robbery, sexual assault, assault, or bribery—compared to 34 percent in Prague, 41 percent in Tallin (Estonia), 44 percent in Rio de Janeiro, and 61 percent in Buenos Aires. Moscow's rate was almost exactly that reported by urban respondents in Finland (26.6 percent) and lower than that for England and Wales (34.4 percent).

Table 2. Percentage of Respondents Who Had Been Victimized by Administrative Bribery, 1996–2000, Major Cities

Albania	59.1	Slovak Republic	13.5
Argentina	30.2	Paraguay	13.3
Indonesia	29.9	Hungary	9.8
Bolivia	24.4	Croatia	9.5
India (Mumbai)	22.9	Estonia	9.3
Lithuania	22.9	Costa Rica	9.2
Mongolia	21.3	Macedonia, FYR	7.4
India (New Delhi)	21.0	South Africa	6.9
Azerbaijan	20.8	Czech Republic	5.7
Belarus	20.6	Philippines	4.3
Colombia	19.5	Botswana	2.8
Uganda	19.5	Netherlands	0.9
Kyrgyz Republic	19.3	Northern Ireland	0.8
Romania	19.2	Denmark	0.5
Brazil	17.1	Scotland	0.5
Russian Federation	**16.6**	Finland	0.4
Georgia	16.6	England and Wales	0.3
Bulgaria	16.4	Sweden	0.2
Ukraine	16.2	Spain (Barcelona)	0
Latvia	14.3		

Source: UN International Crime Victims Surveys, UN Human Development Report, 2002, Table 21, and Alvazzi del Frale and J. van Kesteren, "Some Preliminary Tables from the International Crime Victims Surveys," *Criminal Victimisation in Urban Europe*, UNICRI, Turin, 2003.

Conclusion

Russia's economy is no longer the shortage-ridden, militarized, collapsing bureaucracy of 1990. It has metamorphosed into a marketplace of mostly private firms, producing goods and services to please consumers instead of planners. The economy has been growing at an impressive pace. The country's political order, too, has changed beyond recognition. A few business magnates control much of the country's immense raw materials reserves and troubled banking system, and lobby hard behind the scenes for favored policies. Small businesses are burdened by corruption and regulation. Still, the dictatorship of the party has given way to electoral democracy. Russia's once all-powerful Communist Party no longer penetrates all aspects of social life nor sentences dissidents to Arctic labor camps. Instead, it campaigns for seats in parliament. The press, although struggling against heavy-handed political interventions, is still far more professional and independent than the stilted propaganda machine of the mid-1980s. In slightly over a decade, Russia has become a typical middle-income, capitalist democracy.

So why the dark—at times almost paranoid—view? Why the hyperbole about kleptocracy, economic cataclysm and KGB takeovers? Why are Russian conditions often portrayed as comparable to those in Zaire or Iran, rather than to the far more similar realities of Argentina or Turkey?

Although many factors may have been involved, we believe that the exaggerated despair over Russia was fueled by a fundamental and widespread misconception. Many Western observers thought that, as of the early 1990s, Russia was a highly developed, if not wealthy, country. With its brilliant physicists and chess players, its space program and its global military influence, Russia did not look like Argentina or South Korea. Thinking that Russia started off highly developed, these observers saw its convergence to the norm for middle-income countries as a disastrous aberration. The same misconception informed some academic analyses. One recent paper, for example, makes the remarkable observation that although institutions to support the rule of law are imperfect in all countries, "between Russia and most other developed, capitalist societies there was a qualitative difference." Indeed, there was a qualitative difference. Russia was never a "developed, capitalist society."

Such misconceptions have important consequences for western policy toward Russia. They predispose decision makers to overreact to the inevitable volatility of Russian economic and political life. The result is extreme mood swings in the West's approach to Russia. When things go "well," markets and political leaders respond with enthusiastic rhetoric, ratcheting expectations up to ever more unrealistic levels. When things go "badly," western Russia-watchers are prone to panic or denunciations and too ready to consider changing course completely. The discourse changes in a matter of days from one of partnership to one of isolation and containment. Such exaggerated swings are not helpful to either Russia or the West.

What does the future hold for Russia? Some see the sudden spurt of growth over the last five years as an indicator of more to come and expect Russia soon to join Hungary and Poland in the community of poor developed countries, leaving behind the middle-income developing ones. They emphasize the country's advanced human capital, its reformed tax system and its mostly open economy. Others see a serious barrier to growth in the bureaucratic regulations and politicized interventions. In politics, optimists anticipate continuing expansion of democratic competition and the emergence of a more vigorous civil society. Pessimists see an accelerating slide toward an authoritarian regime that will be managed by security service professionals under the fig-leaf of formal democratic procedures.

None of these predictions can be ruled out. However, thinking about Russia as a normal, middle-income country suggests the implausibility of extreme forecasts. Middle-income countries rarely revert from democracy to full-fledged authoritarianism, although they often renegotiate the boundary between the two. Their democracies are incomplete, unpredictable and subject to temporary reversals. When they grow at all, middle-income countries tend to grow in spurts that are often interrupted by financial crises. Russia has probably destroyed enough of the vestiges of central planning to stay a market economy, albeit one with flawed institutions and much counterproductive state intervention. Its bureaucracy will remain corrupt, although it will become less corrupt as the country grows richer.

That Russia is *only* a normal middle-income democracy is, of course, a disappointment to those who had hoped for or expected more. But that Russia today has largely broken free of its past, that it is no longer "the evil empire," threatening both its own people and the rest of the world, is an amazing and admirable achievement.

4.2

The Triumph of Bureaucratic Capitalism

Lilia Shevtsova

The economy Putin is leaving to Russia looks impressive and might be the envy of previous Russian and Soviet leaders. The gross domestic product has risen during his presidency from $200 billion in 1999 to $920 billion in 2006 (in current dollars); gold and currency reserves have risen from $12.7 billion in 1999 to $303.86 billion in February 2007. The reserves of the stabilization fund, into which oil revenues are deposited, have reached $70 billion. In 2006 the trade proficit was more than $120 billion, and the budget proficit is 7.5 percent of the gross domestic product. The Russian economy is now the twelfth largest in the world. In macroeconomic terms, as Anders Aslund argues, Russia "is very strong": no G7 country can compete with Russia in fiscal responsibility. Although economic growth has been slowing since 2005 (from 10 percent in 2000 to 6.8 percent in 2006), it still looks fairly impressive (economic growth in the first half of 2007 amounted to 7.8 percent). A boom is continuing, not only in the extractive sectors of the economy but also in construction, trade, and the service and banking sectors. Russian business has shown that it is able to organize large-scale production, successfully competing against international corporations. Russia, which in the 1990s had to beg humbly for loans, repaid its debt to the Paris Club ahead of schedule. The number of major businessmen in Russia is increasing more than twice as fast as in the United States. In 2005 the number of dollar millionaires in Russia grew by 17.4 percent compared to a 6 percent increase in the United States.

However, as with everything else in Russia, the economy has a false bottom. The causes of the economy's success give no grounds for optimism, mainly because the success is due to high oil prices and has been achieved partially by sectors protected from foreign competition. A collapse of the oil price could plunge the Russian economy into a recession, and people remember what a fall in the oil price means. Gaidar has emphasized that the sixfold decrease in the oil price in 1986 led to the collapse of the USSR and the twofold fall in 1998 caused a financial crisis that almost finished off a barely breathing Russian economy. The government technocrats try to reassure the public that the economy would

---

Source: Lilia Shevtsova, "The Triumph of Bureaucratic Capitalism," Russia--Lost in Transition: The Yeltsin and Putin Legacies. Carnegie Endowment for International Peace, 2007. 118–131.

Note: Notes and references have been removed from this article.

survive even if the oil price fell to $25 a barrel, but then they also claimed that the Russian economy was stable in 1998, immediately before its collapse.

Independent Russian economists, like Andrei Illarionov, Putin's former economic adviser, constantly warn that current growth is not based on solid foundations. Many predict an inevitable devaluation of the ruble, which may result in another crisis. They warn that wages and incomes in Russia have been growing systematically faster than productivity. As a result, the share of consumption in GDP has increased at the expense of investment (gross investment amounts to no more than 20 percent of GDP).

There are other causes for concern. The government cannot bring inflation down below 10 percent, and the banking system is not fulfilling its role as mediator: financial flows in the raw materials sector are not being transmitted to other sectors. The banks siphon money off into the shadows, and they service rentiers living off their dividends and sometimes even criminal gangs. The government has no idea what to do about the negative impact of the flood of petrodollars, evident primarily in a strengthening of the ruble that stimulates imports and hits Russian industry. Russia has managed to pay off its national debt (in 2006 it amounted to $48.1 billion), but the corporate debt of Russian companies has risen from $30 billion in 1998 to $159.5 billion in 2006 (that amounts to 16.2 percent of GDP) and the corporate debt of Russian banks in 2006 has increased twofold, amounting to $100 billion. Russia's foreign trade accounts for 45 percent of GDP (in China this indicator is closer to 70 percent), which warns us that the Russian economy is cut off from the rest of the world and that its goods are not competitive.

Russian investors prefer to invest abroad. The number and the scale of deals in which Russian companies acquire assets abroad are quite amazing. This trend is now called "the export of capital." In 2006 investments in the Russian economy amounted to $150 billion and Russian "export of capital" reached $140 billion (according to unofficial sources, more than $60 billion has been transferred from Russia to Britain in the past six years). The names of the people responsible for Russian "export of capital" can be found on the Forbes "rich list." In 2006 foreign direct investments (FDI) into the Russian economy amounted to $31 billion (two and a half times more than in 2005). Still, this constituted only 3 percent of GDP, whereas a good proportion should be 5 to 6 percent, which would give the economy a boost. In 2005 up to 90 percent of FDI was directed into the energy-related areas and in 2006, 60 to 70 percent. (However, the plunging of investments in the commodity areas was a result not of diversification of the economy but of growing risks). Capital inflow in the first half of 2007 amounted to a record-breaking $67 billion (capital inflow for the first half of 2006 was a respectable $42 billion), but most of it was made up of loans and speculative operations.

The World Economic Forum confirmed that in 2006 Russia had fallen from 62nd to 72nd place in its rating for the level of use of information technology. Analyzing the difference between China and India on the one hand, and Russia and Brazil on the other, the observers pointed to the fact that "the former are competing with the West for 'intellectual capital' by seeking to build up top-notch universities, investing in high value-added and technologically intensive industries. Russia and Brazil are benefiting from high commodity prices but are not attempting to invest their windfall in long-term economic development." At the beginning of 2007 Yegor Gaidar maintained that Russia has to deal with two parallel trends: the gradual depletion of the state's revenue sources and increasing social obligations, which may bring a crisis as early as 2015.

That proves that the Kremlin team has no ground for complacency. Indeed, unresolved issues are accumulating for which no one in the Kremlin has a solution. How can Russian business be stimulated? What strategy should be adopted for economic development? How should Russia insure itself against a fall in the price of oil?

There is no more argument about what economic model—dirigiste, liberal, or populist—is developing in Russia. Putin's team has chosen dirigisme, and during his presidency a bureaucratic capitalism has been established that serves the interests of the bureaucratic corporation. The share of the private sector in Russia's gross domestic product shrank from 70 percent in 2004 to 65 percent in 2005 and continues to fall. In 2004–2006 the state's share of the capitalization of the securities market increased by one and a half times to 30 percent of the total, amounting to $190 billion. The state, in the form of the bureaucracy, has not only become an aggressive player in the economy but is also the regulator deciding the rules, which it naturally sets in its own favor. This undermines market principles. The predominance in the Russian economy of "sharks"—state- or partially state-controlled financial and industrial corporations—dents the prospects of small and medium businesses. There are only six small businesses per one thousand of the population, against no fewer than thirty in the European Union. Some 15 million people, about 20 percent of the workforce, are employed in this sector of the economy. That is between three and three and a half times less than the European level. Small-and medium-sized businesses account for only 13 percent of Russia's GDP, which reflects the business atmosphere in the country. Monopolization by sharks rules out diversification of the economy, which requires an abundance of small- and medium-sized fish.

It is surprising that these problems appear not to disturb in the slightest the majority of economic analysts—Russian or Western—who have been in a state of euphoria over the success of the Russian economy for several years now. They have some serious arguments to support their optimism. Dividends are increasing, economic growth continues, initial public offerings (IPOs) are bringing billions of dollars to Russian companies. The total is expected to be $30 billion in 2007, twice as much as in 2006. It might seem that in Russia the economy and politics are quite separate areas, functioning independently of one another, and indeed, for the time being, the negative processes in politics are not preventing people from making money. The moment is approaching, however, when inefficient government will inevitably take its toll in a highly destructive manner—not least on the reputation of optimistic economic analysts.

There is, of course, a logic in the fact that a monopoly of political power in Russia is accompanied by state monopolism in the economy. The tradition of the regime's swallowing property has again prevailed, which testifies to the fact that a personalized regime never tolerates competition in any sphere and seeks absolute control over its environment, even if it damages economic efficiency. I am not by any means saying that all state expansion is a bad thing. We are looking here at intervention in the economy by a particular kind of state, one that does not respect the rule of law and operates on the basis of slippery, unofficial rules. Even these rules the state does not observe consistently. The expansion of a state not based on the rule of law makes corruption inevitable and clear principles inoperable, driving business into a gray area. In fact, in the case of Russia, we are dealing with a bureaucratic corporation that privatized the state structure and through it controls the economy. Ironically, the collapse of communism has allowed the bureaucratic apparatus to use state power in its interests more effectively. Privatization of the state, which is the key economic regulator, does not leave any room for observing property rights or economic laws. No amount of economic reform can stimulate business activity while the state is the servant of the bureaucratic corporation and refuses to operate in a competitive environment.

One of the reasons given by the ruling elite for expanding the state's role in the economy is that Russia needs to create mega-companies capable of competing successfully in world markets, or "national champion companies," as they are called. The elite also considers it a matter of prestige to create gigantic companies in order to confirm Russia's claim to a global role. The creation of national champion companies is proceeding apace, with Gazprom and Rosneft swallowing smaller companies, Aeroflot buying up regional airlines, and companies that design and construct aircraft (Sukhoy, Mig, Irkut, Tupolev, and Ilyushin) merging. Rosoboronexport is monopolizing the arms trade, Transneft is preparing to merge with Transnefteprodukt in the oil industry, and so on. This trend toward creating mega-companies is to be observed also in China, India, and Brazil. There is clearly a pattern here that suggests that countries trying to make a breakthrough create gigantic companies of this kind that can attract capital and technology. Gazprom plays almost the same role in the Russian economy as Tata

Group does in India, where its profits amount to almost 2.6 percent of GDP. Experience has shown, however, that gigantic companies supported by the state limit competition and lead to stagnation of the economy. India is managing to prevent this, but in Russia the giant companies controlled by the bureaucracy are holding back economic growth.

The centralization of the economy also partially results from a simplistic understanding of how innovation arises. It is widely believed in Russia that only large companies can make breakthroughs in innovation. In reality, as research by the World Bank has found, innovation comes to a significant extent from small businesses operating in a competitive environment. By delegating economic powers to provincial authorities, China has achieved a dramatic improvement in its business climate and in innovation. The centralization of power in Russia, however, and the regime's support for its megacompanies, is leading to stagnation and a preoccupation on the part of economic players with rent-seeking behavior.

While the state is busy reestablishing itself in the economy no one thinks about reform. This lack of reform effort confirms that a centralized regime is incapable of creating a dynamic and diversified post-industrial economy. Its primary concern is to safeguard its own interests through a pact between the authorities and a section of big business loyal to the regime. Anything threatening that—competition, the inalienability of private property, open court hearings, the transparency of decision making, business ethics, or freedom of the press—must be restricted. Such restriction shuts off the air supply that would enable a normal market to develop. Personalized power, as it ponders ways of surviving beyond 2008, is most certainly not willing to introduce reforms that might cause instability in the run-up to the elections. The price of oil is also at work, enabling the regime to relax and forget reform. Reforms are introduced only in response to a crisis, not when petrodollars are raining down from the skies and you can live, as in the Soviet era, with subsidized consumption.

The functioning of the economy under direct or indirect state control is entirely predictable. "Our state is currently inefficient, and consequently so are the overwhelming majority of state companies," the minister of economic development, German Gref, once admitted. The inefficiency of Russian bureaucratic capitalism is widely acknowledged. "The economy is now at the limit for developing under the existing model," admitted Alexander Shokhin, the president of the Russian Union of Industrialists and Entrepreneurs. [. . .]

Forecasts are being downgraded. The technocrats within the government admit they are unlikely to get inflation down to 2 to 4 percent before 2010, which would allow interest rates to fall to a level where enterprises could borrow to invest. In practice this means that Russians are unlikely to see investment-driven growth and that the economy will continue to function on the basis of consumer demand. Inflation, however, is already reining in this consumer demand, which indicates that the economy is gradually losing its engines of growth and has nothing to replace them with.

These obvious signs of stagnation fail to cool the optimism of the supporters of dirigisme. In search of sustaining arguments, they like to refer to the success of state capitalism in East Asia and China. Perhaps they do not realize that they are calling for Russia to continue along the path that the Asian Tigers abandoned after their model led to crisis. Russia's supporters of a dirigiste economy also prefer to ignore the fact that China's 11 percent economic growth rate is due not to the state sector but primarily to the private sector and low labor costs. China's economic success also results from a low level of social development and the fact that the state does not concern itself with social welfare. If it tries to imitate the Chinese scenario, Russia will risk not only sliding back to the level of a preindustrial society but also of failing to insure against upheavals. By giving the bureaucracy a free rein in the economy the Kremlin has reverted to a point the world has left behind, with the exception of underdeveloped countries, most of which are dependent on the export of raw materials.

It is perfectly true that when Charles de Gaulle, whom some Russian supporters of state capitalism like to mention, came to power, he increased state intervention in the economy. The president of France had his representatives in every ministry and in every province, but they were there to promote reform, not to maintain the status quo, and quite certainly none of them was engaged in a personal "redistribution of economic resources." No less relevant is the fact that French dirigisme was being implemented in the context of an industrial economy.

The Russian bureaucracy, while regaining control of oil, which is the main source of its revenues, does not overlook other natural resources and sectors of the economy in its efforts to get its hands on successful private companies. The regime instills in the minds of people the notion that Yeltsin's privatization was unfair, which indeed it was, but it does so not in order to encourage respect for the concept of hard-earned private property. The ruling elite is preparing public opinion for renationalization, probably selective and with a further redistribution of property. We cannot, however, rule out the possibility that, after the changeover of power in the Kremlin, at least some of today's bureaucrat-oligarchs might be forced out of their positions as managers and heads of the boards of companies, to be replaced by the members of the new ruling team. The old guard is aware of the looming threat and will most likely attempt to convert its current positions into property. A number of bureaucrat-oligarchs might privatize their mega-companies where they sit on boards, trying to get their hands on real money. Lots of it. Accordingly, a new kind of privatization could be expected, one that will create a new generation of billionaires. The new beneficiaries of privatization are unlikely to develop their own businesses since theirs is the psychology of a parasitic class. There is no certainty that the new round of privatization will be seen as fair, and it is unlikely to be the last as property in Russia continues to change hands. Yet, controlling the capital flows of the state companies through affiliated private structures will remain the preferred means of survival for the Russian elite, which means that bureaucratic capitalism will remain the key economic model, unless the system is restructured.

The expansion of the Russian state's role in the economy raises a number of questions. Society loses out from the transition to bureaucratic capitalism, not least because this expansion of the state's activities is funded by ordinary taxpayers. In order to buy out Yuganskneftegaz and Sibneft, the government had to dip not only into the exchequer, but also to borrow money abroad. These debts will be repaid by Russia's citizens. Society loses out also because state companies pay less tax to the treasury and are less efficient managers of property than private companies. It is clear enough who is losing, but it seems reasonable to ask who is gaining. After Ukrainian metallurgy giant Krivorozhstal was privatized by India's Mittal Steel group, the Ukrainian budget received a bonus of $4.8 billion. Russia, in contrast, paid out $13 billion for Sibneft and it is unclear to whom the money was paid. This raises further questions, this time about the legitimacy of Russian nationalization (and privatization as well) and whose interests it serves. There is more. Incapable of handling its growing obligations, the state hands over its resources to be managed by middlemen, who turn out to be exactly the same bureaucrats or people from their entourage or members of their families. As a result, the ownership of property becomes entirely nontransparent. In formal terms it is owned by the state, but the revenues and control over cash flows are in private hands.

Let us not, however, unduly dismay the Western investor with this description of bureaucratic capitalism. He has a place in the Russian market, and still would even if the entire economy were suddenly to be taken under state control. Russia needs the West, not only because bureaucratic capitalism needs financing and modern technology. The Kremlin needs the West to enhance the status of the ruling team and to ensure international acceptance of Russia's merging of the regime and property. Western investors should, however, keep their appetites within bounds. The Kremlin is already grumbling about such participation of Western capital in the Russian economy as the marriage of Lukoil and Conoco Phillips, which until recently was regarded as more or less acceptable. The authorities will try to further reduce opportunities for Western capital to influence the management of state companies. The main problem for Western investors, however, is less the reduction of opportunities than the question of how far the Russian state will follow its own rules. At this point we have some bad news for Western business people: Russia develops in cycles, and the end of each cycle brings a change of the rules, although they can, of course, be changed several times, even within a cycle.

The Kremlin has changed its mind more than once about which strategically important companies Western investors are barred from investing in. Decisions have been changed and postponed many times regarding the privatization of the Svyazinvest telecommunications monopoly. When operating within the framework of bureaucratic capitalism, the regime prefers to keep the rules vague so that they will be open to a variety of interpretations. Legislation itself always provides the scope for revising agreements with a Western partner, so there is never any certainty that a particular company will not repeat the fate of Sibir Energy, seized by Sibneft, which has in turn been absorbed by the state-owned Rosneft, or the history of Shell, Mitsui, and Mitsubishi, whom the Kremlin forced to sell their shares in the lucrative Sakhalin-2 project or the experience of BP-TNK, which under pressure from the Kremlin had to sell its stake in Kovykta gas field to Gazprom.

In the 1990s the state and Russian big business had an interest in attracting foreign investment, both because of a lack of resources of their own and in order to establish the free market nature of the Russian economy. Now, however, the Russian elite faces a dilemma. The operations of foreign companies may reduce the dividends produced by Russian business, and the bureaucrat—oligarchs find it more difficult to help themselves to dividends under the watchful eyes of foreign investors. It is also the case that they no longer need Western investment as desperately as they did in the 1990s. But at the same time, the Russian elite and Russian business continue to need the West not only for investment purposes, but also to become integrated into the global economy, which, they feel, is the only way to prosper. [. . .]

Russia has been actively expanding in Western markets. The commodity-sector champions are most active in expanding outside Russia (in 2001–2006, the total amount of their investments abroad increased fivefold). Russian business is buying not only into the West's gas and oil distribution networks, but showing growing interest in joining other Western business projects. The first attempt by Russian business to gain control of one of the world's leading companies was the skirmish in which the owner of Russia's Severstal, Alexey Mordashov, tried to take over Arcelor. The attempt failed because Western shareholders were wary and suspicious of doing business with the Russians, who do not have the best of reputations in Europe. This foray, however, showed that Russia has developed an appetite for aggressively playing in the top league. The new Russian expansionist projects "are rolling in." Roman Abramovich, one of the few old oligarchs still close to the Kremlin, has begun—evidently on instructions from Putin's team—creating Evraz Group, a giant metallurgy company, which is aiming to take over American companies. One of the leading Russian banks, Vneshtorgbank, bought 5 percent of the shares of the Franco-German aerospace company EADS and tried to expand its holdings, throwing European shareholders into disarray. French newspapers wrote in a panic, "The Russian cannibal wants to snack on our national property." In response, Putin, while in Paris in the fall of 2006, could not refrain from commenting irritably on the West's anxieties, "People are afraid of us because we are rich and very large." In Munich he soon continued a charm offensive to persuade Western investors that there was no need to be worried about Russia: "The Russians are coming, not with tanks and Kalashnikovs, but with hard cash, and they want to buy rights." The Russian president has said on more than one occasion, in injured tones, that the West would prefer only to buy natural resources from Russia and prevent it from developing and expanding. In Moscow the West's anxiety is seen as a fear of increasing Russian competition, and even liberals share this view.

The expansion of Russian business sometimes triggers conflicts and misunderstandings and very often provokes anxiety in the Western community about the Russian corporate mentality and the fusion between Russian economic and political interests. The Russian ruling class does not understand that what the West is afraid of is that Russia will continue to behave like a bull in a china shop, which Russia often does.

Meanwhile, integration of Russian business into global networks is the most effective way for it to learn the new rules of the game. Both sides, Russia and the West have to find ways to sort out mutual concerns; Russia's membership in the World Trade Organization (WTO) and further integration of Russia into the global economy could help transform the mentality and behavior of Russian companies.

In this context, a rather peculiar characteristic of the Russian economic model should be mentioned. The Russian state tries to limit the presence of foreign capital in the so-called strategic branches (not only in the military-industrial complex, but in the commodity sector as well), whereas in the food industry and services, FDI constitutes half of the total investment. Russian business in these areas is reluctant to invest heavily. Thus, Russia defends its natural resources, tries to export capital, and at the same time leaves (so far) its consumption market to foreign capital. Possible consequences of this type of development including social and political implications, have to date been underestimated.

4.3

Comrade Criminal

Stephen Handleman

Seran Akopyan opened his tiny grocery store on Moscow's Krasnoprudnaya Street in the spring of 1992, soon after municipal authorities gave private citizens the right to lease state retail shops. A few months later, he bought a gun.

"It's just a gas pistol," Akopyan smiled, pulling it from the bottom drawer of his desk. "It can't kill anybody. But it's useful in this neighborhood."

In more than five years as a correspondent in the Soviet Union, I could not remember ever meeting an ordinary, law-abiding civilian with a weapon. But I could see Akopyan's point. His business was within bullet range of one of the roughest districts in the capital. The nearby Central Market was a haven for drug dealers. A few blocks away, the Kazan, Yaroslavl, and Leningrad railway terminals attracted runaway children, beggars, drunks, con men, thieves, and prostitutes.

When the stations were built in the early years of the twentieth century, they had been magical additions to the Moscow skyline. Today, their clock towers and soaring fairy-tale roofs look forlorn against the hustle and grime of New Russia.

Akopyan's grocery was a more fitting monument to the new age of Russian capitalism than the railway stations. Most Soviet food stores were grim, cluttered places, where a pushing mob of customers faced sour-looking clerks over counters filled with largely unrecognizable merchandise. Beyond the heavy glass doors of Akopyan's food emporium, however, was a new world. The shelves and floors were briskly swept clean of litter. Clerks in spotless aprons stood in front of rows of tinned food, imported vegetables, and jars of pickled spices—all neatly sorted by category and size. Cellophane-wrapped packages of meat and poultry were piled invitingly in a large, modern freezer, a sight unimaginable in a normal Moscow *produkty* store. Akopyan's store radiated enterprise and profit.

But the shopkeeper's gun was proof that the businesslike atmosphere inside his establishment offered no protection from the predatory world outside. "The other night, there was a shoot-out outside my door," he said. "A bunch of guys

Source: Steven Handleman, excerpts from "Comrade Criminal," and "The Criminal State," from *Comrade Criminal: Russia's New Mafiya*. Yale University Press. 1995.

Note: Notes and references have been removed from this article.

just opened fire on each other, like cowboys, and when we came to work the next morning, there was blood all over the sidewalk."

He bought the weapon following an unpleasant encounter with the neighborhood mafiya. A pair of hoodlums walked through his door one evening when the shop was nearly empty and the storekeeper was counting the day's receipts. Smiling at Akopyan, they complimented him on the success of his new business. They wondered whether he would be interested in a long-term "protection" arrangement.

Akopyan is small and wiry, with a black mustache and a combustible temper. When the hoodlums emphasized their point by methodically kicking over chairs and sweeping his papers to the floor, he cursed and lunged at them. Years of lifting heavy crates had put strength in his arms and shoulders. To his surprise, his visitors fled into the night.

As he recounted the story, Akopyan was disconcertingly casual. "Most of the mafiosi in this area don't make trouble for me," he said. "They even bring me some of their stolen goods—imported tape recorders, that sort of thing—and ask me to sell them. I tell them no, and they go away. But some of the groups are not easy to handle, even for me."

According to the mutual friend who introduced us, Akopyan was among the few private businessmen in the city who did not have to worry about satisfying mafiya greed—and it wasn't because he carried a gun. My friend hinted that Akopyan had powerful mob connections.

"He's the biggest food distributor in north Moscow, and he knows everyone," he said. Lowering his voice meaningfully, he added, "To have a food business in Moscow is to have power in a hungry country like ours—and he knows how to use his power."

Akopyan did not mind being perceived as having a secret, darker dimension. "I have always known influential people," he said grandly. "Everyone knows me in this region."

Was the shopkeeper a minor crime lord, as my friend tried to suggest? Or was he an honest man trying to make his way in a world which could be cruel and unforgiving to the timid?

As I continued talking with him, it was apparent that the quest for profit in post-Soviet Russia required a businessman to play both roles. For instance, he soon found a way to discourage further visits from the gang that had tried to pull him into an extortion racket. The same hoodlums returned to his store a few weeks later, but this time Akopyan was ready. Several large, powerful men were waiting inside his office, and as soon as the gangsters stepped inside, they overwhelmed them in a melee of fists and sticks. The shopkeeper merely had to watch.

Who were these men? Akopyan described them, with an uneasy smile, as his "friends." He said that after the attack he had formed an "association" of 120 strong young fighters, including former policemen, black-belt karate experts, and wrestling champions. "From now on, if I'm in trouble, I know I can always call my friends," he said, "and in ten minutes they will be here to help me." The shop-keeper had evidently learned valuable lessons from Uganov, the Armenian *vor* who had impressed him as a child in Karabakh, in the art of overcoming the obstacles Russia threw up to its citizens—and of profiting from them. [. . .]

A few weeks after he developed his private security force, Akopyan was in Grozny, the capital of Chechnya (and the national home of the Chechen mob). When he prepared to board the airplane for his homeward flight to Moscow, an airport official informed him that there were no seats—a transparent attempt to extract a bribe. Strengthened by the newly "found" friends he could call on, Akopyan played the gangster.

"I told the guy he had two choices," Akopyan boasted. "He could let me on the plane and then go home, and I'd be sure to guarantee he had some wine and nice things. Or he could keep me from boarding—in which case he would spend the rest of his life trying to earn enough money to pay his medical bills." Akopyan boarded the plane.

With his "association" behind him, Akopyan no longer feared anyone. "The mafiya provide certain services," he said. "If you need goods, they can find them quickly," he said. "If you're having problem, they solve it so that you can be sure no one else will get in your way. People need protection. What does it matter who provides it, or who they pay?"

But this picture of the "evolution" of an honest shopkeeper into an aggressive participant in gangster economics was incomplete. There was another reason why the mafiya held no terrors for Akopyan; its tactics were simply an extension of the system he had been working in most of his life.

When Seran Akopyan decided to become a capitalist, at the age of forty-five, he was already manager of one of the city's largest state road warehouses. He tried playing by the rules established under the government's 1992 privatization plan. He wrote a formal letter of application to participate in the bidding for a lease; he paid the registration fee; he obtained references from a bank. But he was getting nowhere.

Then a municipal official he had known for years arrived one night at his door. The two men spent an hour chatting over glasses of *tutovka,* Akopyan's favorite throat-searing cognac from his native Karabakh, in the Caucusus Mountains. Finally, Akopyan's visitor cleared his throat.

"That shop you want on Krasnoprudnaya Street," he began. "It can be arranged that you get the lease. But, you know . . . it has to be bought first."

Akopyan understood immediately. "How much?" he asked.

"Two hundred thousand rubles."

As he conducted me on a tour of his establishment, Akopyan gave me a further education in the ethics of post-Communism. He proudly pointed to a corner of the room where ten-pound bags of rice were stacked.

"In your country, all you need to do is ring up some distributor and say I want so much rice; please bring it around next week," he said, and then he smiled. "That's not how it works here."

Akopyan mimicked someone handing over a bottle.

"So only the person who pays a bribe gets the goods?" I asked.

Akopyan laughed. "No, not necessarily. You have to be known and trusted. Even though I may have the money to pay, that doesn't ensure I will get what I need. Personal sympathy, that's what counts."

He went on to explain. "If you are starting a shop, you still need to get approval for everything you do, even after you come up with the money to buy it. The local district committee wants to see your remodeling blueprints. The regional food ministry official has to approve the purchase of machinery, and there's the health inspector. But when you go to see the bureaucrat, he's reluctant. He tells you that he's busy, and that things could take a lot of time.

"So you tell him you happen to know there is really good beer for sale at such and such a shop. He's interested. Everyone knows there's a shortage of beer. You ring the shopowner who happens to be a friend of yours, and you tell him to set aside some beer, and of course you tell your friend not to take any money from this bureaucrat but to put it on your account. He goes along with it because he knows someday you could help him. It works perfectly—and you get your approval."

Akopyan smiled again. "People exaggerate when they say you need thousands of rubles to get things done," he continued. "It's often just a question of fitting in with someone's interests. As I said, it's all based on personal sympathy."

Twenty years earlier, Akopyan was considerably less cynical. When he first arrived in the capital from the Caucusus, he was a fervent believer in the system.

"I actually wrote a statement to my bosses on my first Moscow job, saying I thought our life in the Soviet Union was the most correct way of life," Akopyan laughed. "I wanted to live like a real Communist, and I even told them I didn't want a big salary, just enough so my family could live. I got those ideals from my father, who was a military engineer—one of those crystal-pure souls who believed that to be a Communist was the best thing in the world. I believed everything he taught me. But it didn't take me long once I came to Moscow to see what was behind all that propaganda."

Akopyan's first job in Moscow was on an assembly line, producing jet engines for Russian MIGs. He worked hard—too hard, he said. His bosses were irritated to discover that their zealous apprentice was earning more in bonuses than they were. They made his life uncomfortable, and he finally left the factory to work as a forwarding agent in a food warehouse. There, he received his initiation in the system's brand of corruption.

"We would get an order to ship 120 kilograms of sausage to some shop, but the shipments we sent out contained only 100 kilograms," Akopyan remembered. "Where were the other twenty? They were shifted into the manager's private stock so he could sell them for his own profit. It was up to us to cover the loss."

The "private stock" made its way into the black market. But the so-called shadow economy was more than a vast private supermarket. It was also the only place real work ever got done. Some Russians now say that the phrases "black market" or "shadow business" are misleading, because they convey a system that thrived on the edges of the real economy. According to Lev Timofeyev, a former Soviet dissident who became active in the reformers' movement in the 1990s, the market was not "black," but "universal." "In the last decades in the USSR, not a single product has been manufactured and not a single paid service has been performed outside the confines of the black market," he wrote in a book published after the fall of Communism, called *The Secret Rulers of Russia*. "[It was] the living blood circulating in a dead organism." The black market is a key to understanding the history of the Soviet Union as well as the trauma of post-Communist Russia. "The entire Soviet system—everything without exception—was nothing more than an enormous black market," Timofeyev observed. [. . .]

The rise of cooperatives and small businesses not only offered a way to launder black-market profits; it also directly contributed to a rise in crime, thanks to the conditions under which the country's new businessmen were forced to work. Food suppliers, for example, were prohibited from selling produce to a private restaurant at the cheap subsidized prices available to state-owned restaurants. This was supposedly intended to prevent competition from "destabilizing" the market, but it was actually designed to cushion the monopoly held by bureaucrats who were already selling subsidized food for windfall profits. The profiteers of the black market flourished, as desperate restaurant owners and small businessmen came to them for supplies. A clothing cooperative, for instance, found that no state manufacturer could sell him denim. But the same denim became available at astronomical prices in the shadow economy, where the factory manager had secretly helped underwrite a "private" production line.

The small businessman was also vulnerable to extortion rackets, which appeared at the same time. Mobsters provided a unique form of protection to these seedlings of free enterprise. They were happy to help a businessman collect his bills or stave off unfriendly creditors, but; they were also quick to punish any who resisted their help. In the late 1980s, a wave of firebombings and assaults hit dozens of cooperative restaurants and businesses in Moscow and other cities.

"Cooperative owners, even the legitimate ones, had to get involved with illegal activity in some form—they had no choice," said Aleksandr Gurov. "If they wanted office space, they would have to bribe officials; if they needed a loan, there were no banks to go to; and if they tried to get money from customers who didn't pay their bills, there were no courts to come to their side. The only businessmen who didn't go bankrupt were the ones who were associated with the mafiya."

The peculiar nature of perestroika *bizness* was missed, or ignored, outside the Soviet Union, where any form of enterprise that bore a resemblance to capitalism was treated as a brave departure from the command-administrative economy. Western investors who rushed into Moscow to cultivate what they believed were the first shoots of Soviet free enterprise quickly discovered that unless the "new businessmen" they found as partners for their joint ventures were able to pay for bureaucratic or mob protection, or were disguised bureaucrats themselves, the partnership would soon evaporate.

The relaxation of the command-administrative system had done little more than allow enterprising apparatchiks and black marketeers to convert the wealth they earned through the manipulation of the system into "real" money. The bureaucracy showed no interest in making things easier for ordinary entrepreneurs: a competitive marketplace would not only reduce their opportunities for private gain, but also challenge their power. Instead of laying the groundwork for a free market, perestroika merely reinforced the operating methods of the black economy.

Some argued that it had an even worse long-term effect. Long after perestroika had faded into history, one of the former Soviet Union's most prominent political figures said that the government's failure to regulate the black market had doomed the chances for genuine reform. Vadim Bakatin, minister of internal affairs in the Gorbachev government until 1990—and Aleksandr Gurov's boss—admitted that bureaucrats and mobsters not only shared a common interest in blocking the creation of a competitive open market, but had joined forces in terrorizing independent businessmen as well. "The foundation of today's organized crime was the shadow economy, but the roof was our own bureaucratic system," Bakatin ruefully explained to me in 1993. "Our bureaucrats, police, procurators, judges, even the KGB, were merging with the underground world. It was a critical change in the development of crime in our country."

The inevitable consequence was the rise of the unique post-Soviet gangster-bureaucrat: the comrade criminal.

In 1993, I was shown one of Russian law enforcement's most secret, and most embarrassing, documents: a list of eighty leading criminals in Moscow and the surrounding region. Their faces stared triumphantly out of the grainy police mug shots, as if they were celebrating the fact that they were all still at large. But what was especially interesting was that less than a quarter of them were acknowledged *vory v zakonye.* The majority were men in their late thirties and early forties, whose occupations were listed as industrial manager or business director. [. . .]

But the most telling evidence that the gangster-bureaucrat continued to squeeze legitimate business enterprise after the Soviet collapse was in the uninterrupted flourishing of the black market, years after there was any apparent reason for it to exist—at least if one took seriously Russia's proclaimed intention of moving toward a free economy. In 1992, the estimated size of the shadow economy—that is, goods and services for which no taxes were paid—was 2.5 trillion rubles (then worth about 1.3 billion dollars). According to a confidential paper prepared by Russian law enforcement agencies, this post-Communist black market already accounted for 15 percent of the Russian volume of goods and services by the end of 1991.

Comrade criminals, and the shadow economy they manipulate, continue to affect the way Seran Akopyan does business. The Party bosses he once dealt with as a bureaucrat have turned up in Moscow's privatized retail trade as either administrators or practitioners.

"Compared to people like myself, they are the sharks," Akopyan told me. "Everyone operates in the same way as in the old days. The networks haven't changed. I estimate that 40 percent of the old bureaucrats are still there—they're not interested in ideology, but business. For instance, if I ring the Ostankino sausage factory for an order, they might bring me three or four varieties of sausage; but to another [shopowner] they might send ten types." The determining factor was "personal sympathy," Akopyan repeated. "It doesn't matter to the factory that I could do a better job of selling the sausages," he said. "In our country, the producer is not interested in selling his goods fast."

After several conversations with Akopyan, I came away with a grudging respect for the oasis he had created on Krasnoprudnaya Street—and for what it cost to maintain it. Akopyan survived from day to day on the strength of his ability to get along with the city's comrade criminals.

In the middle of one of our chats, an old woman walked into his office, carrying a container of powdered cleanser. She handed the detergent to Akopyan without a word, and he kissed her on each cheek and stored the container away in the same desk drawer where he kept his gun. The woman stalked out, mumbling angrily beneath her breath.

Akopyan noticed my mystified stare and started to laugh.

"We have a special arrangement," he said. "That woman works in a house next door, and she steals the stuff for me because I can't get any myself from the people I know. Tomorrow, I will give her a nice imported chicken."

The shabby edifice of the Soviet Union may have collapsed—but the moral ambiguities it fostered have survived on the New Russia's frontier.

★ ★ ★ ★

The Criminal State

In the heady weeks following the defeat of the August, 1991, coup, Moscow was in an uproar. Crowds roamed the streets day and night, pulling down the statues and slogans of the old regime. The city was swept by rumors of an imminent ban on the Soviet Communist Party. An angry mob gathered behind police lines in front of the offices of the Central Committee on Staraya Ploshchad (Old Square), calling out threats to frightened secretaries and office workers. Inside the building, a high-ranking Party official sat down to write an urgent memo to one of his assistants.

"I've taken one hundred million rubles," the memo said. "Hide it." In the midst of its worst disaster, the world's largest Communist Party was reverting to its clandestine habits. In Moscow, and around the country, Party leaders were shredding records and files and making preparations to go into underground opposition. Even in forced retirement, though, the Party had better prospects than it did nearly a century earlier, when the threadbare bands of Marxists in Geneva, Minsk, and St. Petersburg first began plotting the overthrow of the czarist empire. In fact, many Soviet Communist Party leaders looked less like reluctant pensioners than like bandits fleeing the scene of a crime: they were moving off the stage of Russian history with a fortune worthy of a czar.

After seventy-four years in power, the Party was one of the world's richest organizations—controlling property and investments abroad worth, by some estimates, billions of dollars. Although the extent of its actual cash reserves was unknown—some insiders maintain that it was; much less than critics believe—it possessed the unchallenged ability to treat the Soviet state's financial resources as its own. Greed and corruption marked its final years in power to an extent scarcely suspected abroad. The truth did not become apparent until records of the Politburo and Central Committee—the Party organs that effectively governed the Soviet Union—became accessible to researchers after the aborted 1991 coup.

A complete account of the secret wealth of the Communist state may never be possible, but the impact of that wealth on post-Communist society is just beginning to be clear. There is evidence to suggest that the money now underwrites both left-wing and right-wing opposition to reforms that would open the Russian economy to greater competition and restrict the comrade criminal's ability to plunder the state. Even more ominously, Party funds have contributed to the criminalization of life after Communism. But that is merely a testimony to the enduring influence of Russia's largest and most sinister mafiya organization.

In the 1970s and early 1980s, a series of revelations about murder and corruption in high places shook the Soviet Union. The newspaper accounts and summaries of court cases of the time read like true-crime tales. The cases had one common denominator: they all involved officials who were influential members of the Communist Party.

The mayor of Sochi, for example, amassed such a huge private fortune from bribery and kickbacks that he was able to build a fantasy mansion with a singing fountain that emitted different notes, depending on the height of the water. In the nearby resort spa of Gelendzhik, several high-ranking officials were murdered just before they were to give evidence to investigators about massive influence peddling in the region. Sections of the exclusive vacation compounds in southern Russia and the Baltic states reserved for the Party elite and their families were turned into brothels. Senior bureaucrats even dabbled in drug trafficking and the distribution of pornographic videos.

One of the most riveting scandals came to light in April, 1983, when a search of the home of an official in the fabled Central Asian city of Bukhara revealed a treasure trove of one million rubles, nearly a mile's length of gold brocade, and piles of diamonds, rubies, Swiss watches, and jeans. The official admitted that his wealth came from a complicated kickback scheme that involved falsifying reports about the production of cotton.

Moscow had decided several years before to turn Central Asia into a vast cotton plantation. After a few bumper harvests, the weakened soil could no longer produce enough to fulfill the quotas set by the planning ministries. The region's leaders, however, were not bothered by those details. With the collusion of the Moscow bureaucracy, which feared admitting any failure in agriculture, they continued to report huge crops and were paid anyway. Moscow bureaucrats, who took a cut of the profits, were happy with the arrangement. Everyone could become rich while advancing socialism. The conspiracy spread to include hundreds of officials across Central Asia and reached into the higher levels of the Soviet establishment. Among those eventually implicated in the scandal were Yuri Churbanov, deputy minister of the Soviet Ministry of Internal Affairs (and son-in-law of the late Soviet leader Leonid Brezhnev), and Sharaf Rashidov, the Party boss of Uzbekistan, a candidate (non-voting) member of the Politburo and a close Brezhnev ally.

Some of the Central Asian and Moscow bosses arrested as a result of the investigation were shot, and others received jail terms. But police inquiries never penetrated deeper into the system. The affair was officially regarded as a "deviation" from the moral code of Bolsheviks, and the establishment closed ranks behind the culprits. Yet no one could have any doubt that this scandal, like many others, was traceable directly to the Central Committee of the Communist Party.

"The Central Committee was like a czar's court," said Yevgeni Myslovsky, a former senior investigator in the office of the Moscow procurator (public prosecutor), who worked on the cotton scandal and other cases. "There were about five thousand people employed there, but twenty-five of them were the real unofficial organizers of the corruption that was going on around the country. They weren't really top officials, just deputy heads of departments, special [Party] instructors, those kinds of people. But they acted like a mafiya clan."

It was a mafiya that could dictate which of its members would be prosecuted. As in the cotton scandal, the leadership decided how far any investigation could go. "Every time we wanted to prosecute a corruption case against a bureaucrat, we had to bargain with these people at Party headquarters," Myslovsky recalled. "As soon as we got close to someone they wanted to protect, they removed all the evidence. They had terrible power. They seemed to me like a special caste."

Aslambek Aslakhanov, chairman of the Russian parliamentary commission on law and order until 1993 (and a former investigator with the Soviet Ministry of Internal Affairs), told me a similar story about his efforts to prosecute top officials in the 1970s. After arresting a senior Party figure on bribery charges, a man who boasted of having "three friends" in the Politburo, Aslakhanov was assured by the justice minister that there would be no interference. But the justice minister was fired, and the corrupt bureaucrat was released from prison the next day. "They even showed him on television as a hero," Aslakhanov recalled bitterly.

The special caste that senior officials belonged to—the nomenklatura—was officially unmentionable in Soviet public discourse. Yet no one was untouched by their power.

The nomenklatura were the governing class of the old empire. Occupying the privileged center of Soviet politics, they were to ordinary civil servants what sharks are to goldfish. They numbered, by some estimates, nearly 1.5 million people, and their special authority came from their place on a secret list prepared by the Central Committee containing the names of the most worthy Party members. From this list all the top officials of the state were chosen, from regional and municipal Party secretaries to ambassadors and senior government ministers. The nomenklatura constituted a private club of individuals whose loyalty to the Party transcended any other obligation. And it was their chief, the general secretary of the Communist Party, the first name on the list, who led the Soviet state.

Over the years of Soviet power, the nomenklatura adopted an internal system of rewards and punishments that was as carefully graded as any Sicilian mafia clan's. Relatively innocent gifts, like fruit or flowers, were required to establish key relationships. Raisa Gorbacheva was said to have presented a necklace to Galina Brezhneva, wife of the late Soviet leader, when the couple came to Moscow after her husband had been appointed agriculture chief at the Central Committee. Party memberships went for higher prices. In Krasnodar, they cost between 3,000 and 3,500 rubles; in other regions, the cost of securing a leading position could be as high as 6,000 rubles— then the equivalent of about two years' wages for an average Soviet worker. [. . .]

The system knew how to repay the loyalty of its members. In the 1970s, a senior Party worker named Kulakov received on his retirement the right to free hospitalization for his family, a country dacha, and private cars for as long as he lived. His grandchildren were awarded a monthly seventy-ruble stipend. In a revealing note of cynicism, an anonymous Central Committee official headed the document approving Kulakov's retirement plans, "Easing the Panic of Comrade Kulakov."

The nomenklatura not only took care of its own; it also kept its ranks firmly off-limits to politically incorrect outsiders. Children of high officials went to the same schools and holiday camps, and intermarried with each other. "The *apparat* tried to set up a system of inherited power. . . through an exclusive system of education and then through a system of appointments and promotions," Arbatov wrote, adding that, like corruption, the nepotism originated at the top. Brezhnev's son, for example, became deputy minister for foreign trade.

Despite the titillating revelations of scandal in high places, the Party bosses set clear limits on what the Soviet public could be told about the extent of their criminal activity. When the popular national magazine *Krokodil* published an exposé in the early 1980s which linked Communist officials in the Ukrainian city of Dnepropetrovsk with local gangs, the issue never appeared on local newsstands. Dnepropetrovsk happened to be Brezhnev's political base, and allegations of corruption touched sensitive nerves.

Corruption was imprinted in the system's genetic code. "The old administrative-command society [was] organically connected with corruption," wrote Arbatov afterward. "[We had] an enormous and parasitic *apparat* [that] gives or takes away, permits or prohibits, takes care of everything, can fire anybody, demote anybody, often even throw him in prison or, on the contrary, raise him up. And who with such power at his disposal can resist temptation?"

But no one really guessed how lucrative the temptation was. "The budget of the Communist Party of the Soviet Union [CPSU] was always marked 'top-secret,'" said Aleksandr Kotenkov, a state legal official who defended the Russian government's ban on the Party in a 1992 trial. "But we have evidence showing that the CPSU spent hundreds of millions of dollars of the state's money for its own needs alone every year."

To back up his charge, Kotenkov made public at a Moscow press conference documents showing that the Party regularly plundered the state treasury to underwrite foreign Communist groups and terrorist organizations. "There would be a decision of the Politburo on financing a particular group," Kotenkov said. "Then an instruction would come from the Central Committee to the [Soviet] State Bank for a delivery of hard currency. A man would come around from the bank to Old Square with the cash, and it would then be handed over through KGB channels."

There are other versions of how the money went abroad. Former Party insiders have told me that the money was sent directly from the Central Bank to KGB station chiefs overseas. I have also seen memos from the Central Committee archives authorizing the direct transfer of millions of dollars to Communist Party leaders in Europe and North America. (No detail was too small: one 1970s memo authorized the purchase of an expensive fur coat for a loyal Canadian party worker.) The disclosure of such transfers embarrassed the recipients, but no one was surprised by them. The secret flow of cash was central to the Soviet goal of winning friends and financing clandestine movements abroad. The troubling issue raised by Russian investigators later, however, was how many millions went into private foreign bank accounts held by Party officials rather than the pockets of designated "friends" of the international proletariat. The nature of the clandestine process made it impossible to verify how the money was actually spent. It was not nearly as hard to figure out where it came from. "The Party always insisted that everything it had came from membership dues," Kotenkov said. "But our documents show that the source of all the Soviet Communist Party's wealth came from state property."

In other words, Party and KGB officials were raiding the government treasury for their overseas operations. Formally, this was a violation of Soviet constitutional provisions that separated Party and state. But it was the least of the illegalities associated with the establishment's behavior. "We had," said Aslambek Aslakhanov, "a mafiya of the supreme organs of power." [. . .]

But the Party possessed an advantage undreamed of in the *vorovskoi mir*: it was the ruling class of the society it ravaged. In the absence of any serious check on its power, it was free to do whatever it wanted, to whomever it wanted.

"In Soviet conditions the decisive mafia [*sic*] role is played by politicians," wrote Arkady Vaksberg, a prominent Moscow journalist who, in a book called *The Soviet Mafia*, described the inner workings of the Party and government bureaucracy in the 1970s and 1980s. "[They used] criminal methods to preserve their jobs and their strongholds."

Vaksberg compared the conspiracy of silence surrounding the nomenklatura to the Italian mafia's code of *omerta*, the blood oath committing each member to take the secrets of the clan to his death. A number of top officials committed suicide during the late 1970s and early 1980s, when the KGB, under the ambitious Yuri Andropov, launched a crackdown on corruption. For example, Gen. Nikolai Shcholokov, a Brezhnev ally and minister of internal affairs, was found shot to death on December 13, 1984. Shcholokov had been at the center of a scandal threatening to involve even more senior figures in the hierarchy. According to one widely circulated version of his death, he was visited in his apartment the night before by agents of the Moscow procurator's office and handed his own service revolver. The officials then silently departed to let him draw the obvious conclusion. [. . .]

In the Party's final days in power, another rash of suicides claimed the lives of leading *apparatchiki*. Boris Pugo, then minister of internal affairs and one of the leading plotters of the coup, shot himself and his wife to avoid arrest. Nikolai Kruchina, financial and property administrator of the Communist Party, jumped to his death from the balcony of his fifth-floor Moscow apartment on Aug 26, 1991, only days after the botched coup—and a few weeks before an investigation of Party finances was scheduled to open. In his suicide note, he explained that he was killing himself out of "fear of the future."

It was an intriguing phrase. Kruchina evidently believed that he could not participate in a future without the Communist Party. But the treasurer may also have sacrificed himself in the hope of taking to the grave the secrets of how the Soviet mafiya had guaranteed its own future. Unfortunately for Kruchina, the story—or most of it—is now in the public domain.

The Party's private insurance program effectively began after February 5, 1990. On that date, at a historic plenary session, the Communist Party's governing Central Committee voted to revoke the privilege granted to the Party under Article Six of the Soviet constitution as the state's only legal political organization. The Party did not easily consent to the removal of its seven-decade-long monopoly on political power. It took a tough speech by Mikhail Gorbachev to persuade reluctant Central Committee members that it was "time for us to understand the age we live in." Few in the leadership saw anything but trouble ahead as a result of the decision.

"The whole system was held together by the nomenklatura," said Vadim Bakatin, who, as Soviet minister of internal affairs from 1988 to 1990, was present at that meeting. They knew if you pulled one nail out, the whole thing was in danger of falling apart. The decision to abolish Article Six was the nail. It was the moment when the Communist Party lost its time-honored right to steal.

"The Party no longer had easy access to state funds," Bakatin told me in 1993. "Now money had to be found somewhere to pay the bureaucrats who had no other jobs apart from Party work. We were faced with a huge financial crisis. The central bureaucracy and the Politburo were already in terrible financial shape. Even the income from Party dues was reduced because so many members were leaving. So instructions came [from the leadership] to invest Party money in commercial structures."

Within months of the February 5th meeting, huge sums of money were quietly being transferred out of Party coffers. Documents from the Central Committee archives made public after the coup have provided a graphic illustration of the Party's miraculous conversion to capitalist enterprise.

In June, 1990, the first of many private banks was established with Party funds. Some thirty-one million rubles (about 1.2 million dollars at commercial 1990 rates) were placed as start-up capital for an operation envisioned as leading to large-scale credit and investment transfers at home and abroad. Officials reported that they planned to transfer an additional five hundred million rubles (about twenty million dollars) from the Party's reserves to the account by that autumn, because of what they called "the deterioration of the economic and political situation in the country." Eight months later, Party treasurer Nikolai Kruchina was so pleased with the bank's work that he deposited, in the name of the Central Committee, another fifty million rubles, at an interest rate of 6 percent.

The banking operation blithely ignored a law of the Russian Federation that restricted the ownership of commercial banks to state bodies. As a political group, the Party did not formally qualify. But this was a minor quibble compared to the arrogance with which Party officials ignored their own ideological proscriptions against "profiteering" from bank interest. [. . .]

The Soviet Union's military empire overseas was an early source of dividends. According to the Moscow crime newspaper *Kriminalnaya Khronika*, the sale of military property in East Germany during the early 1990s produced huge amounts of Soviet rubles, which in turn were exchanged for East German marks at the artificial rates set by COMECON, the moribund socialist trade market comprising the Soviet Union and its East European satellites. After German unification, the East German currency was exchanged for West German deutschmarks at an enormous profit.

The newspaper claimed that it had proof of an even more notorious scheme in which several Communist-established "private" banks in Russia accepted huge dollar deposits from Panamanian and Colombian drug dealers, converted them to rubles, and then reconverted them to dollars, transferring the money overseas again in return for a hefty commission. "The Soviet Union," the paper said, "was operating as a colossal launderette."

There could be no doubt the Party was aware that its commercial activities were a betrayal of the state it purported to lead. The August 23rd Politburo resolution expressly ordered that the financial structures created under its scheme were to have "minimal visible ties" to the Communist leadership. "Anonymous organizations [will] mask direct links to the Party when launching commercial and foreign economic Party activity," the resolution instructed, with the aplomb of a mafiya syndicate creating front groups.

The fast track to capitalism was authorized at the highest levels. A classified Politburo resolution dated June 11, 1991, which approved the transfer of six hundred million rubles to commercial organizations and banks established by Party bodies such as the Komsomol, was signed by Communist Party general secretary Mikhail Gorbachev. According to the resolution, the funds were to serve as seed money for investment in "modern forms of economic activity, such as shareholding companies and small enterprises." These funds were also to be made available to "reliable" foreigners willing to establish joint ventures with Party enterprises.

Lenin's heirs were not only concerned with preserving their communal wealth. According to evidence presented at the 1992 trial involving the Yeltsin government's ban on the Communist Party, Gorbachev also signed another document just a few weeks before the coup recommending that Party property around the country be transferred into the name of trustworthy "private" owners—all presumably members of the nomenklatura. Officials testified that there had not been time to carry this recommendation out, but the attempt to protect the Communist patrimony was already well under way.

Long before the coup, the nomenklatura's eleventh-hour switch to capitalism produced maneuvers that made the black-market buccaneers of Yekaterinburg look like lowly bank robbers. The paper trail left in the archives shows that top state officials positioned themselves very early for a struggle over the control of post-Communist Russia's financial and industrial base. In one case, senior bureaucrats at Gossnab, the Ministry of State Supply, arranged to buy 142 government-owned dachas outside Moscow for the equivalent of about seventy-five thousand dollars, at prevailing rates, in 1990. A year later, the buildings as well as the land had an estimated value of more than four million dollars.

For those nomenklatura separated by distance and rank from the financial schemes under way in Moscow, there were other means of assuring a secure future. In the final years of the regime, the entire system echoed to the thud of bureaucrats parachuting into comfortable private-sector jobs.

In August, 1990, Igor Gorbunov, then the regional party chief of Bashkiria—a region southwest of Yekaterinburg—received two million rubles from the Central Committee to establish a small cooperative bank. A few months later, the bank moved to Moscow, where it was relocated in a building owned by the Lenin District Party Committee. After the coup, Gorbunov and other Bashkirian Communist Party officials landed jobs at the bank, with monthly salaries of up to eighty thousand rubles, several times the average worker's wage.

What helped these officials enormously, of course, was the fact that they were writing the new rules as they went along. "For a brief time, the. . .nomenklatura both acquired the freedom of private initiative and preserved their entire distributive power over state property," observed Lev Timofeyev.

The measures taken under perestroika to liberalize the economy and reduce state control promoted first and foremost the interests of the Party elite. A Soviet pun in the early 1990s recognized this when it transformed *privatizatsiya*, "privatization," into *prikhvatizatsiya*, "grabbing." One of the major beneficiaries of the government's privatization program turned out to be the KGB. A maverick KGB general named Oleg Kalugin disclosed later that the agency "virtually controlled" the privatization program in the final years of the Soviet regime. This was confirmed by Yevgeniya Albats, a Moscow journalist, whose investigation of the spy agency's activities showed that it invested three billion rubles (about 120 million dollars) in six hundred newly established commercial firms and banks around the country.

Taking advantage of new rules permitting the establishment of "foreign economic associations" with the right to trade abroad, the agency created a Moscow-based export firm named Santa, whose board members were all active reserve officers of the KGB. The general director was a reserve KGB colonel identified only as V. Belousov. Santa lived up to its name. Within a few months, it was distributing generous gifts of cash to other newly created commercial firms inside the Soviet military-industrial complex. [. . .]

The KGB was an important secret player—perhaps the most important—in bridging the criminality of the old regime with the criminality of post-Communist era. On January 5, 1991, the KGB Third Main Department, the division responsible for military counterintelligence, sent a classified telegram to Soviet army and navy bases around the country. The message, discovered by Russian researchers in the agency's archives and listed as document 174033, relayed coded instructions from then KGB chairman Vladimir Kryuchkov for the establishment of private commercial firms to sell military technology overseas. Document 174033 triggered one of the most important domestic operations in KGB history. Kryuchkov, citing the "deteriorating domestic political situation," outlined the plan's three strategic aims in dry, bureaucratic language. The new companies were to serve as "reliable covers for [KGB] leaders and the most valuable [KGB] operatives, in case the domestic. . .situation develops along East German lines; to provide financial means for the organization of underground work if 'destructive elements' come to power; and to create conditions for the effective use of foreign and domestic agent networks during [a period of] increased political instability." [. . .]

Before Russia's new democratic leaders could get their economic priorities in order, they were faced with a group of powerful opponents who looked disturbingly familiar. The nomenklatura bureaucrats who had invested in the private sector were now among Russia's most influential bank managers, company directors, and heads of commercial enterprises. The Communist Party's well-timed investments had assured the nomenklatura of political influence as well as personal wealth in the era that succeeded them.

"Some of my old friends in the Party are today chairmen of banks and stock exchanges, and they keep calling me up to cut me into deals," said Vadim Bakatin. "They always have something going in Siberia, or Odessa, or some other place. When I say no, they take pity on me. They say, 'Vadim, can I give you a car, for God's sake, you are in a bad way.' I just keep saying, 'No thanks, don't give me anything.'"

Bakatin used to command magisterial offices as a senior member of the nomenklatura. He had been a minister in Gorbachev's cabinet and Boris Yeltsin's chairman of the KGB. When I met him in 1993, his working quarters were so small that if he shifted his big frame slightly, he could reach the pot of withered flowers on the windowsill overlooking the Moscow River without getting up from his desk. He made a modest living, working for one of the handful of "foundations" that have provided safe perches for perestroika veterans. A map of the former Soviet Union, hanging on one wall, provided the only color in the room.

Bakatin, a genial man whose liberal attitudes and square-jawed good looks made him a poster boy for perestroika in the West, typified the best and the brightest of the nomenklatura. Like Arbatov, he had risen on the strength of his intelligence. But once inside the inner circle of power, he became a victim of its ruling ethic. From October, 1988, to December, 1990, Bakatin was the Soviet Union's chief policeman. As minister of internal affairs, he was given the impossible task of keeping law and order in a system that was gradually unraveling. Bakatin read Aleksandr Gurov's research paper and was so impressed that he set up the ministry's special division on organized crime—and made Gurov its head. But he was never allowed to challenge the guiding principles that made the job futile. When he tried to push through some of his ideas about legalizing the black economy to counter organized crime in the late 1980s, he was told by the Party secretariat not to make waves. "They said we didn't need any more problems," he recalled.

He had one accomplishment to be proud of. Throughout his career, which included an unsuccessful run for the presidency of Russia against Yeltsin in 1991 and a brief five-month appointment as chairman of the KGB following the coup, he was never tarnished with any corruption scandals. But that made him all the more defensive about the other members of his class.

"I don't like all this talk about the corruption of the old system," he told me. It is true we ran the economy ineffectively, and there was an elite which enjoyed limitless wealth. But you can't really call that corruption. The senior Party leaders were gods and czars. They already lived under Communism. They could get whatever they wanted from abroad. They didn't need to take bribes, but it was the order of things that people gave gifts. It was the way power was organized then. But it was a less corrupt system than what we have now.

Bakatin was right in a sense. The scandals of the Soviet regime pale beside the massive corruption and crime of the present era. But like most members of his generation in the former leadership, he is reluctant to acknowledge the formative role played by the nomenklatura in the development of post-Soviet crime.

Other Russians, however, have had no hesitation about doing so. "The criminal party has left the stage, but the criminal state has remained," declared Pavel Voshchanov, a commentator for *Komsomolskaya Pravda* who became Yeltsin's press secretary, in the summer of 1992. Mafiya habits, embezzlement of public funds, and corruption remain the norms of social relations and penetrate the atmosphere in which the country and each of our citizens lives. Our efforts to present [the defeat of the coup] as a victory for democracy are nothing more than self-deception. On the whole, Communists were defeated by other Communists.

Within a month of the coup, there were as many schisms inside the nomenklatura as there were inside the Russian underworld, as Communists continued to fight Communists for a share of the Party legacy. Aleksandr Muzikantsky, an official appointed by the Russian government to deal with the expropriation of Party buildings, complained that rival bureaucrats were scrambling over each other in a race to "grab state property."

At a press conference on August 30, 1991, the exasperated Muzikantsky held up a letter he had received from Mikhail Gorbachev demanding title to a building owned by the Institute of Social Sciences, on Moscow's Leningradsky Prospekt. Gorbachev claimed that he needed the quarters for his presidential staff now that he no longer had access to his former offices at Central Committee Headquarters. Gorbachev was not the only top official eager to stake out his claim. Muzikantsky received a curt demand from the new Russian government for transferring ownership of the luxury apartment blocks that had belonged to the Central Committee to the new Council of Ministers. "We need to make sure that property is not handed over from one set of bureaucrats to another set of bureaucrats," Muzikantsky pleaded. "This kind of thing has to stop."

It didn't. The secret financial deals of the last years of the Soviet regime blossomed into open chicanery in the hospitable environment of post-Communism. As one long-term foreign resident put it succinctly following the coup, "There are only two kinds of people with money in Russia: ex-Communist officials, and the men who bribed them."

The two classes remain the principal combatants in the struggle over the spoils of the Soviet system—a struggle whose outcome will determine the future power balance of Russia. "The struggle for power in our country is the struggle for property," Len Karpinsky, editor of the liberal newspaper *Moskovskiye Novosti* wrote in March, 1993. "Capital and wealth are the key to position in the power structure. . . . If the [former] bureaucrat continues to be pivotal to the system, we may well find ourselves living under 'nomenklatura capitalism,' whose despotism will not be inferior to the planned socialist system."

The "nomenklatura capitalists" have financed their struggle with the funds transferred or embezzled from the former Communist state. Long after the coup, laundered Party money was turning up in every sector of the new Russian economy. Russian government investigators found evidence showing that Communist Party money financed more than one hundred commercial enterprises in Moscow and some six hundred across Russia. The investigators traced to the Central Committee more than one billion rubles deposited in Russian banks alone. An estimated fifty billion rubles was believed hidden around Russia and abroad. Considering the senior nomenklatura's freedom to do what it wanted without fear of scrutiny, this may be the tip of the iceberg. According to the Russian Ministry of the Economy, the Soviet Communist Party held 453.5 billion "hard-currency" rubles (freely convertible to dollars) in its accounts between 1981 and 1991, and some one billion dollars in cash. There were many powerful interests anxious to keep that money secret.

Inspector Vladimir Kalinichenko, on special assignment from the government to track Communist funds abroad, ran into the wall of silence erected by the nomenklatura capitalists almost as soon as he began his investigations. When I first called and asked for an interview with him in the summer of 1992, he insisted on meeting me away from his offices in the old Gosplan building, which had once housed the powerful Soviet planning agency, near Red Square. "Too many people listening up there," he said cryptically.

He brought along his aide, Nikolai Emelyanov, one of the few colleagues on the commission he trusted. Hunched like conspirators over a table in the nearly empty coffee shop of the Intourist Hotel on Tverskaya Street, the two men talked in rapid-fire sentences, frequently interrupting each other. The astronomical sums they tossed over the coffee and heavy pastry sounded fantastic against the claims of bankruptcy made by the new Russian government.

"While our leaders go to the West and beg for a few million dollars in aid, I would say many more millions, even billions, are being transferred back and forth through our country," Kalinichenko said.

"We know businessmen who in the course of a month can get together three hundred billion rubles for a deal," said Emelyanov. "I don't think you can collect that much money in the States over a month, but here they can. . ."

"In no time at all," cut in Kalinichenko. Then they go to the West and change the rubles for dollars. Even at a cheap conversion rate, it still comes back as pure profit. And they know how to use it. The president of one bank came to me and said that if we left him alone we could just name our bank account and he would transfer fifty million dollars to it. That's the kind of money moving around this country now.

"And that's why it's foolish to keep looking for Party money abroad. We'll never get that back, but the money that counts now is all around us."

The investigations begun by Kalinichenko and Emelyanov were filed away in oblivion when the government anti-corruption commission they worked for was closed down. Subsequent commissions met the same fate. It had become politically impossible to acknowledge the sheer volume of corruption that overtook Russia in 1992 and 1993. According to the two former investigators, the "dirty" money that financed the purchase of a New York skyscraper and numerous other properties in the United States and Europe came from the same secret treasure chest that finances the nomenklatura's growing interests at home. [. . .]

The former Communists have enlisted new allies. In the wreckage of Soviet Communism, the *vory* and the nomenklatura have grown closer together. "We can no longer talk about links between the old mafiya underworld and the bureaucrats," Kalinichenko grumbled. "We have to talk about mergers."

The two criminal societies made a natural fit. Already strikingly similar in organization, they presided over the two major streams of capital available to post-Communist Russia: black-market profits and the wealth of the Communist Party. The old formal barriers between the *vorovskoi mir* and the Party hierarchy were erased by new alliances of convenience. The process was most visible in Russia's regions, where the crime lords and the bureaucrats shared the common aim of resisting the attempts of the central authorities to break the power of the large state enterprises. This was what Yeltsin meant by "nomenklatura separatism."

As in Yekaterinburg, regional and local officials turned their fledgling coalitions with former black marketeers and the criminal world into a new power base. In nearly all the seventy-eight regions of the Russian Federation, former bureaucrats became the most outspoken proponents of de-centralization—a fashionable notion in the West, but in Russia a code word for local resistance to Moscow-imposed economic reforms.

Mikhail Poltaranin, former Russian minister for press and the mass media, warned in 1992 that the coalition of crime lords, former Communist managers, and local authorities represented a "fifth estate." By that year, they were already strong enough to defy Moscow's authority. Local governments withheld tax revenue, appointed their own justice and customs officials, and committed thousands of other violations of federal rules during 1992, and the country's chief law officer filed more than two hundred thousand formal protests against violators of local authority. No one expected the trend to be reversed. By 1993, some provincial bosses were mounting even more pointed challenges to Moscow. Yekaterinburg, for instance, became the focus of efforts to set up an "independent" Urals Republic.

When the new Russian government, in an early burst of reformist zeal, abolished the central industrial ministries and gave enterprises the right to deal directly with suppliers and customers instead of going through Moscow, it played directly into the local bosses' hands. Freed from Moscow's scrutiny, they took control of the huge state enterprises in their jurisdiction and blocked further efforts to turn them into private companies.

But the regional axis of power was only one of the combinations threatening political and economic stability in Russia. Connections between the nomenklatura capitalists and criminal groups have turned up at the central-government level. On October 18, 1992, a former Party colleague of Vadim Bakatin's named Anatoli Melnik was sentenced to five years in prison for smuggling. Melnik was associated with an Armenian crime lord who imported nearly seventeen thousand bottles of liquor from Germany designated as "humanitarian aid." With new labels identifying the bottles as containing mineral water, the liquor was reexported to Poland and Germany and sold at a profit of nearly 400 percent. According to evidence presented in court, Melnik bribed one of his contacts in the Russian Customs Department to let the shipment leave the country on forged waybills. At the time, Melnik was head of the Russian Interpol office; previously, he had held the rank of colonel in the Ministry of Internal Affairs, to which he had been promoted by Bakatin.

Until he was arrested, Melnik belonged to the circle of Russian government insiders who comfortably administered the transition from Communism to capitalism. He even lived in the same exclusive Moscow building as top officials of the Ministry of Russian Security. Clearly, not every member of the bureaucracy was corrupt. Was it fair, then, to condemn all former nomenklatura because of the excesses of a few? Even the comrade criminals, after all, might well be tomorrow's Russian Rothschilds, Rockefellers, and Morgans. Considering the risks of the Russian marketplace, who could better assure the country's stable passage toward the future than the guardians of the old order? The situation bears an ironic resemblance to the earliest period of the Soviet state, when the leadership recruited czarist functionaries to keep the country running and the empire's military officers to assure its defense.

"If you look at the social make-up of today's *nouveaux riches*, there are an awful lot of former Party and KGB workers, maybe proportionally more than anyone else," said Bakatin. "But I see nothing wrong with it. If we had a normal economy, things might have been different. KGB and Party *apparatchiki* are the leaders in business simply because they are the people who had more information than others, better contacts, more possibilities of getting hold of supplies. They are not stupid."

It is a depressing argument, all the more so because many Westerners appear to have conceded the point on the grounds, perhaps, that no one can keep an old car on the road better than those who know what it looks like under the hood. But it is circular reasoning. The fact that there was no "normal economy," in Bakatin's phrase, to produce an efficient, non-partisan managerial class and civil service capable of presiding over the transition from Communism is hardly an accident of history. Although the czarist functionaries were eventually purged by the Soviet leadership, they never posed a serious threat of subversion to the new order. In contrast, yesterday's nomenklatura—enriched by the Communist fortune and reinforced by its mob contacts—does have the power to subvert the new Russian democracy. And it has had the extra advantage of advance planning.

"The nomenklatura knew years ago that the system would come tumbling down," said Aslambek Aslakhanov. "They prepared themselves for that, and they have obviously been successful. But no matter how high a position they occupy in our country, I still consider them ordinary criminals, because they put their own interests above the interests of the state, just as they did when the Party existed."

Lev Timofeyev, the former dissident, went a step further in his book with a warning that the code the nomenklatura lived by, and which it now shared with its underworld partners, was poisonous to Russia's hopes for a normal economy. "The danger isn't that a former member of the *apparat* becomes a bank president," he wrote. "The trouble is, rather, that this person is. . .bound hand and foot to his social class—[to] the apparat, the military-industrial complex, and the KGB. He is dependent on that trinity in everything he does, because he obtains his property rights from them for a price: a silent oath of loyalty. If he breaks that oath, he will not remain a property owner for long."

Timofeyev went on to predict that those forces that preserved their economic monopoly while holding on to government power would move into positions of greater political authority in Russia and other Commonwealth states. After the December, 1993, Russian parliamentary elections, his prediction was borne out. By February, 1994, the majority of senior cabinet posts in the Yeltsin government was occupied by former Communist officials with deep ties to powerful state industrial and agricultural interests. Russia was well on its way to a form of state capitalism in which former Communists played the commanding roles.

In post-Communist Russia, as in the former Soviet Union, the boundaries between crime and politics have been blurred. That is one reason why Russia's comrade criminals do not represent a law-and-order problem in the accepted Western sense of the term. The comrade criminal carries with him the baggage of the criminal state.

Aslakhanov could find only one reason for reassurance as he surveyed his country's surging corruption and crime. "Russia is still too big and disorganized for there to be one Al Capone," he said. The spirit of independence is strong among all our different criminal groups. While the chaos continues, they would rather act on their own without having to submit to one criminal chieftain who is in charge of everything.

"The real problem may start when the state actually manages to come to grips with organized crime—when our law enforcement agencies work the way they're supposed to, and when we begin to control corruption. Then the criminal clans and the political clans may try to elect someone who can lead them."

If Aslakhanov is right, the entire "transition period" may be little more than an interregnum between Russia's previous oppressors and its as-yet-unidentified future ones. It is all the more important, therefore, to look at the multifarious and often imaginative ways Russia's comrade criminals are advancing their political and economic fortunes.

5

The Executive and the Legislature

After coming to power in 2000, Vladimir Putin concentrated immeasurable power into his hands in an executive branch heavily populated with members of the security services, who as a rule have had no tolerance for the practices or principles of open politics. As a result, there is no transparency, no account-ability, and little in the way of opportunity for the Russian people to effect change. As one government official put it in 2004, "Democracy is finished in this country."[1] That executive power dominates all spheres of political life in the country. Within the legislature, within the executive branch, and in relations between the two branches, politics in Russia lacks the transparency, account-ability, competition, or representation to justify using the word "democracy" in relation to that country.

This was hardly an inevitable outcome. Russia's legislature in the 1990s was one of the most active and interesting places in the world. Indeed, it so chal-lenged executive power in the first two years after the fall of the Soviet Union that it forced a hostile struggle between the Supreme Soviet, a carryover of the Soviet period, and the executive branch. At the center of the dispute was which entity would exercise control over the government ministries. Articles 87 and 104 of the Russian Constitution[2] anointed the Supreme Soviet and its overarch-ing Congress of People's Deputies as the "highest organ of state power," and the chair of the legislature understood his position as carrying "the same responsibil-ity as the President for all that occurs in the country."[3] The president, of course, also claimed to hold authority as head of the executive branch. While Supreme Soviet Chair Ruslan I. Khasbulatov and President Boris N. Yeltsin both claimed executive authority, at least one constitutional expert argued that neither held authority over the government![4] Within the legislature and in relations with outside entities, Khasbulatov consistently attempted to challenge and thwart presidential authority. In October 1993, the nearly two-year power struggle burst into the streets, as an informal militia cobbled together by the Supreme Soviet attempted to seize power. They battled with military units deployed by and loyal to the president. This was a traumatic convulsion, to say the least, in which at least 146 people perished.[5]

It was in the wake of that tragedy that President Yeltsin and his closest advisors, consumed by the overriding objective of preventing another such struggle between political institutions, in a series of secretive moves, effected subtle changes to the constitution. These changes, noticed by few between their introduction and the adoption of the constitution in a national referendum in December 1993, destroyed any balance of power between the branches and created a super-strong presidential system highly vulnerable to authoritarian abuse.[6] They bestowed upon the president virtually unchecked authority over the government and over the legislature.

For the remainder of Yeltsin's term in office during the 1990s, the new legislature, the Russian State Duma, remained a highly engaged, influential, and interesting body. Although Yeltsin had created a super-presidency in the constitution, during his tenure, this constitutional situation was of astonishingly little significance. Yeltsin had no interest in waging another battle with the legislature, nor did he wish to dominate it. In fact, he genuinely wished to work with the legislature and insisted that his government ministers do the same. From his perspective, the reason for the constitutional changes was to compel the legislature to work with the executive and prevent it from waging battle like the one the country had just experienced.[7] So, the Duma worked to legislate both internally and in relation with the executive branch. For example, under the Kremlin's orders and at the new State Duma's insistence, the government went from being months late in submitting its annual budgets to submitting them on time and even early.[8] Even more significant, under Yeltsin, the budget itself dramatically expanded from a total of one or two pages lacking any specificity in revenue or spending priorities to several hundred pages of detail on each government department's budget.[9] It was an increase in transparency and accountability that fostered hope for legislative–executive cooperation.[10] A fairly safe argument can be made that the annual budget is the most important piece of legislation an effective legislature engages in, and from 1994 to 1999, the Russian State Duma was the site of an active legislature wielding influence on the annual budget. The same spirit carried over to other types of legislative activity. Yeltsin was dedicated to working with the new legislature and to forging collaborative relations between the branches.

However, this collaboration did not mean that Russia was on its way to a stable democratic system with institutional checks and balances—far from it.

The reality of the new constitution was that Russia fit the definition of dictatorship: How the political system would function depended entirely on the personality of the individual occupying the position of president. Yeltsin sought collaboration and cooperation. His handpicked successor was of an entirely different mind. Vladimir Putin sought executive dominance under a firm hand, using the enormous powers the constitution grants to the Russian presidency to emasculate the power and influence of the legislature. Almost immediately upon taking power, Putin began chipping away at the legislature's autonomy. Part of this effort he achieved by eliminating political competition, exiling, imprisoning, or otherwise eliminating serious political contenders and disbanding or marginalizing opposition parties. The Duma, which in its first two sessions had influenced and attempted to provide oversight on policy, had become a ghost town. Members marched in lockstep with their president. Within a few years, legislators so lacked autonomy or independence that they were required to receive permission from the president if they wished to speak to the media, which he was also moving to silence. The halls and chambers of the legislature, once vibrant with policy debate, questioning of government officials, and lawmaking had been literally silenced; the Duma transformed into a rubber stamp of government policy. The Duma now ratifies but does not legislate; it does not question government ministers or provide oversight; indeed, it lacks any of the components of an effective legislature.[11]

Some scholars, following lessons derived from the study of established, effective legislative bodies, such as the United States Congress, found increased "party discipline" and "cohesion" in the Russian State Duma after 2000.[12] But, Russia is not a democratic system marked by open, competitive politics. Studies such as these use legislative votes as their primary measure, but legislative votes in a legislature lacking meaningful authority fail to tell a meaningful story. What is significant is not that there is cohesion. What would be significant, in Russia's context, is if there wasn't! Chaisty's selection included in this chapter, "Majority Control and Executive Dominance," is also reflective of this approach that looks to Putin seeking stabile majorities to reinforce support for his power. A look beyond legislative votes, to include the nature of elections, of information and political association, and of executive behavior, underscores the view that Putin has used his power to ensure the impossibility of meaningful checks on or opposition to executive authority. This is the approach of Shevtsova's, "Liberal Technocrats as an Adornment of the State" and Kryshtanovskaya and White's "Inside the Putin Court."

Putin runs the country with an increasingly iron fist. As president and, since 2008, as prime minister (his handpicked successor Dmitry Medvedev is widely recognized to be marching to Putin's drum), Putin has restored one-party rule, reinstituted state control over the media, eliminated competitive politics, silenced political opposition, and in short, has restored a dictatorship. The potential of the massive executive power enshrined in the constitution has come to fruition in Russia, with nothing in place to balance that power.

For Further Reference

Books

Peter Baker and Susan Glasser, *Vladimir Putin's Russia and the End of Revolution*, Scribner: 2005.

Timothy J. Colton and Stephen Holmes, eds., *The State After Communism: Governance in the New Russia*, Rowman and Littlefield: 2006.

Eugene Huskey, *Presidential Power in Russia*, ME Sharpe: 1999.

Joel M. Ostrow, *Comparing Post-Soviet Legislatures: A Theory of Institutional Design and Political Conflict*, Ohio State University Press: 2000.

Joel M. Ostrow, Georgiy A. Satarov, and Irina M. Khakamada, *The Consolidation of Dictatorship in Russia: An Inside View of the Demise of Democracy*, Praeger: 2006.

Lilia Shevtsova, *Russia—Lost in Transition: The Yeltsin and Putin Legacies*, Carnegie Endowment for International Peace: 2007.

Kathryn Stoner-Weiss, *Resisting the Russian State: Reform and Retrenchment in Post-Soviet Russia*, Cambridge University Press: 2007.

Brian D. Taylor, *State Building in Putin's Russia: Policing and Coercion After Communism*, Cambridge University Press: 2011.

Journal Articles

M. Stephen Fish, "Stronger Legislatures, Stronger Democracies," *Journal of Democracy*, Volume 17, No. 1 (2006).

Henry Hale, "Russians and the Putin-Medvedev 'Tandemocracy'," *Problems of Post-Communism*, Vol. 57, No. 2 (2010).

Joel M. Ostrow, Conflict management in Russia's Federal Institutions, *Post-Soviet Affairs*, Vol. 18, No. 1 (2002).

Novel

Vladimir Sorokin, *Day of the Oprichnik: A Novel*, Farrar, Straus and Giroux: 2011.

NOTES

1. See Ostrow, Satarov, and Khakamada, *The Consolidation of Dictatorship in Russia: An Inside View of the Demise of Democracy* (Praeger, 2007), p. 123.

2. This refers to the RSFSR Constitution, much amended but originally adopted in 1977.

3. See Joel M. Ostrow, *Comparing Post-Soviet Legislatures: A Theory of Institutional Design and Political Conflict* (Ohio State University Press, 2000), especially pp. 86–90.

4. Ibid.

5. The figure is the official Kremlin tally, but the credibility of the figure is widely disputed. The best account, bar none, of the October 1993 crisis is Veronika Kutsyllo, *Zapiski iz Belogo Doma: 21 sentyabrya - 4 oktyabrya* (Moscow: Izdatel'skiy Dom 'b', 1993).

6. See Ostrow, Satarov, and Khakamada (2007), especially Chapter 3.

7. Ibid, p. 38; also see Ostrow (2000), Chapter 6, especially pp. 183–189.

8. See Ostrow (2000), pp. 177–180. From 1997 to 2000, the budget arrived at the Duma either by or prior to the legal deadline.

9. Ibid, pp, 160–164 and 181–183.

10. See Ostrow, "Conflict-Management in Russia's Federal Institutions," *Post-Soviet Affairs*, Vol. 18, No. 1 (2002), pp. 49–70.

11. Ostrow, Satarov, and Khakamada (2007), pp. 100–102 and 107–109. On effective legislatures, see Nelson W. Polsby, "Legislatures," *Handbook of Political Science*, Vol. 5, eds. Fred I. Greenstein and Nelson W. Polsby (Addison Wesley, 1975).

12. See Thomas F. Remington, "Presidential Support in the Russian State Duma," *Legislative Studies Quarterly*, Vol. 31, No. 1 (January, 2006), pp. 5–32; also Paul Chaisty, "The Legislative Effects of Presidential Partisan Powers in Post-Communist Russia," *Government and Opposition*, Vol. 43, No. 3 (Summer, 2008), pp. 424–453.

5.1

Liberal Technocrats as an Adornment of the State

Lilia Shevtsova

The liberal technocrats in Russia . . . are free marketers who consent to work within a less-than-democratic, or even blatantly undemocratic, system under the direct patronage of the leader. They are to be found in many countries, from Saudi Arabia to China, and from Singapore to Argentina. In most cases they serve a useful purpose, obstructing both the expansion of the bureaucracy and populist policies. In a transitional society they play a crucial role as the only group capable, if supported by the leader, of carrying out painful reforms without having to worry about their popularity or political future. Their role is constructive, however, only if there are other political forces with a developed liberal democratic sensibility to mitigate the technocrats' social insensitivity and excessive managerial zeal. Technocrats can make for a social breakthrough, but they can also be destructive. The success of the reforms of Leszek Balcerowicz in Poland and Václav Klaus in the Czech Republic was due to the fact that the local technocrats were operating in societies with powerful democratic movements. Technocrats without redeeming democratic support operate equally well in the interests of authoritarianism or oligarchy. In Chile, the Chicago Boys were a mere tool of the oligarchy. They played a crucial role in the coup that brought Pinochet to power, only then to work efficiently under his orders and against the oligarchy.

In post-Soviet Russia the technocrats (the most prominent being Yegor Gaidar and Anatoly Chubais), faced with the weakness of the democratic movement, became politicians. They not only created a free market system, but also, as Democratic Party Yabloko's leader Grigory Yavlinsky rightly notes, facilitated the development of oligarchic capitalism. In 1996–1997 the technocrats, under the leadership of Anatoly Chubais, who, with Yeltsin ailing, was the unofficial ruler of Russia for a time, could have played a different historical role. The popular governor of Nizhni Novgorod, Boris Nemtsov, had been invited by Yeltsin to join the government and, with a popularity rating in 1997 of nearly 40 percent, could have eased the transformation of the technocrats into a liberal democratic force capable of changing the rules imposed by the bureaucracy. The technocrats failed to reform either the regime or themselves. The role of the technocrats

Source: Lilia Shevtsova, "Liberal Technocrats as an Adornment of the State," from *Russia—Lost in Transition: the Yeltsin and Putin Legacies*. Carnegie Endowment for International Peace, 2007. 113–117.

Note: Notes and references have been removed from this article.

under Yeltsin has yet to be thoroughly researched. One question to be answered is how far they facilitated reform and how far they assisted in the consolidation of personalized power under the guise of liberalism. So far, the Russian experience shows strong evidence that the first generation of Russian technocrats has been much more effective in undermining, albeit often unconsciously or unwittingly, liberal democracy than in building it.

During Putin's presidency the technocrats' scope and potential have been limited by the regime's priority of maintaining the status quo. Gref, Kudrin, Zhukov, Mikhail Dmitriev, Arkady Dvorkovich, and other technocrats in the Putin government have found it far more difficult to promote reforms, understanding that reforms might undermine the stability of the system and regime they have been working for. Their room for maneuver has certainly been less than that enjoyed by the Gaidar team in the first years of Yeltsin's presidency, or of Anatoly Chubais and Boris Nemtsov in its final stages, if only because the current Russian system has evolved in a way that rules out reforms that might introduce any element of competitiveness. The new echelon of technocrats must be aware of that. One occasionally has the impression that they are perfectly content to be the liberal adornment of an illiberal, undemocratic regime. The sole achievement of the government liberals has been their success in maintaining financial discipline, but, in the run-up to the elections in 2007–2008, even that achievement might become a victim of the regime's populism.

Today there are two groups of interlinked technocrats: those within the government and those within the party framework of the Union of Right Forces. I have already expressed my doubts about the reform potential of the government technocrats. As regards those in the Union of Right Forces, they are evidently technocrats seeking a political niche that will enable them to survive without being wholly in the president's pocket. The origins of the Union of Right Forces as a free-market party favoring cooperation with the regime make it doubtful whether it has any longer-term, independent prospects. After a purging of the political scene that has removed not only opposition movements but also those that showed signs of vacillation, the Union of Right Forces has found itself obliged to swear allegiance to the Kremlin in order to continue in legal politics. If it strays from the rules laid down by the Kremlin, the Union risks expulsion from official politics. That is something the liberal technocrats are keen to avoid.

At the earlier stages of Putin's presidency, the Union of Right Forces could no longer afford to criticize the regime, although for some time its leaders and ideologists had allowed themselves mutterings of discontent, which had been the only way to retain credibility. The increasing rigor of the regime forced them to seek a compromise and, one cannot help but wonder whether heading into the parliamentary elections of December 2007, their leaders (official leader Nikita Belych and unofficial leader Anatoly Chubais) signed up on the side of the Kremlin. The evolution of that party from mild and hesitant grudges and disagreements with the Kremlin policy to support of the regime merely confirms that it cannot emerge from the Kremlin's shadow. Another reason is that the unofficial leader of the Union of Right Forces, Anatoly Chubais, is the chair of the monopolist RAO UES (which manages the Russian electricity grid). He is not only the godfather of the Russian oligarchy, but also a pillar of the ruling bureaucratic corporation, which includes, in various capacities, all the other technocrats who continue to serve the regime. The fact that, during the run-up to the regional and parliamentary elections in 2006–2007, leaders of the Union of Right Forces were constantly seen on television, where news output is agreed upon with the Kremlin, made it abundantly clear that the Union of Right Forces had surrendered to the regime and in return was being allowed to participate in public politics. In fact, its leaders could not behave differently because its membership base and supporters are mostly loyal to the authorities. In any case, technocrats have agreed, some knowingly and some perhaps not, to act as a smokescreen for the current system as they try to remain in politics. Liberals like Boris Nemtsov who, for some reason remains in the leadership of the Union of Right Forces and continues to oppose the Kremlin, are in the minority, and sooner or later they will be forced into submission or will have to leave the Union of Right Forces.

With the crackdown on dissent, the technocrats have given up sitting on the fence and will most likely end up either loyal to the Kremlin lapdog party or as one of the semi-opposition factions within the chameleon-like governing party. When this occurs it will no longer be possible to doubt that the presence of technocrats with their liberal phraseology on the Russian political scene—both in the government and outside it, serving an illiberal regime—is one of the reasons there is no real liberal movement in Russia, and why bringing together liberalism and democracy has proved so difficult.

A revival of liberalism as an ideology, and of liberal democracy as a political movement, is impossible without a proper understanding of the part played by the technocrats' "liberalism." It may well be that in the future some of the technocrats will join a new democratic movement, but only if they leave the Union of Right Forces, which historically has proved to be one of several "parties of power" despite the fact that it includes a faction of opposition to the regime. Collaboration between the opposition-minded members of the Union of Right Forces and Yabloko in the Moscow Duma elections in 2005, showed that a united front of liberals and democrats is theoretically possible. But the chances of forming a viable liberal—democratic movement in Russia that includes the technocrats, will be nil if the process is again presided over by the Kremlin. Liberalism will have no prospects if those who claim to be its adherents once more try to argue that democracy is a hindrance, or that it will be the next stage after capitalism is established. Despite the complexity of the link between liberals and democrats, neglecting democracy, as the 1990s showed, causes liberalism to degenerate.

5.2

Inside the Putin Court: A Research Note

Ol'ga Kryshtanovskaya and Stephen White

IF THE SOVIET SYSTEM OF GOVERNMENT centred on the General Secretary of the CPSU Central Committee, the Russian system has been based on the powerful executive presidency that was established by the 1993 Constitution. Given his relative obscurity before his appointment as prime minister in 1999, the world was understandably anxious to know 'Who is Mister Putin?' By the end of his first term of office, the outlines of an answer had become reasonably clear. Central authority would be vigorously reasserted; the Chechen war would be prosecuted without compromise; the oligarchs would be 'liquidated as a class'; and the mass media, particularly television, would be placed under the control of the state authorities. It was a 'managed democracy' that found little favour in Western capitals, but one that allowed Putin to win an overwhelming victory in the 2004 presidential election and to retain a level of popular support that could be described as 'Turkmenia'.

The composition of the ruling group became clearer as the new president advanced his supporters and marginalised those who had less reason to be beholden to him, particularly the El'tsin 'Family'. The Putin elite in the early years of the new century was about the same age as its El'tsin predecessor but less likely to hold a postgraduate degree, somewhat more provincial, even more overwhelmingly male, more likely to come from the business world, and more likely to come from St Petersburg. There had also been a change in the career background of the ruling group, and particularly in the proportion that were *siloviki*—that is, who had served or were currently serving in the armed forces, state security, law enforcement or one of the other 'force ministries'. By the start of 2005, on our data, the *siloviki* had fallen slightly as a proportion of the top leadership but were still close to a quarter (24.7%) of the total, and they were continuing to advance in the national government (up to 34.2%) and in both houses of the Russian parliament (up to 18.3% in each case).

Formal position has always counted for relatively little in Soviet or Russian politics, and even career background is an imperfect predictor of attitudes—although a ruling group with a substantial component of *siloviki* is certainly consistent with the

---

Source: Ol'ga Kryshtanovskaya and Stephen White, "Inside the Putin Court: A Research Note," *Europe-Asia Studies*, Vol. 57, no 7. November 2005. 1065-1075.

Note: Notes and references have been removed from this article.

broad direction of public policy since Putin's accession, with a greater emphasis on 'patriotic' education in the schools, attacks on foreign NGOs, a dominant position for the state in the control of natural resources, restrictions on the freedom of scholarly inquiry, and a generous increase in budgetary support for the armed forces themselves. Accordingly, we need an approach that goes inside the 'black box' of Russian policy formation. What are the patterns of informal association? What are the patterns of interaction between other members of the ruling group and Putin himself, and between the presidential administration, the government and other institutional actors? And what, going further, are the ties between informal coalitions and policy positions? Why should it matter which clan is dominant, and which is in retreat?

A modest body of literature has already begun to address some of these questions, although it rests on limited empirical foundations. In what follows we take these matters further by drawing on a substantial new body of evidence, in particular a series of interviews with elite members themselves. The elite is defined, for our purposes, in positional terms: members of the Security Council, senior officials within the presidential administration, members of the government and both houses of parliament, heads of regional executives, presidential envoys, federal inspectors and the business elite. In all, we conducted 150 interviews with members of the elite itself or those closely associated with them, including 20 with staff of the presidential administration, 22 with Duma deputies, 11 with members of the Federation Council, 53 with senior officers of the force ministries, 18 with staff from the government apparatus and nine with staff attached to individual ministries. In addition, we conducted 50 interviews with highly-placed informants, and used our own access to elite circles to refine our understanding of the attitudes and policy orientations that prevail at the highest levels.

Patterns of Elite Decision Making

On the evidence available to us, the authority of the central executive is in practice devolved to a series of small and informal groups around the President himself. Putin prefers to work not with formal institutions but with *ad hoc* groups that are not defined by institutional boundaries. Various people are invited to his meetings in the Kremlin, but scheduled meetings of the entire membership of the government or of the Security Council are relatively infrequent. Even the State Council meets as an 'inner circle' of the governors that have been chosen by Putin to serve on its Presidium.

In these circumstances it is not easy to identify a strategic elite who take the most important decisions and formulate national policy. To identify a group of this kind we used the following methods:

- we analysed the composition of all meetings in which the President participated directly;

- of these, we identified the meetings that were conducted on a regular basis; and
- on this basis, we identified an 'inner circle' of people who took part in practically all of Putin's meetings.

This analysis showed that the President works publicly with two teams of officials, who meet regularly in his Kremlin office to adopt strategic decisions. There is also a smaller group of friends, who meet with him at his dacha. The President conducts these two sequences of meetings on Mondays and Saturdays respectively; the Monday meetings are, in effect, 'meetings of the President with members of the government,' the Saturday meetings are 'meetings of the heads of the force structures.'

The Monday governmental meetings take place in one of Putin's Kremlin offices, with members of the presidential administration in attendance. These meetings are reported regularly in the press, and shown in part on national television news. The composition of these meetings is subject to some variation; most often, however, the Monday meetings include the following:

Putin himself

Mikhail Fradkov (prime minister)

Alexander Zhukov (deputy premier)

German Gref (minister of economic development and trade)

Mikhail Zurabov (minister of social welfare and health)

Sergei Naryshkin (head of the government apparatus)

Igor' Sechin (deputy head of the presidential administration)

Dmitrii Medvedev (head of the presidential administration)

Sergei Ivanov (defence minister)

Sergei Lavrov (foreign minister)

Rashid Nurgaliev (interior minister) and

Andrei Illarionov (presidential adviser).

Other, more occasional participants include ministers Aleksei Gordeev (agriculture), Yurii Trutnev (natural resources) and Igor' Levitin (transport), and Sergei Yastrzhembsky from the presidential administration. It is immediately apparent that there are many ministers who do not take part in these 'meetings of the government', and that at the same time there are other officials who do attend but who do not have ministerial rank (Illarionov, Sechin and Medvedev).

The business of these meetings is reported reasonably fully in the press. In February 2005, for instance, the pay of military servicemen was under discussion; Putin asked for the 'resolution of the problem to be accelerated'; Sergei Ivanov and German Gref responded with positive assurances. A meeting in April focused on preparations for the summit with the European Union that was to be held the following month, and considered the question of membership of the World Trade Organisations.In May there was another of these 'traditional Monday meetings with members of the government' at which Putin discussed the gas pipeline from Taishet to Nakhodka with Viktor Khristenko, minister of industry and energy, and discussed the pensions problem with Mikhail Zurabov, minister of social development and health.Prime minister Fradkov conducts a separate meeting, also on Mondays, at which the social and economic development of the Russian regions is considered.The seating pattern of the most regular participants at these Monday meetings of 'members of the government' is set out in Figure 1.

Figure 1. Monday Meetings: The Participants and Where they Sit

On Saturdays Putin assembles a smaller and rather different group of people, usually no more than eight in number. As with the Monday group, the typical composition of these meetings does not coincide with bureaucratic boundaries. As well as the heads of the force ministries and the Secretary of the Security Council, these Saturday meetings are generally attended by prime minister Fradkov and presidential chief of staff Dmitrii Medvedev. Sometimes the media refer to these Saturday gatherings as 'meetings of the Security Council,' but they are more accurately described as 'meetings of the President with members of the Security Council.' Even when the Security Council meets in its formal capacity there are several members who are not normally in attendance.

The Saturday meetings are further evidence of the President's tendency to avoid formal meetings with people with whom he finds it difficult to work, or who do not have his entire confidence. Those who attend typically include:

Putin

Mikhail Fradkov (prime minister)

Sergei Ivanov (defence minister)

Sergei Lavrov (foreign minister)

Dmitrii Medvedev (head of the presidential administration)

Igor' Ivanov (Secretary of the Security Council)

Nikolai Patrushev (Federal Security Bureau)

Rashid Nurgaliev (interior minister) and

Sergei Lebedev (foreign intelligence).

In addition, Viktor Ivanov (a presidential aide), Igor' 'Sechin (deputy head of the presidential administration) and Vladimir Ustinov (Procurator General) are normally present. The published record makes clear that 'various questions of domestic and foreign policy' are discussed at these meetings as well as defence and national security. The seating pattern at these Saturday meetings is shown in Figure 2.

According to our informants there is also a third group, which might be called the 'tea-drinking group'. This consists of Putin's personal friends, who meet informally at his official residence. Nothing is known of the frequency of such

Figure 2. Saturday Meetings: The Participants and Where they Sit

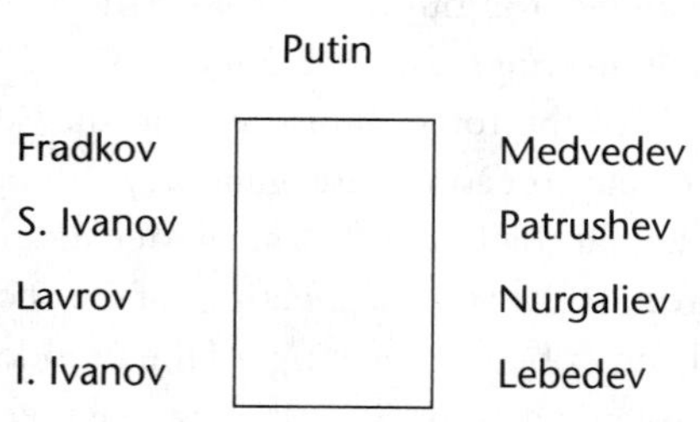

Putin

Fradkov		Medvedev
S. Ivanov		Patrushev
Lavrov		Nurgaliev
I. Ivanov		Lebedev

meetings, and every precaution is taken to ensure that even the names of those who are admitted into this inner circle are not made public. This 'tea-drinking group' is overwhelmingly composed of leading officials who—like Putin himself— were born in Leningrad and graduated from its university. They include Sergei Ivanov, Igor' Sechin, Dmitrii Medvedev (a former member of the university's teaching staff), federal narcotics board head Viktor Cherkesov, presidential envoy Dmitrii Kozak (a Leningrad University graduate though not a native of the city), presidential aide 'Vladimir Kozhin (born in the Chelyabinsk region but a graduate of Leningrad Electrotechnical Institute), German Gref (born in Kazakhstan and an Omsk University graduate but a postgraduate law student at St Petersburg, where his father had been a professor), and Georgii Poltavchenko (presidential envoy in the central federal district, born in Baku but a graduate of Leningrad Institute of Aviation Equipment).

All three groups coincide to some extent. Fradkov, Medvedev, Sergei Ivanov, Lavrov and Nurgaliev, for instance, are members not only of the Monday but also of the Saturday group. Only two of them, however, are central to each of the three groups: Medvedev and Sergei Ivanov. These two (and after them prime minister Fradkov) should accordingly be regarded as Putin's closest associates, with whom he discusses all the key issues of domestic as well as foreign politics.

Kremlin Clans

These patterns of interaction are underpinned by less formal patterns of informal association, or 'clans'. On the evidence of our informants, there are now essentially two of these clans, which can be labelled *'siloviki'* and 'liberals' respectively (see Table 1). The *siloviki* are those in uniform, whether in the army, police or security. The liberals, by contrast, are committed to Western values, including the principles of a market economy, and support what they regard as a democratic path of development. This simple binary division is modified by a variety of cross-cutting allegiances, and by a constant process of horizontal and vertical mobility in which individuals constantly move between positions, and sometimes into or out of the ruling stratum as a whole. Not only this, but their political orientations are not as different as might at first sight appear, with very little opposition in either case to a 'strong' or even authoritarian state. This is an understandable position for *siloviki* to take; liberals support it for rather different reasons, arguing that the population is unready for democratic reforms and that the government has no alternative but to introduce them from above, by executive authority. Putin appears to have deliberately retained both of these groups in his immediate environment in order to avoid becoming dependent on either of them.

Table 1. 'Siloviki' and 'Liberals' in Government Structures, 2005

	Siloviki	Liberals
Presidential administration	Sechin, Viktor Ivanov	Medvedev, Surkov, Illarionov
Government	Fradkov, Sergei Ivanov, Lavrov, Patrushev, Nurgaliev, Lebedev, Cherkesov, Shoigu	Gref, Kudrin, Zubarov, Trutnev, Gordeev, Reiman, Naryshkin
Presidential envoys	Poltavchenko, Latyshev, Kvashnin, Pulikovsky, Klebanov	Kozak, Kirienko
Other institutions	Ustinov, Stepashin, Primakov	
Party leaders	Gudkov (People's Party)	Gryzlov (United Russia), Rogozin (Rodina)

The Siloviki

Over the years of the Putin presidency, the *siloviki* have become not only more numerous but also more differentiated. There are *siloviki* in security itself, *siloviki* who have moved into politics (such as those who head the federal districts), and *siloviki* who have moved into business (for instance, within Gazprom). [. . .]

The *siloviki* may also be divided into those who are concerned with questions of domestic politics and those who are concerned with Russia's international security. The first group is concentrated around Igor' Sechin, and is currently the most numerous and influential in Russian politics. Its unquestioned leader is Sechin himself, deputy head of the presidential administration and a languages graduate who worked for military intelligence in Angola and Mozambique before establishing an association with Putin through his service in the foreign economic relations department of Leningrad city. Sechin, according to our informants, has direct access to the President and enjoys his absolute confidence. Apart from Sechin the most important members of this group are presidential aide Viktor Ivanov (who also has direct access to the President and is particularly influential in personnel matters), Procurator General Vladimir Ustinov, banker Sergei Pugachev, and the head of Rosneft' Sergei Bogdanchikov. Ustinov is related to Sechin (their children are married, and there are grandchildren), Pugachev is one of Putin's personal friends, and Bogdanchikov is friendly with Sechin as well as Viktor Ivanov.

Defence minister Sergei Ivanov may be considered the leader of the other group, which is focused on international security. This group includes SVR director Sergei Lebedev, foreign minister Lavrov, the president's foreign policy adviser Sergei Prikhod'ko, and the head of the General Staff Yurii Baluevsky. Prime minister Fradkov, whose background is in foreign trade and who is regarded by our informants as a Sergei Ivanov protege, may also be assigned to this group; his function is to promote the policies of the *siloviki* within government. The 'foreign relations *siloviki*' are less unified than their internal counterparts, and are less closely associated at a personal level; they are distinguished more by their allegiance to the President himself than to Sergei Ivanov. The defence minister is generally identified as Putin's closest confidant and most likely successor, though he has himself disclaimed such a role.

The 'liberals'

The other Kremlin clan can be described as 'liberal' in only the most qualified of terms, as it includes people with very authoritarian views about Russia and its future. The leader of this group is Dmitrii Medvedev, head of the presidential administration since October 2003, together with his deputy Vladislav Surkov, presidential envoy Dmitrii Kozak, Gazprom head Aleksei Miller, ministers Gref, Kudrin, Reiman, Gordeev and Trutnev, presidential aide Igor' Shuvalov, presidential counsellor Andrei Illarionov, Vladimir Kogan of the St Petersburg Banking House, and others. Medvedev, like FSB director Patrushev, is believed to have a difficult relationship with Sechin, and on some accounts he did not support the seizure of Yukos assets in late 2003; on the other hand his published statements have left little doubt that he shares the *silovik* diagnosis that Russia could 'disappear as a state' unless the elite preserves its unity, and that state ownership and management have 'far from exhausted their potential'. The position of the Medvedev group has been strengthened by the recent appointment of his classmate from Leningrad University, Anton Ivanov, as the new chairman of the Higher Arbitration Court.

Clans and Policy

Siloviki and liberals have few differences about the concentration of power: they are both agreed that Russia needs a 'single vertical' of executive authority. They are much more divided in their views about the economy. The 'liberals' do not object to the partial renationalisation of natural resources, but believe any changes of this kind should be carried out in accordance with the law and over a relatively extended period. In their view, Russian business will not revive until it has a greater degree of entrepreneurial freedom; they are annoyed by the peremptory actions of the *siloviki*, which have damaged investor confidence, and believe they cannot be entrusted with management of the economy as a whole. The *siloviki*, on the other hand, are convinced that privatisation has inflicted great damage on Russian national interests and take the view that 'strategic' enterprises, especially in the energy sector, should be returned to state control.

It had become conventional during the El'tsin years for officials of ministerial rank to occupy positions on the boards of state-owned companies. Rather different practices have come to prevail under Putin: it is no longer ministers but Kremlin *siloviki* and senior officials from the presidential administration who have been entering the boardrooms. The head of the presidential staff, Dmitrii Medvedev, himself chairs the board of Gazprom, a company with an annual turnover of $30 billion, and Igor' Sechin heads the board of the state oil company Rosneft', with an annual turnover of $4 billion. Viktor Ivanov heads the boards of Almaz-Antei, the country's largest producer of anti-aircraft defence equipment, and of Aeroflot. Sechin's counterpart in the presidential administration, Vladislav Surkov, chairs the board of another oil company, Transnefteprodukt, and the President's foreign policy adviser, Sergei Prikhod'ko, chairs the board of an armaments firm. The president's press secretary Aleksei Gromov is a member of the board of the country's most important television company, First Channel, and presidential aide Igor' Shuvalov has joined the board of Russian Railways.

At the same time, ministers of a more liberal orientation have been losing their places in company boardrooms: Kudrin left Unified Energy Systems and Gref resigned his positions in Rosneft', Sheremet'evo, Svyaz'invest and Aeroflot, although vice-premier Aleksandr Zhukov has remained chairman of the board of Russian Railways and industry and energy minister Khristenko chairs the board of oil company Transneft'. A few oligarchs of the El'tsin period have however maintained their position by establishing good relations with the *siloviki*: these include the heads of such companies as Surgutneftegaz (Vladimir Bogdanov), Severstal' (Aleksei Mordashev), Lukoil (Vagit Alekperov) and Interros (Vladimir Potanin). Our interview with an FSB officer suggested that the *siloviki* had at least one guiding principle in their dealings with individual oligarchs: whether or not they were 'nationally oriented'. 'Good oligarchs' were people like Mordashev or Bogdanov ('they're Russians'), but not the others: 'all Jews are traitors, oriented towards the West. That's how it's always been'.

Divisions between *siloviki* and liberals have underlain at least two of the central issues in recent economic policy: the ownership of oil, and the attempt to double GDP and 'catch up with Portugal'. [. . .] Liberals accused the *siloviki* of incompetence, and of policies that would make it impossible to achieve their longer-term objectives (capital flight, for instance, was four times as great in 2004 as it had been a year before, which was an understandable reaction to the seizure of Yukos assets). The *siloviki*, for their part, accused the liberals of undue pessimism, and suggested other ways of resolving the problem that made greater use of the state itself. As one of our interviewees noted, this was another conflict with important political implications, because if the *siloviki* were able to achieve their objectives, extending state control and their own role in its management, they would have no alternative but to seek an extension of Putin's presidential term in order to protect themselves against the possibility that a future head of state might choose to make other arrangements.

A range of other divisions separate liberals and *siloviki* on matters of domestic politics. The *silovik* ideology is as follows. The state is the basis of society; therefore, the state should be strong. A strong state controls everything. The supports of the state are the *siloviki* and law enforcement agencies in general. Accordingly, they occupy a certain position in society. They need a special status—material and legal. Security agents who risk their lives in the service of the state, for instance, should be beyond the reach of courts of law. A strong state should also control the economy, at least its natural resources, which cannot be allowed to remain in private hands. Pluralism of opinions is dangerous as it undermines the state from within. There is still an external enemy—the West—and this means that a strong army is needed, and a powerful armaments industry. The state, accordingly, should spend heavily on defence, and on research into new weapon technologies. Society should be passive and obedient, and not impede the strengthening of the state; and the aim of Russia itself should be to be feared, as only those who are feared are respected.

The 'national project' that is implicit in this diagnosis has been summarised as follows: patriotism; anti-Westernism; imperialism; Orthodox clericalism; militarism; authoritarianism; cultural uniformity; xenophobia; economic dirigisme; and demographic pessimism. The central element is the revival of the Russian state, understood in the traditional sense: as a patrimonial, monocentric form of authority, in which every citizen is a subject of the supreme ruler. The revival of the state is understood as the elimination of anything that weakens its power, above all the separation of powers, an effective parliament, independent media and an organised opposition. Moreover, it is a project that has domestic and foreign opponents. Its external enemies are all who do not wish or even fear a strong Russia, the USA in particular. Internal enemies, by extension, are those who support the West and share its values. [. . .]

[These] assumptions were apparent in the contribution of a businessman close to the Kremlin, Mikhail Yur'ev (a former Yabloko member and vice-speaker of the Duma). He identified Russia's enemies very precisely:

> Anyone who calls for negotiations. . .with Maskhadov, . . . or whoever says that it was not necessary to storm Dubrovka or Beslan—is an *enemy*. Anyone who suggests repeating Khasavyurt is an *enemy*. Anyone who proposes practically liquidating the army because the mighty West supports peace on

the planet is an *enemy*. Anyone who suggests that our economy and political system should be organised in the way and only in the way that Western countries and all kinds of IMFs tell us is an *enemy*. Anyone who pines for Gusinsky's NTV and shouts about a dictatorship because there is not a single channel on which you can see Russia being attacked and insulted is an *enemy*. Anyone who says it is unnecessary to imprison the billionaires who have seized power because it is bad for the investment climate is an *enemy*.

Putin invited Yur'ev to the Kremlin to continue the discussion; as he later told the radio station Ekho Moskvy, they talked for three and a half hours. [. . .]

As statements of this kind make clear, the tensions between rival Kremlin clans is likely to have a very direct bearing on the domestic and international policies that will be followed by the Kremlin during and indeed beyond the Putin leadership.

5.3

Majority Control and Executive Dominance: Parliament—President Relations in Putin's Russia

Paul Chaisty

Since the collapse of Communism, Russia's presidents have enjoyed varying degrees of success when governing through parliament. Although the 1993 constitution laid the foundations for executive dominance, the political control required by the president to realize these powers has oscillated depending on the strength of presidential support within the Federal Assembly. Boris Yeltsin's inability to build a stable and disciplined presidential majority post-October 1993 produced a weak form of what Arend Lijphart might term 'consensual' as opposed to 'majoritarian' parliament—president relations. Although legislative politics endured periods of adversarial conflict, such as the impeachment vote of 1999 or numerous votes of confidence, the executive was forced to bargain and compromise with the assembly. Institutional innovations during this period served to mitigate intra—and inter—branch conflict: arrangements for sharing power between parties within the lower house of the Federal Assembly, the State Duma, and the creation of consensus-seeking bodies like the 'Council of Four'. These developments assuaged fears that the paralysing inter-branch conflict of the early post-Communist period would reappear. However, the transaction costs of building majority support for policy initiatives from many different constituencies of interests—partisan, corporate, administrative, and regional—weakened the executive's capacity to impose its agenda, particularly during Yeltsin's second term.

The Putin presidency has changed the dynamic of parliament-president relations in Russia. The relationship between the parliament and the president has become more majoritarian, which has in turn advanced executive dominance in the policy sphere. The Kremlin's strategy is majoritarian in that it seeks the creation of narrow decision-making majorities—ideally confined to one disciplined party—as opposed to broad majorities composed of different interests. The formation of a dominant and disciplined government party has therefore been central to the Kremlin's desire to assert greater executive control over the parliamentary agenda. From the early months of Putin's presidency, the preference for party was

Source: Paul Chaisty, "Majority Control and Executive Dominance: Parliament–President Relations in Putin's Russia," *Leading Russia: Putin in Perspective,* Oxford Scholarship University Press, 2005. 119–139.

Note: Notes and references have been removed from this article.

demonstrated by the introduction of a law 'On Political Parties', which was intended to consolidate Russia's emerging party system. However, executive control over Russia's legislators has not just taken a partisan form. The reform of the composition of the upper house of the Federal Assembly, the Federation Council, has produced what one writer calls a *nomenklatura* method of composing majorities. Although Putin's reform gave regional executive and legislative branches of government the power to appoint 'senators', in practice, presidential officials at both the federal and regional level have strongly influenced the process of appointment.

The result of both the majority-building approaches is that Putin has established a basis of political support not enjoyed by his predecessor. In this chapter the partisan, institutional, and policy effects of this move toward majoritarianism will be assessed. First, the problems faced by the executive during Yeltsin's presidency are examined. Second, the measures taken by the Kremlin to address these problems are explored, and finally the impact of the new arrangements on political behaviour in the assembly and policy outputs is considered. Although it is important to note that some of the developments observed predate Putin, the evidence presented shows a marked change in the nature of inter-branch relations. The executive's dominance in the legislative sphere is not absolute, however. Putin is still constrained by particularistic interests that encumbered Yeltsin's presidency. But the conflicts on legislation that previously spilled out on to the floor of the assembly are now largely confined to the government's party, United Russia. This development is indicative of the Kremlin's more effective management of parliamentary politics under Putin.

Parliamentary Resilience in Russia's Early Transition

President Yeltsin struggled to impose his will on the Russian parliament in the aftermath of the Soviet collapse. Lacking the institutional power over, and political support within, Russia's first post-Communist parliament, the Supreme Soviet (1990–3), Yeltsin was unable to bring Russian legislators to heel. A constitution that placed significant powers in the hands of the parliament, such as control over the composition and survival of the government, and limited executive influence over the parliamentary agenda, constrained the presidency in the early post-Communist period. These constitutional obstacles were further augmented by half-hearted presidential efforts to build a political basis of support in the legislature. President Yeltsin's reluctance to give parliamentary democrats a say on executive appointments and policy matters undermined attempts by pro-Yeltsin deputies to create a parliamentary 'Coalition for Reforms'.

The introduction of new constitutional arrangements after the crisis of October 1993 moved legislative power into the president's orbit. The new constitution conferred on the executive significant legislative powers of initiation, veto, scrutiny, and decree, and gave the president key powers in relation to the composition and survival of the government and parliament, such as the conditional power to dissolve the lower house, the State Duma. In addition, the introduction of a mixed electoral system devised to strengthen political parties was intended to enhance executive support in the lower house. However, whilst these arrangements produced more constructive executive-legislative relations in the post-October 1993 period, Yeltsin never acquired the political control needed to subordinate the two houses of the new parliament. In the first two Dumas, Russia's new electoral system failed to deliver a cohesive parliamentary majority for pro-Yeltsin parties, and the method for selecting members of the upper house, the Federation Council, produced a 'governors' club', which proved itself capable of acting independently of the president's wishes. Without a powerful presidential party to control the parliamentary agenda, deputies enjoyed a significant degree of legislative autonomy.

During Yeltsin's rule, power was dispersed between a number of institutional actors and interests within the legislative branch. In the Supreme Soviet, leadership officials, notably the chairman of the Supreme Soviet, and the heads of the assembly's standing committees competed for influence over the legislative agenda. Although parliamentary chairman, Ruslan Khasbulatov, used his considerable powers and institutional resources to steer the direction of policy in the assembly, the system of law-making was too fragmented to allow the chair undivided control. Committees and their chairs exerted a high degree of influence over the Supreme Soviet's legislative work, and became the main focus of ministerial lobbying within the assembly. In the post-1993 Federal Assembly, agenda control was divided between different forces in each house. The Duma's internal arrangements gave political parties formal power over the legislative agenda. However, in the absence of a cohesive parliamentary majority, parties shared control over the assembly's chief presiding organ, the Duma Council, and its main leadership posts: the chair and his deputies, committee chairs, and their deputies. In practice, such power dispersal weakened the rule of both party leaders and the executive over the assembly's legislative priorities. The Duma Council was relatively ineffective in preventing the assembly's committees and its deputies in plenary sessions from diluting its legislative plan; the parliamentary chairman enjoyed a significant degree of autonomy from his party's leadership; and the Duma's committees and its deputies were susceptible to extra-parliamentary lobbies. The particularistic character of legislative behaviour was even more marked in the upper house, the Federation Council. In contrast to the Duma, political parties were not part of the Council's organizational structure. Regional interests predominated in the upper house under Yeltsin, and the work of the assembly was steered by its leading officials: the chair and his deputies, the heads of the legislature's committees and commissions, and the chamber's *apparat*, its standing bureaucracy.

Parliamentary institutions therefore posed obstacles to executive dominance in the early years of Russia's post-Communist transition. Although Yeltsin stacked the rules in the executive's favour after his victory in October 1993, the absence of coherent and stable parliamentary presidential majorities weakened his ability to govern through parliament. Unlike De Gaulle's Fifth Republic, Yeltsin's constitution did not give the Russian executive the power to determine the parliamentary agenda, and the option of rule by decree had its limitations. As a consequence, Yeltsin struggled to impose his will on the direction of reform. The passage of legislation necessitated extensive bargaining with partisan and regional forces, as well as with departmental and corporate interests that exploited the opportunities provided by the parliament's dispersed structure of decision-making; the corollary was a comparatively low proportion of laws initiated by the executive. As Yeltsin explained in his 1997 annual presidential address to the Federal Assembly:

> Out of nearly 750 bills introduced into the State Duma in 1996 the government initiated only 188. Of these, 53 were bills concerning the ratification of international agreements and treaties. At the same time, lobbying of this or that bill by departments flourished behind the scenes. Several of these bills contradicted the policy direction, defined by the president, and even the position of the government.

[. . .] Under the new constitution, a more deliberate effort was made to increase the executive's influence over the parliament's legislative direction with the formation of the United Commission for the Coordination of Legislative Activities in November 1994. This Commission, formed as part of the process of Social Accord' in the aftermath of the October 1993 crisis, involved the executive more directly in drafting the parliament's legislative plan, but the parliament's effectiveness in realizing its priorities continued to be hampered by countervailing pressures. Weak political control was at the heart of the problem. Without the party political levers to discipline legislators, the existing institutional arrangements lacked force. Under Putin, the executive finally acquired those partisan controls.

The Move Toward Majoritarian Control

The recognition of parliament's importance in achieving executive dominance has been a notable feature of Putin's presidency. Political strategies aimed at building a parliamentary basis of support, and institutional changes centred on curtailing the dispersed system of parliamentary agenda-setting, have been employed to considerable effect. The Kremlin's determination to play a more central role in parliamentary affairs was evident from the start of Putin's rule. In contrast to Yeltsin, Putin paid greater attention to building alliances with parties in the Duma, and used flexible tactics in doing so. During his first term, Putin was not averse to making deals with the Communist opposition on procedural and substantive issues. At the start of the Third Duma (2000–3), the Kremlin-backed party, Unity, cooperated with the Communist Party to undo the power-sharing 'package' method for dividing up key leadership and committee assignments in the assembly. The exclusion of smaller parties from the assignment process revealed a desire by the larger parties to assert their dominance, which had been present in previous Dumas but was never fully realized.

The Kremlin was also more effective in uniting centrist forces in the lower house. In the spring of 2001, a majority coalition consisting of Unity, People's Deputy, Fatherland-All Russia (OVR), and Russia's Regions was formed in the Duma. Although the 'coalition of four' was far from united on many issues, and the Kremlin continued to engineer cross-party alliances on many key votes, it produced a further shift toward majoritarian control. In the spring of 2002, the pro-government bloc achieved a procedural majority with the support of several parties outside the coalition, and finally managed to break the package regime by successfully forcing the expulsion of seven Communist committee chairs. Alexander Mitrofanov, a leading member of the Liberal Democratic Party of Russia (LDPR), captured the essence of majoritarian governance when he warmly welcomed Unity's assault on the Duma's power-sharing arrangements in the corresponding parliamentary debate:

> You know, it's possible to talk a lot about professionalism, but this [the assignment process] is a political thing. Those people who currently wish to make these changes in the Duma are simply larger in number, do you understand? In America, with just a majority of one the whole apparatus becomes theirs, all the committee chairs become theirs, and the speaker theirs, without discussion, do you understand? With just one additional person! Therefore, every vote is fought for. But we have got used to the idea that the minority is entitled to equal treatment. Why is this the case? . . . I'll tell you what's needed: the victors should get everything, that's politics. We absolutely agree that professionalism is preferable. But democracy is that kind of game.

The landslide election victory of the Kremlin's United Russia party in December 2003 consolidated majority rule in the lower house. With seats in excess of 300, United Russia comfortably enjoyed the simple majority needed to institutionalize the executive's control over the Duma's internal arrangements, and acted decisively to translate its electoral success into institutional power. The ability of independent deputies to form 'groups' in the assembly, thereby profiting from internal rules that gave groups the same rights as 'factions', was restricted. By raising the number of deputies required to form a deputy group from 35 to 55, United Russia precluded the creation of deputy groups at the start of the Fourth Duma. This measure cajoled office-seeking independents into joining United Russia, and prevented the leftist opposition from forming 'satellite' groups to increase their representation in the Duma Council—a tactic used effectively by the Communist Party in previous Dumas.

United Russia also gained almost total control over the key leadership posts in the assembly. Previous arrangements that gave each party leader one vote of equal weight within the Duma Council were replaced by a new composition, consisting of the chair of the Duma and his deputies. United Russia gained the majority of these posts, and also acquired control of the overwhelming number of senior committee positions. In contrast to previous Dumas, the assignment process was heavily loaded in favour of the largest party, with the minority confined to nominal representation on the Duma Council and a share of deputy committee chairs (see Table 1). The Duma's rules were also changed to allow party leaders to hold leadership positions in the assembly. This rule change enabled the leader of United Russia, Boris Gryzlov, to become Duma chair. Moreover, the leaders of various subgroups within United Russia each gained a deputy chairmanship. Consequently, the relative autonomy that parliamentary leaders had enjoyed from their parties in previous Dumas was reversed; the leadership of the Duma was now the leadership of the dominant party: United Russia.

The parliamentary minority was, with the exception of LDPR, left extolling the virtues of consensual democracy. Motherland leader, Sergey Baburin, argued 'democracy is not the power of the majority, democracy is respect for the rights of the minority, it is about finding a balance of forces and interests'. Ironically, Communist presidential candidate Nikolay Kharitonov warned of a return to one-party rule:

> Yes, there were 202 patriotic voices [Communist supporters] in the Second Duma, but it was never permitted to shut up the minority in such a way! . . . I appeal to all colleagues and to the praesidium: after we have seen the business of democratic centralism—which today the constitutional majority has permitted—we should introduce into the constitution Article 6 of the constitution on the leading and guiding role of the party.

However, the new majoritarian arrangements belie United Russia as a homogeneous and ideologically cohesive party. United Russia is a presidential coalition comprising different partisan, regional, corporate, and administrative interests. The existence of four intra-party subgroups, each coordinated by a Duma deputy chair, illustrates the party's different constituencies: former Unity members (*medvedy*) comprise the Vladimir Pekhtin group; former members of OVR (*luzhkovtsy*) are represented by the group of Vyacheslav Volodin; deputies representing regional administrative interests (*shaimievtsy*) are led by the Oleg Morozov group; and corporate interests compose a group led by former head of the Duma's Energy Committee, Vladimir Katrenko. [. . .]

Nonetheless, the decision not to divide United Russia into several parliamentary groups following its election victory, which was anticipated by some commentators, reduces the transaction costs the Russian government faces when governing through the lower house. The Kremlin is not required, as in previous Dumas, to consult separately the leaders of different parties, but just one party; United Russia. Although the party's leader, Boris Gryzlov, does not enjoy the undivided loyalty of party members, as evidenced by disagreement within United Russia on substantive policy issues, the establishment of one-party rule has empowered the government to tighten its control over the parliamentary agenda. In ways reminiscent of other states in transition, party dominance has provided a vehicle for executive control over the internal activities of the legislature. This is highlighted by a number of procedural innovations.

Under the Duma's new arrangements, the parliamentary leadership is more directly involved in the coordination of legislative activity with the executive branch. An additional first deputy post was created to strengthen the leadership's capacity to coordinate work on legislation between the various branches of government. Most significantly, first deputies are charged with regularizing the informal practice of 'zero readings' in the legislative process. In effect, 'zero readings' reconcile conflicts between the executive and parliamentary leaders on legislation before its official 'readings' (first, second and third) in the assembly, thereby increasing the likelihood that legislation will be passed without the serious delay or amendment that hampered government bills in the past. Such 'readings' were originally introduced in the Third Duma to iron out disagreements on government budget bills, but following the expulsion of Communist committee chairs in the spring of 2002, they were extended to other legislation. Since 2003, the executive has sought to integrate 'zero readings' into the legislative process. According to Chairman Gryzlov, this development will enable the parliament to realize the 'strategic aims of the president.' [. . .] In theory, such 'readings' are open to all parties, but in reality the main purpose of this innovation appears to centre on the resolution of conflicts on legislation within United Russia.

A further measure aimed at controlling the law-making process concerns the gate-keeping powers of committees. In earlier Dumas, the Duma Council struggled to impose the assembly's legislative plan. In addition to laws assigned 'priority' status, deputies initiated large numbers of bills that inhibited efforts to streamline the Duma's work. At the Second Duma, the volume of bills in the legislative system was on average nearly double the number originally planned. Although the assembly considered most of this legislation, it was rarely enacted, and as a consequence it clogged up the legislative timetable of committees. In the Third Duma, for example, the assembly enacted just 10 per cent of such bills, but scrutinized over 50 per cent. Responding to this problem, United Russia

Table 1. Duma Posts Assigned to the Largest Party or Coalition (1994–2004)

	First Duma: (1994–5)	Second Duma: (1996–9)	Third Duma (2000-March 2002)	Third Duma (April 2002- December 2003)[*]	Fourth Duma (2004–)
Party/Coalition (Seats %)[†]	RC (17)	CPRF-APG -PP (49)	CPRF- AIDG (29)	Unity-OVR- RR-PD (52)	UR (68)
Leadership: Duma chair and deputy chairs (%)	17	43	30	40	73
Duma Council (%)	10	50	30	44	73
Committee chairs (%)	17	50	39	68	100
Committee deputy chairs (%)	17	31	25	61	66

Key: RC (Russia's Choice); CPRF (Communist Party of the Russian Federation); APG (Agrarian Party Group); PP (Popular Power); AIDG (Agro-Industrial Deputy Group); OVR (Fatherland—All Russia); RR (Russia's Regions); PD (People's Deputy); UR (United Russia).

introduced a rule change in March 2004 that gives committees the power to propose the rejection of any bill already approved in its first reading that is considered to have 'no prospect' of passage. Aimed principally at clearing up a backlog of bills (in excess of 1,000) under consideration from the previous parliament, this measure seeks to restrict lobbying activity within the assembly. In practice, it may also limit the capacity of minority parties to introduce legislation. The combination of greater executive control over the parliament's agenda, plus United Russia's dominance over the Duma Council and the chamber's legislative committees, imposes significant constraints on the legislative influence of minority parties. According to one commentator, key ministers now meet only with the leaders of United Russia on a regular basis: 'Members of the government now consider it superfluous to build relations with the leaders of other factions.' [. . .]

The Effects of Executive Dominance

Although the view is frequently expressed that legislative politics under Putin has become more executive-centred, it is too early to examine systematically the impact that majority control has had on the Federal Assembly. It is also problematic to attribute all of the changes that have occurred under Putin to the measures introduced since he came to power. Nonetheless, there is evidence of an exponential tightening of executive control over the parliament's internal activities, in particular since the spring of 2002 when the Kremlin majority asserted its majority power over the internal organization of the assembly. This can be illustrated with reference to both the partisan and the policy effects of majoritarianism.

Partisan Effects

One indicator of the impact of the Kremlin's influence over Duma parties is the extent to which its coalition-building initiatives have produced more cohesive government parties. The consolidation of parties within the assembly and the growth of party discipline is a development that predates Putin. However, the creation of the 'coalition of four' and the assertion of its institutional power in the spring of 2002 appears to have contributed to higher levels of discipline among government-supporting parties, albeit with some interesting variation. By securing a stable basis of support within the assembly, the presidency's effectiveness in building winning coalitions has been enhanced. Consequently, parliament-presidential relations have been less confrontational under Putin.

Two measures of the voting discipline of government parties are considered: voting cohesion and the level of absenteeism on key and contested votes. The Rice Index is used to indicate voting cohesion on a scale from 0 to 100. The cohesion score moves towards 0 as the difference between aye and nay votes within a party increases; a score of 100 indicates unanimous voting by party members. The data for deputies who were absent on individual votes was treated as a separate indicator of the capacity of government parties to mobilize their members on key issues. Although non-voting is used strategically by some parties in the Duma, notably LDPR, the motivation for not voting is often unclear, and few examples of unanimous non-voting by government parties were found. Hence, non-votes were not recoded as 'nay' votes.

The results of this analysis for all government parties since 1994 are summarized in Figure 1. The findings show that the voting cohesion of the main government parties—Russia's Choice (First Duma, 1994–5), Our Home is Russia (Second Duma, 1996–9), and Unity (Third Duma, 2000–3)—has steadily increased. In the latter half of the Third Duma, Unity came close to achieving unanimous voting on the key votes selected. However, the general trend toward more cohesive government parties since 1994 is mirrored by most opposition parties and therefore cannot be attributed solely to the leadership of Putin. In addition to the presidential administration's role in engineering more cohesive government parties, factors such as the mode of election, institutional benefits, and intra-party arrangements have all played an important role in raising discipline. More striking is the decline in the percentage of Unity members absenting on key votes since 2000. Unity had higher voting participation rates than both of its predecessors—Russia's Choice (RC) and Our Home is Russia (NDR)—according to this set of data. Moreover, absenteeism for Unity members was lower than for

Figure 1. Rice Cohesion Scores and Absenteeism
Rates for Government Parties (1994–2003)

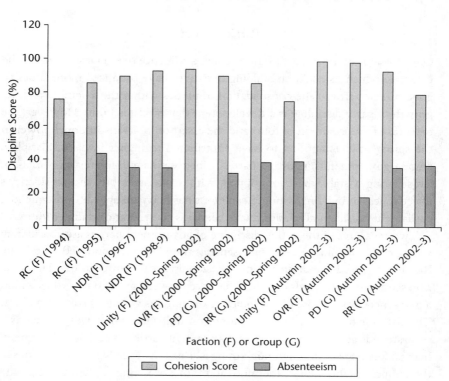

Faction (F) or Group (G)

□ Cohesion Score   ▨ Absenteeism

all other parties. While on average 34 and 27 per cent of party members in both periods of the Third Duma were absent for the votes analysed, Unity had an absenteeism rate of just 11 and 13 per cent.

The formation of the 'coalition of four' had a notable impact on voting discipline within Fatherland—All Russia (OVR). Although relations between OVR and Unity were strained at first, the consolidation of the coalition's institutional power in the spring of 2002 contributed to far higher levels of discipline. Both the Rice cohesion score and the level of absenteeism illustrate this development. However, for the other parties in this coalition, People's Deputy (PD) and Russia's Regions (RR), the results were mixed. As in previous Dumas, Russia's Regions continued to register low levels of cohesion. Composed of single-mandate deputies representing the interests of regional authorities, members of this group were more susceptible to parochial pressures on certain issues. By contrast, People's Deputy, which was more closely aligned with the Kremlin, achieved far higher levels of voting cohesion after the formation of the Kremlin coalition. Yet both groups continued to show high levels of absenteeism, which hampered efforts to convert the 'coalition of four' into a disciplined voting bloc. With a majority in single digits, the Kremlin alliance was vulnerable to defections. Nonetheless, the 'coalition of four' established a solid basis on which to construct winning majorities. Data on voting affinity between Unity and its coalition partners found Unity's allies to be more reliable toward the end of the Third Duma (see Figure 2). Moreover, the Kremlin received important support from other parties on key votes, notably LDPR and SPS, and as a consequence became less reliant on dealing with its principal opponent: the Communist Party. This is a luxury that Putin's predecessor did not enjoy.

Policy Effects

Following the collapse of Communism, the Russian executive struggled to impose its legislative priorities on the parliament. Corporate, regional, and departmental lobbying all contributed to a bloated legislative agenda, and the law-making organs empowered to steer the assembly's legislative activities, such as the Duma Council, proved to be relatively ineffective. Reflecting on the difficulties facing the Duma Council in the Second Duma, Russia's Regions head, Oleg Morozov, revealed the scale of the problem:

Figure 2. Variation in the Voting Affinity of Duma Parties to Unity, 2000–3

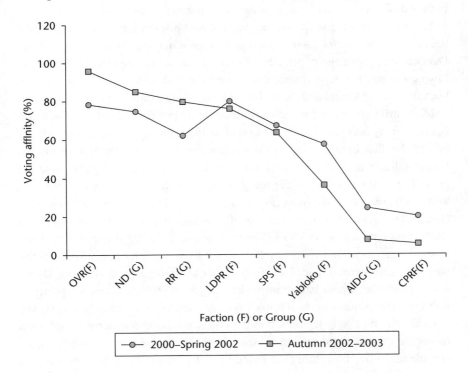

. . .we must reject the principle of mechanically combining all the proposals of parties. This principle exists today and produces a gigantic calendar, often making it difficult to determine which [bill] should receive primary attention, and which secondary. A lot depends on how smart those who propose legislation are.

The steps taken to tighten executive control over the Duma's legislative activities do appear, however, to have had an impact on the size and content of the Duma's plan, and the effectiveness of legislators in realizing their legislative priorities. Aggregate data on the volume of 'priority' laws introduced since 1996 shows a marked decrease during the Third Duma. In the first five sessions of this Duma, an average 150 bills were scheduled for priority consideration in each session, and following the assertion of the 'coalition of four's' majority power in the spring of 2002, this figure fell to an average of around 130 bills. These figures contrast favourably with the Second Duma, when on average more than 250 bills were considered to be of priority importance in each session. Such streamlining of the assembly's legislative priorities suggests that the Duma Council was more successful in curtailing the ability of committees and individual deputies to acquire priority status for their legislative projects. This development cannot however be attributed directly to the establishment of a pro-government majority. Initiatives to raise the effectiveness of the Federal Assembly's law-making process, and the concomitant decline in the number of priority laws, predate the formation of the 'coalition of four'.

Yet the Duma's capacity to scrutinize and pass priority laws was enhanced by the institutional control gained by the government majority in the spring of 2002. Data on the percentage of priority bills scrutinized and passed by the Duma following the route of Communist committee chairs shows a notable increase on both the Second Duma and the earlier sessions of the Third Duma (see Figure 3).

More striking are the data on the authorship of priority legislation. The number of priority bills initiated by the executive dramatically increased in the latter half of the Third Duma, and this trend has continued into the Fourth Duma. Figure 4 illustrates this development with reference to priority legislation in the area of economic policy. While the gap between the number of priority laws initiated by the executive (government and president) and the Federal Assembly (Duma deputies and Federation Council) averaged less than 10 per cent in both the Second Duma and the Third Duma (up to and including the spring 2002 session), the gap increased to around 70 per cent following the renegotiation of the package agreement. These data suggest that the reorganization of the Duma along majoritarian lines had an immediate impact on the executive's capacity to influence the content of the Duma's agenda. At the same time, however, the volume of non-priority legislation in the Duma's various committees continued to rise. In the last three sessions of the Third Duma, the volume of bills under consideration by committees increased by over 100 per cent. It is too early to know how effective the new rules strengthening the gate-keeping powers of committees have been in curtailing this outlet for legislative autonomy, but

Figure 3. Percentage of Priority Bills Scrutinized and Passed (1997–2003)

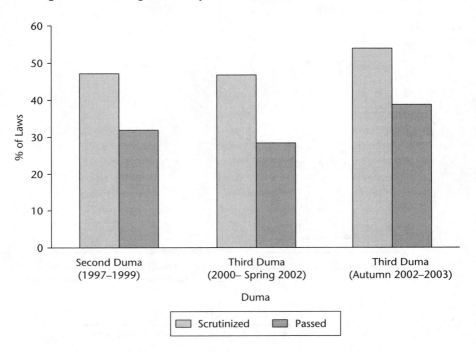

government critics revealed that much of the Fourth Duma's early work was concerned with clearing this backlog of laws from the legislative process. By constraining the legislative activity of deputies in this respect, the executive appears to be acquiring further control over the Duma's timetable.

Another indicator of the policy effects of majoritarianism is the impact that executive control has had on the parliament's capacity to veto legislation. For the Federation Council, the power to veto bills is a key source of legislative influence. Although the Council can initiate legislation, in practice this power has been used to a limited extent. Vetoes provide members of the upper house with a more fruitful opportunity to shape the content of legislation. The 'conciliation commissions' formed to resolve conflicts on vetoed bills between both houses, and the 'special commissions' that are created to reconcile disputes between both houses and the executive, give regional lobbies a say on the content of legislation. Conciliation commissions dealing with financial matters, in particular budgetary and taxation legislation, were most common during Yeltsin's tenure.

Under Putin, inter-cameral and inter-branch relations have certainly become less confrontational. The number of Duma bills vetoed by the upper house has fallen significantly since 2000. In the First Duma, one third of all Duma bills were initially rejected by the Federation Council; this figure fell to around a quarter in

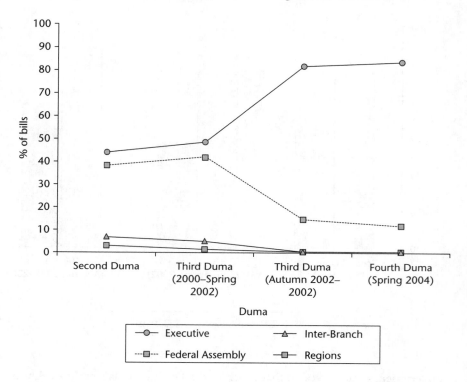

Figure 4. Authors of Priority Economic Legislation, 1997-2004

the Second Duma, and in the Third Duma to less than 10 per cent. Early evidence from the Fourth Duma shows a further decline in the use of Federation Council vetoes. [. . .] The relative timidity of the upper house under Putin is further illustrated by cases when 'senators' followed the Kremlin on legislation that clearly undermined the powers of regional authorities, such as new laws on regional elections, and the rejection of legislation empowering regional legislators to determine the level of the minimum wage at the local level.

The Duma's willingness to confront both the upper house and the executive has also been tempered. Data show that the number of Duma bills that remained vetoed by both the upper house and president has declined: from 102 bills in the Second Duma to just ten bills in the Third Duma. Interestingly, no Duma bills were vetoed by both the Federation Council and President Putin after the institutional consolidation of the executive's Duma majority in spring 2002. [. . .]

Conclusion

Parliament-president relations have become more majoritarian under Putin. The Kremlin has acquired majority backing in both houses of the Federal

Assembly, and this political support has been used to strengthen the executive's influence over the internal legislative arrangements of both houses. New techniques for resolving conflict on legislation, such as the use of 'zero readings', have shifted the centre of law-making from the legislative branch to the executive, and the policy effects of this development appear to be supported by data on legislative decisions in the latter half of the Third Duma.

It would be inaccurate to attribute all these achievements to Putin. Proposals to rationalize and streamline law-making in Russia have been present since the early years of transition. In Khasbulatov's Supreme Soviet, and in earlier State Dumas, a number of initiatives were proposed to address the problems caused by particularistic lobbying and legislative overload. The difference under Putin is that more effective political control has enabled this desire to be transformed into reality. However, it is premature to talk about total executive dominance in Russian legislative politics. Although the proportion of priority bills initiated by the executive has increased under Putin, the executive continues to be responsible for a comparatively low proportion of all enacted legislation, and the new majoritarian arrangements belie United Russia as a homogeneous and ideologically cohesive party. In the first session of the Fourth Duma, tensions emerged within United Russia on nationalization and welfare legislation, and deputies representing regional interests proposed ways to increase internal party discussion on legislation as a way of mitigating the effects of 'zero readings'.

So long as Putin remains the dominant force in Russian politics, these tensions are unlikely to jeopardize the Kremlin's majority. However, Putin is still required to appease a range of views within what is a very broad presidential coalition. The division of United Russia into subgroups, each with their own leader and seats in the Duma Council, and the use of the Duma's assignment process to distribute patronage, provide a means of managing the heterogeneous preferences within this party. Further measures are being prepared to enhance executive dominance. At the time of writing, proposals to create a fully proportional system for elections to the State Duma appeared aimed at strengthening party control. By removing deputies elected in single-mandate districts from the lower house, the voice of regional representatives within United Russia could be further weakened. Yet, the heightening of executive power carries risks. Future governments will struggle to blame policy failures on an obstructive parliament, and United Russia may be held to account for potentially unpopular measures, such as housing and welfare reform. Splitting United Russia into its constituent parts is always an option if a new party in power is required, but this could undermine efforts to consolidate executive control in Russia.

6

Political Parties

Quite a bit of time and effort has been devoted to studying political parties in postcommunist Russia in terms of their emergence, organization, consolidation and influence.[1] The reason scholars have focused so much attention here is fairly straightforward. A functioning and stable party system is essential to democracy. Democracy is a system of popular control over the state under conditions of transparency, accountability, and free and open competition for political power. Political parties are central to this. They structure competition for political office and serve as training grounds for future political officials.[2] They provide a means for the public at large to participate, to elect representatives to government, to communicate with those officials, and to hold them accountable. For these central reasons and others, political parties and a stable party system are core features of any democracy.

Constitutional designers and lawmakers in any state wishing to create a democratic political system, then, must consider the implications that a host of rules and institutional configurations will hold for the development of political parties. It is hard to conceive of any democracy without an array of stable political parties—organizations that last over time; organizations that have roots in society with real members upon whom they can call upon to vote, to mobilize the vote, and to support candidates; and organizations with identifiable and complex structures, with policy platforms they seek to advocate and to implement. Where they are absent, we see authoritarianism, dictatorship, or absolutism.

Many of Russia's new leaders immediately after the fall of the Soviet Union, and those advising them, understood this. However, they faced a massive roadblock. For three quarters of a century, the Communist Party of the Soviet Union (CPSU) was "The Party." This "party of a new type"[3] held important legacy implications for postcommunist Russia. The CPSU was a state party, a ruling party in a one-party state whose edicts were compulsory for the entire population. The

Party's "correct line" could not be questioned; it carried the force of law and the status of universal truth. It was mandatory for all. If not membership in, at least adherence to the Party and its edicts was a universal requirement.

For much of the population, having lived through decades of political repression under the Party's totalitarian rule, which for millions meant no choice but to be *partiiniy*—a party member—for purposes of career and even personal security, after the communist collapse, political parties were something to be despised. The term *partiiniy* was hurled as an epithet rather than a status to be sought. People sought to avoid parties, not to join them. For those who actively sought the end of communism, being non-*partiiniy* was a central part of the liberation. "Democracy," in this respect, came to mean the absence of not just "The Party" but of any party. It meant not only liberation from fear but from hypocrisy and political control. Fish generally described the "hyper-democracy" of the early 1990s, and this was one aspect that was destructive of long-term democratic prospects, that an institution so universal to democracy was so reviled.[4] Among those who decided to remain aloof of parties was President Boris Yeltsin, who publicly refused membership or to support any of the party organizations even during elections.[5] He set the example for a wary people that a political party is something undesirable, to be suspicious of, and to avoid.

In the scramble that followed the collapse of communism, the alignments of candidates in the elections of the 1990s were incredibly fluid. Any label of "political party" to all but one or two of the organizations that fielded candidates in elections in that decade is grossly exaggerated. In 1993, thirteen groups ran in the Duma election. In 1995, of these thirteen, only five remained, but many of their members had bolted to other groups. In all, in 1995, thirty-eight electoral blocs contested the Duma election, and in 1999, the number was twenty-six. Most of these organizations appeared just weeks prior to the election and disappeared after. While the Duma had rules nominally designed to foster the longevity of parties, notably the inclusion of their leaders in the agenda-setting and organizational leadership council, in fact, they spurred fluidity and a "go-it-alone" mentality.[6] Because the Duma Council was so powerful, leaders wanted a place on it and so formed their own organizations in an effort to win their own spots at the table rather than consolidating efforts to form wider majorities across the legislature as a whole. These political "factions" existed to serve their leaders; they were individual personality cliques, not political parties in any meaningful sense of the word. As a rule, they lacked any nationwide or even regional organization, lacked members, lacked policy platforms, and in the end, lacked longevity. Outside of the Communist Party and perhaps the Liberal Democratic Party of Russia (LDPR), none of the organizations possessed any of the qualities of a political party.

In this weak and fluid space, and with the extraordinary powers of the office behind him, a president so inclined could reestablish the essentials of a one-party state. By emasculating competitive politics and creating his own organization of security services personnel, this is precisely what Putin has achieved.[7] As part of his strategy for reestablishing a highly centralized system of power in the country, Putin eliminated any independent political competition by changing the rules of political engagement and pursuing an aggressive policy of closing access. With attacks on independent political organizations and on individual politicians, he achieved this goal and has made it virtually impossible for independent political parties to organize or to compete. Putin's centralization of authority and creation of a new ruling party has denied potential competitors access to funding because any who would dare fund them face reprisals. Forming or funding political parties is, under the regime Putin has consolidated, not a legitimate use of one's resources and constitutes a challenge to the state. The state's attacks on Boris Berezovsky, Vladimir Gusinsky, and Mikhail Khodorkovsky have made clear the message that politics is not an acceptable arena for action, and attempting independent political organization will lead to arrest, exile and seizure of assets. Politicians who are vocal and honest and demonstrate prospects for rising popularity and successful organization have been arrested or worse. And, to ensure the outcomes that Putin mandates, rather than free elections, Russia has "operations" in which the outcomes are rigged in advance.[8] Political parties do not exist, and they have no hope of developing until and unless the rules and the framework for those rules—the constitution—are changed.

In the view of Putin and his United Russia organization, any voice that diverges from the voice of the state is hostile. It is the role of business, of politicians—of everyone—to support the state. The agenda of the state, in turn, comes from its leader. In form, this is quite similar to the old communist party correct line. The substance is entirely different—there is scope for entrepreneurship, profit making, private property, and privacy, all of which were officially banned or heavily regulated under communism. But, the public sphere is again dangerous and highly regimented, and there is no scope for independent political action. The reality is that serious organization of political parties independent of the state is impossible because Putin and his followers will brook no competition to themselves personally or to their agenda politically.

Yet, every election has multiple parties running. How can one say there is no political competition? Putin tolerates the remaining Communist Party and the eccentric LDPR as both explicitly support Putin's program and that of Putin's organization, United Russia. Vladimir Zhirinovsky, the ultra-nationalist figurehead atop LDPR, openly supports the restoration of dictatorship. The Communist Party supports the order and obedience orientation. They are not, in fact, opposition at all. Remaining organizations in the legislative elections and candidates in the presidential elections are tolerated as they have no prospect of winning. They serve the purpose of the facade of political competition; any real threat to the dominance of United Russia or of Putin himself are simply prevented from organizing or running. Indeed, those who do run have likely been fostered by the Kremlin itself to help create the democratic facade.[9] Again, without any potential donors to fund their efforts—the threats of exile or imprisonment in Siberia are well known—would-be politicians have no ability to pursue their political ambitions outside of the ruling party.[10]

The selections in this chapter detail the shift from competitive to hierarchical politics and the closing off of political space. Where Yeltsin was a populist politician who was not afraid of political competition or of multiparty politics, his successors have proven to be of an entirely different orientation.

For Further Reference

Books

Timothy J. Colton and Michael McFaul, *Popular Choice and Managed Democracy: The Russian Elections of 1999 and 2000*, The Brookings Institution: 2003.

M. Steven Fish, *Democracy Derailed in Russia: The Failure of Open Politics*, Cambridge University Press: 2005.

Grigorii V. Golosov, *Political Parties in the Regions of Russia: Democracy Unclaimed*, Lynne Rienner: 2004.

Henry E. Hale, *Why not parties in Russia?: Democracy, Federalism and the State*, Cambridge University Press: 2006.

Stephen E. Hanson, *Post-Imperial Democracies: Ideology and Party Formation in Third Republic France, Weimar Germany, and Post-Soviet Russia*, Cambridge University Press: 2010.

Vicki Hesli and William Reisinger, eds., *The 1999–2000 Elections in Russia: Their Impact and Legacy*, Cambridge University Press: 2003.

Robert G. Moser, *Unexpected Outcomes: Electoral Systems, Political Parties and Representation in Russia*, University of Pittsburgh Press: 2001.

Richard Rose, William Mishler, and Neil Munro, *Popular Support for an Undemocratic Regime: The Changing Views of Russians*, Cambridge University Press: 2011.

NOTES

1. See Robert G. Moser, *Unexpected Outcomes: Electoral Systems, Political Parties, and Representation in Russia* (University of Pittsburgh Press, 2001); Michael McFaul, *Russia's 1996 Presidential Election: The End of Polarized Politics* (Hoover Institution Press, 1997); McFaul, "Explaining Party Formation and Nonformation in Russia Actors, Institutions, and Chance,"

Comparative Political Studies, Vol. 34, No. 10, pp.1159–1187; and Richard Rose, Neil Munro, and Stephen White, "Voting in a Floating Party System: The 1999 Duma Election," *Europe-Asia Studies*, Vol. 53, No. 3 (2001), pp. 419–443. These are just a few of dozens and dozens of books and articles devoted to the subject.

2. See William Nesbit Chambers, *Political Parties in a New Nation* (Oxford University Press, 1963); Mosei Ostrogorski, *Democracy and the Organization of Political Parties* (Quadrangle Books, 1964); Giovanni Sartori, *Parties and Party Systems* (Cambridge University Press, 1976); and Larry Diamond and Richard Gunther, eds., *Political Parties and Democracy* (Johns Hopkins University Press, 2001) on the critical role of political parties in democratic states.

3. See V. I. Lenin, *What Is To Be Done?* (International Publishers, 1984).

4. M. Steven Fish, *Democracy From Scratch* (Princeton University Press, 1995).

5. See Ostrow, Satarov, and Khakamada, *The Consolidation of Dictatorship in Russia: An Inside View of the Demise of Democracy* (Praeger, 2007), especially pp. 57–58.

6. See Joel M. Ostrow, *Comparing Post-Soviet Legislatures: A Theory of Institutional Design and Political Conflict* (Ohio State University Press 2000), especially pp. 100–106. Also see Rose, Munro and White (2001).

7. Stephen Sestanovich, "Putin's Invented Opposition," *Journal of Democracy*, Vol. 18, No. 2 (2007), pp. 122–124. Also see Julie Anderson, "The Checkist Takeover of the Russian State," *International Journal of Intelligence and Counterintelligence*, Vol. 19, No. 2 (2006), pp. 237–288; and the selection by Kryshtanovskaya and White in this volume.

8. See Ostrow, Satarov, and Khakamada (2007), pp. 108–112.

9. See Sestanovich (2007).

10. Such has been the fate of Gregoriy Yavlinsky and his "Yabloko" group, of Irina Khakamada and her liberal followers, and of others.

6.1

Party Politics in Russia:
From Competition to Hierarchy

Vladimir Gel'man

IN THE 1990S, POLITICAL PARTIES IN RUSSIA SUFFERED FROM THEIR under development. By contrast, in the 2000s they became major actors in the electoral and parliamentary arenas, both at the national and sub-national level. However, party competition—the very heart of democratic politics—virtually disappeared in Putin's Russia. Instead, all political parties became effectively controlled by the Kremlin and incorporated into the formal and informal hierarchy of Russia's government. While the major opposition parties were about to become extinct, the party of power, United Russia (*Edinaya Rossiya*), overwhelmingly dominated the landscape of party politics. Still, by the end of Putin's second term Russia's political regime combined some elements of both personalist and party-based authoritarianism. I will analyse the formation of the new party system in Russia in the 2000s, with a special emphasis on the role of political elites and institutional engineering in the building of the dominant party and centralised control. The prospects for a party-based authoritarian regime in Russia are also discussed.

Trends in Russia's Party System

On 17 December 2007 the congress of United Russia (UR), Russia's leading party, which had just received 64.3% of the vote and won 315 out of the 450 seats in the State *Duma* elections held two weeks before this event, met in Moscow. The congress nominated UR candidates for the three top posts in Russian officialdom: the president (Dmitry Medvedev), the prime minister (outgoing president Vladimir Putin), and the chairman of the *Duma* (Boris Gryzlov). Besides that, 65 out of 85 regional chief executives and four members of the cabinet of ministers during the 2007 elections ran on the UR party list, which was led by Putin. Another top official post, the chairman of the Federation Council, was occupied by Sergei Mironov, the leader of another pro-Kremlin party, Just Russia

---

Source: Vladimir Gel'man, "Party Politics in Russia: From Competition to Hierarchy," *Europe-Asia Studies*, Vol. 60, Issue 6, August 2008, 913–930.

Note: Notes and references have been removed from this article.

(JR, *Spravedlivaya Rossiya*), and yet another member of the cabinet of ministers ran on the JR party list. This was clear evidence of the spectacular rise of the influence of party politics (if not party government) in Putin's Russia in comparison with Yel'tsin's period.

Russia's party system in the 1990s demonstrated several distinctive features in comparison with post-communist party systems in Eastern Europe. First, Russia's party system was greatly fragmented, because all segments of Russia's electoral markets were over-supplied. Second, the very high level of electoral volatility demonstrated great elasticity in voter demands. Third, non-partisan politicians who possessed resources other than party support (mainly backed by regional or sectoral interest groups) also played a major role in national and especially sub-national electoral politics. For these reasons, Russia's party system is correctly regarded as unconsolidated. In the 2000s, trends in party politics were quite the opposite. Parties became the only legitimate actors in the national electoral and parliamentary arena, and non-party politicians no longer competed with them. Instead of the bizarre competition of dozens of small parties and coalitions, only four parties enjoyed parliamentary representation over two consecutive legislative terms (2003–2007 and 2007–2011), and together received almost 92% of the vote in the December 2007 elections. Finally, both national and sub-national executives, who in the 1990s stayed above and beyond party politics, became loyal partisans by the late 2000s.

To a certain degree, the dynamics of party politics in post-Soviet Russia demonstrated a pendulum-like effect. After breaking the equilibrium of Soviet-style one-party rule, Russia's party system switched to hyper-fragmentation in the mid-1990s, when 43 parties competed for popular votes during the 1995 parliamentary elections. During the 2000s, the pendulum swung back to low fragmentation against the background of the monopoly held by the party of power. According to the data presented in Table 1, the effective number of legislative parties in the State *Duma* after 2003 dropped to 1.97 and then to 1.92. Therefore, all parties other than UR acting together do not have enough potential to form a meaningful alternative to it. In other words, Russia's party politics in the 2000s developed as an amalgamation of two inter-related trends: the emerging dominance of the party of power at the electoral and parliamentary levels; and the continuing decline (if not a total extinction) of opposition of different kinds (see Table 2). Unlike in the post-communist party systems of Eastern Europe or those in post-Soviet Moldova and Ukraine, the pendulum of Russia's party system raced through the position of democratic equilibrium (involving moderate fragmentation of the party system) to a new non-democratic equilibrium: rather, the decline of party fragmentation led to decline of party competition, which is the necessary (although not sufficient) condition for democracy.

Table 1. Effective Number of Parties in Russia, 1993–2008

Year	Electoral parties[*]	Parliamentary parties
1993	7.6	
1994–1995		8.53
1995	10.7	
1996–1999		5.7
1999	6.8	
2000–2001		7.8
2001–2003[**]		4.7
2003	5.34	
2003–2007		1.97
2007	2.25	
2007–2008		1.92

Notes: The effective number of parties is calculated as: $= \frac{1}{\sum_i v_i^2}$ ' where 'v' is the share of votes (or State *Duma* seats) for each respective party. The effective number of electoral parties is based upon the results of respective State *Duma* elections, and the effective number of parliamentary parties is based upon the actual composition of parliamentary parties in the State *Duma* in respective years. The data draws heavily upon Gel'man (2006, p. 546).

[*]Calculated on the basis of party list voting.

[**]After the establishment of United Russia, four parliamentary parties—Unity, Fatherland-All Russia, Regions of Russia and People's Deputy—are calculated as a single party.

After the triumphant 2007 State *Duma* elections, UR finally turned into a dominant party. This can be defined as a party that is established by and closely tied to the rulers of an authoritarian regime; freely employs state power and resources to maintain its dominance; and uses extra-constitutional means to control the outcomes of politics during elections and beyond. The rise of UR as a dominant party coincided with the sharp destruction of Russia's major democratic institutions, including (although certainly not limited to) competitive elections. Domestic and international observers widely regarded them as unfair. The blatant abuse of state resources for election purposes, one-sided media coverage, administrative pressure and intimidation toward voters, and (last but not least) electoral fraud, became routine in Russia's electoral politics, which, alongside many other states in the world, has been dubbed 'electoral authoritarianism.' One may conclude that while Russia's nascent political regime in the 1990s (whether democratic or not) was by and large non-party-based, Russia's emerging non-democratic regime in the 2000s became increasingly party-based. Political scientists are largely agreed on the 'indispensability' of political parties for democracy, but the same argument might be relevant for some non-democracies, too, as Russia's Soviet and post-Soviet politics suggests.

Why and how did Russia experience this turn in party politics? Why did political parties as such and, especially United Russia, known as 'the party of power', become major tools of the ruling elite? And what are the prospects for a dominant party-based authoritarian regime in Russia? This contribution seeks answers to these questions. First, I examine varieties of authoritarian regime building in the post-Soviet context and analyse the strategies and choices of Russia's leaders within this framework. Second, I present an analysis of the dynamics of party politics under Putin, with a special emphasis on features of the new party system and the role of political and institutional factors in its formation. Then, I draw some parallels with party-based authoritarianism in Mexico under the Institutional Revolutionary Party (PRI) and focus on similarities and differences with Russia's trends and prospects. Finally, the effects of party politics on political regime dynamics in Russia will be considered.

Why party?: Strategies of Authoritarian Regime Building and the Kremlin's Choice

All rulers in the world would like to govern their countries without checks or balances. In established regimes, however, they are faced with constraints that are based upon institutions or other influential actors (both domestic and international). No wonder that leaders in newly established states and nations are often more successful in authoritarian regime building from scratch if they are able to remove these constraints and eliminate alternatives to their governments. Comparative studies of authoritarianism offer a useful distinction between personalist, party-based and military authoritarian regimes, which form on different power bases and employ different strategies of dominance. Upon the collapse of the Soviet Union, post-Soviet states demonstrated a wide spectrum of personalist authoritarian regimes, although some of them were destroyed in the period 2003–2005 during the wave of so-called 'colour revolutions' in Georgia, Ukraine and Kyrgyzstan. In this respect, Russia exhibited a rather distinctive pattern of authoritarian regime building. While its 'hybrid' regime under Yel'tsin in the 1990s was largely personalist, despite several unsuccessful attempts to establish pro-Kremlin 'parties of power', Russia's authoritarian turn under Putin in the

Table 2. Results of the State *Duma* Elections, 1999–2007

Elections Party/block	1999			2003			2007		
	Number of lists	*Party list vote, %*	*Seats, total (PR + SMD)*	*Number of lists*	*Party list vote, %*	*Seats, total (PR + SMD)*	*Number of lists*	*Party list vote, %*	*Seats, total (PR)*
Turnout, %		61.8			55.75			63.66	
Fatherland-All Russia (FAR)		13.3*	68 (37 + 31)						
Unity		23.3**	73 (64 + 9)						
United Russia (UR)					37.6	225 (120 + 105)		64.30	315
LDPR		6.0***	17 (17 + 0)		11.5	36 (36 + 0)		8.14	40
Motherland					9.0	37 (29 + 8)			
Just Russia (JR)								7.74	38
KPRF		24.3	113 (67 + 46)		12.6	52 (40 + 12)		11.57	57
Yabloko		5.9	20 (16 + 4)		4.3	4 (0 + 4)		1.59	0
Union of Right Forces (SPS)		8.5	29 (24 + 5)		4.0	3 (0 + 3)		0.96	0
Other parties below threshold	20		25 (0 + 25)	17	15.5	33 (0 + 33)	5	4.59	0
Independent candidates			105 (0 + 105)			60 (0 + 60)		N/A	
Total	26	94.7	450	23	94.5	450	11	98.9	450
Parties over 5% (7%) threshold	6	81.2		4	70.7		4	91.75	
Against all lists		3.3			4.7			N/A	
Invalid votes		2.0			0.8			1.1	

Sources: McFaul (2005, p. 69) and http:\\www.vybory.izobirkom.ru. accessed 12 January 2008.

Notes: *Taken over by 'United Russia'.

**Transformed into 'United Russia'.

***Listed as 'Zhirinovskii's Block'.

2000s coincided with the spectacular rise of United Russia, the 'party of power', which dominated the electoral and parliamentary arenas by the end of Putin's rule. In the course of the 2000s, the Kremlin invested deliberate and thorough efforts into building a dominant party, which greatly contributed to the continuity of Russia's authoritarian regime beyond the leadership succession in 2008. Given the fact that party-based authoritarian regimes are usually the longest-lived in comparison with personalist and military regimes, this Kremlin strategy might be very rational in the long-term.

Why did the Kremlin choose this strategy after Putin's unexpected rise to power in 1999 and 2000? To a great extent, this choice was driven by the learning effect from Russia's own experience under Yel'tsin as well as from other post-Soviet states. Yel'tsin's personalist regime was heavily unpopular in the eyes of Russia's citizens due to its poor performance, but it was faced with a deeply fragmented elite, which was organised around multiple cliques and clans of oligarchs and regional leaders. This constellation left Yel'tsin room for manoeuvre, using 'divide and conquer' strategies, but it was rather risky in terms of leadership succession, as the experience of some post-Soviet states (especially the Ukrainian 'orange revolution') suggests. In Russia, presidential turnover produced a shift in loyalty of formerly subordinated elites, which established a loose coalition 'Fatherland—All Russia' on the eve of the 1999–2000 parliamentary and presidential elections and threatened the very survival of Yel'tsin and his entourage. Even though the Kremlin then was able to avoid this outcome due to successful electoral campaigning and manufacturing its own political vehicle, Unity (*Edinstvo*), the post-Yel'tsin elites had little intention of falling into the same trap. Beyond these short-term considerations, Putin and his associates sought to establish long-term bases for the stability and continuity of Russia's emerging political regime. This task was three-fold. First, they had to monopolise and strengthen the instruments of their administrative control over the political and policy agenda in order to impose their will on all segments of the elite. Second, they had to prevent any opportunities for alternative coordination among elites by the demolition or co-optation of all independent organisational entities (such as parties, interest groups, NGOs and the media). Third, they had to ensure the long-term loyalty of elites and masses to the status quo regime, irrespective of its performance, personal qualities of leadership and the like.

From this perspective, a 'soft' version of a personalist authoritarian regime, which had emerged in Russia by the early 2000s, was the least useful instrument, because regimes of this kind are most vulnerable to lose their equilibrium in comparison with other authoritarianisms. Thus, Russia's rulers had to choose between two different strategies of long-term authoritarian regime building.

One option was a 'hard' version of personalist authoritarianism, in the manner of Belarus or Turkmenistan, which would base the loyalty of elites and masses through the intense use of coercion toward them. But this strategy would be costly for the Kremlin: quite apart from the need for huge investment in a large-scale coercion apparatus, which would diminish the threat of major disobedience, such regimes could be faced with the danger of international isolation and political turmoil in case of leadership succession. And also, given the fact that elites in 'hard' personalist authoritarian regimes could become victims of repression more often than ordinary citizens, Russia's ruling class had no incentive to launch such a risky enterprise.

In the terms elaborated by Robert Dahl, in Russia's post-communist setting the costs of repression were incredibly high. An alternative to a 'soft' party-based authoritarian regime looked much more attractive for both the Kremlin and the various segments of the elite. It could successfully solve all three above-mentioned problems: the establishment of monopolist control, the prevention of alternative coordination, and the building of long-term loyalty; but was less coercive and thus less costly for the Kremlin than 'hard' personalist authoritarianism. Indeed, it could lower the regime's costs of toleration without the risk of the loss of power due to open political contestation. Also, a 'soft' party-based authoritarianism would be very functional and instrumental for rulers in three other respects: it could enhance the regime's legitimacy due to both efficient political patronage and discouragement of alternatives to the status quo; it could effectively and flexibly perform policy adoption and implementation due to the non-ideological nature of the dominant party; and it would maintain elite consolidation and recruitment through mutually reinforcing bureaucratic and political mechanisms of control.

However, while the choice of this strategy of authoritarian regime building might bring long-term and large-scale benefits to the Kremlin, it also required a significant amount of political investment with a relatively long compensation period. Even though the political environment of Putin's Russia was very advantageous for the Kremlin's authoritarian regime building due to the recentralisation of the Russian state, unprecedented economic growth and the monopolisation of control over major economic assets, political and institutional engineering as well as organisational efforts were vital for this venture. The turning of a non-party-based regime into an emerging party-based authoritarian dominance was achieved as a result of the following deliberate and conscious steps.

In 2001, the party of power, United Russia, was established in the form of a 'hostile takeover' of the formerly regional-based coalition 'Fatherland—All Russia' (*Otechestvo–Vsya Rossiya*) and two small parliamentary groups by the

Kremlin-sponsored movement, Unity. The newly-born party gained a majority in the State *Duma* and unequivocally supported virtually all bills proposed by Putin and his government. Thus, UR established its parliamentary dominance. In 2003, the United Russia party list received 37.6% of votes during the State *Duma* elections, but the implicit coalition policy of the party of power in single-member districts and further institutional changes of internal parliamentary rules led to the formation of a 'manufactured super-majority': UR soon acquired more than two-thirds of the seats in the national legislature. Not only was UR's parliamentary dominance strengthened, but also alternatives to it became irrelevant.

In 2001–2003, the Kremlin and the State *Duma* launched a reform of regional electoral systems in order to improve the performance of UR in regional legis-latures and win centralised political control over the periphery (Golosov 2004a). Despite the fact that in 2003–2004 UR gained a significant share of votes in many regional legislative elections, it represented only a limited success for the party of power: its local branches performed well if they were captured by regional governors and served merely as their (rather than the Kremlin's) political vehi-cle. Also, governors often based their support on parties other than UR or on nonparty entities. But after the abolition of gubernatorial elections in early 2005, the incentives were reversed: the appointment and further survival of regional chief executives largely depended on their loyalty to UR. No wonder that most of them either voluntary or forcefully joined the ranks of the party of power. United Russia, in turn, established majorities in almost all regional leg-islatures and by 2007 achieved regional dominance: with some exceptions, regional politics no longer produced meaningful alternatives to UR.

From 2003 the Kremlin initiated a new wave of institutional changes, which were oriented toward further shrinking the field of party competition. The elec-toral threshold for parliamentary representation in the State *Duma* and most regional legislatures increased from 5% to 7%. The new federal law on political parties toughened many organisational and membership requirements for political parties, which had to re-register according to the new conditions. This reform significantly raised the entry barrier to Russia's market of party politics: the formation of new political parties has become very difficult, while only 15 out of 46 previously existing Russian parties by 2007 managed to squeeze in according to these rules and were able to participate in the December 2007 State *Duma* election. Also, pre-election party coalitions (blocs) from 2005 were pro-hibited altogether, thus rendering the survival of small party entities very prob-lematic (Wilson 2006). Finally, the recent reform of the State *Duma* electoral system (the shift from mixed to party list representation), not only increased UR's own party discipline and loyalty to the Kremlin, but also helped the party of power in gaining its electoral dominance during the 2007 parliamentary elections. While many factors, ranging from unfair campaigns to the high approval rate of Russia's President Vladimir Putin ensured UR's success, no other party could present a viable electoral alternative to the party of power.

The emergence of parliamentary, regional, and electoral dominance of the party of power made questionable the use of traditional classifications of parties in democratic polities such as 'left versus right parties', 'mass versus cadre parties', 'programmatic versus clientelist parties', and the like in conditions of a party-based authoritarian regime in Russia. Rather, Russia's new party system is better understood through the criteria of parties' loyalty to the Kremlin. While this (purely *ad hoc*) classification would be based on continuum and not on dichotomy (in fact, no political party in today's Russia is fully independent of the presidential administration), for the sake of further analysis I will take the liberty to present Russia's party system as a kind of multi-layered pie, with three hierarchical layers: first, the dominant party, United Russia; second, its satellites, which include JR, Vladimir Zhirinovskii's LDPR (Liberal Democratic Party of Russia, *Liberal'no-demokraticheskaya partiya Rossii*), and some other small 'pocket parties'; and third, its enemies, which include the Communist Party of the Russian Federation (KPRF, *Kommunisticheskaya Partiya Rossiiskoi Federatsii*), the Union of Right Forces (SPS, *Soyuz Pravykh Sil*) and *Yabloko*.

The New Party System in The Making: United Russia, its Satellites and its Enemies

Most political parties in the world were created by politicians in order to gain public office through a popular vote. The genesis of Russia's parties of power was essentially different: UR, as well as its predecessors, Our Home is Russia (*Nash dom Rossiya*) and Unity, was crafted by top officials in order to maximise their control over political arenas. This distinction undoubtedly affected major features of the party of power in Russia in three important aspects—party organisation, party ideology, and party government.

If one compares party organisation with those of firms, two basic models could be easily traced in a comparative perspective. In many well-established political parties in the world, a party's own managers (or party apparatus) established its bureaucratic control over nominations, electoral strategy, policy agenda and the like. These trends were dubbed as 'oligarchy' almost a century ago: in fact, they are similar to managerial control in corporate governance. An alternative, typical for many nascent parties in new democracies, is a clientelist intra-party organisation, which is based on personal loyalty and favouritism—a model similar to a family-run business. Unlike these two models, UR's party organisation developed in a rather different way: it could be described as Kremlin-based 'external governance', which was independent of the party leadership. While UR party officials were merely in charge of everyday routine management, the key Kremlin officials served as extra-party rulers, who controlled strategic decision-making. Thus, the party of power can be compared to a firm whose assets are owned not by its management but by a large multi-sectoral holding company, which hired its management and personnel and could easily replace them from time to time. [. . .] 'External governance' soon turned the party of power into a highly disciplined and centralised organisation: no internal dissent or factionalism is tolerated, and even discussion within the party is strictly regulated by the Kremlin. One might speculate, though, that if Fatherland—All Russia had defeated Unity during the 1999 electoral conflict, the party of power would likely have had few chances to follow the model of 'external governance': rather, it would have become a loose coalition of clientelist-based factions.

The genesis of the party of power also affected its lack of ideology. Top state officials needed UR as an instrument for the preservation of the status quo but not as an instrument of political change. No wonder that UR openly and deliberately manifested its loyalty to Russia's political regime and personally to Putin, while its position on major policy issues remained vague and indefinite. During the 2007 State *Duma* election campaign, UR's major slogan was 'Vote for Putin's plan!' ('*Golosui za plan Putina!*'), without specific reference to the content of this 'plan'. Some critics have argued that party ideology is necessary for long-term regime maintenance; however, in the short run UR's non-ideology was an asset rather than a liability, because it contributed to the success of the party of power. Against the background of a decline in transitional uncertainty, the role of ideology as a product in Russia's electoral market has shrunk. An in-depth analysis of the programmatic rhetoric of Russia's parties in the 1995–2003 parliamentary elections demonstrated the trend for policy positions to converge. Under these circumstances, UR enjoyed the merits of the median voter orientation of its policy positions: it is located near the zero point on the left—right continuum between pro-statist and pro-market parties. This is also true for any other axis of issue dimensions (for example, pro-Western vs. anti-Western issues). The lack of ideology gave UR wide room for political manoeuvre that was unavailable for the disunited opposition. Indeed, the large policy distance between these parties creates major obstacles for the formation of a negative anti-regime consensus coalition, which would include the KPRF, on the one hand, and *Yabloko* and SPS, on the other. In a comparative perspective, opposition parties under dominant party regimes (whether authoritarian or not) would also prefer the preservation of the status quo (continuity of dominant party rule) rather than the breakthrough to power of their ideologically distant counterparts; Russia was not an exception here.

Finally, the genesis of the party of power doomed it to play a subordinate role in policy adoption and implementation: to put it bluntly, the top Kremlin officials needed party politicians as obedient followers rather than as autonomous partners. This produced a great asymmetry in terms of party government: while top federal and, especially, regional executive officials joined UR, rank-and-file party members (even its MPs) were only occasionally rewarded by executive posts of secondary importance due to their personal fortunes rather than to party affiliation. Moreover, beyond the parliamentary and electoral arenas, the role of the party of power remains rather limited despite the aspirations of UR leaders. In February 2004, upon the resignation of Mikhail Kasyanov's cabinet of ministers, UR announced its intention to be actively involved in the process of cabinet formation, but when Putin proposed the virtually unknown Mikhail Fradkov as the new prime minister, who formed his cabinet without any serious influence on the part of UR, the party of power had no choice other than unanimous support, and its presence in the government was merely symbolic. During Fradkov's (2004–2007) and Viktor Zubkov's (2007–2008) governments, four members of the cabinet (deputy prime minister Alexander Zbukov, and ministers Sergei Shoigu, Alexei Gordeev and Yuri Trutnev) were members of UR, but they held these posts by subordination to the president rather than to UR, and by no means exercised party influence on governmental policies. Quite the opposite, it was the party of power which pushed governmental policy through the State *Duma* and was forced to take up the challenge of political responsibility for unpopular policies, such as social benefits reform launched in January 2005. [After this reform, UR's performance in regional legislative elections was the lowest ever.] The negligible effect of UR on policy making to a large degree was a by-product of Russia's institutional design and its notoriously overwhelming presidential power, which diminished the role of other actors and agencies. It was similar to that in Mexico, where presidentialism coincided with a party-based authoritarian regime for decades. The dominant party, PRI, despite the pervasive presence of its members in all levels and branches of government, merely approved proposals initiated by the president and his cabinet of technocrats (*'technicos'*) rather than serving as a key active actor in the policy-making process. In a similar vein, Putin's approach to government and policy making was ostensibly technocratic, thus leaving little room for party politics.

These features of United Russia as a dominant party—'external governance', non-ideology, and its secondary role in policy making—produced certain consequences for Russia's emerging party-based authoritarianism. In sharp contrast to the Soviet experience of Communist Party rule, which was best characterised as a 'party-state' regime, UR dominance could be labelled as 'state-party': not only did the dominant party itself informally serve as a branch of the presidential administration, but party politics as a whole in Russia performed the same role.

Satellites: Just Russia and Others

Post-communist Russia exhibited a strong record of active involvement of top executive officials not only in the building of dominant parties but also in the building of loyal or fake alternatives to them. These Kremlin-driven 'projects' served two basic—and not mutually exclusive—goals: first, to form a reserve or substitute to the party of power and avoid placing too many eggs in one basket (especially given the background of transitional uncertainty); and second, to weaken the oppositions of various colours by splitting their votes by spoiler parties. Attempts to pursue the first goal were demonstrated several times between the 1995 State *Duma* elections ('*Blok Ivana Rybkina*') and the 2003 parliamentary campaign (the People's Party of the Russian Federation). Manifestations of the pursuit of the second goal have also been numerous, and the Kremlin used a wide array of political technologies. They ranged from the encouragement of dissident factions of opposition parties to form their own party lists [such as the SLON party led by the former deputy chair of *Yabloko*, Vyacheslav Igrunov, which ran in the 2003 State *Duma* elections against his former party-mates], to a hostile takeover of formerly non-Kremlin parties (such as the *Democratic Party of Russia*, which ran in the 2007 State *Duma* elections under the slogan of Russia's prospective membership in the European Union, aiming to split the vote for liberal parties).

In the 2000s the Kremlin, facing an oversupply of potential satellite parties, was very active in 'inventing the opposition'. Under its auspices, small left and nationalist parties established the 'Motherland' ('*Rodina*') coalition before the 2003 elections, which was led by popular politicians, Dmitri Rogozin and Sergei Glaz'ev. Its well funded and much publicised campaign under nationalist and populist slogans was oriented towards diminishing the vote for the Communists, and its electoral success exceeded initial expectations: 'Motherland' won 9.1% of the eligible vote and established a parliamentary party in the State *Duma*. Soon after this, however, the leaders of 'Motherland' escaped the Kremlin's control: without permission, Glaz'ev ran in the presidential election of March 2004 and was expelled from the party's ranks. [. . .] [I]n 2006 Rogozin was forced to resign from the post of party leader. He was replaced by the businessman Alexander Babakov, who was completely subordinated to the Kremlin.

The precipitate rise and fall of 'Motherland' led the Kremlin into another venture, a satellite party, which was intended to act both as a reserve to the party of power and to split the communist vote. In 2006, the Kremlin initiated the merger of three previously established satellite parties—the Party of Life (*Partiya zhizni*), led by Sergei Mironov, the post-Rogozin 'Motherland' party, and the Party of Pensioners (*Partiya pensionerov*) (whose leadership was also replaced due to the uncontrolled political activism of the party chair, Valerii Gartung). The formation of the new party, Just Russia, which declared its leftist policy position and employed extensive socialist rhetoric, has been perceived as a major step towards the establishment of a 'managed' two-party system in Russia. Vladislav Surkov, the chief Kremlin political strategist, even announced that while UR should remain the major Kremlin vehicle, or its 'right leg', JR would act as its substitute in the manner of its 'left leg', 'if the right leg becomes numb'. When Vladimir Putin announced his decision to lead the UR party list in October 2007, it dealt a huge blow to JR prospects: Mironov and his party lost the major basis of their criticism toward UR, given their unquestionable personal loyalty to Putin. Although in the December 2007 election JR received 7.74% of the vote and became established as a parliamentary party, and (alongside UR and two other satellite parties) endorsed Medvedev's nomination for the 2008 presidential election, its future as the Kremlin's reserve became unclear.

Among satellite parties, the LDPR (*Liberal'no-demokraticheskaya partiya Rossii*) was probably the most valuable and long-standing Kremlin asset. From the very beginning, this party successfully combined nationalist and populist rhetoric with its fully fledged loyalty to the Kremlin. In fact, Zhirinovskii and his allies played two important roles. First, they endorsed major presidential and governmental proposals in the *Duma* and, more importantly, blocked several initiatives of the opposition (such as the attempt to impeach the president in May 1999). Second, they presented an image of a fake nationalist party, which was attractive to a number of voters without threatening the status quo. With the establishment of the parliamentary dominance of UR, the Kremlin no longer needed LDPR's services in the *Duma*, but its presence on Russia's electoral arena remained important given certain demands among voters and the effective use of the LDPR in the Kremlin's negative campaigning against selected targets (be they 'oligarchs', communists or somebody else). Yet, besides LDPR as fake nationalists, a number of fake left parties as well as fake liberals were always at the Kremlin's disposal.

[. . .] Party politicians beyond UR were faced with a difficult choice between complete subordination and (relative) autonomy from the Kremlin: in fact, this was a choice between survival and possible extinction. Still, some parties that sought political autonomy remained in Russia's political arena.

Opposition: Is there Life After Death?

In the 1990s, political opposition (first anti-communist, and later communist) had a decisive impact on the emerging Russian party system. By contrast, in the

2000s both communist and liberal political oppositions not only dramatically lost their influence but appeared ready to disappear from the political arena, in the manner of a dying species. Two major factors affected the collapse of Russia's opposition parties, which became evident after the 2003 State *Duma* elections and continued over time. First, the institutional background of strong presidentialism was unfavourable for opposition politics by definition and was accompanied by the institutional changes of the 2000s, such as an increase in the threshold for parliamentary representation, tough rules for party registration, and the prohibition on electoral coalitions. Second, in the 2000s, political competition in Russia became very limited due to the 'imposed consensus' of elites; the Kremlin and UR dominated Russia's political scene, and all remaining elite sections have had to agree on their subordinated role or have lost their elite status as such. While elite fragmentation and conflict is likely for opposition-induced political protest, the 'imposed consensus' left the opposition with no choice: it became co-opted or damaged, located at the periphery of the political arena, and no longer played the role of political actor. Under these circumstances, neither the KPRF, *Yabloko* nor the SPS were able to resolve the 'classical problem of any opposition. . .how much to oppose and by what means': the choice of opposition strategies lies between 'exit', 'voice', and 'loyalty', (Hirschman 1970), but none of them brought Russian opposition parties any success in the 2000s.

The Communist Party of the Russian Federation exhausted its potential of 'voice' (of decisive anti-regime mass mobilisation) as early as 1996, and then they turned to 'loyalty' to the status quo regime under the slogan of 'growing into power' ('*vrastanie vo vlast*'). Since then, the KPRF attempted to be a junior partner of the ruling group; in 2000 the communists even reached an agreement with the Unity faction about sharing the chairships of parliamentary committees and still controlled the position of State *Duma* chairman. But bargaining gains were minimal: in fact, the very existence of a Kremlin-controlled majority in the State *Duma* undermined the position of the KPRF, which turned into a 'cosmetic' opposition. During the 2003 State *Duma* elections, the KPRF became a major Kremlin target: vicious attacks on the communists, including large-scale negative coverage on television, Kremlin pressure on pro-communist governors and businesspeople, and the splitting of the electorate through the nomination of alternative party lists, led to the sharp electoral decline of the KPRF. It lost almost half of its vote in the 2003 State *Duma* elections, and KPRF success in regional elections after 2000 also declined. But even these conditions did not change the KPRF's strategy: its policy positions, organisation and leadership remained nearly the same as in the 1990s. The party's appeal to voters was oriented toward 'back to the USSR', the party was led by Soviet-style second-order bureaucrats, and party activists rejected any major innovations that could provoke major party changes. In fact, this immobilism helped the KPRF to preserve its organisation and electoral bases from a total collapse: the communists received 11.57% of the vote in the 2007 *Duma* election, and its performance in regional elections was relatively strong. At the same time, it pushed the KPRF into a narrow electoral 'ghetto' without any prospect of serious influence on politics and policy making: the Kremlin's drive for exclusion of the KPRF from the political arena could provoke the communists to adopt an 'exit' strategy probably leading to their subsequent marginalisation.

Unlike the communists, Russia's major liberal party, the SPS, as well as its predecessor, Democratic Choice of Russia, always occupied a niche of semi-opposition, which was not represented in the government, but which sought to join it without any significant changes in the political regime and/or of major policies. This strategy bore the SPS some fruit in the 1999 State *Duma* election, when the liberals backed Vladimir Putin and his military actions in Chechnya. Thanks to Kremlin support and positive TV coverage, the SPS received 8.5% of the vote. However, given the emerging parliamentary dominance of UR, the Kremlin needed liberal allies in the *Duma* only occasionally, while the influence of the SPS on decision making was fairly limited. The liberals' gains were minimal. Despite the SPS 'loyalty' strategy, the party of power still received the lion's share of political benefits. In the 2003 State *Duma* election the SPS was unable to squeeze above the 5% threshold, and this failure brought the party to organisational collapse. Although some previous leaders and activists left the party's ranks, the SPS was able to reinvent itself: in 2005 liberals elected the new party chair, Nikita Belykh, hired a new campaign manager (the energetic Anton Bakov), and (despite the party's name and official policy positions) actively used leftist rhetoric during regional legislative elections. Still, the most influential wing of the SPS coalesced around the architect of 1990s privatisation and the major party sponsor Anatolii Chubais and remained loyal to the Kremlin at any cost. In the course of the 2007 State *Duma* election, however, the SPS suddenly shifted from 'loyalty' to 'voice'. The party blamed Putin and UR for the authoritarian drift of the country, vigorously defended political freedoms, and even joined anti-regime protest rallies organised by the radical non-partisan units such as Gary Kasparov's United Civic Front (*Ob"edinennyi Grazhdanskii Front*) and Eduard Limonov's National Bolsheviks (*Natsionalnaya Bolshevistskaya Partiya*) (previously, the SPS stayed away from such activities). However, this 'voice' was raised in vain: the Kremlin argued that it was an attempt to seek revenge by those actors who had unsuccessfully ruled Russia in the 1990s, and initiated a massive negative campaign. The remaining voters of the SPS were disoriented while a new Kremlin satellite party, the Civic Force, split the liberal electorate (it received 1.1% of the vote at the polls against 0.96% for the SPS). It is too early to predict whether the SPS will survive as a political party or whether it will transform into something else. But it is clear that

the very project of liberal semi-opposition has failed: Surkov was absolutely correct when he announced immediately after the 2003 State *Duma* elections that the
liberals' historical mission was exhausted.

Finally, *Yabloko*, the major (if not the only) democratic opposition party in Russia, suffered most from the political changes of the 2000s. From the very beginning,
Yabloko remained a small party, whose resources were insufficient to achieve electoral success. In a parliamentary system such a party could become a useful ally for
a governmental coalition, but in Russia's presidential system opportunities for
coalition building were fairly limited. At the same time, the Kremlin actively
offered *Yabloko* various forms of informal coalition in order to 'swallow up' this
party via a hostile takeover. Due to these constraints, the 'exit' strategy was the
only viable path for survival: in the 1990s *Yabloko* systematically and unequivocally
opposed virtually all presidential and governmental proposals. Under conditions of
multiple crises and fragmentation of elites this strategy brought *Yabloko* some
short-term benefits, but the long-term costs were much higher. Despite its significant investments in party building, in the 2000s *Yabloko* faced a deep organisational
crisis: several *Duma* deputies and regional activists left the party ranks, it lost the
financial support of major sponsors, and the threat of a hostile takeover became
more dangerous. These hardships drove *Yabloko* to a change of strategy: from 'exit'
to 'loyalty' to the Kremlin. However, it was useless: *Yabloko* gained little benefit
from its consultations with the Kremlin, while the arrest of the major party sponsor, Mikhail Khodorkovskii in 2003 was the last blow against the party's hopes.
Yabloko's defeat in the 2003 State *Duma* election, when it failed to cross the 5%
threshold, was a natural consequence of this strategic shift. Subsequent events,
such as the party's grand failure in most regional legislative elections, clearly indicated that *Yabloko's* electoral potential was exhausted. [. . .]

As one can see, none of opposition parties was able to secure their positions
during the 2000s. At best, they found their place at the bottom of the multi-layered pie of Russia's party system. Their symbolical presence in national and/or
regional legislatures, weak mobilisation potential and low profile in public perceptions demonstrated the deep stagnation of opposition politics. Even though
these trends provoked the rise of disloyal non-party oppositions, whose street
protests became visible in Russia's major cities, such an activism cannot be seen
as an effective substitute for competitive party politics. To summarise, the Kremlin's thorough and comprehensive control over political parties might even
result in the extinction of the opposition parties in the long run. However, what
is good for the Kremlin is not equally good for Russia's political development.

Conclusion: between Mexico and the GDR?

The early development of competitive party politics in Yel'tsin's Russia could be
seen as the manifestation of the protracted growing pains of the nascent political

regime. By contrast, the demise of party competition and the emergence of a dominant party in Russia under Putin could become symptoms of it having a chronic disease. Given the lack of alternatives, one might assume that the current trends in Russia's party system could be maintained over time. In his speech before UR party activists in February 2006, Surkov announced the Kremlin's intention to preserve UR dominance at least for the next 10–15 years (Surkov 2006) and compared this kind of dominant party system with those in Japan under the Liberal Democrats or Sweden under the Social Democrats, which are usually labelled as 'uncommon democracies'. However, critics of the new party system draw many parallels with the authoritarian regime in Mexico under PRI, and former State *Duma* deputy Vladimir Ryzhkov even dubbed it a 'Dresden party system', openly referring to the experience of East Germany under the GDR's communist regime, which was familiar to Vladimir Putin during his KGB service in the 1980s.

While many dominant party systems under democratic and authoritarian regimes exhibit some similarities, the crucial difference lies not only in the degree of party competition, but also in the degree of autonomy of party politics from the state. While in 'uncommon democracies' politics beyond the dominant party is rarely damaged by the state officials, party-based authoritarian regimes tend to tolerate non-dominant parties only if they do not challenge the status quo regime. Yet, Mexican party-based authoritarianism was not overly repressive, and some autonomous parties like the right-wing National Action Party (PAN) actively operated in the political arena for decades (even though without major achievements). However, party-based authoritarianism in the GDR was probably one of the most repressive regimes in Eastern Europe, which completely excluded organised political activism beyond the dominant and satellite parties. In this sense, Russia's party system, with its Kremlin-controlled hierarchy of a dominant party, its pocket satellites, and weak and impotent opponents, could be placed somewhere between Mexico and the GDR, but certainly not alongside the 'uncommon democracies'. Despite the fact that the current state of Russia's party system cannot be easily changed without major exogenous shocks, the comparative experience of both communist and non-communist party-based authoritarian regimes demonstrates that these party systems cannot survive indefinitely. In the long run, exogenous factors such as economic and social modernisation or international 'linkages' tend to erode one-party dominance. But whether or not a return to party competition in Russia will happen under the political generations of Putin and Medvedev remains to be seen.

6.2

Political Opposition in Russia: A Dying Species?

Vladimir Gel'man

In the classic 1966 volume *Political Oppositions in Western Democracies*, the chapter on France in the early years of Fifth Republic was entitled "France: Nothing but Opposition." A similar chapter about Russia in the mid-2000s would have to be called "Russia: Anything but Opposition." In fact, after Vladimir Putin's first term in office and the 2003–2004 parliamentary and presidential elections, all political actors who claimed to form an "opposition" were about to disappear or, at least, seriously lose their influence. As one observer put it: "There is no opposition today in Russia's political system—neither system opposition, which is oriented toward a shift of a country's rules, nor antisystem opposition, which is oriented toward changing the overall rules of the game." According to surveys done by the Levada Center, Russia's best-known opinion pollsters, the number of Russians who believed that political opposition exists in the country declined from 53 percent in mid-2002 to 42 percent in mid-2004. Simultaneously, the number of Russians who believed that political opposition is needed dramatically increased.

Yet the sharp difference between the political oppositions in two post-crisis political regimes under charismatic leadership (De Gaulle's France and Putin's Russia) is interesting in itself. For the current analysis, however, it may be considered rather as a point of departure for another question: why is the role of the political opposition in Russia in the mid-2000s so drastically diminished in comparison with the previous 10–15 years? In the 1990s, political opposition (first anti-communist, and later communist) had a decisive impact on the supply and, to some extent, on the demand on emerging Russia's political market. By contrast, in the 2000s, the former political oppositions had nearly disappeared without successors.

The major explanations put forward by observers for the decline of political opposition in Russia are, at minimum, insufficient. On the "supply" side of the political market, many analysts focus unconvincingly on *ad hoc* factors such as the lack of coalitions between liberal political parties (notably Yabloko and the

---

Source: Vladimir Gel'man, "Political Opposition in Russia: A Dying Species?" *Post Soviet Affairs,* Vol. 21, No. 3, 2005, 226–246.

Note: Notes and references have been removed from this article.

Union of Right Forces), the crucial role of some events, such as the "Yukos affair," or the personalities of political leaders. On the "demand" side of the political market, sociological determinism is overwhelming. Scholars of survey research explain the failure of the opposition by referring to the high popularity of Vladimir Putin and the improvement of economic conditions in the country. Although these factors are important, they do not lead *per se* to the extinction of political opposition, as the French experience suggests. Some culturally oriented scholars are deeply concerned about the negative influence that embedded non-democratic features (such as statism and anarchism) in Russian political culture exert on the construction of effective democratic institutions, including political opposition. But this approach, most popular among Russian observers, is poorly grounded empirically, since survey data show a very different picture.

Sociological determinism is also poorly grounded theoretically, being implicitly based on the assumption that the political regime—or at least the party system (in the context of electoral democracy)—largely reflects the distribution of societal preferences. On the contrary, research has shown that both political regimes and party systems are often autonomous of popular values and attitudes, and display their own logic of political development. Moreover, during the early stages of the development of political parties, the supply side of the political market decisively affects the demand side, not vice versa. In other words, political actors and political institutions, or humanly devised "rules of the game," shape the direction of mass preferences and determine the dynamics of the political regime and of oppositions. This does not, of course, mean that mass preferences do not matter at all, but, realistically, the masses matter in politics only as much and for as long as political elites permit (or do not permit) them to do so.

Accordingly, we should aim to explain opposition as a political phenomenon through the prism of political factors, rather than by concentrating on general societal processes. This political science approach has been successfully applied to the analysis of some post-Soviet political transformations, and will be employed in this article. I first present a theoretical framework for analyzing political opposition in Russia and elsewhere. Then I focus on the impact that the structure of the political elite and political institutions had on the evolution of political opposition in Russia from the late 1980s to the mid-2000s. On the basis of this, I analyze three cases of the most visible political parties that claimed to represent the political opposition in Russia: the Communist Party of the Russian Federation (KPRF), the Union of Right Forces, and Yabloko. Finally, tentative conclusions on the prospects for political opposition in Russia will be considered.

Political Opposition: A Conceptual Map

The study of political opposition is by no means a popular field in contemporary political science. Most recent publications are heavily descriptive, and the number of theoretical monographs is very limited. Review articles published in the 1980s and 1990s demonstrated the lack of progress in research in this area. As Eva Kolinsky rightly points out, the fact that political opposition remains neglected among scholars is the other side of the coin of the popularity of the study of government, in the same way that common interest in the losing team in the final of a sporting event suffers because of interest in the winning team.

Some established theoretical schemes, however, are not always useful analytical tools. Most empirical typologies either are *ad hoc* categories based on single case studies. Or are overloaded by different dimensions, so that their explanatory potential for comparative studies is insufficient. Therefore, the analysis of political opposition in Russia as well as in other "hybrid" regimes requires not only a new typology, but a more general framework—or, so to speak, a conceptual map. This map should be useful not only for making distinctions among the various types of political opposition, but also for understanding their political dynamics in a post-communist regime.

The construction of such a conceptual map is based on two major dimensions of political opposition: their ends and their means, as Dahl and Smith rightly suggest. The various ends or goals of the opposition might be represented in the form of a continuum. Those parties, politicians, cliques, and clans that are not present in the government, but would like to join it without any significant changes in the political regime and/or of major policies, are located at its minimalist pole. As Linz noted in his study of opposition in Spain under Franco, these actors could be regarded as a "semi-opposition"; simultaneously, they play the role of "quasi-opposition." At the other extreme, political actors whose goals require total control over power resources, usually to effect radical change of the political regime, are located at the maximalist pole of this continuum. Those actors, according to Kirchheimer, are the "principal" opposition. Some other forms of opposition, such as "non-structural" opposition, which is oriented toward a change of major policies as well as "structural" opposition, which is oriented toward a change of political regime but accommodates power-sharing, could be located at intermediate points on this continuum.

Classification of the means of political opposition is a more difficult task. We could rely upon Linz's distinction among loyal, semi-loyal, and disloyal oppositions, although Linz underlines the ambiguity of this typology and the residual nature of the category of "semi-loyalty." Two major criteria of the loyalty of political opposition, according to Linz, are acceptance of legal means for political struggle and rejection of political violence, while the use of purely illegal or violent means (or the threat thereof) is typical of disloyal opposition. With some reservations, these criteria might be used for an analysis of opposition in a broader context. Thus, various political oppositions under different types of political regimes (whether democratic or not) could be located on a two-dimensional conceptual map of ends and means (see Figure 1).

Figure 1. Conceptual map of political opposition

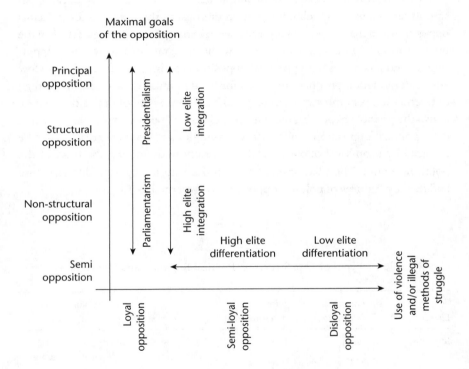

Having specified types of political oppositions, let us now address factors involved in the formation and transformation of political oppositions. The key role is played by the characteristics of the political regimes to which these oppositions must relate, such as their competitiveness and the nature of their political institutions. The competitiveness of a political regime is related to the structure of the political elite. An "elite" is broadly understood here as a set of actors who could affect politically meaningful decisions. The "elite structure" is defined by the levels of elite integration (the capacity of various elite segments to cooperate with each other) and elite differentiation (functional and organizational diversity of various elite segments and their relative autonomy *vis-à-vis* the state and *vis-à-vis* each other). On this basis, Higley et al. produced the following typology of elite structures: (1) *ideocratic elite* (high integration, low differentiation); (2) *divided elite* (low integration, low differentiation); (3) *fragmented elite* (low integration, high differentiation); (4) *consensual elite* (high integration, high differentiation). The first type of elite structure is associated with stable non-democratic regimes, while the last is associated with stable democracies.

We can now relate these types of elite structure to the types of political opposition they spawn. High elite integration diminishes the potential for principal opposition and makes more likely a cooperative bargaining strategy between the opposition and the government, while low elite integration provides more opportunities and incentives for a principal opposition to form. At the same time, low elite differentiation produces no room for loyal political opposition, while high differentiation is in most cases unlikely to breed disloyalty of opposition. There is also the possible hyper-fragmentation of elites, or "polarized pluralism", when loyal political opposition, under certain conditions of political crisis, might be replaced by semi-loyal opposition, thus possibly undermining the basis of the political regime. The relationship between the various types of elite structure and the key features of political opposition is presented in Table 1.

Table 1. Types of Elite Structure, Political Regimes, and Oppositions

Elite structure	Elite Integration	Elite differentiation	Political regime	Predominant opposition
Ideocratic	High	Low	Stable non-democratic	No opposition or disloyal opposition
Divided	Low	Low	Unstable non-democratic	Principal disloyal opposition
Fragmented	Low	High	Unstable democratic	Principal loyal or semi-loyal oposition
Consensual	High	High	Stable democratic	Loyal structural or non-structural opposition

Source: Author's reconstruction based on Higley et al. (2003, p. 15)

As for the effects of *political institutions* on the opposition, the most important distinction is between parliamentary and presidential systems, which appears to be decisive for the emergence of various types of political opposition. Presidential and presidential-parliamentary systems are commonly criticized for their basic "winner takes all" principle, so it is no surprise that they are likely to produce a principal opposition. On the other hand, under parliamentary and/or premier-presidential systems, political oppositions are offered more incentives for bargaining on the basis of coalition-building and/or corporatism. In this connection, Kirchheimer noted the "vanishing" of opposition. In the same way, proportional-representation (as opposed to majoritarian) electoral systems, as well as decentralization and federalism (rather than unitarism and hyper-centralization), also diminish the likelihood of a principal opposition forming. Thus, we might predict that the type and evolution of elite structures and political institutions determine the evolution of political oppositions.

Opposition Dynamics In Russia, 1989–2004

The evolution of political opposition in Russia can be interpreted through the prism of the conceptual map outlined above. During *perestroika*, increasing elite differentiation as well as the installation of partially free, semi-competitive elections and the emergence of parliamentarianism promoted the formation of a loyal structural opposition in the form of a democratic movement along with the emergence of some left-wing and nationalist proto-parties. But the potential of the opposition plummeted after the breakdown of the Soviet Union in 1991. The Soviet ideocratic elite was replaced by a divided elite, exemplified by the conflict between President Boris Yel'tsin and the Supreme Soviet. The over-concentration of presidential power relative to the legislature logically resulted in zero-sum conflict. Under these circumstances, the disloyal principal opposition that dominated before October 1993 lost heavily. The outcome of this conflict between the government and the opposition was fixed in the 1993 Constitution.

Subsequent events have had a contradictory impact on the development of political opposition in Russia. On the one hand, the broad and ill-defined powers of the executive within the "super-presidential" system led to winner-take-all conflicts and a strengthening of principal opposition, while the ability of other political institutions to mitigate conflict was negligible. On the other hand, a deep economic recession and multiple political crises (including the Chechen wars) contributed to fragmentation of the elite structure. To a large degree, elite fragmentation in the 1990s was a by-product of the fragmentation of the Russian state and the decline of its capacity because of "state capture" by economic interest groups and spontaneous decentralization. Although political opposition of different colors flourished in Russia during 1993–2000 (resembling to some extent the notion of "nothing but opposition"), the oppositional strategies remained unsuccessful.

Segments of the opposition were unable to find a solution of the "classical problem of any opposition. . .how much to oppose and by what means. If the opposition does not oppose—does not present alternatives and struggle energetically for them—then the representative powers of political institutions—their capacity to mobilize and incorporate—is weak. . . . But if the opposition does oppose vigorously, democracy may be threatened." The problem affects not only the ideological and organizational development of opposition parties, but also their political strategies. According to the well-known typology of reactions to crises elaborated by Albert O. Hirschman, the choice of opposition strategies lies between "exit," "voice," and "loyalty," represented, respectively, in the form of doing "petty things," (i.e., oppositional activities without serious challenge to the status quo), mass mobilization (mainly electoral), and bargaining with the ruling group and consequent cooptation ("implementation into power"). Although Russian opposition parties tried to use all these strategies, none of them brought about significant achievements. For a principal opposition, the only way to attain their goals was to win presidential elections. Neither legislative dominance (in the case of KPRF in the State Duma in 1996–99) nor influence on the composition and policy of the government (in the case of Prime Minister Yevgeniy Primakov's cabinet in 1998–99) helped to achieve the opposition's ends. As for the semi-opposition, which tried to serve as a junior partner of the ruling group, it lost mass support in conditions of political and economic crisis. In fact, while the potential of the disloyal opposition was fairly limited, the impact on the political regime of the loyal principal opposition (which pursued either "exit" or "voice"), not to mention the semi-opposition, was also negligible.

Putin's presidency changed the structure of the elite dramatically, which had a decisive impact on political opposition in Russia. Simultaneously, elite integration sharply increased and elite differentiation became very limited as a result of the "imposed consensus" of elites. Thanks to these developments, the new ruling group around Putin overwhelmingly dominated Russia's political scene, and all remaining elite sections (parliamentary factions, political parties, media, business, and regional leaders) had to agree on their subordinated role or lost their elite status as such. This loss of autonomy and/or resources by segments of the elite led to a diminution of political opportunities for the opposition. Previous opposition strategies resulted in heavy losses. For the principal opposition, the "exit" strategy produced marginalization and a lack of opposition influence, while opportunities for "voice" were limited because of the scarce resource base and the threat of use of force from the ruling group. For the semi-opposition, cooptation into the regime resulted in the loss of its distinctive identity *vis-à-vis* the ruling group. Thus, the "imposed consensus" of Russia's elites left the opposition with no choice: it became co-opted or damaged, located at the periphery of the political arena, and lost its role as a political actor. The massive defeat of all opposition parties in the 2003 Duma elections and the lack of meaningful alternatives to Putin in the 2004 presidential elections serve as the most dramatic examples of these trends. The dynamics of change sketched above are displayed in Table 2.

Table 2. The Dynamics of Political Opposition in Russia, 1989–2004

Period	Elite structure	Political institutions	Predominant opposition
1989–1991	Breakdown of ideocratic elite; rise of elite differentiation	Emergence of parliamentarism	Loyal structural opposition
1991–1993	Divided elite (low integration, low differentiation)	Presidential-parliamentary conflict	Disloyal principal opposition
1993–1999/2000	Fragmented elite, hyper-differentiation	Super-presidential system	Loyal principal opposition
2000–?	Re-emergence of ideocratic elite, rise of elite integration, and decline of elite differentiation	Super-presidential system	Extinction of principal opposition and semi-opposition

We will now apply this general logic of the rise and decline of political opposition in Russia to the evolution of opposition parties, which differ in their genesis, ideology, and organizational development. Although the most popular typology of Russian political parties identifies liberals, left-wing, nationalist parties, and the "party of power", I will add one further distinction. According to some classifications of ideologies in Russia, liberals—free-marketers who consider democracy just one of several possible means—should be separated from democrats—supporters of democratization who consider the market economy to be important but not the only means of economic coordination. Liberals and democrats tend to be close in their policy positions, but their ends and means during the process of regime change in Russia were very different. The liberal trend in Russian politics in the 1990s and 2000s was represented by Russia's Choice, Democratic Choice of Russia, and the Union of Right Forces, while Yabloko was a prime example of the democratic trend. Along with the KPRF, these parties claimed to be the major opposition actors in Russian politics. I will therefore focus on the communists, liberals, and democrats, examining the evolution of their oppositional roles and the reasons they recently lost their influence and are about to disappear from the country's political scene.

The KPRF: between Principal Opposition and Semi-Opposition

The organizational and ideological development of the KPRF is widely described in the literature. Its trajectory on our conceptual map of opposition looks like a zigzag from disloyal opposition (during the period when it was banned in 1991–92), through ambivalent semi-loyalty during the violent conflict of September—October 1993, then, after December 1993, to loyal opposition within the framework of parliamentary and electoral politics, and to principal opposition since 2000.

The KPRF claimed a monopoly on representation of left-wing and nationalist voters, so the party's policy positions proved to be inconsistent. The party needed to maximize mobilization of its supporters in order to take control of powerful positions as well as to preserve both its dominant position on the political market and the party's own organizational unity. Hence, the KPRF presented itself as a "real" opposition to the power of non-communist incumbents. But the communists proved unable to secure the main prize: victory in the 1996 presidential elections was impossible, owing to tough resistance from Yeltsin's clique (including the threat of a *coup d'etat*) but also because of the radicalism of the KPRF, which was unacceptable to many voters. For these and other reasons, after the 1996 presidential elections the KPRF leaders announced a change of approach toward greater accommodation of the ruling group. The communists delegated representatives to the government and regional administrations, were deeply involved in bargaining with the ruling group on both political and policy issues, and tried to find a balance between the poles of principal opposition and semi-opposition. But this was not a conscious attempt to combine "voice" and "loyalty" as a means of coming to power. Rather, the KPRF refused to choose between loyal and disloyal opposition, in hopes of preserving the status quo within the party and its position on the political market. In terms suggested by Hirschman's followers, by default the communists adopted a strategy of "neglect", and systematically rejected taking any meaningful decisions. This was the case with their behavior during the failed no-confidence vote in then—Prime

Minister Viktor Chernomyrdin's government in 1997, the legislative approval of Sergey Kiriyenko as prime minister in 1998, and the failed attempt at impeaching the president in 1999. The KPRF campaign during the 1999 parliamentary elections was based on the same lack of strategy, or on a strategy of simply securing the status quo.

In tactical terms, the "neglect" strategy brought some gains to the KPRF, but the communists lost strategically. Although the share of the KPRF votes in 1999 slightly increased (24.3 percent against 22.2 percent in the 1995 elections), the communists could not consolidate their dominant status in the legislature. After that, the KPRF attempted to act as a junior partner of the ruling group, reaching an agreement with the Kremlin-created Unity faction about sharing chairmanships of parliamentary committees and retaining the position of State Duma chairman. But the potential of the opposition had been weakened and bargaining gains were merely symbolic. In fact, the very existence of a non-communist majority in the legislature undermined the position of the KPRF. The communists could not shape major parliamentary decisions, so they soon lost the role of "veto group" and turned into a "cosmetic" opposition. And when the KPRF tried to return to a "voice" strategy and actively opposed some Kremlin-induced bills, it was effectively punished. In April 2002, United Russia—the "party of power"—and its supporters revised the distribution of committee chairmanships in the legislature, and pushed the KPRF out of those positions. Some communist leaders, including State Duma Chairman Gennadiy Selyeznev, chose loyalty to the ruling group and were expelled from the party's ranks. The communists also lost some of their potential for electoral mobilization. Their success in regional gubernatorial and legislative elections after 2000 was more modest.

The grand failure of the KPRF in the 2003–2004 national elections was a logical extension of this process. The communist opposition was a major Kremlin target during the parliamentary election campaign, including large-scale negative coverage on television, Kremlin pressure on pro-communist governors and businessmen, and dilution of the communist electorate through the nomination of alternative party lists—of which the Motherland list, which garnered 9 percent of the votes, was the most effective.

But even these conditions did not change the KPRF "neglect" strategy: its policy positions and organization remained nearly the same. After the December 2003 elections, when the KPRF got only 12.6 percent of the votes and 52 seats, the communists finally lost their leading role in the opposition. [. . .]

It is hard to say why the communist strategy of "neglect" in 1996–99 was so ineffective. In all probability, the KPRF leaders wrongly assumed that against a backdrop of permanent political and economic crises, they could come to power almost by default. Also, some rumors about a possible coalition between the communists and the ruling group—especially in the wake of their informal bargaining with the leaders of Fatherland—All Russia before the 1999 parliamentary elections—were not groundless. But in general, political institutions and elite structure limited the political opportunity structure for the KPRF. Because of the impossibility of a communist victory in presidential elections, political institutions provided a strong incentive for the KPRF's movement toward semi-opposition. But the change in elite structure after 2000 toward a new "ideocratic" elite has led the KPRF toward principal opposition without any significant chances of success.

Liberals: Semi-Opposition

Among Russian liberals—proponents of the free market and minimalist state—the key ideological and organizational positions were overwhelmingly occupied by a group of economists led by Anatoliy Chubais. They proposed a large-scale program of authoritarian market reforms to Gorbachev as early as 1990. When, in late 1991, the liberals were promoted to leading posts in the Yel'tsin government, their program lost all relevance because of the breakdown of the Soviet Union. Nevertheless, the liberals consistently pursued these ideas and vigorously supported the elimination of the Supreme Soviet in October 1993. During the 1993 parliamentary elections, they organized the coalition Russia's Choice (VR), which combined the status of a "party of power" with an ideology of radical market reform, and they inherited some of the resources of the former democratic movement. Soon after the relatively unsuccessful campaign, the coalition was reorganized into the party Democratic Russia's Choice (DVR).

DVR was a typical semi-opposition. The party represented itself as moderately critical of some governmental policies (notably the Chechen war) but unequivocally backed the Kremlin on major decisions, of which Yel'tsin's 1996 re-election bid was the most important. Also, some party leaders, including Chubais, secured positions in the executive branch. But the strategy of "loyalty" did not bring benefits to the liberals, owing to the extremely unfavorable socioeconomic context, while the costs of this strategy were significant. The liberals backed the ruling group but did not affect its composition and only partly affected some policies. Yet the general public saw them as responsible for government failures, and they soon lost popular support. For these reasons, the mobilizing potential of DVR was undermined, the party's influence in Kremlin circles weakened, and in 1994–95 many politicians deserted the DVR and VR parliamentary factions. DVR responded by trying to claim the leading role among liberal and democratic parties, and by trying to weaken its major competitor, Yabloko. This did not succeed. During the 1995 parliamentary elections, DVR lost heavily and seemed to have been relegated to the "minor league" of Russian politics.

However, thanks to the hyper-fragmentation of Russia's elites in the 1990s, not even the liberals' major electoral failure led to their total breakdown. Quite the opposite. The liberals' success during Yel'tsin's 1996 electoral campaign, as well as appointments of some liberals to key posts in the government in 1997–98, helped them to re-establish their status as the leading reformers among the ruling group. In this period, they effectively used patron-client ties and access to financial resources, including Western aid secured through intrigues among Kremlin cliques around Yel'tsin. After the financial meltdown of August 1998, most liberals were forced to resign from government posts, and their chances of political survival seemed to be disappearing.

Faced with this major threat, the liberals displayed an organizational cohesiveness that served them well for purposes of political survival. On the eve of the 1999 State Duma elections, they created a new coalition of minor parties and organizations called the Union of Right Forces (SPS). The context of the 1999 campaign was more favorable for the liberals, who openly backed Vladimir Putin and his military actions in Chechnya. Thanks to Kremlin support and unlimited positive coverage on national television, SPS got 8.5 percent of the vote and 32 seats, defeating its principal opponent, Yabloko. Soon after the elections, the SPS transformed itself into a full-fledged party with a more-or-less coherent program and organizational structure.

During the third State Duma, the SPS remained a semi-opposition, as DVR had been in 1994–95. But the crucial distinction was that, after 2000, the new ruling group needed liberal allies in the parliament only from time to time, while the influence of the SPS on executive and parliamentary decision-making was limited. Although the SPS backed Putin during the 2000 presidential elections, only a few of its representatives were rewarded with prominent posts—and even so, they broke ties with their own party. Even liberals in the government, such as Aleksey Kudrin and German Gref, remained loyal to the Kremlin and oriented toward an alliance with the "party of power." Although the policy positions of SPS and United Russia were not always the same, liberals only partly criticized the Kremlin's major policies in certain areas, such as military reform. Nevertheless, the SPS explicitly backed the Kremlin's major anti-democratic proposals, such as its hostile takeover of the independent television channel NTV and its banning of referenda on the eve of national elections. But the liberals' gains were minimal. Besides their loyalty in the context of Russia's economic recovery, the "party of power" got the lion's share of the political benefits. In addition, in 2001–02 the SPS unsuccessfully attempted to eliminate its democratic opponents from Yabloko in the manner of a hostile takeover—as VR and DVR had tried to do previously in 1993–95.

The same strategy predominated during the 2003 parliamentary elections. The Union of Right Forces did not even try to maximize its own vote, but rather tried to steal Yabloko votes. The response of its opponents was similar, as a result of which both parties undermined their positions. The Kremlin's attacks on big business during the campaign also weakened the SPS. The failure of the SPS in the 2003 elections was similar to DVR's results in the 1995 electoral campaign, and brought the party to the brink of organizational collapse. The co-chair of the SPS, Irina Khakamada, resigned from her post and ran in the 2004 presidential elections as an independent candidate, after which she established her own party. Along with some SPS activists, she announced her intention of creating a new opposition, but the most influential wing of the SPS around Chubais remained loyal to the ruling group. As a result, SPS was unable to elaborate a definite position for the 2004 presidential elections and in fact did not back any candidate. It is too early to predict whether the SPS will survive as a political party or will transform itself into something else. But it is clear that the very project of liberal semi-opposition has failed.

Paradoxically, by the mid-2000s the liberals had become victims of the success of their own reform proposals of the early 1990s. The re-establishment of an integrated elite and the re-emergence of a dominant ruling party were a great help to Putin's re-launch of marketizing reforms. But to pursue this policy, the Kremlin seeks only technical assistants, rather than even partly autonomous junior political partners. The fragmented elite of the 1990s had left space for political opportunities for semi-opposition. But the new ideocratic elite that consolidated after 2000 no longer needed even a semi-opposition. The deputy head of the Kremlin administration, Vyacheslav Surkov, was correct when he announced immediately after the 2003 State Duma elections that the liberals' historical mission was exhausted. Nevertheless, as long as the ruling group in Russia does not turn into an organizational monolith, new attempts at building a liberal semi-opposition can be expected, even though their chances of success are extremely limited.

Democrats: From Principal Opposition To Semi-Opposition (And Back)

Since its emergence as an electoral coalition in 1993, Yabloko, unlike the liberals, presented itself as a principal democratic opposition, and it explicitly criticized not only governmental policies but also the political regime itself. During the first State Duma, because of high party fragmentation, Yabloko was able to affect some legislative decisions and used its parliamentary status to articulate alternative proposals. This was of great help to Yabloko, which in early 1995 transformed itself into a party with visibility not only on the national level, but also on the regional level. However, unlike the KPRF, which tried to achieve its goals through electoral victory, Yabloko remained a small party, whose resources were insufficient for electoral success. Yabloko's scant electoral appeal became very apparent during the 1995 parliamentary and, especially, 1996 presidential elections, when the party, in the words of its Duma deputy Viktor Sheynis, found itself "a relatively small boat between two large ships" (i.e., the KPRF and the "party of power"). The democratic opposition was pushed into an electoral "ghetto". [. . .]

Although Yabloko could not affect the outcomes in these cases, these and other moves increased its popular support. Nevertheless, Yabloko refused to delegate its representatives to the government, and those politicians, such as Mikhail Zadornov and Oksana Dmitrieva, who joined the cabinet immediately lost their party affiliation. In circumstances of permanent crises and hyper-fragmentation of elites, this strategy brought Yabloko some short-term benefits, but the long-term costs were much higher. The party looks like semi-responsible opposition, i.e., a party that could never be in government. This provides few selective incentives for participation of mid-range activists and prevented attraction of new voters. To put it bluntly, in the eyes of its activists and supporters, Yabloko was not a party that could implement its own goals.

In the face of this threat, Yabloko's leaders invested serious efforts in building up the party organization, but were inconsistent because of an internal schism. Before the 1999 parliamentary elections, regional party branches were rearranged, and some experienced politicians ran on the Yabloko ticket: former Prime Minister Sergey Stepashin, Minister of Nationalities Affairs Vyacheslav Mikhailov, and some regional candidates. According to some sources, Yabloko also tried to reach a compromise with Fatherland—All Russia and proposed itself as a possible junior partner for this potential coalition, But in the context of the 1999 campaign, after the apartment-building bombings in Moscow and Ryazan and the beginning of the second Chechen war, Yabloko's strategy was completely out of place. Yavlinskiy's proposal for negotiations with Chechen leaders was heavily criticized in the media and strongly attacked by the liberals, who were competing with Yabloko for votes. After a weak performance in the 1999 State Duma elections (17 seats, compared with 45 in 1995) and Yavlinskiy's unsuccessful presidential campaign in 2000, Yabloko's electoral perspectives became gloomy. In 2000–01, Yabloko faced a deep organizational crisis. Several Duma deputies and regional activists left the party ranks, it lost the financial support of major sponsors, and the threat of a hostile takeover by the liberals loomed larger. Finally, after the takeover of NTV by state-owned Gazprom in April 2001, Yabloko nearly disappeared from national television screens.

These hardships drove Yabloko to a change of strategy: from "exit" to "loyalty" to the ruling group. During the third State Duma, Yabloko only slightly opposed some governmental policies and mostly just supported Kremlin proposals; its criticism of the president and the political regime seriously softened. Yabloko backed the Kremlin even in several dubious cases, such as the hostage crisis at a Moscow theater in October 2002 (while a semi-oppositional SPS criticized the Kremlin). At first glance, this allowed Yabloko to minimize losses in party-building. On the eve of the 2003 State Duma elections, Yabloko found a new major sponsor in the oil company Yukos; Yukos nominees, meanwhile, occupied key positions in the party list. At this time, Yabloko left the niche of principal opposition to avoid political marginalization. But the democrats had little chance of becoming a semi-opposition either. First, this niche was already occupied by the liberals. Second, the ruling group needed the democrats as allies even less than it needed the liberals. Third, the democrats by then had limited impact on decision-making and on public opinion. In fact, Yabloko's electoral tactics were based on fruitless consultations with the Kremlin; the "Yukos affair" and the subsequent arrest of Yukos head Mikhail Khodorkovskiy were the last shots against Yabloko's prospects. The party's failure in the 2003 parliamentary elections was a natural consequence of this strategic shift, although the explanations proffered by Yabloko representatives point to the unfairness of the campaign, electoral fraud, and the like. [. . .]

Is There a Future for Political Opposition in Russia?

The extinction of political opposition in Russia after the 2003–04 national elections resulted in bitter self-criticism among politicians; Khodorkovskiy's letter from prison was also a reaction to the new circumstances. There have been efforts toward further coordination of the residual opposition parties: the formation of an umbrella organization called Committee-2008, led by some liberals and democrats; and joint anti-Kremlin protests by communists, democrats, and some liberals—particularly by the youth organizations. The rise of anti-democratic trends in Russian politics might produce incentives for the emergence of a coalition of negative consensus among virtually all segments of the opposition, as happened during the anti-communist mass mobilizations of 1989–91. Without denying the role of these efforts, we should focus not only on the opposition's activities, but also on its external environment, which determines its political opportunity structure. This structure is unfavorable for opposition of any kind. Moreover, the most recent institutional changes, adopted by the Russian parliament in 2005, aimed to diminish the political opportunity structure as much as possible. The increase of electoral threshold in the State Duma and in regional legislative elections from 5 percent to 7 percent, the prohibition of establishment of electoral coalitions, the tougher rules for registration of political parties, and the minimization (if not total elimination) of the role of electoral observers at the polls would all inhibit oppositional chances in electoral politics. But does this mean that the window of opportunities for the emergence of new opposition in Russia is closed forever?

Some observers have suggested that prospects for opposition in Russia might improve as a result of possible regime destabilization in the wake of its ambitious modernization project, including tough social reforms. As yet, this has not materialized, even in the wake of the neo-liberal reform of social benefits in 2004–2005; popular protest then was relatively limited, and oppositions of different kinds were unable to mobilize the masses under any political slogans. Even major policy failures of the Russian government have not yet led to anything akin to the "Orange" or "Rose" revolutions experienced in Ukraine and Georgia. Even if such a scenario is still possible, in this case it would not be the loyal principal opposition that has the best chance of success, but rather the semi-loyal or disloyal opposition. Although parties and movements in the latter category are relatively negligible at present, their potential has not yet been revealed. Minor groups—such as the National Bolshevik Party, led by Eduard Limonov, who serves as one of the most vocal opponents of the Kremlin's reforms in 2004–2005—merely use symbolic violence as a tool of their protest activities. But they could be easily replaced by actors who would use real violence in its crudest forms, ranging from terrorism to pogroms—as happened in Russia in the early twentieth century. The Kremlin is aware of this threat, and its recent attempts to establish a puppet-like "opposition" based on the left and nationalist camps (around the Motherland party) as well as around loyal liberals aims to split and thus weaken possible protest.

The prospects for a resurgence of loyal opposition may hinge on a breakdown of the "imposed consensus" of Russian elites, perhaps in the wake of the 2007–2008 national elections. New intra-elite conflicts could lead to the appearance of influential opposition allies among elites. If intra-elite conflicts cannot be resolved, this will produce favorable political opportunities for an opposition. This scenario is not fanciful, for the simultaneous rise of elite integration and decline of elite differentiation under Putin is not based on a unity of elite goals and means. The "imposed consensus" of Russia's elite became possible because of the Kremlin's tactics of selective punishment of some elite sections and selective cooptation of others. Such a cartel-like equilibrium might be stable only if the resource bases of elites support the purchase of loyalty to the status quo. As yet, the resource inflow is sufficient for Russia's elites, thanks especially to high oil prices on the world market. However, elites could mobilize additional resources through political engineering. An example is the Kremlin's ongoing efforts to establish a mechanism of elite organizational continuity with the help of a monopolist "party of power". If sustained and successful, such efforts could marginalize political opposition for decades, as happened in Mexico. But that assumes a degree of elite unity that may prove difficult to sustain.

Russia's Client Party System

Stephen White

Introduction

Party development in Russia reflected that of other European countries but lagged notably behind it in the years up to the First World War. Parties and other public organizations began to be formed in the late nineteenth century, but they had no legal existence until the Tsar issued his October Manifesto in 1905 as part of the move to a more constitutional form of monarchy that followed the revolutionary events of that year. Under the detailed regulations that were issued the following year, all such organizations were strictly limited in their scope and activities; they could not exist at all if their aims and objectives were judged to represent a threat to public morals, and the police could close their meetings at any time if they appeared likely to "incite hostility between one section of the population and another." Parties had relatively few members under these circumstances—no more than 0.5 per cent of the population during the years before the First World War, and up to 1.5 per cent during the months leading up to the October revolution. In spite of these restrictions, more than 40 parties were active on a country-wide basis in the early years of the century, and more than a hundred catered for the Empire's numerous minority nationalities. The political left, organized in the Russian Social Democratic Workers' Party, was a member of the Second International and took part in its regular congresses in other European countries.

The Bolshevik revolution of October 1917 brought these early developments to an end and ushered in more than two generations of single-party dominance. Formally, there was no limit on the number of parties that could be created; the Bolsheviks were in coalition with the radical Left Socialist Revolutionaries for some months after the revolution, and other parties continued a de facto existence until the mid-1920s. But fairly soon, the boundaries of political contestation began to be narrowed: factions were banned in the Bolshevik party itself in 1921, and opposition leaders were marginalized, or in a few cases (in 1922) put

Source: Stephen White, "Russia's Client Party System," in *Party Politics in New Democracies*, Oxford University Press, 21–51.

Note: Notes and references have been removed from this article.

on trial. According to the new orthodoxy, the working people had a single interest; that single interest was expressed through the Communist Party, which had a unique understanding of the laws of social development; and with the establishment of public ownership of productive resources there was no social basis for the kind of political divisions that were to be found in capitalist countries. The Communist Party was one of the USSR's many "voluntary associations." under legislation of 1932, although it was already dominant. The 1936 constitution spelt out its role more fully when, for the first time, it acknowledged the party as the "vanguard of the toilers" and the "leading core of all organizations". The 1977 constitution, adopted during Leonid Brezhnev's leadership, made still more comprehensive provision for the party's political dominance when it defined the Communist Party in its sixth article as the "leading and guiding force of Soviet society [and] the nucleus of its political system".

The Gorbachev years, in the later 1980s, saw the dissolution of the Communist monopoly and the emergence of an "informal" and then an organized opposition. The first largely competitive elections took place in 1989, with a choice of candidates in most seats if not yet a choice of parties. Then in February 1990 the Communist Party agreed to relinquish its leading role, and the constitution was amended accordingly the following month. In October 1990 a new law "on public organizations" provided a legal basis for what had already become a multiparty society, although it was one within which the CPSU remained the most important source of political authority. The collapse of an attempted hard-line coup in August 1991 led to the suspension and later the banning of the party entirely (Gorbachev had meanwhile resigned as leader), and then in December 1991 the state itself dissolved into fifteen independent republics. The constitution of the Russian Federation, which was the largest of these successor republics, included a formal commitment to "ideological diversity" and "multiparty politics", provided the constitutional order was respected and that no attempt was made to incite social, racial, national, or religious animosity (Art. 13). The new Russia, evidently, would be multiparty: but what kind of multiparty politics remained unclear and, indeed, still does.

The elections of December 1993, at which the new constitution was adopted, were the first in modern times to take place on a formally multiparty basis. They incorporated a number of principles that remained in place for more than a decade. The new parliament, first of all, was to be a bicameral one. [. . .] [T]he lower house, the State Duma, would be elected in two ways. Half of its 450 members would be elected by constituencies of roughly equal numbers of electors formed throughout the federation, with not less than one seat for each of its constituent units; nominations could be made by electors themselves as well as by parties and other organizations. The other half of the Duma would be elected by a national party-list system, with scats allocated proportionately to the parties or movements that cleared a 5 per cent threshold. From 2007, according to changes that became law in May 2005, the Duma was to be elected entirely on this party-list basis.

The 1993 election regulations included parties among the "electoral associations" that had the right to put forward candidates in the national party-list contest. Political movements had the same right, and both of them might combine in "blocs" with other national organizations for the same purpose. At the same time it was clear that those who had framed it intended that the list system would encourage the development of a multiparty system in place of the single-party monopoly of the communist past. Their expectations, so far, have not been entirely fulfilled (Table 1). One reason is that independents, rather than party nominees, have enjoyed a great deal of success in the single-member constituencies. In 1993, 1995, and 1999 they won the largest number of single-member seats (in 2003 the second-largest), and in the 1993 election they won more seats than all the party-sponsored candidates put together. But the parties themselves have also been an unstable element, frequently splitting, merging, or disappearing entirely. The result is what Rose, Munro, and White have called a "floating party system", one that leaves little opportunity for the electorate to pass judgement on a party's record since the previous election and in this way ensure the accountability of those who govern to those who elect them.

The 1993 constitution established two other principles that are basic to the operation of Russian parties. In the first place, it provided for a legislature with relatively little influence over the conduct of government. Under the 1993 constitution, the prime minister surrenders his powers to a newly elected president, not to a newly elected parliament. The government as a whole was required to be non-party, under the legislation on state service that applied until 2003, and it need not command the confidence of a parliamentary majority, although the president can dismiss it at any time. [. . .] There is accordingly no "party government" in post-communist Russia, and although there were moves in that direction in the early years of the new century, the parties that secure a majority of seats at Duma elections can hardly be said to have "won power".

The second major change that was introduced by the 1993 constitution was a substantial enhancement in the powers of the president (how, indeed, could it be otherwise when the president had crushed what he defined as a "parliamentary uprising" and submitted his own draft for popular approval?). [. . .] The president is subject to popular election, and can hold office for a maximum of two consecutive four-year terms. But he is almost entirely free of parliamentary constraints, as the procedure for impeachment is so complicated that it is unlikely ever to be successfully initiated. The present incumbent, Vladimir Putin, assumed office after winning the first round of the March 2000 presidential election, and was re-elected with a still more convincing majority in March 2004.

Table 1. Russian Duma election results, 1993–2003

	1993				1995				1999				2003			
	List (%)	List seats	SMC Seats	Total seats	List (%)	List seats	SMC Seats	Total Seats	List (%)	List seats	SMC seats	Total seats	List (%)	List seats	SMC seats	Total seats
LDPR	22.9	59	5	64	11.2	50	1	51	6.0	17	0	17	11.5	36	0	36
RC	15.5	40	30	70	3.9	0	9	9	–	–	–	–	–	–	–	–
CPRF	12.4	32	16	48	22.3	99	58	157	24.3	67	46	113	12.6	40	12	52
WR	8.1	21	2	23	4.6	0	3	3	2.0	0	0	0	–	–	–	–
AP	8.0	21	12	33	3.8	0	20	20	–	–	–	–	3.6	0	2	2
Yabloko	7.9	20	3	23	6.9	31	14	45	5.9	16	4	20	4.3	0	4	4
PRUC	6.8	18	1	19	0.4	0	1	1	–	–	–	–	–	–	–	–
DPR	5.5	14	1	15	–	–	–	–	–	–	–	–	0.2	0	0	0
OHR	–	–	–	–	10.1	45	10	55	1.2	0	7	7	–	–	–	–
Unity	–	–	–	–	–	–	–	–	23.3	64	9	73	–	–	–	–
FAR	–	–	–	–	–	–	–	–	13.3	37	31	68	–	–	–	–
URF	–	–	–	–	–	–	–	–	8.5	24	5	29	4.0	0	3	3
UR	–	–	–	–	–	–	–	–	–	–	–	–	37.6	120	103	223

(Continued)

Table 1. (Continued)

	1993				1995				1999				2003			
	List (%)	List seats	SMC Seats	Total seats	List (%)	List seats	SMC Seats	Total Seats	List (%)	List seats	SMC seats	Total seats	List (%)	List seats	SMC seats	Total seats
Rodina	–	–	–	–	–	–	–	–	–	–	–	–	9.0	29	8	37
Others	8.7	0	8	8	34.0	0	32	32	12.2	0	18	18	12.5	0	23	23
Indepts	–	–	141	141	–	–	77	77	–	–	105	105	–	–	67	67
Agst. All	4.2	–	–	–	2.8	–	–	–	3.3	–	–	–	4.7	–	–	–

Source: Central Electoral Commission, incorporating amendments up to July 2005 (*Vestnik: Tsentral'noi izbiratel' noi komissii Rossiiskoi Federatsii* no. 8, 2005:215–19).

Notes: Figures show share of party-list vote, party-list seats, single-member constituency (SMC) seats, and total seats won by parties that in any election exceeded the 5% party-list threshold. In 1993, 1999, and 2003 there were no valid results in six, nine, and three single-member constituencies, respectively; these were filled in subsequent ballots. Turnouts (ballots cast as a percentage of the registered electorate) were 54.3, 64.4, 61.7, and 55.7, respectively. The 1993 results were reported by the CEC in relation to the total valid vote; in other cases, vote share and turnout are calculated in relation to total (valid and invalid) vote. Figures for the effective number of electoral parties (ENEP) have been calculated on the basis of the share of the party-list vote cast for each party and for "against all"; this yields results of 9.35 in 1993, 9.28 in 1995, 6.75 in 1999, and 5.35 in 2003. Party abbreviations are LDPR—Liberal Democratic Party of Russia (competing, in 1999, as the Zhirinovsky Bloc); RC—Russia's Choice (in 1995, Russia's Democratic Choice); CPRF—Communist Party of the Russian Federation; WR—Women of Russia; AP—Agrarian Party; PRUC—Party of Russian Unity and Concord; DPR—Democratic Party of Russia; OHR—Our Home is Russia; FAR; Fatherland-All Russia; UR—United Russia; and URF—Union of Right Forces. There were thirteen parties, "electoral blocs" or "electoral associations" on the ballot paper in 1993, forty-three in 1995, twenty-six in 1999, and twenty-three in 2003.

Russia's early post-communist experience has given rise to a range of issues, some of which are reminiscent of party-related discussion elsewhere and some of which are more distinctive. Perhaps the clearest difference from party systems in established democracies is the role that is played by the political executive at all levels in framing the rules of competition and forming parties themselves. In Russia, and many of the other former Soviet republics, this takes the form of a regime-sponsored "party of power". In 1993 the Kremlin vested its hopes in Russia's Choice, led by former acting Prime Minister Yegor Gaidar and with many other ministers in its list of candidates. Russia's Choice, however, failed to justify expectations, and in 1995 the Kremlin chose a different vehicle through which to promote its interests, Our Home is Russia, led by then Prime Minister Viktor Chernomyrdin. With a modest 10 per cent of the party-list vote, it was another disappointment. At the following election, in 1999, a hastily formed grouping, Unity, enjoyed much more success, and after the election it merged with the Kremlin's main challenger, Fatherland-All Russia, to form a still larger party of power under the name United Russia. The task of the new party, declared its leader Sergei Shoigu, was to "unite the society around the creative policy pursued by the president and around the head of state himself", and there was a "tumultuous standing ovation" when Putin appeared at its inaugural congress. Helped by the Kremlin's control of the mass media, it won by far the largest share of the vote at the December 2003 Duma election and established a dominant position in the new Duma, including chairmanship of all of its committees.

Viewed from this perspective, one of the largest issues that arises in present circumstances is indeed the extent to which parties will remain derivative of powerful interests, including the state itself. The law on political parties that was adopted in the summer of 2001, for instance, advantaged the larger parties that were represented in the Duma, and gave the Kremlin considerable powers to regulate their activities—including, in certain circumstances, the right to suspend their activities. It also provided for the state funding of political parties in a manner that reinforced the position of the largest, as support would be directly proportional to vote totals. The new law on elections to the State Duma, adopted in 2005, abolished the single-member constituencies, which had offered opportunities to the smaller parties as well as independents, and raised the threshold for representation from 5 to 7 per cent, which was again more likely to benefit the larger competitors. The Kremlin has not disguised that its longer-term ambition is to forge what Putin has called a "normal, civilized" party system with two, three, or at most four parties represented within it.

Parties that depended on the support of the regime itself, however, would find it difficult to oppose Kremlin-sponsored policies, even if they were unpopular and ill conceived. Depending more on favours from the authorities than the active support of members, internal party activity might often atrophy. Collecting dues might appear a slow and ineffective way of raising funds when commercial sponsors could more readily be obtained. The priorities of members and of a wider constituency might take second place when the party leadership in the Duma traded its votes for various kinds of pay-offs, including direct ones. But the more a party became the client of powerful interests or of the regime itself, the less ordinary people would regard it as an effective means of advancing their own concerns. They would have no reason to join a party of this kind, or trust it; they might not vote at all, or they might vote "against all", which was a distinctive and increasingly popular option on the Russian ballot paper until an amendment to the law removed it in 2006. In December 2003 nearly three million exercised this option, which was enough to make it the fifth most popular "party" of the twenty-three that were in contention, and more than twice as many voted "against all" the candidates in the single-member constituencies. Many, denied the opportunity to articulate their preferences through the political parties and—from 2007—by voting against all of them, were likely to move outside the party system entirely, and to engage in strikes and other forms of unofficial action. The Western literature on "disengagement" has considerable resonance in Russia and most of the other post-Soviet republics; indeed the survey evidence suggests most Russians believe they have even less influence on government, in spite of multiparty elections, than they did in the late Soviet period. Recovering a role for political parties that allows them to represent citizens to government is accordingly a task that has much wider significance than for the parties themselves.

The Popular Legitimacy of Russian Political Parties

Parties in modern Russia operate in the difficult circumstances of a former single-party regime, which to a large extent appears to have compromised the concept of "party" itself. According to the national public opinion research centre, more than half the population see parties as a "source of nothing but harm" (52 per cent); another 17 per cent believe party leaders are concerned only about their own well-being, and 10 per cent believe quarrels between the parties undermine social stability. Russians, it was reported in 2006, have very mixed feelings about the multiparty politics they have enjoyed for more than fifteen years. Fully a quarter (25 per cent) would still prefer a "single national party, permanently in power"—in effect, another CPSU. Rather more (29 per cent) favour "two or three mass parties", but another 20 per cent believe there is no need to have parties at all, in current circumstances—better a few "real leaders", like the Liberal Democrats' Vladimir Zhirinovsky. Indeed almost half (49 per cent) believe that "weak, small parties" should have no right to exist at all.

A more direct measure of party legitimacy is the extent to which respondents are willing to "trust" political parties as compared with other institutions. The national public opinion research centre has asked questions of this kind since the early 1990s (see Table 2). Consistently, the church and the armed forces enjoy the highest levels of confidence. The presidency, after a bad patch in the later Yeltsin years, exceeded them both in the early years of the new century but might not continue to do so. Local government was normally more widely respected than central government, and the media were more widely respected than the agencies of law enforcement, which were more often associated with corruption and maltreatment than with the administration of justice. Political parties, however, have consistently come at the bottom of the list, below even the parliament in which they are represented. And these are findings that are replicated in other investigations; the only case in which political parties have not been the least trusted civic institution appears to have been when respondents were asked, on a single occasion, to express their confidence in a list that included the investment funds that had (for the most part) defrauded ordinary citizens of the vouchers they had obtained as a result of the privatization of state property. [. . .]

Table 2. Trust in parties and other institutions, 1998–2006

	1998	*1999*	*2000*	*2001*	*2002*	*2003*	*2004*	*2005*	*2006*
President	2	2	45	54	61	59	62	54	56
Church	32	37	39	38	40	37	41	44	38
Army	28	35	35	33	28	27	28	30	20
Media	24	25	26	24	23	22	26	25	22
Security organs	18	20	21	23	23	23	20	23	23
Regional govt.	15	19	20	22	19	13	19	20	19
Local govt.	18	22	19	21	21	15	18	16	16
Courts	12	11	12	14	16	13	13	16	14
Government	4	8	20	22	24	16	12	14	14
Trade unions	11	9	11	11	13	13	10	12	9
Parliament	7	4	10	11	11	9	9	10	11
Parties	4	4	7	6	7	5	5	4	4

Source: Derived from All-Russian Public Opinion Research Centre (VTsIOM) and (from 2004) Levada Centre data as reported in *Monitoring [later: Vestnik) obshchestvennogo mneniya*, various issues.

Note: "Courts" from 1998 to 1999 refers to law enforcement generally (courts, police, and procuracy); references to "parliament" from 2001 are for the State Duma. Figures report percentages who "completely trust" a given institution.

Table 3. Levels of support for Russian parties, 2000–7

	2000	2001	2002	2003	2004	2005	2006	2007
United Russia	14	13	16	17	33	21	29	26
Communist Party	22	23	18	20	11	11	9	10
Liberal Democrats	4	4	5	8	6	6	6	6
For a Decent Life	–	–	–	–	–	1	3	–
Yabloko	5	6	3	6	1	1	2	2
Rodina	–	–	–	–	3	2	2	4
All others	15	14	15	12	6	8	6	5
Against all	8	8	7	8	7	5	5	–
Do not know	17	15	19	17	12	16	18	20
Would not vote	15	18	18	12	22	22	14	17
Might or might not vote	–	–	–	–	–	7	7	8

Source: VTsIOM/Levada Centre data consulted at www.russiavotes.org on 5 April 2007; figures are for May in each year, but for August in 2000, in rounded percentages.

Notes: United Russia figures for 2000 and 2001 are for its predecessor, Unity, Rodina figure for 2007 is for its successor. Fair Russia. The question wording was "For which of the following parties or blocs would you be most likely to vote if there were elections to the State Duma next Sunday?"

There have been different views about the extent to which partisan identifications have developed in post-communist Russian politics. These variations stem, not least, from the different question wordings that have been employed, and from the different time-periods in which surveys have been conducted (in particular, immediately subsequent to an election or at a time of greater political tranquillity). Among the most "optimistic" assessments are those that have emanated from the University of Iowa, extending not only to Russia but also to Ukraine and Lithuania. Respondents, in their surveys, are asked if there is a particular party that "expresses your views better than any other party". If the answer is yes, the next question asks which party the respondent has in mind, and how close the respondent feels to that party. On this basis, "survey data collected in 1992, 1995 and 1997 reveal a significant growth in party identification among elites and ordinary citizens". In Russia, at the mass level, party identification increased from 16 per cent in 1992 to 52 per cent in 1995 and then "skyrocketed" to

61 per cent in 1997. The question, however, assumes that at least one of the parties will reflect the opinions of respondents, rather than asking whether any of the existing parties can do so; and responses will also have been raised by the decision to show respondents a list of parties from which to make their choice.

Other studies have asked somewhat different questions and have come to rather different conclusions. White, Rose, and McAllister, for instance, using data that were also gathered in the mid-1990s, speak of the "absence of party identification", basing themselves on the low proportion—just 22 per cent—that are prepared to "identify with any particular political party or movement". But this, others have objected, assumes respondents will know what it means to "identify" in this way. Miller, White, and Heywood, in a study that extended across Russia and four other post-communist states, asked respondents if, "generally speaking", they thought of themselves as a "supporter of any political party"; no more than 26 per cent did so, in Russia, a lower level than almost everywhere else. Colton, in his examination of the 1995 and 1996 elections, used another question entirely, asking respondents if they felt any party or political movement was "my party, my movement, my association?" This was a broadly worded prompt that might have been expected to draw a positive response from a wider constituency than those who associated themselves with a political party as conventionally defined. Nonetheless, on this basis only 14 per cent were "strong" and another 15 per cent were "moderate partisans"; no other respondents were prepared to identify any of the parties or movements as "their own", although a small proportion (20 per cent) were prepared to identify one of the parties or movements as more likely to reflect their "interests, views, and concerns" than the others.

In a 2005 survey, the author and associates asked two different questions: whether respondents considered themselves to be "a supporter of a political party", and whether they thought there was "a political party that was closer to you than others in its policies (*po svoim pozitsiyam*)". Almost a fifth (19.6 per cent) thought of themselves as party supporters; rather more (29.6 per cent) thought there was a party that was closer to them in its policies than others. But although almost all party supporters thought there was a party with whose policies they could identify (91 per cent), not nearly as many of those who thought there was a party with whose policies they could identify were party supporters (60 per cent). Measures of partisan identification have not been uncontroversial in the established democracies, and here also much depends on the wording of the question. When all allowances have been made, however, it remains difficult to contest that Russia has low levels of partisanship in broadly comparative terms, still more so in comparison with established democracies such as the UK (where 86 per cent have some form of partisan identification) and the USA [where nearly 92 per cent identify with either of the two main parties. [. . .]

The individual-level evidence also suggests that there is a greater degree of change in party support than in the established democracies—even among the parties that are on the ballot paper in successive elections. The only party to retain even half of its 1993 vote in the Duma election two years later was the Communist Party of the Russian Federation, which kept 68 per cent of its earlier support. The two other parties that contested the 1993 election and secured at least 5 per cent of the vote in 1995 were the Liberal Democratic Party, which retained 47 per cent of its earlier support, and Yabloko, which retained 43 per cent; but at the other extreme, just 19 per cent of Russia's Choice voters in 1993 opted for Russia's Democratic Choice two years later (the ephemeral nature of the parties makes such calculations problematic, even across two elections). A level of volatility of this kind points to a number of the distinctive features of post-communist politics, not just in Russia, particularly the fluidity of social structures, of popular attitudes, and of parties themselves, all of which made it difficult to sustain continuing patterns of support. As a consequence, levels of volatility are much greater than those in Western Europe, and greater even than those in other European countries at the stage of development in which their party systems were taking shape.

The Organizational Strength of Russian Parties

The organizational context within which political parties operate is defined by the law on political parties that was adopted in the summer of 2001. The debate raised a number of controversial issues. One of the issues that attracted most discussion was the minimum number of members that would be required. Without rich sponsors or support from government structures, it was argued, many of the prospective parties might find it difficult to attract as many as 10,000 members, which would deny political representation to a substantial section of the society. Any restriction upon the right to form regional or local parties, in addition, would limit the rights of ordinary citizens in a manner that might well be unconstitutional, and would certainly operate to the advantage of the powerful interests that had the most widely extended national networks. But supporters of the draft insisted on the importance of a "single political space", otherwise local parties using the levers of influence that were available to their governors might squeeze out the regional sections of national parties, which would encourage the development of regional separatism and reduce the ability of the federal government to influence developments throughout the country. The chairman of the Central Electoral Commission certainly left no doubt that so far as the regime itself was concerned, there could "only be all-Russian parties".

The introduction of state funding of political parties was a particularly controversial development. There was a risk, some thought, that this would undermine the parties' independence, and it would certainly be unpopular with Russia's long-suffering electorate, which would damage the position of political parties even further. If they were unable to pay teachers their hard-earned salaries, objected a deputy from the Union of Right Forces, how could they possibly defend the funding of political parties? Others argued that the sums involved were insufficient in any case: either there should be adequate funding, or none at all. But Communist deputies took a different position: all the parties in the world, explained their leader Gennadii Zyuganov, took money from the state, and this made them independent of oligarchs. The presidential view was very similar: that state funding would help to free parties from the wealthy sponsors that would otherwise control them. In the end, a funding formula was agreed, which would take effect immediately after the December 2003 Duma election; but an amendment was adopted that allowed parties to do without state funds if they wished, and the Union of Right Forces (which had more access to private support than almost all the other parties) made it clear that it would make no call on the funds that would be placed at its disposal.

The law, as adopted, regulates all aspects of party activity. In order to register, a party must have a membership of at least 50,000 (the law had originally specified 10,000, but was amended in December 2004). In addition, it must have branches in more than half of the Russian regions, each of which must have a membership of at least 500, and any other regional party branches must each have at least 250 members (Art. 3). The main aims of a political party, under the terms of the law, are the formation of public opinion, political education, the articulation of the opinions of citizens on any question of public life, and the nomination of candidates at elections to representative institutions and elective office at all levels. As in many other countries, parties are not allowed to advocate extremism, or to incite social, racial, national, or religious antipathy; nor may parties be formed on an occupational, racial, national, or religious basis (Art. 9). Parties must be registered by the state at national, or local level on presentation of the appropriate documentation (Art. 15); they must have a statute (Art. 21) and a programme (Art. 22). Members must be at least 18 years old, and may belong to no more than a single party (Art. 23). Parties, under the law, may take part in elections and referendums, hold meetings, and otherwise propagate their views (Art. 26). Parties, in fact, are the only bodies that are allowed to put forward their own candidates at elections, although individuals could also be nominated in the single-member constituencies that accounted for half of the seats in the Duma between 1993 and 2007 (Art. 36); and if they fail to do so over a five-year period (in other words, in two consecutive elections), they are dissolved on the instructions of the Supreme Court (Arts. 37, 41).

The 2001 law also defines the various sources from which a party may draw its material support, including membership dues, donations, and income from its activities, including commerce (Art. 29). Donations from private individuals in any year may not exceed ten times the minimum wage that prevails the previous March (in 2006 this meant that they could not exceed 8,000 roubles or approximately $280). Donations may not be accepted from foreign states, companies or citizens, or from Russian companies with more than 30 per cent foreign ownership, from international organizations or government bodies, from military or police units, from charities or religious organizations, or anonymously. No donation in a single year from a single body may exceed a hundred thousand times the minimum wage, and the total from all sources may not exceed ten million times the minimum wage (Art. 30). The law introduced a new system of state support for political parties, although on a modest scale. The total sum available, under the amended legislation that was adopted in July 2005, is 5 roubles ($0.17), multiplied by the total electorate; individual parties are able to claim the same level of payment provided they obtain at least 3 per cent in the national party-list contest, or if their candidate wins the same share of the vote in a presidential contest. Payments are annual, following each Duma election, or once only, in the case of presidential elections, and are indexed to take account of inflation (Art. 33).

Overall, just over 1 per cent of the adult population regarded themselves in our 2005 survey as a member of a political party; this compared with 2 per cent who were members of a residential association, 3 per cent who were in a musical or artistic society, 6 per cent who were in a sports club, and 12 per cent who were members of a trade union. Comparatively considered, these are very low levels of membership. The figures made available by the parties themselves vary widely and are often problematic. Indeed there was some evidence that parties maintained three different lists of members: one for public consumption, another for the Ministry of Justice, and a third for internal use. The Liberal Democratic Party, for instance, told the Justice Ministry it had 19,100 members, but claimed 600,000 in its public statements. The Communist Party, similarly, claimed 19,300 in its registration documents, but 500,000 in its official statements; and United Russia appeared to maintain another, fourth column, for reporting to its Kremlin masters (it had promised a million members by the end of 2002 but had fallen short). Specialized firms were available that would take care of all of these arrangements, including a statute and members, for a payment of $200,000; many of these parties were likely to secure fewer votes in national elections than the number of members they had nominally recruited.

Membership totals have also varied over time. The Communist Party, in the early years of the new century, was the largest, with half a million or more; but its membership has steadily drifted downwards, and by the time its records had been scrutinized by the Ministry of Justice at the start of 2006 it could claim no more than 184,000. United Russia, by contrast, claimed a membership of 300,000, all of whom had been enrolled since its foundation at the end of 2001, and by 2005 it had enrolled more than a million members; but many had evidently been recruited in a somewhat "Soviet" manner, on the basis of directives passed down from above. In a shopping complex in the Moscow region, for instance, each retail unit had been told it would have to provide two members; in the town of Velikie Luki, local employees were being fired or had their wages withheld unless they took out membership.

All the parties had to demonstrate they had at least 50,000 members by November 2006, failing which they would be de-registered. In the event, just nineteen parties satisfied the Federal Registration Service of the thirty-five that had been in operation at the beginning of the year (see Table 4). The number fell further when three of the newly registered parties—Rodina, the Russian Party of Life, and the Russian Party of Pensioners—merged shortly afterwards into a new grouping, "Fair Russia", which conceived of itself as a "Social Democratic Party in the European sense of the word" and based itself on the Russian Party of Life as its leader was a "personal friend of the president", which ensured the administrative support of the state apparatus. The head of the Central Electoral Commission predicted that no more than about ten parties were likely to be in a position to contest the December 2007 parliamentary election, completing the move to a party system that was more coherent than at any time in the post-communist period but also more subordinate to the Kremlin authorities.

Members, as elsewhere, represented one of the parties' most important sources of income; but the financing of Russian parties, as President Putin complained in his parliamentary address in the spring of 2003, remained a "secret under seven seals" for many electors. In practice, there were several sources from which Russian parties could draw the resources they needed. For those with the largest membership bases (most obviously the Communist Party), the dues paid by individual members were a significant source of income. A further source of support, as we have seen, was the state funding that was made available to parties that enjoyed a given level of support at Duma or presidential elections (the first such payment at the new level of 5 roubles a vote was made in March 2006, a total of nearly 270 million roubles—or about $9.5 million—divided among the nine parties and blocs that had secured at least 3 per cent of

Table 4. Russian parties after registration, November 2006

Name of party	Membership (as of 1 January 2006)
United Russia	943,000
Rodina	135,000
Communist Party of the Russian Federation	134,000
Agrarian Party	133,500
Russian Party of Life	108,000
Russian Party of Pensioners	97,200
Liberal Democratic Party of Russia	86,000
People's Party	74,200
Democratic Party	60,200
Patriots of Russia	59,400
Party of Peace and Unity	57,300
Union of Right Forces	56,900
Yabloko	55,300
Free Russia	55,000
People's Will	53,400
Socialist United Party	51,900
Greens	51,700
Party of Russian Revival	51,600
Party of Social Justice	50,700

Source: Kommersant (27 October 2006: 2).

the vote in the December 2003 Duma election. More controversially, parties could be directly supported by individuals or corporate bodies. The law on political parties limited the nature of this support, but its provisions could easily be evaded, and the most important source of support for most parties was more often than not the country's wealthiest corporations and individual oligarchs. How much the parties were paid, by whom, and in return for what kind of favours has been a matter of (sometimes quite extravagant) speculation. [. . .]

Russian parties have many other opportunities for increasing their revenues—their votes, for instance, can be traded by party leaders in return for favours from business, and in some cases it has been suggested that they have established a relationship with organized crime. An "index of the corruption of political parties" was made public in early 2006 by a group of independent scholars; it took no account of United Russia, the "party of power", because its subordination to the Kremlin and high degree of centralization provided very little scope for private enrichment. The most corrupt of the other parties, on a 10-point scale, was the Communist Party (8.6 points), followed by Yabloko (7.9), the Union of Right Forces (7.3), and Rodina (6.5). The conclusion was that "the oppositional political structures that claim[ed] to be trying to make things better [were] infected by the same ailments as officialdom itself", and there was little prospect of improvement apart from far-reaching and unlikely changes among the opposition parties and more open methods—primaries—of selecting their lists of electoral candidates. [. . .]

The Russian media, as in other industrial countries, are dominated by television, and television in turn is dominated by the state itself, which largely or entirely owns the first two national channels and exercises a powerful influence over the others. This has meant that election coverage, up to the present, has been strongly biased towards the parties and candidates that are most loyal to the Kremlin. The December 1999 Duma election saw a particularly blatant use of state television to boost the position of Unity and to damage the standing of Fatherland-All Russia, which appeared to represent a serious challenge to the Yeltsin "Family"—a term that came to be used in something like its Sicilian sense. The independent channel NTV, which had been more supportive of opposition parties and particularly of Yabloko, was taken over by the state gas monopoly in the spring of 2001 (its owner, oligarch Vladimir Gusinsky, was imprisoned and then forced into emigration). At the following election, in December 2003, international monitors found a "clear bias" in favour of United Russia and against the Communist Party, and that state television—which had by far the largest national coverage—had "openly promoted United Russia".

The balance was to some extent redressed by the daily press, although circulations were much lower than in the Soviet years and the political influence of an individual title was rarely significant. There was, however, a party press, and it allowed some degree of communication among members if not necessarily with a wider public. The Communist Party was the best placed to make use of these opportunities, not least because of its membership base and its inheritance of large-circulation dailies from the Soviet period. The party paper *Pravda* had a circulation of about 65,000 in 2000, and about a third of its copies were produced outside Moscow with an insert of regional news. *Pravda Rossii,* originally an insert in the paper *Sovetskaya Rossiya,* appeared weekly with a circulation of about 74,000, addressed mainly to members. The regional party press issued 800,000 copies weekly, and what the party called the "left-patriotic" press as a whole had a circulation of more than 2 million. There was a party-aligned radio station, and in 1997 a party website was established that had received half a million visitors by 2000 (party leader Zyuganov had a site of his own).

With the possible exception of the Communist Party, it was difficult to argue that parties as such had much organizational strength in post-communist Russia. The state itself was dominant in almost every way, particularly through its control of the electronic media, but also through the "administrative resource" that allowed it to use the apparatus of government in support of its favoured parties and candidates. This might include office transport and secretarial services, meeting rooms, printing and publicity services, and the ability to distribute public investment in such a way as to "reward" local officials in regions that had been strongly supportive of the Kremlin and its favoured parties and candidates, and to "punish" those whose efforts had been less successful. An element of pluralism was introduced by the oligarchs, who could use their private resources to sustain parties and movements that were independent and sometimes critical of the Kremlin: Boris Berezovsky, another political exile, was able to use his considerable fortunes to establish a party known as "Liberal Russia" (from which he later parted company), and he retained a presence among the print media. But the arrest of Khodorkovsky, followed by an eight-year prison sentence in 2005, was a clear warning; and he had neither established a political party of his own, nor funded a media outlet that was openly oppositional.

The Systemic Functionality of Parties in Russia

Given their formal powers, and the membership and the organizational resources on which they could draw, what part do Russian parties play in the process of government? To what extent do they form administrations, recruit a political class, and shape the process of political articulation and aggregation? To what extent, indeed, do they allow their own members to choose party leaders and influence the formation of party programmes? The short answer must be: to a very limited extent; but there is considerable variation by party and level of government, and the regime itself is engaged in an attempt to reshape the political system in a way that would, deliberately, give political parties a more central role in the future. The Russian experience, accordingly, is relevant to more general questions of "institutional design", and the extent to which government can be provided with a party basis in an environment in which parties are otherwise relatively weak.

Governance

Parties, up to the present, have not been central to the Russian process of government or of policy formulation. The key issues in Russian public life, complained the journalist Otto Latsis at the end of 2001, such as foreign debt or the country's demographic crisis, "should be the subjects of public debate and accordingly should be included in the programmes being proposed to society by various parties". But thanks to the Kremlin, Russia had "come under the sway of a different political style, under which all these things [were] decided without the involvement of political parties". In this sense, he went on, there were "no parties in the generally accepted meaning of the term"; and the prevailing view in the governing apparatus must be that "this [was] the most convenient way of running the country". It was indicative of this situation that neither Boris Yeltsin nor Vladimir Putin had a declared party affiliation (although Putin did make clear his personal sympathies before the 1999 and 2003 Duma elections); equally, that Putin's successors as prime minister did not belong to any of the parties in the Duma, least of all the party that had won the largest number of seats.

There were several reasons for the relatively low salience of parties in the process of government in the early years of the new century. One was certainly the constitutional framework. Government was not accountable to parliament, but to the president which meant that Russian parties were unable to "win power" at a parliamentary election, and in no position to compel the formation of a government that reflected the composition of a new Duma. When Prime Minister Chernomyrdin's party, Our Home is Russia, won just over 10 per cent of the vote in the 1995 parliamentary election, he did not resign but told journalists that the election result would make no difference to the composition of the government or the policies it pursued. When Boris Yeltsin dismissed the entire government three times in 1998–9, equally, it had nothing to do with a change in the party balance in the Duma, still less a national election. Under the terms of the law on state service that applied until 2003, indeed, ministers were classified as "category A" public officials and required to have no party affiliation, and under the law on the government until it was amended in 2004 they were not allowed to hold office in a party or public organization; this reflected the Soviet view that the business of government was to administer affairs of state, but not to set national priorities. In the Soviet period policy was determined by the leadership of the Communist Party, and then implemented by government; after 1991 the "main directions" of foreign and domestic policy passed into the hands of the president, whose powerful position was a consequence of its elective nature as well as of the provisions of the constitution. [. . .]

Interest Articulation and Aggregation

Parties have enjoyed no monopoly of the right to nominate candidates at local or national elections. In the first Duma elections in 1993 a whole series of public organizations put forward candidates within the framework of a larger association, including the All-Russian Society of Invalids, the Chernobyl Union, the Union of the Women of the Navy, and two trade unions. In 1995 the Russian Union of Advocates and the Union of the Residential-Communal Economy put forward their own lists of candidates in the party-list contest, and many more formed part of a larger bloc of candidates, including the Union of Afghan Veterans, the Tatar Centre for Cultural Enlightenment, and the Association of Independent Professionals. In 1999 another varied set of public bodies formed part of a larger bloc of candidates, including Jurists for a Worthy Life, the Movement for the Support of the Army, Defence Industry, and Military Science, and the Union for Support and Assistance to Small and Medium Business. After 2001, only bodies that had registered under the law on political parties and whose objectives included the nomination of candidates at elections would be able to do so; but independents could still contest the single-member constituencies, and they accounted for a large proportion of the candidates that successfully contested them.

One reason for the continued strength of independents was that very few of the party-list contenders put forward candidates in more than a minority of the 225 single-member constituencies. In 2003, 32 parties put forward candidates, a total of 1,689 as compared with 1,338 independents. But none of the parties put forward a candidate in every seat, and only 7 put forward candidates in a majority of the 225 seats. The most active were the Liberal Democrats (186), all of whose candidates were unsuccessful, followed by the Communist Party (175); United Russia put forward 144, and Rodina, the other party that secured party-list representation, just 55. The United Russia won 103 of the single-member seats, but independents won 67; and independents, across all the single-member seats, took 26.3 per cent of the vote, more than all the other parties (calculated from the constituency returns).

The outcome of an election was in any case a very approximate guide to the composition of the Duma over the course of its four-year term. The Duma is organized on the basis of "fractions" and smaller "groups" of deputies, which are formed when the new parliament assembles. But even fractions based directly on political parties do not necessarily correspond to the seats the same parties have notionally won in the preceding election. After the 1995 election nearly all the independents joined one of the organized groupings, some of them established after the election had taken place, while at the same time some of the deputies that had been elected on a party ticket chose to become independents; and there were party fractions that gained deputies that had been elected under entirely different auspices. In 1999, almost a third of the seats had changed hands by the time the new Duma assembled in January 2000; nearly all the independents joined one of the organized groupings, and two new ones were formed after the parliament had been elected. In 2003, similarly,

United Russia won 223 seats at the election but had 300 at its disposal when the new Duma convened for its first meeting, as newly elected members traded their vote for the patronage of a party that would evidently be able to offer them the support of the regime itself, and by the summer of 2006 its numbers had increased to 309.

Political Recruitment

In these circumstances, parties have been of marginal significance in terms of political recruitment, not just nationally but also locally. Parties served as vehicles of legislative recruitment, but up to a third of the seats were won by independents; party lists were not necessarily composed of party members; and in any case "parties in parliament" diverged substantially from election outcomes. Only in a limited sense, moreover, were there "parties in government": governments did not necessarily correspond to the party balance in parliament and ministers were not selected from among the party leaders, nor chosen for their various portfolios by the parties themselves, as for instance, in Australia. The same was true for lower-level institutions of government (see Table 5). Of the executive heads of regions (governors or presidents), a very small proportion had a party-political background. The proportion with a party background, moreover, was declining rather than increasing; and where party-sponsored candidates competed with independents, it was the party-sponsored candidates that tended to lose ground. Parties were slightly better represented in regional legislatures; but again their share was falling, and there was a similar tendency for party-sponsored candidates to lose ground to independents.

Table 5. Political parties and regional government, 1995–2000

	Number of candidates	Of which Party-nominated	Number elected	Of which party-nominated
Executive heads				
1995–7	424	80 (18.8%)	70	10 (14.3%)
1998–2000	724	53 (8.4%)	67	5 (7.6%)
Legislatures				
1995–7	17,906	4,452 (24.9%)	2,870	533 (18.6%)
1998–2000	14,794	2,602 (17.0%)	2,066	311 (15.1%)

Sources: Derived from *Vybory* (1997: 42–8, 1998: 587–9, 2001, vol. 1: 86, 72).

Parties have, however, been important in structuring political recruitment at least in one important characteristic: the representation of women. There are consistent differences, first of all, in the gender balance of deputies returned through party lists as compared with the single-member constituencies. Conventionally, women are expected to do better under proportional than majoritarian systems. One reason is that parties are likely to make some effort to balance their lists of candidates in order to appeal to all sections of the electorate, whereas the outcome of individual elections in single-member constituencies need have no overall logic. Globally, women account for 10.8 per cent of deputies in majoritarian systems, 15.1 per cent in mixed systems, but 19.8 per cent in proportional systems, making women "twice as likely to be elected under PR [as under] majoritarian electoral systems".

The fortunes of women candidates in Russia have also been influenced by whether they stand on a party list or in a single-member constituency. All the parties are obliged to provide "equal opportunities" for men and women in drawing up their lists of candidates. The most important single variable, however, was whether Women of Russia, with an exclusively female list of candidates, had reached the 5 per cent threshold. In 1993, there were fifty-nine women deputies (13 per cent of the total); thirty-four represented a party list and twenty-one Women of Russia, who also won two single-member constituencies. In 1995, however, the Women of Russia vote fell from 7.6 to 4.6 percent, which meant that they secured no party-list seats at all although three of the party's candidates won individual constituencies. Overall, female representation fell to forty-five (10 per cent of the total), fourteen through a party list but more than twice as many in single-member constituencies. In 1999 the Women of Russia vote dropped to 2 per cent and female representation fell still further, to 8 per cent, although once again more women were elected in single-member constituencies than on a party list; in 2003 Women of Russia did not put forward a party list of its own, although female representation recovered slightly to forty-five (10 per cent). This still left Russia well below the global average for lower houses of 15.6 per cent, and below all other parts of the world except the Arab countries.

Increasing numbers of women, in fact, were being nominated as candidates (they accounted for 7 per cent of all party-list candidates in 1993 but 16 per cent in 1999. What made the difference, as in other systems, was whether women were well represented on party lists that had a chance of exceeding the 5 per cent threshold. In Russia, it was clear that larger parties with the best chance of doing so were in fact less likely than others to include women in their lists of candidates. The Zhirinovsky Bloc were the least likely of all to include women in their list of candidates, with just 3 per cent; and only one of the larger parties, the Union of Right Forces, included a woman in one of its top three places, which maximized the chances that she would be included in the party's allocation of seats. [. . .]

Political Participation and Communication

Levels of activism within Russian parties are not particularly high in comparative terms, although they exceed levels of membership. In our 2005 survey, no more than 1.1 per cent regarded themselves as members of a political party; nearly three-times as many (3.2 per cent), however, devoted some proportion of their spare time to party activities. There were relatively few age or gender differences but very large differences by party, with the most active overwhelmingly concentrated among those who had voted for the Communist Party at the previous election.

Levels of activism, as in other countries, are defined in part by the rights with which members have been entrusted under their party rules. Many of the rules, in fact, are reminiscent of those of the Communist Party of the Soviet Union, and not just those of its obvious successor, the Communist Party of the Russian Federation. The rules of United Russia, for instance, took "a great deal of their content" from the rules of the CPSU: "But then", asked newspapers, "where else could they have got it from?". Members of United Russia, as in the CPSU, have to pay dues, take part in the work of a party branch, implement the decisions of the leadership, and undergo party instruction. As in the CPSU, they have somewhat vaguely defined rights to "receive information" about the party, to appeal against the decisions of higher party bodies, to "express their views freely", and to "address questions" to party organs at any level; they can also take part in "party referendums" whenever they are held. Members are obliged to take an appropriate part in election campaigns on the party's behalf, and if they are elected themselves to a legislative body they have to join the party fraction and act in accordance with the party's instructions. The party, commented newspapers, clearly intended to "keep its members on a short leash".

The rules of the Communist Party are the most directly inspired by those of the CPSU, and for obvious reasons. The CPRF bases itself, as the CPSU had done, on democratic centralism, including the obligation on lower party bodies to carry out the decisions of those above them. It also provides for the right of criticism, and of a minority to set out their views and have them considered in the taking of a decision. The principle of "constant renewal" was to be observed in party elections (not less than a fifth of all elected bodies should be replaced on each occasion). All the major parties elected their leadership indirectly; in the Communist Party, for instance, the Central Committee, elected by the Congress, elected the party chairman. The liberal party Yabloko shared many of the same organizational principles, including the binding character of higher-level party decisions and the indirect nature of the election of its leadership, although it also allowed for the possibility of a "preliminary all-party vote" before the choice of a party leader or presidential candidate. Yabloko, as well as United Russia and the Union of Right Forces, had "supporters" as well as ordinary members; these were citizens who supported party policy but were not bound by the rights and duties of formal membership. The Union of Right Forces appeared to be the only party that allowed members the right not to fulfil decisions with which they were not in agreement, although they could not oppose their implementation.

There has so far been relatively little research into levels of activism within Russian parties, and of the ways in which members engage with their organizations at local level. A study of three regions in the middle Volga—Samara, Tatarstan, and Ul'yanovsk—is likely to be broadly representative of "middle Russia". Overall, interview and survey evidence suggested that the Communist Party was the "most open to internal debate", and the party that "most directly encourage[d] the contribution of members to discussion of party business". The Liberal Democrats were the "least receptive to the views of its members", with the other three parties that were considered—Fatherland-All Russia, the Union of Right Forces, and Yabloko—"somewhere in between". There were corresponding differences in levels of engagement, with Communist Party members involved in some form of party activity at least weekly, "and in a majority of cases practically every day", while Union of Right Forces members were, for the most part, only very occasionally engaged. This strengthened the impression that the Communist Party was the one with the "firmest base of activists".

The same impression emerged from the pattern of responses to a question about "how close" members were to their party. Nearly two-thirds of the Communist Party members, at least in these central Russian regions, had a "very strong" relationship with their party (62 per cent), and another 29 per cent had a "strong" relationship. Members of the Union of Right Forces were again at the other extreme, with only 19 per cent who declared a "very strong" relationship (slightly more—21 percent—had no identification at all). Overall, there appeared to be "two quite different types of members: loyal communists of many years" standing, most of whom were already members of the CPSU and the vast majority of whom seemingly joined on their own initiative; and a more detached URF membership which identified weakly with the party and joined in response to social group networks and television advertising'. There were, as this suggested, many ways in which members could engage with their party of choice: the

Liberal Democrats, for instance, operated a women's and a youth movement, sports clubs, and even a farm.

Conclusion

Political parties in modern Russia operate within what is perhaps a uniquely adverse environment. The long experience of misrule by the Communist Party of the Soviet Union was scarcely an encouragement to the development of the multiparty politics for which the 1993 constitution provided; indeed it seemed almost to have discredited the very word "party", as appeared to be implied by the way in which so many Russian parties found other labels with which they could describe themselves. As we have seen, parties are viewed with scepticism, or even hostility, by the mass public. Given a chance to vote for a party-sponsored candidate or an independent, in the single-member constituencies, party-sponsored candidates lose ground. There is only a loose relationship between election outcomes and party representation in the Duma; and the Duma itself has little to do with the composition of government apart from its ability to reject nominations to the premiership and to declare its lack of confidence in the government as a whole, both of which would normally lead to an early general election. Parties have relatively few members, and they can draw on relatively few human or material resources apart from the covert support of the richest corporations and individual oligarchs. Most important of all, the contest for the presidency itself—in a system in which the head of state enjoys unusually extensive powers—is conducted on an almost entirely non-party basis.

Parties, at the same time, provide the main vehicle through which candidates can stand at elections to the Duma or to regional assemblies. And under the Putin presidency, as we have seen, efforts have been made to give them a more prominent role as part of an explicit attempt to engineer a "managed democracy". Parties, first of all, have a monopoly of the right to nominate candidates under the law on political parties. But parties can register only if they have a substantial membership drawn from a large number of republics and regions, and to secure representation within the Duma they will have to secure an increasing share of the party-list vote. The largest parties have been the principal beneficiaries of the funds the state began to make available because the level of funding is directly proportional to their electoral support, and they are likely to be well represented among the parties that reach the threshold in future Duma elections. This means they will be able to nominate a presidential candidate in the future without collecting the signatures that would otherwise be necessary.

But how far could a party system be shaped from above, in the interests of the regime itself? Across Europe, there was a generalized crisis of political engagement: turnouts were falling, parties were losing members, and political institutions were losing the trust of ordinary citizens. In the former communist countries, and particularly in the former Soviet republics, memberships remained very low, parties were more distrusted than all other institutions, and substantial numbers at elections were voting "against all" candidates where they had an opportunity to do so, or not voting at all. Russia had a number of factors that might ordinarily have been expected to encourage political engagement, including high levels of education and a substantial pool of professionals. But the long experience of communist rule had choked off the development of a civil society—of independent forms of association that could help to sustain a viable party system—and there was little sign of its emergence in the first decade or more of a post-communist administration. It was possible, even probable, that the continuation of a "top-down" approach to the development of Russia's post-communist parties would deny them the organizational autonomy that would be necessary before an authentic citizen politics could hope to develop.

6.4

Symptoms of the Failure of Democracy in Russia

M. Steven Fish

Limitations on Association

Control, manipulation, and repression are not limited to communicative interaction. Restrictions on associational freedoms also characterize official action and policy.

In conformity with Dahl's point seven, free formation of political parties and interest groups is possible in Russia. During the early post-Soviet years, restrictions on associational rights were fairly light. But some types of organizations have come under increasing, systematic official pressure since the mid-1990s. These include most religious associations other than the Russian Orthodox Church. Since the mid- and late 1990s, the Orthodox Church has enjoyed official "protection" and has been used ever more frequently by political leaders as a tool for enhancing their own legitimacy and for building a new Russian nationalism. "Protection" for Orthodoxy has included new laws that restrict "alien" religious associations. Rights of organizations other than the Orthodox Church to hold bank accounts, publicize activities, and hold meetings have eroded. Restrictions hem in not only evangelists from abroad but also organizations made up of Russian citizens if those groups are deemed "alien"— that is, not Russian Orthodox. Strictures on religious organizations have not returned to the wholesale persecution of the Soviet period. But the trend has clearly run in the direction of less, rather than more, associational freedom. By the end of the 1990s, it was impossible to speak of full freedom of association for religious purposes in Russia.

During the Putin era, restrictions on association have grown more acute and have been tethered to the constriction of communication. During the 1990s, surveillance of private citizens' communications and lives—a hallmark of the Soviet regime—fell off dramatically. But since 2000, the monitoring of those whom officials consider opponents—be they Committees of Soldiers' Mothers, the nationwide network that fights official mendacity on casualty counts in Chechnya, or opponents of incumbents in regional elections—has returned with a vengeance. Proving such activity is always difficult, but the behavior of political actors themselves is instructive. As the

Source: M. Steven Fish, selections from "Symptoms of the Failure of *Democracy in Russia*," *Democracy Derailed in Russia: The Failure of Open Politics*, Cambridge University Press, 2005.

Note: Notes and references have been removed from this article.

Nations in Transit report for 2003 notes: "Many environmental and political activists. . .now eschew e-mail for sensitive communications in favor of faxes and face-to-face meetings." Under such circumstances, associational life is cramped at best. The report concludes that "whether the authorities have the resources to monitor the burgeoning flow of information is unclear."

In my own experience and that of many political activists in Russia with whom I have contact, the state indeed has the necessary resources, or at least enough to chill associational life. At the beginning of the 2000–2001 academic year during my stay as a visiting professor at the European University at St. Petersburg, little state presence was visible, with the occasional exception of the uniformed police officer who stopped by the next-door café for a cup of tea and a snack. By the end of the academic year, 10 months later, FSB agents were prowling the halls and squeezing administrators for information on foreign students and Russians who associated with them. Such activity is as socially degrading as it was during the Soviet period. So too is it as wasteful and useless—unless the intended effect is again to draw a blanket of quiet intimidation over associational life, a cover that has a familiar feel to anyone raised in Soviet times.

The Putin government's push to bring "order" to political party competition also threatens free association. In mid-2001, the Duma passed a Kremlin-sponsored bill that required a political party to have 10,000 members and a substantial presence in at least half of Russia's 89 provinces in order to maintain the legal right to exist. As of this writing, the effects of this provision are still unclear, but several parties have already been denied registration on dubious grounds, and it is obvious that only a handful of parties will pull through. The measure is pure and typical Putinism. First, target an arena of political life for takeover. Second, justify takeover by claiming that it is needed to rectify a pathology that most reasonable people do, in fact, regard as a pathology. In this case, the pathology is the whole realm of diminutive, short-lived parties that crowd the political arena during elections but that represent no one's interests and contribute nothing to structuring political competition. Third, redress the apparent pathology by issuing a rule that prima facie makes good sense but that in practice opens limitless possibilities for abuse by officials who answer to the president alone. In the case of the law on parties, the Putin government claims only to seek the consolidation of small, weightless parties and the formation of larger, stronger organizations that are better able to structure political competition. But the law essentially gives the state—in practice, the executive—the right to decide who gets to compete. If Putin intends to establish state control over political competition and participation, the new law will enable him to do so. It would not be surprising if Putin's intentions run in such a direction. According to Vladimir Pribylovskii, the director of the Panorama think tank in Moscow: "The law on political parties potentially gives the authorities the power to decide who will be allowed to participate. The Kremlin wants to have a stable of tame parties that cover the spectrum—including tame communists, tame democrats, and tame patriots." [. . .]

7

Elections

No single aspect of Russian politics since 1992 has been more studied or analyzed than its elections.[1] They have certainly been interesting, in some cases even entertaining. However, in no instance have they been truly free and fair. Rather than open competition, more often than not and consistently since 2000, they have been closed and rigged.

The mechanism for choosing political leaders is central to understanding any political system. Bowing to the recognition that direct democracy in the manner of the ancients is no longer practical, modern democracies incorporate systems of representation by officials who are selected through elections. Elections of representatives are the means by which all citizens participate, express their voices, and ultimately exercise the power of the people that underlies the word "democracy." It is central to democracy as elections are the process by which representation becomes possible; they are the means by which the people choose leaders and hold them accountable for their actions in office.

For this reason, elections and democracy go hand in hand. But, they are not synonymous. Far too many succumb to the temptation of equating the mere holding of elections, regardless of the rules under which they are held or the circumstances surrounding them, with the existence of a functioning democracy.[2] This has been the case with most analysts of Russia since 1991. Equating elections with democracy is often a highly dubious position. One may also question the often-expressed contention that elections, however flawed, are better than none at all.[3] After all, the Soviet Union regularly held elections for a wide array of positions, but it would have been ridiculous to have called that country a democracy. Those elections were properly understood as a farce, with single candidates for each office, all from the Communist Party of the Soviet Union (CPSU), and outcomes preordained. This is not to say such exercises are useless; quite to the contrary, they may serve important legitimization functions for the regime and did so in the Soviet experience.[4] But, they had nothing to do with democracy. Even when the ballots feature multiple candidates for positions, that is not sufficient to declare a country a democracy. Multicandidate elections may also be rigged, noncompetitive, or otherwise fraudulent, and when this is the case, it becomes fair to ask whether there is any significant difference, from the perspective of democracy, from single-candidate elections.

Some scholars are impressed with the pervasiveness and decisive nature of elections in Russia. They note that scheduled elections are always held, that they have multiple candidates, and that the candidate with the most votes wins. Rules, they argue, are established, widely known and accepted, and followed. While the details may have become more problematic since Putin's rise to power, the fact that Russia continues to hold elections as scheduled is, for these authors, sufficient cause for optimism about the country's democratic, even if somewhat flawed, credentials.[5] These studies conclude not only that "elections still matter," but that they retain meaning and consequence as well.[6]

Others, including the authors of the selections in this chapter, find the evidence overwhelming that Russia's federal elections, at least since 1996, have been fundamentally corrupt, increasingly closed, and rigged. Local and regional elections, when held at all, are even worse. Elections in Russia are neither free nor fair. In 1996, President Yeltsin and his advisors aggressively plotted and rigged the election by controlling the media and institutionalizing corruption. Since then, direct state interference has been the hallmark of all federal elections in Russia. In 1999, as Yeltsin's term wound to a close, he torpedoed a burgeoning multicandidate, competitive campaign for the country's leadership and instead handed power over to a little-known successor. Once ensconced in power, Putin then tightly controlled the outcome of the election that formally installed him to a full term. In the following three years, Putin moved to cancel elections for a variety of offices and outlaw competition by eliminating parties and politicians who criticized or opposed his policies. In the end, he named his own successor while de facto remaining in power by sliding into the prime minister position. All the while, he stacked the parliament—again under highly controlled election processes—with his own followers, largely security service personnel rather than politicians who simply rubber-stamp Kremlin policies.

The former position, that elections are still meaningful, is simply impossible to sustain. As the selections that follow detail, Russia's leaders have used crises, real or contrived, to foment fear and use questionable methods to exclude candidates they opposed. Russia is a system in which the leadership does not tolerate opposition and holds periodic elections as legitimizing exercises to confirm their power and provide a sense of popular rule. But, there is no real competition, no real debate, no ability to present alternative policy platforms, and certainly no freedom for aspiring politicians to run or for the people to hold leaders accountable. Because the popular impression remains that Russia is an electoral democracy, this chapter includes articles that seek to debunk this fallacy.

Myagakov and Ordeshook nicely brand the notion of Russian elections as "an oxymoron of democracy." As they put it, "only Kremlin apologists and Putin sycophants argue that Russian elections meet the standards of good democratic practice." Ostrow, Satarov, and Khakamada detail the connections between the rigging of the 1996 elections and the subsequent squelching of political competition, which have turned elections in Russia into farcical exercises. Fish finds the manipulation of elections since 1996, characterized by "mischief" and "fraud," to represent the "symptoms" of democratic failure. Through a system of laws and administrative orders, and a web of formal and informal rules and norms, officials loyal to the Kremlin systematically prevent aspiring candidates from running, fledgling parties from forming, wealthy and interested potential donors from giving, and in the end, a population from effectively participating. And, indeed, the expectation and practice of systematic election fraud in Russia is only expanding with each round of elections. Sacrificed, among other important political values, is any semblance of transparency or accountability.

For Further Reference

Books

Timothy J. Colton, *Transitional Citizens: Voters and What Influences Them in the New Russia*, Harvard University Press: 2000.

Timothy J. Colton and Jerry F. Hough, eds., *Growing Pains: Russian Democracy and the Election of 1993*, The Brookings Institution: 1998.

Timothy J. Colton and Michael McFaul, *Popular Choice and Managed Democracy: The Russian Elections of 1999 and 2000*, The Brookings Institution: 2003.

Michael McFaul, *Russia's 1996 Presidential Election: The End of Polarized Politics*, Hoover Institution Press: 1997.

Richard Rose, William Mishler, and Neil Munro, *Popular Support for an Undemocratic Regime: The Changing Views of Russians*, Cambridge University Press: 2011.

Stephen White, ed., *Russia's Authoritarian Elections*, Routledge: 2012.

Journal Articles

Ian McAllister, " 'It's the Economy, Comrade!' Parties and Voters in the 2007 Russian Duma Election," *Europe-Asia Studies*, Vol. 60, No. 6 (2008).

Richard Rose, "How Do Electors Respond to an 'Unfair' Election? The Experience of Russians," *Post-Soviet Affairs*, Vol. 25, No. 2 (2009).

NOTES

1. See Stephen White, Richard Rhodes, and Ian McAllister, *How Russia Votes* (Chatham, 1997) and their related website, www.russiavotes.org, which includes a lengthy list of publications on Russia's elections and electoral system; Timothy J. Colton and Jerry E. Hough, eds., *Growing Pains: Russian Democracy and the Election of 1993* (Brookings Institution, 1998); Timothy J. Colton, *Transitional Citizens: Voters and What Influences Them in the New Russia* (Harvard University Press, 2000); Robert G. Moser, *Unexpected Outcomes: Electoral Systems, Political Parties, and Representation in Russia* (University of Pittsburgh Press, 2001); and Henry E. Hale, Michael McFaul, and Timothy J. Colton, "Putin and the 'Delegative Democracy' Trap: Evidence from Russia's 2003–04 Elections," *Post Soviet Affairs*, Vol. 20, No. 4 (October–December, 2004), pp. 285–319.

2. Kenneth Wilson, "Party-System Development Under Putin," *Post-Soviet Affairs*, Vol. 22, No. 4 (2006), pp. 314–348; Henry E. Hale, "The Origins of United Russia and the Putin Presidency: The Role of Contingency in Party-System Development," *Demokratizatsiya*, Vol. 12, No. 2 (2004), pp.169–194; and Michael McFaul and Nikolai Petrov, "Introduction" in Mcfaul and Petrov, eds., *Between Dictatorship and Democracy, Russian Postcommunist Political Reform* (Carnegie Endowment for International Peace, 2004) are three representative samples of the assumption.

3. See, for example, Michael McFaul and Nikolai Petrov, "What the Elections Tell Us," *Journal of Democracy* Vol. 15, No. 3 (2004), pp. 20–31.

4. Stephen White, "Non-Competitive Elections and National Politics: the USSR Supreme Soviet Elections of 1984," *Electoral Studies*, Vol. 4, No. 3 (1985), pp. 215–229.

5. See Michael McFaul, "The Electoral System," in White, Gitelman, and Sakwa, *Developments in Russian Politics 6* (Duke University Press, 2005). McFaul has easily been the most prolific and vocal in defending Russia's democratic credentials in these terms and in hailing the importance and significance of elections as evidence confirming that status. See also Henry Hale, "Eurasian Polities as Hybrid Regimes: The Case of Putin's Russia," *Journal of Eurasian Studies*, Vol. 1, No. 1 (January 2010), pp. 33–41; and Richard Rose's numerous articles at www.russiavotes.org and in Richard Rose, William Mishler, and Neil Munro, *Russia Transformed: Developing Popular Support for a New Regime* (Cambridge University Press, 2006).

6. McFaul, "The Electoral System," and McFaul and Timothy Colton, *Popular Choice and Managed Democracy: The Russian Elections of 1999 and 2000* (The Brookings Institution, 2003).

7.1

Corrupting the Elections: Enter the Oligarchs

Joel M. Ostrow, Georgiy A. Satarov, and Irina M. Khakamada

In any state hoping to create a democratic political system, competitive politics pose a challenge to the leaders. Where no recent experience with peaceful leadership change exists, or in countries like Russia where there is no such experience at all in history, the rise of organized and serious political competition as elections approach presents dilemmas for those in power. Even with a balanced constitution in place, the laws on paper guarantee nothing in terms of performance. Precedent matters, behavior matters, in short, leaders matter.

In Russia, five years after the fall of communism and two years under the new constitution, serious political questions confronted President Yeltsin and his advisors as his first term in office neared its end. For the first time, Yeltsin faced a hostile public, which gave him deeply negative ratings, at the same time that a range of new groups had appeared with strong political interests. The drop in popularity was expected as a result of the societal pain associated with the myriad economic changes taking place. The strain many segments of society felt from the economic transformation guaranteed a decline in support, as it had previously for the new leaders in every postcommunist state that implemented market reforms. In Russia, violence, corruption, and hardship all hit people hard. The streets of large cities often resembled conflict zones, as entrepreneurship merged into organized crime. Price liberalization and the rapid, often disorganized privatization brought skyrocketing inflation, while the government was cutting many of the social services the public had become accustomed to under communism. Across the country, millions of people lost everything they had to pyramid schemes, bogus "mutual funds," and corrupt financial pirates who promised astronomical earnings to investors but instead deposited the money into private offshore accounts, often disappearing altogether themselves. Much of the public had come to equate "democracy," the label under which all of these reforms had taken place, with theft, impoverishment, corruption, and disorder.

Source: Joel M. Ostrow, Georgiy A. Satarov, and Irina M. Khakamada, selections from Chapters 3 and 4, *Consolidation of Dictatorship in Russia*, Praeger, 2007.

Note: Notes and references have been removed from this article.

As the first presidential and parliamentary elections under the new rules neared, Russia faced a crossroads. How would Russia's leaders handle the challenge presented by the rise of strong political opposition? Would free and fair, truly open and competitive elections decide who would lead Russia for the next four years? Would unfettered democratic contestation set the precedent for the future? Would the incumbent leader allow a fair contest for power in which he would potentially lose? Or would such a prospect tempt the incumbent to rig or otherwise control the outcome to prevent such a possibility? In short, would the first elections chart a democratic course under the new constitution?

Free and fair elections were not to be. The new structures could not guarantee them, and the leaders were not prepared to enforce them. Yeltsin and his team chose a course that would set the precedent of controlling electoral outcomes, with tactics that would hold long-term consequences nobody at the time seems to have considered. The 1996 Russian election cycle featured numerous violations of the basic democratic principle that national elections be free and fair, and made evident the authoritarian potential in Russia's new political system. That the conventional wisdom in much of the world is that this election was free and fair, that it was a positive step forward for democracy in Russia, defies logic and reason. The most prominent Western analysts of and major media covering Russian politics conveyed the message that Yeltsin won because he "ran the right kind of campaign." In "historic" fashion "this emerging democracy" had purportedly shown its mettle, abided by its new institutions and rules and had a competitive election for the leadership of the country; this was true progress! Elections were now supposedly "the only game in town," and the "precedent-setting election" promised a "democratic renewal in Russia." [. . .]

Except for the part about setting precedents, the rest was so much tripe.

[. . .] [T]he 1996 elections in Russia violated many requirements of free and fair elections, and of the country's own election rules. [The] 1996 presidential campaign [. . .] dealt [a] severe blow to hopes for a democratic future. Among the most consequential actions were reestablishing Kremlin control over that media and using it to savage an opposition afforded no opportunity to respond, and inviting the wealthiest and most criminal business elite into the highest circles of power where they infused billions of dollars of laundered money pilfered from the state to finance not only Yeltsin's victory but also their ascension to positions of political power and continued access to state resources. Yeltsin, as the incumbent responsible for his own campaign, was responsible for that campaign's violation of the rules and violation of democratic principles. [. . .]

This was hardly preordained. The alternatives clearly existed to enable open political competition, with a variety of political candidates, organizations, and interests represented, in the 1996 presidential campaign. The legal framework was in place, both in electoral law and in media law, as were a range of opposition organizations with several viable presidential candidates, notably Gennady Zyuganov, leader of the Russian Communist Party, Georgiy Yavlinsky from the small but fairly well-organized social-democratic party Yabloko, and the charismatic former General Alexander Lebed. Russia could have had a freewheeling, spirited campaign to determine the leadership of the country going forward, five years after the collapse of the Soviet regime. In other countries, these elections brought the ouster of the first postcommunist leaders without a return to a communist past, even where former communists emerged victorious. [. . .]

Yeltsin and his advisors chose a different path that proved antidemocratic in the precedents it would set. Even those among the political elite who actively promoted democratic development in Russia consistently confused the victory of their preferred candidates who accepted and trumpeted the shorthand label "democrats" with the victory of democracy itself. There was a general failure, in Russia and the West alike, to distinguish between preferred individual candidates and the political system. Moreover, these same officials tended to categorize candidates and parties according to these preferences, actively opposing and fearing a wide spectrum rather than actively working for unity around the principles of open, democratic politics. The damage this orientation caused to democratic development is difficult to overstate.

In 1996, Yeltsin and his advisors endorsed a philosophy of "win at any cost," political or financial, regardless of what the law might say or the long-term consequences might be. Fear was the motivation that generated the "win at all costs" mentality. In the face of rising competition and opposition, Russia's leaders chose a path that amounted to stealing the election with the help of the criminal, corrupt, and newly superrich business elite. They enabled Yeltsin to circumvent all financial restrictions, to close the press to the competition, and as a result to corrupt the elections by violating rules for competitive democratic politics. This attitude to the first presidential elections under the new constitution legitimized and ultimately institutionalized an assault on press freedom, official accountability, responsible government, and free and fair elections. It undermined the prospects for a democratic future rather than being a signal of democratic consolidation. [. . .]

Fear as a Motivator

[. . .] [F]ear served in 1996 both as a motivating factor inspiring the leaders to act and as a weapon in their hands. Fear, real and imagined, guided the main figures involved in the corruption of Russia's 1996 presidential election. Different motivations drove different actors. For some it was, paradoxically, fear of Yeltsin that fueled the no-rules approach to getting him reelected. As Yeltsin's popularity dropped into the single-digits just three months before the election, the prospect loomed of an electoral defeat. As no such transfer of power had ever occurred before in Russia, advisors who genuinely fought for democracy feared Yeltsin might not cede power should he lose. [. . .] Reflecting the doubt among his own advisors about what Yeltsin would do in the event of electoral defeat were rumors that ran rampant throughout the media and society in early 1996 that Yeltsin would never cede power to the communists, or to anyone. [. . .]

Such were their fears, and they were not necessarily unfounded. Yet these supporters of democracy were unbending in their insistence that elections were absolutely necessary. There was only one conclusion available to them: Yeltsin had to win, even if in the end the elections themselves were for the sake of appearances, to allow Yeltsin to make a claim to honestly remaining in power. This was the path they saw to defend democratic development in Russia. Yeltsin remained, for them, the only viable guarantor of democracy in Russia.

These individuals were outnumbered by the self-serving. They were Yeltsin associates who, having played a role in shaping policies, some having gotten rich off of them, feared for their own safety. It remains in political Russia a widely accepted, though never verified, truth that the leaders of the October 1993 Supreme Soviet uprising in October 1993 maintained a list of individuals to be "liquidated" in the event that their coup proved successful. This rumored list consisted of present and former members of Yeltsin's government and circle of advisors, as well as liberal-minded journalists, business people, politicians, and activists. Because it was merely rumored, anyone could have placed themselves on that list in their own mind, and many did. It was also a common, though deeply-flawed shorthand to equate the Communist Party under Zyuganov in 1996 with the organizers of the violent opposition in 1993. [. . .]

Some had good reason to fear arrest under a communist return to power, or for that matter under the rule of law were this to emerge in Russia. Loss of access to a continued stream of graft would not have been the only consequence of a Yeltsin defeat. There would also have been the real possibility of punishment for deep corruption for billions of dollars swindled away, by officials in government ministries, members of the Yeltsin administration, and business magnates with whom these officials were in cahoots. The rampant corruption in government in Russia has been well documented in scholarly books with titles like *Tragedy of Russia's Reforms: Market Bolshevism Against Democracy*, *Comrade Criminal: Russia's New Mafiya*, and *Godfather of the Kremlin: The Decline of Russia in the Age of Gangster Capitalism*, and in pioneering studies by the Russian NGO INDEM.

The mutual, if different, fears of those who had crafted the reforms and those who profited off them led to a marriage that would win Yeltsin's reelection while doing long-term harm to democratic development. [. . .] "No one in this [business] elite wanted to see Yeltsin lose a presidential election" because they "owed [their] existence and riches to the state." The common presence of fear among the political and financial elite about the consequences of Yeltsin not remaining president propelled a direct alliance between the wealthiest and most corrupt, if not criminal, business leaders with the innermost circles of the Kremlin. [. . .]

Enter the Oligarchs

Throughout the first half of the 1990s, associates of Russia's wealthiest financial bosses had been killing each other on the streets of Moscow and Russia's other large cities. Cars, stores, restaurants, and sidewalk kiosks would suddenly blow up. People would be shot in the back entering their apartment buildings at night. Few were ever arrested. Boris Berezovsky, head of a network of automobile dealerships, quasi-banks, and media outlets had openly sought the murder of Vladimir Gusinsky, head of a rival network of quasi-banks, media outlets, and other commercial properties. Though they had never met, they were in virtual war with each other and Berezovsky has not denied suspicion that he at one point had a contract out on Gusinsky's life. In January 1995, many of Russia's new, rich business leaders attended the annual World Economic Forum in Davos, Switzerland. In addition to Berezovsky and Gusinsky, Vladimir Potanin, Aleksandr Smolensky, Vladimir Vinogradov, Mikhail Khodorkovsky, Rem Vyakhirev, and Roman Abramovich, the heads of all of the private banks and largest privatized industries, all attended. Chubais, their closest patron in government, joined other government officials in Davos, and Communist Party leader Gennady Zyuganov.

Berezovsky took a momentous step in Davos by approaching Gusinsky about the danger of the then upcoming election. They quickly agreed they had "no choice" but to set aside their differences and work together to prevent a communist victory. Common fears of what that victory would bring trumped mutual dislike. Berezovsky then approached the other financiers, who all agreed. In short order, he had brought together the wealthiest Russians, a group of heretofore mortal enemies, to work together and suspend their wars with each other. They agreed they had to cooperate to prevent a communist return to power, or risk losing the spectacular wealth they had amassed, and perhaps more.

Berezovsky knew firsthand, and it was widely known, that Yeltsin's reelection effort had been managed to then by incompetent buffoons. A group of drab hardliners, including longtime Yeltsin security aide Aleksander Korzhakov, FSB Director Mikhail Barsukov, and Deputy Prime Minister Oleg Soskovets, controlled the campaign plans and coffers. Under their direction it was like a ship without a rudder, "it burned fuel, made noise, vented steam, created waves around itself, but stood still." These men were in fact opposed to elections, and were already counseling the president to cancel them. Berezovsky, as an acquaintance of Yeltsin's daughter and son-in-law, was part of a wider circle included in the campaign strategy sessions, and could see all of this for himself.

Zyuganov, with his seemingly insurmountable lead over Yeltsin, went to Davos to introduce himself to the West. Zyuganov played the role of Social Democrat, striking poses that rang familiar to Western business elite. Communists-turned-social democrats had won elections across Eastern Europe, appealing with messages of increased welfare programs to a public that had been slammed by radical neoconservative market reforms. From Estonia to Poland to the Czech and Slovak Republics to Hungary, they had furthered the development of democracy and the building of market economies. To many at Davos, it appeared Zyuganov would follow suit. Indeed, one could interpret his very presence in Davos as indicative of his interest in maintaining good relations with the leaders of the capitalist business world, and perhaps of having Russia join the ranks of leading capitalist economies.

Others saw a smoke screen, convinced Zyuganov remained an unreformed communist in the Stalinist tradition. The Zyuganov at Davos was not necessarily the Zyuganov who would have been president. In the State Duma and in interviews inside Russia he presented a distinctly hard-line communist message. Such an impression was reinforced by the company he kept.

Was he simply putting on a face to calm the West? Would he in fact have wrenched Russia back to the past? In the end, we will never know what Zyuganov would have done had he become President of Russia. The oligarchs and Yeltsin made sure of that.

Berezovsky and Gusinsky agreed at Davos to work together to guarantee that Yeltsin remain in office. Together with the other financiers, including Potanin, Vinogradov, and Khodorkovsky, they agreed to use all resources available to prevent any change in power in the Kremlin. They then approached current and former members of government, including Deputy Prime Minister Yevgeniy Yasin, Moscow Mayor Yuriy Luzhkov, Chubais, and a wider group of

Russian business people, all of whom agreed to take any necessary measures to prevent a Yeltsin defeat. They agreed on the need to wake Yeltsin up to the danger, in particular to the danger residing in his own campaign team. Chubais was a key figure, because without him some of these individuals would have refused to set aside their differences merely at the instigation of Berezovsky. The distrust and dislike were too fierce. Chubais had been essential to the enrichment of each of these figures. Berezovsky used Chubais as a conduit, to help unite this financial front and to make the appeal to Yeltsin. One account has the financiers promising support only on the condition that Chubais be installed as head of the campaign.

Berezovsky also had Yeltsin's daughter's cooperation, through their mutual direct observation of the incompetence of the campaign staff, to influence Yeltsin. It was she, Tatiana Dyachenko, who organized a meeting between the financiers and the president, to warn him of the dangers and the need to make changes. There is no doubt that the financiers offered the president their full support, and that they expected benefits in return. Whether those were explicitly or implicitly spelled out remains unclear, but the benefits most certainly were realized.

Virtually simultaneous to these events, Yeltsin received a letter from some of his top staff that contained the same basic message. While Yeltsin's rating plummeted and the security triumvirate plotted a shady course to disaster, Yeltsin's analytical staff, strong advocates of democratization to this point marginalized from the reelection planning, became distraught. [. . .]

Satarov [. . .] set to work with Chief of Staff Viktor Ilyushin and others to urge Yeltsin to overhaul his campaign, warning him that "normal staff work had not yet even begun," and that without changes there would be disastrous consequences for him and for the country. They were stunned to learn Yeltsin, due to the falsehoods coming from Soskovets and Korzhakov, believed he remained enormously popular.

The simultaneous pressure from the financiers, his daughter, and his aides did push Yeltsin to make a change. He put Ilyushin in charge of the campaign staff and Chubais in charge of the "analytical group" planning campaign strategy. Berezovsky and the financiers, meanwhile, continued to meet and with Chubais, Dyachenko, and others to coordinate their efforts. They controlled the major electronic and print media outlets, and had virtually unlimited finances. Dyachenko played the key role as intermediary between the various interested circles—the campaign staff, the financiers, and her father. However, changes meant changes, and staff changes were far from Yeltsin's only option. Another tempting option beckoned: why hold an election at all?

The Charge to Cancel the Elections

Yeltsin was inclined to take drastic steps. [. . .]

Yeltsin instructed his staff on March 17, less than three months before the scheduled elections, to provide him the legal basis and a draft decree on dissolving the Duma, banning the Communist Party and suspending the elections. [. . .]

He gathered Chief of Staff Ilyushin, legal advisors Baturin and Shakhrai, political advisor Satarov, and other aides and instructed them to develop decree language and legal justification. An order from the president is an order from the president, and the advisors saw no choice but to carry it out. Their choice in *how* to carry it out demonstrates their unwavering commitment to democratic principles. Focusing on the legal aspect, they compiled a list of reasons why the idea was a bad one, in a document they called "Counter-arguments and Alternatives." First, they expressed extreme doubt that any legal basis existed for doing what Yeltsin had requested. [. . .] Yeltsin's staff indicated a number of alternative steps, including working with the Federation Council on a ruling that the Duma had created circumstances making elections impossible, and delaying them for two years.

Yeltsin was far from satisfied, and barked, "Why is there no text of a decree? In 1993 two people figured it out." [Decree No. 1400, which annulled the old Supreme Soviet and ultimately led to conflict in the streets.] He ordered them again to write the decree and sent them out of his office. He also met with his ministers to prepare them for the steps ahead. The president had been telling selective ministers about his plan to dissolve the Duma, ban the Communist Party, and cancel the elections, instructing them to prepare measures related to their spheres of activity. At each meeting he told the official in question that everyone else supported this plan. Believing this to be the case, each thought "if everyone else is in favor then I better agree with them." Only the Minister of Internal Affairs, Anatoly Kulikov, after hearing the president out asked him to wait a few hours before issuing a decree, so that he could "provide [him] with several proposals." Kulikov was also under the impression that everyone else was on board. But when he saw the justice minister and Chair of the Constitutional Court, and revealed that he had deep reservations, he found them similarly concerned. These three decided to develop a list of arguments in support of the radical steps Yeltsin was seeking, and a list of arguments against those steps. Together they would bring these to the president.

Each group saw the other as leading the president astray. The president had told his aides that everyone else supported his idea, and believing this they glared with disdain at Kulikov, Yuri Skuratov and Vladimir Tumanov as they crossed paths in the president's office. In reality, the latter group had just told the president exactly what those staff members had told him earlier, that "We have thought long on this and we are of the opinion not to proceed." Yeltsin was irate that Kulikov had not told him of his opposition when they first met. "I am not happy with you!" he said. When Kulikov tried to protest that it was his job to fully inform, Yeltsin interjected, "No! That is all! You will carry out my orders! You will get the decree." As Interior Minister, after all, his job was to receive and implement orders to guarantee security inside the country.

An angry Kulikov went straight to Ilyushin, who was huddled with the rest of the analytical staff, and said, "So, you are writing the decree?" The staff, in turn, glared at him again. Kulikov handed them the notes the president had so energetically rejected, and they handed theirs to him. They were practically identical, and both groups were now on to Yeltsin's game. Realizing they all opposed, rather than supported, the demand, they united their efforts. Just then, Chubais entered Ilyushin's office and started lecturing them that the author of the decree, regardless of the president's signature on the document, would bear responsibility. All that would remain for them is their resignation, as this would be the political death of the president. They merely handed Chubais their work and found another ally. Meanwhile, the president had left for his dacha, instructing Ilyushin to bring him the decree in one hour.

This was at 10 P.M. Instead, they drafted a joint note to the president, in which they wrote, "The decree could not be written, since no legal basis exists for taking such action. . .and would risk a civil war." Not even 11 P.M. yet, they called the president, learned he was already asleep, and decided to wait until morning.

Yeltsin saw the note at 6 A.M., in a meeting with his security ministers and chief of staff. He asked who wrote it. Ilyushin named, among others, the president's main analytical staff (himself, Baturin, Shakhrai, and Satarov) Chubais, the interior and justice ministers and Chair of the Constitutional Court. Fifteen minutes later, Kulikov attended a meeting with Yeltsin, Prime Minister Viktor Chernomyrdin, Deputy Prime Minister Nikolai Yegorov, Barsukov, Soskovets, and Ilyushin. The president decided against using force, announcing instead that he would go ahead with the elections as planned. Military maneuvers in the Moscow region were brought to a halt the next day. Apparently, they had been preparing to move on the issuance of a decree.

The decision not to use force, and to proceed with elections as called for by law and by the constitution, reflected the pro-democratic alternative chosen at this critical juncture. Clearly, other options were on the brink of being chosen, and in fact had been ordered by the president. [. . .] Sadly for democracy, however, this was only one piece of the puzzle.

The democratization literature overemphasizes formal elections, and the literature on Russia since the collapse shares this flaw. The mere holding of this election meant less than how the elections were conducted. The future of democratic development and the performance of the new constitution and legal framework still hung in the balance. First precedents are important. Indeed, one can say that if cancelling scheduled elections because of fear of defeat is not merely a real but a central consideration, it is difficult to speak of democracy. The question really was whether these first presidential elections would help to put democracy back on course after the jarring effects of 1993.

The decision to bring in the financiers made sure this would not happen, as it, in effect, ensured that the elections were not free and fair. The alliance brought massive violations of virtually every important law regulating the campaign and deeply corrupted the presidential election process. While Berezovsky did not take over campaign operations, in fact he only appeared twice in the offices of the campaign staff in the Presidential Hotel, he did help to control the outcome. Chubais and Dyachenko kept the oligarchs informed on the progress of the campaign informally, but the oligarchs' most important work was behind the scenes. It is in the heavily laundered money and the direct control over a national propaganda machine where the election was truly stolen.

(Not) The Oligarchs' Money

The half-dozen or so most influential oligarchs were all highly skilled in the shadowy art of money-laundering. Currency transactions brought them their spectacular wealth. Much of that wealth they siphoned off from the state coffers, depositing billions of dollars into foreign bank accounts for purported business purposes. After several transfers, each involving large siphons as kickbacks to themselves, they took out the remaining money as cash and transported it back to Russia, by then untraceable to the original source or purpose. During the campaign, they simply branched off the siphon to create a loop, putting state funds they had received directly into the president's campaign treasury. In essence, the conspirators devised a classic money-laundering scheme to disguise state budget funds as private donations into the Yeltsin campaign. The exact figures most likely will never be known, and, because the actions were so patently illegal, the true figures may not even be possible to know. While rumors that it amounted to billions of dollars are probably inflated, Chubais is on record describing the legal limit of $3 million as "an insignificant sum" compared with what was in fact spent. [. . .]

While the use of money from rich financiers in democratic elections is seldom illegal and widely practiced, this was different. In the American robber-baron period, for example, Henry Ford, J.P. Morgan, and others frequently corrupted elections and politicians at all levels with their money; however, it is impossible to argue that their wealth was entirely parasitic and extractive. They were independent actors, contributing to a growing industrial base and economic development. Their economic activity was independent of the state, and their political activity was independent of the state. They were not simultaneously members of Congress or of the president's cabinet. While corruption existed, parties changed power, incumbents lost, competitive politics continued. Moreover, they invested back into the American economy and were the engine for its growth. They bought politicians and elections, clearly antidemocratic and illegal activities. Eventually, the legal system put a halt to the effort. Antitrust legislation broke up their monopolies. Again, they were independent of the state.

All of this was different in Russia. The oligarchs' association with the Kremlin was not independent—it was semiofficial. Their assistance on the campaign came with *quid pro quos* of government positions and direct decision-making power. Their access would be direct, the line between government and business thoroughly blurred. This was institutionalized corruption in the making, corruption of government itself, and of the procedures necessary for democracy to have any hope. They were not just lending money to the campaign, they were becoming the campaign and taking over the administration, or rather, that is what it all meant. [. . .]

Erosion of Press Freedom and Fair Access

Gusinsky's Independent Television Network (NTV) offered the highest-quality news coverage in the country, by far. Perhaps the most objective praise possible of the quality of NTV programming comes from Berezovsky. "You can say anything you want about Gusinsky, but he created a unique television station. Unique, and not only in the Russian context. Compared to the Western television I have seen, and I have seen a lot, NTV was in those years a highly-quality, professional product both in terms of news and entertainment." Coming from Berezovsky, Gusinsky's fierce rival and owner of Channel 1 (ORT), this comment speaks volumes. NTV News was a fiercely independent, genuinely informative news program on which talented journalists conducted quality investigative reporting, and where informed and intelligent hosts offered insightful and enlightening programs on subjects related to politics and policy, economic and social. NTV was the network to turn to for information.

The 1996 campaign set in motion events that would ultimately destroy the network and its owner. In Spring 1996, having joined forces with the Yeltsin campaign, Gusinsky assigned NTV Director Igor Malashenko the additional task of running advertising and public relations for that campaign. He similarly delegated other NTV staff to work on the campaign. In retrospect, given the Kremlin's seizure of control over electronic media and the restoration of censorship across the press, it might appear that this was Yeltsin taking direct control of the media. It was not, but it did create conditions that paved the way for Putin to restore this control. In 1996, the oligarchs who orchestrated the financing and overhaul of the campaign happened to own the major television networks and newspapers. In essence, they donated these to the campaign and, as a result, closed off competition and guaranteed a Yeltsin victory. What became an oligarch—Kremlin marriage under Yeltsin opened the door to direct control by the next president.

Yeltsin, however, was not seizing media assets. He did not close publications or networks, or censor the wide range of viewpoints across the print media, which ranged from fascist to Trotskyite. The best journalists in the major media, and the owners of those outlets, feared a Yeltsin defeat just as the rest of the political, power, and business elite feared it. To them, Yeltsin was the guarantee that they could continue to work as journalists. Throughout Yeltsin's first term, investigative reporting on government and society flourished, and the dedication of young journalists served as one of the best hopes for a democratic future for the country. Under Yeltsin, Kremlin backlash to reports it did not like could sting, but there was no crackdown. Gusinsky, for example, tried before Spring 1996 to expand his network's access to the airwaves from a few hours to a full twenty-four hours. He shared Channel 4 with the Sport channel. Unfortunately for Gusinsky, Yeltsin and his security chief Korzhakov liked the Sport channel, and instead of more time for NTV Yeltsin issued a decree giving more time to Sport. Gusinsky was furious and had NTV unleash a torrent of attacks on Yeltsin and his staff, with angry private exchanges between Gusinsky and the staff ensuing. It is quite probable that Berezovsky, the owner of ORT Channel 1, had a hand in this sequence, working through Dyachenko and Yumashev to prevent NTV from receiving more broadcast time. But through the scandal and the critical reports there was never a crackdown. Yeltsin never tried to censor or exert direct control over press content. Journalists worried that their freedom to report and investigate would disappear should Yeltsin lose the election and communists again occupy the Kremlin offices. To prevent this, they willingly and actively promoted Yeltsin while savaging his opponent. They sacrificed objectivity hoping to preserve their freedom. The choice ultimately cost them both.

The media owners viewed themselves as independent political players, and were so viewed by public officials. They behaved not merely as observers and watchdogs, but as active participants in political battles with their own political objectives. From the very first thoughts about the 1996 campaign, Yeltsin's advisors understood that "any hope for success would depend on a close and friendly union with the mass media." The 1996 presidential campaign substantially strengthened this tendency and blurred the line between the Kremlin and the media into the future. The oligarchs had their media outlets go not merely lockstep for Yeltsin, they openly campaigned for him. Only Yeltsin received prime-time air coverage on television, despite the law's demand for equal air time for all major candidates. Channel 1 simply did not show Zyuganov other than to air scandals about him. Not only was there no coverage of his campaign, Zyuganov was not afforded paid commercial time during prime viewing hours. Any straight reporting of the Zyuganov campaign or running of advertising spots took place in the wee morning hours, to ensure the smallest possible viewing audience.

This policy was carefully organized between the campaign staff and the media owners and directors, as indeed these entities overlapped. The media "became vehicles of the Yeltsin publicity campaign, resulting in a blurring between the line that separates political advertising from news." Media executives did not limit themselves to creating that advertising campaign. They assisted in creating branches of the president's communications office across the country, to promote coverage of the president in the regional press. They used these structures to bring provincial reporters to Moscow, to meet with members of the Administration in the Kremlin on fully paid junkets. There were also reports that the Kremlin spent millions of dollars bribing journalists around the country for articles and reports favorable to the president. To an individual writer for a provincial newspaper, $100 for a story was a mammoth sum.

This media and advertising effort for the Yeltsin reelection campaign was made possible by the decision of the president and the oligarchs to unite their efforts. The president welcomed the financiers in, and they made possible a media monopoly for the president. Together, in close cooperation with staffs merged, they crafted a propaganda onslaught that overwhelmed the electorate and made a mockery of laws on spending or fair use. The controllers of the media violated the law and were rewarded, not punished.

For those close to Yeltsin, advocating enforcement of the law to allow Zyuganov equal time on television was counterintuitive. The law was clear: the media had to provide equal coverage and equal access to all candidates. But television time of any sort was advertising, and the Yeltsin team was not going to force the media to advertise Zyuganov, whom they saw not merely as a political opponent but as an enemy. The law was not in their interests, which they equated with the country's interests, and so they ignored it. They had convinced themselves that the imperative was to prevent a return to communism. The free press became a casualty of this mind set, though few, if any, supporters of democracy saw any such danger at the time. Their fears of the danger of a Yeltsin defeat blinded them to these other risks. One of Russia's most respected and talented young journalists, Sergei Parkhomenko, told the *Los Angeles Times*, "This is not a game of equal stakes. That is why I am willing to be unfair. That is why I am willing to stir up a wild anti-Communist psychosis among the people." This reporter and others like him knew exactly what they were doing. And they did it well.

Fear as a Tool

The problem the newly overhauled campaign staff faced was how to raise a mass of people to vote for Yeltsin, given his ratings in early 1996 stood at less than 10 percent. If the vote were seen as a referendum on his performance, Yeltsin faced almost certain defeat. They had to make Yeltsin seem like the safe, stable choice. The strategy they adopted was to demonize Zyuganov, who continued to poll around 30 percent. As noted above, many among Yeltsin's staff, as among the broader political and business elite, really did fear for the future were Zyuganov to win. Fearful themselves, they knew the mass populace either was in fear or could be made to fear. Relentless exaggeration was the recipe, and with the media then at their disposal the task was straightforward.

They cast Zyuganov as a demon, representing a demonic ideology. The media began to consistently portray him as wild, an uncontrolled buffoon prone to dangerous outbursts. Nightly broadcasts on every network portrayed Zyuganov as a monster. Reporters, interviewers, documentaries, and other programs fomented fear of a restoration not merely of the Soviet system, but of full-blown Stalinism should Zyuganov win. The formula was simple. Zyuganov was the Communist Party leader, the Communist Party had created the gulags and ruled by terrorizing the populace, so a Zyuganov victory would mean the return of the gulags, the end of private enterprise and property, in short a return to the dark days of Stalin's Russia. It would mean famine and terror. These messages aired in the oligarch-controlled media and were reinforced throughout the campaign in slogans, posters, badges, letters to voters, in every conceivable format. Every format, except for one. Yeltsin never directly attacked Zyuganov; instead, he continued to issue campaign promises and dole out pork at every stop he made. He mostly ignored his opponent.

The propaganda turned the choice presented to the public as being between catastrophe and stability. This was exactly the choice the campaign wanted, knowing the electorate would always choose stability. While most voters might see it as a choice between the lesser of two evils—between the president you know though may not like, or the Communist who may bring famine, terror, and civil war—the choice would be Yeltsin. Voters, once convinced that this was indeed the choice they faced, found it a simple one to make. The barrage media and propaganda blitz effectively "made a mishmash" of the peoples' brains.

There were few public complaints from any pro-democracy or free press advocates in Russia or abroad at the time. On the contrary, these constituencies enthusiastically supported what was hailed as Yeltsin's energetic revival, and rescuing the country from the danger of a communist restoration. They acted as if they bought into the campaign propaganda hook, line and sinker. Journalists demonstrated no sense of fear that the same tactics could be used against them in the future, no sense that precedents were being set that could come back to haunt them. Yeltsin would be the victor, and freedom would be protected. [. . .]

The problem was, of course, not the negative strategy. Election campaigns in established democracies are often fiercely negative and always have been. It is the democratic requirement that all candidates have the ability to campaign, have equal access to the media, and have an ability to respond to statements made by opponents. This is all required for free and fair elections, and this is precisely what the marriage between the oligarchs and the Kremlin prevented. The requirement of equal access demands that news coverage give equal time in reports on candidates. It also requires equal access to advertising time and space, that any candidate willing and able to pay receives air time and that there be no discrimination in the offering of time slots.

The 1996 Russian campaign was not free or fair in any of these respects. When candidates lack equal access, a mishmash is indeed made of the electorate's brains. The oligarchs denied Zyuganov access throughout the onslaught. No major outlet would afford him advertising spots or provide him a chance to respond in news interviews. The only times offered and the only news coverage of his campaign were between the hours of midnight and 6 A.M. The networks closed access to Zyuganov during main viewing hours. Zyuganov simply did not have an opportunity either to present his own message or to fire back against Yeltsin. The Central Election Commission, ostensibly set up to oversee elections and ensure adherence to election laws, never stepped in, hardly a surprise as it is staffed by and answers to the Kremlin.

It was this closure of media access that set the antidemocratic precedent for the future. The decision to wed the Yeltsin campaign to the oligarchs effectively stole the campaign. It ensured that there would not be a free and fair election, the most basic and necessary element of democratic politics. The oligarchs, and thus the campaign, controlled the media, they denied Zyuganov access to that media, and they used the media to whoop up a frenzy of fear about both Zyuganov and anyone affiliated with him.

More shadowy processes may also have been at work. On June 11, five days before the election, a bomb exploded at the Tulskaya metro station in Moscow, killing four and injuring more than a dozen passengers. There were no claims of responsibility, and no arrests were ever made. At the time, rumors of official involvement seemed so wildly unfounded as to not be taken seriously. In retrospect, given similarly timed deadly blasts in each future national election, never with any claim of responsibility and never any assigned in the form of arrests, the rumors seem less wild. Suggestions that the FSB (Federal Security Service, the successor to the KGB) had a role in the June 1996 bombings place among the variety of motivations the desire to create a state-of-emergency situation put the security forces back at the center of Kremlin power, and realize the earlier desire of Korzhakov and Barsukov, detailed above, to cancel the elections altogether. None of that happened, of course, however Yeltsin did use the bombings both to confirm the fear the campaign had generated and to call for stability in the face of that fear. "Don't give in to provocation," he said. He condemned efforts "toward destabilizing the situation in the capital and creating an atmosphere of uncertainty and fear in Russia," and said, "The best answer to the extremists is to vote on June 16, vote for civil peace, for stability and for the future of Russia." In other words, vote for Yeltsin, or there will be worse to come. Even if it was a pure terrorist attack, the results held lessons for future unsavory acts out of the Kremlin.

The strategy of generating fear to win votes worked spectacularly well. Having fomented fear of a return to communism, Yeltsin's team prevented a Zyuganov victory, by 35–32 percent in the first round, and 54% to 40% in the second. Fear won, by uniting much of the political elite, all of the major mass media, and the newly superrich business class. By polarizing the campaign and exaggerating the danger, the combination of the oligarchs, the media, and the administration ensured a second term for Yeltsin. Yeltsin fell gravely ill immediately after the election and spent much of the next four years in hospitals and rest homes. He was never the same, never at full strength in his second term. However, the oligarchs were then firmly entrenched in the Kremlin, and as a result had a victory far greater than they could ever have imagined. Nobody could touch them, because anyone in a position to do so was an accomplice.

Payback and Precedent

The first presidential election under the new constitution set an "at-all-costs" precedent, one in which the incumbent in the Kremlin controlled the outcome.

There was a vote, there were several candidates, but the process leading up to that vote was not free and fair. Together the staff and the oligarchs violated without consequence all media laws on fair access. They obliterated legal limits to campaign spending and transparency. A decade later, Russia has yet to have a national election that could be termed free, fair, and truly competitive. That first election could have set a different precedent. Other options were available, some of them even worse for democracy. However, the most basic necessary component of democracy—free and fair elections—has never been met under Russia's new system, and that as much as anything is responsible for the dictatorship that has emerged.

In the short term, it meant a thoroughly corrupt regime. The close association between the president and the oligarchs in the campaign brought institutionalized corruption as a consequence. After the election, the oligarchs wanted their pay-back. Having set aside their differences, having promised their assistance to the president to get him reelected, and having delivered, they expected substantial rewards for that support. Given the propaganda of the campaign, they could argue they saved Yeltsin, saved market reforms, and saved the country, and who in the Kremlin could refute those claims? Indeed, they saw the victory as theirs, and they expected rewards and sought to collect them. These they received in spades.

The payback was swift and extraordinary. Yeltsin immediately named Potanin and Berezovsky to major posts in the new government. Potanin became deputy prime minister in charge of overseeing the economy. Berezovsky was appointed to the National Security Council, where he eventually would become secretary. At the same time they, like all the others who joined the government, continued to hold their corporate positions, running their businesses while serving in government. They could now use their public office to further their private gain. Potanin's first task was to reform the bank system that had been so profitable to him and his Uneximbank, and to the other oligarchs. He had no interest in making the banking sector more open, competitive, or fair! Indeed, his efforts were to close rather than open the banking sector. Beyond official titles and making policy in their own interests, other benefits accrued as well. Gusinsky received his expanded time on Channel 4 for NTV. The oligarchs secured state resources and freedom from tax burdens, and won new government projects.

And so grew the practice of buying politicians and policy, and of placing loyal subjects in positions of power. In government, Berezovsky, Potanin, and the others pushed their own projects, their own interests, and their own people. The most lucrative project was the new loans-for-shares scheme in the next wave of privatization, which put the energy and utilities sectors in their hands at a fraction of their actual value. Corruption in government was extraordinary and complete.

The oligarchs' deal with the Kremlin in 1996 brought the precedent of the purchase of cabinet posts that continues to this day. It triggered also the purchase of officials throughout government, as the other oligarchs sought to counterbalance the inside influence of Potanin and Berezovsky by purchasing their own allies in other positions. Almost anyone of any significance in the Russian government "belonged" to someone.

Those who did not, those loyal to the cause of creating a market democracy, did try to effect a counterattack, to attempt to limit their reach. The ill-fated Kiriyenko government, in particular, tried to isolate the oligarchs from policymaking, and Chubais made an effort to assert his political independence and future by initiating a crackdown on the oligarchs' influence. These efforts failed spectacularly. With the assistance of Dyachenko and Yumashev, the oligarchs joined the inner circle in the Kremlin that came to be known as "The Family," that close and corrupt circle of oligarchs, relatives, and two or three personal advisors that defined Yeltsin's final years as president. Anything and anyone requiring the ailing president's attention went through his daughter Dyachenko, or his son-in-law Yumashev, or his new Chief of Staff Aleksander Voloshin. They were the people with regular direct access to Yeltsin. Through their close connections and influence, the group of bankers frequently named ministers and deputy ministers, the formation of and changes in the government.

A recent major study on corruption indicates that corruption in government has reached epic proportions in Russia. Positions in government are sold for enormous sums. To become a deputy minister today costs upwards of $500,000, with a price scale ranging from several times more for cabinet level positions all the way down to rank-and-file posts. In 2005, seven men from President Putin's close circle controlled nine monopolies with assets over $220 billion, or 40 percent of Russia's gross domestic product. Corruption defines the Russian government.

If the institutionalization of corruption in government was the most significant short-term consequence, the loss of independence for the media held grave long-term consequences. Those consequences were not visible right away. Having succeeded in warding off a communist return, the journalists went back to their job of investigative and independent reporting. NTV went back to its role of being a watchdog. Newspaper reporters began writing about corruption and the president's fading health in a critical fashion. That the former was a direct consequence of the campaign events in which they were a part, and the latter was easily predicted, was beside the point. As journalists in a free press they reported on the problems in the government. As for the election, Yeltsin was indebted to them, not they to him, or so they saw it. There was no reason to continue to lavish praise. This was the case for many individual journalists.

But they were exposed in ways that were not immediately apparent. The media were deeply compromised, as an institution. The campaign "exposed the dangers of reinstalling state control over the media and of turning it into a vehicle of support for the President, the Government, the State." The Leninist concept of the media as a weapon, as a tool in the hands of politicians, reemerged with a vengeance. Despite continued Western press accounts still casting him as the best hope for democracy, in fact Chubais was behaving as if in authoritarian control. According to one account, he called leading media executives—editors and producers—to the Kremlin and blasted them for daring to critique him and his policies, and threatened them physically should they continue. Direct intimidation for unflattering reports helped fuel a growing censorship. The Kremlin expected the journalists to behave, for their bosses were part of the government. They were all on the same team, right?

More generally, the media in Russia do not and never have viewed themselves as part of civil society, are not observers, and are not a conduit between government and society. There was a chance for the Russian press to move in that direction, and it was beginning to do so, but 1996 changed all that. The media were now not oriented to informing and reaching the citizens, but rather to reaching one viewer, the president. In this way, though not immediately evident, they came to work for the president. It was a precarious position to be in, to be sure. All their eggs lay in the personal predilections of the holder of that office. [. . .]

In short, the 1996 presidential election brought institutionalized corruption in government that paved the way to destruction of the media as an independent voice. But tragic and monumental as each of these would prove to be, neither represented the deepest blow to hopes for democracy. This was the first election under the new constitution. Under that constitution, for elections to be free and fair requires a president and an administration that wants them to be so. Yeltsin's 1996 campaign actively violated the main laws intended to make them free and fair: laws on access to media and laws on financing. It did so with impunity. Wary of competition and fearing defeat, they made a choice to take any action whatsoever to avoid the former as a means to prevent the latter. No means existed to prevent such transgressions. But alternatives did exist. Democratic elections hinged on the inclinations of the incumbent and his advisors to want them, to allow competition and embrace the possibility that the electorate would choose someone else. It required a president willing and able to put trust in the citizens as sovereign. Such a president could have chosen to allow a freewheeling campaign for the presidency. Yeltsin did not choose that democratic path in 1996. Nor would he ever choose it. As the first president, he set the course for future attitudes toward elections. The course he set in 1996 undermined them, and in 1999 he used another election to slam the door shut. [. . .]

★ ★ ★ ★

Abandoning Democracy: Anointing a Successor

Boris Yeltsin often liked to think of himself as Russia's George Washington. He knew about Washington, admired him, and speech writers and staff were aware of his desire to be remembered in the same light. He wanted to be remembered as a great political figure in Russia, one "without whom history would be very different." In some respects Russia's first elected president explicitly emulated the first American president. His decision not to associate himself with any political party [. . .] may have been the most important example of this sporadic emulation. Washington made a conscious strategic decision to "stand above the fray" of daily partisan politics, crafting for himself the air of leader of the country as a whole and serving "as a symbol of national unity." As one authority on Washington put it, "[What] he cared about most passionately, [was] his reputation as the 'singular figure' who embodied the meaning of the American Revolution in its most elevated and transcendent form." This is who Yeltsin wanted to be for Russia. He rejected any party affiliation and never actively supported any political organization after his departure from the Communist Party, aiming to present himself as standing above politics. However, Yeltsin was selective in his emulation and ignored the most important lesson. In so doing he forfeited any hope of being remembered as Russia's Washington. The last important decision Washington made as president was perhaps the most important for the development of democracy in America: to depart at the end of his second term and allow the people to choose their next president without interference from himself. Every new democracy faces the dilemma of leadership succession and how to handle the problem of leadership change. Yeltsin chose a different path, one that, combined with the earlier decisions, closed the door on democratic development.

Democracy requires an open, free, and fair contest in which the population plays a direct role in selecting its leaders. "Democratic norms require a willingness to accept political defeat: to leave office upon losing an election, to follow rules even when they work against one's interests." The decision whether to allow step down, and under what terms, is one that every first leader in a democratizing country must confront. It is a particularly difficult decision to make where no tradition or precedent exists for voluntary, peaceful leadership change or democratic leadership selection. Such was the case in Russia, as it was in the early United States and in any state lacking a democratic history.

Washington made several decisions at the end of his presidency around which the future of American democracy would pivot. He rejected, and made clear he considered insulting and repulsive, pressures from a variety of circles to anoint himself King George the First. The pressure came from those who feared the potential of chaos, instability, and even war that may result from unbridled competition for the top political position in the country. Cries for stability and order accompanied the suggestion that Washington remain in office indefinitely. He rejected these calls, as he rejected similar suggestions that he become "president-for-life." Instead, Washington made a momentous decision to retire, quietly exiting the political scene. But equally important to this decision was his behavior in light of it. Washington refused to appoint a successor, and even refused to state a preference in the competition that ensued. He stayed out of the campaign to succeed him, despite his own vice president's candidacy. He considered it inappropriate even to comment much less take an active position on who the next President of the United States should be. It was for the people to decide. Even in his private communications he did not express a position on the raging campaign. While still holding the office, he watched as a normal citizen with the rest of the country as a freewheeling campaign ensued between his vice president, John Adams, about whom he was lukewarm, and Thomas Jefferson, whom he despised. Some suggest that had Washington been inclined to appoint a successor it would have been neither Adams nor Jefferson, but one who never became president, Alexander Hamilton.

Though few authors focus on the point, it is indisputable that Washington's decision as a sitting president to stay out of the campaign to determine his successor set a tremendously important precedent. He was "the first head of a modern state to hand over the reins to a duly elected successor," and his momentous decision set an example that enabled future presidential elections to proceed smoothly, and made it more difficult for the defeated to contest results or for future presidents to cling to power. As one authoritative history puts it, "The most weighty factor of all in 1796 was George Washington . . . Hardly a step in the process of nation-building nine years before at Philadelphia would have been what it was were it not for the expectation, universal in every sense, that George Washington would be the Republic's first Chief Magistrate. What, then, would happen when Washington made his departure? Scarcely a citizen in all the Republic had more than the remotest idea." Had he held office until his death, or tried to direct the outcome, "subsequent presidential successions would have been more difficult" and democracy in America may not have survived. Allowing the people to decide was one of the most important steps in entrenching a democratic path for the country. His enemy King George III is reported to have said that if Washington retired and went back to his farm, "he will be the greatest man in the world." The specific precedent holds to this day: Ronald Reagan was not active in the 1988 campaign that resulted in the election of his vice president, George Bush; Bill Clinton did not participate in his vice president's controversial and ultimately unsuccessful campaign in 2000. It is, in the United States, considered improper for a sitting president actively to engage in the electoral process over his succession. They stay out.

This is relevant for Russia because, according to his speech writer, this was a history about which President Yeltsin was aware and on which he was well read. In the end, however, he chose not to let that history guide his own actions. Rather than stand aside and allow a competitive campaign and open democratic election to determine his successor, rather than be the first head of state in Russia to hand power to a freely elected successor, Yeltsin made the decision for the country on his own. He preempted the campaign by naming his successor, handing the presidency to a little-known former KGB officer, Vladimir Putin, on December 31, 1999. His decision was antidemocratic in both form and content, and in the important precedent it set. While Yeltsin's action may have adhered to the letter of the Russian Constitution, it did violence to the spirit, as it did to remaining prospects for democratic development.

Yeltsin's decision restricted political competition. It compelled the liberal wing of the Russian political spectrum to capitulate in support of the chosen successor, with no hope left of making its case to the country in a spirited contest for the direction of Russia's economic and political future. It compelled centrist groups to drop out altogether, lacking any hope of organizing a campaign in the shortened timetable and against a new incumbent. It was thoroughly undemocratic and set precedents that Putin has used to consolidate dictatorship.

[. . .] The uncertainty regarding new procedures for leadership change presents a critical juncture in the development of any political regime. As democracy is predicated on particular procedures, above all on open, free, and fair competitive elections, the precedents set in the first instance of leadership change hold particular significance for the potential development of a democratic political system. [. . .]

The Search is on: Everyone is a Successor

That the matter of who would follow Yeltsin was a central concern in the Kremlin was obvious from the dizzying rotation of prime ministers during his second term. Each change brought proclamations that the new incumbent was the sure presidential front-runner. The administration, the press, and the public were acutely aware of the problem attendant to leadership change, and the prolonged buzz around this issue was unlike any other since the collapse of the communist system. For their part, Yeltsin's staff began considering "operation successor" immediately after the 1996 elections, and Yeltsin personally became involved in earnest after the economic default of 1998. In large part, the matter stemmed from Yeltsin's earlier decision to remain unaffiliated with and not actively to promote political parties. Had he done so, one might have expected a party nomination process would have been devised to determine the candidates who would compete. But in the absence of such a system and being resolutely disassociated from parties altogether, Yeltsin was left to be an independent player in the determination of his successor. In the final months of 1999, meanwhile, The Family became intensely worried about the possible outcome of a freewheeling campaign to decide who would be the next president of Russia. They had no intent of allowing it to occur, and made one of their tasks, indeed their primary and most important task, to select that individual themselves.

The authors of the constitution envisioned this possibility as early as 1993. While transfer of power to the prime minister and early elections were supposed to be emergency provisions on the death, incapacitation or removal of a president, some also envisioned a hand over of power and even considered it desirable. "We understood that we needed to know how to transfer power," says former Yeltsin legal advisor Sergei Shakhrai. Voluntary resignation and hand over of power was "part of the political discussion" at the inception of the constitution. Open, competitive elections free from interference by those holding power is a minimal prerequisite of democratic politics. Aversion to and fear of the outcome of an open, competitive, and free political process is, at its heart, antidemocratic. However, the 1996 election had already set a precedent for circumscribing free competition, and by 1999 a commitment to open political competition was not present in the Kremlin. Indeed, Yeltsin's close advisors, which after the 1998 economic default no longer included the pro-democracy voices, opposed such a prospect altogether. Instead, they would choose.

They had a convenient and built-in mechanism for vetting possible successors. Because the constitution gave the president exclusive power over his prime minister, a president could observe and evaluate heads of government as possible successors. In his final months Yeltsin turned the prime minister post into a revolving door of potential successors, with each occupant hailed as Yeltsin's handpicked successor to assume the presidency upon his departure. [. . .]

The Family and the oligarchs genuinely feared for the future of economic policies that had enriched them, for the future of their own amassed wealth, and for their physical futures. They would not risk democratic politics in the form of open electoral competition to choose the next president. Secret Kremlin machinations would control the outcome.

When Yeltsin named him prime minister and declared him his presidential successor on August 8, 1999, Putin became the sixth head of government in just seventeen months. Because Russia's president names the prime minister, it is reasonable to assume that the latter enjoys the president's trust and support.

Accordingly, each of Yeltsin's prime ministers in his final months in office carried for the media, the public, and Kremlin insiders alike, the presumed tag of president-in-waiting. The certainty with which the claim was made only increased each time Yeltsin made a change. Viktor Chernomyrdin (twice), Sergei Kiriyenko, Yevgeniy Primakov, and Sergei Stepashin each had his turn as the universally proclaimed favorite and Yeltsin's hand-chosen successor to become the next president of Russia. With so many faces in such a short period of time, it was as if everyone was Yeltsin's preferred successor.

The dizzying turnover makes it difficult to believe that "Operation Successor," as the hand over of power to Putin became known in Russia, was planned out in its specific contours long in advance, despite some suggestions that the FSB secretly manipulated the political situation to bring one of its own to power. [. . .]

What explains this revolving door that embodied both the prime minister post and the presumed position as presidential successor? Why did Yeltsin chew through so many so rapidly? Why, indeed, was there a notion of "successor" at all under a constitution that called for free and fair elections to the top elected office in the country? More than anything else, fear and self-interest again moved Yeltsin to snuff out an open campaign for president.

Protection

The intersection of fear and greed drove antidemocratic decisions in the Kremlin. An open political competition would have risked election of a president hostile to The Family, who might launch a campaign of recrimination against and punishment of those who worked in and profited during the Yeltsin Administration. To some, "it was clear that there would be a revenge, and then Yeltsin, The Family and everyone would die," and so "a scheme was needed for handing over power to a strong [president] who would guarantee Yeltsin his personal security."

Yeltsin's daughter, Tatiana Dyachenko, was central to the final decision to hand power to Putin. She was instrumental both to the president's decision and to his emphasis on protection. As Yeltsin's health declined, Dyachenko played an ever-increasing role as advisor, gatekeeper, and confidant. She and her fiancé, Valentin Yumashev, had much at stake if their fears came to pass, for they had facilitated bringing the oligarchs into the highest circles of power, and therefore stood to be at the center of attention of any unfriendly president. It is not so much that Yeltsin sought to protect individuals such as Berezovsky, indeed there is evidence he resented the oligarchs' influence over personnel and policy in his administration and was conflicted about their presence and their role. However, Yeltsin in failing health was unable to focus on combating their growing influence. Rather, he was increasingly dependent upon and concerned about a smaller inner-circle that included his daughter, Yumashev, and perhaps one or two other aides. It was they who, in turn, watched out for their wealthy friends. The latter simply had nightmares about what might become of their fortunes and of themselves.

[T]he consequences of those first decisions in 1992 rippled through Russian politics. The effort to create a market economy without putting into place democratic political and legal institutions resulted in institutionalized corruption at the apex of power in the Kremlin. Neoliberal economic reforms without political mechanisms for accountability and legality corrupted the new system to the core. When Yeltsin's second term neared its end, fear of reprisals for that corruption moved those around the president to maneuver to install a new leader not on the basis of competence or policy, much less electoral legitimacy, but rather for the promise of protection and even the hope that they themselves might secretly control their puppet.

Yeltsin also became preoccupied with assuring his and his family's—however one wishes to interpret that word—safety. The political consequence of the 1998 default was to clean out his administration, removing those who devised his economic reform policies, such as Gaidar, Kiriyenko, and Nemtsov, as well as his political and legal staff from speech writers on down. These were replaced overwhelmingly by those with backgrounds in the various security services such as the interior ministry police, the military, and the old KGB, now the FSB. Yeltsin's search for a successor would be limited to those with military or intelligence training, who would be unquestionably loyal to Yeltsin personally. Why the security services? Because one with such a background could offer a more plausible guarantee to be able to control those with the guns, to control that sprawling security apparatus. Such control was a necessary component to being able to protect Yeltsin and his circle.

The revolving door Yeltsin created in his government reflected his search for the right person, the most trustworthy, from among those with security service backgrounds. Primakov initially seemed an obvious choice for a handpicked successor. He was in a position to protect Yeltsin and his family, as not only did he have the KGB background but also he enjoyed support from the center and left of the political spectrum, from where the greatest danger would presumably have come. Primakov was known for his independent politics, his desire to be independent of the oligarchs, and was not himself corrupt. A longtime Soviet bureaucrat, Primakov had a biography closest to Yeltsin among likely presidential hopefuls in an election, and was close in manner and of the same generation. While these attributes did not describe the oligarchs or advisors close to the president, they did describe Yeltsin himself. And this all appealed to him.

Yeltsin, however, came to doubt Primakov's loyalty. In part it was his fierce independence, but more troubling to Yeltsin was that the heart of Primakov's political support was the communist left and the nationalist right. Those were Yeltsin's main enemies. Even worse for Yeltsin was that Primakov displayed obvious ambition, he openly pined for the presidency and as he assumed more control over decision making and cemented his power as prime minister, Primakov's actions increasingly appeared threatening. Putin confirmed to a reporter at the time what many already suspected, that Primakov, with Yeltsin in a weak physical and political state, had assumed most of the functions of the presidency. Primakov "never hid his political ambitions," which made him appear more out for himself than committed to Yeltsin. The ambition, independence, and power base made Primakov for Yeltsin "an unloyal successor who was absolutely unacceptable." Whether the next president would be a heavyweight or not was less important than that the individual not be threatening to Yeltsin personally.

Primakov fell out of favor with The Family by trying to remove the oligarchs from the Kremlin. He launched investigations into their activities, part of his strategy to expand his own popularity and power. While not threatening to Yeltsin directly, who may even have approved, the oligarchs obviously wanted Primakov out. They appealed to their patrons, above all Dyachenko and Yumashev, to convince Yeltsin to make a change. The Family wanted Primakov out, and so he was out.

Primakov's strength and popularity, however, made removing him a problem. The trick would be to replace him with someone who would not be damaged by being associated with Primakov's removal. As a first step, The Family convinced Yeltsin to remove his Chief of Staff, Nikolai Bordyuzha, who increasingly appeared oriented toward the presumed successor. Bordyuzha fought back, warning Yeltsin of the massive corruption in the Kremlin, and that as a military man dedicated to serving Russia he could not continue to serve as head of the Security Council, as Yeltsin had offered. He implored Yeltsin to reconsider, and instead dismiss from the Kremlin not only the oligarchs, but also Yumashev, Voloshin, and his daughter. Whether Bordyuzha's gambit was self-interested or followed genuine ideals, it presented Yeltsin with an opportunity, another choice point that would help define the process of leadership change in Russia. Had Yeltsin chosen to follow Bordyuzha's path, it could have led to an open electoral process. He appeared noncommittal at first, saying, "Ok, I will think about this." But within hours Yeltsin dismissed Bordyuzha from all of his posts. An open electoral process was not to be, and two months later Primakov met a similar fate.

Yeltsin told Primakov, "You have fulfilled your role; now, it is clear, you will need to resign. Make this easy and sign your letter of resignation, indicating any reasons you choose," Primakov refused to do so. "I don't want to make anything easier for anyone," he said. "You have every constitutional power to sign such a decree if you wish, but. . .you will be making a huge mistake. The issue is not me but the cabinet, which has worked extremely well." Indeed, it had. Russia had emerged from default and balanced its budget. Agreement was pending with the IMF, and the government was popular both in the Duma and with the public. But for Yeltsin, Primakov had in a sense performed too well, had become too strong, and now he was threatening both the oligarchs and their benefactors. Primakov was initiating investigations into their past activities and maneuvering to remove them from positions of power. Dyachenko leaned on Yeltsin to remove Primakov, which the president did, replacing him with Stepashin.

The sigh of relief from The Family was almost publicly audible. Stepashin had held many positions and long served under Yeltsin. Surely, Yeltsin had decided to anoint his close, longtime ally to succeed him. In fact, Yeltsin used Stepashin, considering him more of a loyal soldier deployed to fill a role in a larger play than as a man with long-term leadership ability. Stepashin was also popular, but his tenure lasted a mere three months before Yeltsin replaced him with Putin, whom he immediately declared as his choice to be the next president.

Yeltsin had already decided on Putin as his preferred successor when he appointed Stepashin, but recognized that the dismissal of Primakov would be wildly unpopular in the Duma, among much of the political elite, and with the general public. He needed a sacrificial lamb to buffer the sting of Primakov's firing. Prior to naming Stepashin, in fact, Yeltsin asked legal experts whether the constitution permitted him to name an interim prime minister for a defined period. Told it did not, the constitution nevertheless permits the president to dismiss prime ministers at will, so Yeltsin named Stepashin to be an interim prime minister without telling anyone. He never intended to leave Stepashin in the post for more than a few months, relying on his devoted political friend whom he could trust to pave the way for Putin.

Yeltsin did not reward Stepashin's loyalty by informing him of his intentions. [. . .] When Yeltsin told Stapashin after less than three months in office that he was being removed, Stepashin "acted uncharacteristically for a fired premier and asked the president, 'For what reason?'" Yeltsin accused him of being weak and failing to counter political attacks from Primakov and Moscow Mayor Yuriy Luzhkov. It was a flimsy argument at best. Stepashin argued with the president, laying blame with Chief of Staff Aleksander Voloshin, a Berezovsky loyalist who, by attacking Gusinsky, propelled his media empire into the Primakov camp.

Stepashin gave Yeltsin pause and inclined him to investigate. Criminal investigations of Berezovsky and other oligarchs had exploded at the international level, such as the Bank of New York and the Harvard Institute for International Development scandals that featured millions of dollars of theft by individuals in or close to the Yeltsin Administration. Chubais tried to the last to protect Stepashin and prevent Putin's rise, having become wary of him as secretive and hard to read even though he was responsible for Putin's initial move to the Kremlin. Yeltsin had decided, however, steadfastly avoided Chubais and three days later told Stepashin, "You are free. Clean out your office for Putin. Good bye!"

Primakov and Stepashin sealed their political demise by threatening to take action against the oligarchs. The criminal investigations constituted attacks not only on the oligarchs, but by extension on their patrons. Primakov openly told the president of his intention to isolate, remove from government, and prosecute the oligarchs at the time of his dismissal. His investigations into Berezovsky and Abramovich, in particular, and his attempts to remove the oligarchs from positions of decision-making authority, proved threatening to both Dyachenko and Yumashev. It was they who ultimately convinced Yeltsin to make a change and believed Stepashin, a longtime ally, would not upset the status quo. However, Stepashin continued the investigations Primakov had launched, and confronted The Family on several occasions despite his short stint in office. It was for their stands against the oligarchs, not weakness, that both men ultimately paid.

Perhaps Primakov and Stepashin suffered also the weakness of ambition. The office of Prime Minister of Russia brought with it presumed front-runner status in the presidential election, and the presumption of Yeltsin's support for he controlled the occupant of the prime minister's office. That front-runner status naturally would make one think like a candidate, and appearing strong against the loathed oligarchs would go a long way to claiming the votes of the centrist masses in Russia. What neither seemed to grasp was that they could never sway Yeltsin to go against the wishes of his daughter and closest confidant. Yeltsin was concerned for the future safety of his family; the weakness he feared was not in the realm of decisiveness of action, but in the realm of personal loyalty. Primakov's and Stepashin's weakness was in not understanding that their actions against the oligarchs threatened Dyachenko, who would prevail upon her father to make a change. It came across as being disloyal.

Putin, however, had demonstrated that he understood the concept of unwavering loyalty toward a political patron in his protection of St. Petersburg Mayor Anatoly Sobchak. [. . .] What made Yeltsin take such special notice of this unassuming bureaucrat were his activities shortly after arriving in Moscow, in mid-1996. Local FSB investigators in St. Petersburg had begun investigating Sobchak shortly after his election defeat. The new mayor, Vladimir Yakovlev, having defeated Sobchak was now pursuing revenge. This is just what The Family feared on a much larger scale at higher levels. During a series of interrogations Sobchak took ill, suffering a heart attack. Putin went to Yumashev, saying he was trained in special operations and wanted to protect Sobchak. Yeltsin approved, and Putin organized Sobchak's escape from a St. Petersburg hospital to Paris, where he remained in exile until shortly before his death, and only after Putin was in charge of the FSB.

Yeltsin and The Family noted both the loyalty and the continuation of the peculiar Russian tendency for new leaders to take action against their predecessors. Putin later waged a scathing campaign to discredit the Prosecutor General, Skuratov, producing a videotape of him naked in a hotel room with two prostitutes. None of the identities of those in the fuzzy video could be confirmed, but the damage was done, the prosecutor's career was over. He had rid the oligarchs of a prosecutor investigating their activities, and they certainly took note. The Family, which hoped for a future president who would protect them, was most impressed that this attack against Sobchak emanated from Putin's own agency. Putin had proven himself to be loyal to those who helped him, and able to direct the forces that could protect them. It seemed clear that Putin would prioritize personal loyalty over institutional or other loyalties. As Putin arrived in Moscow a virtual political unknown, those who promoted his rise to the apex of power hoped to reap such similar rewards from their client. They believed if they promoted Putin, he would be entirely in their debt, under their control, and they would all be safe. When Yumashev asked a skeptical Igor Malashenko of NTV to support Putin as Yeltsin's successor, he assured Malashenko, "He didn't give up Sobchak. He won't give us up." In the end, this could not have been more wrong, at least as it pertained to the press.

Putin is not a politician and shows little in the way of traditional political skills. Initial reports describe a man extremely uncomfortable and not particularly skilled in public political settings. Most notably, he had absolutely no competence or real interest in dealing with members of the media. He conducted himself less like a politician than he did as an intelligence officer, a spy, or a bureaucrat. Unlike Primakov, Putin did not demonstrate any political ambitions because he likely had none. At the time of his appointment as prime minister, his popularity rating stood at 2 percent, largely because nobody knew who he was or for what he stood. His purpose was to serve those above him. As for political views, Yeltsin knew little more about Putin than anyone else in the country did, which is to say, he did not know much at all. Yeltsin most wanted, as was the case in 1996, to prevent Zyuganov and the Communist Party, or anyone who would threaten him and his family, from coming to power. Promoting Putin did just that. [. . .]

If there were any doubts about Putin's control of the guns, within weeks of his taking over as prime minister several explosions rocked apartment buildings in Moscow and other cities, killing over 300 people and injuring several hundred more. As with the 1996 Moscow apartment bombings, no credible explanation exists regarding who was responsible for the explosions. But the events conveniently served to send Putin's approval rating skyrocketing upward as he presented a military face to the country and a promise of an overwhelming response. The perpetrators were never found, but the results benefitted the new leader, and claims abound that the explosions were the work not of Chechen terrorists but of Russian security officials conducting special operations on behalf of their bosses. Whether these were the work of Putin, Berezovsky, or the FSB remains unknown.

What is known is that from political oblivion, Putin used the bombs as a pretense to launch a second war against Chechnya and he garnered near-universal support. Unlike the first war, the initial weeks the new campaign, while equally savage, appeared far more successful. Russian troops swarmed into Chechnya and quickly seized control of the capital, Grozny. Putin trumpeted Russia's strength, military prowess, security and order, and doing all of that in a successful war he could present as punishing terrorists, whom he famously promised to wipe out "even if we catch them in the bathroom." The air of competence and the focus on restoring order and strength to the country all appealed to a public tired of disorder and malaise.

On the day of Putin's appointment as prime minister, Yeltsin openly declared him his preferred successor. When asked about Putin's chance of becoming president, the experienced political analyst Aleksey Volin found the notion laughable. The only scenario he could construct that would "enable a hopeless client, with such low ratings and no public face" to become president was, "A small winnable war." Putin's ratings after the explosions and start of the war against Chechnya rose several percentage points each week.

The Decision to Hand the Presidency to Putin

Appointing Putin prime minister, indicating a preference, and supporting him in a presidential election would have been one thing. Though hardly consistent with Washington's precedent of staying out of the fray, a fair and competitive election was theoretically possible. Handing Putin the presidency was another thing altogether. This was neither necessary nor preordained. It was another conscious decision, and an extraordinary one in the face of the available alternatives. Yeltsin could have completed his term and waited out the campaign, or he could have remained in office but announced early elections. He could have overseen, even ensured, an honest campaign and vote to determine the next president, and left a lasting, pro-democratic legacy. Instead, he chose to hand the leadership of Russia to Putin, a momentous decision that left a legacy of a final blow to democracy.

The people of Russia still have never selected their political leader in a free and open competition, nor experienced an open transfer of power.

The story of how Yeltsin decided to sidestep electoral competition and hand power to Putin remains murky to this day. Few details are known, and many may never be known. In some respects it bore the stamp of a typical Yeltsin decision. First, Putin was now wildly popular, with the Chechen war an apparent success with Russian troops overrunning the secessionist forces. He presented a strong and confident face, particularly next to the infirm Yeltsin. He had shown unfailing loyalty to those who had supported him in the past and could be hoped to do so for Yeltsin and his circle in the future. As prime minister he already enjoyed presidential powers with control over the military action in Chechnya. He was capable, loyal, and popular, and Yeltsin may have decided that the task was done, so why wait?

Second, Yeltsin himself was visibly weak; his speech slowed and slurred, his attention span short, he had not been able to fulfil the duties of his office for much of his second term. The aesthetics and theatrics provided by a millennium hand over of power offered the finishing touch to the decision, but not the basis. What was clear to everyone else was likely also clear to Yeltsin: his control over his administration and government was anemic at best. [. . .] The reality of still being president but influencing little likely became intolerable to him. The rigging of the 1996 election left Russia with a president who lacked the energy needed for the job.

Third, and perhaps the most important, a powerful attraction to Yeltsin was the desire to decide for himself, and on his own terms, the moment and method of his departure. The written process in the constitution and election laws seemed arbitrary and forced. The idea of "a nice political exit" was more appealing and a hand over offered him the ability to create just such an exit. As he had no right to another term, said one of the constitution's main authors, "to sit for a year and wait, even less than a year, this would have been stupid." Yeltsin "is also one who loved theatrical actions. He loved to plan things ahead. So that he was the author of the situation, so he could dictate the conditions." The popularly accepted end of the millennium on December 31, 1999, provided an opportunity for a poetic end to the Yeltsin era, a chance to leave not merely on his own terms but with an unprecedented flourish, with fireworks and parties around the world the likes of which had never been seen. Yeltsin liked a party, and here was a party like no other. He would add to the bang.

Dyachenko, Yumashev, and Voloshin wrote Yeltsin's final address to the country in which he announced his decision. [. . .] But it was Yeltsin himself who made this decision. It came as a surprise to virtually everyone, including those inside the Kremlin, up to the last minute. [. . .]

Elections as Window Dressing

The methods used to erode free competition in the 1996 elections concentrated overwhelming electoral resources and access squarely in the office of the president. As a result, when Yeltsin handed Putin the office, he also effectively handed him the election. Putin now enjoyed overwhelming resources and a shortened electoral time line, for the law required that the election take place within three months of Yeltsin's resignation, that is, three months earlier than would have been the case under the standard election rhythm. The hand over predetermined the outcome in favor of Yeltsin's chosen successor.

It need not have happened this way. Yeltsin, the dominant political figure in Russia for a decade, was exiting the stage. Anticipation was high for an election campaign with an equal playing field, with a number of prospective presidential candidates such as Primakov, Stepashin, Yavlinsky, Zyuganov, and others. It had the potential to be an election like none Russia had yet experienced, a truly competitive race in which the people would decide who would lead the country. The six months leading up to the June elections could have been an open and free-wheeling campaign, raucous and exciting. Had Yeltsin stood on the sidelines, completed his term and allowed society to choose the next president, Russia's future may have looked entirely different. Even had Putin run as prime minister, with Yeltsin remaining on the sidelines while a campaign proceeded, it could have been an open contest. [. . .]

But the hand over of power to Putin prevented that open process. From inside the Kremlin, with Berezovsky committed to guaranteeing his victory, Putin now controlled the media and overwhelming financial resources. Following the 1996 script, he and his loyalists trumped up scandals and systematically annihilated all potential opponents, including Primakov and Moscow Mayor Yuriy Lyuzhkov. Potential candidates immediately saw the futility of trying to oppose this onslaught. Similarly, mysterious and unsolved apartment bombings and murders in advance of the elections, again eerily similar to 1996, including murders of journalists critical of Putin, whipped up demands for order and lifted the popularity of the former-KGB agent. It all foreshadowed the most disturbing aspects of the coming authoritarian regime. And it all followed an exaggerated version of the precedent set in the 1996 election cycle. Putin left no doubt about the outcome. Russia still has not had an open, democratic election for its national political leader.

Academics and journalists in the West, however, blinded by their desire to see democracy proclaimed Russia's first free and fair democratic, constitutional leadership change. McFaul was most influential, and on television and in print he trumpeted the March 2000 coronation of Putin as the triumph of Russian democracy. Not wishing to see an authoritarian hand over of power, to an obscure KGB official no less, he and others chose to see that there was a vote, that there was more than one candidate, that the votes were counted and that the one with the most votes won. Elections were now the "only game in town," the constitution had rules for elections that were followed. This was enough for those desperate to see democracy to proclaim its triumph, ignoring the effects of Yeltsin's handing the office to Putin.

Elections were not even the most important game in town, much less the only one, and they were certainly not democratic. Both the campaign and the election carried clear authoritarian warnings. For example, although no proof was offered and none has since been forthcoming, Putin immediately blamed the numerous apartment bombings around the country on Chechen terrorists and used them as a pretext to launch a new war against Chechnya. Former presidential candidate, National Security Advisor, and regional governor General Aleksander Lebed is reported to have been "convinced" that the Kremlin was behind the bombings as a pretext for launching an invasion of Chechnya in advance of the election. The Russian public wildly approved, propelling Putin's popularity rating skyward. As with the 1996 apartment bombings, the government never offered any proof of any individual or group responsible, and never brought anyone to justice. Evidence of FSB involvement and Kremlin complicity, however, is strong enough to demand it not be brushed aside as wild conspiracy theory, particularly in the absence of evidence to support Putin's claim. As one Putin critic put it:

> Putin was a nobody; he became president and a hero simply as a result of an enormous television crusade, using the war in Chechnya as an instrument. They offered a simple thesis: "They are bombing us in our homes—here is a man who can defend us." And this effectively broke the spine of any possible opposition. Remember how they destroyed such mastodons as Primakov and Lyuzhkov. This was all organized and planned, this entire project of Putin's had an absolutely primitive goal from the point of view of Yeltsin's clan, to prevent the coming to power of the Primakov and Lyuzhkov clan.

Berezovsky's network portrayed Primakov as senile and Lyuzhkov as stupid. The entire political elite that had been rallying behind Primakov "got scared and accepted these rules of the game, and said, 'No, we don't need this Primakov when we have Colonel Putin who is all we need.'" It was essentially the same with Gusinsky, whose rival NTV network also savaged Primakov, Lyuzhkov, and their electoral alliance, though Gusinsky as always backed Yavlinsky's Yabloko.

What did "Yeltsin's clan" have to do with all of this? It was The Family that wished at a minimum to gain protection and perhaps even to remain in power. Certainly Berezovsky wished for both. The sudden creation of a hero in Putin, in the face of an emergency, created a hysteria similar to the one this same team created in 1996, one that would destroy any remnants of Primakov's popularity and cement Putin's. Whether or not they created the crisis, there can be no doubt that the crisis was beneficial politically and that the Kremlin pounced on the opportunity to make every use of it. In later years, independent investigators into Putin's role have been arrested or, as in the case of Aleksander Litvinenko, killed under suspicious circumstances, as have prominent politicians such as Sergei Yushenkov, who had detailed knowledge of the evidence and was outspokenly critical of Putin. Berezovsky, who certainly was in a position to know, went public with accusations and evidence, including supporting a documentary film produced by two French journalists after Putin moved against his media and financial holdings and forced him into exile.

Berezovsky knew what he was talking about because he had helped bring about and was firmly behind Putin's promotion, and he led the effort leading up to the campaign. He came up with the idea of a party and the name "Unity," at a meeting of The Family—Yumashev, Dyachenko, Berezovsky, and others—at which Putin is reported to have remained silent. Putin built on the 1996 experience of Kremlin involvement with the media, using Berezovsky and his control over the largest television network to savage his principle opponents. Berezovsky installed Sergei Dorenko in the news anchor chair at Channel One, from where he hammered away at Putin's opponents while affording them no chance to respond. He accused them of murders, of bad health, and of corruption, all under direction from and coordination with the Kremlin. The onslaught was so badly damaging in the parliamentary elections that Primakov and most other serious candidates opted out of the presidential elections after Yeltsin resigned. Only Zyuganov remained among the candidates who could garner significant votes, and he would meet the same fate as in 1996. Primakov and Lyuzhkov's Fatherland alliance went from favorite to a distant third place finish in the Duma elections in the wake of the personal attacks and scandals of questionable accuracy. Gusinsky, supporting as always in parliamentary elections Yavlinsky's "Yabloko" party, unwittingly aided and abetted Putin's ultimate triumph by piling on in the attacks against the two erstwhile favorites.

As if to remove any doubt that the results had been fixed, Dyachenko was oddly nonchalant about Putin's rapid turnaround from a 3 percent rating to electoral victory in a matter of a few weeks, telling a journalist, "What unexpected results are you talking about? We had this all completely figured out from the very beginning." In addition to the war and the media control, Putin and his supporters apparently rigged the vote itself. On the day of the parliamentary elections, Kremlin officials fed the results of their victory to "their" media outlets.

Boasting, "See how we work!" a giddy Yumashev presented a text message of the results on his pager to a correspondent, dated early morning of election day. The results, not surprisingly, proved exceedingly accurate. They had been written up before the voting had even begun. Broadcast of results before the close of all polling stations was illegal, "But there was simply nobody around to bring the victors to justice." The reports early in the day quite likely had the effect of boosting Unity's victory, as those who may have voted for others stayed home, already having been told that their preferred representatives had lost. It also helped to reward SPS for its capitulation, by helping it to cross the 5 percent barrier and thereby gain a few seats in the Duma. Whether Dyachenko's claim of strategic prowess was bravado or not, there is little room to doubt they rigged the election.

By exerting control over the media, launching a war under possibly sinister circumstances, undermining election campaigns using similar tactics, and meddling with election results, Putin ensured victory in the parliamentary and presidential elections for himself and his handpicked group of KGB and security officers who would respond to his bidding. The processes introduced in 1996 had ballooned to such an extent as to make farcical any notion that what was taking place was either free or fair.

Of course, Putin also presented the population with a figure they were prepared to embrace, a leadership style they were amenable to be swayed toward. He offered a stark contrast to Yeltsin in his strict nature, decisive language, and his emphasis on discipline and order. This phenomenon was familiar across the postcommunist space. While Putin was not the candidate of the Communist Party and did not actively trumpet a return to socialist values, he was KGB, promised a strengthening of the state, and represented a familiar image that proved attractive to a large segment of the population. He exploited these sentiments to the fullest in his dizzying rise to the apex of Russian politics.

Dictatorship as a Consequence

The consequences of the hand over of power were grave both for the constitution and even for the most basic hopes of a bare minimum electoral democracy. The 2000 election cycle, by repeating the 1996 precedents of creating crises and hysteria and exerting Kremlin control over the media, institutionalized these practices. It also established that the presidency in Russia changes with a hand over, rather than an open electoral competition for the most important office in the country. [. . .] These are not trivial issues; they are the cornerstones of Russian authoritarianism.

As for the constitution, Article 92 spells out the procedures for when a president resigns, dies, is incapacitated, or removed from office upon impeachment. The prime minister is to become acting president, and elections must be held within ninety days. Resigning six months before the end of a term to hand power to a chosen successor violates the spirit of the provision. It violated any pretense to democracy by choking the regular rhythm of presidential elections. Yeltsin invoked extreme, emergency provisions to effect a desired political outcome. Shakhrai suggests that he and others who had a hand in crafting the constitution intended the provision as a loophole to allow for a hand over of power, which he claims also to have advocated. It is not possible to have it both ways. Either the constitution is intended as a document to foster the development of a democratic system and Yeltsin violated the spirit of the document, or democracy was never intended in the first place.

[. . .] Within a few months, Putin's actions made it plain to see that Russia was heading not toward, but further and further away from democracy. It is an authoritarian system and the future bodes even worse.

7.2

Russian Elections: An Oxymoron of Democracy

Misha Myagkov and Peter C. Ordeshook

Introduction

On the basis of official election returns, the late Alexander Sobyanin argued that vote counting in Russia's 1993 constitutional referendum had been falsified to push turnout above the fifty percent threshold required for ratification and that the balancing of the books necessitated by the falsified figures accounted for the surprising success of Vladimir Zhirinovsky's LDPR in the parliamentary election held in conjunction with the referendum.

Three years later, in the 1996 presidential contest, Boris Yeltsin, rising seemingly from the 'political dead' as judged by his single digit approval ratings, won reelection after being forced into a runoff by his Communist opponent, Gennady Zyuganov—an election that saw some incredulous reversals in official voting statistics between rounds that favored Yeltsin.

In the next presidential contest, in 2000, a then obscure KGB bureaucrat from St. Petersburg, Vladimir Putin, succeeded Yeltsin after being elevated to the post of prime minister and after the Kremlin's party (Unity), with 23.3 percent of the vote, upset a seemingly 'sure thing' in the fortunes of Moscow mayor Yury Luzhkov and ex-prime minister Yevgeny Primakov's party (Fatherland-All Russia, with 13.3%) a few months earlier in 1999 parliamentary contest.

In 2004 an admittedly popular Putin won reelection by the largest margin in post-Soviet voting in an election in which, as we argue elsewhere, officials awarded upwards of 10 million or more suspicious votes on his behalf. Finally, after all explicitly anti-Kremlin opposition had been muffled, barred from the ballot, jailed or cowered into submission in 2007, Putin's party, United Russia, won a landslide victory and secured enough seats to amend the constitution and override the veto of any succeeding president.

Source: Misha Myagkov and Peter Ordeshook, "Russian Elections: An Oxymoron of Democracy". NCEEER Study. April 2008.

Note: Notes and references have been removed from this article.

Measuring Fraud and its Significance

Only Kremlin apologists and Putin sycophants argue that Russian elections meet the standards of good democratic practice. As ex-Premier Mikhail Gorbachev said, "Something is wrong with our elections." However, the question arises as to whether Russia's post-Soviet elections are but part of a flawed yet gradually maturing political system in which fraud and electoral skullduggery in various forms are mere irritants in a still-imperfect transition or whether fraud of a more malignant type has increased in extent and severity to where the idea of a democratic election in Russia is now an oxymoron.

In asking this question we emphasize that the fraud that concerns us is not the sort normally cited by observers or journalists, such as ad hoc barriers to the registration of parties and candidates or state sanctioned limits on access to the media. Rather, our concern is with acts of a more criminal nature—the stuffing of ballot boxes, explicit intimidation of voters, and the manipulation and whole-sale fabrication of official vote counts. Here we argue that fraud of this sort has now infected and metastasized within the Russian polity to such as extent that we must also assume that the powers that be in the Kremlin either has no control of their own politicians in their competition to please Putin or it no longer cares whether the West or anyone else judges their elections as free and fair or whether they are in fact a transitional democracy at all.

It may have been that in initially facilitating the formation of a party, Just Russia, to compete against his own, Putin preferred to encourage the image of a competitive democracy. But trends in official election returns are now consistent with the proposition that Russian policy is dominated by the view, "To hell with the West—they need our oil and gas too much to object to anything we say or do." Regardless of whether it is a loss of control or a shift in policy to one that ignores the West and definitions of democracy, this essay examines one indicator of aberrant official election data to argue that the 'oxymoron hypothesis' is a sustainable one.

1995 Through 2003

Let us begin, not with 1995, but with the presidential election of 1996 since it, unlike any other, generated a unique set of data by requiring a runoff between the top two challengers—Yeltsin and his Communist Party opponent, Zyuganov. The immediate background to this election was Yeltsin's apparent vulnerability prior to the first round, which made it difficult for regional officials to know who to back if they wished to curry favor with the eventual winner (and throughout Russian history it has rarely been a good or healthy thing to back someone other than whoever ultimately controls the Kremlin).

Yeltsin's competition came not only from Zyuganov but also from the then popular general Alexander Lebed and the pro-reform Grigori Yavlinski who, minimally, threatened to siphon off enough votes to raise the possibility that Zyuganov might ultimately prevail. Nevertheless, reflecting in part the power of the oligarchs who supported him and the significant share of the Russian electorate that, then at least, sought to avoid a return to their communist past, Yeltsin led the field with 35.3 percent of the vote, followed by Zyuganov with 32.0%, Lebed with 14.5%, Yavlinsky with 7.3% and the ultra-nationalist Zhirinovsky with 5.7%.

Despite the closeness of the vote, it was apparent that Yeltsin would most likely prevail in the runoff. With Boris Berezovsky and his media empire leading a cadre of oligarchs strongly opposed to a Zyuganov victory and Lebed no longer on the ballot, not only was Yeltsin likely to win a majority of Lebed's vote and virtually all of Yavlinsky's, but the power of the oligarchs to resurrect Yeltsin's viability was now evident to those regional political bosses who had otherwise sat on the fence or even initially backed his opponents. If there was, then, an incentive to commit to and make special efforts for Yeltsin, it came between rounds with the supposition that Zyuganov was approaching the ever-lower 'glass ceiling' of support thru which no Communist candidate could pass.

"Special efforts", though, come in a variety of forms. They vary from simple endorsements to biased media coverage to outright fraud in the form of stuffed ballot boxes and manipulated official election returns. That fraud in the classic criminal sense was not wholly absent in 1996 is attested to by the example of the rayon (county) in Tatarstan that officially reported 2,064 and 7,461 first round votes for Yeltsin and Zyuganov respectively, but which subsequently awarded 8,512 votes for Yeltsin in the second round and a mere 2,050 for Zyuganov. Even if we assume that everyone who supported some third candidate in the first round returned to the polls in the runoff to vote for Yeltsin, fully 73 percent of Zyuganov's initial vote (5,411 voters) would have had to switch to Yeltsin in order to account for the official numbers. Then we have the rayon, also in Tatarstan, that gave Yeltsin and Zyuganov 7,436 and 10,841 votes respectively in the first round, but reported 21,777 votes for Yeltsin and a mere 1,428 for Zyuganov in the second, thus requiring that no less than 87 percent of the communist's vote (9,413 voters) switch sides between rounds. Such switches, of course, strain credulity and it is more reasonable to suppose that these official numbers bore little relation to actual ballots.

Such examples occasion two questions when tracing the progression of electoral fraud. First, how pervasive are such reversals? And second, where did they arise? The answers are straightforward, at least for 1996. Although the magnitude of 'incredulous switches' is nearly matched in several other rayons of Tatarstan and the republic of Dagestan, of the 2,327 rayons in our 1996 data set, only 194 saw Yeltsin's vote increase between rounds and Zyuganov's decrease. And on the flip side, only 30 rayons reported an increase in Zyuganov's support in conjunction with a decrease in Yeltsin's. Thus, even if we ignore the fact that many of these reversals are of insignificant magnitude and do not match our earlier examples, only 224 rayons, or less than ten percent of the total, yield a suspicious pattern.

Moreover, the reversals that do raise suspicions are concentrated almost exclusively in Russia's ethnic republics—regions that are rarely identified with good democratic practice. For example, of the 194 rayons reporting reversals that favored Yeltsin, only twenty three (12%) occur in oblasts as opposed to republics. The remaining 171 reversals occur in ethnic republics, and are most heavily concentrated in the "usual suspects": Tatarstan, Dagestan and Bashkortostan. Slightly more than half of Bashkortostan's rayons report reversals favoring Yeltsin (53%), while fully 85 percent of rayons report such reversals in both Tatarstan and Dagestan. Thus, these three republics account for fully two thirds of all reversals in the ethnic republics.

In all other regions, in contrast, the shift in votes seems unexceptional. In Moscow, for instance, Yeltsin won 2,861,258 votes in the first round and 3,629,464 in the second—a 27 percent gain over his initial support—while Zyuganov won 694,862 votes in the first round and 842,092 in the second—a 21 percent gain over his initial vote. Surely there is no surprise that Yeltsin did appreciably better than his opponent in Russia's most urban and reform-minded region in 1996, yet even here Zyuganov captured some votes in the runoff that went to other candidates in the first round.

There is another way to look at this data that is especially useful when comparing elections and which moves us to an assessment of fraud in the form of stuffed ballot boxes, voters coerced into voting, or manipulated and even wholly fabricated official totals. Suppose an electorate consists of two types of election districts—those that, for one reason or another, are susceptible to fraud in this form and those that are not. Assume that absent fraud, the distribution of turnout for both types looks approximately identical and normal in the statistical sense (i.e., some districts report higher turnout than average, some report lower turnout, but the bulk report turnout near the average and both averages roughly coincide). The overall distribution of turnout nationally, then, will also be approximately normally distributed (i.e., unimodal).

Now suppose that in districts susceptible to fraud, fraud occurs in the way previously cited—the stuffing of ballot boxes with falsified ballots, compelling voters to vote who otherwise might prefer to stay home via various threats and forms of intimidation, or by simply adding to a candidate's total in official summaries without regard to votes actually cast. The distribution of turnout for those districts, then, will be shifted to the right, with the initial effect of creating an 'elongated right tail' for the overall distribution. That is, if falsifications of this sort are 'slight', the national distribution of turnout will appear skewed left. But as falsifications increase in magnitude so that the shift in the district subsample increases, that 'tail' will become a second mode to the right of the original one so as to render the overall distribution bimodal.

Now consider Figure 1, which graphs the turnout distributions for all of Russia's national elections between 1995 and 2003, where we restrict the data to rayons from its oblasts. Clearly there is nothing here of a suspicious nature: All distributions are approximately normal without discernable perturbations. Indeed, the distributions for the three presidential ballots (the first and second rounds of 1996, and 2000) are nearly identical and are about as perfect a match to a normal distribution as we are likely to find in any set of empirical data.

Figure 1. Distributions of Turnout, oblasts

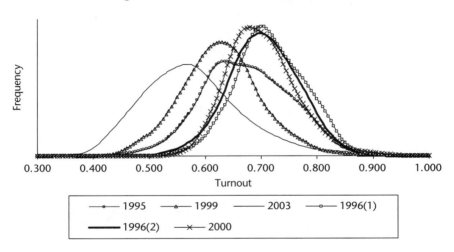

But now consider Figures 2a and 2b, which replicate Figure 1 using data from Russia's ethnic republics, although now we separate presidential and Duma contests to make trends more evident. Here we see two things: First, the distributions are no longer normal; there is a discernable "bump" in each. And second, with respect to trends, the bump increases in severity in both figures as we move from 1995 to 2003. These data, then, are consistent with two hypotheses: (1) whatever manipulations of turnout occurred in Russia between 1995 and 2003 occurred for the most part in its ethnic republics; and (2) the severity of those manipulations increased incrementally over time.

The graph in Figure 2b for the 2003 Duma vote is interesting for another reason. Notice that in addition to becoming bimodal, the left-most node—corresponding ostensibly to those republic rayons in which there were little or no outright falsifications—diminishes significantly in size. Thus, not only do Figures 2a and 2b suggest that artificially augmented turnout grew more severe in specific suspect republics, but that its scope expanded to include republics that were previously untouched by such malfeasance.

Figure 2a. Distribution of turnout, Presidential elections, republics

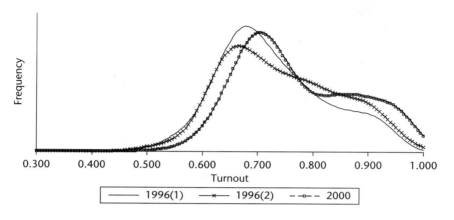

Figure 2b. Distribution of turnout, Duma elections, republics

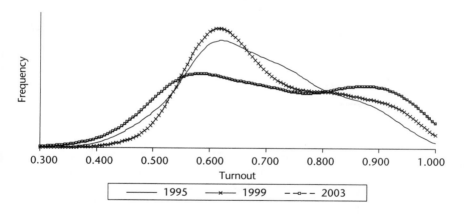

The 2004 Presidential Contest

A word of caution is warranted here. Deviations from normality in the distribution of turnout can arise, of course, if there is significant non-homogeneity in the data— if one subset of precincts or districts owing any number of demographic reasons has a 'normal' higher rate of turnout than another subset. Differences in turnout among urban and rural regions, for example, then, might occasion non-normal distributions when those districts are mixed. For this reason, then, the trend in the data that Figures 2a and 2b suggest are especially important since we know of no demographic shift within Russia's ethnic republics that might explain the appearance of a right mode in the distribution of turnout. Nevertheless, the preceding data are subject to two benign interpretations. First, with respect to Russia's oblasts, although political elites there may have used various 'administrative resources' to support one candidate or party or another between 1995 and 2003, whatever advantage they established was not so great or of a form to discredit the process. If there was fraud in the oblasts our method fails to detect, it seems to have remained a constant—neither increasing nor decreasing over time. Second, with respect to Russia's ethnic republics, a skeptic (or Kremlin apologist) we might argue that the trend we observe is merely the acceleration of differences between, say, republics of one type with as yet undiscovered distinguishing characteristics as that type adapts to democracy and as the other type lags behind in its democratic development. This 'explanation' though is undermined first by the evident examples of fraud (e.g, 100% turnout rates and 100% support for a specific candidate or party) in republics we know *a priori* are permeated by fraud (e.g. Tatarstan and Dagestan) and is undermined as well by the sudden upsurge of turnout in other self-evidently corrupt republics (e.g., Chechnya) which cannot be accounted for by any shift in demographics. Nevertheless, at worst, fraud of a magnitude that might cause us to question the overall legitimacy of an election appears to have remained largely isolated in a subset of republics so that an apologist might reasonably argue that Russia compared favorably with voting in the early 1800s in an evolving American republic where counties in, for instance, New Jersey often reported turnout in excess of 100%.

The presidential election of 2004, though, is quite different. Riding a wave of approval over his handling of Chechnya, feeding off the fears of bomb blasts in Moscow of suspect origin, and enjoying the resources afforded by rising energy prices, Putin's reelection was a forgone conclusion from the start—a fact confirmed by his garnering of 71.3 percent of the vote as compared to his closet rival, the Communist Party's nominee, Nikolay Kharitonov with 13.9 percent. Indeed, the writing on the wall was sufficiently clear that Kharitonov sought to withdraw from the race, but was kept on the ballot by the Central Election Commission, presumably because some opposition was deemed necessary to give the election the semblance of legitimacy.

Naturally, Putin's inevitable victory impacted the strategic imperatives of regional bosses in an unambiguous way: Support the incumbent or suffer the consequences. We can even say that regional bosses were trapped in a Prisoners' Dilemma: With no boss wanting to show less support for Putin than any other (aside from a few quixotic figures), each was compelled to exert the maximum effort to that end, fair or foul and regardless of how absurd official returns might appear. We have, for instance, Nurlatinski rayon in Tatarstan (again) in which, of 43 precincts, 33 reported turnout of 100 percent, and of those 24 awarded Putin 100% of the vote. More generally, the consequence of the strategic imperative occasioned by a sure winner is illustrated in Figure 3.

Figures 3. Distribution of turnout, 2004 compared to 2000

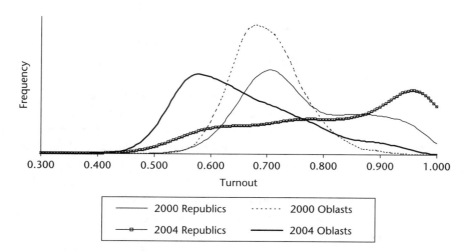

As before, this figure graphs the distribution of turnout after we separate republics from oblasts, and the most evident fact here is that despite the overall national decline in turnout (from 69 percent in 2000 to 64 percent), we see a dramatic shift to the right of the distribution for republics. The explanation for that shift lies in the fact that, in addition to habitually suspect Tatarstan, Dagestan and Bashkortostan, we now have the republics of Ingushetia, Kabardino-Balkaria, North Ossetia and Chechnya all reporting turnout in excess of 90 percent, with Putin, in Soviet-era style, being officially awarded, respectively, 98, 97, 91 and 92 percent of the vote (one wonders how many mujahideen came down from their mountain hideaways disguised as babushkas, circumvented a Russian military with orders to shoot to kill, and cast ballots for their nemesis so as to raise his Chechnya vote twenty one points above the national average).

The election of 2004, however, is not a critically important juncture in Russian politics simply because of the unambiguous pervasiveness of fraud in the republics. The change in the turnout distribution among oblasts, although nowhere near as dramatic as among republics, is also important. Looking again at Figure 3 we see an overall general shift left in that distribution, corresponding to the national decline in turnout for an election that was a forgone conclusion. However, we also see a 'sticky' or elongated tail that makes the distribution begin to approximate what we observed for republics in 1995 and 1996. In other words, a number of oblast rayons were not a part of the general decline in turnout and a few even reported increases in participation.

We can, in fact, identify the type of rayons most susceptible to fraud. Regional bosses in rural areas hold the greatest sway over voting since it is areas removed from urban centers that afford them a near monopoly on information and, oftentimes, on the employment of local bureaucrats. With this in mind, consider Figure 4, which graphs turnout for 2004 as before, but separates urban from rural rayons in the republics and oblasts. The picture here is striking: In the oblasts, the 'sticky tail' identified in Figure 3 is most noticeable among rural oblasts, and the distortion in the distribution of turnout within republics occurs most dramatically among rural rayons as well.

Figure 4. Turnout distribution, 2004, urban vs. rural rayons

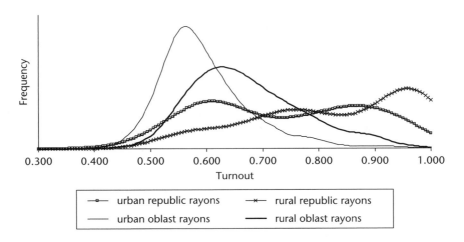

Figure 4 reveals another pattern: A nearly symmetric bimodal distribution among urban republic rayons, which is consistent with approximately half of those districts resisting fraud in some way while the other half succumb to reporting artificially augmented turnout. As to when this effect was first felt, Figures 5a and 5b provide an answer. Although we can see slight perturbations in the right tail of the distributions in Figure 5a for presidential elections prior to 2004, they are far too small to be significant. Figure 5b, on the other hand, shows that the parliamentary election of 2003 represents a break with the past. Thus, it was in the middle of Putin's first administration, before the 2004 presidential campaign officially began that fraud's scope expanded to infect not only the republic's rural areas, but their urban centers as well.

Figure 5c adds an interesting caveat to this story. There we again graph the distribution of turnout among rural oblast rayons, but now we compare that distribution to 1999, 2000, and 2003, whose distributions follows a logical and unexceptional pattern: Turnout is greatest overall for the 2000 presidential contest and shifts left-wards in 2003 to a level below that of the competitive parliamentary vote of 1999. However, all three distributions are unexceptional. It is only the distribution for 2004, with its elongated right tail, that looks suspicious. The

Figure 5a. Presidential turnout distribution, urban republic rayons

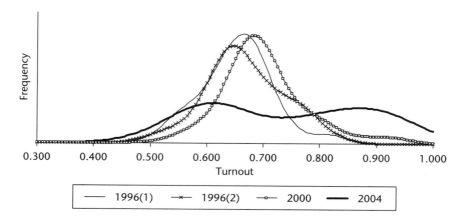

Figure 5b. Duma turnout distribution, urban republic rayons

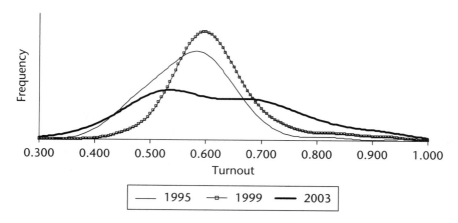

implication here, then, is that although the parliamentary vote in 2003 presaged 2004 in the republics with respect to manipulations and falsifications, such effects appeared in rural oblasts only in 2004.

We are hardly surprised that a discernable level of outright falsification of ballots and official summaries did not wait until 2004 to expand in scope among the republics. Russian parliamentary elections are little more than primaries for the forthcoming presidential contests, and in 2003 it was evident that United Russia was Putin's new party of power and the parliamentary vote but a prelude to his recoronation. If regional bosses were to demonstrate their loyalty to the Kremlin, they had little incentive to wait until 2004 and every incentive to jump on the

Figure 5c. Turnout distribution, rural oblasts

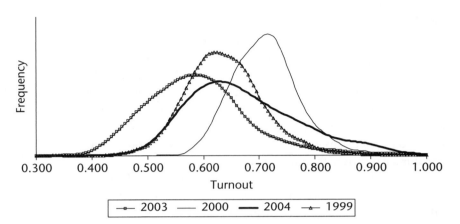

bandwagon as soon as possible. What is surprising is that the evidence of fraud within rural oblasts is weak to nonexistent in 2003 (as judged by our method). Nevertheless, regardless of the explanation for this differential timing, the fact remains that as we move into 2004 we see the sometimes gradual and sometimes accelerated increase in the scope and magnitude of fraud over time in both republics and oblasts.

The 2007 Duma vote

Setting aside trends within Russia's republics, we want to emphasize that, as Figures 3 and 4 suggest, our assessment of turnout suggests that fraud in 2004 began to infect parts of Russia—its oblasts—that previously gave the appearance of a reasonably fair counting of ballots (which isn't to say, of course, that other 'administrative measures' weren't applied to favor one candidate or another). We also should note that there is little journalistic evidence to prove or even suggest that fraud in 2004 was directed or even explicitly sanctioned by the Kremlin. It may have been that Putin still sought to wear a democratic mask but found himself unable to control the actions of regional bosses and elites who, as we note above, had a clear incentive to ensure a solid victory for him in the areas under their control. Even if they knew the Kremlin would be less than overjoyed to have examples of blatant electoral irregularities brought to the attention of Western governments and media, they also knew that inflating Putin's vote would hardly yield negative legal or political consequences. And with regional governors now being appointed rather than directly elected, it was far more personally dangerous to operate with restraint or to allow any effective opposition to Putin.

Suppose, however, that rather than reign in regional elites and pressure them to avoid the electoral excess of 2004, in 2007 Putin chose a different strategy—one designed to assert Russia's independence from the West, and to demonstrate to others the West's (specifically, the European Union's) impotence and dependence on Russia. What better way to do that than by reverting back to a Soviet-era electoral style wherein regional elites are allowed to operate as before, election observers from OSCE are pointedly denied access, and with bluff and bravado, officials are directed to assert that Russia's elections are as free and fair as anyone else's—and then to simply ignore the sarcasm of journalists and the grumblings of Western politicians and bureaucrats who are more concerned with the flow of natural gas than of fraudulent ballots?

That fraud again occurred in 2007 in the form of stuffed ballot boxes and falsified official summaries is self-evident. We can only conclude on the basis of official returns that the mujahideen of Chechnya again descended from their mountain hideaways to vote, this time in greater numbers than before, so as to raise turnout to a remarkable 99.2 percent with 99.4 percent going to Putin's United Russia. Thus, of the 580,000 registered voters in Chechnya, only 3,000 are reported not to have participated.

Then there is the republic of Ingushetiya which replicated its remarkable turnout from the previous election of 98 percent. This time, however, the dissident website ingushetiya.ru began a campaign of collecting the signatures and passport numbers of registered voters who certified that they hadn't voted. As of December 23, 2007, fully 57,898 certified signatures had been collected, representing 36 percent of the republic's registered electorate! And while, with the returns from Chechnya in mind, the Western media may have chuckled at the assertion of Vladimir Churov, chairman of Russia's Central Election Commission, that he knew of "no serious violations in the course of polling day", there is also the rayon in the republic of Karachaevo-Cherkessia in which *all* 15 voting stations reported 100 percent turnout (17,779 voters) with 100 percent of the vote going to United Russia.

These Soviet-era type numbers, though, do not tell us about overall trends. Thus, Figure 6a graphs turnout for 2007, comparing the distributions for republics and oblasts against what we observe for 2003. The differences are striking. Not only is there a virtual explosion of rayons with turnout in excess of 90 percent, and although the change in the distribution among oblasts is nowhere near as extreme, we still see the overall right-ward shift in that distribution with a not insignificant share of oblast rayons reporting turnout in excess of 80 percent.

Indeed, as Figure 6b reveals, patterns of turnout in 2007—essentially an 'off year' election for which turnout usually declines relative to presidential contests—closely match what we observe for 2004. Specifically, in 2003, 2004 and 2007, the percentage of republic rayons reporting turnout in excess of 90 percent increased

Figure 6a. Turnout distributions, 2007 vs 2003

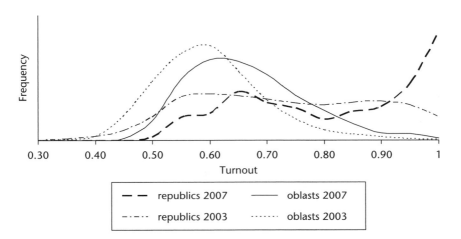

from 14 to 33 to 39 percent while the percentages for oblasts went from 0.4 to 3 to 2 percent. Similarly, the percentage reporting turnout in excess of 85 percent went, in republics, from 23 to 44 to 48 percent, and in oblasts from 1 to 6 to 4 percent. Conversely, the percentage of republic rayons reporting turnout less than 65% went from 31 to 11 to 12 percent but in oblasts declined from 64 to 37 to 39 percent.

Overall, then, the message conveyed by these numbers in conjunction with Figures 6a and 6b is that the 2007 parliamentary election bears a closer correspondence to the 2004 presidential contest than it does to the preceding parliamentary vote in 2003. The 2003 vote may have presaged the corruption and fraud that permeated voting and vote counting in 2004—notably, the continued deterioration of democratic standards in the republics and the increasing turnout of rural oblast rayons that is explicable only with reference to artificially manipulated vote counts. But if there is a clear difference between 2004 and 2007 it is only that an even greater number of republic rayons had their turnout augmented in 2007.

Moscow

The conclusion seems inescapable, then, that whatever fraud infected oblast rayons for the first time in 2004 largely remained in place thereafter. This fact is no more strikingly revealed than when we begin to examine data at the precinct level. We know, of course, that any aggregation of data necessarily loses

Figure 6b. Turnout distributions, 2007 vs 2004

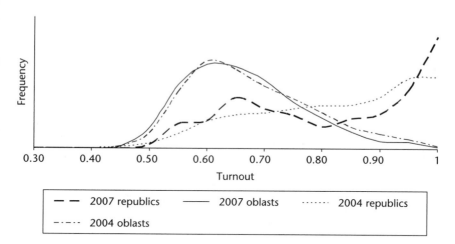

information—summary national data hide patterns in regional statistics, regional data hide patterns in rayon level numbers, and rayon level data hide patterns at the precinct level.

Fortunately, we also have data on a select number of precincts and it is informative to look at one Moscow rayon in particular (Presnya) since it reveals how fraud has now infected even Russia's capitol. Figure 7 graphs the distribution of turnout by precinct in that rayon for the 2003, 2004 and 2007 elections. The results are striking. The distribution for 2003 looks utterly normal, without a hint of malfeasance. In 2004, on the other hand, it is as if we are dealing with two separate elections or two separate countries. There is a massive upsurge of turnout, but only among a subset of precincts whereas the remainder looks much like it did in 2003.

The net result is that the overall distribution of turnout looks as if it were made of two wholly disjoint distributions. Finally, in 2007, there seems to be some "backsliding" among a subset of previously corrupted precincts, but not so great as to return them to where they had been in 2003. And in the remaining subset, there is virtually no backsliding at all. Overall, whatever fraud we attribute to 2004 in this urban Moscow rayon persisted to a significant extent in 2007.

These data need to be understood in context. If international observers had access to polls and polling stations, that access was greatest in Moscow. Still, in 2004, nearly half the precincts of this particular rayon saw a remarkable upsurge in turnout, all to the benefit of Putin. And while a Putin apologist might argue that all we are seeing here is a manifestation of his popularity, we also need to keep in mind that Moscow rayons are demographically homogeneous (nor are we aware of any temporal demographic process that would result in such a

Figure 7. Presnya rayon, Moscow

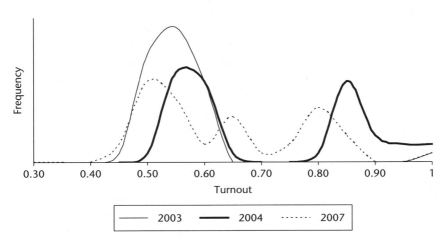

change in distributions over the course of a few months). So that leaves unexplained why voters at a majority of polling stations did not share in this enthusiasm. And it leaves unexplained why whatever mechanisms that were implemented in 2004 to pad turnout and the vote for Putin persisted into 2007.

Surely the Kremlin was well aware of what occurred in 2004, but Figure 7 leads us (somewhat cynically) to ask why it so pointedly discouraged outside observers from monitoring its elections in 2007: After all, monitors, at least in the Moscow rayon of Presnya, seemed to have had little impact in 2004 (or is that why not all precincts reported turnout in excess of 80 percent?). It is almost as if the Kremlin was challenging the West to officially deem its election illegitimate, knowing that it would not do so, and thereby demonstrate that Gasprom's vote counts more heavily in international affairs than does that of the Russian electorate.

Conclusion

There are two conjectures to be considered here: Either the Kremlin has deliberately orchestrated the fraud that permeates its electoral process or that process is not under its control but a system of incentives exists whereby regional political elites have, as their primary incentive, that of currying favor with the Kremlin. Reality is almost a mix of the two. On the one hand we see officials within the Kremlin unapologetically defending an electoral process that consistently produces self-evidently absurd outcomes (e.g. Chechnya), no evident attempt at any serious policing of the polling process itself, and officially sanctioned Stalinist style harassment of political opponents.

On the other hand, we also understand the incentives established by such "reforms" as the appointment rather than the direct election of governors embedded in a political-economic system where nearly all resources and power are centered in Moscow. Is not unreasonable to conjecture, in fact, that the incentives established by the institutional changes implemented under Putin have created a Frankenstein monster that the Kremlin can no longer control.

Regardless of the ultimate source of electoral corruption, our analysis of turnout distributions suggests that it is now widespread and growing. Although we have thus far refrained from offering an estimate of the number of falsified ballots in 2007, we should keep in mind that in a deeper analysis of the 2004 contest using a variety of methods, we estimated no fewer than 10 million suspect or fraudulent votes. Figures 6a and 6b give us no reason to suppose that fraud was significantly less prevalent in 2007. Almost surely United Russia's greater-than-two-thirds majority in the State Duma derives from an artificial inflation of its vote, and that the 2007 contest, like the 2004 vote (and surely the 2008 presidential vote as well), is a democratic oxymoron.

A final comment now on our methods: First, we appreciate that a study of this sort is much like a criminal investigation, wherein all available evidence needs to be gathered before an indictment is arrived at. Here we look at only one indicator of fraud and there are certainly many others—statistical, journalistic, and from first hand observations of an electoral process. Our objective, however, is merely to illustrate the application of one forensic indicator with, admittedly, significant substantive (i.e., policy) implications. Other indicators should also be applied if only to refine our methods for detecting electoral fraud. Second, we also appreciate that various tests can be applied to assess the 'statistical normality' of data. We have eschewed such tests since we believe that, for the data at hand at least, a simple visual assessment is sufficient (especially when examining, say, Figures 6a, 6b and 7). Admittedly, we might prefer a deeper assessment of the demographic correlates of variations in turnout here, but data of the type necessary for such a study is in rather short supply or availability in Russia. This, of course, is but an argument for the further development of indicators of electoral malfeasance of the sort introduced here.

7.3

Symptoms of the Failure of Democracy In Russia

M. Steven Fish

Our local electronic media here are completely under the sway of the administration. The government controls what's aired. And the electoral commission—that's under the administration's control too. We're on the Putin model here.

> - Viktor Ostrenko, staff director, Center for Social Development "Vozrozhdenie" (an NGO dedicated to democracy promotion), Pskov, July 11, 2001

Putin is no enemy of free speech. He simply finds absurd the idea that somebody has the right to criticize him publicly.

> - Ksenia Ponomareva, deputy chief of Vladimir Putin's presidential campaign staff in 1999–2000, March 26, 2001 (reported in the *St. Petersburg Times*, March 27, 2001)

Russia held four elections for parliament and three elections for president between 1993 and 2004. Elections have been carried out on a regular basis for officials at subnational levels. Control over government is constitutionally vested in elected officials, which means that Russia satisfies Robert Dahl's first criterion for polyarchy.

Dahl's other six criteria specify the conditions that ensure that election results express popular preferences. None of these other conditions is met in Russia. Dahl's second and third criteria specify that "elected officials are chosen in frequently and fairly conducted elections in which coercion is comparatively uncommon" and that "practically all adults have the right to vote in the election of officials." In practice, elections are carried out frequently and at regular intervals, but they are not conducted fairly and coercion is common. Furthermore, while all adults have the right to vote, this right is hollowed out by practices that prevent votes from counting equally—or from being counted at all. The regularity of fraud and coercion in elections prevents Russia from fulfilling Dahl's second and

Source: M. Steven Fish, selections from "Symptoms of the Failure of Democracy in Russia," *Democracy Derailed in Russia:* The Failure of Open Politics, Cambridge University Press, 2005. 30–81.

Note: Notes and references have been removed from this article.

third criteria for an open polity. His fourth criterion, which requires that "practically all adults have the right to run for elective offices in the government," is met in strictly legal terms. No portion of the population is de jure disenfranchised. In practice, however, an important segment of adults—namely, those who pose a serious challenge to incumbents—often find themselves barred from seeking office. Thus, Dahl's fourth criterion, while met on paper, is not fulfilled in practice. Finally, the communicative and associational rights that he specifies in his fifth, sixth, and seventh conditions for democracy are sharply circumscribed.

This chapter examines Russia in light of each of Dahl's criteria. On each condition, with the exception of the first one, Russia comes up short. [. . .]

Funny Numbers

If deduction is all one has to detect foul play in some cases, it is sometimes also all one needs. The result in the Iraqi referendum of 2003 provides an example. Another is provided by balloting in Tatarstan in the 1996 presidential election. According to the official results, in the first round of voting, Boris Yeltsin received 38.3 percent to Gennadii Ziuganov's 38.1 percent, though this result transpired only after initial press reports announced that Ziuganov had won a plurality in the republic. Then, in the second round when the field was narrowed to only two candidates, Ziuganov's vote declined in *absolute* terms, from 38.1 percent to 32.3 percent, while Yeltsin received 61.5 percent. In the first round, Ziuganov won absolute majorities in 19 rural districts; in the second round, he lost every one of these to Yeltsin. In Bavlinskii district, Ziuganov's vote total went from 45.3 percent in the first round to 5.9 percent in the second. In some districts, turnout exceeded 99 percent. Mintimer Shaimiev, Tatarstan's president and an election-day ally of whoever controls the executive branch in Moscow, clearly managed to deliver the proper result for Yeltsin. As the numbers suggest, he overdid things a bit.

How can such obvious mischief occur in a supremely important national election that involves open competition among multiple viable candidates and no marauding goons stealing ballot boxes or blocking roadways leading to polling places? How can it happen, moreover, in a major country that is under the scrutiny of the whole world? Some answers are to be found in a few arcane but consequential matters of electoral procedure. Examination of the 2000 presidential vote, which Vladimir Putin won with 52.9 percent in the only round of balloting, sheds some light on these problems.

In this contest, as in all national elections in Russia, each of the country's 94,864 voting precincts writes an official document, called a protocol, which records the results. The precincts tally the votes immediately after the polls close (usually at 8 pm), record them in the form of the protocols, and send their protocols up to the territorial electoral commissions, which number several hundred. Territorial commissions send their tallies to the regional electoral commissions, one of which is located in each of Russia's 89 provinces. The regional commissions then report their results to the federal Central Electoral Commission (CEC) in Moscow.

By law, the protocols are supposed to be made public at each precinct immediately after votes are tallied. This measure is meant, in principle, to check abuses higher up the chain. Each precinct's results, in theory, also can be looked up in the vote count of the territorial commissions and compared to the results recorded in the protocol. Crucially, however, the precinct captains usually do not make the protocols available to the public after the vote. Independent efforts to obtain them from the CEC in the days and months after the vote normally meet only official stonewalling. Usually the CEC claims that there is no need for it to publicize the protocols since the latter were—despite actual practice—freely available to all interested parties at the precincts on election night.

Reporters from the *Moscow Times*, who conducted a major investigation of the 2000 election, managed to obtain 245 of Dagestan's 1,550 protocols. By law, obtaining all the protocols should have been easy, but getting a hold of just one-sixth of them was an investigative coup. Comparing the protocols that they were able to obtain with the territorial commission's reported totals, the *Times* found 87,139 fewer votes for Putin in the former than appeared in the latter.

The votes cast in these 245 precincts accounted for 16 percent of Dagestan's precincts. If the rate of overreporting for Putin in the 84 percent of the precincts that the investigators did not have access to was the same as it was in the 16 percent on which they did manage to gather data, 551,287 votes of the 877,853 that Putin officially won in Dagestan would have been attributed to him wrongly. These extra votes alone would equal one-quarter of the 2.2 million votes that stood between the 52.94 percent that Putin officially received and the 50 percent-plus-one that he had to receive to avoid a second round. Such an extrapolation may not be accurate; the actual number of votes falsely attributed to Putin in Dagestan might have been much lower than this. So too might it have been much higher. [. . .]

The CEC's reporting of results on election night provides grounds for further speculation about what happens to votes as they move up the hierarchy of electoral commissions. According to the CEC, as of 6 pm, 59.2 percent of Dagestan's registered voters had cast their ballots. By the close of voting at 8 pm, however, that number had surged to 83.6 percent. A skeptical Russian sociologist who examined the data noted of the reporting: "Normally most people come in the morning, then attendance decreases slowly and in the end, there is a small rise, but not a vertical skyrocket of visitors". Indeed, a rise of a few percentage points would have been expected, and an increase of up to 10 percent would have been plausible. But the surge recorded by the CEC contradicts normal voting behavior. Election days are holidays in Russia; no voters must rush to the polling place from their workplaces to cast their ballots before the polls close in the evening. At any rate, the lion's share of these latecomers must have weighed in for Putin, since the then-acting president, according to the final official tally, captured a whopping 81 percent of the republic's vote.

According to the analyst just cited, "'ghost voters' or 'dead souls' created by electoral commissions" almost certainly accounted for a large portion of the voters in Dagestan who allegedly rushed to the polls in the closing two hours of voting. Such apparitions appear to have played a substantial role in the government's efforts in 2000. The country's voting rolls, according to the CEC, expanded by 1.3 million voters between the parliamentary elections of December 19, 1999, and the presidential vote of March 26, 2000. The number grew from 108,073,956 to 109,392,046. Unlike the United States, Russia does not have a system of voluntary voter registration. By law, all people are added to the voting register when they turn 18 years of age—and, of course, are supposed to be removed when they die. The official numbers suggest a major surge in the size of the voting-age population over the course of 14 weeks. The remarkable demographic phenomenon caught the attention of some observers. The explanation that the CEC offered after the election included some interesting statements. In a written response on the question, Aleksandr Veshniakov, the head of the CEC, said that 550,000 Russians had turned 18 between the elections. One of his spokespersons, Taisiia Nechiporenko, said in a separate statement that immigration into Russia from other former Soviet republics had augmented the rolls.

The numbers are intriguing. The birth rate has lagged behind the death rate in Russia for many years, yielding a decline in population that has averaged about 800,000 people per year over the past decade. Numbers from Goskomstat (the State Statistics Committee) show that consistent with this long-term national trend, Russia lost 235,100 people to the differential between the birth rate and the death rate during the first three months of 2000, which was offset by 53,000 immigrants from abroad. Thus, in the period between the elections, Russia experienced a net loss of 182,100 people, most of them presumably of voting age. It is conceivable, albeit not likely, that even while the population contracted, the pool of voters expanded due to a dramatic spike in births in 1981 and 1982 that would have flooded the rolls with many hundreds of thousands of people who turned 18 between December 19 and March 26. The CEC, as just noted, claimed that 550,000 new 18-year-olds joined the ranks of voters during the 14-week interval. Yet in separate statements, Murray Feshbach, an American demographer, Evgenii Andreev, a demographer at Russia's Institute of National Economic Forecasting, and Irina Rakhmaninova, head of the Goskomstat's department that tracks national trends in population change, noted that there was no baby boom in the early 1980s. All three concluded that the CEC's claims do not stand up to any reasonable demographic assessments.

Indeed, the CEC's behavior after the vote left room for question about the integrity of even the highest-level and highest-profile electoral commission. After the 2000 election, the CEC publicized every aspect of the results—except the protocols. That is to say, the CEC published everything but the one set of documents that would make possible a systematic investigation of falsification. The CEC often sang the virtues of transparency and posted the election results on its website shortly after it announced the final tally. The protocols data, however, were not published; nor did the CEC help observers denied protocols at the precincts to gain access to them. Furthermore, in August 2000, soon after some observers began publicly questioning the unexpected expansion of the voting rolls just discussed, all data on the presidential election vanished from the CEC's website.

In Chechnya, whether use of "dead souls," some other means of fraud, or the actual mass expression of highly counterintuitive preferences stood behind the result must be left to question. There, Putin captured 50.6 percent. The outcome, if accurate, represented either a magnificent spirit of forgiveness or an intriguing display of masochism on the part of people whose homes had been decimated by a military campaign associated closely with Putin himself. Similarly peculiar sentiments were even more strongly evident in the Ingush Republic, which has been sorely affected by the war in neighboring Chechnya. In the Ingush Republic, 85.4 percent cast their votes for Putin. By analogy, one must imagine George W. Bush winning smashing victories in the District of Columbia and Massachusetts.

In these cases, suspicions arise due to a clash between commonsense reasoning and official results. Yet evidence on fraud comes not only from such deductive inference but also from direct observation. Though most fraud is invisible, many naked eyes have witnessed abuses that corroborate what can be inferred through extrapolation. Yet monitors in Russian elections are often hobbled by powerlessness and timidity. Powerlessness is commonly experienced by domestic observers and stems from official intransigence and manipulation. Timidity is often found among foreign observers and arises from counterproductive habits of thinking, fear of the consequences of candor, and lack of self-confidence bred by ignorance.

Spectacles of Mischief and Failures of Monitoring

A half-dozen mundane but telling anecdotes culled from recent elections illustrate the difficulties that monitors face. They show that if electoral officials and incumbent politicians are resolved to rig the results and unwilling to provide redress, election monitors may find themselves in the place of United Nations peacekeeping troops—acutely aware of the disorder and utterly unable to cure it.

As mentioned, while the law calls for making protocols publicly available at each precinct immediately after the votes are counted, in practice, precinct captains often ignore this rule. In fact, precinct officials may go well beyond simply failing to provide information; they may also shunt observers aside. Doing so obviously eliminates any possibility of effective parallel tabulation of votes by observers. One observer in 2000, a teacher at a local school of agriculture, recounted such an experience in Makhachkala's Kirovskii district. Her story puts the flesh of real experience on the bones of the curious numerical results discussed earlier. The observer, who called herself "Natalia," recalled: "When they turned the ballot boxes upside down, there were two big packets of ballots there on top. Clearly they had been inserted altogether—and one even had a sheet of paper around it. I rushed on them, grabbed both packets and saw they were all filled in for Putin. I pressed them tightly to my chest. The [other observers] were astonished. I said, 'Each person must vote separately, these are fake.'" The hapless teacher quickly found that some observers had more authority than others. Observers representing Putin's campaign took the packets of ballots from her and, she recalled, "spread them over the pile. They all got mixed together." Not only did Putin's observers prove to be highly effective advocates whose authority apparently transcended mere observation, but the precinct election commission also proved unequal to the rigors of counting all the ballots. Once ballots cast for each candidate had been divided into separate piles, members of the electoral commission took the stack of votes for Ziuganov, which Natalia estimated to be about 15 centimeters thick, into a separate room. The officials emerged a short time later with a much smaller stack.

An election observer from the village of Priiutovo in Bashkortostan, Klavdiia Grigorieva, recounted how things worked in the same elections at her polling station, No. 514. Unlike in the case from Makhachkala just recounted, apparently no stuffing or robbing of ballot boxes took place. Like in Makhachkala, however, electoral officials themselves perpetrated fraud.

In Bashkortostan, precinct officials doctored the protocol. Grigorieva watched the vote count and recorded the results: 862 votes for Putin, 356 for Ziuganov, 24 for Vladimir Zhirinovskii, 21 for Konstantin Titov, and 12 for Grigorii Iavlinskii But the precinct's protocol, which the precinct chief wrote up, listed 1,092 votes for Putin, 177 for Ziuganov, and no votes for anyone else. Grigorieva lodged a formal complaint with the CEC, but never received a response.

Grigorieva's account is especially interesting because it reveals precisely the type of vote counting illustrated in Table 3.1, which provides data on Dagestan, though the fraud was perpetrated by electoral officials at different levels in the two cases. In the Dagestani results shown in Table 3.1, precinct officials may have been honest, but electoral officials at the territorial level cooked the results. In Bashkortostan, the results were fixed at the precinct level. In both cases, however, cheating took the form of inflating Putin's total, reducing Ziuganov's—and discarding the votes for the other candidates. In most of the Dagestani precincts shown in Table 3.1, as well as in Grigorieva's precinct in Bashkortostan, artlessness—indeed, laziness—is evident in the work of the election officials, who simply threw out the odd votes for candidates other than Putin and his main challenger. Results that show zero totals for Zhirinovskii and/or Iavlinskii are especially suspect. Each is a household name in Russia, a long-standing standard-bearer of a major political camp (nationalism and liberalism, respectively), and the head of a major political party (the Liberal Democratic Party of Russia [LDPR] and Iabloko, respectively). Doctoring the numbers in a way that took account of these facts and thereby presented more plausible-looking totals, however, apparently was not worth the effort for some of the numbers fixers. [. . .]

Denying citizens access to protocols, cooking numbers during tabulation, stuffing ballot boxes, drawing on reservoirs of "dead souls," and disappearing with carloads of ballots en route to delivery might not be the stuff of elections in Russia if electoral commissions were immune from the blandishments that the presidential, governmental, and gubernatorial apparatuses might offer them. But in practice, electoral commissions are often under the sway of incumbent executives. In many cases where the opposition insists on a seat at the table, the incumbents simply exclude it with impunity. In the fall of 2001, as Moscow prepared for its elections for the municipal Duma, local electoral authorities under the sway of the mayor, Iurii Luzhkov, denied representatives from the leading liberal parties their places on the city's electoral commissions. By law, the representatives of all major parties had the right to sit on the commissions. But Arkadii Murashev and Natalia Borodina, leaders of the Moscow organizations of the liberal Union of Right Forces (URF; SPS in Russian) and Iabloko, respectively, reported that their parties' representatives were barred from participation.

If any doubt about the politicization of electoral commissions persisted after the national elections of 1999 and 2000, the CEC's decision of November 2000 on the proposed referendum on nuclear waste dispelled them. During 2000, a grassroots movement in Russia organized a petition drive to reverse a law that allowed importation of spent nuclear fuel into Russia for long-term storage. The Putin government planned to import several tens of thousands of tons of spent nuclear fuel from around the world. It saw the usage of Russian land for the purpose as a cash cow that promised to generate billions of dollars, but popular opposition was stiff. Environmental groups, led by the Russian chapter of Greenpeace, gathered about 2.5 million signatures—about a half million more than the 2 million needed by law to trigger a referendum on the issue. But the CEC recognized the legitimacy of slightly fewer than 2 million—1,873,216 to be exact. The rest of the signatures the CEC rejected on the basis of technicalities. As Thomas Nilsen, a researcher at a major Norwegian environmental group that supported the referendum drive, noted of the chairman of the CEC and his relationship with the Putin government: "Veshniakov did as he was told".

The probity of the officials in charge of elections is, in any polity, the first and best check on electoral fraud. It is also a necessary condition for free elections. If electoral commissions are corrupt, meaningful elections are unlikely. Those who run the electoral machinery need not be professionals, intellectuals, experts, or even nice people; but if they are not shielded from politicians' pressures and inducements and committed to preserving the integrity of the vote, the prospects for free and fair elections are slight.

Lack of autonomy and honesty on the part of electoral commissions might not completely undermine efforts to deter falsification if election observers, investigators, and candidates themselves could obtain a serious hearing with high-level electoral commissions, such as the CEC, or other bodies. But redress is rare. The individuals named in the preceding few paragraphs—"Natalia," Grigorieva, Zaripov, Borodina, and Murashev—did complain. In fact, more than 2,000 complaints and 200 lawsuits were filed in connection with the 2000 election alone. But, true to the norm, few complaints received any meaningful response. Inquiries lodged by prominent citizens at high levels are sometimes answered, but in the form of logically indefensible or even ludicrous claims, such as those that Veshniakov and Nechiporenko offered the demographers who questioned the startling growth in the voting-age population between December 1999 and March 2000. Observers may report suspected fraud, but when their complaints disappear into a morass of official stonewalling, their influence amounts to naught. [. . .]

I was present in Russia during every major national election during the 1990s and encountered the problem myself. An example may provide illustration.

I served as an international observer in the 1995 parliamentary elections. I was part of a small group headed by a prominent scholar whose observational acumen and knowledge of Russian politics and society (not to mention language) far outstrip my own. One of our stops included a polling place at an army base just outside Moscow. We arrived at midday, four hours after voting commenced and eight hours before polling places were to close.

Merely gaining access to the precinct was difficult. We were held up for 15 minutes by an army officer who disputed our right to enter the polling place even after we presented our credentials, which entitled us to inspect any polling place at any time during the vote. After gaining entry, we saw that no voting was taking place at all. Several men in army uniform stood by a large container, which, we were told, held the ballots already cast. The precinct head told us that the polling place had already closed—though by law all polling places were to remain open until 8 pm—and that all eligible voters had already cast their ballots. He informed us that people around the place were early risers. In fact, everyone had already voted by 9 am.

It is impossible to establish whether the circumstances we observed were evidence of fraud. We knew that closing the polling station early constituted an infraction, but was it hard evidence of falsification? I felt discouraged by my own inability to tell. I could take comfort only in my much better informed colleague telling me during our drive back to central Moscow that he did not know what to make of the situation either. He promised to make a note of the (very) early closing of the polling station in our report (which he wrote). Still, we could not assert confidently that we had witnessed fraud.

Yet the experience helped prepare me for a result that otherwise would have left me stunned. Several days after the election, the Defense Ministry announced that throughout Russia as a whole, fully three-fifths of all officers and enlisted personnel who voted in the election chose Our Home Is Russia (OHR; NDR in Russian), the party that then-President Boris Yeltsin supported and that then-Prime Minister Viktor Chernomyrdin led. The party's stellar performance among the military contrasted with the one-tenth of the vote it received overall. The figures were so extravagant that they would be suspect even had OHR been especially attractive to military personnel. But the party had no such special allure. What is more, independent surveys conducted after the elections contradicted the official results. They found that the CPRF and the nationalist LDPR each far outdistanced OHR in support among the military.

Does Falsification Really Matter?

These examples raise several issues that are sometimes overlooked, glossed over, or misunderstood. The first regards the impact of falsification on electoral outcomes. It may be natural to assume that despite falsification, things roughly even out in the end. According to such logic, perhaps the military's vote for OHR was greatly inflated in the 1995 parliamentary elections; but surely the CPRF "compensated" for such abuses elsewhere. The CPRF, after all, has its own stalwarts among regional elites. Does falsification really matter if "everyone does it"? A leading Russian social scientist quipped in personal conversation on the eve of the 1999 parliamentary elections that he anticipated "full pluralism of falsification." This meant that "every conceivable technology of falsification and hiding falsification will be used" and that "every party that has any support among those holding power anywhere will engage in it."

As it turned out, this analyst's prediction was almost certainly on target. But it is important to bear in mind something that is not always well understood: Pluralism of falsification does not wash out the effects of falsification. Perhaps both OHR and the CPRF benefited from fraud in 1995. But the chances that they benefited equally are remote. And parties that do not wield great clout among regional leaders, such as Iabloko, will always lose from it.

In some elections, moreover, small numbers make a great difference. In 1995, fully six parties received more than 3.75 percent on party-list balloting but still failed to reach the 5 percent threshold required for representation in the Duma. These included the ultraorthodox Communists-Working Russia, the liberal Democratic Choice of Russia (DCR), and the centrist Women of Russia. The presence of one or more of these parties in the Duma would have affected the legislature's complexion between 1996 and 1999.

Not only does "pluralism" not necessarily neutralize the effects of falsification; it also does not wash out the stain of falsification, meaning the blot of illegitimacy that fraud leaves on the political process. Putin was the most popular candidate for president in 2000. Even if he did rely on fraud to put him over the 50 percent-plus-one mark needed to avoid a second round, he probably would have beaten Ziuganov in the second round had the event taken place—even had it been a squeaky clean affair. Putin did not need fraud to win. But the presence of widespread mischief in the first round—on a scale that may well have been decisive in eliminating the need for a second—damaged the legitimacy of the electoral system. Establishing procedures for selecting rulers that are respected and regarded as fair by the citizenry as a whole is no mean problem, particularly where institutionalized humiliation of the people by the powerful has long marred political life. Even when it is not "decisive," electoral fraud perpetuates the overlordship, hoodwinking, and injustice that characterized political life under the Soviet monocracy.

The consequences are hard to measure precisely, but may nevertheless be significant. In a study of eight African countries, Jorgen Elklit and Andrew Reynolds found that individuals' perceptions of the conduct of elections directly affected their sense of political efficacy and the legitimacy of the political regime. The matter is of great importance in Russia. In a major public opinion survey carried out in Russia in late 1996, shortly after Yeltsin's reelection, 87 percent of respondents said that it is "important" that "honest elections are held regularly," but only 36 percent said that their country actually holds "honest elections". There is little evidence that opinion has since turned toward greater faith. In another major survey carried out in 2002, two-thirds of respondents said that they regarded elections as window dressing. Such surveys must be taken as just one bit of evidence. But it merits note that an overwhelming majority of Russians consistently say that their country's elections are not honest or even determinative of who rules.

Falsification in Russia is not as severe as it is in countries, such as Azerbaijan and Belarus, where elections are charades. Still, it occurs on a scale that gravely compromises the elections' "fair conduct," Dahl's second criterion for an open polity.

Election-Related Coercion

Soft Coercion and Abuse of "Administrative Resources"

A second problem that violates Dahl's requirement for meaningful elections and thus open politics, election-related coercion, is rife in Russia. Like falsification, coercion is often difficult to observe and measure. But as with falsification, neglecting or glossing over the problem for that reason would be a mistake.

Some forms of coercion are "soft," insofar as they do not involve the commission of violence. In Russian electoral politics, soft coercion often takes the form of playing on individuals' and communities' economic dependence, threatening dissenters with loss of employment, intimidating people with threats of violence, and using voting schemes that do not necessarily qualify as falsification but that nevertheless ensure powerholders' control over blocs of votes.

People who depend on the state for their subsistence in Russia frequently hear from their bosses, who in turn are under the influence of government officials, that their sustenance depends on their vote. A secretary of the CPRF in Mordovia, Valentina Liukzaeva, recounted after the 2000 elections: "In the village of Permievo, where I am from, the head of the collective farm told villagers that if they vote for Ziuganov, he would find out—and they would not get tractors for sowing, or wood, or food. The villagers, most of whom are old women, of course got frightened and voted for Putin." Rinat Gabidullin, a secretary of the CPRF in Bashkortostan, reported that observers as well as voters came under similar pressure: "In many polling stations our [the CPRF's] observers were threatened that they would not receive food and fodder packages." Gabidullin has argued that such pressure is so extensive in small towns and rural areas that villagers as a class have effectively been cut out of the electoral process. Communists are not the only source of such complaints and sentiment. Viktor Sheinis, a prominent academic, parliamentarian, and leader of Iabloko, argued after the 2000 vote: "I think this [bullying] has affected the final results of the presidential elections more than even direct falsification of votes." Particularly outside the large cities, the influence of the ballot is readily annulled by local and regional powerholders. According to Sheinis: "If some babushka comes to vote, and she is completely dependent on the administration chief for getting wood and fodder for her animals, she will of course vote the way he tells her to". Indeed, as one elderly woman resident of Mesker-Yurt, Chechnya, remarked of her village after the October 2003 election for the president of that republic: "Only pensioners went [to vote], and those who are getting children's or unemployment allowances, because they were told by our administration that if they didn't go and support [Akhmad] Kadyrov [the Kremlin's favored candidate], they would stop getting their money".

During the first post-Soviet decade, I frequently heard such stories from people from every major region. For example, several weeks after the December 1999 parliamentary elections, I interviewed four prominent political activists from the city of Tiumen. Two were from the liberal URF and two from the CPRF. I spoke with them as a group in a lengthy conversation in Moscow. Each insisted upon anonymity. Each worked in the parliamentary campaign for their respective parties, as well as for candidates for single-member district seats. Both the liberals from the URF and the communists from the CPRF reported that local officials in Tiumen raion, one of the four districts in the city of Tiumen, informed large groups of people in workplace meetings that if they did not support Gennadii Raikov in his reelection bid for the Duma, wages in arrears would be withheld indefinitely and local budgets would be revised to the detriment of the district's workers. Threats were not always economic in nature, nor were they always delivered to large collectives. Several of the activists also recounted that they had received ominous personal warnings during the election campaign, delivered anonymously over the telephone or on the street, including threats against their children.

Those who challenge incumbents may find their jobs as well as their persons and families in jeopardy. One of the interviewees from Tiumen was a teacher at a local institute whose boss told her that her political activism would cost her her job. On this score, officials often do little to mask their actions. Displaying fealty to higher-ups is usually more important than demonstrating loyalty to fair process. In the run-up to the 2000 elections, Tatarstan's President Shaimiev made clear to his subordinates that their jobs depended on delivery of the proper result. Rashid Khamadeev, mayor of Naberezhnye Chelny, recounted after the vote:

> Mintimer Sharipovich [Shaimiev] collected us, the heads of local govern-
> ments, and said approximately this: "If [Evgenii] Primakov had put for-
> ward his candidacy, we would call on Tatarstan's people to vote for him.
> But as he has declined to do so, today the republic urges its citizens to
> vote for Putin. Today I earnestly urge our leaders to create initiative
> groups headed by heads [of enterprises], and to organize public recep-
> tions at every enterprise to support Putin's candidacy. Of course if [a local
> leader] does not desire to do so, he may refuse. But after the elections, I
> have a great desire to analyze the quality of work of each [enterprise
> director or local leader]. We will take the results of each polling station
> and see how many people came and how they voted. And we will see
> how each local leader worked—and in whose favor? And is it worth it to
> keep him in his post?"

No one ever accused Shaimiev of political ineffectiveness; as noted earlier, Putin racked up 68.8 percent in Tatarstan. Placing the jobs of local officials, enterprise directors, and sundry others on the line was, unsurprisingly, a good way of ensuring that the "caterpillars" functioned properly and that turnout was extraordinarily high—and even included many nonexistent residents who occupied nonexistent apartments. [. . .]

In sum, "soft" coercion does amount to coercion, and it is not a normal part of politics in democracies. The soft coercion that permeates post-Soviet politics, moreover, bears a striking resemblance to what some democratic-movement activists suffered during the elections of the late Soviet period. The stories activists now tell hardly differ from those I heard in the Russian provinces at the end of the Soviet period. The manipulation of people's dependence on the state for employment and access to the material means of survival, as well as threats of violence delivered by anonymous callers, were commonplace during 1989–91. [. . .]

Hard Coercion

While soft coercion and manipulation are staples of Russian elections, so too is hard coercion. Politically motivated assault and murder are ordinary occurrences in Russia, even if they are rarer than violence motivated by conflict over commercial affairs and even if they seldom draw major international attention. What is more, politically motivated violent crimes are almost never solved, and only very rarely are perpetrators brought to justice.

Journalists are particularly vulnerable. Beginning at the time that he came to power as head of Primorskii krai in 1993, Evgenii Nazdratenko regularly deployed both the police and private thugs to pummel any journalist who irritated him. By the time of his highly dubious reelection in 1999, what at the beginning of the decade had been a freewheeling regional press had been quite literally beaten into submission.

Primorskii krai was by no means unique or exceptional. To cite just a few other examples: In late November 1999, during the closing weeks of the election campaign, a leading journalist in Kaliningrad, Igor Rostov, who took a critical stance toward the governor, Leonid Gorbenko, was badly beaten by a band of thugs. Igor Rudnikov, a Kaliningrad city legislator and editor of a local newspaper that had also criticized the governor, was beaten nearly to death in an attack in 1998. One of Rudnikov's associates had earlier been attacked as well, and the newspaper's offices finally moved to Lithuania after being bombed twice. Just a few days before Rudnikov was savaged in Kaliningrad, Sergei Bachinin, the editor of a newspaper critical of local and regional officials in Kirov and in 1996 the main opponent of the city's mayor in municipal elections, was assaulted, sustaining extensive skull and brain injuries.

Candidates for office themselves, along with their staffs, are often in danger as well. Challengers to incumbents are usually in the greatest danger. In some cases, incumbents who run against Moscow's—that is, the president's—favored candidates or against candidates who control the agencies of coercion are also vulnerable. In the run-up to the election for the governor of Smolensk oblast in May 2002, a large portion of the staff of Aleksandr Prokhorov, then governor, suffered attack. Prokhorov was challenged and defeated in the election by Viktor Maslov, the head of the regional Federal Security Bureau (the successor agency to the KGB). Although the source of the violence was—unsurprisingly—never authoritatively identified, Maslov appears to have made effective use of his offices in his election bid. In the period before the election, the dachas of two members of Prokhorov's election staff were burned, the son of Prokhorov's lawyer was attacked and beaten, and Prokhorov's election headquarters was bombed. Days before the election, the car of Anatolii Makarenko, Prokhorov's deputy, was attacked by gunmen. Makarenko's bodyguard was wounded and his driver killed in the attack.

The cases discussed here are not isolated incidents. They are frequent, entirely normal events in Russia. In many places they are an integral part of the conditions under which elections are held. Coercion of many types, as well as some types of what is often called "abuse of administrative resources," violate Dahl's second condition for an open polity, which posits that "elected officials are chosen in frequently and fairly conducted elections in which coercion is comparatively uncommon."

Arbitrary Exclusion from Electoral Participation

Dahl's fourth criterion for polyarchy, which stipulates that "practically all adults have the right to run for elective offices in the government," is also regularly violated. Unless by including "practically" Dahl meant to provide a loophole to excuse the exclusion of candidates who threaten the reelection of incumbents, which is doubtful, then the arbitrary disqualification of such people constitutes a violation.

Russia is not Iran; candidates are not screened for their political or religious views. By law, anyone has the right to run for office. But the law and actual practice are two very different things. A few examples will illustrate the problem.

Evgenii Nazdratenko's campaign for reelection as governor of Primorskii krai in late 1999 provides one. Using his powers as incumbent and his grip on regional courts, Nazdratenko disqualified a leading opponent, Svetlana Orlova. Orlova was removed from contention just two days before the vote after it became clear that she threatened to attract substantial support. According to the court, Orlova had failed to list a plot of land she possessed on her declaration of personal property, a document that candidates are required to furnish. The same court that announced Orlova's disqualification also banned Nazdratenko's political archenemy, the former mayor of Vladivostok, Viktor Cherepkov, from running for the Duma. Cherepkov was scratched from ballots on the grounds that he had supposedly failed to provide campaign spending information in time. In a final touch of absurdity, the court also canceled mayoral elections in Vladivostok, thereby leaving a close Nazdratenko ally in office, on the grounds that the city did not yet have a charter. That elections had been held previously in the city despite the absence of a "charter" did not figure in the court's reasoning.

The courts' disqualification of candidates does not always favor the incumbent. If the incumbent has fallen afoul of the president, the former may attract the zealous gaze of the judiciary or electoral commissions and fall prey to disqualification. In October 2000, one day before the gubernatorial elections in Kursk oblast, a regional court barred Governor Aleksandr Rutskoi from seeking reelection. The court was responding to complaints lodged by Viktor Surzhikov, a KGB officer and Putin's main federal inspector in the oblast. The violation that prompted Rutskoi's disqualification: In his declaration of personal property, the governor had failed to mention his sale of a six-year-old Volga automobile. He no longer owned the vehicle, but he had neglected to de-register it and had simply transferred the ownership papers to the new owner. Alas, the roadster was still registered in his name. In comments to the press about the case, the CEC's Veshniakov intoned that a candidate "should not give erroneous information about income and property." Georgii Poltavchenko, the presidential representative to the Central District (which includes Kursk oblast), weighed in on the side of virtue as well. According to Poltavchenko, Rutskoi "should have known the law." Rutskoi had long been an antagonist of the Kremlin. He had broken with Yeltsin, whom he served as vice president, in 1993, and had angered Putin in 2000 by launching a program to help the families of the seamen who were killed in the disaster that befell the *Kursk* submarine. [. . .]

8

Nationalism and Chechnya

In 1993, in the proportional election that allocated half the seats in the new legislature, the State Duma, Vladimir Zhirinovsky's Liberal Democratic Party of Russia (LDPR) garnered 21 percent of the vote, nearly twice the total of the second-place finisher. Observers inside and outside of Russia were shocked and worried. Most expected the "reformist" or "liberal" wing—the assumed democrats who allegedly wished to build a liberal, capitalist democracy in Russia—to run away with this vote on the heals of the triumph over Ruslan Khasbulatov and the others who led the attempted coup from the vanquished legislature, the Supreme Soviet.[1] Zhirinovsky and his followers were neither liberal nor democratic; in fact, they were xenophobic nationalists. The result of the vote seemed to reflect the weakness of the liberal message and the strength of the appeal of nationalist sentiments in Russia. While LDPR's electoral showing has tapered off to roughly 10 percent in subsequent elections, this is largely because other political groupings, most notably Vladimir Putin's United Russia, have expropriated and widely expanded the nationalist message and captured followers sharing those sentiments.

Concerns about Russian nationalism, particularly in Europe, are nothing new. The echoes of nationalism and xenophobia were clearly present at the time of the Soviet collapse. This was perhaps natural and understandable. A people used to being part of a superpower, a great country with designs on spreading its system and ideology across the globe, had suddenly seen that country and that status wither away. Out of the humiliation of this remarkable collapse emerged, in some, a desire to blame, to oppose, to strike back.[2] Such a sentiment was and remains clearly evident in Zhirinovsky's bluster, in his promise to punish those responsible for Russia's tailspin, and to rebuild the Russian Empire in a *Last Dash to the South,* as he titled a book outlining his designs. It similarly marked actions such as those of former Mayor of Moscow Yuriy Luzhkov, who in the mid-1990s ordered the search and deportation of any in the capital city with dark skin, essentially blaming those from the Caucusus regions for the decline of the country and for the surge in violence around the city at that time.[3] That violence, in reality, was overwhelmingly the work of wealthy ethnic Russians as they consolidated their mafia-like, quasi-commercial organizations.[4] To the extent that such activities involved those from the Caucusus, it was because the bosses had employed them to do the dirty work or had partnered with them in various retail ventures. But, reality was of little concern; any excuse to remove the dark-skinned non-Russians was sufficient.

And, most destructively, the urge has marked two deadly wars in Chechnya, one of Russia's federal republics in the tumultuous Caucusus region. The first was nominally to prevent the disintegration of Russia along ethnic lines following on the disintegration of the Soviet Union into its 15 constituent, ethnic-based republics. No doubt, the prospect of several dozen independent states on the territory of present-day Russia would be a nightmare scenario economically and strategically for the world in general and for Europe and Asia in particular. The second war, however, served as much to propel Putin into the presidency and provide a convenient excuse to clamp down on openness and political competition.[5] It also was designed to, and has largely served to, mobilize and unite the people around a nationalist message of Russian exceptionalism.

The nationalist message is increasingly pervasive, for under Putin, the Kremlin began sponsoring a variety of programs. Among the most aggressive are the new youth summer camps around the country. The consistent theme in the messages delivered at these camps is a combination of crisis and of Russian national pride. Central to the camps is a program of ideological indoctrination designed to pit *Nashi* (our people, that is, ethnic Russians) against perceived enemies inside and out. The youth are taught to "vanquish" these enemies as threats to the Russian people. Students are, among other things, encouraged to propagate more white ethnic Russians in large numbers from a young age as part of an overall plan to combat a spread of alternate messages and the growing populations of non-Russian ethnic groups. From manipulation to intimidation to violence, this new cult promotes Putin's nationalist message and program. Indeed, these "Putin Youth" are that program.[6]

At the same time, the situation should not be overly exaggerated. Some observers stress the weakness of nationalism in Russia, particularly when judged against some widely accepted stereotypes that caricature Russian culture as xenophobic and nationalist. The appeal may be wide, but it is not deep. Attempts to rally the people on strong nationalist messages have fallen flat, suggesting that the communist internationalist propaganda after seven decades penetrated somewhat into the culture and that racism and "other" branding is less accessible or appealing to most Russians today.[7] Certainly, some degree of "nation building" was necessary in the wake of the disorienting nature and suddenness of the Soviet collapse.

The extent of nationalism in Russia, the degree of its appeal, and the threat it poses are all questions that have interested and will continue to interest students of that country. There is little new about this debate; it is one that is as old as the study of Russia itself. The questions and the concerns are as relevant today as ever. In the selections that follow, the late Anna Politkovskaya, a journalist murdered by the regime for her investigative reporting on the Chechen wars, offers vignettes of the suffering of the people of Chechnya at the hands of the Russian Army. Her courageous reporting exposed the consequences of that war and the ravages that nationalist pursuits can wreck on a society. Khachaturian elaborates the use of nationalism as a political tool to strengthen Putin's agenda to bolster central authority and the dangers such a strategy holds for Russia itself given the attendant risks that the nationalist sentiment could spin out of control.

For Further Reference

Books

Dominique Arel and Blair A. Ruble, *Rebounding Identities: The Politics of Identity in Russia and Ukraine,* Johns Hopkins University Press: 2006.

Matthew Evangelista, *The Chechen Wars: Will Russia Go the Way of the Soviet Union?,* Brookings: 2003.

Marlène Laruelle, *In the Name of the Nation: Nationalism and Politics in Contemporary Russia,* Palgrave Macmillan: 2009.

Andrew Meier, *Chechnya: To the Heart of a Conflict,* WW Norton: 2004.

Anna Politkovskaya, et al., *A Small Corner of Hell: Dispatches From Chechnya,* University of Chicago: 2007.

Ronald G. Suny, *The Revenge of the Past: Nationalism, Revolution, and the Collapse of the Soviet Union,* Stanford University Press: 1993.

Journal Articles

Mark Kramer, "The Perils of Counterinsurgency: Russia's War in Chechnya," *International Security,* Vol. 29, No. 3 (2005).

Dmitry Gorenburg, "Nationalism for the Masses: Popular Support for Nationalism in Russia's Ethnic Republics," *Europe-Asia Studies,* Vol. 53, No. 1 (2001).

Anatoly Lieven, "The Weakness of Russian Nationalism," *Survival,* Vol. 41, No. 2 (2005).

Novels

Arkady Babchenko, *A Soldier's War in Chechnya,* Portobello Books: 2007.

Film

Alexandra

NOTES

1. On Khasbulatov, see the introduction to Chapter 5 of this volume. On elections, see Chapter 7, and on the 1993 election, see Timothy J. Colton and Jerry F. Hough, eds., *Growing Pains: Russian Democracy and the Election of 1993* (Brookings Institution, 1998).

2. On the connection between humiliation and such urges, see Isaiah Berlin, "The Bent Twig: A Note on Nationalism," *Foreign Affairs*, Vol. 51, No. 1 (1972), pp. 11–30, especially p. 28; and Adam Jones, *Genocide: A Comprehensive Introduction* (Routledge, 2006), pp. 268–270.

3. See Donald N. Jensen, "The Boss: How Yuri Luzhkov Runs Moscow," *Demokratizatskiya*, No. 1 (2008), pp. 83–122.

4. See Stephen Handelman, *Comrade Criminal* (Yale University Press, 1997).

5. Several investigative reports have made a convincing case to this effect, notably *Tovarish Prezident*, directed by Pavel Shirov (2004; Moscow, Russia: independent film). Also see Yuri Felshtinsky and Alexander Litvinenko, *Blowing Up Russia: Terror From Within* (Liberty Press, 2001). Also see *Assassination of Russia*, directed by Jean-Charles Deniau and Charles Gazelle (2000: Transparences Productions).

6. See a brilliant PBS Frontline investigative report, "Russia: Putin's Plan," *Frontline*, reported by Victoria Gamburg (February 26, 2008: PBS).

7. See Anatol Lieven, "The Weakness of Russian Nationalism," *Survival*, Vol. 41, No. 2 (1999), pp. 53–70.

8.1

The Specter of Russian Nationalism

Rafael Khachaturian

When he was named acting president of Russia on December 31, 1999, Vladimir Putin inherited a country still reeling from the Soviet Union's breakup: economic woes caused by the rapid privatization of state assets and the August 1998 financial crisis, ethnic unrest and war in Chechnya, and Russia's demotion from superpower status. Over the next seven years, the Putin government introduced a series of national reforms aimed at making Russia once again a major player on the world stage. Dmitry Medvedev's election as the new president means that his term will be a continuation of the policies set in place by his predecessor and mentor, who stays on as prime minister and seems literally prime—"first in rank, authority, or significance," as the Oxford English Dictionary says.

Putin's time in office has left its mark. Until recently, the economy had grown steadily for ten years, largely because of Russia's oil and natural gas reserves, which make up around 60 percent of its export earnings. Gazprom, the energy monopoly once chaired by Medvedev, supplies a quarter of Europe's natural gas. The inflow of foreign investment capital contributed to growing prosperity in large cities like Moscow and St. Petersburg; reflecting this growth, for the last three years Moscow has been ranked as the world's most expensive city. According to *Forbes*, it is also the world's billionaire capital, with seventy-four; the total number of billionaires in the country is eighty-seven, second only to the United States. However, this economic growth has slowed since the summer because of the global decline in oil prices, as well as the war with Georgia, which made foreign investors wary and caused a capital outflow of thirty billion dollars within just a month of the end of the conflict.

Despite these sobering prospects, recent times have been a far cry from the tumultuous years under Boris Yeltsin, and the result is wide-spread support for Putin, Medvedev, and their United Russia party. In the eyes of many Russians, Putin represents a stabilizing force, ready and able to advance the national interest after the country was eclipsed by the West for too long. Although much has been written about his consolidation of power, silencing the opposition, and curbing the free media, it can't be denied that he retains a high degree of popularity

Source: Rafael Khachaturian, "The Spectre of Russian Nationalism," *Dissent*, Winter 2009.19-24.

Note: Notes and references have been removed from this article.

among young and old. A candidate like Medvedev, almost completely unknown and never having held elective office before, could never have won the presidential election without Putin's backing.

With Russia's reemergence and Putin's popularity, there are more than enough factors to worry any democratic observer. Aside from the steady accumulation of power—the Kremlin authorities call it "sovereign democracy"—there is a revival of populist nationalism at home that coincides with Russia's increasingly hard-line foreign policies. The looming presence of nationalism in Russia's public discourse has gone hand in hand with the Kremlin's stance toward the former Soviet republics, Western Europe, and the United States. The political climate is increasingly anti-American, the world increasingly polarized, in Putin's representation of it, into an irreconcilable opposition between Russia's national interests and those of the West. Suspicious popular sentiment is focused on American expansion into Ukraine and Georgia under the guise of NATO. The result is a growing parallelism between nationalism at home and the renewed effort to build regional and international influence.

The question of Russian national identity is far from new. Anticipating the key internal struggle over the next two centuries, Rousseau remarked in the *Social Contract* that Peter the Great went wrong because "he wanted to make Germans and Englishmen, when he should have made Russians." While the nation's cultural and literary life bloomed during the nineteenth century, the intelligentsia was unable to agree on the extent to which Russia was part of the West, eventually ceding to the crash-course westernization of the Bolsheviks. During the Soviet period and under the guise of Marxist internationalism, Russia asserted its cultural dominance over its neighbors. However, the *perestroika* years of Mikhail Gorbachev allowed for the revival of ethnic identity politics among the people of the republics, resulting in an upsurge of nationalism that contributed to the fragmentation of the Soviet Union. It was during that time of sociopolitical crisis that Russians once again began to seriously think about their own national selfhood.

Under Yeltsin in the 1990s a wave of xenophobia began that remains today, particularly with regard to the ethnic groups from the Caucusus and Central Asia. The influx of these people into Russia, either as refugees or laborers looking for work, was met with hostility by many Russians. For example, the notorious Vladimir Zhirinovsky, leader of the Liberal Democratic Party of Russia, spent much of the past decade calling for state patriotism and Russian territorial expansion in Asia. It is true that Zhirinovsky values statist over ethnic nationalism and accepts the multi-ethnicity of the Russian nation. This past spring, in a sign of things to come, he appeared on the popular debate show *K Barieru!* (*To the Barricade!*), arguing for Russian military involvement in the breakaway

Georgian region of Abkhazia to protect Abkhazians who were granted Russian citizenship—a tactic that the Georgians saw as a step toward annexation. Even then, for Zhirinovsky the interests of the "Russian people" are the driving force of the country's policies.

Other right-wing organizations that appeared in the nineties were even more threatening. An extreme example is the disbanded Russian National Unity, which was the closest group that post—Soviet Russia has seen to a true fascist paramilitary group. Its members adopted a modified swastika and other Nazi symbols, while simultaneously portraying themselves as marching in the footsteps of the Black Hundreds, the pre-1917 monarchist and Orthodox reactionaries. The ethno-racial nationalist ideology of the RNU appealed to mostly unemployed and working-class urban youth who had experienced the social disintegration of the Gorbachev and Yeltsin years. Formed in 1990, the group grew rapidly in size, and although membership estimates ranged from 15,000 to 50,000 according to different sources, it is known that it infiltrated high ranks in certain government agencies, most notably the Ministry of Internal Affairs.

The RNU also found official support in regional administrations, particularly in the Stavropol and Krasnodar territories of southern Russia, where substantial numbers of ethnic immigrants from the Caucusus lived. RNU members "patrolled" public parks and harassed demonstrators, gradually becoming an arm of the regional governments. However, in 1998, Moscow's mayor, Yuri Luzhkov, a nationalist sympathizer himself and a Putin ally today, forbade a planned RNU gathering, as part of a larger federal anti-RNU campaign. The group's influence began to wane after that, and two years later it split into a number of smaller factions, which are still active today.

Violence against minorities and foreigners has risen in recent years. Small but well-organized neo-Nazi skinhead gangs stage random attacks on unsuspecting civilians—mostly people of darker complexion. The SOVA Center, a Russian nongovernmental organization that tracks radical right-wing organizations, reported that from 2004 to 2007 there were 1,049 racially motivated attacks in Moscow and St. Petersburg alone, with 140 fatalities. While the government officially condemns these acts, victims complain that too often the police response has been nonexistent. Indeed, police often tacitly support anti-immigrant discrimination. Racially motivated attacks by skinheads are often recorded as minor incidents of hooliganism rather than serious offenses. People of foreign appearance are also consistently targeted for passport and registration checks. In the fall of 2006, when tensions between Russia and Georgia were rising, the Russian government cracked down on Georgians living in the country, deporting hundreds of people and urging Moscow schools to produce lists of students with Georgian names for local police. Instances like this show that although there may not be an outright link between racial violence and the Russian state, there is an ideological convergence based on a crude nationalism that has created an environment conducive to xenophobia.

Paradoxically, one of the ways that Putin's government has attempted to redefine national identity at home is by invoking Russia's struggle against fascism. Authorities have used the "fascist" accusation as a rallying cry against any opposition, whether it comes from actual neo-Nazi groups or democratic reformist parties such as *Yabloko* (Apple). The word designates a sort of bogeyman, a coalition of secret conspiratorial forces striving to undermine the country for their own benefit. The government youth movement *Nashi* (Ours), founded in 2005 in the wake of Ukraine's "Orange Revolution," which has gained attention in the West for being something of a Putin personality cult, claims to be an anti-fascist movement. Its 120,000 members have staged demonstrations against British and Estonian diplomats, protested against the adoption of Russian children by Americans, and clashed with demonstrators from other parties—all under the pretense of combating fascist forces. *Nashi*'s allegiance lies with the Kremlin, and its mission always falls in line with the political needs of the governing elite. Its members have also held rallies against neo-Nazi groups' persecution of minorities, showing that *Nashi* is a nationalist, not a racist, organization. What is troubling is that in today's Russia the line separating the two has become unclear.

As of now, Kremlin policy has been to oppose neo-Nazi violence—in order both to save face on the international scene and to maintain state authority over public life. But the state's overt nationalism is indirectly spurring radical activity at home, something that it has been reluctant to acknowledge. *Nashi*'s ideology taps into the hostility that many young Russians already feel toward America and Europe, reaffirming it with a dose of Manichaean patriotism. *Nashi* not only provides an emotional outlet for the young but also gives them the opportunity to ascend the government ladder by making important connections—much as the *Komsomol* did during the Soviet era. While this year the government has announced plans to scale back and reorganize *Nashi*, it remains an active organization that reveals the state's new focus on promoting nationalism and Russian identity.

The forms of nationalism in Russia are not limited to a single, state-endorsed ideological movement. They derive from diverse and sometimes obscure intellectual sources. One such source is Aleksandr Dugin, a philosopher and public intellectual whose work ranges from historical reflection to myth and occultism. An outspoken admirer of the Italian traditionalist philosopher Julius Evola, he has also on more than one occasion sympathized with the left (Strasserite) branch of National Socialism. Virtually unknown during the nineties, Dugin's ideas now reach a wide audience. He is a regular guest on the country's most popular political shows. More important, Dugin is known to be an especially close adviser to

Vladislav Surkov, a top Kremlin insider currently serving as the deputy chief of staff and the government's chief ideologue. Dugin's 1997 book *Osnovy Geopolitiki* (*Foundations of Geopolitics*), with its promotion of a neo-Eurasianist doctrine, has generated an ongoing debate about Russia's role in global politics.

Influenced by the work of the German geostrategist Karl Haushofer and the Russian historian Lev Gumilev, Dugin has revived the idea that Russia is a unique geographical entity culturally affiliated more with Asia than Europe, which therefore must seek its own path. World politics is a recurring confrontation between the commercial materialism of the maritime West and the organic spiritualism of the Eurasian heartland, of which Russia is the center. His fascination with traditionalism and mysticism leads him to trace this opposition to a prehistorical and elemental origin, but Dugin's prescriptions for Russia remain concrete. Eurasian geopolitics must serve the interests of the states involved; there must be an undemocratic order so that leaders preserve the right of decision-making; Russia must seek to expand itself into a new Soviet space, not only in eastern Europe and central Asia but also in China; and an alliance must be formed with Germany, Japan, and Iran, to act as the Eurasian counterbalance to the Atlantic powers, mainly the United States and United Kingdom. Despite his intellectual affinities with far right thought, Dugin does not propagate an explicitly ethno-nationalist or pan-Slavist position. Instead, neo-Eurasianism is a doctrine based on a nationalist patriotism and the necessity for the state's survival in today's global alignment. But empire and expansionism are at work here, as Dugin argues for a campaign of coercion and political maneuvering (although not necessarily military force) to extend Russia's influence across the two continents while simultaneously blocking Western encroachment.

Since 2005, Dugin has criticized Putin for not taking a firm enough stance against the United States. As Russia has become an increasingly important economic force, the Kremlin's foreign policy has split into a pragmatic desire for Western integration and a rhetorical anti-Western nationalism. This is not a contradiction but the product of the economic liberalization of the post-Soviet era (which has brought great material gain) and the simultaneous ideological backlash against the perceived loss of national prestige. There is undoubtedly a "realist" element in the Kremlin's current policies that will displease the autarkic neo-Eurasianists. The prospects of Western capital, especially with Russian energy companies reaping massive profits from sales to Europe, are too enticing for the Kremlin elite. This means that Russia under Medvedev will continue to be a key player in the world economy, despite the anti-Western rhetoric of its government and the political tensions that result from it. Nevertheless, it is clear that Russia looks to solidify its presence in both Europe and Asia, maybe not to a full-fledged Eurasianism but to a more assertive foreign policy.

The Georgian crisis remains the clearest example of Russia's new involvement within the former Soviet sphere. The short August war over the breakaway regions of South Ossetia and Abkhazia has brought relations between Russia and the West to a post—cold war low. Georgia's hope for NATO membership heightened Russian fears of Western encirclement, and after years of mounting tensions and Georgian-Ossetian skirmishes, the conflict rapidly escalated. Russia's swift invasion, which not only secured the disputed regions but also led to a partial occupation of Georgian territory, has shown the West that the country will take drastic measures to reclaim its traditional sphere of influence. The long-term effects remain to be seen, but South Ossetia and Abkhazia are on the way to becoming Russia's new satellite states. The war has brought new instabilities, yet it demonstrates Russian opposition to what Medvedev calls a unipolar world that is itself "unstable and fraught with conflict."

Russia has claimed that NATO's 1999 war in the Balkans and Western recognition of Kosovo's independence from Serbia provide moral precedents for its own involvement in the Caucusus. According to *Time*, the Russian government recently purchased a 51 percent stake in *Naftna Industrija Srbija* (NIS), Serbia's national oil company, further expanding its dominance over the East European energy supply. Russia's relations with another Slavic nation, Belarus, have in recent years oscillated between distrust and cooperation, but last year the controversial Belarusian president, Alexander Lukashenko, named Putin prime minister of the Belarus-Russia Alliance. Like other former Soviet states under Russian pressure, Belarus faces an important question: will it be able to enter such an alliance without effectively giving up its sovereignty to its huge neighbor?

There are other instances of Russia's renewed involvement in nearby regions. When, in the wake of the Georgian War, the Polish government reluctantly agreed to host U.S. missiles on its territory, the reaction from Moscow was fierce and threatening. Now Ukraine finds itself in a tug-of-war between the West and Russia on the issues of NATO membership and possession of the Crimea. The uneasy coalition government of pro-Western president Viktor Yushchenko and pro-Russian prime minister Yulia Tymoshenko collapsed in September, almost four years after the Orange Revolution that first swept Yushchenko into office. Elsewhere, the Moscow-Tehran axis spoken of by Dugin is solidifying, with Russia acting to delay UN imposition of sanctions on Iran, to which it has been selling weapons and nuclear technology. For Russia, Iran is a valuable counterforce to American interests in the Middle East.

Russia's military presence in what is known as Transnistria, an unrecognized breakaway republic in Moldova, is little known but emblematic of Kremlin policy. This tiny sliver of land bordering Ukraine and cut off from Moldova by the Dniester River declared its independence in 1992 after a short war. Although there is comparatively little ethnic tension among the population—composed in almost equal proportions of Moldavians, Ukrainians, and Russians—the region is potentially volatile due to alleged human rights violations, organized crime, and arms trafficking. The Russian Army currently maintains 1,200 troops there, which were initially part of a temporary peacekeeping force. In 2004, however, the army halted its withdrawal. Citing Kosovo's independence, the Kremlin has denounced the West for its hypocrisy in recognizing a breakaway region only when it is politically useful.

All this brings us back to Russian nationalism. The rise to power of the Kremlin elite colloquially known as the *siloviki* (approximately, "the forceful")—composed of former Soviet military and intelligence operatives with ties to Yeltsin and Putin—has led to a new era of statist conservatism in Russian politics, emphasizing stability over democratic proceduralism. The *siloviki* promote an economic nationalism where the state controls the distribution of natural resources in the name of the Russian people—countering the privatization of the nineties. The state takeover of numerous oil and gas industries has come with a dose of xenophobic rhetoric. For example, one agent of the FSB (the institutional heir to the KGB) was quoted as categorizing the Russian oligarchs in two groups—the good, ethnically Russian ones and the foreign elements: "All Jews are traitors, oriented toward the West. That's how it's always been."

The increasing corporatism of the Russian state, where government officials, bureaucrats, and business officials together form the insider elite, has made policies that are good for profit centrally important. Some observers have argued that this means Putinism is ideologically empty and that the government remains fundamentally realistic and pragmatic when balancing between Western integration and nationalist posturing. Yet it would be a mistake to overlook the role that nationalism plays in the Kremlin's strategy of building popular support for its geopolitical aims. In fact, there has been a noticeable attempt by the government to make modern Russia the focus of patriotic sentiment in the national consciousness. One small example of this is the introduction of a new holiday, the Day of People's Unity, first celebrated in 2005, to replace the official commemoration of the Bolshevik Revolution. Meant as a celebration of the expulsion of Polish-Lithuanian forces from Moscow in 1612, its patriotic message of homeland resiliency against foreign antagonists has allowed far right-wing organizations to appropriate it for their own cause. During the first year of celebration, some thousand members of these groups rallied in Moscow, chanting "Russia for Russians!" and "Russia against occupiers!" The following year Luzhkov banned such demonstrations, showing that the government's top priority regarding nationalist sentiment is to cultivate it through its own official means but not to condone radical groups that could potentially challenge its rule.

Even the fledgling liberal opposition to these developments has not avoided contamination by one or another form of nationalist politics. In 2007, chess master Garry Kasparov, the face of liberal opposition to Putinism in the Western media, entered into an alliance with the fascist writer and countercultural icon Eduard Limonov and his National Bolshevik Party. The National Bolsheviks—for whom Dugin was the chief ideologue before breaking with Limonov in 1998—have acquired a reputation as a group of extremist hooligans, adopting a Nazi tricolor flag but replacing the swastika with a sickle and hammer and featuring Limonov's own taste for radicalism on both ends of the political spectrum. Not surprisingly, the government has attempted to outlaw the party in the last few years. Indeed, one of the purposes of creating *Nashi* was to crack down on the NBP and counter its activist presence. United in their mutual dislike of Putin, Kasparov and Limonov joined with a small number of other parties to create the Other Russia coalition. The liberal anti-Putin parties, *Yabloko* and *Soyuz Pravykh Sil* (Union of Right Forces)—with no representation in the state Duma—refused to cooperate because of their concern over the inclusion of such radical elements. Kasparov fired back that the URF was Putinist as well. The coalition was prohibited from registering in time for the December 2007 presidential election, but its efforts highlighted the fragmented nature of democratic opposition in Russia's stifling political atmosphere. Kasparov's choice to align himself with Limonov and the NBP reduces the already marginal chances for a liberal or social democratic movement untainted by questionable alliances. Unfortunately, it seems that questionable alliances are necessary for any opposition to United Russia.

More than ever before, nationalism is a political tool that makes for an increasingly volatile Russian society. Under mounting pressure, the government has stepped up its efforts to prosecute hate crimes and prevent any further activity by far right groups. But these measures by themselves will not be enough to suppress xenophobia and chauvinism in which the government is itself complicit. Even more troubling is the chance that the line between the more "benign" nationalism of the Kremlin and the violent ultra-nationalism of the fascist groups will begin to blur. There is certainly some overlap between the ideology of the far right and the general feelings of some members of the government elite about the meaning of Russian patriotism. And if Dugin's gradual ascension from the radical fringes to the center stage of national politics is any indication, a further shift toward a radical nationalism by the government is not out of the question.

Nationalist ideology in Russia has a constantly shifting purpose, determined by the political ends toward which it is applied. There is no single, large-scale nationalist movement uniting the Kremlin elites and the far right neo-Nazi parties; ideologically they are too disparate ever to be completely reconciled. Even a populist demagogue like Zhirinovsky, known for his xenophobic attitude toward minorities, was an eager supporter of Russia's policy of handing out passports to Abkhazians, because he saw this as an opportunity to expand Russia's influence. Russian fascists are unlikely to accept such a policy: for them a true Russia means one purified of all foreign elements. Despite this divergence, both groups have actively perpetuated an aura of hostility and mistrust, which has only been intensified by the government's rhetoric. Nationalism is a dangerous political tool, and the Kremlin's resentment over its loss of empire and the encroachments of the West into its traditional sphere of influence makes for a dangerously virulent politics.

Although Medvedev was not counted as a member of the *silovik* group prior to his election and was thought by some to be a more moderate and "liberal" figure, his allegiance clearly lies with the Putinist Kremlin. He may be a more pragmatic face to the West, but the political machine behind him is firmly in place, with Putin as prime minister, pushing for a more aggressive Russian foreign policy and beating the nationalist drum.

8.2

Chechnya: A Dirty War 1999–2002

Anna Politkovskaya

[Editorial Note by John Pilger]

Unlike the wars in the former Yugoslavia, the war in Chechnya has been all but ignored by the West. Although Russia's behaviour in Chechnya has been condemned by human rights organisations, the Putin government continues to enjoy membership of the Council of Europe, is a signatory to the European Convention for the Protection of Human Rights and is answerable to the European Court of Human Rights.

The dissolution of the Soviet Union was relatively non-violent—except in Chechnya, where calls for autonomy led to a war with Russia in December 1994. Fierce Chechen resistance, mounting casualties and a small but articulate opposition in the Russian parliament and media forced President Yeltsin to reach an agreement with Chechnya's leaders in August 1996.

Three years later, the war resumed when two Chechen warlords, Shamil Basayev and Khattab, staged an armed rebellion in neighbouring Daghestan. The new Russian prime minister, Vladimir Putin, once head of the counterintelligence service FSB, successor of the KGB, ordered an uncompromising response and Russian troops attacked two Islamic villages in Daghestan. In response, bombs tore apart a Russian Army compound in Daghestan, then killed more than 200 people in Moscow and southern Russia. On 1 October 1999, Russian forces attacked Chechnya.

This time, following a wave of anger at the explosions inside Russia, military intervention in Chechnya appeared to have broad popular support. Russian propaganda linked the attacks to 'international terrorism' and to Osama bin Laden, who at that time was wanted by the United States for attacks on American embassies in East Africa. Doubts remain, however, that the bombings were the work of Chechens; there is the strong possibility that Islamic militants from Daghestan and Russian provocateurs played a part. Certainly, the main beneficiary of these events was Vladimir Putin, who now emerged as Russia's new autocrat.

Putin's 'anti-terrorist campaign' destroyed the Chechen capital, Grozny. The civilian population fled to the neighbouring republics of Daghestan and Ingushetia, where they live today under appalling conditions in refugee camps. Although the war has been declared officially over, Russian soldiers continue to shoot civilians for no discernible reason. Torture is commonplace, 2,000 civilians have 'disappeared' and there seems to be no accountability for Russia's 'excesses'. Moreover, the maltreatment of the civilian population has bred a culture

---

Source: Anna Politkovskaya, "Chechnya: A Dirty War 1999–2002" in John Pilger, ed, *Tell Me No Lies: Investigative Journalism that Changed the World,* Thunder's Mouth Press, 2005, 409–433.

of revenge: the rebels are replenishing their ranks with new recruits from decimated families. More than 4,000 Russian soldiers and many more Chechens have been killed.

Russia has refused Western mediation, pointing to NATO's compromising attack on Serbia. Although the Council of Europe had temporarily suspended the voting rights of the Russian delegation, Tony Blair invited Putin to London at the height of the fighting, with his spokesman claiming that Russia was facing a 'terrorist insurrection' in Chechnya. Having demonstrated his ability to keep post-Soviet Russia under control, Putin was Washington's and London's man, and in return received carte blanche in troublesome Chechnya.

Most Russian journalists reported the war from the point of view of Moscow. The most honourable exception was Anna Politkovskaya, writing for the independent Novaya gazeta. Politkovskaya visited Chechnya thirty-nine times, doggedly uncovering atrocities and human rights abuses. In her dispatches from July 1999 to January 2001, she concentrated on the civilian victims of war caught between the Chechen fighters and the Russian Army. 'Both sides support the same ideology,' she wrote. 'Neither one or the other has any pity for the civilian population.' Reporting from the refugee camps in Daghestan and Ingushetia as well as from the front line in Chechnya, she has shown that, through the use of indiscriminately applied firepower, the civilian population has become the main target of the Russian 'antiterrorist operation'. Still, she treats both the victims and the victimisers with compassion and describes the plight of the rank-and-file Russian soldiers as hungry, abandoned cannon-fodder.

Politkovskaya is outraged that the suffering in Chechnya has been ignored in Russia and the West. She likens the refugee camps in Daghestan and Ingushetia to the Nazi concentration camps and compares the branding of the Chechens as a 'nation of criminals' to the Nazi treatment of the Jews. The destroyed Chechen capital of Grozny is an 'appalling contemporary Stalingrad'. Not surprisingly she has made powerful enemies. When, in February 2001, she investigated a Russian Army torture centre, she was detained overnight and repeatedly threatened with rape by senior Russian officers. She has received numerous death threats, including an attempted poisoning in 2004. She lives and works in Moscow.

The following dispatches are followed by her remarkable reporting from a Moscow theatre captured by Chechen guerrillas in July 2002.

Chechnya: A Dirty War

You probably think I'm writing all this to stir your pity. My fellow citizens have indeed proved a hard-hearted lot. You sit enjoying your breakfast, listening to stirring reports about the war in the North Caucusus, in which the most terrible and disturbing facts are sanitised so that the voters don't choke on their food.

But my notes have a quite different purpose, they are written for the future. They are the testimony of the innocent victims of the new Chechen war, which is why I record all the detail I can.

4 November 1999

We know of instances when air-force pilots jettisoned their bombs into the river on the outskirts of villages so as not to commit the sin of bombing their peaceful inhabitants.

We know cases of quite the opposite kind. The pilots deliberately fired on the Rostov-Baku Highway when refugees were fleeing along it from the war zone, and then flew past a second, third and even a fourth time when they saw that someone below was still moving. The war is rapidly acquiring two faces and each potential victim hopes and prays that they will be lucky and meet the 'kind' face of this war.

Asya Astarmirova, a young twenty-eight-year-old inhabitant of the Katyr-Yurt village in the Achkhoi-Martan (district, has looked at both the one and the other. She survived physically because some soldiers saved her. But she is now dead to the world because other soldiers carried out a dreadful and cynical atrocity before her very eyes.

On 16 November Asya was bringing the body of her husband Aslan back to be buried in Katyr-Yurt. He had died in the Sunzhensk district hospital from the wounds he received when he came under fire. With her in the car were her children, six-year-old Aslanbek and two-year-old Salambek. In another car were Aslan's older sister Oeva, a mother of two, and their two uncles who were no longer young men. At the checkpoint between Achkhoi-Martan and Katyr-Yurt they were stopped and, without a word, the soldiers opened fire on both vehicles. When the first burst into flames Asya and the little boys leapt out. 'For Allah's sake, save us!' they cried. The contract soldiers in their bandannas, who were not raw youths, continued shooting and told her: 'There's no Allah, you Chechen bitch! You're dead.'

They fired directly at her and the children. Aslanbek fell unconscious, Salambek screamed and Asya saw the car and her husband's body burn. Young conscripts observed the whole scene from a distance. When the contract soldiers had finished and went off to rest, the conscripts loaded the wounded Asya into an armoured vehicle and took her away. After several hours driving across the fields, avoiding the military posts, the soldiers unloaded the wounded family outside Sunzhensk hospital and without a word to anyone they left.

Asya is still in a state of shock. She gazes blankly round ward No. 1 where she and the children were placed. Her mother Esita Islamova asks each new visitor, 'How can I tell anyone after this that we belong together, that we're citizens of Russia? I can't!'

I try to stroke tiny Salambek's hair—his right leg is encased in plaster where fragments hit him—but the boy begins to scream and cry. He turns away and hides in the pillow.

'He's afraid,' Esita explains. 'You're a Slav, like the contract soldiers.'

'But what about the conscripts, they're also Slavs?'

'He's only a child. . .It's what he remembers and that's what he's reacting to.'

Our losses are immeasurable as we let the army get out of hand and degenerate into anarchy. By allowing such a war to be fought in our own country, without any rules, not against terrorists but against those who hate their own bandits perhaps even more strongly than we do, we are the losers and the loss is irreversible.

28 November 1999

She was lying on her back, arms by her side, shoulders square, like a soldier on parade, unaware of anything in the world around her apart from her pain. Some people came up, threw back the sheet, and looked at the eleven bullet holes scattered across her slight, girlish body and sewn together by the doctors. But even then Mubarik Avkhadova did not react. Her enormous dry eyes were fixed on the ceiling. Her arms lay helplessly by her side. Her only link with the world was the drip running into her vein.

For the third week twenty-two-year-old Mubarik has hovered between life and death. No one will give any guarantees. No one who visits her in Ward 8 of the Nazran republican hospital talks about the future. And everyone looks away when, worn by her struggle to keep alive, this once cheerful and carefree fourth-year student at the languages faculty in Grozny university suddenly shifts her gaze from the ceiling and stares at them as they repeat their meaningless phrases.

What happened? By current standards it was a very ordinary case. The Russian Army were advancing on the village of Alkhan-Yurt, only a kilometre from Grozny. Mubarik, the younger daughter, had stayed there on Suvorov Street with her elderly parents, her mother Tumish and father Ali, convinced until the last that the soldiers would not open fire on peaceful civilians and residential areas. On 1 December Ali decided that they could wait no longer and, stopping a passing *Zhiguli*, which already contained six people, he persuaded them to also take his wife and daughter. He stayed behind.

Round midday the vehicle with a white flag tied to its radio aerial was moving towards Goity. The village is now overflowing with refugees and it was there, a few days earlier, that Mubarik's elder sister, Aiza, had gone with her four small children. Two kilometres down the Goity road, off the main Rostov-Baku Highway, a plane began to pursue the unfortunate *Zhiguli* and finally opened fire.

An old woman and her grown-up daughter died immediately. To this day their names are not known. Mubarik and a thirteen-year-old girl, the old woman's granddaughter, were wounded. While the plane prepared for a second swoop, Tumish dragged the girl and her own daughter out of the car and shielded their bodies with her own, already bleeding from a number of wounds. She feverishly tucked their arms and legs under her and when the plane returned and again fired it only killed Tumish. On the evening of 1 December it was announced on TV that the air force had destroyed a *Zhiguli* full of Chechen fighters who were trying to flee. Only on 11 December, on a Saturday, was Aiza able to get her wounded sister to hospital in Ingushetia, after bribing each and every post now set up on the Rostov-Baku Highway. (At Goity the village elders had collected 3,000 roubles to help her.)

And what about Mubarik's village? On 9 December the federal forces arrived at Alkhan-Yurt. What did they gain there at the cost of such torment to this pretty young woman?

The same day that Mubarik was brought to Ingushetia, 11 December, the area around the village was swarming with soldiers and their officers, tanks and armoured vehicles. At first sight it looked exactly the way the books describe the front line in a war or the fictional versions of the present Chechen campaign that they show, hour after hour, on every TV channel. Machine-guns, bullet-proof jackets, mud, and helicopters boastfully zooming overhead.

The closer you look, however, the stranger the sights you see. The officers, for instance, are standing with their backs to the front line. Whoever heard of such a thing? The soldiers follow their example. They sprawl over their armoured vehicles in such a way that they cannot possibly observe the territory of their opponent because it is located directly behind them.

'Where's the front then?'

'Over there.'

All cheerfully pointed to a pile of tree trunks that have been chopped down and laid straight on the road to Grozny. This means that from where we're talking to the front line, beyond which there was fierce fighting, is at most fifty metres. You could hit the trees with a slingshot, let alone a machine-gun or a sniper's rifle.

'And the fighters are over there, in that belt of trees,' the officers continue, with no concern for the absurdities they themselves are offering me.

'But we're no distance from them, and you're not even wearing bullet-proof jackets? Why aren't the fighters firing? Where are those snipers that everyone is so scared of? We're sitting ducks here.'

The ordinary soldiers are even more open targets on this strange front. Contemptuous of the dangers concealed in the surrounding area (if, that is, one believes this talk of a front outside Grozny), they stand on the roofs of the ugly concrete bus-shelters and seem in no fear for their lives.

So where are the Chechen fighters? Are there any here at all, and were they ever here? It all feels like some show put on by the military and not really the front line in an uncompromising struggle with international terrorism. What physical evidence can we see here of the fierce war that Russia's forces already, in their tens of thousands, have been waging in the North Caucusus since mid-December?

The refugees are unanimous. They talk today of a slaughter only of the civilian population, and the death of children, pregnant women and old men, instead of Basayev and Khattab. That is why I am here to record such testimony from those around Alkhan-Yurt. This is the area the military call the front. We know that here, one kilometre from Grozny, there were particularly fierce battles and pitiless operations to 'cleanse' the territory. I want to understand the reason why the nameless passengers of that *Zhiguli* on the Goity road lost their lives, and Mubarik was shot.

I want to know why twenty-three people died here in Alkhan-Yurt between 1–8 December: farmers, their wives and children. Only three died as the result of bombing, the rest perished during a check on 'ID documents and residence permits' (information from Human Rights Watch). [. . .]

How are we to go on living after this? Who is our friend or enemy now?

On the eve of Constitution Day the 'liberated' Chechen settlement of Alkhan-Yurt was as empty as a film-set in the middle of the night. There was not a single human being anywhere, not a cow, a chicken or a goose. Not a single living thing, nor any sound that might distantly suggest a mooing or clucking. If someone had been weeping, shouting or lamenting it would have been less frightening.

Silence. On the hill a churned-up graveyard. The officers tell me that Chechen fighters had dug themselves in there, so they had to fire straight at the graves. But where then are the dead fighters' bodies or the prisoners?

'Where they should be,' the officers reply.

Perhaps it would be better to show them to everyone. To put the survivors on trial. Then that would really be the triumph of the legitimate authorities over international terrorism.

The silence that greets these elementary proposals is the most telltale sign of this war. We continue gazing in silence at Alkhan-Yurt. The cupola of the mosque has been turned into a sieve. A few jagged rafters are all that remain, at best, of the roofs of hundreds of houses. The walls are like some worn and discarded garment, with gaping holes of all sizes (depending on the calibre of weapon the officer chose to shoot with). Alkhan-Yurt lies quiet and deathly still in the tight grip of the encircling armoured vehicles. If people can be wounded, so can the villages they leave behind them.

So this is the 'fierce struggle with the Chechen fighters'. The army tells us, 'We are not shooting at people's homes', and the result is a devastated village and not one piece of evidence that the fighters have been there. And the front? There are no fighters there either.

But where are all the people? There must be someone on the front line in Alkhan-Yurt. Where is Mubarik's father, Ali, who couldn't get into the *Zhiguli* on 1 December and stayed behind at their house on Suvorov Street?

The commanding officer issued a very straightforward order. The civilian population has the right to leave their cellars and basements only between 11 a.m. and 1 p.m., carrying a white flag. If there is no white flag, they will be shot and also if they come out after 1 p.m. But why, I ask? The village has already been 'liberated'. And why only at those times, why not from 9 a.m. to 9 p.m.? The military here prefer to answer every question with a brief and clear 'Because'. That's how General Shamanov, our newly decorated Hero of Russia, has taught his subordinates to reply when asked about his imposition of this twenty-two-hour curfew, an unfathomable addition to the theory of military strategy at the close of the twentieth century.

That is why they do not allow journalists here who have not first been thoroughly tested and processed by the press service of the combined forces in Mozdok. Without such ideological preparation the picture is all too clear. They call it the front, but it's nothing of the kind. And there can be no justification for the sufferings of Alkhan-Yurt. Who then are they fighting against? When the remaining inhabitants are allowed back, to walk again through their village and fields as they wish, they will know the soul-wrenching answer. Well, what would you say if you found yourself in the position of these hunted and tormented villagers who have been deprived of every human right?

The answer is obvious. But let me offer one more picture, this time from the 'liberated' northern areas of Chechnya, a region opposed to Maskhadov, Dudayev, Basayev and all of their kind. The snapshot comes from Goragorsk on 10 December. This large and once unbelievably beautiful village, spread out like Moscow over 'seven hills', lies roughly eighty kilometres north-west of Grozny. There were also fierce battles here and people died on both sides. A great deal of destruction is evident, as are the fresh graves. A rough-hewn cross commemorates Private Alexei Mitrofanov, who died fighting for Goragorsk, and stands next to the vast and gaping holes left in the oil tanks by heavy artillery shells. This speaks more eloquently than any briefing: Mitrofanov died for someone else's oil.

You can't help noticing that they took particular and malicious delight in targeting the mosque in Goragorsk. It has been reduced to its foundations. The villagers give a welcoming smile to all visiting 'persons of Slav nationality', but their silent response came during the night. The statue of the Unknown Soviet

Soldier, which stands as always in the central square, was neatly decapitated. No one can find the head. There are those here who fought the Germans in the Great Patriotic War, but even that did not halt the villagers who have driven inwards their feelings of hate and desire for revenge.

The memorial itself suffered from the fighting nearby. The words NO ONE IS FORGOTTEN, have fallen off; the words NOT ONE DEED IS FORGOTTEN remain.

16 December 1999

The Independent Expert Legal Council in Moscow, at the request of the Memorial Human Rights Centre, has recently provided its analysis of certain aspects of events in Chechnya. This voluntary group of lawyers, headed by Mara Polyakova, has spoken out firmly and clearly, as international law and Article 2 of our own Constitution ('the rights of the individual take priority over all other values') demand.

There can be no talk of a guilty nation that must answer for the actions of certain of its members. The Criminal Code and Russia's law 'On the Struggle against Terrorism' both define a terrorist action as a specific event. An anti-terrorist operation is therefore an action taken against specific individual criminals. Any restrictions on the rights and liberties of the population as a whole can only be imposed by the law 'On the State of Emergency'. In this case, that law has not been invoked. Additional Protocol No. 2 of the Geneva Conventions (to all of which Russia is a signatory) is expressed in even more uncompromising terms: 'collective punishment for a specific crime is categorically prohibited'.

Are we witnessing an anti-constitutional putsch? Without a doubt. When you carelessly congratulate yourself that we have just had democratic elections to the Duma, stop and think for a moment. We are living under a Constitution that has in part been revoked and now functions only in those parts that continue to receive the approval of the Kremlin. If they then take a dislike to other articles they will toss them aside, just as they will quickly deal with any of us. Yet what will Chechnya look like in the year 2000? We are moving towards the creation of some anti-constitutional territory, a reservation jointly controlled by the harsh military rule of the federal authorities and the so-called police force of the Gantamirov band. This reservation has been set aside for people of an inferior status, Russia's Red Indians of the late twentieth century, who are guilty of having been born in the Chechen Republic. Russia, it seems, cannot live without a Pale of Settlement. At the end of the last century the Jews were thus confined and, as a consequence, they provided many of the young revolutionaries and terrorists of Bolshevism. By creating a reservation for the Chechens we are preparing an inevitable rebellion, led by the hot-headed youths who will grow up there.

27 December 1999

Picture a classroom. Children sit on their small chairs. One is scratching her leg, another picks his nose, while over there a boy in ragged sports trousers examines a gaping hole in his shoe as if no one else exists.

What can you expect? They've only been going to school for three years and are still little children by ordinary standards. They have just written a composition on the most universal school subject of all: 'My Homeland'. Which of us has not done the same, and committed the minor offence of filching wise words from some book or other?

But as I read through this pile of papers I was horrified. This hackneyed subject produced a series of burning revelations. It proved so wounding and painful a subject for those gathered in that classroom that I could hardly bring myself to call them children, let alone small children. Outwardly eight- or nine-year-olds, tragic circumstances had filled them with an adult and fully formed view of the world. Moreover, there were no exceptions, it affected each and every one.

But before you read about 'My Homeland' I should set the scene. We are in Ingushetia on the outskirts of the village of Yandara, not far from the Chechen border, at a refugee camp called 'Goskhoz' (State Enterprise). Tents, sheds and dugouts. Nothing to eat, nowhere to sleep, no clothes to wear and nowhere to wash, not even once a month. Nothing to provide any cheer. Yet the school is working and, an unbelievable luxury by local standards, it has been given several tents.

Officially we are in 'Tent School No. 8'. Almost 500 children are taught by twenty-one volunteer teachers. Of course they are not being paid, though there have been a great many promises. The admirable young director, Minkail Ezhiev, is devoted to his profession and, until September, was Head of School 21 in Grozny. Today that school is nothing but ashes.

Class 3C. Russian Language. Composition. Jamila Djamilkhanova, the young teacher from Grozny, speaks a faultless literary Russian; she does not conceal her surprise and pride at the patriotism of her pupils.

There's nothing else to add. I did not select the best compositions. There were only twelve altogether because the classes in the school are small. The tents are not large and many children cannot attend regularly; they have nothing to wear. As a rule, one member of a family attends school today, and tomorrow a different child goes. No one complains if they miss their studies; no one calls in the parents for an explanation.

There is something else distinctive about these compositions. The girls are usually more lyrical, but the boys are severe, single-minded and uncompromising. It's frightening, isn't it?

The first important discovery: not one of the children said that the Russian Federation was their homeland. That's all finished! They have cut themselves off from us.

Second, and equally important: these texts are the work of small children and so they have made quite a few mistakes. Their teacher Jamila has given them all full marks, however, no matter what errors they made in spelling or grammar.

'In our situation could you possibly say to one of them: "I'm giving you top marks for love of your homeland," and tell another, "You're only getting three out of five?"' she asks. 'I thought I could also learn some patriotism from them, and so could many other adults. Full marks are a very small reward for the suffering through which these children have learned to love Chechnya. Not one other child in Russia has had a comparable experience.'

She handed me the flimsy scraps of paper. Condensed emotion. Undeniable proof and material expression of their love. It does not get any more truthful than this.

And in the short interval before her next lesson we talked: you can still do something about hatred (for instance, by using superior force to overcome it) but, we agreed, there is nothing you can do about love. The only reaction is one of resignation and acceptance.

'I'm giving you these compositions,' concluded Jamila, 'with one purpose in mind: so that people in Moscow will finally understand.'

And their authors seem to be talking to us; even in the pages of our newspaper you can feel how much they want to make us listen.

Abdelazim Makhauri:

I have only one homeland. Grozny. It was the most beautiful city in all the world. But my beautiful city was destroyed by Russia and together with it, all Chechnya and the people living there. The people that Russia had not yet managed to destroy went to Ingushetia, as I did. But I miss my home. I so terribly want to go home although I know already that my house has been bombed to pieces. All the same, I want to go . . . Why do I want to live at home? So I can have the right to do what I want, and no one would tell me off.

LEAVE US ALONE, RUSSIA. WE'RE ALREADY FED UP WITH YOU. There were only a few Chechens before you started. GO HOME and put things in order there, not in our country . . .

Ali Makaev:

I always wanted to see my country Chechnya free from terrorism. Now here I am studying in a cold tent while Russian children can work on computers in warm schools. . .I do not know if Putin has a heart. But if he did he would not have started such a war. Putin thinks that human life is worth fifty kopecks. He is deeply mistaken. He is stealing these lives from people. I'd like Putin to know that we are also human beings. Until war came Chechnya was more beautiful than Moscow. I would like to go home and live there to the end of my life.

Islam Mintsaev:

I very much miss my school, my friends and all that I know and love. We don't live badly here in Ingushetia. We go to school in a tent settlement. But Ingush children go to big schools, to a three-storey building like we had in Grozny.

At night I often wonder when this cursed war will come to an end and we can go home. Grown-ups say that the houses are no longer beautiful there: everything has been destroyed and each day young people and our furniture are carried away on APCs [armoured personnel carriers]. They take the young people to Mozdok and torture them there like in the worst films. When I hear the roar of aeroplanes I again feel terrified, just like when we were at home. Again they are bombing my homeland. How many of our relatives have died? And how many are left homeless?

[no name]:

I love my homeland, the village of Urus-Martan because it is the most beautiful village in the world. Now I miss it very much. At night I dream that I am running with my satchel in my hands and my girl friends to our own school.

Here in Ingushetia planes and helicopters often fly past and I get scared, as though I am at home again. During the last war the soldiers from Russia killed my father. Mum searched for him everywhere. Finally she found a dead, mutilated body buried in the ground. I was six then, my brother was eight and my younger sister was eleven months old. After everything that happened I thought, the war has ended for good. But in a short time it all started again.

Now every day I hear the grown-ups weeping and telling of their murdered relatives. I would like to live under a peaceful sky! But will there be such a thing?

Marina Magomedkhadjieva:

My city Grozny always radiated beauty and goodness. But now all that is gone like a beautiful dream and only memories remain. The war is blind, it doesn't see the city, the school or the children. All this is the work of the armadas from Russia, and therefore not only our eyes are weeping but also our tiny hearts.

Now we have nowhere to go to school, to play and enjoy ourselves. Now we run back and forth and don't know what to do. But if they asked us we would say: 'That's enough bloodshed. If you do not stop this senseless war we shall never forgive you.' Soldiers! Think of your children, of your own childhood! Remember the things you wanted in childhood and what your children want, and you'll understand how sad and difficult it is for us. Leave us alone! We want to go home. [. . .]

Hospital No. 9 is the only accident and emergency hospital in Grozny. You come here to be saved or to die. All emergencies end up here, from appendicitis to a stab-wound in the chest. Most of its patients, though, are people wounded by mines. Not a day passes without an amputation, because the main scourge of the city are the anti-personnel mines that were scattered everywhere and today turn up in places where they were not to be found yesterday. During June there were forty-one amputations, not counting the patients who did not survive. Ilyas Talkhadov in Ward 3 was blown up on a route he had safely used the day before, driving to collect hay from the '60th October Revolution Anniversary' collective farm. The six neighbours travelling with him were torn apart. Both Ilyas' legs are broken and his hip joints were smashed to pieces. The only hope for him is Hospital No. 9. However, there is nothing here today apart from healing hands and souls. Nothing that could distinguish a hospital of the early twentyfirst century from a rural dispensary of 100 years ago. The only modern equipment is an X-ray machine that works one day in two because the electric current is unreliable and the machine itself is old.

A diesel engine roars fiercely outside the office window. The military donated it so that the hospital could occasionally have some electric light. Abdul Ismailov, deputy chief surgeon of the hospital, explains why the engine has just started: the relatives of a patient have finally found some fuel and the doctors have begun to operate.

Another way of operating is described by Salman Yandarov, a middle-aged and highly qualified specialist. Today he is the chief traumatologist and orthopaedic surgeon of the Chechen Republic, having recently returned, after appeals from his colleagues, from St Petersburg where he had everything: a professorship, students, respect and a very good position in a famous clinic (not to mention a salary).

'This is my native country, so I gave up everything. But what can I offer people who are blown up by mines every day? The hospital is not functioning, it simply exists,' he says. 'For instance they often bring in someone who has lost both legs and needs urgent amputation if they're not to die. I carry in the battery from my car, connect it to the X-ray machine and take an X-ray. Only then do we operate. When the relatives don't have any money to buy diesel I again go and get my battery, rig it up to my car-lamp and operate. It's shameful . . .'

'But they've surely been bringing you some equipment from Moscow?'

'Yes,' replies the doctor, who has the hands of a pianist and the manners of a gentleman. 'They donated three operating tables. I can tell you, they are so out of date that no self-respecting hospital in Russia would accept them today.'

To begin with I thought how senseless everything happening here was. If you look at it from the state's point of view, why scatter a vast number of mines around the city and receive in return an astronomic growth in the number of disabled people, who require tons of medicine, artificial limbs and so on? And then scatter more mines. And again ferry in medicine, etc. Now it's clear what the state is up to. Its concern for the situation is purely virtual; the only reality is the scattering of mines. No matter how much we want to believe the reverse, or attribute everything to our chronic disorder or thieving, the reality is that the inhabitants of Grozny have been sentenced to this fate. Evidently, the ultimate aim is to ensure that as many people in the city as possible are either left without legs—or dead. Perhaps this is a new stage in the 'anti-terrorist operation', an unhurried punitive mission directed against one ethnic community, which now requires hardly any more ammunition, just the patience to wait for the inevitable outcome.

It all fits together. Why bother to rebuild if there is no fundamental need to rebuild? Why feed people if there is no fundamental reason for them to be fed . . . ?

27 July 2000

On 23 October 2002, Chechen guerrillas stormed a Moscow theatre and held 750 people hostage for four days. In the rescue operation staged by Russian special forces, at least sixty-seven hostages (the official figure is 128) and all fifty Chechens were killed. On the third day of the siege, Anna Politkovskaya returned to Moscow from exile and entered the theatre. Her aim was to save the hostages. This is her report.

I Tried and Failed

'I am Politkovskaya, I am Politkovskaya,' I cried out at about 2 p.m. on 25 October, when I was entering the theatre at Dubrovka seized by terrorists. I had no expertise under my belt, absolutely no experience of negotiating with terrorists. If I did have something, it was my desire to help the people who were in trouble through no fault of their own. And also, as the terrorists had chosen me as a person they wanted to talk to, I couldn't refuse.

My soles squeaked on the floor of the theatre, and the sharp noise made by my feet on the broken glass will always reverberate painfully in my heart. I kicked spent cartridges as I walked, tossing them up. My legs felt like rubber from fear. 'Why have I, a woman, got myself into this hellish situation?' I thought. 'We have macho men at every crossroads, just whistle for them. Why did I have to come here?'

'I am Politkovskaya. . .Is there anybody here?' I cried. 'Hello, I am Politkovskaya. . .I have come to meet the commander. Reply!'

It was completely silent and calm around me. To my right, the theatre's cloakroom was filled with raincoats and jackets. Coats but no people, and no people sounds. It felt like walking into a school while all the children were sitting quietly in their classes.

I walked up the stairs to the second level, still crying out. I stepped into the half-lit area, without a soul in sight. Finally, a man wearing a black mask and carrying a sub-machine-gun appeared. 'I am Politkovskaya. I have come to meet with your commander,' I said.

'I will call him right away,' he replied. He looked me up and down and we exchanged a few words.

'Where are you from?' I asked him.

'From Tovzeni.' (A big village in the Chechen mountains.)

'I have been there.'

'You have? How was it? Did you like it there?'

I shrugged. We had already been waiting for fifteen or twenty minutes. What were they up to? I thought I heard a rustling noise coming from behind the green door just a couple of metres away, where I imagined hundreds of people were sitting trapped and frightened, the people whose plight I had come here for. Then the green door opened. Another masked person led out a frail teenage girl with a bluish-whitish face, wearing a yellow blouse. She was led past me, then they came back, and I plucked up my courage and asked, 'How are you doing?'

'What?' the girl replied.

And that was it; she was pushed away with a sub-machine-gun, back behind this damned dark-green door. With all my expertise and education, I was still totally unable to help the child. The helplessness was terrible.

Masked people were going to and from, talking to each other and asking me, 'Are you Politkovskaya?' Curious heads bent down from the third-level balcony. I could see through the mouth slits that they were smiling behind their masks. In order to shake off the heavy weight of silence, I tried talking to them.

'Your mothers. Do your mothers know about this?'

'No, but we have gone past the point of return. Either the war stops, or we will blow up the hostages.'

'When will the commander come?' I asked.

'Wait. Are you in a hurry? Don't hurry. You'll have everything right away,' one of them replied. The words made me tremble again.

What's next? Will they kill me? Will they take me hostage?

Soon, someone entered from that door, behind which were the hostages, and told me to follow him. A minute later, we were talking in a dirty room with no windows, adjoining the hall. There was light in here, and for the first time I could see everything properly. The chief negotiator from their side turned out to be a twenty-nine-year-old man called Abubakar, who introduced himself as deputy commander of the subversion and intelligence battalion. At the beginning, the conversation was strained. Abubakar seemed nervous at first, but then calmed down. He became angry when he talked about his generation of Chechens, aged twenty to thirty, who had been through the two wars and knew nothing except fighting.

'You won't believe it, but for the first time in many years we feel calm here.'

'In the theatre?'

'Yes. We will die here for the freedom of our land.'

'You want to die?'

'You won't believe it but we want it very much. Our names will remain in the history of Chechnya.'

I am, of course, a very poor negotiator. I had no idea what to say. And he— who had lived for half a life without taking off his military uniform and with a sub-machine-gun in his hands—he didn't know how to do it either. That is why we kept slipping into conversations about the meaning of their life, for instance. Some of the other rebels came in to listen.

Abubakar became calm again, put aside the sub-machine-gun and said he wanted to clear his soul before death. I listened to him attentively but also tried to interject about the plight of the hostages.

'Let the teenagers out,' I suggested.

'No. We suffered at the hands of your people. Now let your people suffer. And the parents there, outside the theatre, let them feel what it was like for our parents.'

'At least let us feed the children.'

'No. Our children are hungry—let yours also go hungry.'

Abubakar said he did not expect mercy and that he dreamed of dying in the battlefield. I think he was being honest and frank with me because he was in the presence of a woman the age of his mother. And that is what I told him—that he was the same age as my son and that even in the worst nightmare, I would not see my son cornered by people.

'If he were a Chechen, he would be. And he would also wish to die like myself because of everything that you are doing to us in Chechnya.'

'And if you have to die tomorrow?'

'Praise be to the Almighty.'

Finally, we decide it is time for us to part. We have not agreed on much and I'm not convinced that the talks were in any way effective. But I am no negotiator. We had only agreed that in the coming hours I would carry water and juice into the theatre and I would try to bring them enough for almost 700 people.

I left the theatre in complete silence. Again, I had the feeling that there was no one around me. Lonely jackets and raincoats watched my steps. It was cold, very cold in this dreadful theatre—and there has never been a theatre in the entire world so stuffed with explosives. I just said to myself, 'Go and get the juice, look for it, do now only this and don't think.'

Had I done a lot or a little? A little, of course. But I could not do more. When the place was stormed, all the terrorists I had spoken to died. And with them died sixty-seven of the hostages who had drunk my juice before death. Let war be damned.

Guardian, 30 October 2002

8.3

[Conclusion]

Marlène Laruelle

Nationalism as Political Posture

During perestroika and the first years of the 1990s, Russian society was torn apart by considerable ideological conflicts in which the political class showed remarkable disdain for a public opinion that it considered too conservative and unenthusiastic about the liberal changes under way. In response to this, the *posture* of nationalism that emerged during the second half of the 1990s has aimed at achieving reconciliation. Nationalism has made it possible to proclaim that the leaders and their people have regained their unity: for the first time since perestroika, the political class is speaking the same language as the population and is proposing a vision of society with which the latter is in agreement. Nationalism, then, cannot be understood as a phenomenon forcibly imposed from *above* without the consent of those *below*: on the contrary, it can be argued that the movement went in the opposite direction, since the authorities themselves were seeking to find a language in common with society and came to interpret societal demands in terms of a need for identity. This at least partially explains the populations' vote of allegiance to Vladimir Putin, who personifies the long-awaited consensual atmosphere, as well as the rather compliant acceptance of a limited political chessboard on which opposition parties no longer propose competing social projects. Moreover, this nationalist posture reinforces the mix-up between the state as a mediator of the general good and the ruling elites: the search for an identity between the people and its main leader weakens the importance granted to elective institutions of representation, which has allowed United Russia to occupy the field largely unchallenged.

Nationalism can therefore be likened to a highly strategic tag, the acquisition of which is controlled by the Kremlin, which uses it to govern the authorized political repertoire: refusing the nationalist posture results in self-exclusion from the public sphere, but proclaiming it can also prove difficult, since the authorities consider themselves to be the only ones entitled to determine its content. Thus, a battle of words, symbols, and postures is being played out between United Russia, the

Source: Marlène Laurelle, [Conclusion], *Nationalism and Politics in Contemporary Russia,* Palgrave MacMillan, 2009. 193–203.

Note: Notes and references have been removed from this article.

so-called constructive opposition that the CPRF has become, dissident movements stemming from the defunct Rodina, and extra-parliamentary milieus such as the Movement Against Illegal Immigration. The primary stake in this battle is the ability to decide where the line between "true" and "false" nationalism passes, not to mention the line between competing rivals. It enables the division, to be passed over in silence, that actually structures the political scene in Russia between supporters and nonsupporters of the presidential apparatus, shrouded because of a black-and-white, binary division separating patriots and nonpatriots. "Managed democracy" has therefore given rise to a "managed nationalism": the Kremlin has created a nationalist demand and, at the same time, seeks to co-opt or eliminate every nationalist mobilization that it has not fomented or cannot control.

The nationalist posture might conceal political oppositions even among the ruling elites; however it does not suffice to efface them. In point of fact, United Russia, just like the Communist Party of the Soviet Union, has become a pluripartite party, encompassing multiple unofficial fractions, interest groups, professional corporations, and ideological convictions. What this consensual atmosphere masks is that only having a role in the state apparatus secures the compliance of each of these actors with the rules of the real game.

Nationalism as an Ideology of Domination?

Nationalism has become an ideology of domination, precisely in the sense that it was understood by Marx or Bourdieu: domination is all the more effective in that it conceals the alienation of specific social groups by an ideology that veils relations of power. By fabricating legitimacy for the representation of power, nationalism justifies the social order: the economic system implemented in the 1990s, which the population resented as profoundly unjust, is henceforth justified. Indeed, Vladimir Putin's political restoration has as its bottom line to legitimate the market economy. Whereas other elements from the 1990s have been put into question, the rules of the market economy, the right to entrepreneurship, and the principle of private property stand unchallenged. Although the recentralization of power means that the large sectoral corporations, in particular energy-related ones, again fall under the control of the state and its secret services, nonetheless they continue to be governed by a capitalist commercial logic (to make profit) rather than by the logic that prevailed during the Soviet period (to fulfill the plan). Here again it is illusory to imagine that there has been a return to the past, insofar as the Russian economy can no longer be thought of as an autarky, but only in interaction with the rest of the world.

Nationalism, therefore, justifies the interests of the ruling class, which by promoting confusion between the public and the private has succeeded in carving up the most profitable political, bureaucratic, and economic functions. Its being an ideology of domination is substantiated by its conservative framework: one of nationalism's focus comprises questions of morality and values. But while nationalism involves multiple appeals to respect the traditional norms of the family, heterosexuality, and religion, it cannot express Russian society's autonomy and it reveals the state's inability to understand the social realities, cultural diversification, and multitude of lifestyles in contemporary Russia. Moreover, this domination through alienation is not as strong as it professes to be. The Kremlin no longer conceives society in the way it did in Soviet times: its right to legitimate violence is limited, as is its power of coercion. The ruling elites consider that the price to pay for implementing a new repressive apparatus would be too high; here again, Russia is rather far from a supposed return to Stalinism. The borders are open, new technologies have a strong presence, and impartial information is still available for those with the courage to seek it out. The prospect of large social movements like that of 2005, of an international economic down-turn affecting the middle classes, or of the resumption of emigration as a sign of social discontent, would put the Kremlin at risk of appearing that it does not know where to turn next.

An Ideology Without Any Doctrine of the Nation?

Although the Kremlin's political technologists are far from lacking imagination and innovative ability, the available repertoire upon which to build a consensus appears limited. Having rehabilitated symbols of the motherland and institutionalized a patriotic "brand", the Kremlin seems hesitant about giving it a doctrinal formulation. It understands nationalism as a determinant factor in its ability to structure the political field over the long term. Justified or not, this reading of the situation threatens to lead United Russia into a position of discursive rigidity, which could provoke internal dissension among the ruling elites or rejection by a society that is hardly keen on relearning a political cant and may refuse new indoctrination.

To date, the patriotism promoted by the Kremlin has turned out to be nothing more than a protean container largely devoid of content. As Ivan Demidov states, the authorities do not intend to establish a "barometer of patriotism" (patriotismometr): from the moment that one accepts the reconciliatory dynamic under the Kremlin's guidance, any discourse on the nation, regardless of its theoretical assumptions, has a right to speech. The themes this imprecise patriotism advocates are fairly general: that Russia again become a great power with a voice on the international stage; that it speak on equal terms with other world powers in the diplomatic, energy, and military domains; that it modernize the imperial tradition by defending Russia's right to have a say in matters concerning the Near Abroad; that it protect its fragile demographic situation by implementing probirth measures; that the country be recentralized by lifting taboos on the russification of Russia; that a halt be put to all attempts to undermine central power, perceived as a threat to the integrity of the state itself; and that the historical continuity of the state be foregrounded over and above differences in political regime and border alterations. Once this level of generality is exhausted, however, consensus gives way to divergences of opinion.

Two key issues focus and divide the ruling classes, namely migration policy and nationalities policy. Both issues involve distinct definitions of national identity that affect differently the choice of foreign and domestic policy. In fact, both issues raise the question of Russia's national identity in a way that is not just *theoretical* but also *practical*. The federal nature of the country is in fact slowly being erased in favor of a proclaimed russification that may well result in the emergence of a bill decreeing Russians (*russkie*) the eponymous people of Russia. This russification conceals multiple objectives. First, it is an act of national affirmation, since Russia is increasingly being conceived in terms—hitherto nonexistent in Russian history—of an ethnic homeland. Second, it is a vector of normalization in which the nation-state is perceived as the modern framework par excellence. And third, it is construed as a guarantee of the state's political and economic effectiveness, the logic being that centralization is a factor of modernization.

While the question of the country's national diversity is receding, leaving the North Caucasus issue at an impasse, the "Russianness of Russia" is being undermined by the phenomenon of migration. This issue divides the political class: for some, Moscow's standing as a great power must be backed up by an open migration policy, while others consider that the country and its eponymous people are in danger of being swamped by a flood of migrants. The Kremlin has hedged its bets: while new bills have been drawn up to promote the settlement of millions of foreign workers, the authorities are proliferating discourses on the need for a russification of the country. But the supposed dilemma between ethnocentered and imperial visions of Russia is once again invalidated by the parallel rehabilitation of the terms "nation-state" and "empire," both of which are conceived in opposition to a civic Russian nation (*rossiiskii*) that is dismissed on account of its abstraction. Instead, what is at work here is a concentric logic in which all those who assert their "Russianness" in one way or another are assured a place: ethnic Russians make up the inner core, followed by the national indigenous minorities (and here again there are more concentric circles: the Siberian peoples are for example closer to the core than those of the North Caucusus); the Russophone "diaspora" settled in the former Soviet republics; communities of Russian émigrés around the globe; and the citizens of CIS states who are invited to come and work in Russia and, by such migratory means, to preserve Moscow's role as the driver of Eurasian space.

Nationalism as Conformism or as Social Mobilization?

Nationalism is much more than a simple political posture; it is a general label enabling the construction of social legitimacy. In Russia today, nationalism is promoted as the ideological armature of the politically correct, and yet it remains subject to the contradictions of the contemporary Russian regime. A declaration of patriotism is a conformist gesture by which each citizen confirms his or her acceptance of the rules of the game. It signals a form of depoliticization, since discussions on the political and economic orientation of the country are rendered practically nonexistent, or decreed nonpertinent in public space. In fact, by proclaiming his or her patriotism, every Russian citizen shows an interest in the *res publica* without this affecting private life or necessitating any modification in the practice of everyday life. If this ambivalent social contract functions, it is essentially due to its implicit character: citizens are encouraged to abandon the political field to the ruling elites in exchange for the right to invest in their private lives free of state interference.

However, the Kremlin's will to depoliticize citizens in the name of the reconciliation process is at variance with its desire to remobilize society. United Russia has understood that its long-term political project will not come to life without society's somehow being repoliticized to its own advantage. The Kremlin stands for a rejection of feelings of humiliation and self-depreciation that aims to foster economic revival (for example, national priority projects, in particular in the agricultural domain) as well as to reorganize society on a self-sufficient basis. Nationalism, that is, aims to arouse in citizens a capacity to "stand up" for themselves; which means, for instance, completing their military service of their own accord, having children, being united with elderly persons, stopping drinking, engaging in acts of charity, and doing so in order to make up for the incompetence, not to mention the almost complete absence, of the state in these social domains.

This conformism, which is as depoliticizing as it is mobilizing conceals profound antagonisms and does not guarantee that the state can model society as it intends, which is evident, for example, in the discrepancy between the patriotic declarations of the youth and their massive rejection of military service. So, even though, as Egor Kholmogorov, an ideologist close to the Kremlin, affirms, "nationalism [is] a specific technology of working with the nation," does this mean that the Russian state is really able to control the direction society takes? Insofar as the ruling power has responded to rather than provoked the social demands relating to nationalism, it will be able neither to control their spread throughout society nor to ascertain the degree to which nationalism itself conditions and produces changes in social practices. The consensual character of nationalism is partially illusory: the convergence between the objectives that the Kremlin has assumed and the very real expectations of the citizens are probably only temporary. Though the Russian population seems immensely appreciative of the authorities' willingness to rehabilitate the national narrative, this by no means implies that it is ready to make sacrifices in the name of a new mobilizing ideology.

Nationalism as Nostalgia for a Mythologized Soviet Union

Contemporary state nationalism is directly inspired by the famous triptych "Autocracy, Nationality, Orthodoxy," formulated in the nineteenth century by Sergei Uvarov (1786–1855), during the reign of Nicholas I (1825–1855). By these three terms Uvarov defined the doctrine of the Tsarist regime, namely its conservative character in the areas of politics, the nation, and religion. Uvarov was a staunch supporter of a state nationalism centered on dynastic fidelity to the Romanovs. His triptych stood in contrast to the Slavophiles, who were also in search of a national identity, but who gave priority to the people as the source of the nation. The newly operative nationalist ideology, which is centered on the state, is also conceived in partial opposition to those currents that emphasize the people, ethnicity, or race. Indeed, the Kremlin is the direct inheritor of a tradition of Soviet patriotism born in the 1930s, when the idea of socialism in one country and authoritarian modernization were established. It fits perfectly with Stalin's definition, as of 1934, of the Soviet Union as a motherland (*sovetskaia rodina*) as well as his talk of "mother Russia" (*matushka-Rus'*), which he carried out in terms that would not have displeased defenders of Russian uniqueness.

Soviet nostalgia constitutes the structuring content of the nationalist consensus. Nevertheless, it is not the Communist regime but the *country*, its everyday culture and its borders, that are rehabilitated. The Soviet referent is drawn from a fund shared by the whole population; it transcends social and ideological divisions, and even, though to a lesser degree, different age groups. Indeed, for the young generation that will soon take command of Russia, the Soviet regime is practically, if not entirely, unknown to them. As Yuri Levada explains, these youths "have not chosen anything, they have not gained anything after a hard-fought struggle and they have no need to adapt to anything at all . . . they basically constitute, after the entire last century, the first generation of pragmatists that have no (institutionalized) social memory." For this youth, the Soviet past seems particularly remote: it thinks of Communist Russia's various eras, from Stalin to Brezhnev, in rather uniform fashion, and has no knowledge of the personal suffering and inter-familial division that rallying to or refusing Communism could cause. This absence of affective involvement in the regime and the increasing pacification of memories enable the Soviet Union to be integrated into a largely depoliticized national imaginary in which Stalin is nothing other than the winner of the Second World War and the incarnation of Russia at the pinnacle of its power.

The Soviet referent offers a range of identifiers plastic enough to allow the contradictions inherent in the USSR and its interpretation, such as the nature of the regime, Stalinist repression, or the ambiguous status of Russian preeminence, to be blotted out. In this way, it is possible for everyone to share the same consensus on national, military, and civil heroes, on the foundational myths (the Second World War and the conquest of space), and on cultural production (cinema, variety shows, and literary classics) from the Soviet era. In its search for unity, the Kremlin's use of the Soviet heritage has enabled it to project a capacity for social mobilization that it would not otherwise know how to express. In addition, notwithstanding the discourse of "tabula rasa," the Soviet regime itself also managed to recreate a sort of continuity with the regime preceding it: indeed, it rehabilitated a specific Tsarist past, in particular via historical reconstitutions devoted to the greatness of Russia, that was decreed compatible with the values of the Soviet Union. This sterilization no doubt helped pave the way for a certain imperial past, effaced of its political specificity, to return within the contemporary historical imagery alongside the Soviet Union and without arousing monarchic nostalgia.

The idea of reconciling contraries thus came to take precedence over sentiments of the insurmountable divides between historical epochs, political and moral values, and ideologies and national heroes. Sociological studies confirm that it is possible, for instance, to attach importance to both Stalin and Sakharov and not to see any contradiction. Indeed, the construction of the symbolic resources of the nation does not respond to logics that an external observer would declare rational. National sentiment is made possible precisely by foregrounding certain references and obscuring others to create a consensus of memories. Impressions of unity and historical continuity in France or the United States obey the same logic and may be shown to be equally artificial and contradictory. Nevertheless, in the current Russian context, the basis of the consensus is not the sentiment that disagreements are natural and constitute part of the social contract, but the restoration of a form of self-censorship, one stemming as much from society as from the authorities, which motivates the internalization of normative discourse on the legitimacy of the nation and the referents that embody it.

Nationalism as the Driving Force of Westernization?

It would, however, be one-sided to see this nationalism as no more than a cult of the past, for it also attempts to project onto the future a specific community of destiny. It is likely here that we see one of the main differences between the nationalism of the 1990s extolled by the opposition—from the extra-parliamentary groups to the Communist Party—and the nationalism of United Russia. Turned toward the Soviet or Tsarist past, the first nationalism is that of the defeated. It expresses a refusal of the post-Soviet world and of the pauperization resulting from the reforms of the early 1990s. It does not signal a form of consensus but a need to compensate for social difficulties by exulting identity values. On the contrary, the satisfied nationalism of United Russia is that of the winners, of those who have profited from the changes of these last two decades. It expresses a satisfaction with the current situation, gives support to the reforms under way, and displays a desire to make the most of a promising future. The first sort of nationalism has not disappeared; it can be seen with the development of the skinheads and the Movement Against Illegal Immigration. After its main battle theme, national identity, was revived by the authorities, this first nationalism shifted its focus onto a second object, namely the migration question, with the aim of mastering its own discursive field and therefore of establishing its own autonomous public space. Nevertheless, the overall growth of ethnophobia in Russia also leads to progressively effacing the socially "anomalous" character of this first nationalism. This latter in fact tends to be systematically overlapped by the second, winners' nationalism, which means it has more difficulties in making its voice heard in the present nationalist polyphony.

The Kremlin's nationalism does not dismiss the heritage of perestroika, nor even that of the 1990s liberal reforms, but gives them meaning within a *longue durée* that effaces their most salient traits and is no longer centered on the need to "catch up" with the West. In this vein, Vladislav Surkov's insistence on the fact that the Soviet Union ceased to exist not as a result of its defeat in the Cold War, but because Russian citizens themselves had adjudged it ineffective, is revealing of this will to integrate a disputed Yeltsinian heritage into the course of national history. This assumption is inscribed into the conviction that the Russian state bears a fundamental historical continuity over and above political ruptures. Such ruptures are not considered pertinent insofar as the "essence" of Russia is said to lie not in its political regime—imperial, Communist, presidential republic, and so forth—but instead in the country's greatness, in its place on the international stage, in the existence of a sphere of influence over its neighboring countries, and in its sense of a world mission. It is therefore difficult to talk of ideology, in the sense that this would imply a well-defined body of ideas, but one cannot but notice the progressive constitution of a coherent set of assumptions and visions of the world.

It also ought to be mentioned that, over the last two decades, the discourse on the "Russian Idea" has been distinctly Westernized. Based on its position between West and East, between capitalism and socialism, theories about Russia's *Sonderweg* continue to be largely accepted. However, at the same time, these theories are—depending on the group—rivaled or doubled by the idea of a community of origin and of destiny with Europe. In the first place, this introduction of Europe into the nationalist argumentative spectrum can be put down to the success of the most radical movements in displacing the axis of the enemy from the West onto the migrant. Fears of immigration and of a "clash of civilizations" indeed enable Russia's confrontation with the West to be put in a different light: as a struggle internal to the "white world," it ought to be bracketed whenever a greater danger threatens from the outside. Alexander Dugin is therefore no longer the only one arguing for the Westernization of Russian nationalist doctrine: he is now rivaled by movements modeling themselves on the White Powers and wanting to establish dialogue with specific sections of American culture or with the Western European extreme right wing.

The growing Europeanness of Russian nationalism is also perceptible in the Kremlin's discourses, echoed by the presidential party, about Russia's belonging to Europe. Contrary to the opinion of some researchers who think that the assertion of Russia as a great power goes hand in hand with Eurasianist theories on the Asian nature of Russia, the Russian authorities promote great power by rooting it in Europe. The Kremlin rather contends that it is possible to be of European culture but not be subordinate to the European Union, to develop a globalized economy without sharing the viewpoint of the United States, and to join the club of world leaders while preserving a specific culture, as in the case of Japan or China. The Europeanization of ideological references is also evident in the terminological evolutions under way. If the official discourse still employs the Soviet division of patriotism vs. nationalism, these terminological boundaries are in the process of changing. An ever-greater number of doctrinaires close to the Kremlin desire, as Egor Kholmogorov puts it, "to found the right of Russians in nationalism." The undermining of the taboo of *nationalism* attests once more to the ambivalent Westernization of the Russian national narrative.

By virtue of these inherent paradoxes, the Kremlin promotes an explosive mixture of Soviet nostalgia, focused on past greatness and the victory of 1945, and the call for Russia to assume a leading role in the twenty-first century, at the forefront of globalization. This conjunction is supposed to encourage the society to reunify around the advocacy of consensual symbolic referents. It therefore gives the impression of a political power continuously manipulating contradictions and toying with multiple identity strategies: allusions to Russia as a fortress surrounded by external and internal enemies, and bound to the historical values of empire and faith, combine with convictions of an open and globalized Russia that seeks to acquire a new role in world leadership. The Kremlin, then, has to deal continually with the conflict between Russia's international integration and the protection of its national autonomy. In this domain of national identity, the United States' experience of multiculturalism has reinforced the feelings harbored by some of the Russian political class who claim that the model to follow, the brother-enemy worthy of comparison, is the United States and not a European Union that dreams of overcoming national identities. The slogan "believe in Russia, believe in yourself!" symbolizes, for instance, the individualization of nationalism and appears to be modeled on the American principle of achieving national success through that of its citizens.

Thus, as paradoxical as it may at first seem, the Kremlin interprets nationalism as an instrument in the service of Russia's triple goal: modernization, normalization, and Westernization. This "enlightened patriotism" is aimed at facilitating a top-down modernization, inspired by the Soviet Union but following a capitalist model. Nationalism is also called upon to accelerate the process of normalization, identified both with the passage to the nation-state and the return of an imperial memory. Finally, nationalism promotes an indirect Westernization, even if this is achieved by military or authoritarian means, as once occurred under Peter the Great. Born in the Middle Ages, the Western European model according to which the national identity resides in the capacity of the citizens to govern their discords—one argues precisely with those with whom one shares something—cannot be taken for granted in contemporary Russian culture. The feeling that division (political, cultural, or ideological) imperils the collectivity and ruptures national unity instead of strengthening it, is very widespread. The current social contract in Russia is therefore not built on the idea that clashes of opinion and interests are natural, but on the effort everyone makes to shore up the consensus by recognizing the need to reconcile one with another. This phenomenon thereby has to be understood by avoiding the essentialist pitfall according to which Russia is in principle unable to adopt the values of the West, as well as the linear and directive pitfall according to which it is only a matter of time, that Russia is simply *behind* relative to a model of society conceived of as unique and atemporal. Multiple modernities and modalities of citizenship are summoned to coexist.

9

The Media

———•——

Glasnost, or openness, was the policy that catapulted Soviet leader Mikhail S. Gorbachev to popularity in the West. He was not only a younger, more energetic leader compared to his several predecessors, but he had lifted the shackles of censorship off of the Soviet people, sparking a renaissance in literature and the arts. The excitement was palpable, both inside Russia and out. Gorbachev's new policy, intended to help the regime to reduce economic waste and inefficiency, triggered a blossoming in society.[1] Suddenly, singer Boris Grebenshikov, the Russian Bob Dylan, could perform, record, and distribute his music. The writer Anatoliy Ryabakov could finally publish his lengthy exposé of the arbitrariness of Stalin's purges. The director Yuri Lyubimov could stage Bulgakov's "Master and Margarita" and other avant-garde plays at the Taganka theater.[2]

As time went on, writers became more bold as it became clear that anyone could publish on any subject. This was no Khrushchev-era "thaw;" it was a real opening. As freedom of the press surged and became codified in law in 1990 and in the new constitution in 1993, it seemed self-evident that glasnost was irreversible.[3] Independent newsletters, pamphlets, and other works proliferated on the streets of major cities, entirely free of official influence or control. Underground crosswalks, street corners, and subway stations were bustling with every sort of publication including a wide range of news. From old-style propaganda voices like *Pravda*, the mouthpiece of the Communist Party, to the steady and reliable news source *Izvestiya*, to hard-hitting investigative news reporting new voices such as *Nezavisimaya Gazeta* and Segodnya, to an unlimited supply of pure smut, there was a literal explosion of published works. And, a people accustomed to being information starved absorbed it all with a seemingly insatiable appetite. Newspapers were worth reading, plentiful, highly partisan, and entertaining and provided a wide range of information.[4] The television and radio airwaves were no less vibrant, with call-in shows, Claymation satires, and a range of other innovative programming offering news commentary and incisive news reporting on several networks, including but not limited to the independent NTV.[5] An energetic pack of young parliamentary and Kremlin correspondents from dozens of these outlets took their jobs seriously and attempted to create a watchdog media that they properly understood was essential to any hopes for a functioning democracy.

Most of this is now just a distant memory. Upon assuming power in 2000, President Vladimir Putin worked methodically to end this press freedom, and he succeeded. The media are no longer free. Censorship is heavy and spreading, most oppressively on investigative and political reporting. Investigative journalists are murdered at a rate of more than one per month since 2000, killed in their line of work, because of their work, with no investigations or arrests made. Among those killed is Anna Politkovskaya, whose work on Chechnya is included in this volume. Suspicion lies heavily on the state for the circumstances of these deaths.[6] There are no longer independent electronic media. Since 2004, all television stations are again state owned, and all but a tiny number of radio stations that broadcast news are state owned as well. Glasnost proved, in fact, to be reversible.

In Putin's world, the news, like everything else, exists to serve the state and the interests of the state, where the word "state" means "the Kremlin leadership." It is difficult to overestimate the seriousness of the impact that the loss of media independence has had on Russia, its politics, and its people. The relationship between a country's public officials and its media says a lot about the nature of politics in that country. Throughout the first decade of the century, for example, it was a truism that Putin was enormously popular among the people. How, then, could one complain about electoral results reflecting that popularity? However, as Georgiy A. Satarov once put it, "one should beware of putting too much stock in polling data gathered on a population that has been hypnotized." The reestablishment of Kremlin control of the media and the messages in that media are central pieces in that process of hypnotization. The scope for corruption, the image of the government institutions, the relationship toward political organizations, the outcome of and attitudes toward elections, and mass sentiments including nationalism all are related to the nature of the media and influenced by government control over and censorship of that media.

Freedom House, in 2009, ranked Russia 174th out of 195 in terms of press freedom, with a designation of "not free." To offer some perspective here, that ranking placed Russia below Sudan, whose president the International Criminal Court has twice indicted for genocide in Darfur, and just barely ahead of Iran.[7] In a virtually identical ranking, Reporters Sans Frontiers (Reporters Without Borders) ranked Russia 153rd out of 175 with trends indicating a sharply downward trajectory.[8] By all accounts, the media and journalists in Russia are in dire straits, their ability to report sharply curtailed, and journalists, editors, and publishers regularly harassed or worse. Being an investigative reporter in Russia is one of the most dangerous jobs in the world. That, alone, says more about the current status of Russia's political system than anything else possibly could.

The selections that follow detail the plight of the Russian media under President Vladimir Putin. The chapters by Ostrow, et al., and Masha Lipman detail the connection between Putin's strategy for centralizing authority and his crackdown on the media at all levels. Most remarkable is just how quickly Putin was able to reverse glasnost and restore controls over the press. Within a few years, all independent electronic media outlets had been closed or taken over by the state, and newspapers face a harsh regime of censorship buttressed by fears of violence against reporters and editors who dare to challenge the new reality. The selections by Panfilov, Satter, and Sidorov all detail specific examples of this reality and the dangers writers and editors face on a daily basis. The elimination of investigative reporting has left the regime with no important check on its power, lifting limits that may have otherwise held on the behavior of officials. Abuse, corruption, and control have been restored in large part thanks to the crackdown on the media.

For Further Reference

Books

Peter Baker and Susan Glasser, *Vladimir Putin's Russia and the End of Revolution*, Scribner: 2005.

Birgit Beumers, Stephen Hutchings, and Natalia Rulyova, eds., *The Post-Soviet Russian Media: Conflicting Signals*, Routledge: 2009.

Maria Lipman, *Media Manipulation and Political Control in Russia*, Chatham House: 2009.

Ellen Mickiewicz, *Television, Power, and the Public in Russia*, Cambridge University Press: 2008.

Anna Politkovskaya, *Is Journalism Worth Dying For?*, Melville House: 2011.

Stephen White, *Media, Culture and Society in Putin's Russia*, Palgrave Macmillan: 2008.

Ivan Zassoursky, *Media and Power in Post-Soviet Russia*, ME Sharpe: 2004.

Journal Articles

Jonathan Becker, "Lessons From Russia" *A Neo-Authoritarian Media System*, Vol. 19, No. 2 (2004).

Katherine Ognyanova, "Careful What You Say: Media Control in Putin's Russia— Implications for Online Content," *International Journal of E-Politics (IJEP)*, Vol. 1, No. 2 (2010).

NOTES

1. For the unintended consequences, see Ostrow, "Glasnost Gutted the Party, Democratization Destroyed the State" in Chapter 2 of this volume.

2. See Ed A. Hewett and Victor H. Winston, eds., *Milestones in Glasnost and Perestroyka* (Brookings Institution, 1991); and Stephen F. Cohen and Katrina vanden Heuvel, *Voices of Glasnost* (WW Norton, 1989).

3. Leon Aron, "Boris Yeltsin and Russia's Four Crises," *Journal of Democracy*, Vol. 4, No. 2 (1993), pp. 4–16; Stephen White, Rita Di Leo, Ottorino Cappelli, *The Soviet Transition: From Gorbachev to Yeltsin* (Frank Cass, 1993); Ellen Mickiewicz, "Institutional Incapacity, the Attentive Public, and Media Pluralism in Russia," in Richard Gunther and Anthony Mughan, eds., *Democracy and the Media: A Comparative Perspective* (Cambridge University Press, 2000); and David Wedgwood Benn, "The Russian Media in Post-Soviet Conditions," *Europe-Asia Studies*, Vol. 48, No, 3, pp. 471–479.

4. On the diverse range of information available in the print media, see Ostrow, "The Press and the Campaign: Comprehensive but Fragmented Coverage," in Colton and Hough, eds., *Growing Pains* (The Brookings Institution, 1998), pp. 237–265.

5. On electronic media coverage, see Laura Roselle Helvey, "Television and the Campaign," in Colton and Hough, eds., *Growing Pains* (The Brookings Institution, 1998), pp. 211–235.

6. The Glasnost Defense Foundation remains the most thorough and best site for information on the conditions surrounding the Russian media. See www.gdf.ru for information and explanation of their data, which varies heavily from international organizations such as Freedom House, whose overly conservative approach grossly underestimates the gravity of the situation facing Russian journalists.

7. See Freedom House's "Freedom of the Press 2009 Global Rankings" at http://www.freedomhouse.org/template.cfm?page=495&year=2009.

8. See Reporters Sans Frontiers, "Press Freedom Index 2009," at http://en.rsf.org/press-freedom-index-2009,1001.html.

9.1

Dictatorship Becomes the Only Game in Town

Joel M. Ostrow, Georgiy A. Satarov, and Irina M. Khakamada

It Turns Out Glasnost *Was* Reversible

In the late 1980s, Soviet leader Mikhail Gorbachev introduced *glasnost*, or political openness, as a spark to generate public critique of inefficient economic practices. His initiative to jump-start the economy by exposing the inefficiencies of the stagnant Stalinist economic system rapidly spiraled out of control, as intellectuals seized on the thawing of censorship to examine everything. When the Soviet Union collapsed in 1991, it appeared that press censorship would be a thing of the past in Russia, as young, talented, and energetic journalists dominated a thriving print and electronic media. During Yeltsin's presidency, the media were often a raucous and fiercely critical watchdog on policy and politics.

Under Putin, those seeking news need not turn on the television, and the print media are not much better. Putin has destroyed media independence in Russia to such a degree that he has earned the label "enemy" and "predator" from global organizations committed to a free press. The 2006 Annual Report of Reporters sans Frontieres (RSF) paints a damning picture:

> Working conditions for journalists continued to worsen alarmingly in 2005, with violence the most serious threat to press freedom. The independent press is shrinking because of crippling fines and politically-inspired distribution of government advertising. The authorities' refusal to accredit foreign journalists showed the government's intent to gain total control of news, especially about the war in Chechnya. . . . The lack of broadcasting diversity and closure of several independent newspapers crushed by huge fines is alarming. The government tightly controls distribution of state advertising, which amounts to blackmailing independent papers that dare to discuss the war in Chechnya. TV stations, now all controlled by the Kremlin or government associates, are also subject to very strict censorship.

Source: Joel M. Ostrow, Georgiy A. Satarov, and Irina M. Khakamada, *Consolidation of Dictatorship, Consolidation of Dictatorship in Russia*, Praeger, 2007. 114–123.

Note: Notes and references have been removed from this article.

Even this may be an understatement. Putin has overseen the destruction of media independence, termination of private ownership of electronic media, persecution of media owners, harassment and murder of journalists, and reinstatement of censorship and self-censorship across the Russian press. In a democratic society, a free press serves as the peoples' watchdog over the activities of public officials. Free and competitive elections are intermittent events offering ultimate accountability—removal from office. A free press is a continuous check on government, a tool for transparency and a source of information and ideas independent of the authorities. As such, a free press serves as a fourth branch in democratic states.

Putin behaves as if a free press were a fifth column. RSF consistently ranks Russia in the bottom third in the world, next to Singapore, Yemen, and Colombia. Freedom House has been slightly more forgiving of Russia's transgressions of press freedom, recording it as having a "partly free" press until 2003 when it fell into the "not free" category, where it has remained.

Most troubling are the violent attacks against journalists. Consider just one case, that of Anna Politkovskaya. By all accounts she was a controversial figure, but her courage and persistence are indisputable. Her most important investigative reporting was on Russia's two wars in Chechnya. Not only did she question the wisdom and motivations for the military campaigns, but also she critiqued the strategies and tactics. She exposed the devastation to Chechen civilians, the savage targeting of those civilians and human rights abuses on both sides, in often gruesome detail. The extent of knowledge of human rights abuse in Chechnya owes much to her work. As an unrelenting critic of War in Chechnya and of the Putin regime generally, she made an enemy of the president. Her poisoning and arrest trying to cover the Beslan school tragedy in 2004 was just one of many incidents in which authorities physically harassed her. They must have tired of her tenacity. On October 7, 2006 she was shot four times in the head after entering her apartment building elevator, and the killer left the weapon at her side. It was a professional job, carefully planned, and the killer escaped without a trace. Less than six weeks later, Litvinenko, who was conducting an independent investigation of the murder, was killed in signature FSB style, poisoning by polonium-210, an obscure and devastating radioactive substance. These are typically called contract murders, but there is no evidence that they, or [. . .] other political figures mentioned [. . .] who have been murdered, had contracts on them. The phrase "contract killing" suggests the sort of violence that engulfed major cities in Russia in the 1990s, as organized crime coincided with the growth of private business activity. For Russian journalists killed while investigating the actions of those in government, there is less reason to suspect mob-like contracts and more reason to suspect orders from political authorities.

While the data vary, all reports on violence against Russian journalists are horrifying. Investigative journalists are routinely murdered, and no justice is ever served. It is one thing to have a closed media, quite another for the murder of a journalist to become routine. The CPJ (Committee to Protect Journalists) reports twelve murders of journalists in Putin's first five years as president. RSF's annual reports, meanwhile, indicate twenty-five such murders from 2001 through 2005. However, the reality facing Russian journalists is even worse. According to the FZG (Glasnost Defense Foundation), eighty-seven investigative journalists were murdered between 2000 and October 2006. The variation stems from differing criteria for classifying a murder as being "in the line of work." RSF and CPJ data only count victims whom the Russian State Prosecutor qualifies as having died as a result of their work as a journalist. FZG, however, counts in its statistics any investigative journalist murdered, unless the Prosecutor certifies otherwise.

Since Putin took office, an average of one journalist a month has been killed in a politically motivated murder. Given the suspicious circumstances surrounding these killings, and the fact that none of the killers of these eighty-seven has ever been identified, the onus is properly placed on the state to investigate and solve these crimes. When prosecutors make no effort or turn up nothing, the murder is quite reasonably classified as political. As FZG's founder and director Aleksei Smirnov argues, given the authorities themselves are the ones under suspicion for responsibility for these murders, to rely on those self-same authorities to certify the nature of the murders makes no sense. In the case of a random killing, during a robbery for example, FZG does not include that death in its statistics. The organization does still consider context in its research, and probably is itself underreporting.

The timing, style, and nature of Politkovskaya's execution, and the fact that none of the other journalists' murderers has ever been caught, all point to security service involvement. That Putin, after international public outcry, declared he would personally take charge of the investigation does little to reduce suspicion. Other investigative journalists have been shot in the back of the head, hacked with axes, bludgeoned with hammers, or poisoned; most of the murders have taken place in the victims' own apartment buildings, and not one of the killers has been caught or punished. There is absolutely no reason to believe Politkovskaya's murderer will be sought, much less caught.

When it is journalists conducting investigations into corruption, ineffectiveness, or other wrongdoing who are murdered, this raises suspicion the murders are the work of authorities supposedly entrusted to protect civilians and constitutional guarantees of press freedom. That the increase in murders coincides with the ascension of the secret services into every branch of government only raises suspicion further. Even the lower figure, that two investigative journalists are murdered annually without anyone being punished, makes Russia the deadliest country in the world for journalists outside of Iraq. One per month puts Russia beyond the pale.

Journalists covering corruption or problems in government are threatened, harassed, attacked, and killed. The state launches criminal proceedings against journalists to quiet their probes into public officials. Yuri Shchekochikhin, a Duma deputy and editor at *Novaya Gazeta*, a publication critical of Putin and the war in Chechnya, was killed under mysterious circumstances that remain unclear but had the typical KGB signature of poisoning with a rare substance, radioactive Thallium, bearing resemblance to the dioxin poisoning one year later of Ukrainian presidential candidate Viktor Yushchenko. Somewhat ominously, Shchekochikhin, like Yushenkov and Litvinenko, whose murders were detailed above, had also been investigating the series of apartment bombings surrounding elections. [. . .] Another investigator of these events, Mikhail Trepashkin, has been arrested, jailed, reportedly tortured, and arrested again. Elena Tregubova, an enterprising young Kremlin reporter and author of the first investigative account of Putin's rise to and first years in power, was forced into seclusion after an explosion outside of her apartment building nearly took her life, just days after her editor succumbed to Kremlin pressure and fired her. Her book *Tales of a Kremlin Digger*, which triggered these attacks, tells of the system of censorship enforced by Putin's press office, which uses threats both professional and physical to prevent critical reporting. Shortly before the 2004 presidential election, Aleksei Venediktov, editor of the radio station Ekho Moskvy, received a call on a private cell phone number known only to his immediate family. The caller told him "to think about my son, to think about what I was doing." Countless direct threats and acts of violence, more than three per day each of the last three years according to FZG, mark Putin's relentless onslaught to end press freedom.

Data on other forms of violence against journalists are staggering. Between 2001 and 2004, RSF reports that eight journalists were kidnapped or disappeared. From 2001 through 2003, 38 journalists were arrested and jailed, 48 were physically attacked, and there were 124 reported instances of physical obstruction or pressure on media outlets. By 2005, there were too many instances for RSF to list individually. Their report simply stated, "Once again, a large number of journalists were physically attacked throughout the country during the year, without anyone responsible being punished." Again, the FZG reports more numerous attacks, including ninety-six cases of physical attack in 2003, and more than sixty each year since. More disturbing, FZG reports over one thousand "conflicts" between journalists and officials each year since 2003, including violent physical attacks, arrests and imprisonment, threats, censorship direct and indirect, removal from employment, and other forms of pressure.

Putin's crackdown on the independent media began with his inauguration. His arrest of Gusinsky, four days after the inauguration, culminated with the most successful media mogul in the country fleeing into exile and NTV, his

Independent Television Network, placed under Kremlin control as ownership was handed to Gazprom, the gigantic state gas producer. Putin did not have the prosecutor deal with Gusinsky in prison, but the press minister, who informed Gusinsky that the price of his freedom would be to relinquish his company to the state. Anticipating further action against him he obliged, and fled to Israel. Most of NTV's most dedicated and respected journalists left for TV6. Putin promptly seized that network too, with trumped-up legal charges and rigged court procedures. Then, when Berezovsky-owned Channel One offered critical reporting on the handling of the Kursk submarine crisis, Putin seized that network for the Kremlin as well. Within months of taking office, Putin had seized all national television networks under his control.

Putin abolished independence of the electronic media in less than two years. After the 1996 campaign, and the marriage of the Kremlin with the oligarchs, the Kremlin viewed the media as its weapon, just as Lenin had viewed it during the Bolshevik Revolution. Putin simply dispensed with the inconvenience of dealing with the oligarchs as an intermediary, restoring direct Kremlin control over the networks, their employees, and content. Soon this reality befell electronic media across the country, the only exceptions being small radio outlets, as long as they remained nonpolitical.

Putin has restored state control over information, with harassment and violent crackdowns awaiting any who cross the Kremlin. Less than two decades after open political reporting began under Gorbachev in the late 1980s, Putin had restored censorship to Russia's mass media. Already in early 2001, it was the case that "the media, already overwhelmingly state-controlled, have consolidated around the Kremlin. If there are no fewer newspapers, television networks, and Internet web sites than a year ago, the range of views that could be aired has certainly narrowed." They have since narrowed considerably further.

That censorship has returned is not surprising given the physical risks involved. Direct censorship is evident during crises, such as the Beslan hostage tragedy. Russia's security services certainly carried out a "special operation" in Beslan, an operation against journalists. Almost immediately after the terrorists entered the school, the Kremlin instructed television and newspaper editors how to word their reports. Putin was not to be mentioned, to prevent any potential for the public to associate him with the events and to limit any affect on his popularity. No information was allowed on troop deployment, names of witnesses, relatives, or the hostages themselves. The Kremlin even banned them from using such phrases as "suicide bomber" and "War in Chechnya." Officials arrived in Beslan to control rather than share information, establishing no press center, confiscating tapes, preventing access to information, and instructing police to detain journalists. Politkovskaya and Babitsky were poisoned, beaten and detained, preventing them from covering the crisis. An *Izvestia* reporter was fired for his report and photographs. Two months after Beslan, when demonstrations broke out in several regions protesting Putin's elimination of election of governors, the Kremlin warned the media not to report on those protests. Editors and publishers got the message. Local media remained silent, and the protests fizzled. Under intense government pressure, when murders of investigative journalists are left unsolved, self-censorship has returned.

Journalists, editors, and publishers are now "worried about what the Kremlin may think about [their stories]: if the story may affect their career in the media or if they are going to lose their job." Journalists, such as *Izvestia's* Editor-in-Chief who was fired for his reporting on the Beslan massacre, are routinely fired for their reporting. Leonid Parfyonov, a prominent broadcaster and one of the only journalists to stay with NTV after the Kremlin takeover, was sacked for protesting censorship by the security services, who banned his interview with the widow of a Chechen rebel leader. That the Kremlin would move against a popular journalist who stuck with NTV, enabling the Kremlin to claim the legitimacy of its takeover, indicates the extent to which it is determined to exert control.

In 2004, five of six national and 20 percent of local newspapers were still privately owned. However, they were all dependent upon state-owned printing and distribution facilities. Privatization never reached these media intermediaries, and officials are able to exert pressure direct and indirect. When content appears in newspapers critical of the Kremlin, the reaction is swift and final. Censorship is again widespread, and the most oppressive form is self-censorship. Recently, a poetry web site informed authors of a list of taboo subjects reminiscent of the old KGBs *Glavlit* list of items not to be published. The list included criticism of Putin, the government, members of United Russia, or the pro-Putin youth movement, anything about the war in Chechnya or specific government policies. Explained the web site's director, "it is easier to limit publications of such works than to try and guess what the president may or may not like." Content filtering on the web and in print is extensive.

The once-thriving Russian journalism profession has suffered immensely. As one Moscow journalism professor explains, Russian journalists now have to please two masters: the Kremlin and their owners. They "have lost the freedom to examine society, government, politics and business issues." As a result, "it is impossible to understand what is really going on in this country." Chechnya, corruption, and crises do not make the news, or, if they do, only the "official" Kremlin line gets reported without question or investigation, "to avoid trouble." With no objective or investigative analysis possible, the Russian people lack information about the government and rumor again substitutes where reliable information is absent.

For ending press freedom, for systematically restoring state control over the electronic media and censorship in all media, and for persistent harassment of and violence against reporters, RSF placed Putin on its list of "predators," political leaders most violently hostile to journalists. He joined leaders of Burma, China, Iran, Libya, and Uzbekistan on the "most wanted list," RSF wrote, for "using his training as a former KGB official to continue bringing all the country's media to heel. The government controls the written press and radio and TV stations. . . . Putin appears more and more on TV these days and even lectures his ministers there. Those who ordered the 2004 murder of Paul Klebnikov, editor of the Russian edition of the US magazine Forbes, have still not been identified and punished." CPJ placed Putin in 2001 on its list of ten "enemies of press freedom" that includes Ayatollah Khamenei of Iran, Jiang Zemin of China, and Charles Taylor, Liberia's former henchman now facing trial for crimes against humanity in The Hague. One can only agree, in the face of the evidence, with Politkovskaya's assessment that Putin has failed to transcend his origins and stop behaving like a lieutenant-colonel in the KGB. . . . ", he persists in crushing liberty just as he did earlier in his career.

9.2

Symptoms of the Failure of Democracy In Russia

M. Steven Fish

Constriction of Civil Liberties

Restrictions on Communication

In terms of Dahl's fifth, sixth, and seventh criteria, which enumerate several basic rights, Russia again comes up short. First, many citizens do no "have the right to express themselves without the danger of severe punishment on political matters broadly defined" (Dahl's point five). Journalists—the very individuals who supply and interpret public information—are often deprived of this right, as reviewed earlier. Here, the problems of political coercion and freedom of expression are joined, underlining the intimate interdependence of political voice and civil liberties. The harsh pressures faced by many journalists who oppose or expose officials violate Dahl's points two (on freedom from coercion) and five (on rights of expression). Election-related coercion of journalists was discussed in a previous section. Such violence and intimidation is not, however, limited to election time; it occurs regardless of the political season.

Several cases of official repression of journalists in Russia have received attention in the West. The abuse of Anna Politkovskaia, Andrei Babitskii, and other journalists who attempted to continue covering Chechnya after the resumption of hostilities in the summer of 1999 has been reported in some Western media. So too was the sensational case of Grigorii Pasko who was imprisoned for treason for reporting on radioactive pollution. The Putin government has made no secret of its intentions to shut down press coverage of the war in Chechnya and anything else that it determines to be a matter of national security. Politkovskaia, Babitskii, and Pasko broke no laws, but they ran afoul of the central government's policy. From reading the Western press alone—or for that matter, the increasingly closed Russian press—one might think official abuse of journalists is limited to matters that involve national security.

Source: M. Steven Fish, selections from "Symptoms of the Failure of Democracy in Russia," *Democracy Derailed in Russia: The Failure of Open Politics*, Cambridge University Press, 2005. 30–81.

Note: Notes and references have been removed from this article.

But these high-profile cases represent a trifling portion of the coercion that journalists endure. Far more typical are the innumerable instances of abuse that happen away from the gaze of Western press agencies and that have nothing to do with national security. In February 2001, Rashid Khatuev and Vladimir Panov, the editors of *Vozrozhdenie*, a newspaper in Cherkessk, the capital of the Karachaevo-Cherkes region, were badly beaten in their workplace by attackers armed with guns and rubber truncheons. Khatuev and Panov's paper had been critical of the republic's president, Vladimir Semenov. The assailants, who were dressed in special police force uniforms, destroyed computers and broke journalists' bones. Criticism of local officials ended even more tragically in Reftinskii, a town in Sverdlovsk oblast. Eduard Markevich, the editor and publisher of *Novyi Reft*, which exposed malfeasance among local officials, was severely beaten at home in front of his family in 1998 and detained for 10 days in 2000 by the local prosecutor's office for defamation. The defamation charge stemmed from an article he had published that questioned the propriety of a large government contract that the former deputy prosecutor of the town had received. In May 2001, Markevich's treatment prompted Vladimir Ustinov, the federal prosecutor general, to reprimand the local prosecutor in Reftinskii for violating Markevich's constitutional rights. Faced with the prospect of drawing more unwanted attention, local authorities decided to do away with the problem altogether: In September 2001, Markevich was found dead after having been shot in the back. A series of threatening phone calls had foretold his death, but true to what had become his courageous style, Markevich had not heeded the warnings to cease his investigation of local officials.

As Markevich's story shows, reporting on public prosecutors can be especially dangerous. In another such case, Olga Kitova, a reporter in Belgorod who wrote for *Belgorodskaia Pravda* as well as for the Moscow-based national newspaper, *Obshaia gazeta*, was repeatedly assaulted, threatened, and finally prosecuted for her writings that raised questions about the legitimacy of the Belgorod prosecutor's case against several university students. In March 2001, 10 police officers surrounded Kitova outside her home, forced her into a police car, and beat her unconscious. The local prosecutor's office then launched an investigation against Kitova for insulting and using force against the police officers who had abducted her. In May she was arrested again, and in December convicted of insulting an individual's honor, obstructing justice, using force against state officials, and insulting state officials.

In April 2003, Dmitrii Shvets, deputy to the general director of a television station in Murmansk, was shot to death near the headquarters of the television company. Shvets's colleagues said that he had been subject to death threats and that his car had been torched shortly before his death. The station at which Shvets worked had been critical of the mayor.

Journalists who air their work on the Internet rather than traditional media are also vulnerable. In January 2003, Dmitrii Motrich and Lada Motrich of the

Internet publication *kandidat.ru*, which is associated with the group Democratic Russia, were attacked by a group that beat them and seized a bag of documents. The editor in chief of *kandidat.ru* remarked after the attack that the publication had experienced pressure since its inception, and that the violence was probably backed by politicians that the publication had criticized.

Such events are not at all unusual. On average, between late 1991 and 1998 one journalist was murdered for political reasons every 10 weeks in Russia. In 1996, Reporters Without Borders named Russia and Algeria as the most dangerous countries for journalists. The pace doubled during the current decade: In the first three years of the 2000s, 40 Russian journalists were murdered for political reasons and 4 others disappeared. Many times more were subjected to crippling assaults but survived. The Paris-based World Association of Newspapers reported in 2001 that after Colombia, Russia was the world's most dangerous place for journalists. The report highlights the enormity of the problem in Russia, though the judgment that Russia is less dangerous than Colombia is open to dispute, since on a per capita basis, slightly more journalists have been killed in Russia over the past decade than in Colombia. Most coercion occurs not over matters of national significance, such as the war in Chechnya, but in response to reporting that power holders do not like, as in the cases of Khatuev, Panov, Markevich, Kitova, Shvets, Motrich, and Motrich recounted here. Crimes against journalists are almost never solved in Russia; the powerful act against those who criticize or embarrass them with impunity. Thomas Dine, the president of Radio Free Europe/Radio Liberty (RFE/RL), remarked in January 2003: "Russian authorities have shown little interest in solving these crimes, perhaps because the trail of culpability too often leads back to the boardroom, the police station, or the city hall."

The courts often do come into play in conflicts between power holders and journalists, but the latter nearly always find themselves in the role of defendants. Suits for libel and criminal proceedings against journalists for defamation were common during the 1990s, but the first three years of the Putin presidency witnessed the initiation of more criminal cases against journalists than were seen during the entire Yeltsin era. The 1992 Law on the Mass Media and the 1991 Law on the Protection of Citizens' Honor, Dignity, and Business Reputation make libel a criminal offense, and power holders can usually rely on the courts to deliver verdicts that define unflattering commentary, revelations, or allusions as insults to dignity and honor. Kitova's prosecution in Belgorod represents an example. So too does the sentencing to a year of corrective labor of Iiulia Shelamydova, the editor of *Simbirskie izvestiia*, for publishing an article that criticized some associates of the governor of Ulyanovsk, Vladimir Shamanov.

As one might expect, the combination of violence, harassment, and the threat of legal action severely restricts the flow of political communication. Dine notes: "In a climate such as this, when independent journalists face everything from lawsuits to jail to death, it is almost a miracle that anyone is willing to do journalism at all. In fact, fewer and fewer are willing." Uncommon bravery and integrity are requirements for those who seek to provide the public with unprejudiced information about politics. Russia does not lack such journalists. Eduard Markevich, the publisher from Sverdlovsk oblast who published *Novyi Reft*, continued to displease the authorities despite threats on his life, beatings, and detentions. After Markevich was shot dead, his widow took up the task of publishing the paper. Such extraordinary individuals enjoy some organizational support in society. The Society for the Defense of Glasnost, a union of journalists, teachers, and lawyers, organizes training programs to foster professional ethics and help journalists resist the bribes and the blows of officials and private interests. The organization, however, obviously finds itself in a lopsided battle that favors those who control the agencies of administration prosecution, and coercion.

When embarrassing publications make it to the newsstands despite all good efforts to stop their dissemination, officials can take other actions. One popular technique is seizing the newspapers. During 2001 and 2002, Governors Sergei Darkin of Primorskii krai and Boris Govorin of Irkutsk oblast and President Valerii Kokov of Kabardino-Balkar autonomous republic, to name three examples, regularly sent the police to the vendors to confiscate and destroy runs of the one or handful of newspapers left in their bailiwicks that published unflattering articles.

These practices by provincial officials obviously violate Dahl's point six, which requires that "citizens have the right to seek out alternative sources of information. Moreover, alternative sources of information exist and are protected by law." They amount to trivial harassment, however, compared to the national government's policy toward the media since the onset of the Putin era. During his first three years in office, Putin shutdown or took over all private television networks with national reach. By the middle of 2003, serious criticism or scrutiny of the president in the electronic media had become as scarce in Russia as in the dictatorships of Central Asia. Anything resembling thorough or balanced coverage of the war in Chechnya had disappeared. Parliament was fully complicit in the statization of the airwaves, even though the president, and not the legislature, assumed control of the flow and content of information. Provincial officials took their cue from the chief executive. Local television stations and newspapers that previously enjoyed some autonomy increasingly came under the control of provincial executives. Aleksandr Prokofev, the mayor of Pskov between 1996 and 2000, noted shortly after leaving office: "The national leadership sets the tone in Russia, as it always has, including in the treatment of opposition. The provincial leaders take their cues from the center. They mimic it even when they don't obey it." Based on his in-depth research in Iaroslavl' oblast, Sakhalin oblast, Primorskii krai, Khabarovsk krai, and the city of St. Petersburg, Jeffrey Hahn concluded that only in the last of these five regions did a trace of meaningful freedom in the local media survive into the third year of the current decade. Even in St. Petersburg, the local electronic media are in the governor's hands and, through the president's sway over the governor, under the control of the central government.

Television was not the only medium to undergo statization. While some nonstate newspapers continued to publish, the most incisive independent print media, notably the daily newspaper *Segodnia* and the weekly news magazine *Itogi* (which was copublished with the U.S. magazine *Newsweek*), were taken over by the government. Putin has wrapped his every move against the media in a web of pretense about the outlet's financial insolvency, inadmissible business practices, or illicit dealings or connections. He has relied on state-owned corporations, the courts, and the police to do the dirty work, always coyly denying personal interest and involvement. Ann Cooper, the executive director of the Committee to Protect Journalists, a leading international press watchdog organization, remarked in May 2001: "President Putin pays lip service to press freedom in Russia, but then maneuvers in the shadows to centralize control of the media, stifle criticism, and destroy the independent press." To use Dahl's formulation, "citizens have the right to seek out alternative sources of information" in Russia; the problem is that the chances of actually finding such sources, not to mention enjoying regular, reliable access to them, became increasingly slim during the first half of the 2000s. "Alternative sources of information exist and are protected by law": This portion of Dahl's sixth point is met in Article 29 of the Constitution, which explicitly guarantees freedom of speech and information. The catch is that the Putin government simply ignores Article 29 in practice.

Some sources of political information are still difficult for the state to control. The Internet is one potentially important source; others include the *Moscow Times* (and its sister paper, the *St. Petersburg Times*) and Radio Free Europe/Radio Liberty (RFE/RL). Such sources have become increasingly important as the government has methodically eliminated independent outlets. Indeed, researchers such as this author, as my citations make clear, must rely on them, as well as on personal interviews and on international agencies, such as the Committee to Protect Journalists, the World Association of Newspaper

Journalists, and Journalists Without Borders. Valuable as they are for the researcher, however, such sources are not readily accessible to most people in Russia, and they certainly cannot be as influential as conventional media outlets. The *Moscow Times* is accessible only to people who read English and is difficult to obtain outside Moscow, St. Petersburg, and a handful of other large cities. The number of Russians who have a computer at home is rising rapidly, but in 2003 it was still only 7 percent of the population. By contrast, 97 percent of Russian households have a television. As in most of the world, people get their political information from TV. It is little wonder that the government has focused on it with particular intensity. RFE/RL broadcasts its radio programs in Russian and is widely accessible. This fact has not been lost on the government: In October 2002, Putin cancelled an August 1991 decree that guaranteed the legal rights of RFE/RL to operate in Moscow. At the time of the 1991 revolution, Yeltsin regarded the outlet as a valuable source of independent information. He issued the decree to protect RFE/RL from governmental or commercial manipulation. True to form, the Putin government claimed that the move was a strictly technical measure designed to give equal status to all foreign media outlets in Russia. The ruling's ultimate consequences are, as of this writing, still unsettled. But one need not be a rocket scientist — or even a political scientist—to predict them.

Putin's policies have degraded freedom of expression in Russia, but the downward trend was already evident during the second half of the 1990s. During the Yeltsin period, Article 29 was not a dead letter. Some pluralism in mass communications obtained at the national level and in many regions. Critical scrutiny of officials, including the president, was common. But the growth of the national electronic media's slant toward Yeltsin was palpable in the 1990s. In 1996, the chief of NTV, then the main private television station with national reach, also served as the director of media operations in Yeltsin's presidential campaign. The presidential administration probably had to do little beyond allowing Ziuganov, Yeltsin's communist opponent, to serve up his warm accounts of Soviet life to ensure that most journalists would rally behind the incumbent. Still, even granting a great deal of leeway for the possibility that bias did not result from official pressure, it is hard to escape the conclusion that the national electronic media severely distorted the political process during the second half of the 1990s. It is impossible to establish a clear threshold beyond which systematic media bias undermines fair competition, but for the observer who lived in Russia during election campaigns, it was obvious that some such threshold was habitually crossed.

While all political parties are allowed to buy television advertisements, most discussion relevant to campaigns takes the form of coverage on political news reports and talk shows. Such programs occupy a larger portion of total air time in Russia than they do on the major commercial networks in the United States. By the middle of the 1990s, pro—government candidates and parties received an abundance of flattering coverage, while opposition parties and candidates encountered virtual embargoes. In the presidential election of 2000, television coverage of Putin reached Soviet levels of sycophancy, with tender reporting on the acting president's recreational activities crowding out coverage of politics. One could easily have surmised that one was watching television during "normal" times in Belarus, Azerbaijan or Kazakhstan, where the chief executive's virtues are slavishly extolled as a matter of course.

Thus, even before Putin's victory in March 2000, the medium in which the vast majority of voters get their political information was so thoroughly preferential that alternative voices were often drowned out or not represented. Putin's full-blown assault on the independent media represented a new level of state-led constriction of communication, but state interference in the free formation of popular political preferences was evident during the Yeltsin period as well.

Figure 1 illustrates Russia's press freedom scores between 1994, when Freedom House began publishing its analyses of press openness around the world, and 2003. The numbers capture the deterioration in openness during the second half of the 1990s, as well as the continuation of closure in the 2000s. Countries are scored on a 100 point scale. In the ratings as published by Freedom House, lower scores represent greater freedom. Here, I reverse the scale for more intuitive presentation. As the figure shows, press openness has declined

Figure 1. Freedom House Press Freedom Ratings in Three Countries, 1994–2003

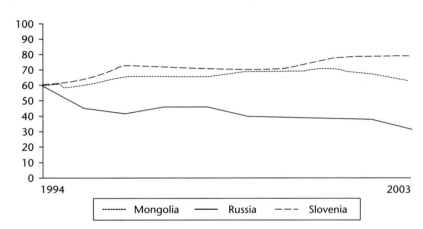

substantially. In 1994, Russia received a score of 60, which placed it in the "partially free" category. A decade later, Russia's score had fallen to 34, leaving it in the "not free" category. For comparative purposes, the figure also includes graphs for Slovenia and Mongolia. These two countries (and, in the postcommunist region, only these two countries) received scores in 1994 that were identical to Russia's in the same year. The graphs show the divergence between Russia and the other two countries. Press freedom in Mongolia improved moderately in the late 1990s and the beginning of the 2000s but then fell back a bit in 2003 it received a score of 64. In Slovenia, press freedoms improved steadily and markedly, in 2003 it received a score of 81. While Russia began the period on the same level of openness as Slovenia and Mongolia, in 2003 its score was the same as Singapore's, 8 points worse than Pakistan's, and just 3 points better than Kazakhstan's.

9.3

Constrained or Irrelevant:
The Media in Putin's Russia

Masha Lipman

The Soviet Union had an enormous number of newspapers, but no independent media. Objective reporting, working with a source, investigative journalism, news itself were unfamiliar concepts. Competition, advertising, profitability were unheard of. Holding the government accountable on behalf of the public was not an issue: the Soviet press was an arm of the state, and it preached to the public on the state's behalf.

One of Lenin's pronouncements that adorned many a street and square of Soviet cities proclaimed that "a newspaper is not only a collective propagandist and agitator, but also a collective organizer". And sure enough through the decades of communism the Soviet press—and later television—fulfilled that mission. Every word printed or broadcast for a mass audience was to be authorized by Communist party censors; all periodicals and broadcasting agencies (like all property) were owned by the state; all important appointments had to be approved by the Communist party. The party produced and disseminated ideologically appropriate opinions on every issue, and even provided ideologically correct wording.

In the late 1980s the press started to open up, and soon thereafter the era of preliminary state censorship came to an end. This was the beginning of revolutionary change: in 1990, a year before communism collapsed and the Soviet Union followed suit, the first nongovernment periodicals in 70 years began to take shape. When Boris Yeltsin, the first Russian president, took the helm, private mass media and professional modern-day press and television not controlled by the state came into existence.

Less than a decade later the Russian government undertook its first major crackdown on press freedom. In the spring of 2000, within days after President Vladimir Putin's inauguration, the government launched a campaign to take influential media under state control. The campaign began with a raid by masked security men on the offices of Media-MOST, the largest privately owned media

---

Source: Masha Lipman, "Constrained or Irrelevant: The Media in Putin's Russia," *Current History*, October 2006, 319–324.

group; three years later all national television networks were controlled by the state. In recent years the Kremlin's control over media has tightened further.

Compared to the Soviet era, today's Russian media still enjoy considerable freedom. They are predominantly commercial institutions, and even on state-controlled national television constraints apply almost exclusively to politically sensitive coverage. The days of total prepublication censorship have securely become a thing of the past. Yet, if one looks back five years ago rather than twenty, the picture is of a Russian media scene significantly constrained.

Taking Control

In 1994–1995, at the time of the Russian government's first war in Chechnya, reports by the privately owned television network NTV helped to shape public opinion in much the same way as American media did during the Vietnam War. The atrocities and horrors of the Chechen War entered the homes of the Russian people as those of the Vietnam War seeped into the living rooms of Americans, and before long this yielded a similar effect: the war grew so unpopular that President Yeltsin had to stop it—otherwise he ran no chance of winning reelection for a second term in 1996.

Such a result today would be inconceivable. With all national television networks tightly controlled by the Kremlin, nothing that government authorities deem "inappropriate," unexpected, or unpleasant may appear on the television screens of the major networks. In the summer of 2004 the last live TV political talk show was shut down, as well as the last political satirical show. Technically the top manager of the channel made the decision, but there was little doubt he was acting on orders from the government. The Kremlin keeps "stop lists" of individuals (political opponents, uncompromised critics) who are barred from national television. The coverage of sensitive issues is thoroughly filtered to ensure that the picture of Russian life delivered to viewers is not politically disturbing or provocative.

In their recent book, *Kremlin Rising: Vladimir Putin's Russia and the End of Revolution, Washington Post* Moscow correspondents Peter Baker and Susan Glasser cite an insider's description of how government control over television coverage is implemented: "The Kremlin convened meetings each Friday with the top television directors at which Putin aide Vladislav Surkov, Kremlin consultant Gleb Pavlovsky and others handed out weekly talking points. Over time, the agenda became nakedly political, aimed at supporting Putin and his political party. . . . At each session, a written agenda was handed out with the week's expected news topics and recommended approaches."

By the time he emerged as Russia's president, Putin was well aware of the political power of television. In late 1999 Boris Berezovsky, a businessman, media tycoon, and political operator, used his television channel to destroy Putin's political rivals. A sophisticated smearing campaign significantly reduced their popularity, thus clearing Putin's path to the presidency. After this experience it was only natural for Putin to desire that a tool as powerful as television rest under Kremlin control and not in the hands of business tycoons whose loyalties he could not trust. Print press was of much less importance: the distribution of mainstream dailies and weeklies is confined to a few large urban centers (mostly Moscow) and their circulation rarely exceeds 100,000 copies. National television networks reach over 90 percent of the Russian population of over140 million people.

Acts of Disloyalty

Bringing the television networks fully into submission proved a complicated and time-consuming task. In the meantime, Russia lived through a variety of dramatic developments and crises, and at least some of the journalists covering them were driven by professional instincts developed during the earlier post-communist years: they repeatedly sought to unveil what the government was anxious to conceal.

Such was the case of the submarine *Kursk* catastrophe in August 2000, which took the lives of all 118 sailors aboard. The media exposed officials' lies and cover-ups while a furious and frustrated Putin lashed out at journalists, blaming them for subverting the Russian army and navy. Another example was the October 2002 attack at a Moscow theater in which about 900 people were taken hostage by Chechen terrorists. A botched rescue operation that used knockout gas but failed to provide adequate and timely medical help left 130 hostages dead.

Journalists did their best to investigate these events, while Putin accused them of cynical profit seeking: they are taking advantage of the tragedy, he said, in order to attract more public attention and thus more advertising money. Shortly afterward, the top manager of the television network whose coverage especially enraged Putin was replaced by a loyal director, to whom the Kremlin's instructions were a much higher priority than the ethics of the journalistic profession.

Each act of "disloyalty" by the media served as additional proof of the need to keep television firmly under control, in the government's view, and the Kremlin has worked to tighten the constraints. By the time the hostage-taking tragedy at a Beslan school occurred in September 2004 the Kremlin was fully protected against the detrimental effects of professional journalism, at least as far as national television was concerned. As soon as the storming of the school was over, so was television coverage of one of the world's most horrible terrorist attacks, which took the lives of more than 300 people, most of them children. There were no survivors' accounts, no stories of desperate people who lost loved ones, no independent experts' analysis, and no public discussion whatsoever.

Indeed, national television has become a tool for maintaining Putin's popularity and the political dominance of his administration. Tame television certainly came in handy for the past election cycle (parliamentary elections in December 2003 and Putin's reelection in the spring of 2004). Secure control of national networks ensured that campaign coverage was fully in favor of the pro-Kremlin party Edinaya Rossiya (United Russia). International observers from the Organization for Security and Cooperation in Europe evaluated the campaign as generally free but unfair and accused the state-controlled media of showing bias toward pro-presidential parties and the incumbent president.

There is no doubt that the forthcoming election cycle in 2007–2008 will see the Kremlin take full advantage of its control over television. The ruling elite is anxious to preserve the political status quo, and television is invaluable when it comes to clearing the political scene of genuine competition—granting fully uncritical coverage to the incumbents, while barring and smearing the undesired candidates.

Limited Access

Control instead of competition has been the trademark of Putin's government. Under his tenure decision making has been concentrated in the Kremlin inner circle and fully shut off from the public eye. The Kremlin strongly limits access to "public" briefings and never has them televised. The Kremlin spokesman is not a familiar face, except for a small group of trusted and loyal journalists included in the so-called Kremlin pool.

Putin himself holds one press conference for Russian journalists a year, with over 1,000 reporters from all over the country. This is more a gala public relations event than a format for asking pressing policy questions. In fact, asking urgent policy questions of the Kremlin has become an extinct genre in today's Russian journalism. As a result, decision makers enjoy full unaccountability. To cite just one example: when FSB (Russian state security agency) chief Nikolai Patrushev appeared on television for the first time after the terrorist attack in Beslan (this was about one month later), the interviewing television reporter did not ask him a single concrete question about the episode. He would not even inquire where Patrushev was at the time. (Rumors had it that he did arrive in North Ossetia—the Russian republic in which Beslan is located—but never appeared in public so as to avoid responsibility for what was emerging as a horrible tragedy.) It should come as no surprise that at Putin's yearly press conference in late 2004, the issue of Beslan was never raised. The atmosphere in today's

Russia suggests there was likely no need to instruct the journalists not to ask this question—they know better than to antagonize the president.

With no autonomous, private ownership of national television networks, self-censorship among journalists has become pervasive. As for the top television managers, they are willing and skilled promoters of Kremlin policies who eagerly and creatively cooperate with Kremlin aides.

Media Weakness

In the late 1980s, at the time of perestroika, there was tremendous enthusiasm for free words. Print runs of periodicals skyrocketed. Press articles stirred passionate public debates. Gradually, a liberated press helped the Russian people shed their long-abiding fear of the state and eventually free their country of communist oppression.

President Yeltsin did not interfere with the free press, even if at times it caused him serious trouble (for instance, when media coverage of the first Chechen war reduced his popularity and forced him to sign a humiliating agreement with Chechen leaders). Yeltsin seemed to genuinely value press freedom, in part because it was one of the democratic liberties he secured for Russia, and also because liberal journalists were his natural allies in the fight against fierce Communist opposition, a struggle that lasted throughout his rule. Even if Yeltsin or some in his inner circle had wanted to restrain freedom of speech, his weakened government most probably would have lacked the capacity to do so.

Unfortunately, although Yeltsin's government did not directly attack press freedom, the fundamental principles that make it possible—just like the principles of other democratic institutions—were compromised during his tenure before they had a chance to take root in the Russian soil. Problematic ownership of media assets, murky business practices, and institutional weakness all helped to erode the foundations of an independent media.

Russia's unprecedented transition from a fully nationalized economy was associated with legal anarchy and get-rich-quick schemes in which the most entrepreneurial and the best connected enriched themselves at state expense. Big businessmen, media tycoons included, were engaged in murky relations with government officials, thus gaining access to resources such as lucrative contracts, exemptions, or easy loans. Media owners may have been powerful and independent, but their autonomy was shaky: it lasted only until the government gained enough strength.

The flaws of state institutions, the prevalence of secret collusion over open political competition, the large-scale lobbying unregulated by law, and the growth of corruption all had an effect on the activities of mass media during the

1990s. Paid-for articles and advertising disguised as news became common in the news media. So did the publication of smearing and compromising materials to undermine political and economic rivals. (These materials generally were provided by the "client"; the journalist would make no effort to probe or verify. Among other detrimental effects this practice has undermined the development of professional investigative journalism in Russia.) Of course, these activities were not universal. The best publications, television stations, and journalists retained their passion, curiosity, and ethical principles and perfected their skills. Yet their professional mastery could not address the main problem: the declining credibility of the media and reputation of the journalistic profession. Owners not averse to using their influential outlets to further their own political and business goals caused further damage to the media's image.

Just like other democratic institutions—the parliament, political parties, the judiciary—mass media tried to follow the time-tested Western models, yet none of them made good progress. Disillusioned with a democracy that failed to meet their expectations of a better life, and abhorring the new rich as well as greedy officials, the Russian people resumed their habitual attitude: a deeply ingrained mistrust of the government and of each other, supported by apathy and cynicism. The mass media failed to evolve as a means of advancing public politics in part because the sphere for vigorous debate was gradually reduced and because few Russians sustained hopes of using the media to hold authorities accountable.

The Kremlin's Strategy

The Kremlin did not shrink from seizing advantage. In 2000, however, when Putin and those around him identified the mass media—and first and foremost national television—as a target for expanding state power, Russia still had a variety of actors who defied the central government. Business oligarchs, unruly local governors, and liberal opponents in the parliament remained politically powerful (though not cohesive). The government thus had to act carefully.

The Kremlin did not harass journalists or editors. Attacking individuals armed with weapons as innocuous as writing skills and a computer could have promoted public sympathy for those persecuted. The Kremlin did not intend to conduct a bloody repression, and harassment of journalists one by one was more likely to encourage than to intimidate them. Instead, the Kremlin went after media owners. Their outright negative public image made them a better target. Besides, they were more vulnerable. All of them were engaged in questionable business practices in the early stages of Russian capitalism; with huge property holdings they stood to lose a lot more, and thus were more easily intimidated. Finally, the television network owners were a tiny group, so pushing them out was a more secure way to take all national television under control.

This was how the Kremlin embarked on a sophisticated campaign against its first media target—Media-MOST. Founded and owned by Vladimir Gusinsky and shaped in the mid-1990s, Media-MOST was the largest non-government media group. It included a popular radio station, a few high-quality periodicals, and, by far the most important asset, NTV, Russia's highest-quality national television network, which was politically influential and enjoyed the public's affection.

Media-MOST was hugely indebted to the giant gas monopoly Gazprom, in which the state held a large share. The Kremlin targeted Gusinsky in part because he refused to pledge allegiance to Putin during his presidential campaign. Also, his debt to Gazprom made him vulnerable when the gas company's management, once closely tied with Gusinsky, switched loyalties and abetted the government's attack on the bold media tycoon.

The campaign combined business litigation with personal intimidation. Gusinsky was threatened with criminal prosecution and even briefly jailed. The public, expectedly, had little sympathy for the media magnate. Neither would the rich and the powerful stand up for him, for fear of falling out with the Kremlin: they realized they were in no way immune to similar troubles. The Kremlin spinmeisters vehemently denied that the campaign against Gusinsky and his media group had anything to do with press freedom and state control over coverage. They did everything in their capacity to persuade the public that this was merely business litigation.

The campaign took longer than the government expected and turned out to be fairly costly, both in terms of state resources and Russia's image in the West. Yet eventually the Kremlin had its way. Gusinsky was forced to flee the country, and his television network was taken over by the government surrogate Gazprom. Another business and media tycoon, Boris Berezovsky, who controlled Russia's largest national television network, followed Gusinsky's path a short time later.

The Sound of Apathy

The public may have felt sorry for its favorite journalists, some of whom chose to go off the air rather than work under the Kremlin's command, but the protest was not powerful enough and quickly faded away. Although the eviction of the two biggest media tycoons and the takeover of their television networks meant the end of political diversity on television, most Russians did not appear to regard the government's efforts as an infringement on their rights.

After the takeover of two major networks, the Kremlin elite felt more confident in further tightening control over national television. Two attempts to launch nongovernment national television channels proved unsuccessful; both were shut down with little regard to legality and barely any public reaction. As the Kremlin infringed deeper and deeper on the public ground and wiped out all non-government national television in Russia, the Russian people easily gave in. Freedom of choice and an alternative to government opinion were not valued: in a national poll conducted in the fall of 2003, 36 percent said increased state control was beneficial for mass media, 25 percent thought it was detrimental, and the rest had no opinion.

Those precious few television journalists whose talent, professional ethics, or political beliefs put them out of tune with the general atmosphere of self-censorship and compliance quit or were fired. Several shows were taken off the air altogether.

If the journalistic community was unhappy about these developments, its reaction remained fairly timid. In 2004 the Russian Television Academy awarded its annual prizes to several non grata journalists and terminated shows; some academy members in a public letter expressed concern about the political censorship of television. They suggested that the letter be read at the award ceremony, but other members would not take the risk. The letter ended up in the low-circulation liberal press. There a couple hundred thousand Russians could see it, instead of an audience of many millions for the National Television Awards ceremony.

Pockets of Freedom

While strategically targeting television, the Kremlin left the print press largely alone. Until recently, the government would not bother with minor media outlets: about a dozen mainstream dailies and weeklies, a smaller television channel, a popular radio station, and a few high-quality political websites have maintained liberal and critical editorial lines.

The picture of Russian life that emerges from these outlets is quite different from the one provided by the national television networks. Yet all these outlets remain at the mercy of the Kremlin. With politics under state control, there is no political force or sufficiently powerful public group capable of opposing a crackdown on the remaining nongovernment media, should the ruling elite deem it necessary. Some outlets are especially vulnerable, since they are owned by the same evicted tycoons whose television properties were taken over by the state.

Liberal outlets have small audiences. The largest mainstream daily newspaper, *Izvestia,* has a press run of 250,000; others rarely exceed 100,000. And these runs have not gone up since national television came under tight control—a significant sign of low public interest in liberal media. Declining circulation of high-quality mainstream periodicals may be a worldwide trend, but in Russia, with a population over 140 million, the existing runs are especially low, and the distribution is generally limited to Moscow and a few major urban centers. Some Internet-based publications maintain a liberal and critical editorial line and offer high-quality news and analysis. But the Internet's penetration of the public, though growing fast in recent years, still remains relatively low. (The number of regular users is under 10 percent of the population.)

Meanwhile, the habit of reading newspapers in order to be politically aware is largely lost in Russia. The incredibly high press runs of the perestroika era evaporated as soon as the economic reforms of the early 1990s liberalized prices and newspapers became too expensive for the vast majority of Russians. National distribution systems, which crashed after the collapse of the Soviet Union, have never been properly reestablished, with most periodicals distributed by retail sales rather than subscription. As a result, even *Izvestia* is read by only 2 percent of the national audience and 4 percent of Muscovites. None of the other high-quality mainstream print media has a national audience of more than 1 or 2 percent.

Since most of the fragmented dailies and weeklies do not pick up each other's stories, even an important news piece creates little public resonance and fails to become a politically significant event. Occasionally, a publication will produce an excellent article disclosing important information, yet the impact is essentially absent.

To provide just a few examples: several years after the *Kursk* submarine disaster, a high-quality weekly (with a circulation of about 60,000) published revealing facts about official inaction during the first hours after the submarine had sunk. There was no response from the public, or military authorities, or from other publications. Similarly, two members of parliamentary commissions investigating the Beslan tragedy spoke to the same weekly, reporting outrageous facts about the storming of the school. This disclosure also caused no response. And a business daily, *Vedomosti*, exposed the financial intricacies of the purchase by a state-run oil company, Rosneft, of Yugansneftegaz, the most valuable asset of the convicted tycoon Mikhail Khodorkovsky's oil company Yukos. President Putin had earlier referred to this transaction as purely a market deal in full compliance with the law. Yet, according to the *Vedomosti* story, it involved unlawful use of government funds. No government official bothered to deny the information that challenged the president's credibility.

Empty Space

The problem with today's media in Russia is not just that the Kremlin controls national television, but also that those publications that remain uncontrolled do not make a difference, since they operate in a virtually empty public space. The real public space is that of national TV, where Kremlin loyalists shape the news.

Even so, the Kremlin more recently seems to be extending its control over smaller-circulation media. It orchestrated a change of ownership in *Izvestia* and a television company with a relatively small audience and a liberal editorial line. For the time being, the coverage and editorial perspectives of both outlets remain unchanged. But with their new, fully loyal owners, the Kremlin may be confident that both will prove useful if and when the Kremlin might need to use them for its political purposes. The most obvious purpose is ensuring the desired outcome in the next election campaign.

9.4

Russia: Why Do Journalists Die?

Oleg Panfilov

Press advocates need accurate information, not inflated death figures, to shed light on the real threats to Russian journalists. Joel Simon, executive director of the Committee to Protect Journalists (CPJ), during a general meeting of the International Freedom of Expression Exchange held in Oslo in early June, called for organizing a global conference on impunity. Simon put forward the idea after presenting a report on murders of journalists. He stressed that such crimes remain unsolved in many countries.

Simon is not the first person to raise the issue of impunity for crimes against reporters. The International Federation of Journalists (IFJ) unveiled today in Moscow the results of its research based on data from the CPJ, the Center for Journalism in Extreme Situations (CJES) and the Glasnost Defense Foundation. This will be the first attempt to analyze systematically why so many reporters are killed in Russia and identify the causes of attacks. The study aims to find out which of the victims were killed in connection with their profession.

Morbid Competition

Ever since 1991, when the first attacks on journalists took place (some reporters might have been assassinated in the Soviet Union, but this is impossible to find out), media watchdogs have reported different figures. Even the Russian Union of Journalists (RUJ) cannot tell the exact death toll. For instance, it reported 201 journalists killed in 2006, while five years earlier, in 2001, the body count was in excess of 250. The numbers contradict the RUJ director's statement that "the list gets longer by 10-20 names every year."

Discrepancies do not add credibility to watchdogs' conclusions about media freedom in Russia. The RUJ does not have a monitoring service and uses data from other organizations. The inconsistency may be a result of internal disputes in the RUJ leadership, as higher death tolls make its mission look more important

Source: Oleg Panfilov, "Russia: Why Do Journalists Die?" *Transitions Online*, June 16, 2009.

in the eyes of the international community: If so many journalists are being killed, the union needs more financial support. But can it help change the situation?

Nearly all press advocacy groups doing research in Russia are involved in this competition of numbers. Reports from the leading organizations shed little light as to what happens to journalists, while victim numbers—and even names— differ. Reports by four prominent organizations for 2006, for instance, name from one to four journalists killed in the line of duty, and only Anna Politkovskaya's name appears on all four lists.

Discrepancies are often explained by the use of different criteria for determining the causes of murders. The criteria are normally based on a superficial examination of media reports about each case and accounts of fellow workers or relatives.

In reality, every year in Russia typically some 20 to 25 journalists die of non-natural causes not connected with their profession, including those killed in air crashes and traffic accidents. Journalists lose their lives through domestic violence, robberies, and attacks by hooligans. Russia has a high crime rate and its journalists often get in trouble, just like ordinary people.

In 2006, in all, 29 journalists died from non-natural causes: one drowned in a river, five were killed in drunken brawls, nine in road accidents, four in apartment break-ins, four in holdups, one while climbing a mountain, another in an air crash, and one was run over by a train.

No doubt, the murder of Anna Politkovskaya in 2006 was politically motivated. The CJES also probed the fatal beating of Vagif Kochetkov but failed to unearth conclusive evidence that his death was connected with his work. Indeed, he wrote about sensitive issues, but his suspected assailants were acquitted.

The CJES collects information about all journalists who die violent deaths and monitors the course of investigations. Even air crashes and road accidents can come under suspicion as relatives and colleagues may allege that the victim's vehicle was tampered with or a hit-and-run was plotted.

International organizations also are to blame for publishing inflated numbers or unchecked accounts to create new heroes—"courageous journalists" who perished for freedom of expression in Russia.

Regretfully, this discredits journalism, as weak and immature as it is in Russia. In this light, every crime against a journalist is seen as a political assassination even if it is not linked to his or her job. In my view, the number of professional and courageous journalists in Russia is out of proportion to the reported number of victims (20–30 a year).

Murder is a grave crime. An official or crime boss would hardly dare to kill a journalist even if his or her writing harmed that person's financial or political interests. There are few journalists pushing the limits in Russia, they are well known and their colleagues are proud of them, while the authorities try to ignore them. Anna Politkovskaya was slain over her investigations in Chechnya and her courageous and uncompromising position. There are very few reporters like her in Russia.

Stark Numbers

The CJES has developed investigative methods that help determine a crime's links to a reporter's professional activities based on an analysis of the victim's writing (a drama critic is hardly likely to be targeted by an enraged director).

An investigation into a murder that is not linked to the journalist's work normally does not take long. Police question witnesses, identify and arrest suspects and the latter go on trial. In sharp contrast, there has been scant progress on most politically-motivated murders of journalists—about 50 in Russia over the last 16 years. A rare exception is the 1998 killing of Larisa Yudina, a journalist from Kalmykia. The suspects were convicted and sentenced to prison. However, the trial gave no clue as to who masterminded the attack.

Not only killings but also assaults give rise to controversies. Between 160 and 180 journalists are physically assaulted in Russia every year, according to CJES data. Half of the attacks are linked to the journalism profession; some victims have been beaten in the presence of many witnesses so that their colleagues also learn a lesson.

I have repeatedly urged my counterparts in international press organizations to get together and discuss statistics and murder investigation criteria. This is crucial for assessing the state of journalism, and not only in Russia.

Press advocates publish their reports and lists of murdered journalists at the beginning of every year, or on the eve of World Press Freedom Day, 3 May. I can well imagine a Kremlin bureaucrat reading a new report and wondering, "Why do you insist that we ensure media freedom? You first need to clarify how many journalists are killed and why, and then call us to account."

9.5

Rebirth of Russian Nationalism

Oleg Panfilov

State Control of the Mass Media is the Principal Cause of the Growth of Xeno-phobia in Russia, with Television the Main Weapon in the Propaganda Armoury.

On 4 November 2005, more than 3,000 activists of nationalist organisations, making Nazi salutes and with stylised swastikas on their banners, marched through the centre of Moscow to Slavianskaia Square between the Kremlin and the headquarters of the FSB (KGB). If the aims of the marchers had not been clear enough from the line of drummers and young people wearing quasi-military uniform, they were soon evident from their slogans: 'Sieg Heil!', 'Hail Russia', 'Russia for the Russians', 'Who owns Russia?—Russians!', 'Russia is All, All Else is Nothing!'

The organisers of the march had been given official permission for the demonstration. Several radical nationalist and fascist organisations, including the skinheads' movement, made no secret of the fact that their main aim was to drive all 'non-Russians' out of Moscow. Anti-Semitic utterances were also to be heard at the meeting.

On that same day, 4 November, the traditional 'grey briefing' took place in the Kremlin for the directors of federal television companies, at which officials of the administration of the President of Russia distributed a 'list of terminology'. The document advises against 'distorting' the Russian language and the employment of 'correct terminology' in television news programmes.

Terms in use	Correct terms
Jamaat	terrorist organisation, grouping
Shahid	terrorist, suicide bomber
Mujahad	fighter, terrorist
amir, emir, imam, sheikh	head of a group formation field commander
Wahhabi	Islamic extremist

Source: Oleg Panfilov, "Rebirth of Russian Nationalism: State Control of the Mass Media Is the Principal Cause Of the Growth of Xenophobia in Russia," *Index on Censorship*, Vol. 35, No. 1. 2006, pp. 142–148.

Terms in use	Correct terms
shahid's belt	belt with explosives
Jihad	terrorist sabotage
Chechen terrorism, Islamic terrorism	International terrorism
Caucasian, North, South etc. fronts, Brigades	Chechen terrorist groupings active in the Caucusus
Chechen separatist fighters' military operation, troop operation of *mujahaddin* emissary of the Chechen separatists (Ahmed Zakayev)	Chechen terrorist, fighter action by terrorist fighters, outrage by terrorist fighters spokesman of the Chechen fighters

At first sight, these events seem unrelated, but there is one very important detail to note: not one of the nationwide federal television stations screened a report on the march of the nationalists and fascists. In all likelihood, that decision was taken that same day in the Kremlin.

Fourth November started a new page in the history of Russia: the rebirth of nationalism. This rebirth was initiated by the government, beginning in 2000, after both personnel changes in the Kremlin administration and the revival of the traditions of Soviet propaganda and xenophobia became a component of official and unofficial ideology. It is manifest in the colourful expressions frequently used by Vladimir Putin, for example: 'beat the crap out [of the Chechen resistance] in the shithouse'; or about men becoming 'circumcised radical Muslims'. Xenophobia is endemic both among the leaders of political parties ideologically close to the Russian government and among those that comprise its opposition.

Russian xenophobia has gradually evolved from being anti-Semitic into being anti-Caucasian and anti-Islamic. The development of xenophobia is encouraged, not only by the public speeches and acts of politicians, but also by the mass media: the state-owned media because it is obliged to broadcast the comments of politicians, and the non-state-owned media because it reflects the general nationalistic mood of society. Only a small proportion of the liberally minded mass media resists the spread of xenophobia. Unfortunately, the influence of a few Moscow newspapers and a few dozen provincial newspapers cannot significantly alter the situation.

Neither can the Internet, despite being completely uncontrolled by the government. The freedom of the Internet has made possible not only the uncontrolled delivery of alternative news, but also the appearance of a large number of nationalistic and fascist websites.

There are several reasons for this reappearance of Russian xenophobia. Researchers usually link Putin's coming to power with the renewed outbreak of the war in Chechnya: the population wanted to see someone with a firm hand in the Kremlin. This is entirely plausible, because many Russian opinion polls in the late 1990s, the last two or three years of Boris Yeltsin's rule, pointed to disillusionment after the first war in Chechnya ended in 1996. Many described the peace treaty with the Chechen President Asian Maskhadov as a 'shameful defeat'.

The 'news war' against Chechnya intensified immediately after the signing of the peace treaty in 1996, and the Russian state-owned mass media increasingly began to refer to 'Chechen bandits' and 'Chechen terrorists'. During this period, however, the independent television company NTV was still functioning, and the Echo of Moscow radio station was developing. The Internet had become widespread and independent newspapers were being published. It was possible to discuss and debate the problem of Chechnya. The levels of xenophobia in the mass media could be seen as a manifestation of popular nationalism unrelated to government policy. Only radical politicians and the military claimed that the only way they could resolve the Chechen problem was by means of military force.

This situation began to change in August 1999 after the Russian army's campaign in Dagestan, a federal republic adjacent to Chechnya where Chechen and Dagestani separatists were organising resistance. This was the first military operation conducted under a news blackout. Almost nothing was known about it, because journalists were stopped at the approaches to Dagestan. Only a few journalists working for independent publications managed to report on the operation and its consequences, and their information differed markedly from officially approved news.

Almost as soon as Putin was appointed prime minister in August 1999, he started to woo journalists. Newspaper editors and the directors of television companies began to receive frequent invitations to the Kremlin. After the first few such meetings, a number of heads of independent newspapers began to publish commentaries on their conversations with Putin. When Putin was elected president in March 2000, he continued to socialise with the heads of the mass media, but in recent years only 'reliable' journalists, who keep their mouths shut and don't give away secrets, are invited to the Kremlin.

When two blocks of flats were blown up in Moscow in September 1999, there was no investigative journalism from the Russian media. Within a few hours, all the television channels were broadcasting interviews with politicians who spoke of 'clear signs of Chechen involvement', but since then, neither the official enquiry nor any other investigation has come up with evidence to suggest the leadership of the Chechen republic was involved. In spite of this, the television channels did what the government needed them to do: they created a public consensus on who was behind the Moscow atrocities.

The Kremlin's policy on news was finalised when, in September 2000, Putin signed a strange document titled 'Doctrine of Information Security'. This is neither a law nor a legally binding document, but is rather a government action programme. The Doctrine refers to the leading role of the state press and makes mention, several times more often than it mentions freedom of speech, of 'news war' and the 'news weapon'.

The provision of news in Russia began to change from 2000 as persecution of the independent television company NTV and of journalists on independent newspapers began; this was accompanied by the creation of new state-owned television companies, newspapers, agencies and websites. Government bureaucrats began routinely to bandy about a new concept, 'unified news provision', which, on closer inspection, proves to be none other than the familiar Soviet concept of propaganda. The main aim has been achieved: Russian society now hears what is going on in Chechnya only from official sources. The government has introduced rigorous controls on Russian journalists, restricting visits to territory where the so-called 'anti-terrorist operation' is being conducted, that is, to Chechnya. Similar controls have been applied to foreign journalists. Journalists who wrote extensively about the First Chechen War have been neutralised by being refused visas and accreditation by the Russian ministry of foreign affairs.

News about events of any description in Russia is now strictly controlled by the government: all the national television companies and radio stations are state-owned. Only a small proportion of news sources, newspapers and the Internet are in a position to deliver alternative news, and their influence on public opinion does not compare with that of radio and TV.

The essential conditions for spreading the language of enmity have been created in Russia. Television is free: it is financed out of the state budget and by advertising revenue. Anybody living in Russia has only to press the button on their remote control to access five national channels, only one of which is dedicated to culture, while the others include news bulletins or news analysis.

There is at present no public service television network in Russia and, to judge by the Duma's postponement of discussion of the legislative proposal, there is unlikely to be one in the near future. Public control of the programming of television companies would be detrimental to the government, since the Kremlin would lose its principal disseminator of propaganda.

Only subscribers to cable television packages can access non-official news from Euronews, BBC or CNN programmes translated into Russian. In 2002, however, there were only 12 million users of cable networks in Russia out of a population of 145 million. Accordingly, more than 90 per cent of the population is dependent on news from programmes broadcast by state television. The independent television companies in the Russian provinces have their own news and news analysis programmes, but are subjected to pressure by the local authorities. For the most part, they try to avoid dealing with topics which might cause trouble.

The situation with radio is much the same. The only independent news radio station is Moscow Echo, which is able to rebroadcast its programmes in 41 Russian cities. This gives it a potential audience of 22,400,000, but obviously not all of them listen to the station's programmes. Probably, as in Moscow, only 8 per cent to 9 per cent tune in. The other independent radio stations (of which there are about 1,000) broadcast music and devote 3–6 minutes in the hour to news. Foreign radio stations broadcasting in Russian—Radio Liberty, the BBC, Deutsche Welle—continue to have a modest following.

The other source of news is, of course newspapers. Traditionally those published in Moscow are considered the most liberal, but their circulations are not large enough to sway public opinion in Russia as a whole. Some idea of their readership is given by counting visitors to their websites. The table below gives figures for the print-run and average number of hits per day on their websites and hosts.

Title	Print run	Daily Web hits/unique visits
Nezavisimaya gazeta	140,000	100,000/28,000
Kommersant	145,500	300,000/40,000
Novaya gazeta (twice weekly)	583,000	40,000/10,000 per issue
Izvestiya	241,000	240,000/53,000

Of course, several dozen liberal newspapers are published in the provinces, but the standard of living and hence the purchasing power of the population is lower than in Moscow. In consequence, the print run of these newspapers is several times smaller than those in the capital.

The government is unwilling to give up its control of television since TV news bulletins and news analysis programmes are crucial in forming public opinion. Statistics for February 2004 on the database of the Public Opinion Institute (*Fond Obshchestvennoe mnenie*), reveal that ORT (the First Channel) is received by 95 per cent of the survey's respondents, RTR (the Rossiya Channel) by 93 per cent. The figures for the remaining television companies are much lower: NTV 69 percent; TVTs 48 percent.

The only area of news provision over which the government has no control is the Internet. As yet there is no law in Russia regulating Internet activity and no statutory obligation to register websites. A large number of nationalist and fascist websites have been created on the Russian Internet (RuNet). Almost every organisation preaching racial or national hatred and intolerance has its own website. RuNet is developing rapidly and is used by 10 per cent to 12 per cent of the population, but only a small number of users appear interested in political information.

Russian legislation makes it an offence to publish materials instigating or aggravating national and religious discord. Russia also has a Public Prosecutor's Office whose job it is to monitor the observance of laws and punish those who flout them. Despite this, hundreds of newspapers daily publish articles whose xenophobic content falls within the provisions of these articles of the Criminal Code: it is extremely rare for cases to be brought on these grounds. The courts deal leniently with those accused of distributing jingoistic publications.

Xenophobic materials are to be found not only in nationalistic publications, but primarily in the popular press, in newspapers like *Komsomolskaya Pravda* and *Moskovsky Komsomolets* with huge circulations of 2–3 million. It is clear that anti-Chechen xenophobia has been whipped up by the authorities, both military and political, who are eager to ensure that society continues to believe in the necessity of the military campaign in Chechnya.

The state's bureaucrats did use propaganda during the First Chechen War, but from the beginning of the Second Chechen War all rhyme and reason disappeared from the news they distributed. Official sources appeared totally unconcerned whether the news they were releasing was subsequently discredited, or was seen to be totally ridiculous, even by those without specialist military knowledge. For example, on 6 October 1999, the ITAR-TASS news agency, quoting one of the leaders of the North Caucusus Military District, announced: 'The Chechen bandits are themselves mining residential blocks and, when federal aircraft appear in the sky, blow them up. This is being done in order to turn the Chechen population against the actions of the federal authorities in the northern Caucusus. At the same time, military sources state that the civilian population is being increasingly disaffected by the actions of the bandit formations.'

Hatred of Chechens is always encouraged, in particular by the Russian military, whose press centres disseminate absurd 'news'. For example, after the Kursk submarine disaster in 2002, ITAR-TASS, citing an anonymous FSB officer, reported that Chechens were planning to hijack a submarine. A year earlier, the intelligence services disseminated a story that the blueprint had been discovered in a cave in the mountains of Chechnya of a Boeing similar to one used by terrorists to destroy buildings in New York on 11 September 2001.

Anti-Chechen propaganda is spread not only via news or news analysis programmes. In the last five years, Russian television channels have shown a large number of feature films in which, as in Indian cinema, the heroes, their characteristics and the ending are already familiar to the audience. These are films about the Chechen war, in which the good guys are invariably Russian soldiers and officers and the bad guys are Chechens or, more generally, Caucasians.

State control of the mass media is the principal cause of the growth of xenophobia in Russia, with television the main 'weapon' in the armoury of Russian state propaganda.

9.6

Remembering Paul Klebnikov:
Journalism Of Intimidation

David Satter

Five years have passed since the murder of *Forbes* editor Paul Klebnikov, and journalists in Russia are, if anything, even more endangered in Russia than they were on the day he was killed.

The problem is that protecting journalists (and, with them, freedom of speech) is simply not a priority in Russia. In January, Anastasia Baburova, a freelance reporter with the independent newspaper *Novaya Gazeta*, was shot dead in broad daylight on a crowded street in the center of Moscow along with Stanislav Markelov, a human rights lawyer.

Markelov was the lawyer for Mikhail Beketov, the editor of *Khimkinskaya Pravda*, a newspaper in the Moscow satellite city of Khimki, who was nearly beaten to death Nov. 13, 2008, by unknown attackers. At the time of the attack, he was about to publish an article about the business activities of the family of the mayor of Khimki. Yet after the demonstrative murder of Markelov and Baburova, no Russian official attended the victims' funerals, and both Russian President Dmitri Medvedev and Prime Minister Vladimir Putin remained silent for nine days before Medvedev expressed perfunctory regrets in a meeting with Dmitri Muratov, editor of *Novaya Gazeta*, and Mikhail Gorbachev, one of the newspaper's shareholders.

There may be attempts by the authorities to use the killing of journalists for their own purposes, for example, by hinting that they were carried out by the regime's political enemies. This is probably what was involved when Putin assured the Klebnikov family that the authorities knew who was responsible for Paul's death. But there is no serious attempt to bring the killers to justice. Most ominously, when underlings involved in the killing of journalists are charged in trials that go nowhere, they turn out to have a maze of connections to the security services themselves.

In the Klebnikov case, the Russians, under intense pressure from the American embassy, charged a group of Chechens with the crime and a closed trial took place in 2006 in a Moscow city court. According to the prosecutor, the organizer of the

Source: David Satter, "Journalism of Intimidation," Forbes Online. http://www.forbes.com/2009/07/07/russian-media-censorship-opinions-dmitry-sidorov.html.

killing was Khozh-Akhmed Nukhaev, the leader of a Chechen criminal group. He was the subject of a book by Klebnikov and supposedly did not like the way he was depicted.

Nukhaev disappeared before the murder and has not been seen since. Two Chechens, Musa Vakhayev and Kazbek Dukuzov, allegedly carried out the killing at Nukhaev's behest. However, Alexander Gordeev, the editor of *Newsweek*'s Russian edition who was with Klebnikov at the time he was shot, said that as he lay dying, Klebnikov said his attacker was a Russian.

Sergei Sokolov, deputy editor of *Novaya Gazeta*, which carried out an independent investigation of the murder of Anna Politkovskaya, the famous Russian investigative journalist who worked for the newspaper, said at the trial of three Chechen brothers accused of involvement in that killing that they were recruited by their uncle, Lomi-Ali Gaitukayev, a self-confessed agent of the Federal Security Service (FSB). Interestingly, Gaitukayev was also in contact, according to Sokolov, with Dukuzov. He and Vakhayev were acquitted of the murder of Klebnikov, but the Russian supreme court overturned the acquittal and a new trial was ordered. In the meantime, Dukuzov fled. The Klebnikov case is no longer being actively investigated.

Seventeen journalists have been assassinated in Russia since 2000. Not in one single case has the person who ordered the killing been found. The reason for this is that law enforcement in Russia is beholden to the very people in the business and political elite who find independent reporting most objectionable.

The tie between the organizations that investigate the killings of journalists and the groups that have an interest in carrying them out may explain a familiar pattern in the investigations. In many cases, the investigation proceeds normally until it shows signs of determining who may be responsible for the crime. At that point, law enforcement officers, typically acting in good faith, find that their efforts have been sabotaged by high-ranking officials and the investigation is ruined.

Such high-level sabotage was clearly evident in the Politkovskaya case. The prosecutor leaked information about the executors of the crime to the press, allowing the triggerman to flee; video footage showing the killer entering Politkovskaya's apartment building mysteriously disappeared; the FSB prevented investigators from seizing the office computer of a former FSB agent who was also charged in the crime. The abuses made an acquittal inevitable. (The acquittal has since been overturned by the Russian supreme court, but this does not necessarily mean there will be justice).

The result is that Russian journalists are seriously intimidated. Every journalist knows that investigating a sensitive story can get him killed, and as a result, much of the crime committed by high-ranking officials and businessmen in Russia goes unreported. The minority of journalists determined to pursue the truth wherever it leads have become accustomed to living in fear.

In the aftermath of Klebnikov's death, various theories popped up in Moscow about the motives for his murder. Few placed any credence in the notion that he was killed because of his negative depiction of a Chechen warlord in one of his books. But in the absence of a serious investigation, none of the other theories led anywhere.

Unfortunately, when it comes to the killings of journalists, theories about what happened have come to replace serious investigations of the crimes. The result is a never-never land in which the very idea of actually solving a crime seems strange. Unfortunately, since Paul Klebnikov's murder five years ago, the situation has become even worse. A Moscow police official, when asked about contract murders, summed up the situation this way:" They solve these crimes only in the movies."

9.7

All The News The Kremlin Thinks is Fit to Print

Dmitry Sidorov

"Why don't you start writing about the weather in America?" a seasoned Russian journalist in Washington asked me a few years ago. His rhetorical question came in response to my numerous complaints about the Kremlin's successfully implemented policy of media control.

He was joking, for the most part. In my case, or rather that of my newspaper—*Kommersant*, Russia's leading business and political daily—the Kremlin's ideological footprint was not so big. Or so we tended to think. After all, we only lost one journalist—our military correspondent Ivan Safronov, who "committed suicide" by falling out of a window in Moscow while investigating Russian arms sales to Arab countries. The true circumstances of his death remain murky.

The newspaper that occupies the unenviable lead in this sad statistic is *Novaya Gazeta*, which has lost at least five journalists over the last five years, including Anna Politkovskaya and Yuri Shchekochikhin. So we have reason to be grateful, even as weekly meetings of newspaper editors continue to take place in the Kremlin.

The Kremlin will assure you that these gatherings are not obligatory, but that's whitewash. Technically, an editor may find some pretext to skip the regular brainwashing sessions. In reality, consequences will follow and just might include a polite request from the Kremlin to the publication's owners to fire the rebellious truant.

Former Secretary of State (and Soviet scholar) Condoleezza Rice said many times that Russia today is not the Soviet Union of yesteryear. In my view, it's worse, at least when it comes to freedom of speech. The communist country I was born in allowed no dissenting opinions at all, but it didn't kill or buy off journalists with such astonishing consistency.

The current regime—whether run by Putin, Medvedev, or both—is much more creative and cruel in its dealings with the press than the USSR ever was. Every journalist who covers Prime Minister Putin, President Medvedev or Foreign Minister Lavrov knows the boundaries. The punishment for crossing them is not death—thank you, dear Kremlin—but rather expulsion from the league of the select.

Source: Dmitriy Sidorov, "All the News the Kremlin Thinks is Fit to Print," Forbes Online. http://www.forbes.com/2009/07/07/paul-klebnikov-murder-opinions-david-satter.html

The fate of those journalists who said or wrote things—often with no intention of being disloyal—that displeased the Kremlin has infected most of the Russian media with a virus of trepidation that has spread like wildfire from television to print. Censorship, self-imposed and policed by editors, in even the most liberal print publications and radio stations is mind-boggling.

I would have been shocked to see the "Echo of Moscow" radio station, supposedly one of Russia's most free-thinking media outlets, taking potshots at its main shareholder, Gazprom, during Russia's recent "energy wars" with Ukraine. But what happened didn't surprise me at all. "Echo of Moscow" director Aleksei Venediktov, routinely praised in Europe and the U.S. as a liberal voice, crudely mimicked a Ukrainian accent on the air, and no one batted an eyelash.

Russian television and wire agencies hardly merit mention. At these places, managers hired by the Kremlin impose old-school censorship with a heavy hand. The watchdogs sometimes go so far as to send correspondents in the U.S. the texts of the stories they are to read when they file reports from Washington.

Everyone feels the pressure to hold down a job, pay the bills and feed the family. Does this excuse shameful behavior? I don't know. But I know about the apologetic phone calls from working Russian journalists to well-known individuals they smeared. "We couldn't say no," they claim, "The order came from on high." The excuses are familiar, and often accepted.

"From on high" means from the owner of a publication. In most cases, this is a Kremlin-friendly oligarch who was either told to buy a media outlet or allowed to keep one purchased before the current regime took over. More often than not, the media moguls get importuning calls from the Kremlin telling them what they should do, or how they can redeem themselves after a misstep.

The latest scandal took place at *Kommersant* a few days ago, when the newspaper published a picture of President Medvedev's press secretary, Natalia Timakova, with her tongue sticking out. The outcome of this particular behind-the-scenes brouhaha remains to be seen. But whenever something like this happens it leaves the owners in a peculiar situation. In most cases their media businesses are merely a sideline—something to provide a public face for their real business, a shield to defend their business or a sword to attack their opponents.

Oligarchs in today's Russia flourish only if they are loyal to the Kremlin. If something goes wrong, their media assets or individual journalists can always be sacrificed. A famous example was the firing of Raf Shakirov, editor in chief of *Izvestiya*, who enraged the Kremlin by publishing troubling pictures of the Sept. 1, 2005, massacre at a school in Beslan.

One can argue that the news still seeps into print in Russia, and I would agree. But information on the domestic front emerges primarily in the course of battles between oligarchs over assets, or their lobbying to push someone into an important post in the federal or local government. The Russian public has long since developed immunity to compromising information leaked for particular purposes. Most stories highlighting individual wrongdoing look merely like an informer forwarding a denunciation to the Kremlin.

With Russian television, most radio stations and print publications genuflecting to the Kremlin on a daily basis, the Internet is the only remaining safe haven in Russia. (Sure, there are a few minimally fettered outfits left standing, primarily to reassure the West that Russian democracy is alive and well.) Why? The answer is simple—political content on the Internet has a small audience and negligible influence, giving it license to run stories that would be unthinkable in mainstream media.

So, hats off to the Kremlin—mainstream political journalism in Russia is more dead than alive, and the profession of political reporter is deadlier than ever. But don't get me wrong. I don't intend to compare Russia to the Central Asian nations, Cuba, North Korea or the Arab dictatorships. They don't even pretend to have democracy and freedom of speech.

The light at the end of the tunnel is dim and hardly visible. I'm still mulling my colleague's advice to start reporting on storms and heat waves. But as Bob Dylan sang more than 40 years ago, "You don't need a weatherman to know which way the wind blows."

ABOUT THE EDITOR

Joel M. Ostrow is Professor of political science at Benedictine University, with a PhD from UC Berkeley (1997). His research focuses on political institutions and political development in Russia, and particularly on the legislative and executive institutions, and more broadly on the political and economic transformation of postcommunist states. He is the author (with Georgiy Satarov and Irina Khakamada) of *The Consolidation of Dictatorship in Russia: The Demise of Democracy* (Praeger, 2007) and *Comparing Post-Soviet Legislatures* (Ohio State University, 2000) as well as a host of peer-reviewed journal articles. He is a former Moscow Correspondent for Crain's Communications and *Advertising Age*, covering business and marketing development in Russia, and a frequent commentator on Russian politics for Chicago-area media.

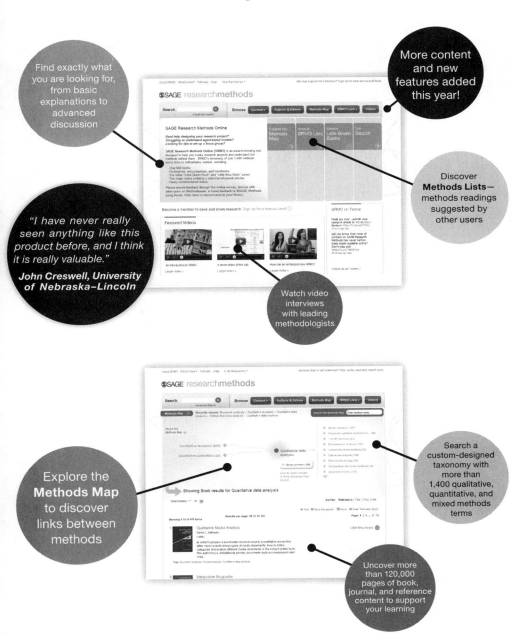